D1559713

THE ELGAR COMPANION TO
SOCIAL ECONOMICS

THE ELGAR COMPANION TO
POST KEYNESIAN ECONOMICS

The Elgar Companion to Social Economics

Edited by

John B. Davis

Professor of History and Methodology of Economics, University of Amsterdam, The Netherlands, Professor of Economics, Marquette University, USA and co-editor of the Journal of Economic Methodology

and

Wilfred Dolfsma

Professor, University of Groningen School of Economics and Business, The Netherlands and corresponding editor of the Review of Social Economy

Edward Elgar

Cheltenham, UK • Northampton, MA, USA

Published by
Edward Elgar Publishing Limited
The Lypiatts
15 Lansdown Road
Cheltenham
Glos GL50 2JA
UK

Edward Elgar Publishing, Inc.
William Pratt House
9 Dewey Court
Northampton
Massachusetts 01060
USA

A catalogue record for this book
is available from the British Library

Library of Congress Control Number: 2008927946

ISBN 978 1 84542 280 6 (cased)

Printed and bound in Great Britain by MPG Books Ltd, Bodmin, Cornwall

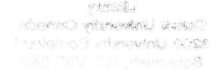

Contents

v

Contributors

Rick Aalbers is a business consultant at Atos Consulting, The Netherlands, where he works in the financial services line of business. He specializes in IT strategy, IT governance and social network analysis. His research focuses on intra-organizational networks and their relation to business performance improvement and innovation. Rick Aalbers received a Master's degree in business administration as well as a Master's in business economics (with honours) from the Erasmus University Rotterdam.

Morris Altman, a former visiting scholar at Cornell, Duke, Hebrew and Stanford Universities, USA, and currently Elected Visiting Fellow at St Edmund's College, Cambridge University, UK, is Professor and Head of the Department of Economics at the University of Saskatchewan, Canada. Past president of the Society for Advancement of Behavioral Economics (SABE) from 2003 to 2006, in 2007 he was elected as vice-president of the Association for Social Economics (ASE) and will serve as president in 2009. Altman is editor of the *Journal of Socio-Economics* (Elsevier Science) and former associate editor of the *Journal of Economic Psychology*. He has published over 70 refereed papers on behavioural economics, economic history and empirical macroeconomics, and three books in economic theory and public policy, and has made well over 100 international presentations on these subjects.

David B. Audretsch is Director of the Research Group on Entrepreneurship, Growth and Public Policy at the Max Planck Institute of Economics, Germany. He also serves as Distinguished Professor and Ameritech Chair of Economic Development at Indiana University, USA, and is a Research Fellow of the Centre for Economic Policy Research, London. His research has focused on the links between entrepreneurship, government policy, innovation, economic development and global competitiveness. His most recent book, *The Entrepreneurial Society*, was published by Oxford University Press in 2007. He was awarded the 2001 International Award for Entrepreneurship and Small Business Research by the Swedish Foundation for Small Business Research.

Pranab Bardhan is Professor of Economics at the University of California at Berkeley, USA, and co-chair of the MacArthur Foundation-funded

Network on the Effects of Inequality on Economic Performance. He has authored or edited a number of books, including *Scarcity, Conflicts, and Cooperation* (MIT Press, 2004) and *International Trade, Growth, and Development* (Blackwell, 2003). He was chief editor of the *Journal of Development Economics* from 1985 to 2003.

Paul D. Bush is Professor Emeritus of Economics, California State University, Fresno, USA. He is a past president of both the Association for Evolutionary Economics and the Association for Institutional Thought, and an honorary lifetime member of the European Association for Evolutionary Political Economy. He has served as a referee for the *Journal of Economics Issues* intermittently since the 1980s, and he is a lifetime member of the International Advisory Board of the *Journal of Institutional Economics*. His research and writing have focused on the theory of institutional change and the pragmatic instrumentalist foundations of original institutional economics (OIE).

José Castro Caldas is a researcher at the Centre for Social Studies of the Faculty of Economics, University of Coimbra, Portugal. He was educated at the Technical University of Lisbon (BSc in Economics in 1988, Master in Operations Research and Artificial Intelligence in 1992) and at the Higher Institute for Labour and Business Studies (PhD in Economics in 2000). He has done research and published on multi-agent simulation applied to economics. Currently his research interests are focused on the moral dimension of economic action involving both the history of ideas and empirical research on decision-making.

David Campbell was educated at Cardiff University, UK (BSc (Econ) 1980), the University of Michigan School of Law, USA (LLM 1985), and the University of Edinburgh, UK (PhD 1985). He is a Fellow of the Chartered Institute of Arbitrators. He is a Professor in the Department of Law at Durham University, UK. His principal recent publications are *The Implicit Dimensions of Contract* (with H. Collins and J. Wightman, eds, Hart, 2003), *Remedies in Contract and Tort* (with D. Harris and R. Halson, Cambridge University Press, 2005), and an edited collection of the works of Ian Macneil (Sweet & Maxwell, 2001). His main current research interests are in remedies for non-performance of contractual obligations and in regulatory theory.

Luís Francisco Carvalho is Lecturer at the Higher Institute for Labour and Business Studies (ISCTE) and Researcher at the Research Centre for Socioeconomic Change (DINÂMIA–ISCTE) and at the Centre for African

Studies (CEA–ISCTE), Lisbon, Portugal. His current research interests include the history of economic thought and development economics.

Metin M. Coşgel is Professor of Economics at the University of Connecticut, Storrs, CT, USA. His research interests include rhetorical analysis of the economy, particularly consumption. He is also interested in the relationship between economics and religion and the economic history of the Ottoman Empire. Recent contributions have appeared in *Explorations in Economic History* (2006), *Journal of Economic History* (2005), *Review of Social Economy* (2004), *Historical Method* (2004) and *Journal of Socio-Economics* (2004). He also maintains a website on the 'Economic History of the Ottoman Empire' (ottoman.uconn.edu). Personal website: cosgel.uconn.edu.

Frank A. Cowell is currently Professor of Economics at the London School of Economics and Director of the Distributional Analysis Research Programme in the Suntory and Toyota International Centres for Economics and Related Disciplines. He has a PhD from Cambridge and is also editor of *Economica*. His books include *Measuring Inequality* (3rd edn, Oxford University Press, 2008), *Microeconomics: Principles and Analysis* (Oxford University Press, 2006), *The Economics of Poverty and Inequality* (Edward Elgar, 2003), *Thinking about Inequality* (Cambridge University Press, 1999, joint with Yoram Amiel) and *Economic Inequality and Income Distribution* (Cambridge University Press, 1998, joint with David Champernowne).

Charlie Dannreuther is from the School of Politics and International Studies at the University of Leeds, UK, and is research area coordinator for Macroeconomic Regulation and Institutional Change of the European Association of Evolutionary Political Economy. He is primarily interested in the political economy of the small firm with special reference to the UK and the EU, and the relationship between SME policy and globalization. From this perspective he has also examined issues relating to risk, social capital and the role of the international in French regulation theory. He is also interested in the practice of economic policy and has worked on EU-related training programmes in pre-accession states including Cyprus, Croatia, Hungary and more recently Turkey and Bosnia and Herzegovina.

John B. Davis is Professor of History and Methodology of Economics at the University of Amsterdam, The Netherlands and Professor of Economics at Marquette University, USA. He is author of *Keynes's Philosophical Development* (Cambridge, 1994) and *The Theory of the*

Individual in Economics (Routledge, 2003), is the former editor of the *Review of Social Economy*, 2008 president of the Association for Social Economics, and currently co-editor of the *Journal of Economic Methodology*.

George DeMartino is an associate professor and the Associate Dean for Graduate Studies at the Graduate School of International Studies at the University of Denver, CO, USA. He received his PhD in economics from the University of Massachusetts and his MA degree in industrial relations from Warwick University, UK. He has written extensively on global political economy (with a particular focus on trade and investment), including his book *Global Economy, Global Justice: Theoretical Objections and Policy Alternatives to Neoliberalism* (Routledge, 2000). He is now at work on his book *I Do Solemnly Swear: On the Need for and Content of Professional Economic Ethics*.

Ashwini Deshpande is Reader (Associate Professor) at the Department of Economics, Delhi School of Economics, University of Delhi, India. Her specific research areas are: the economics of discrimination; inequality and intergroup disparities, with a focus on caste and gender in India; international debt; and aspects of the Chinese economy. She has published several papers in leading economics journals and is the editor of *Boundaries of Clan and Color: Transnational Comparisons of Inter-Group Disparity* (with William Darity, Jr, London, Routledge, 2003) and *Globalization and Development: A Handbook of New Perspectives* (New Delhi, Oxford University Press, 2007).

Wilfred Dolfsma, economist and philosopher, holds a PhD in economics from Erasmus University, Rotterdam, The Netherlands. He is Professor at the University of Groningen School of Economics and Business, The Netherlands. He was 2005/6 research fellow at the Netherlands Institute for Advanced Studies in the Humanities and the Social Sciences (NIAS) and is corresponding editor for the *Review of Social Economy*. His research interests are the interrelations between economy, society and technology, media industries, feminist economics, globalization, consumption, and the developments in and effects of intellectual property rights (IPR). His *Institutional Economics and the Formation of Preferences* (Edward Elgar, 2004) won him EAEPE's Myrdal Prize. His most recent books are *Knowledge Economies* (Routledge, 2008) and *Consuming Symbolic Goods* (ed., Routledge, 2008).

Sheila C. Dow is Professor of Economics at Stirling University, Scotland, UK. She is the author of *Economic Methodology: An Inquiry* (Oxford

University Press, 2002), *The Methodology of Macroeconomic Thought* (Edward Elgar, 1996) and other publications in methodology, history of thought, post-Keynesian economics, monetary theory and regional finance. She is Director of the Stirling Centre for Economic Methodology (SCEME), an associate editor of the *Journal of Economic Methodology*, and special adviser on monetary policy to the UK House of Commons Select Committee. Before becoming an academic, she worked for the Bank of England and the Government of Manitoba.

William M. Dugger is Professor of Economics at the University of Tulsa, OK, USA. He holds the offices of president of the Association for Social Economics, Association for Evolutionary Economics and Association for Institutional Thought. His books are *Alternative to Economic Retrenchment* (Petrocelli, 1984), *Radical Institutionalism* (Greenwood Press, 1989), *Underground Economics* (M.E. Sharpe, 1992), *The Stratified State* (with William Waller, M.E. Sharpe, 1992), *Inequality, Reclaiming Evolution* (with Howard Sherman, Greenwood Press, 1996), and *Evolutionary Theory in the Social Sciences* (4 volumes, with Howard Sherman, Routledge, 2003). He has contributed articles and reviews in *Review of Social Economy*, *Journal of Economic Issues*, *Review of Radical Political Economics* and other journals. He was given the Thomas Divine Award from the Association for Social Economics in 2002 and the Veblen–Commons Award from the Association for Evolutionary Economics in 2005.

Deborah M. Figart is Dean of Graduate Studies and Professor of Economics at The Richard Stockton College of New Jersey, USA. She has published books and articles on social economics topics related to the labour market: pay equity, discrimination, working time, job evaluation, emotional labour, career ladders, employment policies and poverty. From 2006 to 2007, she served as president of the Association for Social Economics. Currently, she is co-editor of the *Review of Social Economy*.

David George is Professor of Economics at La Salle University, USA and is the author of *Preference Pollution: How Markets Create the Desires We Dislike* (University of Michigan Press, 2001). His recent papers have covered such diverse topics as the effect of market values on higher education, the role of introspection in the economic discovery process, and a critical examination of Amartya Sen's analysis of free choice. Long-term plans are for a book that continues his earlier study of the rhetorical practices of economists. He has been a member of the Association for Social Economics for over 30 years and served as its president in 2005.

Ilene Grabel is an economist and Professor and Director of the graduate programme in Global Trade, Finance and Economic Integration at the Graduate School of International Studies at the University of Denver, CO, USA. Grabel has lectured at the Cambridge University Advanced Programme on Rethinking Development Economics since its founding. She has worked as a consultant to the United Nations Development Programme (UNDP)/International Poverty Centre, the United Nations Conference on Trade and Economic Development (UNCTAD)/Group of 24, the UN University's World Institute for Development Economics Research, and with the coalition 'New Rules for Global Finance' and ActionAid.

Shaun P. Hargreaves Heap graduated from Oxford and UC Berkeley and now teaches economics at the University of East Anglia, UK. His current research is on how the membership of groups affects decision-making in trust games and how diversity in the media should be measured and valued. His publications include *Rationality in Economics* (Blackwell Publishers, 1989), *Game Theory: A Critical Text* (with Yanis Varoufakis, Routledge, 2005) and he has recent articles that relate to his current research in the *Economic Journal* (2002), *Cambridge Journal of Economics* (2004), *Economic Policy* (2005) and *Kyklos* (2007).

Geoffrey M. Hodgson is a research professor in Business Studies at the University of Hertfordshire in Hatfield, UK, and editor in chief of the *Journal of Institutional Economics*. He is the author of over 100 articles in scholarly journals and several books, including *Economics in the Shadows of Darwin and Marx* (Edward Elgar Publishing, 2006), *The Evolution of Institutional Economics* (Routledge, 2004), *How Economics Forgot History* (Routledge, 2001), *Economics and Utopia* (Routledge, 1999), *Economics and Evolution* (Polity Press and University of Michigan Press, 1993) and *Economics and Institutions* (Polity Press and University of Pennsylvania Press, 1988). His research is on the nature and evolution of socio-economic institutions and his website is www.geoffrey-hodgson.info.

Max Keilbach is a senior researcher at the research group in Entrepreneurship, Growth and Public Policy. His main research interests are in the area of innovative entrepreneurship and in its economic impact. He uses empirical, econometric and simulation-based approaches in his analyses. He started his professional life as a shepherd, then he studied agricultural engineering in Nürtingen, Germany and economics in Freiburg, Germany, Montpellier, France, and Berlin, Germany. He received his PhD from the Chair of Econometrics at the TU Berlin, investigating causes of spatial agglomeration of production factors and its impact on regional economic growth. Between 1998 and 2002 he worked as a Senior Researcher at the Department of Industrial Economics at the Centre for European Economic Research (ZEW) in Mannheim. There his research focused on the demography of firms and on the development of corresponding databases.

Oliver Kessler is Assistant Professor for International Relations at the University of Bielefeld, Germany. He serves as one of the research coordinator of the Economic Sociology Research Network within the European Sociology Association. His most recent publications include 'From Agent and Structures to Minds and Bodies' in *Journal of International Relations and Development* and 'Space, Boundaries and the Problem of Order: A View from Systems Theory' in *Journal of International Political Sociology* (with Jan Helmig).

Stefan Kesting is a senior lecturer in economics at AUT (Auckland University of Technology), New Zealand. He has previously taught at the University of Bremen, Germany and the University of Missouri, Kansas City, USA. Stefan studied at the universities of Heidelberg and Bremen as well as at the New School for Social Research, New York City. He holds a diploma (MA) and a PhD in economics from the University of Bremen. His main research interests are the interactive and linguistic turn in economic theory, ecological sustainability, gender, feminist and social and institutional economics.

Matthias Klaes is Professor of Commerce at Keele University, UK. His academic background is in engineering, economics and science studies. He is senior research fellow at the Stirling Centre for Economic Methodology (SCEME) which he founded in 2003. His current research interests focus on social framing and identity, gendering of financial markets and, through his involvement in the Health Care Standards Unit (HCSU), health care regulation. Recent and forthcoming publications include 'A conceptual history of bounded rationality' (*HOPE*, 2005, with E.-M. Sent), 'Rationality and its bounds: reframing social framing' (in M.C. Galavotti et al., 2007, *Reasoning, Rationality and Probability*, Stanford: CSLI), and *Transaction Costs* (Cambridge University Press, 2008).

Alfred Kleinknecht graduated in economics at the Freie Universität, Berlin, Germany and holds an economics PhD degree from the Vrije Universiteit, Amsterdam, The Netherlands. He was connected to the Wissenschaftszentrum Berlin (1978–80), the Vrije Universiteit, Amsterdam (1980–84), the Universiteit van Maastricht (1984–88) and the Universiteit van Amsterdam (1988–94). From 1994 to 1997 he was Professor of Industrial Economics at the Vrije Universiteit, Amsterdam. Since 1997 he has been Professor in the Economics of Innovation at TU Delft, The Netherlands.

Edith Kuiper is Visiting Professor at the University of Sassari, Sardinia and Fellow at the Faculty of Economics and Business of the University of Amsterdam, The Netherlands. She is co-editor of *Out of the Margin: Feminist Perspectives on Economics* (Routledge, 1995), author of *The Most Valuable of All Capital: A Gender Reading of Economic Texts* (2001), and co-edited (with Drucilla K. Barker) *Towards a Feminist Philosophy of Economics* (Routledge, 2003) and *Feminist Economics and the World Bank* (Routledge, 2005). She was president of the International Association for Feminist Economics in 2006 and publishes on feminist history and philosophy of economics.

Helena Lopes (PhD in economics in 1994, Université Paris I – Sorbonne, France) is Professor at the Economics Department at ISCTE – Lisbon University Institute in Lisbon, Portugal and researcher at DINÂMIA. Her research interests are in labour economics, ethics and economics, and organizational economics. She has directed several multidisciplinary European research projects funded by Portuguese public bodies and by the 5th and 6th European Union Framework Programme. She has published papers in *The American Journal of Economics and Sociology*, *Revue du MAUSS* and *Économies et Sociétés*.

Anne Mayhew is Professor Emerita at the University of Tennessee, USA, where she was on the faculty from 1968 until her retirement in 2006. During that time she also served as vice chancellor for Academic Affairs and Dean of Graduate Studies, and from 1991 until 2000, as editor of the *Journal of Economic Issues*. She has published work on US economic history and the history of economic thought in a number of major journals and is currently completing a book that compares the growth of John D. Rockefeller's Standard Oil and Sam Walton's Wal-Mart.

Robert McMaster is a senior lecturer in institutional economics in the Department of Management of the Business School at the University of Glasgow, Scotland, UK. He was a senior lecturer in economics at the University of Aberdeen, and has been a visiting scholar at the University of Missouri at Kansas City and Marquette University, Milwaukee, USA. He is a co-editor of the *Review of Social Economy*. Research interests include health care reform and methodological issues in health economics.

Recent publications have appeared in the *Cambridge Journal of Economics*, *Journal of Economic Issues* and *Post-Autistic Economics Review*.

Abid Mehmood is Research Associate with the Social Systems research group at the Institute for Research on Environment and Sustainability (IRES), Newcastle University, UK. He has a PhD in planning. His particular interests include the evolutionary perspectives to socioeconomic development in small islands and peripheral regions. He has worked on a number of UK and European research projects on regional development planning and social innovation, as well as environment and sustainability.

Frank Moulaert is Professor of Planning at ASRO, KU Leuven, Belgium. He is also a visiting professor at Newcastle University, UK and IFRESI–CNRS, Lille, France. He has a PhD in regional science, and has published extensively on topics in urban and regional development, territorial and social innovation, social exclusion, economic policy, spatial planning and institutionalism. He has recently coordinated the FP6 research projects on Development Models and Logics of Socioeconomic Organization in Space (DEMOLOGOS) and KATARSIS. He referees for a number of leading international journals in urban and regional development, and planning. He has served on evaluation panels for various research councils, programmes and international foundations.

Ellen Mutari is an Associate Professor of Economics and Women's Studies Coordinator at the Richard Stockton College of New Jersey, USA. She has published on the theory and methodology of feminist political economy, living wage and working time policies, the gendered impact of the Great Depression, and race- and gender-based discrimination. Mutari is a co-author, with Deborah M. Figart and Marilyn Power, of *Living Wages, Equal Wages: Gender and Labor Market Policies in the United States* (Routledge, 2002). She also co-edited *Gender and Political Economy: Incorporating Diversity into Theory and Policy* (M.E. Sharpe, 1997) and *Women and the Economy: A Reader* (M.E. Sharpe, 2003).

Phillip Anthony O'Hara is Professor of Global Political Economy and Governance at the Global Political Economy Research Unit, Curtin University, Australia. He is on the editorial boards of the *Intervention Journal of Economics*, the *Review of Social Economy* and the *Journal of Economic Issues*. He has published over 80 articles in refereed journals and edited books, and his latest book is *Growth and Development in the Global Political Economy* (Routledge, 2006). He won the Gunnar Myrdal Prize in 2002 for Book of the Year, awarded by the European Association for

Evolutionary Political Economy in Aix-en-Provence; and the Clarence Ayres Award for excellence in institutional economics, awarded by the Association for Evolutionary Economics in Chicago in 1998.

Jouni Paavola is Reader in Sustainability at the School of Earth and Environment, University of Leeds, UK. His research examines the role of institutions and social justice in environmental governance. He has published his research in journals such as *Science*, *Ecological Economics* and *Review of Social Economy*, and has co-edited three volumes on environmental decisions and values. The latest, *Fairness in Adaptation to Climate Change* (edited with W. Neil Adger, Saleemul Huq and M.J. Mace, MIT Press, 2006), was nominated for the Harold and Margaret Sprout Prize of the Environmental Studies Section of the International Studies Association, and was given an Honorary Mention. He is associate editor of *Environmental Values* and a member of the board of European Society of Ecological Economics (ESEE).

Gerben van der Panne graduated in regional economics at the Universiteit van Utrecht, The Netherlands and holds an economics PhD from TU Delft. Since 2004 he has been a lecturer in management economics at TU Delft.

Isha Ray is Assistant Professor at the Energy and Resources Group, UC Berkeley, USA. Her research interests are water and development; technology and development; common property resources; and social science research methods. She is editor (with Pranab Bardhan) of *The Contested Commons: Conversations Between Economists and Anthropologists* (Blackwell Publishing, 2008).

João Rodrigues is a researcher at the Research Centre for Socioeconomic Change (DINÂMIA–ISCTE), Lisbon, Portugal. He is completing his PhD and is currently doing research on the relations between morality, economic theory and the market institution.

Inge Røpke is Associate Professor at the Department of Management Engineering, Technical University of Denmark. Her research examines the history of ecological-economic thought and environmental implications of economic growth, international trade, technological change and consumption. Her ongoing research projects investigate the environmental aspects of changes in everyday life, technology and consumption. She has published her research in journals such as *Ecological Economics* and *Journal of Consumer Policy*, and she has co-edited *The Ecological Economics of*

Consumption (Edward Elgar, 2004). She has been an active member of the International Society for Ecological Economics since its inception.

Hans Schenk is Professor of Economics and Research Fellow at the Tjalling C. Koopmans Research Institute at Utrecht University's School of Economics (USE), The Netherlands. Before his appointment at Utrecht, he was a professor of economics and business at Tilburg University and an associate professor at Erasmus University Rotterdam and the University of Groningen. He has been a visiting professor at universities in the UK, France and China. He graduated from the University of Oregon, USA, obtained his MBA in the collaborative Leuven/Cornell programme and his *summa cum laude* doctorate in economics from Université de Nice–Sophia Antipolis. He has been a consultant to multinational enterprises, employers' federations as well as trade unions, the United Nations, the Dutch and English parliaments, the European Commission, and various governments. He is an associate editor of the *International Journal of the Economics of Business* and the *International Review of Applied Economics*.

Nicolas Sirven was born in 1977 in France. He achieved a PhD in economics at the University of Bordeaux, France in December 2004 and joined as a postdoctorate the Capability and Sustainability Centre (Von Hügel Institute) at St Edmund's College, University of Cambridge, UK. His main work in development and health economics deals with social capital, poverty and living conditions. He is currently research fellow at the Institute for Research and Information in Health Economics (IRDES) in Paris.

Martha A. Starr is a member of the economics faculty at American University in Washington, DC. Before joining the AU faculty, she was a senior economist at the Federal Reserve Board of Governors. Her research is centrally concerned with issues of culture and social values in economic life, and has covered such subjects as consumerism and the media, lifestyle and consumption norms, gender and economic identity, 'self-control' problems in consumer spending, socially responsible investment and consumption, and household saving. She is also a co-editor of the *Review of Social Economy*.

Irene van Staveren is Associate Professor in Feminist Development Economics at the Institute of Social Studies in The Hague, The Netherlands. In addition, she is part-time Professor in Economics and Christian Ethics at Radboud University Nijmegen. One of her research interests is in the capability approach, in particular on the ethics of the approach. She is member of the editorial boards of *Feminist Economics*, the *Journal of Economic Issues*, the *Review of Social Economy* and the *Review of Political Economy*.

John Vail is a lecturer in sociology in the School of Geography, Politics and Sociology at the University of Newcastle, UK. He is the co-editor (with Jane Wheelock and Michael Hill) of *Insecure Times: Living with Insecurity in Contemporary Society* (Routledge, 1999). His critical re-examination of the legacy of Karl Polanyi, *Karl Polanyi: The Paradoxes of the Double Movement*, will be published in 2008 by Routledge. His current research explores two projects: the dynamic processes of market society (market imperialism, market corrosion, market disembedding, market hegemony) using a social mechanisms approach; and the centrality of de-commodification to egalitarian political economy.

Mark D. White is an associate professor in both the Department of Political Science, Economics and Philosophy at the College of Staten Island/CUNY and the economics doctoral programme at the CUNY Graduate Center. His work integrates Kantian ethics into economics, specifically models of rational choice and the field of law and economics, and focuses on Kantian concepts of character and the will. He is currently editing *The Theoretical Foundations of Law and Economics* for Cambridge University Press, as well as a special issue of the *Review of Social Economy* dealing with ethics and economics, both forthcoming in 2009.

L. Randall Wray is a professor of economics at the University of Missouri–Kansas City as well as Research Director, the Center for Full Employment and Price Stability (at UMKC), and Senior Scholar at the Levy Economics Institute of Bard College, New York. He is a past president of the Association for Institutionalist Thought (AFIT) and served on the board of directors of the Association for Evolutionary Economics (AFEE). He has published widely in journals, and is the author of *Understanding Modern Money: The Key to Full Employment and Price Stability* (Edward Elgar, 1998) and *Money and Credit in Capitalist Economies* (Edward Elgar, 1990).

Preface

This *Companion to Social Economics* was initiated in 2004 at the Eleventh World Congress for Social Economics in Albertville, France. Liz Oughton and Jane Wheelock were originally involved in thinking through some of the foundations for this project as co-editors, but had to withdraw for personal reasons. We would like to thank them none the less for their enthusiasm for the project and their generous contributions to its conception.

Wilfred would like to thank the Netherlands Institute for Advanced Studies in the Humanities and Social Sciences (NIAS). Although the hospitality and care offered related to a different project to be undertaken there, he found academic shelter there. John thanks Marquette University and the University of Amsterdam for their support of scholarship that made this project possible for him. For their advice and encouragement we would both like to thank a number of people in particular: Tony Atkinson, Dusan Déak, Rene van der Eijk, Eric Jones, Silke Meyer, Liz Oughton, Antoon Spithoven and Jane Wheelock.

John B. Davis and Wilfred Dolfsma
Amsterdam and Milwaukee, and Utrecht and Maastricht

Social economics: an introduction and a view of the field

John B. Davis and Wilfred Dolfsma

The goal of this *Companion to Social Economics* is to highlight the salient themes and leading ideas of contemporary social economics, particularly as they have been broadly developed in recent research, and as they are likely to contribute to and influence social economics and social economic policy in the future. The last two decades have seen a significant increase in social economics scholarship that has built on earlier foundations (cf. Lutz and Lux, 1988; Lutz, 1990a; Waters, 1993; O'Boyle, 2005), taken new directions, and expanded the horizon of social economics. This *Companion* emphasizes these more recent contributions in order to bring together in one place the fundamental themes and variety of approaches that motivate this new work. Social economics, it should be emphasized, has always included a wide range of perspectives and strategies, and indeed many contributors have multiple theoretical orientations and commitments (cf. Dugger, 1977; Lutz, 1990a; Samuels, 1990). This makes a volume such as this one much needed as it not only demonstrates new cross-connections and linkages between often very different types of research, but also makes it possible to see the changing shape of social economic investigation as a whole.

Social economics has two related domains of investigation. Its origins lie in the investigation of the social economy itself, understood as the third sector in mixed market economies distinct from the private and public sectors, and based on voluntary rather than paid, cooperative rather than competitive, and not-for-profit activities carried out within communities, across national economies and internationally. The social economy is variously referred to as the non-profit sector, the *économie sociale*, the *Gemeinwirtschaft*, and the cooperative economy, and has a long history coincident with the rise of market economies and antedating them as well. But social economics has also come to be concerned with the functioning of the mixed market economy as a whole from the perspective of the role that social values and social relationships play in the economy as well as in economics' representation of it. This social perspective is inspired by the original concern of social economics with the social economy, since there social values and social relationships are prominent and dominate economic values and economic relationships. With regard to the economy as a whole, then, although economic values and relationships occupy the foreground, social economists none the less argue that economic values cannot be separated from social values, and that economic relationships are framed by broader social relationships (DeMartino, 2000; O'Boyle, 2001; van Staveren, 2001; Davis, 2003; Dolfsma, 2004; Finn, 2006). This understanding enables social economists to treat the entire economy as a social economy or to treat the economy as fundamentally social. Social economics in this wider sense investigates the market economy as a social economy; with respect to economics it emphasizes the connection between economics and ethics, where ethics concerns how values are inescapably intertwined with social relationships (Wilber, 1998, 2004). This perspective has clearly motivated social economists to consider the implications for policy of their conceptual and empirical research (Boswell, 1990; O'Boyle, 1996; Figart et al., 2002; Wilber, 1998; DeMartino, 2000). An understanding that everybody needs to be able to provide for themselves has led to a focus on equality and inequality (DeMartino, 2000) and need (Braybrooke, 1987; Doyal and Gough, 1991; Davis and O'Boyle, 1994). Public as well as private organizations can also play their part in promoting equality and meeting needs (Barrett, 2005; Booth, 1998; Ekins and Max-Neef, 1992; Lutz, 1999; Samuels and Miller, 1987; Tomer, 1999; Davis, 2001).

This volume addresses this wider conception of social economics as defined above. Within this broad purview, social economists operate with a variety of strategies of investigation that are interconnected, and which reflect social economics' own development from the investigation of the social economy itself to the investigation of functioning of the mixed market economy as a whole.

First, as befits their original concern with the social economy as a separate cooperative domain within the larger economy, many social economists operate with the concept of boundaries, and ask how the social economy is linked to the market and the state where different principles of organization operate. But just as social economics has broadened its concern to the economy as a whole, the concept of boundaries between domains has been generalized across the economy (Darity and Deshpande, 2003). On this view, the social economic world is made up of a set of relatively distinct domains, each of which operates in a relatively autonomous manner according to principles and values that are characteristic of it. The boundaries between these domains are then where different kinds of human activity come into contact with one another, often creating tensions and conflicts in life and in their (largely) incommensurable discourses that social scientists seek to reconcile. Social economists who work in terms of the concept of domains and boundaries, then, seek to explain cases such as these by pointing to the role that social values and social relationships play in positioning these boundaries.

A second strategy emphasizes the functioning of the mixed market economy as a whole, de-emphasizing the division of the social economic world into relatively distinct domains with boundaries between them. The focus thus moves to the social values and social relationships that underlie and drive all aspects of the market process. One definition of economics that accordingly many social economists hold is that economics is the science of provisioning (Doyal and Gough, 1991; Golden and Figart, 2000; Figart, 2004; Davis and O'Boyle, 1994). Provisioning is an inherently social activity that concerns how people in society organize themselves to produce and consume the requirements of life. Compare this definition to the standard definition of economics as the science of scarce resource allocation. If economic life is restricted to the science of resource allocation, issues such as inequality, environmental sustainability, power and human dignity are all ignored, though economics is clearly central to their understanding. Social economists consequently argue that the scarce resources definition of economics fails to capture the deeper nature of economic activity as inherently social.

A third strategy builds on these two previous approaches, and supposes that because the mainstream economics conception of the economy as a value-free, natural process has been widely influential in the world today, social economic explanations should employ the method of critique whereby mainstream explanations are shown to produce internal contradictions and conflict with empirical evidence. On this approach, alternative social economic explanations are illuminating when accompanied by a dismantling of mainstream misconceptions about the nature of the economy (Danner, 2002; Etzioni, 1988; Samuels and Miller, 1987; Clary et al., 2006). This critical method is sometimes directed towards the functioning of different domains or types of activity within the economy, and is sometimes directed towards dominant conceptions about the economy as a whole, such as the idea that the economy is simply a market process. In either case, this third strategy assumes that people's beliefs about the economy are central to economic behaviour, and accordingly that social economic explanation entails eliminating false belief systems in economics.

The chapters in this *Companion to Social Economics* draw on and often combine these three strategies of investigation as inherited from the historical evolution of social economics. This distinguishes these chapters from other approaches with which social economics is sometimes compared and confused: socio-economics and the 'new social economics'.

Almost two decades ago Mark Lutz (1990b) took stock of the 'cross-fertilization' and 'mutual cooperation' between social economics and socio-economics. His characterization of close connections and fruitful exchanges between the two is still valid today, as both 'emphasize the social point of view'. While both social economics and socio-economics emphasize the role of values in the economy, socio-economics takes a more Kantian perspective. Universal, inalienable values subscribed to by rational human beings are proposed in line with a deontological position in ethics (Etzioni, 1988). Moral considerations tend to be perceived of as a constraint or limitation on the economy, and on profit or utility maximization. This entails a rather precise separation between the economy and society, and, as a consequence, also involves the assumption of autonomous human beings. The more precise separation of spheres in society, of the individual and the social, and of considerations that each individual has, means that a more positivistic approach may be discerned (cf. Lutz, 1990b, p. 313). Social embeddedness is less emphasized in socioeconomics than it is in social economics. The latter uses the concept of (social) institutions more (cf. Waters, 1990), and discusses mutual shaping of social values, institutions, and individuals and their needs and goals (Dolfsma, 2004). A more integrative approach is adopted (cf. Lutz, 1990b). The association that promotes socio-economics, the Society for the Advancement of Socio-Economics (SASE) advertises itself rightly as an interdisciplinary organization. In recent years, socio-economists have increasingly used insights from biology, in addition to psychology and sociology. The association that promotes social economics, the Association for Social Economics (ASE), presents itself as a pluralistic organization that emphasizes the role of social values and social relationships in economics. Social economists have a variety of additional orientations, including institutionalism, Marxism, feminism, post-Keynesian, Kantianism, solidarism, neo-Schumpeterian, environmentalism and cooperativism.[1]

There is also a quite recent literature termed the 'new social economics', which begins with market relationships, and then seeks to add 'non-economic' social content to their analysis (e.g. Durlauf and Young, 2001; Becker and Murphy, 2003; Barrett, 2005). That is, rather than embed the economy in social relationships, these more recent contributions seek to embed social relationships in the market. While some would argue that the ultimate result is the same, social economists in this volume would argue that this more recent approach, in economic imperialist fashion, produces a view of social life as at bottom economic rather than a view of economic life as at bottom social. Further, by beginning with and then enlarging our view of the market process, this new approach casts its explanations in the naturalistic terms that mainstream economists have long used to describe the market process. In contrast, in the long tradition of social economics dating back at least 200 years (Nitsch, 1990), a prior concern with pre-market and non-market cooperative economic relationships puts the social-value-driven character of these relationships at the forefront. Thus the historical evolution of social economics from the investigation of the domain of the social economy to the investigation of the deep underlying social-value principles that encompass and guide the entire social economy offers a distinctive understanding of social economics.

This *Companion* is thus organized to reflect this specific understanding, and to emphasize the social concerns, social relationships and social contexts that embed the economy, the market and individuals themselves. Most contributors see individuals and social structures as mutually influencing one another, and use this overarching conception as a basis for understanding the economy.[2] The economy and markets are thus understood in this wider context. But within this framework there are many different perspectives and types of investigation, and thus to assist readers in seeing the common ground and distinct views of the contributors at the same time, each of the ten parts of the volume is preceded by the summaries for the chapters included in that part. This also makes it possible to quickly compare the different parts to the *Companion* to one another, and thus get a summary sense of the overall thinking that the various contributors to the volume have made to social economics.

This *Companion* obviously builds on many earlier contributions to social economics. Indeed, in the last two decades alone there have been many books, not to mention articles appearing in the *Review of Social Economy*, the *Forum for Social Economics*, the *Journal of Socio-Economics*, the *Socio-Economic Review* and the *International Journal of Social Economics*, that have covered issues we are not able to touch upon in this brief introduction. We see the chapters in this *Companion* as adding to this rich tradition, and further extending the investigation of the underlying social value principles that encompass and guide the entire social economy.

Notes

1. O'Boyle (2005) collects 12 of the best articles published in the *Review of Social Economy* from 1944 to 1999.
2. In this sense social values can be said to exist and exert an influence, countering the methodological individualist critique that 'only individual wants, values, and demands and their interaction' can be seen 'outside of the domain of communism' (Schumpeter, 1908–9, p. 4).

References

Barrett, Christopher (ed.) (2005), *The Social Economics of Poverty*, London: Routledge.
Becker, Gary and Kevin Murphy (2003), *Social Economics: Market Behavior in a Social Environment*, Cambridge, MA: Harvard University Press.
Booth, Douglas E. (1998), *The Environmental Consequences of Growth*, London: Routledge.

Boswell, Jonathan (1990), *Community and the Economy: The Theory of Public Co-operation*, London: Routledge.

Braybrooke, David (1987), *Meeting Needs*, Princeton, NJ: Princeton University Press.

Clary, Betsy Jane, Wilfred Dolfsma and Deborah M. Figart (2006), *Ethics and the Market: Insights from Social Economics*, London: Routledge.

Danner, Peter (2002), *The Economic Person: Acting and Analyzing*, Lanham, MD: Rowman & Littlefield.

Darity, William Jr and Ashwini Deshpande (2003), *Boundaries of Clan and Color: Transnational Comparisons of Inter-group Disparity*, London: Routledge.

Davis, John B. (2001), *The Social Economics of Health Care*, London: Routledge.

Davis, John B. (2003), *The Theory of the Individual in Economics*, London: Routledge.

Davis, John B. and Edward J. O'Boyle (1994), *The Social Economics of Human Material Need*, Carbondale, IL: Southern Illinois University Press.

DeMartino, George (2000), *Global Economy, Global Justice: Theoretical Objections and Policy Alternatives to Neoliberalism*, London: Routledge.

Dolfsma, Wilfred (2004), *Institutional Economics and the Formation of Preferences: The Advent of Pop Music*, Cheltenham, UK and Northampton, MA, USA: Edward Elgar.

Doyal, Len and Ian Gough (1991), *A Theory of Human Need*, New York: Guilford Press.

Dugger, W.M. (1977), 'Social economics: one perspective', *Review of Social Economy*, **35**, 229–310.

Durlauf, Steven N. and H. Peyton Young (eds) (2001), *Social Dynamics: Economic Learning and Social Evolution*, London: MIT Press.

Ekins, Paul and Manfred Max-Neef (eds) (1992), *Real-Life Economics: Understanding Wealth Creation*, London: Routledge.

Etzioni, Amitai (1988), *The Moral Dimension: Toward a New Economics*, New York: Free Press.

Figart, Deborah M. (2004), *Living Wage Movements: Global Perspectives*, London: Routledge.

Figart, Deborah M., Ellen Mutari and Marilyn Power (2002), *Living Wages, Equal Wages: Gender and Labour Market Policies in the United States*, London: Routledge.

Finn, Daniel (2006), *The Moral Ecology of Markets: Assessing Claims About Markets and Justice*, New York and Cambridge: Cambridge University Press.

Golden, Lonnie and Deborah M. Figart (2000), *Working Time: International Trends, Theory, and Policy Perspectives*, London: Routledge.

Lutz, Mark (ed.) (1990a), *Social Economics: Retrospect and Prospect*, Boston/Dordrecht/London: Kluwer.

Lutz, Mark (1990b), 'Emphasizing the social: social economics and socio-economics', *Review of Social Economy*, **48** (3), 303–20.

Lutz, Mark (1999), *Economics for the Common Good: Two Centuries of Social Economic Thought in the Humanistic Tradition*, London: Routledge.

Lutz, Mark and Kenneth Lux (1988), *Humanistic Economics: The New Challenge*, New York: Bootstrap Press.

Nitsch, Thomas O. (1990), 'Social economics: the first 200 years', in M. Lutz (ed.), *Social Economics: Retrospect and Prospect*, Boston, MA/Dordrecht/London: Kluwer, pp. 5–80.

O'Boyle, Edward J. (1996), *Social Economics: Premises, Findings and Policies*, London: Routledge.

O'Boyle, Edward J. (2001), 'Personalist economics: unorthodox and counter-cultural', *Review of Social Economy*, **59** (4), 367–93.

O'Boyle, Edward J. (ed.) (2005), 'The best of the *Review of Social Economy*: 1944–1999', *Review of Social Economy*, **63** (3).

Samuels, Warren (1990), 'Four strands of social economics: a comparative interpretation', in M. Lutz (ed.), *Social Economics: Retrospect and Prospect*, Boston/Dordrecht/London: Kluwer, pp. 269, 288–98.

Samuels, Warren and Arthur S. Miller (1987), *Corporations and Society: Power and Responsibility*, New York: Greenwood Press.

Schumpeter, J.A. (1908–9), 'On the concept of social value', *Quarterly Journal of Economics*, **23**, 213–32.

Tomer, John (1999), *The Human Firm: A Socio-economic Analysis of it Behavior and Potential in a New Economic Age*, London: Routledge.

van Staveren, Irene (2001), *The Values of Economics: An Aristotelian Perspective*, London: Routledge.

Waters, William (1990), 'Evolution of social economics in America', in M. Lutz (ed.), *Social Economics: Retrospect and Prospect*, Boston/Dordrecht/London: Kluwer, ch. 2.

Waters, William (1993), 'A review of the troops: social economics in the twentieth century', *Review of Social Economy*, **51** (3), 262–86.

Wilber, Charles K. (ed.) (1998), *Economics, Ethics, and Public Policy*, Lanham, MD: Rowman & Littlefield.

Wilber, Charles K. (2004), 'Ethics and social economics', *Review of Social Economy*, **62** (4), 421–39.

PART I

SOCIAL CONCERNS IN ECONOMICS

Chapter 1: 'Environment and sustainability', by Jouni Paavola and Inge Røpke

This chapter reviews socio-economic research on the environment and sustainability. The chapter first briefly discusses the core elements of socio-economics, examines how socio-economics has related to the agenda of research on the environment, and assesses how socio-economic research on the environment has become institutionalized. Our contention is that the environment has not been high on the agenda of the core socio-economic research community but that there is, nevertheless, a substantial amount of socio-economic research on the environment in the ecological economics community and in other specialist settings. The chapter then examines two areas of environmental research where socio-economics plays a significant role: the research on institutional sources of environmental problems, and the research on monetary valuation and associated environmental decision-making. The chapter concludes that the admission of both ecological and social embeddedness constitutes a research agenda which could be called 'socio-ecological economics', and for which issues such as sustainable consumption and global environmental change will be important areas of research in the future.

Chapter 2: 'Institutions, culture and values', by Anne Mayhew

Changes in the meaning and importance of three key components of the discourse of social economics, 'institutions', 'culture' and 'values', led to disintegration of a pre-1940 consensus that underlay the strength of social economics within the larger discourse of the social sciences. Lack of confidence in older methods and meanings resulted both from the spread of deductive methods associated with neoclassical economics and from a new and more global socio-economic order. A new consensus based on earlier usage of these terms is required, but study of this new world order will require emphasis on active human agents, an emphasis that may make it difficult to give priority to the use of the tools of descriptive statistics, ethnographic enquiry and historical analysis that are the distinctive tools of social economics.

Chapter 3: 'Insecurity', by John Vail
The chapter highlights the crucial differences between insecurity and risk. To capture the full meanings associated with the term, insecurity is conceived of as three interrelated processes: a cognitive process, an emotional/psychological state of mind and a lived experience. The chapter then identifies four analytical categories by which insecurity can be explored. First, insecurity is generated as the result of the unintentional consequences of human agency. Second, insecurity is inextricably linked to power in society. Third, insecurity is socially constructed by economic, political and cultural forces. Fourth, insecurity may be embraced for its liberating and empowering effects in various aspects of social and political life.

Chapter 4: 'The ethical dimensions of the "globalization thesis" debate', by George DeMartino
This chapter explores the ethical implications of the debate over the 'globalization thesis' – the claim that the global economy today not only dictates economic flows and outcomes but also diminishes substantially the space available for meaningful local and national public policy initiatives. The chapter traces the historical development of the globalization thesis, and argues that it entails a commitment to ontological essentialism that yields methodological reductionism and, as a consequence of this progression, prescriptive rigidity. In this view, political strategies are seen to be dictated by a governing, disciplinary global economy. And this discipline evacuates the ethical space. Hence, how we theorize globalization has vital normative consequences. The chapter then turns to the capabilities framework of Amartya Sen to explore the possibilities for meaningful economic global policy reform. It concludes with suggestions for new avenues of research on globalization that draw equally on insights from socio-economic and post-structuralist economics.

1 Environment and sustainability
Jouni Paavola and Inge Røpke

1. Introduction

Environment and sustainability are issues where many concerns of social economics such as embeddedness, plural values and social justice are highly pertinent. Somewhat paradoxically, there has been relatively little research on the environment and sustainability in the core social economics research community. But this is not to say that social economic research on the environment and sustainability does not exist. The bulk of this research has been generated by scholars who identify themselves with ecological economics or political ecology, and has been published in a wide variety of outlets. Our chapter sets this scholarship in its broader social economic context and examines in some detail some of its core research strands.

In what follows, we will first briefly discuss how we understand social economics, how it has related to the emerging agenda of research on the environment, and how that research has become institutionalized. We will then examine in somewhat greater detail two areas of environmental research where social economics plays a significant role: the research on institutional sources of environmental problems, and the research on monetary valuation and associated environmental decision-making. We conclude the chapter with a brief assessment of the likely future agenda for social economic research on sustainability and the environment.

2. What do we mean by social economics?

Social economics is a more heterogeneous and less integrated academic enterprise than mainstream economics because its practitioners have found their intellectual homes from various heterodox economic traditions, from disciplines other than economics, and from various interdisciplinary research traditions such as ecological economics and political ecology. This means that 'social economics' may mean different things to its different practitioners. Nevertheless, there are some common denominators that most social economists share.

Perhaps most fundamentally, social economists do not see individuals as isolated agents that pursue solely their utility, as in mainstream economics. Social economists emphasize that individuals are interdependent and embedded in a multitude of social groups and networks (Davis, 2003, p. 120). For this reason, the behaviour of individuals is importantly

11

informed by moral concerns other than self-interested utility maximization (O'Boyle, 2005). Social economists also acknowledge that institutions play an important role in economic and social life.

For some social economists, it is the shared moral concerns that underlie and give rise to institutions in the society, while others see that their origin lies in conflicts and their resolution. The former view highlights that the economy and the institutions that constitute and underpin markets rest in part on moral foundations, just as Adam Smith argued in his *Theory of Moral Sentiments* (see Samuels, 1973). That is, markets function only to the extent that they are socially embedded and their operation is supported by morals such as honesty, trustworthiness and equity. The other way round, market and other institutions embody and operationalize particular values that give differential weight to different interests in the society (Samuels, 1977). For example, utilitarian values, which are often used to promote markets and other institutions emulating market logic, have no priority over other values, which may entail a different role and scope for markets. For social economists, the task is to make transparent the value basis of public policies and decisions, and to clarify their differential impacts on differently situated individuals and groups (Dugger, 1977; Samuels, 1977). In essence, equity and social justice are far more central to social economics than they are to mainstream economics.

These core common denominators of social economics are frequently accompanied by other features that social economists share. The emphasis on a broad range of values invites us to acknowledge their incommensurability and plurality (Wilber, 2004; see also Paavola, 2001). This in turn calls for the appreciation of conflicts of values and interests as a central and constructive feature of social and economic life. Conflicts facilitate the clarification of values and drive social change – which is frequently understood as an evolutionary process characterized by cumulative causation, path-dependency and lock-ins. Social economists also acknowledge that scholarship is always informed by values and cannot be value-free (Dugger, 1977).

In light of the most cited articles in *Review of Social Economy* since 1970, social economics has focused on crime, employment, income determination and distribution, financial markets and methodology. The environment and sustainability are not important empirical areas of social economic research despite their increasing social significance. Only a handful of articles (Georgescu-Roegen, 1977; Gowdy, 1981; Daly, 1985; Martinez-Alier, 1995) focusing on the environment are among the 50 most cited articles published in the *Review of Social Economy* after 1970. In what follows, we shall look more closely at the emergence of the environmental research agenda to clarify by whom, where and how the social economic research on the environment and sustainability is carried out.

3.   The environment on the agenda

The environment, as we today understand the term, appeared in the public discourse in the 1960s when Rachel Carson's *Silent Spring* (1962) brought up the alarming impact of pesticides and a social movement opposing nuclear fallout and waste disposal was born. Environmental movements emerged first in the USA and then in other industrialized countries, and the first steps towards the regulation of pollution were also taken. Concerns for the scarcity of resources increased in the 1960s and in the early 1970s because of population growth in developing countries and economic growth in the developed countries. Attention to the scarcity of resources increased particularly with the publication of *The Limits to Growth* (Meadows et al., 1972). Shortly afterwards, the first oil crisis focused the public's attention on energy.

The environment and energy have persisted on the political agenda since the 1970s, but their significance has varied from time to time. The first wave of interest in environmental issues subsided somewhat in the late 1970s, but a new upturn happened in the late 1980s when the *Brundtland Report* (WCED, 1987) increased interest in global environmental problems and popularized the concept of sustainability. This second wave of interest in environmental issues was characterized by the optimistic win–win perspective of ecological modernization (e.g. Cohen, 1997), and it lasted until the late 1990s when a backlash set in. Presently, in the early 2000s, the first signs of a third wave of interest in the environment, related in particular to climate change, are appearing.

The new environmental challenges invited social scientific responses, and several strands of research emerged in mainstream economics, for example. Research on the exploitation and intertemporal allocation of natural resources had existed since the emergence of land economics in the early twentieth century to address issues related to the use (and non-use) of agricultural and other land. Mainstream economics had relatively little to say about land use because it treated land as fully substitutable by man-made capital and considered all resources to be in full use. Land economics acknowledged the role of institutions and explored land-use decisions of practical and policy relevance empirically (see Salter, 1942). In the new situation of the 1960s, land economics had already moved closer to mainstream economics as a result of internal debates, and it expanded its area of research to encompass the newly emerging environmental issues (Castle, 1965).

A new strand of research on the recreational use of the natural environment also emerged in the 1960s (e.g. Clawson and Knetsch, 1963). The increased prominence of pollution in turn led to the revival of Pigou's externality concept and the emergence of environmental economics as the study of the economic system's allocative failures, and private property rights, environmental taxes and tradable permits as their potential remedies. These three strands of economics roughly correspond with the three roles that mainstream economics attributes to the environment: resources for production, assimilative capacity for absorbing pollution and waste, and direct utility from the enjoyment of environmental amenities. These three strands of environmental research are bound together by their shared welfare-economic theoretical framework.

Two distinct heterodox strategies also emerged in the area of environmental research. The first strategy focuses on the relationship between the economy and the environment, whereas the second examines the causation of environmental problems and possible remedies for them. The two strategies can be combined – and many scholars have indeed done so – but they do not have to be combined. The distinction has some bearing on the research programmes that have emerged and that are likely to emerge in the future.

The first strategy – based on the biophysical conception of the economy – was adopted by a small group of economists who were concerned about the scope of environmental problems. They first applied this conception to the economy in the 1960s (Ayres and Kneese, 1969; Boulding, 1966; Daly, 1968; Georgescu-Roegen, 1971). Their starting point was that the economy is embedded in the environment and that it is thus subject to physical laws such as the conservation of mass and increasing entropy. For them, this implied that the economy and economic activities can be studied not only in economic terms, but also in biophysical terms – as flows of energy and matter subject to entropy in a metabolic system.

The biophysical perspective importantly clarifies that externalities are not exceptional but pervasive and persistent characteristics, as production and consumption always generate waste. When the economy grows in physical terms and takes up more space in relation to the environment, the risk of serious environmental destruction increases. Ultimately, economic activities can threaten the life support systems on which human life and life in general depend. In principle, economic growth does not require physical growth: technological change and substitution of natural resources by man-made capital can reduce material intensity and thus the problematic impacts of economic growth on the environment. However, experience shows that this is far from sufficient. Human appropriation of the products of photosynthesis is estimated to have reached nearly 40 per cent of the terrestrial net primary production – the amount of energy left after subtracting the respiration of primary producers from the total amount of energy that is fixed biologically (Vitousek et al., 1986). Another study has found that the humanity now needs 1.3 Earths to sustain its consumption

(Wackernagel et al., 2002). The biophysical perspective also highlights an important ethical dilemma: distributional problems and the problem of population growth cannot be solved by economic growth only. The welfare-economic emphasis on efficient allocation has to be complemented by attention to scale and distribution (Daly, 1992).

Whereas the first heterodox research strategy emphasizes the embeddedness of the economy in the environment ('ecological embeddedness'), the second emphasizes the embeddedness of the economy in social and cultural institutions ('social embeddedness'). The latter social economic strategy is critical of the basic assumptions of welfare economics and tries to develop alternatives to conventional environmental and natural resource economics. Welfare economics concentrates on short-term, static explanations of environmental problems in narrow economic terms, such as the lack of private property rights and market failures at a given point in time, because of which environmental goods and bads are not priced. In contrast, the social economic perspective considers that environmental problems are constructed by irreversible and path-dependent historical processes where social, economic and cultural aspects are all relevant. These processes frequently involve conflicts (Martinez-Alier, 1995; Paavola, 2007), which are obscured by the welfare-economic focus on static efficiency and optimality. The implication of this is that the aims of environmental policies should not be construed narrowly in terms of economic efficiency only: effectiveness in delivering other goals such as environmental preservation and public health is also important, and so are procedural issues such as participation and conformance with the ideals of deliberative democracy. In essence, the social economic research strategy understands that the three pillars of sustainable development are ecological, economic and social sustainability. This means that environmental problems require much wider institutional responses than establishing private property rights and 'setting the prices right'.

4.   Institutionalization of social economic environmental studies

Social economics of environmental issues emerged in the late 1960s but for a while the contributors were few. The Association for Social Economics (ASE) and the Association for Evolutionary Economics (AFEE) had sessions on the environment in their conferences in the 1970s and 1980s, and their journals *Review of Social Economy* and *Journal of Economic Issues* published some papers on the environment. James Swaney (e.g. 1987, 1990) and Peter Söderbaum (e.g. 1982, 1987) were key scholars who kept the environment on the agenda in *Journal of Economic Issues*, and Douglas Booth (e.g. 1990, 1995) played a similar role in *Review of Social Economy*. *International Journal of Social Economics* has also published articles on the environment since the mid-1970s.

The second wave of interest in the environment in the late 1980s emerged at a time when several new academic associations dedicated to the environment were established. One of these was the International Society for Ecological Economics (ISEE), which adopted the biophysical perspective on the economy as a core tenet from the outset. The society was founded by scholars from systems ecology, energy modelling, biophysical economics and environmental economics – a heterogeneous group with a common perspective. Among the founders were also people such as Joan Martinez-Alier, who had a social economic background. In the years following the founding of the ISEE, the society attracted a large number of social economists, particularly in Europe (the development of modern ecological economics is outlined in Røpke, 2004, 2005).

In the 1990s, the heightened interest in the environment was reflected in many social economic associations and journals. In addition to those mentioned already, the European Association for Evolutionary Political Economy (EAEPE) and the Society for the Advancement of Socio-Economics (SASE) featured the environment at their conferences. Social economic study of environmental innovation took off and was published in journals such as *Research Policy* and *Futures*. New journals such as *Ecological Economics* and *Environmental Values* were also established. This process has continued in the recent past during the third wave of environmental interest with the emergence of further new journals such as the *International Journal of Green Economics*.

However, most social economists have concentrated on economic crises, unemployment, changes of capitalism, transition economies and globalization. The environment continued to be an issue of minor importance for them. This was one reason why social economists interested in the environment joined associations such as the ISEE and its regional societies, which were dedicated to the environment. As a result, the social economic associations struggled to maintain a critical mass of environmental research. It is illustrative that there were a number of contributions on the environment in *Review of Social Economy* in the mid-1990s, nearly all of them written by scholars from the ecological economics community. This suggests that although the environment does not have a high priority in social economics associations, their journals remain important publication outlets for social economic research on the environment.

It is noteworthy that social economic research on the environment is not strongly institutionalized in the ISEE despite the fact that many social economists have joined it. The ISEE is diverse and has a broad agenda, and social economic research easily disappears among studies of ecological or mainstream economic bent. But, fortunately, the environment remains alive in ASE and EAEPE as an issue of a lower profile. Thus it can be said that today social economic research on the environment takes place and appears in a wide variety of associations and publications – including those related to other special fields such as feminist economics, development studies, political ecology and innovation studies. However, it has not become institutionalized in any one core organization, nor is it published in any one main publication outlet. We will move on to discuss in greater detail two key substantive areas of social economic research on the environment.

5.   The causation of environmental problems

Social economic researchers are not satisfied with the neoclassical reasoning on the causation of environmental problems. They have presented both critiques as well as alternative approaches in several areas of research, but it is difficult to pinpoint a single, coherent social economic approach to environmental problems. In part for this reason, we will give several examples of social economic contributions on the causation of environmental problems.

K. William Kapp provided an early critique of the externality concept in the 1950s and developed his reasoning further in the following decades (Kapp, 1950, 1970; for overview, see Swaney and Evers, 1989). Kapp used the term social costs 'to refer to all those harmful consequences and damages which third persons or the community sustain as a result of the productive process, and for which private entrepreneurs are not easily held accountable' (Kapp, 1950, p. 14). This may appear similar to the conventional notion of externality, but Kapp used the term social costs to emphasize that they are systemic and pervasive, and not exceptional. Contrary to the neoclassical conception of exogenous institutional structures, Kapp argues that the market system creates new institutions and technologies which in turn give rise to social costs because in a market system firms have an incentive to reduce their costs at the expense of workers, the environment, or the community at large. This cost-shifting is made possible by unequal power relations and institutional structures, and these structures are reinforced by the cost-shifting. This is an instance of cumulative causation – a concept that Kapp adopted from Myrdal (Myrdal, 1957).

Kapp had little success in advancing his views although he tried to communicate with the neoclassical orthodoxy. However, his ideas are echoed in contemporary social economic work. For instance, a session was devoted to Kapp's legacy at the 2007 conference of the European Society for Ecological Economics (ESEE). Kapp's dialectical reasoning has much in common with Richard Norgaard's co-evolutionary perspective (Norgaard, 1994). Norgaard proposes a co-evolutionary approach to environmental history to explain how the environment co-evolves with social systems,

cultural beliefs and values, knowledge and technologies. The various entities of the overall system put selective pressure on the development of the
other entities, and the outcome of the selective processes is highly unpredictable. Norgaard also applies the co-evolutionary perspective to
processes that unfold in the shorter timeframe of decades, such as the co-
evolution of pests, pesticides, politics, policy, the pesticide industry and
integrated pest management. Norgaard's approach highlights the necessity
of a broad social and ecological perspective, and empirical studies of a long
timeframe to uncover how path-dependency shapes environmental problems. That is, for him, the static approach of neoclassical economics – considering externalities at a given point in time – has to be replaced by a
dynamic perspective.

A broad, historically sensitive social economic approach is also important for debates on the 'tragedy of the commons' (Hardin, 1968) and on the
conservation of biodiversity and natural resources more generally. The pioneering works of Bromley and Cernea (1989), Ostrom (1990) and Runge
(1986) brought up a general agreement that it is 'open access' to resources
that leads to their overexploitation, not their common ownership. Open
access resources are owned by nobody and are used on a 'first come, first
served' basis, so there is no incentive for anybody to restrain their use.
Mainstream economists usually consider privatization or the establishment
of private property rights to resources a solution. Social economists
emphasize that common property – under which the resource belongs to a
community which maintains institutional arrangements for their ownership and management in order to avoid overexploitation – is an alternative
to both open access and private property (Gowdy, 1994; Paavola, 2007;
Swaney, 1990; Tisdell, 1991). Paavola (2007) has also argued that many regulatory environmental policies and multilateral environmental agreements
can be understood as examples of collective ownership, which is not fundamentally different from common property.

Social economists have also demonstrated how many cases of overexploitation have been the result of the privatization of common property
resources. Joan Martinez-Alier (1991) refers to these as the 'tragedies of
the enclosure'. Privatization and the subsequent emergence of the market
economy disrupt social patterns that have customarily emphasized social
equity, and replace them with wide social disparities. Social economists
see that privatization and extension of markets are particularly devastat-
ing to local biological resources because they do not conform with the
assumptions of the neoclassical theory. Market decisions about these
resources do not take into account the co-evolution of different species,
the risk of destroying keystone species, the irreversibility of decisions, and
the agents' fundamental lack of information. For these reasons, social

control of markets is needed to prevent loss of biodiversity (Gowdy, 1994, ch. 4).

As indicated earlier in the chapter, ecological economists emphasize that environmental problems should not be seen only as problems of allocation, but first and foremost as problems of scale and distribution. When discussing the causation of environmental problems, they thus focus on the driving forces behind material growth and unequal power relations that enable the rich to increase their standard of living at the expense of the poor and the environment. An important research topic is, for instance, the unequal exchange between and within nations. Older Marxian theories of unequal exchange in terms of labour value have been replaced by theories conceptualizing exchange in terms of energy, materials and land. These studies demonstrate how transfers from developing countries are a precondition for increasing consumption in rich countries (Andersson and Lindroth, 2001; Giljum and Eisenmenger, 2004; Hornborg, 1998; Muradian and Martinez-Alier, 2001). Schor (2005) highlights how unequal power relations lie behind the provision of cheap apparel, fruit and other goods in the globalized economy.

Social economic studies of environmental disruption caused by production and consumption abandon the neoclassical assumptions of exogenous preferences and technology. For example, consumer demands are shaped by social, cultural and material structures, and changes that are endogenous to the socio-economic system – examples include competitive advertising and product development, changing labour market institutions, urban development, gender relations and so on (Røpke, 1999; Sachs, 1992; Schor, 1995). More sustainable consumption can hardly be achieved by relying on individual consumer choice without changing the social conditions for choice, and this requires collective decision-making (Paavola, 2001). In the same vein, technological change is embedded in and endogenous to the socio-economic system, and the development of more sustainable technologies requires regulatory intervention (Kemp and Rotmans, 2004). Recent studies on these issues build on Kapp's legacy and they also have much in common with Norgaard's co-evolutionary approach. However, scholars tend to relate more to the communities working with more specific and limited issues than the development of an overall social economic framework for environmental research.

6. Monetary valuation and environmental decision-making
Monetary valuation of the environment is perhaps the largest area of research in mainstream environmental economics in terms of the number of published articles. In part for this reason, it is an equally important area of work for those who do not adhere to this research strategy. For

mainstream environmental economics, the purpose of monetary valuation of the environment is to determine empirical demand curves for non-marketed environmental goods and bads, so that the contribution of changes in their quality or quantity to consumer surplus and social welfare can be determined empirically. The rationale of this is in turn provided by the normative view that the environment should be protected if and only to the extent that it is economically efficient to do so: that is, as long as environmental protection measures improve social welfare and do not detract from it. This view ties monetary valuation of the environment intimately to cost–benefit analysis (CBA) as a supplier of benefit and cost information.

Social economic research on environmental valuation and decision-making has several strands. The first of these has sought to establish the inconsistency and invalidity of the premises of and arguments for monetary valuation in mainstream environmental economics. The second strand of research has sought to justify, develop and apply deliberative and participatory processes as procedural alternatives to CBA for environmental decision-making. The third strand of research has developed several variants of multi-criteria analysis (MCA) for use as alternatives to CBA in environmental decision-making. In what follows, each of these strands of literature will be discussed and outlined in some detail.

There are several possible starting points for criticism of monetary valuation of the environment. One of them is the denial of the commensurability of agents' values and goals. The assumption of full commensurability is central to mainstream environmental economics: it establishes utility as the common denominator for the satisfaction of different preferences. Although preference utilitarianism embraces ordinalist notion of utility, in cost–benefit analysis money is used as a proxy for utility – a practice that transforms an ordinal conception to a cardinal one. As a result, all choice situations are understood to be instances of utility maximization and further satisfaction of environmental preferences entails having to trade off satisfaction of some other preferences, such as those for ordinary consumer goods. In the light of this assumption, the effect of satisfying environmental preferences can be measured in terms of utility changes and ultimately in pecuniary terms. Moreover, the utilitarian underpinnings of mainstream economic analysis suggest that the effect ought to be measured, so that its welfare contribution and thus desirability can be verified.

Social economists disagree with the commensurability assumption, arguing that values and goals are incommensurable and are only weakly comparable (Martinez-Alier et al., 1998; Paavola and Adger, 2005). Weak comparability means that agents can compare and rank alternatives and choose between them, but that there is no algorithmic method for doing so in an optimizing way. In essence, different decisions belong to different domains where different rationalities prevail (Vatn, 2005), and some of these rationalities do not support optimization or maximization. In this light, issues such as consumption and the environment could be considered to belong to different spheres of rationality, between which calculated trade-offs are not made (Vatn, 2000).

Another line of criticism, informed by institutional economics in particular, has focused on the absent rationale for attributing monetary value to environmental change. Building on the works of Schmid (1967), Samuels (1972) and Bromley (1989), social economists have argued that cost–benefit analysis compares situations characterized by different sets of property rights. For example, a cost–benefit analysis of mitigating the emissions of greenhouse gases compares the *status quo* set of property rights to a hypothetical situation where rights to emit greenhouse gases have been curtailed. The two situations generate different price vectors because property rights – the claims to income streams – differ. Both situations may and are indeed likely to generate Pareto-optimal equilibria and allocative outcomes, but they remain incomparable because of their different assignments of initial entitlements and distributions of income and wealth (Vatn and Bromley, 1994). This is typical of all environmental policy choices: they are not questions of efficiency but rather those of distribution and equity. Therefore, monetary valuation of changes in the quantity and quality of the environment cannot provide guidance for decisions on them.

The reasoning on choices between alternative entitlement structures can also be extended directly to monetary valuation. Willingness to pay (WTP) or willingness to accept compensation (WTA) determinations, on which all monetary valuation methods are either implicitly or explicitly based, entail different hypothetical assignments of property rights which both deviate from the *status quo*, and would entail different price vectors. For this reason, the meaning and indeed the usefulness of results of monetary valuation research remain ambiguous (Vatn and Bromley, 1994). To sum it up, for social economists, monetary valuation of the environment is based on shaky foundations and it cannot provide the guidance it is purported to give (Spash, 2000).

The second strand of research in social economics on environmental valuation and decision-making has examined democratic and participatory processes as alternatives to cost–benefit analysis (see Gregory and Wellman, 2001; van den Hove, 2000; Wilson and Howarth, 2002). This research is informed by a view according to which public environmental decisions are ultimately about what values ought to be decisive, and according to which such decisions are not and cannot be based on pre-existing preferences for different values (see Sagoff, 1998). In essence, the process of environmental decision-making is a process of learning, value clarification and preference formation. In pluralist democracies, such processes are best organized on the basis of public participation because this solution ensures the identification of the best reasons and justifications for the chosen courses of action (see Bromley and Paavola, 2002; Bromley, 2006). Different forms and strategies of participation are examined in the literature, citizens' juries being the most common solution. Perhaps the most interesting cases are the ones where conventional economic studies and participation studies take place in the same setting in parallel or sequentially (see Clark et al., 2000; Kenyon and Nevin, 2001).

The third strand of research has developed multi-criteria analysis (MCA) as an alternative to cost–benefit analysis (CBA) (see Munda, 2004). The literature developing or using MCA is broad, ranging from studies that are quite close to the CBA literature in spirit to others which approach the spirit of the literature on public participation. The more conventional takes on the MCA can be based, for example, on Herbert Simon's arguments on satisficing behaviour (Simon 1955, 1986). For Simon (1955, p. 109), agents may have multiple goals which they seek to satisfy, rather than maximize (see also Paavola and Adger, 2005). In this sense, MCA could be seen as implementing an alternative, multi-goal view of choice behaviour, while otherwise retaining the algorithmic and aggregating strategy of the CBA. In MCA, the performance of alternatives to be compared is just measured in terms of a number of performance criteria. Ranking of alternatives can then proceed either by attributing weights to the indicators for commensuration and aggregation (see, e.g., Joubert et al., 1997), or by using dominance comparisons and ranking across the non-commensurated performance measures (see Gamboa and Munda, 2007).

The other end of the spectrum in the literature on MCA is more in line with the key concerns of social economics, and in particular with the literature on public participation. Participatory MCA can involve key interested or affected groups in the identification and development of alternatives, identification of key performance criteria, measurement of the performance of alternatives, or/and in the ranking of alternatives on the basis of measured performance (see, e.g., Cook and Proctor, 2007). Participatory MCA is often used to provide a science/policy interface between scholars and those vested with a decision-making authority over the addressed issue (van den Hove, 2000, 2007). The science/public interfacing is attempted less often. However, when a broad range of affected and interested parties are involved (see Clark et al., 2000; Dougill et al., 2006), the distinction between science/policy and science/public interfaces becomes blurred and the participatory MCA becomes transformed into a broader participatory or action research strategy.

7. Conclusions: towards socio-ecological economics?

Our assessment of the past social economic research on the environment is that it points towards a new programme of research that we prefer to call 'socio-ecological economics' (see also Jacobs, 1996). This programme of research encompasses both of the broad heterodox research strategies: the one based on the biophysical conception of the economy, and the one seeking a refined and nuanced understanding of the causes of environmental problems which is sensitive to issues of power, conflict and institutions. We do not expect all future research to embrace the whole width of the research agenda which recognizes both ecological and social embeddedness, although some of the research will no doubt do so. The tensions between the different emphases within the dual embeddedness strategy can be seen as a potential source of vitality for the research (see Norgaard, 1989).

The research agenda of socio-ecological economics has potentially a wide applicability to contemporary environmental problems. We see that there are two areas of research in particular which are likely to be important for social economists in the future. On one hand, sustainable consumption is emerging as an area of research where conventional notions of consumer sovereignty are increasingly challenged, and there is a significant policy-driven need to understand consumer behaviour in a far more nuanced way in its everyday context. This is increasingly important as it will be difficult to resolve global environmental problems such as climate change and the loss of biodiversity without changes in the scale and patterns of consumption. Here social economists can make a real contribution, for example by focusing on the systems of provision and the way in which they constrain and facilitate individual choice far beyond what is acknowledged in the mainstream models of consumer behaviour (see, e.g., Seyfang and Paavola, 2008). This is an example of research where the institutional and political economic sources of environmental problems are highlighted.

On the other hand, there will be plenty of scope for research which makes use of the biophysical understanding of the links between the economy and the environment. This model can provide the basis for integrating and mobilizing concepts such as physical limits, social justice and constrained economic optimization to make better sense of issues of emerging importance such as climate change. From this viewpoint, global atmospheric sinks, just like many other environmental resources, have uncertain but clearly limited physical capacity to deliver services (Paavola, 2008). Their sustainable management as global commons will call for consideration of justice in the use of these sinks, and both adherence to physical limits and attainment of justice will ultimately be a matter of crafting and enforcing a set of appropriate institutional arrangements for the purpose.

References

Andersson, J.O. and M. Lindroth (2001), 'Ecologically unsustainable trade', *Ecological Economics*, **37**, 113–22.
Ayres, R.U. and A.V. Kneese (1969), 'Production, consumption and externalities', *The American Economic Review*, **59**, 282–97.
Booth, D.E. (1990), 'In defense of the land ethic and respect for nature', *Review of Social Economy*, **48**, 84–96.
Booth, D.E. (1995), 'Economic growth and the limits of environmental regulation: a social economic analysis', *Review of Social Economy*, **53**, 553–73.
Boulding, K.E. (1966), 'The economics of the coming Spaceship Earth', in H. Jarrett (ed.), *Environmental Quality in a Growing Economy*, Baltimore, MD: Resources for the Future /Johns Hopkins University Press, pp. 3–14.
Bromley, D.W. (1989), *Economic Interests and Institutions: The Conceptual Foundations of Public Policy*, Oxford: Blackwell.
Bromley, D.W. (2006), *Sufficient Reason: Volitional Pragmatism and the Meaning of Economic Institutions*, Princeton, NJ: Princeton University Press.
Bromley, D.W. and M.M. Cernea (1989), 'The management of common property natural resources: some conceptual and operational fallacies', World Bank Discussion Paper 57, World Bank, Washington, DC.
Bromley, D.W. and J. Paavola (2002), 'Economics, ethics and environmental policy', in D.W. Bromley and J. Paavola (eds), *Economics, Ethics, and Environmental Policy: Contested Choices*, Malden, MA: Blackwell, pp. 261–76.
Carson, R. (1962), *Silent Spring*, Boston and New York: Houghton Mifflin.
Castle, E.N. (1965), 'The market mechanism, externalities and land economics', *Journal of Farm Economics*, **47**, 542–56.
Clark, J., J. Burgess and C.M. Harrison (2000), ' "I struggled with this money business": respondents' perspectives on contingent valuation', *Ecological Economics*, **33**, 45–62.
Clawson, M. and J. Knetsch (1963), 'Outdoor recreation research: some concepts and suggested areas of study', *Natural Resources Journal*, **3** (2), 250–75.
Cohen, M.J. (1997), 'Risk society and ecological modernization: alternative visions for post-industrial nations', *Futures*, **29** (2), 105–19.
Cook, D. and W. Proctor (2007), 'Assessing the threat of exotic plant pests', *Ecological Economics*, **63**, 594–604.
Daly, H.E. (1968), 'On economics as a life science', *Journal of Political Economy*, **76**, 392–406.
Daly, H.E. (1985), 'The circular flow of exchange value and the linear throughput of matter-energy – a case of misplaced concreteness', *Review of Social Economy*, **43**, 279–97.
Daly, H.E. (1992), 'Allocation, distribution, and scale: towards an economics that is efficient, just, and sustainable', *Ecological Economics*, **6**, 185–93.
Davis, J.B. (2003), *The Theory of the Individual in Economics: Identity and Value*, London and New York: Routledge.
Dougill, A.J., E.D.G. Fraser, J. Holden, K. Hubacek, C. Prell, M.S. Reed, S. Stagl and L.C. Stringer (2006), 'Learning from doing participatory rural research: lessons from the Peak District National Park', *Journal of Agricultural Economics*, **57**, 259–75.
Dugger, W.M. (1977), 'Social economics: one perspective', *Review of Social Economy*, **35**, 299–310.
Gamboa, G. and G. Munda (2007), 'The problem of windfarm location: a social multi-criteria evaluation framework', *Energy Policy*, **35**, 1564–83.
Georgescu-Roegen, N. (1971), *The Entropy Law and the Economic Process*, Cambridge, MA: Harvard University Press.
Georgescu-Roegen, N. (1977), 'Inequality, limits and growth from a bio-economic viewpoint', *Review of Social Economy*, **35**, 361–75.
Giljum, S. and N. Eisenmenger (2004), 'North–South trade and the distribution of environmental goods and burdens: a biophysical perspective', *Journal of Environment and Development*, **13**, 73–100.

Gowdy, J.M. (1981), 'Radical economics and resource scarcity', *Review of Social Economy*, **39**, 165–80.

Gowdy, J.M. (1994), *Coevolutionary Economics: The Economy, Society and the Environment*, Dordrecht: Kluwer Academic Publishers.

Gregory, R. and K. Wellman (2001), 'Bringing stakeholder values into environmental policy choices: a community-based estuary case study', *Ecological Economics*, **39**, 37–52.

Hardin, G. (1968), 'The tragedy of the commons', *Science*, **162**, 1243–8.

Hornborg, A. (1998), 'Towards an ecological theory of unequal exchange: articulating world system theory and ecological economics', *Ecological Economics*, **25**, 127–36.

Jacobs, M. (1996), 'What is socio-ecological economics?', *Ecological Economics Bulletin*, **1**, 14–16.

Joubert, A.R., A. Leiman, H.M. deKlerk et al. (1997), 'Fynbos (fine bush) vegetation and the supply of water: a comparison of multi-criteria decision analysis and cost–benefit analysis', *Ecological Economics*, **22**, 123–40.

Kapp, K.W. (1950), *The Social Costs of Private Enterprise*, New York: Schocken Books.

Kapp, K.W. (1970), 'Environmental disruption and social costs: a challenge to economics', *Kyklos*, **23**, 833–48.

Kemp, R. and J. Rotmans (2004), 'Managing transition to sustainable mobility', in B. Elzen, F.W. Geels and K. Green (eds), *System Innovation and the Transition to Sustainability: Theory, Evidence and Policy*, Cheltenham, UK and Northampton, MA, USA: Edward Elgar, pp. 137–67.

Kenyon, W. and C. Nevin (2001), 'The use of economic and participatory approaches to assess forest development: a case study in the Ettrick Valley', *Forest Policy and Economics*, **3**, 69–80.

Martinez-Alier, J. (1991), 'Ecology and the poor: a neglected dimension of Latin American history', *Journal of Latin American Studies*, **23**, 621–39.

Martinez-Alier, J. (1995), 'Distributional issues in ecological economics', *Review of Social Economy*, **53**, 511–28.

Martinez-Alier, J., G. Munda and J. O'Neill (1998), 'Weak comparability of values as a foundation for ecological economics', *Ecological Economics*, **26**, 277–86.

Meadows, D.H., D.L. Meadows, J. Randers and W.W. Behrens III (1972), *The Limits to Growth: A Report for the Club of Rome's Project on the Predicament of Mankind*, New York: Universe Books.

Munda, G. (2004), 'Social multi-criteria evaluation: methodological foundations and operational consequences', *European Journal of Operational Research*, **158**, 662–77.

Muradian, R. and J. Martinez-Alier (2001), 'Trade and the environment: from a "Southern" perspective', *Ecological Economics*, **36**, 281–97.

Myrdal, G. (1957), *Economic Theory and Underdeveloped Regions*, London: Gerald Duckworth & Co.

Norgaard, R.B. (1989), 'The case for methodological pluralism', *Ecological Economics*, **1**, 37–57.

Norgaard, R.B. (1994), *Development Betrayed: The End of Progress and a Coevolutionary Revisioning of the Future*, London and New York: Routledge.

O'Boyle, E.J. (2005), 'Homo socio-economicus: foundational to social economics and the social economy', *Review of Social Economy*, **63**, 483–507.

Ostrom, E. (1990), *Governing the Commons: The Evolution of Institutions for Collective Action*, Cambridge: Cambridge University Press.

Paavola, J. (2001), 'Towards sustainable consumption? Economics and ethical concerns for the environment in consumer choices', *Review of Social Economy*, **59**, 227–48.

Paavola, J. (2007), 'Institutions and environmental governance: a reconceptualization', *Ecological Economics*, **63**, 93–103.

Paavola, J. (2008), 'Governing atmospheric sinks: the architecture of entitlements in the global commons', *International Journal of the Commons*, **2**, in press.

Paavola, J. and W.N. Adger (2005), 'Institutional ecological economics', *Ecological Economics*, **53**, 353–68.

Røpke, I. (1999), 'The dynamics of willingness to consume', *Ecological Economics*, **28**, 399–420.

Røpke, I. (2004), 'The early history of modern ecological economics', *Ecological Economics*, **50**, 293–314.

Røpke, I. (2005), 'Trends in the development of ecological economics from the late 1980s to the early 2000s', *Ecological Economics*, **55**, 262–90.

Runge, C.F. (1986), 'Common property and collective action in economic development', *World Development*, **14**, 623–35.

Sachs, W. (1992), *For Love of the Automobile: Looking Back into the History of Our Desires*, Berkeley, CA: University of California Press.

Sagoff, M. (1998), 'Aggregation and deliberation in valuing environmental public goods: a look beyond contingent pricing', *Ecological Economics*, **24**, 213–30.

Salter Jr, L.A. (1942), 'The content of land economics and research methods adapted to its needs', *Journal of Farm Economics*, **24** (1), 226–47.

Samuels, W.J. (1972), 'Welfare economics, power, and property', in G. Wunderlich and W.L. Gibson Jr (eds), *Perspectives of Property*, University Park, PA: Institute for Research on Land and Water Resources, Pennsylvania State University, pp. 61–148.

Samuels, W. (1973), 'Adam Smith and the economy as a system of power', *Review of Social Economy*, **31**, 123–37.

Samuels, W. (1977), 'Reflections on social economics in a diverse and open economics', *Review of Social Economy*, **35**, 113–33.

Schmid, A.A. (1967), 'Nonmarket values and efficiency of public investments in water resources', *American Economic Review, Papers & Proceedings*, **57**, 158–68.

Schor, J. (1995), 'Can the North stop consumption growth? Escaping the cycle of work and spend', in V. Bhaskar and A. Glyn (eds), *The North, the South and the Environment*, London: Earthscan, pp. 68–84.

Schor, J. (2005), 'Prices and quantities: unsustainable consumption and the global economy', *Ecological Economics*, **55**, 309–20.

Seyfang, G. and J. Paavola (2008), 'Inequality and sustainable consumption: bridging the gaps', *Local Environment*, in press.

Simon, H.A. (1955), 'A behavioral model of rational choice', *Quarterly Journal of Economics*, **69**, 99–118.

Simon, H.A. (1986), 'Rationality in psychology and economics', *Journal of Business*, **59**, S209–S224.

Söderbaum P. (1982), 'Positional analysis and public decision-making', *Journal of Economic Issues*, **16** (2), 391–400.

Söderbaum, P. (1987), 'Environmental management: a nontraditional approach', *Journal of Economic Issues*, **21** (1), 139–65.

Spash, C.L. (2000), 'Ecosystems, contingent valuation and ethics: the case of wetland re-creation', *Ecological Economics*, **34**, 195–215.

Swaney, J.A. (1987), 'Elements of a neoinstitutional environmental economics', *Journal of Economic Issues*, **21** (4), 1739–79.

Swaney, J.A. (1990), 'Common property, reciprocity, and community', *Journal of Economic Issues*, **24**, 451–62.

Swaney, J.A. and M.A. Evers (1989), 'The social cost concepts of K. William Kapp and Karl Polanyi', *Journal of Economic Issues*, **23**, 7–33.

Tisdell, C.A. (1991), *Economics of Environmental Conservation*, New York: Elsevier.

van den Hove, S. (2000), 'Participatory approaches to environmental policy-making: the European Commission Climate Policy Process as a case study', *Ecological Economics*, **33**, 457–72.

van den Hove, S. (2007), 'A rationale for science–policy interfaces', *Futures*, **39**, 807–26.

Vatn, A. (2000), 'The environment as a commodity', *Environmental Values*, **9**, 493–509.

Vatn, A. (2005), 'Rationality, institutions and environmental policy', *Ecological Economics*, **55** (2), 203–17.

Vatn, A. and D.W. Bromley (1994), 'Choices without prices without apologies', *Journal of Environmental Economics and Management*, **26**, 129–48.

Vitousek, P.M., P.R. Erlich, A.H. Erlich and P.A. Matson (1986), 'Human appropriation of the products of photosynthesis', *BioScience*, **36** (6), 368–73.

Wackernagel, M., N.B. Schulz, D. Deumling et al. (2002), 'Tracking the ecological overshoot of the human economy', *Proceedings of the National Academy of Sciences of the United States of America*, **99** (14), 9266–71.

Wilber, C.K. (2004), 'Ethics and social economics: ASE presidential address, January 2004, San Diego, California', *Review of Social Economy*, **63**, 426–39.

Wilson, M.A. and R.B. Howarth (2002), 'Discourse-based valuation of ecosystem services: establishing fair outcomes through group deliberation', *Ecological Economics*, **41**, 431–43.

World Commission on Environment and Development (WCED) (1987), *Our Common Future*, Oxford: Oxford University Press.

2 Institutions, culture and values
Anne Mayhew

'Institutions', 'culture' and 'values' have, for more than a century, been key components of the discourse of the social sciences and of social economics. However, what is more interesting than continuity of usage are the great differences in the meaning and importance of the terms within a changing set of sub-discourses. These differences and their evolution will be the focus of this chapter.

Across all of the scholarly discussions that I will describe below there is, and has been, a general understanding that institutions are social norms or patterns of action (behavior) and associated *emic* (which is to say native as opposed to analytical) understandings that vary across time and space.[1] It is also generally agreed that cultures are conglomerations of institutions that are shared by a group of people. Values are aspects of cultures and of institutional patterns.

From roughly 1870 to 1940, as the social sciences took their modern and academically organized form, institutions, cultures and values were defined primarily by methods of study. Working definitions were sufficient given wide consensus about what it was right and important to do as social scientists. In the decades from 1940 until the end of the twentieth century, as this consensus disintegrated, more attention was given to formal definition of the key terms. Given a lack of disciplinary confidence in method, it seemed more important to say what it was that was being studied. In the first decade of the twenty-first century, neither methodological nor definitional consensus has been re-established.

Early use[2]
Modern social science was born at the end of the nineteenth century, the product of dramatic social change stemming from, among other things, the Industrial Revolution, increased commercialization of Western societies, a coalescence of general ideas about evolution and social change, increases in knowledge of variation among human societies, and a widespread commitment to social economic reform. Among academics as well as among non-academic writers and public intellectuals, the organization of human activity was increasingly seen as a consequence of time and place, and of individual human agency within the context of time and place. Older notions of social change as a consequence of individual reason and/or the

unfolding of a fixed scheme of human evolution were replaced by the view that change was contingent and subject to direction through deliberate human action. This understanding was 'Darwinian' in spirit, if not in any actual methodological or definitional detail, and was also crucial to the progressive movement in the USA, as well as to the Fabian Socialists in the UK, and other reform movements of the late nineteenth and early twentieth centuries.[3] The overarching questions were how to describe and discuss *societies*, explain change, understand continuity of systems, and how to direct and/or control both change and continuity.

In order to talk about variation among societies, both across time and across geography, the concepts of 'institutions' and 'culture' were crucial. As social scientists abandoned racial theories, polygenism (multiple human origins), unilinear evolution and pure geographic explanations of observed human variation, the explanatory gap that resulted was filled by the idea of culture, and of mores, folkways and institutions as aspects of culture. The term 'institutions' was used primarily among those economists who, following the lead of Walton Hamilton and J.M. Clark, identified their field of study as 'institutional economics' and 'social economics' (Clark, 1919; Hamilton, 1919). In so doing, neither Hamilton nor Clark nor Wesley Mitchell, also a leading practitioner of institutional economics, gave any clear definition of their eponymous term.[4] In fact, Mitchell wrote that 'institutions' is 'merely a convenient term for the more important among the widely prevalent, highly standardized social habits' (Mitchell, 1924, p. 25). Neither Thorstein Veblen, nor John R. Commons, the widely acknowledged elders of the school of institutionalism, nor any of the other economists of the time who subscribed to the approach, would have argued with Mitchell or with his casual use of the term.

Part of the binding core of the social economic/institutional approach lay, if not in agreement on definition of key terms, in a dedication to critical assessment of the existing order. There was no consensus about the precise shape that a better society and economy would take, but there was consensus that what was, was not the best that could be. The institutionalists, who were the majority of social economists of the interwar period and arguably the majority of US economists as well, took as their responsibility the production of analysis that would be as impartial as possible, but also critical in aid of reform.[5]

Even more important to the strength and cohesion of social economics during this period was common emphasis on, and enthusiasm for, what were widely understood to be the scientific methods of study that would produce impartial analysis, and specifically enthusiasm for the use of descriptive statistics and ethnography or fieldwork. In the same 1923 article in which Mitchell says that 'institutions' was merely a term of convenience, he stressed that it was a 'behavioristic viewpoint' that would 'make economics theory more and more a study of economic institutions' (Mitchell, 1924, p. 25). Mitchell went on to say

> Of course it is mass behavior which the economist studies. Hence the institutions which standardize the behavior of men create most of the openings for valid generalizations. That was true even in Ricardian economics, when the generalizations were made by the treacherous method of reasoning on the basis of imputed economic motives. A much more dependable set of generalizations can be attained as rapidly as objective records of mass behavior become available for analysis. The extension and improvement of statistical compilations is therefore a factor of the first consequence for the progress of economic theory. (Ibid., p. 27)[6]

Of great importance to other social economists was immersion in economic problems via combinations of fieldwork and statistical study.[7] The statistical sources provided today by government bureaux at both the state and federal levels most often originated in the work of the early social economists. But they did more than collect statistics. By contrast to much of the econometric work that characterizes economics today, their work was *emic* rather than *etic*, meaning that the organization of the statistics was derived from the standpoint of those whose activities were being described. Modern econometric studies designed to show the economic rationality of statistically described behavior are *etic* in that analysis is done to show how the statistical series fit categories and expected relationships derived from the standpoint of the analyst. For the social economists of the pre-World War II era, the task was to describe what the participants thought they were doing.

In sociology and in anthropology, and to a lesser extent in political science, there was similar emphasis on *emic* analysis and on fieldwork, and the boundaries between disciplines were sometimes difficult to draw. What did distinguish anthropology from the other disciplines was the emphasis on study of cultures. As with social economists and their casual use of the term 'institutions', anthropologists developed a concept of culture out of the work that they did. The anthropological concept of culture during the early part of the twentieth century was not the older, humanistic notion of the consequences and artifacts of artistic human creativity, but rather the totality of learned behavior of a group of people. A culture was what was described by an anthropologist who undertook the classic year of study of a relatively isolated group of people. The social economists of the early twentieth century had little need to use the concept of culture for they studied parts, not wholes, and the same was largely true for sociologists who focused on studies of their own Western societies.

Although the terms varied across the social sciences and did so in part with variation of assumed disciplinary tasks, it was reasonably clear to all who were engaged in the social science enterprise through the 1930s that the concepts of institutions, mores, folkways, customs, habits and cultures were part of a way of doing social science that held great promise for both understanding and for control of man's fate. World War II, with its multiple causes and consequences, marks the beginning of the end of this consensus.

World War II and its aftermath
Although it is easy enough to find tension in the consensus that had made social economics, and the social sciences in general, a relatively unified and exciting endeavor in the prewar era, there can be little doubt that the domestic and international policy that followed World War II greatly aggravated old tensions and created new ones. In the academic discipline of economics, and particularly in the increasingly hegemonic USA, there was a retreat from the progressive reformism of the prewar period in favor of 'macro' policies of stabilization (Barber, 1985; Mayhew, 1998; Morgan and Rutherford, 1998). In both sociology and anthropology there were increasing doubts about the usefulness of the older concept of culture.[8] Finally, social science as a whole was rocked by a growing emphasis on individuals, rather than society or culture, and its parts, as the locus of explanation and policy.

However, and somewhat oddly, given the way in which things developed through the 1960s and 1970s, the most immediate and obvious aftermath of the war was largely promising for social economics and institutional economists, and for all who hoped for even greater collaboration among social scientists. With increased emphasis placed upon 'economic development', particularly in newly independent nations, there was funding, both private and governmental, for study of economic processes outside of the Western world. Many of those who had been trained in the prewar traditions of social economics became 'development economists' (Neale, 1990; Rosen, 2005). Because the areas studied were those that had been the traditional domain of anthropology, anthropologists were often part of the funded programs.

It was out of this alliance of interests that the concept of values re-emerged as important in the discourse of social economics. During the prewar period there was relatively little mention of 'values', a term that appears to have been associated primarily with the theory of price to which the social economists gave only minor explanatory importance (Clark, 1919; Mitchell, 1924).[9] However, when economic development became one of the most attractive subfields in economics, attracting social economists and the neoclassically trained to funding opportunities and urgent issues, many of the economists were uncomfortable with the methods of social economics that had worked well in study of domestic problems in the prewar period. Statistics were hard to come by, the 'fields' for fieldwork were difficult ones in which to work, and there was pressure for quick answers to policy questions at the 'macro' level (Neale, 1990). The discourse that emerged was one in which the unexpected or perverse outcomes of development projects, usually financed and managed by Westerners, were explained as a consequence of different 'values', where 'values' were deduced rather than directly observed (a point to which I shall return below). This usage allowed communication between those trained in social economics and the other social scientists *and* neoclassical economists because the values could be seen as aspects of institutions/cultures, but they could also be seen by the neoclassically inclined as part of a maximization/minimization process of choice.[10]

Even as debates and discussions about development economics, and the way in which different values characterized different societies, became important, other issues emerged in social economics. One issue that had been around for a long time but had lain largely dormant was the relationship of institutions, culture and human agency. What was the role of 'free will' in the determination of social economic patterns? The issue had occasionally popped up in the earlier period as, for example, in John R. Commons's concern that Thorstein Veblen's conception of 'Darwinian evolution' precluded human agency in aid of reform (Commons, 1934, p. 637). In anthropology and sociology there had been efforts to enhance the role of human agency in theory if not in description (Firth, 1939; Goodfellow, 1939). However, it was not until the 1950s that there was widespread concern that individuals had been left out of social science. With this concern came an increasing assault on the very concepts of institutions and culture as they had developed in prewar social science.

Anthropologists and sociologists had begun to worry that by focusing on cultures and norms, variation among individuals was ignored and, further, and even more damning, that the older focus had been insulting 'in the view that people pattern their lives habitually and unthinkingly in the received wisdom of their elders' (Pelto and Pelto, 1975, p. 1). At least for a time during the 1960s and 1970s, there was considerable interest in the promise that a resurgent neoclassicism in economics held as a solution to this problem. Among economic anthropologists, some sociologists, and especially among a number of political scientists, the rational individual of neoclassical economics, with his/her ability to operate with a numeraire and a well-defined set of priorities across all aspects of life came to be the most prized model of all mankind. Among anthropologists and sociologists, the allure of the economists' individual *homo economicus* gradually faded, at least in practice, if not in high theory, but not so in the field of economics (Mayhew, 1980; Graeber, 2005). For complex reasons, an explanation of which lies well beyond the scope of this chapter, neoclassical economics was indeed successfully resurgent in economics. The kind of work that had been done by social economists in the prewar period, the collection and management of statistics in particular, passed to government agencies or was treated as conceptually complete and no longer of great or rewarding interest, especially as abstract theory came to be more highly prized. As the discipline of economics turned ever more inward and secure in its presumed superiority over the other social sciences, the impact, particularly in combination with government assumption of responsibility for the collection of descriptive statistics, had a profound impact upon social economics. No longer were students who entered graduate training in economics well trained in the other social sciences, and no longer did they receive such training as part of their graduate work. As has been documented many times over, the requirement for and the substance of graduate work was mathematics. Given that social economics had rested heavily upon method which, though quantitative, was not mathematical, the roots of the social economic tradition were considerably weakened. The concept of institutions, and even more so cultures, faded from the discourse of economics, and social economics became increasingly marginalized.

One reaction within the institutionalist tradition was a turning inward with more attention given to definitional matters, but also to the grounds for competition with the now reigning orthodoxy of neoclassical economics in its various manifestations.[11] Concern with definition was given particular shape by the success that advocates of orthodox, neoclassical economic thought had had in laying claim to a universal template for economic efficiency and goodness. During the heyday of social economics, there had been a general, though not always explicit, consensus about the economic good. In the postwar period this consensus gradually evaporated. A loss of faith in technology and science, globalization, recognition of conflicts of interest between generations, concern with environmental sustainability and many other issues made the questions of what constituted progress more difficult. Neoclassical economists offered a model in which market processes (widely conceived to be a more general equivalent of the political processes of Western democracy) could lead to a 'best possible' answer. But what did social economics have to offer?

There had long been a strand of thought among institutionalists that said that 'institutions', because they were habituations or inherited norms, inhibited the progress that could arise for mankind through ever more effective manipulation of the natural environment. Thorstein Veblen had proposed a duality among all humans: a tendency to behave in habitual manner in all aspects of life (workmanship, parenting and emulation, to name three areas that he thought important), but at the same time to be idly curious, particularly in manipulation of the natural world. In Veblen's view it was idle curiosity that drove changes in the way that humans interacted with the natural world, changes that led to alterations in other aspects of human life as well. Habitual behavior was institutionalized behavior; the fruits of idle curiosity led to a continuum of change through learning about nature. Although Veblen remained convinced that change was contingent, with human progress, however defined, most uncertain, his rants about 'imbecilic institutions' gave support to those among his followers who came to see 'institutions' as the problem and 'technology' as the source of continued progress.[12]

In the work of Clarence Ayres, and particularly in the hands of some who had studied at the University of Texas with Ayres and others, most notably Fagg Foster, though not for Ayres himself, 'institutions' ceased to be understood simply as patterns of behavior and came to be understood as part of a dualistic taxonomy that could be used to make generalized recommendations about conditions that would lead to greater economic welfare. Whereas institutionalists had earlier limited recommendations to very specific policies related to very specific parts of the web of institutional arrangements, the neoinstitutionalists, as they called themselves, offered general definitions of better conditions as substitutes for the Pareto optimality of the neoclassical economics (Tool, 1986). For the neoinstitutionalists the message from Veblen through Ayres, as translated by Foster, the interpreter of Ayres who had a great influence on Tool and other neoinstitutionalists, was that institutions were to be decried rather than described.[13]

This shift in point of view created major definitional problems, as 'institutions', even though they might be past-binding and 'ceremonial', and so inimical to technological change, were also 'useful' in that they served to organize human life. Further, it was clear enough that 'technology', the other term of the neoinsitutionalist dichotomy, could not exist without being intertwined with culturally specific 'institutional' or 'ceremonial' elements. Unlike the earlier concept of institutions that developed out of a social scientific approach to description, the concepts of Tool and Foster involved formal and *a priori* definitions, and their use was troubled. For many social economists it seemed impossible to remain true to the evolutionary and contingent sense of the original institutional economics and at the same time offer a standard against which specific institutions could be measured for 'goodness' or 'progressivity', for to do so would require articulation of a non-culturally specific goal. Teleology, a decidedly non-Veblenian characteristic, unavoidably crept in.

Two of Foster's students, Marc Tool and Paul Dale Bush, continued to work on the concept of 'institutions' throughout the 1980s and 1990s. Tool attempted to formulate a 'social value principle' that could be used to distinguish between ceremonial and instrumental behavior and did so largely through discussion of particular policy measures that he advocated. Although his effort to articulate a principle that would definitively support specific reforms was in many ways a departure from past institutional practice, the actual arguments that he advanced were a continuation of earlier social economic advocacy for specific reforms (Tool, 1986).

Bush, however, introduced a more formal and deductive approach, and in doing so he made far greater use of the concept of values than has been common in other institutionalist work.[14] In this approach, institutions are given definition as 'a set of socially prescribed patterns of correlated behavior', and 'values' function as the ' "correlators" of behavior' (Bush, 1988, pp. 126–7). Two separate issues give great importance to values in the Bushian analysis: (1) rejection of the notion that analysis (which is to say *etic* analysis) can never be entirely free of the *emic* perceptions and judgments of the analyst; and (2) a desire to resolve the dilemma inherent in the realization (a realization always present, one should note, in the work of Veblen, Ayres and other institutionalists of the earlier period) that any pattern of behavior involved both the human tendency to behave in both habitual and inquisitive manners. What Bush sought was a way to categorize observed behavior as 'dichotomous' even as he recognized that human behavior is most often (and probably always) 'dialectical', meaning that it involved both 'ceremonial' and 'instrumental' characteristics (Bush, 1988, p. 131). It was his claim that by identifying the nature of the values that warranted or correlated behaviors, patterns of behavior (institutions) could be dichotomously classified. 'Institutional change', Bush wrote, 'takes the form of a change in the value structure of the institution', where such change 'may be measured theoretically by a change in the institution's index of ceremonial dominance' (ibid., p. 149). A reduction in the 'index' of ceremonial dominance would be progressive; an increase regressive.

Although it is clear enough that the Tool–Bush efforts were an attempt to provide for social economics a template that would serve heterodox approaches in the same way that Pareto optimality served neoclassical economics, it is not clear that they were successful. Although what came to be called the 'Veblenian dichotomy' (and should more accurately have been called the Foster–Tool–Bush dichotomy) has been mentioned often in the institutionalist literature, it has not changed the methods of the institutionalist approach, nor has it made advocacy of specific programs noticeably more effective. It certainly did, however, create a dispute as a number of institutionalists found the *emic* analysis upon which social economics rested to be incompatible with the more purely *etic* approach that the neoinstituitonalists had adopted (Samuels, 1990). Unfortunately, the ongoing debate over the meaning of institutions and technology left a lasting impression among many that the core terms of the institutional branch of economics were too ill defined to be useful.

In the meantime, social economists found themselves at least peripherally involved in a major dispute that was challenging the use and understanding of the term 'culture' in anthropology. Matters were made more confusing because this dispute overlapped in some ways with the arguments among institutionalists over whether or not Veblen and Ayres had intended their *emic*-based dialectic to be also an *etic* dichotomy. A corollary of the definition of 'culture' that emerged from the early twentieth-century work that anthropologists did around the world, as well as from the work of sociologists in the USA, was the notion that norms, folkways, institutions could only be understood within the larger context of the cultures within which they existed. This implied what came to be called 'cultural relativism'. To what extent anthropologists of the first half of the twentieth century were ever the strict functionalists who saw cultures as harmonious systems of functionally interrelated parts, or the relativists, that later anthropologists charged, is a matter for dispute. What is more obviously true is that as anthropologists found it increasingly imperative to speak out against some practices of people with whom they worked, as for example against physical torture in whatever cause, 'cultural relativism' came into doubt. The ethical issues were reinforced by the disappearance of isolated groups for whom anthropologists could produce the classic kind of ethnography, and cultures came more and more to be regarded as changing mosaics whose understanding required knowledge of histories and of power relationships among groups. These issues rebounded to social economics and played a particular role among institutionalists in that those who rejected the neoinstituionalist effort to define a universal principle of social value were accused of a kind of amoral cultural relativism that was also under attack among anthropologists (Mayhew, 1987).

At the same time, anthropologists and sociologists adopted different ways of thinking about cultures and societies. As David Graeber describes it, 'structural-functional anthropology' had reached a kind of dead end by the 1950s in that anthropologists could not explain how societies changed, nor could they account for individual conformity to institutional patterns or cultural wholes (Graeber, 2005, p. 445). One way out of the dilemma was to postulate 'values' that guided individual action without dictating unchanging and recurring patterns of action. Values and 'value orientations', or in other formulations of similar ideas, 'symbols', could remain relatively constant but action would vary in different circumstances.[15]

Observed behavior came to be thought of as a situational product of change-resistant values or symbolic systems and shifting contexts through which enculturated individuals negotiated. The growth of 'cultural studies' in a number of humanistic disciplines and colleges of education added to the muddle, or if you prefer, the intellectual excitement of new ways of thinking. Such studies owed little to earlier, which is to say pre-World War II, concepts of culture or of method but were rather applications of the new concepts of situational culture in a world in which even older notions of class as a key explanatory variable were being abandoned.[16]

Within the academic discipline of economics there were also further developments that once again crossed over to add complexity to the larger discourse of the social sciences. Methodological individualism had, as neo-classical analysis developed during the first decades of the twentieth century, placed ever heavier emphasis upon the individual as rational chooser, guided by values that were to be taken as given by the investigator.[17] However, it had become increasingly obvious that 'institutions did matter'. And, out of that recognition, in combination with a continued firm commitment to methodological individualism, the new institutional economics (NIE) was born. The individual, rational chooser was recast to become not only a chooser of inputs and outputs within a given institutional context, but now a chooser as well of institutions (and hence cultures).[18]

NIE shares in a general way the definition of cultures, institutions and values that were given at the beginning of this chapter but differs sharply from the OIE (original institutional economics) and social economics in general in ascribing the source of institutions to active choice by individual agents rather than to inheritance.[19] To the extent that the choices of these agents are culturally influenced they are influenced by 'values' which are themselves a product of prior, but presumably always changeable, institutional choice. Thus the set of institutions becomes a complete and closed set of chosen patterns tending toward equilibrium, but kept in kaleido-scopic change by changing constraints which may include demography, climate, contact with others, or other disturbing factors.

This NIE model of institutions, cultures and institutional/cultural change represents a logical extension of the neoclassical system of economic thought. It has had added appeal in the world of the late twentieth and early twenty-first centuries because individual mobility and well-nigh universal communication networks have provided opportunities for rapidly changing and even multicultural identities (Jones, 2006; Sen, 2006). In a world in which a village boy or girl from India, or China, or any of several African nations can move to London, or Paris, or Little Rock to study or practice medicine, and to choose clothing, food, entertainment of various kinds, it is easy to see 'institutions' or 'cultures' as chosen.

The difficulty, though it is not usually recognized as a difficulty by practitioners of NIE, is to specify the mechanism of choice. The usual recourse is to give acultural (which is to say, non-culturally specific) or, in other words, universal and prior existence to a market mechanism. That there exists such a universal mechanism that is somehow part of 'human nature' has been a powerful political as well as academic assumption for many economists and political scientists in recent decades, one that has played a role in reactions to the collapse of the economies of the former Soviet Union, expectations for post-invasion recovery in Iraq, and the formulation of what are generally thought of as neo-conservative policies. However, in the view of OIE and social economics the market mechanism as conceived in NIE is itself a cultural construct, an institution that was created and extended via a process that can be described using the techniques of OIE.[20] Whether the advocates of NIE or the proponents of OIE and other OIE-sympathetic social scientists are correct about the nature of market mechanisms remains a key point of division.

Not only do many social scientists and advocates of OIE regard the rational choice of neoclassical economics to be a cultural construct on a par with other social constructs; they would also add that actual markets for products such as broccoli or automobiles may not be good analogies for the complex and conflicted processes that cause cultural/institutional change. The complex of power differentials among groups, and inherited ideas of propriety, dignity and need, to name just a few of the factors that are likely to be at work in the creation of new institutions and cultural patterns, are probably not well captured by the simple assumption that values change. Most work in NIE has been done on business firms and other clearly economic agents working in a relatively well-defined economic context. Some practitioners, most notably perhaps Douglass North and Richard Posner, have extended the analysis further, but to date the work has not been done to show the power of NIE to explain institutional choice but rather to assert and argue that whatever is has been chosen. The system, as appealing as it may be in a world of apparently rootless agents, remains tautological. As with the study of 'values', 'symbols' and other mental contructs, it is difficult to see how to proceed as social scientists, except by ascribing the supposedly explanatory variables as consequences of that which must first be accounted for. The *explicandum* becomes the *explicans*.

The resulting muddle
In just over 100 years the social sciences have evolved from a state of general excitement over methods to be used in describing institutions,

cultures and values as key to understanding and reforming human society to a state of considerable confusion over what, if any, meaning the constructs may have. Are cultures and institutions so transitory as to be of little interest? Should social scientists focus instead on the processes of rational choice and on change rather than fixity? There are some who would answer yes (Jones, 2006). And yet the prominence of world divisions along religious and other culturally defined groups, and the association of these divisions with the power of nation-states and other armed groups, has restored interest in persistent cultural patterns. Concern has been raised about a 'clash of civilizations' or a 'clash of cultures'. Within nations 'values' that are more than motivators to choice in allegedly acultural markets have become an important part of the political dialogue. Resistance to Western cultural hegemony has cast a different light upon cultural patterns that might once have been dismissed as of interest only to tourists. The concepts and usages of the early twentieth-century social science, which is to say 'institutions', 'cultures' and 'values', once more seem relevant.

However, much has been learned over the past century. It is absolutely crucial that use of these terms carries with it an understanding that individual human agents simultaneously inherit, use and change the usages that are characterized as institutions. They do so in response to values that impinge on them from other cultural and institutional contexts but also as a consequence of learning. One aspect of the philosophical tradition of pragmatism that emerged with early twentieth-century social science that was, as Clarence Ayres so often argued, downplayed in the evolution of the social sciences was the importance of cumulative learning. Thorstein Veblen tried to capture this as it related to manipulation of nature, and so did John R. Commons, John Dewey and others as it related to human interactions. They were not entirely successful, and what was carried forward into the second half of the twentieth century was a notion of fixity and of culture, institutions and values as chains upon individuals. What was then lost in the rush to correct the errors of the earlier social science/social economics was the empowering notion that mankind, by understanding patterns of behavior, could also change them. If that understanding can be merged with the recognition that we live in a world of considerable individual choice, as well as in a world where every choice is predicated on a set of institutional and cultural expectations inherited from the past, perhaps new, more complex and more powerful notions of institutions and cultures can emerge.

A serious question, however, is whether or not the social scientists of the twenty-first century can reinstate to a central role the tools of their earlier disciplines to serve this end. Actually, many of those tools, which is to say descriptive statistics, ethnographic inquiry, historical analyses, are still in use and robustly so. Studies based on these techniques, however, do not rank well in the reward structures of the various social sciences. They have been replaced in highest regard by formal analyses, polemical exercises, or highly detailed descriptions of very narrowly and academically conceived problems that are difficult for all save a narrow band of scholars to understand. If the terms 'institutions', 'cultures' and 'values' are to be once again understood as important *explanatory* terms, then descriptive methods will need once again to be recognized as not only worthy but essential.

Notes

1. The term *emic* and its antonym, *etic*, are important concepts for the analysis presented in this chapter. And, even though the terms may not be in wide use among socioeconomists it is not, in my view, an exaggeration to modify slightly the words of Thomas Headland, and say that social economics as well as '[m]any anthropologists, in fact . . . owe their jobs to their ability to make the distinction between *emic* and *etic*' (Headland et al., 1990, p. 17). Though used often in anthropological discussion, the terms and the crucial distinction between them originated in linguistics and then spread to anthropology and on to other social sciences. Readers who wish a good introduction to the subtleties involved in the use of the terms should consult Headland et al. (1990). For present purposes it will suffice to say that *emic* refers to the culturally specific or insider view of the world, whereas *etic* understanding is analytical and cross-cultural; it is the 'outsiders' view. When socio-economists began to use fieldwork techniques to understand economic processes they were recognizing the importance of the *emic*, or, in other words, that of understanding the world as seen by the participants in the economic processes themselves. And, although the analytical models offered by most economists from Adam Smith on were founded, ultimately, on their own *emic* notions of the world in which they lived, economists have generally treated their professional knowledge as purely *etic*, without in fact ever making the *emic/etic* distinction. Once crucial characteristic of social economics is the recognition, implicit if not always explicit, of the distinction. The meaning of this assertion will become clearer in the course of this chapter.
2. Primary supporting sources for this section are Davis (2003), Hamilton (1970), Stocking (1968), Veblen (1904) and Mitchell (1924).
3. There is a large literature on the relationship of Darwin and the early social sciences, a summary of which is beyond the scope of this chapter. Suffice it to say that Darwin's name was invoked by a number of the founders of the various social sciences, all of whom were committed to the idea that humans evolved biologically and that societies changed through time as well, though not necessarily as consequence of biological evolution. In 'Darwinian' social evolution, change was not regarded as a simple matter of progression along, or degenerate deviation from, a fixed and natural path. Beyond this there was wide disagreement as to the relationship of biology and race to social evolution, and great variation in explanation of the drivers of change (Morgan and Rutherford, 1998).
4. See Neale (1988) for more on this looseness of definition.
5. Rutherford (2004) and Morgan and Rutherford (1988).
6. Mitchell made the same point in his presidential address to the American Economic Association in 1925.
7. Cookingham (1987) described the wide variety of this kind of work done by social economists at Berkeley; Malcolm Rutherford (2004) describes similar patterns at Columbia; at the University of Chicago until well into the 1930s graduate students were likely to be well versed in the methods of social science in general (Emmett, 1998) and early work on household consumption was carried out there as well. The work of John R. Commons and his students at Wisconsin that led to the system of social security and other legislation is well known.

8. I include sociology in this list because of the work of such as D.H. Wrong. However, I shall spend little time on sociology in this chapter beyond noting now that much good work in the tradition of prewar social science has continued to be done. See for example the essays in Dobbin (2004).

9. It should be said that in some areas of social economics, and particularly in those with close ties to religious traditions and with an emphasis on ethics, there had always been a concern about the relationship of economic processes and value. Further, there had long been debate in economic history about the role that large-scale cultural values such as those associated with Protestantism as opposed to Catholicism played in determining the course of history. However, that discourse had remained largely separated from the work of the socio-economists of the prewar period.

10. One example of this was the considerable attention given by development economists to the possibility of 'backward bending supply curves of labor'. If the 'values' of a people led them to be satisfied with a certain level of income, then higher wage offers, it was argued, would lead to a backward bend in the supply curve of labor, with less rather than more units of labor offered at higher wages. This was an essentially neoclassical way of explaining unexpected failures of wage and employment policies. See Higgins (1968), ch.12, 'Cultural determinism', for considerable discussion of the 'backward bending supply curve' and related issues.

11. I am well aware that there is now considerable debate as to whether economic orthodoxy is neoclassical, whether game theory has beat out the simple maximizing individual of that theory, and indeed whether or not there is any orthodoxy at all. For purposes of this chapter I shall assert that it is sufficient to say that in spite of a variety of doubts and equivocations that can be found in the current literature, there remains a core of theory that is neoclassical and dominant. This is the theory of the small-scale commercial firm as extended to the rational individual who may operate with bounded rationality and a variety of constraints and uncertainties, but is still conceived by most economists as central to social action and organization.

12. See Mayhew (2007).

13. Fagg Foster taught at the University of Denver from 1946 to 1976, during which time most of those who rallied to Tool's neoinstitutionalist approach were students there. Foster himself had been an undergraduate student at the University of Texas in the late 1920s and early 1930s, and later a graduate student, completing his dissertation in 1946. At the University of Denver he developed his own interpretation of the work of Veblen, John Dewey and Clarence Ayres, which, though he published little, he passed along to his students as part of an oral tradition. Foster's ideas, both as expressed in the class-room and in papers presented at meetings, were brought together by one of his students, Baldwin Ranson (1981).

14. This is seen clearly in the contrast between Clarence Ayres's extended discussion of systems of value in *Toward A Reasonable Society* (Ayres, 1961). Ayres argues that because anthropology began as a discipline that focused on differences among humans, a focus that carried over to social economics, systems of value (a term that he prefers to 'values') were largely identified as those that lacked major components of cross-culturally relevant valuation. The exotic rather than common human practice was emphasized and as a consequence there was no general social scientific articulation of the proposition that humans across all cultures share in a process of learning about the physical world in which they live. It is in this way that Ayres makes a sharp contrast between different *processes* of valuation. However, he makes no attempt to offer a formal differentiation between the two systems such as is found in Bush's work.

15. There is a substantial literature on this; a good start is Graeber (2005).

16. To illustrate: in Cashmore and Rojek (1999) cultural theory is presented, the editors tell us, for a postmodernist world in which the idea of society as a grid of relationships among Marxian defined classes has been abandoned, to be replaced by society as a collection of individuals who shift and reshift allegiance as they interpret, via the reading of 'texts' (an all-inclusive set of human products), in a constantly changing world. Cultural theorists are those who seek to understand how this happens. Unraveling the

meaning of this assertion or the complexity of 'cultural studies' is well beyond the scope of this chapter. For more on this see Mayhew (2002).

17.   This approach bore more than passing resemblance to the emphasis that some anthropologists now give to 'symbols' as the constant that guides variation in action. Nevertheless, disciplinary differences remained, with anthropologists continuing to focus on action/behavior while the economists worried over an abstract process.

18.   This should not be confused with the neo-institutionalism represented by the work of Marc Tool.

19.   Oliver E. Williamson, in a review article on NIE, said as much: 'Indeed, although both the older and newer styles of institutional economics subscribe to many of the same good ideas, a progressive research program requires more'. The more that is required being the commitment to use of the tools of microeconomic theory to explain institutions (Williamson, 2000).

20.   Karl Polanyi's 1944 account of the creation of both the actuality, and the justificatory idea, of the kind of self-regulating market that is the neoclassical ideal remains a classic. In the anthropological literature, in the accounts of development economists, and in economic history and OIE-related labor economics one can find many other accounts of the creation of markets and related institutions. One classic is that provided in Barber (1961); see also articles in Dobbin (2004).

References

Ayres, C.E. (1961), *Toward a Reasonable Society*, Austin, TX: University of Texas Press.

Barber, W.J. (1961), *The Economy of British Central Africa*, Stanford, CA: Stanford University Press.

Barber, W.J. (1985), *From New Era to New Deal*, Cambridge and New York: Cambridge University Press.

Bush, P.D. (1988), 'Theory of institutional change', in M.R. Tool (ed.), *Evolutionary Economics*, Vol. 1, Armonk, NY: M.E. Sharpe, pp. 125–66.

Cashmore, E. and Chris Rojek (eds) (1999), *Dictionary of Cultural Theorists*, London: Edward Arnold.

Clark, J.M. (1919), 'Economic theory in an era of social readjustment', *The American Economic Review*, **9** (1), 280–90.

Commons, J.R. (1934), *Institutional Economics*, Madison, WI: University of Wisconsin Press.

Cookingham, M.E. (1987), 'Social economists and reform: Berkeley, 1906–1961', *History of Political Economy*, **19** (1), 47–65.

Davis, J. (2003), *The Theory of the Individual in Economics: Identity and Value*, London: Routledge.

Dobbin, F. (ed.) (2004), *The Sociology of the Economy*, New York: Russell Sage.

Emmett, R.B. (1998), 'Entrenching disciplinary competence: the role of general education and graduate study in Chicago economics', in M.S. Morgan and M. Rutherford (eds), *From Interwar Pluralism to Postwar Neoclassicism*, Durham, NC and London: Duke University Press, pp. 134–50.

Firth, R. (1939), *Primitive Polynesian Economy*, London: Routledge and Kegan Paul.

Goodfellow, D.M. (1939), *Principles of Economic Sociology*, London: Routledge and Kegan Paul.

Graeber, D. (2005), 'Value: anthropological theories of value', in J.G. Carrier (ed.), *A Handbook of Economic Anthropology*, Cheltenham, UK and Northampton, MA, USA: Edward Elgar, pp. 439–54.

Hamilton, D. (1970), *Evolutionary Economics: A Study of Change in Economic Thought*, Albuquerque, NM: University of New Mexico Press.

Hamilton, W.H. (1919), 'The institutional approach to economic theory', *The American Economic Review*, **9** (1), 309–18.

Headland, T.N., Kenneth L. Pike and Marvin Harris (eds) (1990), *Emics and Etics: The Insider/Outsider Debate*, Frontiers of Anthropology, Newbury Park/London/New Delhi: Sage Publications.

Higgins, B. (1968), *Economic Development: Problems, Principles, and Policies*, New York: W.W. Norton & Co.

Jones, E.L. (2006), *Cultures Merging: A Historical and Economic Critique of Culture*, Princeton, NJ and Oxford: Princeton University Press.

Mayhew, A. (1980), 'Atomistic and cultural analyses in economic anthropology: an old argument repeated', in J. Adams (ed.), *Institutional Economics: Contributions to the Development of Holistic Economics*, Boston/The Hague/London: Martinus Nijhoff, pp. 72–81.

Mayhew, A. (1987), 'Culture: core concept under attack', *Journal of Economic Issues*, **21** (2), 587–608.

Mayhew, A. (1998), 'On the difficulty of evolutionary analysis', *Cambridge Journal of Economics*, **22** (4), 449–61.

Mayhew, A. (2002), '(Re)defining culture', *History of Economic Thought and Methodology*, **20-A**, 309–13.

Mayhew, A. (2007), 'The place of science in society: progress, pragmatism, pluralism', in Janet T. Knoedler, Robert E. Prasch and Dell P. Champlin (eds), *Thorstein Veblen and the Revival of Free Market Capitalism*, Cheltenham, UK and Northampton, MA, USA: Edward Elgar.

Mitchell, W.C. (1924), 'The prospects of economics', in R.G. Tugwell (ed.), *The Trend of Economics*, New York: Alfred A. Knopf, pp. 3–34.

Morgan, M.S. and Malcolm Rutherford (eds) (1998), *From Interwar Pluralism to Postwar Neoclassicism*, Durham, NC and London: Duke University Press.

Neale, W.C. (1988), 'Institutions', in M.R. Tool (ed.), *Evolutionary Economics*, Vol. 1, Armonk, NY and London: M.E. Sharpe, pp. 227–56.

Neale, W.C. (1990), *Developing Rural India: Policies, Politics and Progress*, Glenn Dale, MD: The Riverdale Company.

Pelto, P.J. and G.H. Pelto (1975), 'Intra-cultural diversity: some theoretical issues', *American Ethnologist*, **2** (1), 1–18.

Ranson, B. (1981), 'The papers of J. Fagg Foster', *Journal of Economic Issues*, **15** (4), 857–1012.

Rosen, G. (2005), *Globalization and Some of Its Contents*, Xlibris Corporation.

Rutherford, M. (2004), 'Institutional economics at Columbia University', *History of Political Economy*, **36** (1), 31–78.

Samuels, W. (1990), 'The self-referentiability of Thorstein Veblen', *Journal of Economic Issues*, **24** (3), 695–718.

Sen, A. (2006), *Identity and Violence: The Illusion of Destiny*, New York: W.W. Norton.

Stocking, G.W. (1968), *Race, Culture, and Evolution: Essays in the History of Anthropology*, Chicago, IL: The University of Chicago Press.

Tool, M.R. (1986), *Essays in Social Value Theory: A Neoinstitutionalist Contribution*, Armonk, NY: M.E. Sharpe.

Veblen, T.B. (1904), *The Theory of Business Enterprise*, New York: Charles Scribners & Sons.

Williamson, O.E. (2000), 'The New Institutional Economics: taking stock, looking ahead', *Journal of Economic Literature*, **38** (September), 595–613.

3 Insecurity
John Vail

The question of insecurity lies at the heart of social science enquiry. There is hardly an academic discipline – in economics, environmental sciences, geography, international relations, political science, social policy, sociology – that is left untouched by a concern for this subject. In recent decades, however, insecurity has ceased to be merely a matter of academic interest to become one of the most urgent issues in our everyday lives (Vail et al., 1999). The incidence, scope and distribution of risks have shifted dramatically over the past four decades as a consequence of epochal transformations in cultural, economic, political and social life.

Economic insecurity, which had always been the fate of working-class lives, has emerged as the lived experience of the middle classes in the advanced nations as a consequence of mass unemployment, job insecurity, increased work intensity and income volatility. Nearly one quarter of the world's population still lives below the World Bank's one dollar-a-day poverty line and their lives are irrevocably blighted by the persistent scourges of ill health, food insecurity, collective violence, gender inequality and authoritarianism. Family life has become deeply vulnerable and insecure: the past 40 years have witnessed extraordinary upheavals in the social patterns of work, gender relations and sexuality that have ruptured traditional expectations and behaviour and led to unparalleled changes in family arrangements. Environmental risks, encompassing global climate change, water shortages and air pollution, have mushroomed exponentially and are now central to our understanding of the modern world. Despite the hegemony of liberal democracy, political life is more uncertain than ever: governments seem ill equipped to adapt their institutions to the rapidly changing risk environment, their authority is being challenged and undermined by a range of agents from global corporations to terrorist groups, and in an era of declining political participation and fragmenting solidarities, political elites are less able to deliberate about or achieve common goals and the public interest.

It would be impossible to offer a comprehensive account of these social changes in such a brief chapter, so my aim is first to outline what we mean by the term insecurity and then to outline a variety of analytical categories by which the concept of insecurity can be more fully explored.

Insecurity and risk

Insecurity and risk are often used interchangeably in the social sciences, but it is important to highlight the crucial differences between these terms. Risk has come to signify aspects of danger, or threats to people's livelihood which are in theory accessible to some form of calculation; in other words, they are uncertainties that can be transformed into probabilities (Douglas and Wildavsky, 1982; Knight, 1921). This may be applied to any number of areas of social life where the hazards people face need to be estimated and where sufficient information is available and attainable to assign probabilities: the likelihood of getting cancer, or having an automobile accident, or losing a job. However, risk implies a level of abstraction that can distance us from a direct engagement with what we actually fear. Ulrich Beck (1992) has argued that the dominant sensibility of risk virtually requires us to ignore our own senses: dangers are perceived, not by our own immediate perceptions, but by a reliance on scientific expertise that can accurately measure the precise nature and degree of threat. Insecurity, on the other hand, is a form of uncertainty that by its very nature is not amenable to probalistic calculation. Jens Beckert writes in this vein: 'Uncertainty is understood as the character of situations in which agents cannot anticipate the outcome of a decision and cannot assign probabilities to the outcome' (Beckert, 1996, p. 804). It is not merely that there may be crucial barriers that make rational calculation unfeasible – changing circumstances may constitute unique events so no prior experiences to estimate risks exist or accurate information may be lacking – but that in the context of insecurity, the language of probabilities does not aptly capture the full range of meanings associated with the term.

I use the term insecurity to refer to three interrelated processes – a *cognitive* process, an *emotional/psychological* state of mind, and a *lived experience* – each of which is captured by the distinct vocabulary used to characterize insecurity. In the first instance, words such as uncertainty, indeterminancy and unpredictability are often used as synonyms for insecurity. In periods of rapid social transformation, our ability to perceive the contours of change is severely constrained: the pace of change may be so fast that we routinely misdiagnose the nature of the upheaval or the nature of change is so complex that our familiar paradigms of understanding become instantly outdated. This instability and impermanency make it harder for individuals to achieve a sense of order and continuity in their relationships and lives, a condition that Anthony Giddens terms 'ontological insecurity' (Giddens, 1990). The second aspect of insecurity as an emotional or psychological state of mind is illustrated by the familiar terms of precariousness, fear, anxiety, vulnerability, powerlessness. Periods of insecurity are marked by a pervasive societal anxiety, where the old certainties of life are suddenly cast into doubt. 'What is peculiar about uncertainty today is that it exists without any looming historical disaster', argues Richard Sennett about our contemporary insecure times; 'instead, it is woven into the everyday practices of a vigorous capitalism. Instability is meant to be normal' (Sennett, 1998, p. 31). This normalization of risk and insecurity may impose significant emotional traumas, especially when all the familiar certainties of social life such as employment, family life, community, personal identity are being uprooted. The loss of a job can damage self-confidence and self-esteem; a vertiginous drop in family income may make it harder for people to identify their proper place in the world; without stable expectations or a sense of purpose, people find it harder to carve out a predictable narrative about their lives (Newman, 1999). Finally, insecurity as a lived experience refers to the processes in social, economic and political life that take a painful toll on people's lives and reduce their autonomy to pursue the life projects that they value. Insecurity has an immediacy that cannot be avoided or displaced into the realm of probability; an individual who is homeless or out of work, whose children are malnourished and infirm, does not need to calculate the likelihood of disaster striking because they are already living this fate.

Insecurity and unintentional consequences
It is an acknowledged phenomenon of social life that the best-intentioned efforts to ensure security may sometimes increase insecurity instead. Although Western societies have become relatively insulated from the age-old 'natural' insecurities of famine, premature death and illness, human action in modernity has created the potential for even greater insecurity (Beck, 1992). A series of potentially countervailing actions (often referred to as side effects) can be precipitated by human agency, a feature that is extensively documented in the literature on 'risk trade-offs' and the precautionary principle (Graham and Wiener, 1995; Sunstein, 2005). Regulation of the environment often reduces one form of environmental risk only to heighten environmental insecurity in another area: restrictions on air pollution may reduce harmful emissions but lead to higher production of solid wastes that decimate the land; a ban on one noxious substance may only encourage the use of an equally bad one. Charles Perrow argues that the normal functioning of our technologically advanced systems creates a potential for catastrophic disasters such as oil spills, nuclear meltdowns and chemical plant explosions: small mishaps and failures, which taken individually pose no risk but when left uncorrected can accumulate rapidly into a critical breakdown, typically go unnoticed because of the technological complexity and interdependencies of modern life (Perrow, 1999). 'To be modern is to find ourselves', writes Perry Anderson, 'in an environment that

promises us adventure, power, joy, growth, transformation of ourselves and the world – and at the same time threatens to destroy everything we have, everything we know, everything we are' (Anderson, 1992, p. 25).

To put this familiar dynamic into the language of security/insecurity, unanticipated consequences represent optimizing behaviour (to create security) by social actors that unintentionally leads to sub-optimal outcomes (insecurity) (Elster, 1989). A number of combinations can result from this dynamic, as the following examples from industrial relations illustrate. First, a proposal to create security may backfire and generate even more insecurity for the actor concerned: egalitarian wage policies (such as the reduction of wage differentials or the elimination of job classification hierarchies) which European trade unions promoted in the 1970s to enhance solidarity across divisions in the working class unintentionally forged an even larger cleavage between blue collar and white collar workers, who felt their particular interests were not being adequately considered. The fragmentation of interest that resulted made cooperation between the two groups less likely and created a troublesome representation dilemma for unions (Regini, 1992). Second, attempts to create security for one social actor may unintentionally create greater insecurity for a different actor: new technology may be introduced into the workplace by management in order to generate higher levels of productivity but this may worsen existing divisions among workers, weaken worker solidarity and make future mobilization less likely.

Third, a policy for security may lead to greater insecurity for all actors concerned: a firm's attempt to increase productivity by means of an increase in the intensity of work will not only exacerbate the sheer wear and tear on workers' bodies and spirit; it may also violate entrenched workplace norms of fairness that can precipitate higher than normal levels of shopfloor militancy. This could have a substantially negative impact on production schedules and deliveries, thereby reducing productivity and making future cooperation between workers and management much less feasible. Fourth, optimizing behaviour by one group may unintentionally produce greater security for a different group: successful collective action by workers against individual employers can create an incentive for capitalists to devote greater resources to their own collective organization which may allow them to reduce self-destructive competition among firms (Bowman, 1989). Lastly, attempts to make one group secure may indeed make everyone more secure: this is the realm of Adam Smith's 'invisible hand', as when higher job security for workers (through stricter legislation prohibiting unfair dismissals or layoffs) may unintentionally provide firms with distinct advantages by lowering turnover rates and training costs, and thereby increasing productivity as a whole.

The generation of insecurity via unintentional consequences has often been regarded as an endemic feature of the capitalist system. Marx's theory of the falling rate of profit argued that what might be necessary for capital accumulation (the introduction of labour-replacing technology) undermined the possibility of further accumulation in the future by reducing the variable capital (in other words workers themselves) out of which surplus value and hence profit were derived (Marx, 1976). Keynes analysed the same problem from the perspective of the failure of the market to provide for a sustainable form of full employment. Firms, which reduced costs and increased profits by firing workers and bringing in new technology, unintentionally reduced individual spending and savings in the economy, which made future investment less likely and undermined the foundations of economic growth. The same logic underpinned Keynes's analysis of the short-termism and volatile nature of financial markets which he argued made it highly unlikely that sufficient resources would be committed to productive investment without some government intervention (Keynes, 1936).

Karl Polanyi's analysis in *The Great Transformation* of the self-regulating market and the double movement is rooted in a similar logic. The establishment of free trade capitalism and a market society was socially unsustainable because 'such an institution could not exist for any length of time without annihilating the human and natural substance of society; it would have physically destroyed man and transformed his surroundings into a wilderness' (Polanyi, 1944 [1957], p. 3). Against this inherent peril, a system of social protection was implemented to safeguard society against the cannibalistic instincts of a disembedded market economy. Every democratic capitalist state therefore is responsible for two vital tasks: to provide the necessary support and incentives for the successful functioning of a market economy and, at the same time, to shield the wider population from the destructive elements of this very system. These dual roles are complementary but can generate intolerable contradictions. Because control over investment decisions rests in private hands, the state's attempts to influence growth are likely to precipitate planning failures given that state knowledge is bound to be partial and incomplete. The welfare state's strategy for encroachment on the economy (decommodification) may similarly attempt to shape the economy in ways that may be counterproductive to its first task of economic growth (Vail, forthcoming).

Insecurity may equally reflect critical decision-making failures inside the state itself. Government interventions to reduce insecurity may backfire because decision-makers make little effort to consider the range of possible adverse consequences. This may occur because of problems of coordination within the government or the fragmentation of authority within the state. In the US government, as an example, agency jurisdictions are drawn around narrowly focused boundaries that limit oversight responsibilities to a discrete range of activities within single security arenas such as employment, health insecurity and the environment. The potential for neglecting side effects that spill across domains is consequently quite high. Government policy-makers, who have every incentive to ignore the possibility of unintentional consequences, may concentrate their energies on trading off one insecurity against another rather than developing a holistic policy that addresses the consequences of all insecurities at once. Friedrich Hayek famously concluded that given the limits of human cognitive capacity in a world where outcomes are uncertain and unintended consequences are ever-present, any form of government planning was doomed to failure (Hayek, 1948).

Finally, social theorists have viewed this dilemma of insecurity as a paradigm for the modern condition. This has a long lineage stretching back as far as the beginnings of nineteenth-century sociological theory. These writers were witnesses to what could be appropriately called the first 'age of insecurity': the massive upheavals of the century in every dimension of economic, social and political life led to an atmosphere of constant change and transformation where the potential for limitless possibility was matched only by an equal chance of unending misery (Berman, 1982). Marx, as an example, highlighted the 'uninterrupted disturbance of all social conditions, everlasting uncertainty and agitation' that resulted from the relentless expansion of capitalism and the commodification of the market. In the *Communist Manifesto*, he described the prodigious accomplishments of capitalism – 'it has accomplished wonders far surpassing Egyptian pyramids, Roman aqueducts and Gothic cathedrals' – yet insisted that it was equally destructive of self-determination and human talents (Marx, 1848 [in Tucker, 1972]). This theme has resonated in the writings of contemporary theorists as well. Beck sees unintentional consequences as a hallmark of what he calls 'risk society': every institution in society which seeks to legitimize itself through a guarantee of security merely produces even greater possibilities of insecurity. What is particularly frightening in the current context is that unintentional consequences may be global in their impact, especially where local disasters, such as the nuclear accident at Chernobyl, have the potential to unleash horrifying consequences on an international scale, a process Beck calls the 'globalisation of side effects' (Beck, 1992).

Insecurity and power
The question of who is insecure or how they become insecure is intimately related to the nature of power in society. The burden of insecurity typically falls on those who are least equipped to face it: those without economic

resources, those who are marginalized because of gender or racial discrimination, those who are ill or infirm, those who are the least organized or the least mobile. Individuals without power resources are less able to shield themselves from the debilitating effects of insecurity and have a much harder time finding substantive alternatives which allow them to minimize or escape from their predicament. Indeed, the ability to withstand a certain measure of insecurity in the short term in order to further one's long-term interests is a defining feature of social power. One of the crucial determinants in this regard is an individual's opportunity to claim citizenship rights, which are essentially a means of providing security for some (those included within the citizenship umbrella) at the expense of insecurity for others (those denied access to rights). Governments are continually shifting their citizenship boundaries – via tighter immigration policies, restrictions on asylum seekers, expulsion of refugees, denial of welfare benefits – and in this era of mass migration, such policies have become a matter of life and death for millions (Sassen, 1996).

Insecurity may also be the by-product of intentional and purposeful action by economic, social and political actors to enlarge the scope of their own freedom of choice. This autonomy is essentially the power: to opt out of surroundings or situations that impinge on one's interests regardless of how this may generate insecurity for others; to limit the range of freedom that other actors enjoy in the belief that this will enhance one's own security; and to ignore or even condone the consequences (either intentional or unintentional) of insecurity which their actions have generated for others. One of the most important prerogatives of power is the ability to shift the burden of insecurity on to those least able to countenance it. Corporations respond to the uncertainties of a rapidly changing economy by offloading the costs of restructuring on to workers who are less equipped to manage such change. The flexible restructuring of the labour market in the advanced economies is a direct result of these calculations: short-term contracts and reductions of core staff to the bare minimum, subcontracting production or services to smaller firms that bear the brunt of demand fluctuations, flexible hours, more uncertain job tenure, higher unemployment are all manifestations of how the risk of economic change is borne almost entirely by employees (Wheelock, 1999).

Jacob Hacker similarly contends that a 'great risk shift' is intensifying economic insecurity in the contemporary USA (Hacker, 2006). Social protection and collective risk sharing now cover a declining portion of the salient risks faced by citizens: the erosion of heath coverage, retirement plans and income security has meant that many of the most potent risks to life chances are being increasingly borne by families and individuals on their own rather than by collective intermediaries. Government policy has been deeply implicated in this process. Welfare provision has been restructured in particularistic and exclusionary ways with deep cuts in social protection, a decrease in the monetary value of benefits, as well as tighter limits on the duration of benefits such as unemployment insurance or Medicaid. Successive administrations have deliberately blocked reforms of programmes that would allow for a more efficacious adaptation to the new risk environment and have reduced the ability of individuals to find innovative ways of adjusting to social change.

The social construction of insecurity

Insecurity is intimately related not only to how people become insecure, but also to what 'insecurity' comes to mean in everyday experience and understanding. Mary Douglas and Aaron Wildavsky emphasized that the ways in which insecurity and risk are defined, assessed, symbolized and alleviated are inextricably tied to social power (Douglas and Wildavsky, 1982). Perceptions of which insecurities are in most urgent need of redress are heavily influenced by factors such as social class, gender, age, community, and these in turn play an important part in determining the extent to which one group of social actors is willing to recognize the legitimacy of another group's claims to be insecure. For instance, understandings and concerns about personal safety are profoundly influenced by gender and race: the everyday precautions which women are forced to undertake to shield themselves from sexual violence or which ethnic groups use to minimize the likelihood of racial attacks may lead these groups to emphasize specific policies (domestic violence shelters or anti-racist training for the police as an example) which may not have a similar priority among the wider population.

Economic power also exerts immense influence on this process. A bank may unilaterally decide to withhold mortgage financing or small business development loans to individuals who live in an area which they deem to be 'insecure' and a 'bad risk' (this is the practice known in the USA as redlining). As a consequence, other lenders, firms and government agencies may decide to disinvest as well, which assures that the anticipated decay will actually take place as the neighbourhood is starved of funds. Corporations that engage in a frenzy of 'downsizing' are in essence redefining the very nature of what job security should constitute; indeed, the neutral language of the word itself is a way of deflecting attention from the brutal insecurity (poor health, declining incomes, family breakdown, loss of self-esteem) that occurs when people lose their jobs. Louis Uchitelle details how mass layoffs in the USA evolved from a shocking event that once sparked media and political consternation to an accepted fact of life in little more than a generation (Uchitelle, 2003).

Political institutions have the power to systematically influence popular conceptions of what constitutes insecurity or what the established hierarchy of insecurities should be. Political elites engage in various strategies of obfuscation designed to either mitigate or enhance (depending on their specific interests at the time) public awareness of insecurity. Peter Phillimore and Suzanne Moffatt describe a whole series of strategies enacted by a local authority in Britain – what they call a policy of 'convenient misrepresentation' – that generated a false consensus about the local hierarchy of insecurity where concern for jobs rather than pollution dominated. This not only legitimated their efforts at downplaying the impact of environmental concerns; it served their interests as well (Phillimore and Moffatt, 1999). In this context, Howard Becker's concept of the 'hierarchy of credibility', the common-sense assumptions of what 'everyone knows' and the corresponding opportunity for people to be heard in the exercise of this knowledge, has considerable force (Becker, 1967). The power to shape, redefine, manage insecurity is also the power to decide who should be listened to, whose views can be discounted or accepted, whose claim of insecurity can be ignored or denied. European governments have discounted the genuine plight of asylum seekers fleeing political instability, economic hardship, and genocide, and instead have created an illusory 'security' crisis and moral panic where the very presence of immigrants in their countries is deemed to constitute an imminent public danger. Police departments (or local communities for that matter) where institutionalized racism may be systemic have every incentive to discount racially motivated crimes as biased exaggerations or 'even-handed' fights, which can lead them to ignore evidence or dismiss witness statements which would demonstrate the racial basis of these acts. In each case, the dominant hierarchy of credibility is essential for protecting entrenched power and privileges against the claims of subordinate groups.

However, this protective cocoon of ignorance and denial may be becoming less and less feasible at present. Beck has argued that the scale and intensity of modern dangers have escalated to the point where all individuals, regardless of power resources, are equally vulnerable. Smog and nuclear contamination, as he is famous for saying, are 'democratic': they treat the company director, worker, university lecturer, house husband and movie star exactly the same (Beck, 1992, p. 36). The fundamental conflict of industrial society between capital and labour in his eyes has been replaced by this predicament of 'collective self-injury', that what is really at stake is conflict not over the spoils of growth but over the disadvantages of insecurity. An individual's privileges will essentially consist of a reduced disadvantage: reduced by the amount of damages they can manage to shift on to others more marginalized than themselves.

The dialectic of insecurity

If the overwhelming impression so far has been on insecurity as a social relation of power and subordination which should be constrained, it is equally important to explore the multiple ways in which insecurity may be positively embraced by people in their everyday lives for its liberating and empowering effects. The attractions of risk can hardly be overestimated: indeed, one cannot imagine the rich panorama and drama of human life without the interplay of uncertainty and ambiguity. Individuals accept dramatic risks in their personal lives – daredevil sports such as free climbing or hang gliding, drug taking, high risk sexual activity – because they value the attendant pleasure and excitement more than they do the potential costs. Social movement activists are willing to countenance extraordinary dangers and risk personal suffering in order to further their political goals. Uncertainty is a central feature of artistic creation as well; it can be a burden (the lack of predictability in artists' lives or their alienation from normal work life) yet it may also serve as a stimulus for astonishing creativity.

This dialectic of insecurity can be observed in many arenas of social and political life. Risk taking and uncertainty are essential attributes, if not the defining success stories, of the capitalist system. In the felicitous phrase of Joseph Schumpeter, the 'creative destruction' of capitalist accumulation precipitates a veritable gale force of chaos – firms emerge and perish, whole industries arise out of thin air while others are relegated to the scrap heap – but risk taking and entrepreneurial ambition, premised on the lure of unimaginable success alongside a wilful denial of the possibility of failure, is the cornerstone of market dynamism and innovation (Schumpeter, 1954). A firm that wants to make a substantial investment in research and development must estimate the potential profitability over time of the investment (is it likely to generate innovations that will increase profit?) as well as estimating the likelihood of their competitors making similar levels of investment and their probability of success. None of these calculations can be made with any certainty, no company can ever be sure that they will hit the jackpot and, as a consequence, decisions are largely determined by what Keynes called the 'animal spirits' of investors. In financial markets, a successful entrepreneur may be precisely the person who is willing to embrace the most insecurity, for the greater the risk, the greater the potential return on investment (Mandel, 1996). Richard Sennett argues that the work culture of the new capitalism, with its cult of flexibility and incessant occupational mobility, has elevated risk taking to an essential feature of personal character: 'The imperative to take risks is more widely distributed in modern culture. Risk is a test of character; the important thing is to make the effort, take the chance, even if you know *rationally* you are doomed to fail' (Sennett, 1998, p. 90).

The efficacy of uncertainty is also at the core of philosophical work on social justice and the founding of the welfare state. In his groundbreaking work, *A Theory of Justice*, John Rawls argued that in deciding the best principles of justice, one should start behind a 'veil of ignorance': when choosing the appropriate principles to regulate society, people should make their choices without firm knowledge about what position they would occupy in society or what skills or talents they would have allocated. Uncertainty, argued Rawls, is a critical component of this choice process; under conditions of absolute uncertainty, the most rational choice for an individual would be to maximize the worst position which they could conceivably end up occupying. In other words, they should minimize the risk of receiving an unacceptable outcome by making the worst possible outcome as acceptable as possible (Rawls, 1971). This logic underpins Rawl's 'difference principle', which states that social inequalities in the basic structure are permissible but only to the extent that they improve the conditions of the least advantaged. Rawls's work is an ingenious attempt to marry self-interest to social justice, by making individual insecurity and vulnerability to the uncertainties of fate into a rationale for collective support for those who may be more vulnerable.

Indeed, some writers have argued that the creation of the postwar welfare state in advanced industrial societies represented just this sort of fusion of self-interest and social justice (Baldwin, 1990). The development of a system of free and equal access to social services such as education, health care, pensions and unemployment insurance represented a conscious process of collective risk pooling. On the one hand, it enabled people who were labelled as 'bad risks' by private insurers (the elderly, the disabled, those who had suffered major illnesses in the past) to enjoy the benefits of coverage; it also ensured that people who were highly likely to be insecure in the future – as a result of factors beyond their control such as old age, or catastrophic illness, or loss of job – could expect to receive support when they most needed it. Gosta Esping-Andersen maintains that the welfare state in advanced industrial societies is ill suited to address the intense social risks arising from the massive social changes in economic and family life (Esping-Andersen, 2002). In the new knowledge-intensive economies, a continual improvement in human capital (via lifelong learning and skills enhancement) is the only reliable way to ensure equitable life chances, but this will necessitate a new welfare model that provides social protection over the entire life course to prevent citizens from being trapped in permanent social exclusion.

The area of social life where the dialectic of insecurity is perhaps the most celebrated and the most controversial is the family. Family and household arrangements have become increasingly characterized by instability and unpredictability – falling marriage rates, deferred child rearing, high levels of divorce, increase in lone parents, greater numbers of mothers in paid employment – to the extent that it has become a primary location for the creation and negotiation of risk. It is the precipitous rise in marital breakdown that has sparked the most contested debate (Simpson, 1998). Some commentators argue that divorce is essentially a conflict between parents seeking greater freedom and their children, who require stability and security to flourish. Others claim that the primary contradiction of marriage – and hence the reason why the liberating aspects of divorce are most in dispute – is that family security has often been predicated on a veiled inequality, where household and caring work were largely the responsibility of the female partner (Stacey, 1996). A fierce debate has raged in the social sciences for the past decade about the consequences of family insecurity, in particular about what is the most appropriate stance to address the steady rise in the number of divorces in modern societies (Smart et al., 2001; Wallerstein et al., 2001). Clearly, there may be circumstances where one or both parents walk away from their obligations to their children out of convenience or pursuit of personal aggrandizement. Yet divorce continues to be a powerful resource for women (and their children) trapped in abusive or oppressive relationships; it may also be a way to escape the injustices and difficulties of an unequal and unhappy relationship, where the main source of stress is the failure of partners to do their fair share of the household and caring work. However, there is a strong correlation between family instability and poverty (women's incomes after divorce typically plummet while men's improve slightly). Some studies have shown that children in divorced, remarried or unmarried families are at greater risk for a number of behavioural problems than children in conventional families, while others demonstrate that divorce is associated with higher levels of mental and physical illness among the parting couples. There is a growing consensus that a new gender compact and restructuring of family policies, including the maximization of women's employment opportunities, universal provision of child care and income guarantees, is required to alleviate these insecurities (Esping-Andersen, 2002). At the same time, innovative constellations of kinship ties, caring networks and multiple, overlapping household arrangements are emerging to forge new forms of personal security.

References

Anderson, Perry (1992), *A Zone of Engagement*, London: Verso.
Baldwin, Peter (1990), *The Politics of Social Solidarity*, Cambridge: Cambridge University Press.
Beck, Ulrich (1992), *Risk Society: Towards a New Modernity*, London: Sage.
Becker, Howard (1967), 'Whose side are we on?', *Social Problems*, **19**, 239–47.

Beckert, Jens (1996), 'What is sociological about economic sociology? Uncertainty and the embeddedness of economic action', *Theory and Society*, **25**, 803–40.

Berman, Marshall (1982), *All That Is Solid Melts Into Air*, New York: Simon & Schuster.

Bowman, John (1989), *Capitalist Collective Action*, Cambridge: Cambridge University Press.

Douglas, Mary and Aaron Wildavsky (1982), *Risk and Culture: An Essay in the Selection of Technological and Environmental Dangers*, Berkeley, CA: University of California Press.

Elster, Jon (1989), *Nuts and Bolts for the Social Sciences*, Cambridge: Cambridge University Press.

Esping-Andersen, Gosta (2002), *Why We Need a New Welfare State*, New York: Oxford University Press.

Giddens, Anthony (1990), *The Consequences of Modernity*, Cambridge: Polity Press.

Graham, J. and J. Wiener (1995), *Risk Versus Risk: Tradeoffs in Protecting Health and the Environment*, Cambridge, MA: Harvard University Press.

Hacker, Jacob S. (2006), *The Great Risk Shift*, New York: Oxford University Press.

Hayek, Friedrich (1948), *Individualism and Economic Order*, Chicago, IL: University of Chicago Press.

Keynes, John Maynard (1936), *The General Theory of Employment, Interest and Money*, London: Macmillan.

Knight, Frank H. (1921), *Risk, Uncertainty and Profit*, New York: Kelley.

Mandel, Michael (1996), *The High Risk Society: Peril and Promise in the New Society*, New York: Times Books.

Marx, Karl (1976), *Capital*, vol. 1, London: Penguin.

Marx, Karl (1848 [1972]), *The Communist Manifesto*, in Robert Tucker (1972), *The Marx–Engels Reader*, New York: W.W. Norton.

Newman, Katherine S. (1999), *Falling From Grace: Downward Mobility in the Age of Affluence*, Berkeley, CA: University of California Press.

Perrow, Charles (1999), *Normal Accidents: Living with High-risk Technologies*, Princeton, NJ: Princeton University Press.

Phillimore, Peter and Suzanne Moffatt (1999), 'Narratives of insecurity in Teesside: environmental politics and health risks', in J. Vail et al. (eds), *Insecure Times: Living with Insecurity in Contemporary Society*, London: Routledge, pp. 137–53.

Polanyi, Karl (1957), *The Great Transformation*, Boston, MA: Beacon Press.

Rawls, John (1971), *A Theory of Justice*, Cambridge, MA: Harvard University Press.

Regini, Marino (1992), *The Future of Labour Movements*, London: Sage.

Sassen, Saskia (1996), *Losing Ground*, New York: Columbia University Press.

Schumpeter, Joseph (1954), *Capitalism, Socialism and Democracy*, London: Allen & Unwin.

Sennett, Richard (1998), *The Corrosion of Character: The Personal Consequences of Work in the New Capitalism*, New York: W.W. Norton.

Simpson, Bob (1998), *Changing Families: An Ethnographic Approach to Divorce and Separation*, Oxford: Berg.

Smart, Carol et al. (2001), *The Changing Experience of Childhood: Families and Divorce*, Cambridge: Polity Press.

Stacey, Judith (1996), *In The Name of the Family: Rethinking Family Values in the Postmodern Age*, Boston, MA: Beacon.

Sunstein, Cass (2005), *Laws of Fear: Beyond the Precautionary Principle*, Cambridge: Cambridge University Press.

Uchitelle, Louis (2003), *The Disposable American: Layoffs and Their Consequences*, New York: Knopf.

Vail, John (forthcoming), *Karl Polanyi: The Paradoxes of the Double Movement*, London: Routledge.

Wallerstein, Judith et al. (2001), *The Unexpected Legacy of Divorce*, New York: Fusion Press.

Wheelock, Jane (1999), 'Fear or opportunity? Insecurity in employment', in John Vail et al. (1999), *Insecure Times: Living with Insecurity in Contemporary Society*, London, Routledge, pp. 75–88.

4 The ethical dimensions of the 'globalization thesis' debate
George DeMartino

1. Introduction

This chapter explores a set of controversies in political economy that emerged during the 1990s and that continues to attract immense attention today. These controversies relate to the broad and heterogeneous debate over 'globalization'. From the start this debate was normative in a particularly high-profile way. Demonstrators against the World Trade Organization (WTO), the World Bank and related institutions emphasized what they took to be deep ethical failures of the neoliberal world order that had been maturing rapidly during the final quarter of the twentieth century. Many argued that this new global regime threatened to deepen inequality, undermine economic security, destroy cultural autonomy, exacerbate the dependence of the weak on the powerful, degrade environmental integrity and weaken democratic governance. Originating as it did among politically engaged civil society actors rather than among academics, it is hardly surprising that the critique engaged notions of justice and fairness, equality and freedom. And it is certainly the case that the power of the resistance to globalization depended very much on these normative indictments.

These matters have by now been contested at length. But the debate over globalization entails other important elements. My goal in this chapter is to explore some of these. In this connection, I will pursue a set of themes that relate in one way or another to the 'strong globalization thesis'. This is the thesis that the world economy that we inhabit today has been globalized in ways that are deeply consequential for virtually all actors – from states, to corporations, to civil society institutions, to individuals, their families and communities. Those who advocate this thesis contend that globalization forces are not just the principal determinants of economic flows and outcomes today; they are also establishing the context that shapes the viability of cultural practices, political strategies, governing institutions and much else besides. Some advocates of the globalization thesis celebrate these effects; others condemn them. But these adversaries, who stood toe to toe during the Seattle protests against the WTO in 1999, nevertheless share the basic presumption that globalization is today the paramount force of our epoch.

Not all observers hold this view of globalization. Dissenters view the globalization thesis as a collection of overblown claims about what globalization entails and, consequently, about the extent of its force in shaping events. The dissenters have worked to bring the global back 'down to earth', so to speak, in order to better understand international economic processes and to examine what they imply for political practice.

In the first instance the debate over the globalization thesis is 'positive', concerning as it does questions pertaining to what is happening, and with what effects. But there are important normative stakes in play here; these become apparent when the debate is examined through the lenses of social economic, institutionalist, post-structuralist and related perspectives in contemporary political economy. As we shall see, and this is the second important theme of the chapter, advocacy of the strong globalization thesis entails a commitment to a rather severe ontological essentialism that yields methodological reductionism and, as a consequence of this progression of thought, prescriptive rigidity. That is, political strategies are seen to be dictated by a governing, disciplinary global economy. And this discipline evacuates the ethical space. Our obligations come to appear (alternately, depending on the nature of the account) as a duty either to conform or to resist, full stop. In contrast, a holistic, non-reductionist social economic approach that understands the economy to be embedded in (and enabled by) the broader constellation of political, cultural and social institutions reveals the wide and open space available for political intervention. With this expanding space for intervention, of course, comes substantially greater ethical challenges and even confusion.

These insights compel the conclusion that how we choose to theorize globalization has important and even vital normative implications. This point has been made to date most forcefully in a powerful contribution to post-structuralist political economy, and I shall draw on this work (Gibson-Graham, 1996). This approach claims that we theorize ethically about globalization when we not only emphasize the position of those who are most impoverished and vulnerable, and attend to the harms that the emerging regime imposes on them, but when we invoke globalization 'scripts' that look for and therefore find space for meaningful and accessible interventions in pursuit of a more just world. Emphasis is placed in this account on the availability of ameliorative strategies in the here and now rather than on millennial politics that promise justice only in the future.

These arguments then lead to the final substantive goal of this chapter, which I shall perforce treat only briefly in the final section. If we recognize that the global economy lacks the disciplinary power often attributed to it, then we must confront the matter of how social economists might think about the strategy and policy interventions that are available and called for

by increasing international economic integration. Drawing on the important normative contribution of Amartya Sen's capabilities approach, I shall
suggest the need to discover and construct global rules that manage the
nature of international economic flows and competition in ways that ensure
human flourishing – and that expand the space already available for local
practices that seek economic justice. This discussion will suggest future
directions for social economic research in this area.

2.   The globalization thesis – for and against

The outpouring of literature on globalization over the past 15 years or so
has been astonishing. It is pointless to categorize this literature in simplistic ways, and I shall not attempt anything of the sort here. Instead, I shall
identify a striking theme that emerged early on within the most influential
literature and that gave shape to much of the succeeding work. Put simply,
by the early 1990s, prominent observers had begun to proclaim the emergence of a new epoch in world affairs – the epoch of the global economy.

The empirical markers of this new economy are easy to identify. From
the 1970s onward there were pronounced increases in the depth of international economic integration, as registered particularly in trade and
investment flows. During this period, trade as a proportion of total world
economic activity grew steadily. Complementing this trend (and indeed,
contributing to it) was an even more rapid increase in foreign direct investment (FDI) by multinational corporations. Moreover, the nature of FDI
evolved in important ways. Historically, FDI was concentrated in extrac-
tion industries and public and private infrastructure projects; during the
late twentieth century, however, FDI increasingly targeted the establishment of international 'commodity chains' (Gereffi and Korzeniewicz, 1994)
that integrated production of simple and even complex products across
national borders. Finally, during the 1990s there was an extraordinary
increase in international portfolio investment – short-term investment in
currencies, stocks, bonds and other liquid assets. The principal traders in
these markets were large investment funds that by then had begun to consider the whole world as offering viable opportunities for lucrative financial
activity (Dicken, 2003).

The globalization literature presented rather straightforward explanations for this deepening integration. Advocates placed greatest emphasis
on technological advance. Increasingly, wholesalers and retailers, corporate managers and investors could gain information about and monitor
events and opportunities abroad relatively quickly, easily and cheaply.
This increased substantially the field of operation for the traders of
goods, of course, but the impact on corporate managers and portfolio
investors was particularly remarkable. The new information technologies

permitted managers to organize and direct far-flung webs of productive enterprises in a way that would not have been possible just a few decades earlier. The new technologies also propelled the rapid acceleration in financial trading by integrating the world's primary and emerging financial markets.

Although technological advancement biased economic change toward greater international integration, its effects were amplified greatly by government strategies. During the last quarter of the twentieth century, leading states took dramatic steps to promote market-based international integration. On the trade front, operating initially through the General Agreement on Tariffs and Trade (GATT) and later through the WTO and regional and bilateral agreements, states substantially reduced tariff and non-tariff barriers to the international flow of goods and services. Regarding FDI, states enacted strong international protections for corporations – not least through new mechanisms in trade agreements that committed the signatories to protect real and intellectual property rights. Indeed, the investment provisions of ostensible trade agreements by the mid-1990s had come to be a much more important facilitator of deepening international economic integration than were their trade provisions. The North American Free Trade Agreement (NAFTA) is the pivotal agreement in this respect: its investment provisions (Chapter 11) provide for the strongest protections for cross-border investors of any agreement in history. Finally, under guidance of (and substantial pressure by) the World Bank, the International Monetary Fund (IMF), the USA and other national governments during the 1980s and 1990s, states across the globe took steps to eliminate capital controls. These controls had been explicitly provided for in the *IMF Articles of Agreement*, and national governments had imposed controls consistently ever since World War II to protect against rapid inflows and outflows of hot money that could destabilize currencies, trade balances and macroeconomic performance. But over a 20-year period, capital controls fell by the wayside as countries sought to reposition themselves in emerging world financial markets. Why so many states took this rather drastic step (and with what consequences) was contested during the 1990s (see below). But all agreed that the elimination of capital controls, like the reduction in tariffs and the extension of property rights for investors, was vital to the rapid deepening of integration at the close of the twentieth century (Helleiner, 1995; Grabel, 1996; Harmes, 1998).

In the face of such dramatic economic changes many observers came to hail the late twentieth century as a watershed moment of epochal proportions, one that delivered us to a new and unprecedented era of globalization.[1] One prominent commentator, looking out on the crisis of the Soviet Union and anticipating the headlong rush in Central and Eastern Europe to pattern their economies on the capitalist West, famously proclaimed the 'end of history' (Fukuyama, 1989). For many, the competition between diverse forms of economic systems that marked the previous several centuries was over. The liberalized market economy had proven itself; in contrast, state direction of domestic and international economic flows had been discredited. Henceforth there would be 'no alternative' to an integrated, market-based world economy joining free nations that subscribed to a neoliberal governance regime, both domestically and internationally.

It was in this context that the strong globalization thesis took root. Theorists such as Kenichi Ohmae (1994, 1995), Robert B. Reich (1991), Thomas Friedman (2000, 2005) and many others wrote powerfully of the degree to which the economic fate of individuals and their communities was fully determined by the global economy. In this view, economies were now seen to be porous and even borderless, corporations were largely untethered from their home bases and free to roam (and rule) the globe, while finance was completed de-linked from territory (national or otherwise). Advocates viewed these as the consequence of rather natural historical processes in which the combination of market competition and technological innovation drove even reluctant policy-makers to undertake liberal reform. Technological and economic progress was seen to render obsolete institutions and practices that had emerged in earlier eras. For instance, Reich (1991) denigrated the policies that states had traditionally pursued to promote prosperity, such as trade and other barriers, as 'vestigial thought'; Ohmae went so far as to pronounce the 'end of the nation state'. In this he was joined by theorists of the caliber of Susan Strange (1996). More prosaically, many scholars came to explain the shift toward economic liberalization – such as the removal of capital controls – as dictated by technological and economic forces over which governments increasingly enjoyed little control (cf. Goodman and Pauly, 1993). Hence, even if globalization required state complicity, in fact states had little choice but to serve their new global master.

It is important to keep in mind just how extensive was (and is) the embrace of the globalization thesis, even among those who might have been expected to resist its rather grand claims. Let's consider the work of one particularly careful observer of the global economy, geographer Peter Dicken. Through the publication of now five editions of his *Global Shift*, a text that comprises a wealth of data and that draws on findings across the disciplines, Dicken has contributed much to the effort to discern just what is happening in the world economy, and what these developments might imply.

The second edition of *Global Shift* appeared in 1992, and there Dicken proclaimed the arrival of the global economy in rather stark terms:

> The major theme [of the book] is that economic activity is becoming not only more *internationalized* but that, more significantly, it is becoming increasingly *globalized*. These terms are often used interchangeably although they are not synonymous. 'Internationalization' refers simply to the increasing geographical spread of economic activities across national boundaries; as such it is not a new phenomenon. 'Globalization' of economic activity is qualitatively different. It is a more advanced and complex form of internationalization which implies a degree of functional integration between internationally dispersed economic activities. Globalization . . . is emerging as the norm in a growing range of economic activities.
>
> We live in a world of increasingly complexity, interconnectedness and volatility; a world in which the lives and livelihoods of each and every one of us are bound up with processes operating at a global scale. (Dicken, 1992, p. 1)[2]

In this text, the prime mover in facilitating globalization is the transnational corporation (TNC) that marshals technological advance in its global designs. It is the TNC that is engineering the 'functional integration' that Dicken speaks of here; this takes the form of the creation of global supply chains under the direction of the growing ranks of corporate managers. Moreover, globalization processes have no geographical limits: they reach into all of our lives, no matter where we might live.

These sentiments emerged across the disciplines and, notably, even across ideological divides. Advocates of the globalization thesis were to be found among both mainstream neoclassical economists on the one hand and Marxists on the other. Neoclassical economists celebrated the establishment of a liberalized global market economy as the culmination of social progress. Marxists, in contrast, identified in globalization the predictable (and, indeed, predicted) inexorable global expansion of the circuits of capital. Industrial capital sought increased rates of exploitation by relocating to countries where the value of labor power was lower, and thereby also sought to weaken labor organization and resistance in the developed countries. Finance capital sought to establish international circuits that escaped regulation (and taxation) by the nation state. All of this threatened civil society and, for some, the state – with the effect of expanding the control by capital of politics, the economy and society (Tilly, 1995). A kinder, gentler capitalism that had emerged during the postwar period at least in the developed countries now gave way to a far crueler and more dangerous global order in which wealth became increasingly concentrated in fewer and fewer hands (Wilks, 1994). But despite this fundamental disagreement over the nature and effects of the global economy, both camps presumed that globalization was a fact to be reckoned with.

For some, the strong globalization thesis yielded predictions of global convergence – in private and public institutions and in political and economic strategies, practices and outcomes. Those who viewed convergence as benevolent emphasized processes of emulation, in which best practices were readily imported by policy-makers (populating 'epistemic communities') across the globe that now faced the same challenges and opportunities. For Thomas Friedman, states had no choice but to conform to the only available set of strategies that could promote prosperity – in his evocative phrase, states must put on the 'golden straitjacket' to ensure success (2000). In contrast, critics argued that global competition forced states to adopt weak labor and environmental standards so as to create and sustain an attractive business environment that would ensure the success of local corporations. From this perspective, convergence took the form of a regulatory 'race to the bottom', which now appeared inevitable owing to the power of global markets and global corporations.[3]

The dissenting view

The globalization thesis attracted the attention of critics even as it began to take root in the academic and popular press. Dissenters came to contest the characterization and interpretation of international economic developments as portrayed by the thesis. In short, the critique had the effect of rescuing the notion of the embeddedness of the economy in society, and the continuing salience of politics, place and context. Indeed, the critique embraced core social economic principles (even though many of the contributors were not economists). And this, as we shall see, had enormous normative implications.

One way to trace these intellectual developments is to compare Dicken's early views (summarized above) with the views he expressed later on, in subsequent editions of his book. A subtle change in attitude was already apparent in the 1998 edition. In that text Dicken paraphrases the claims of some of the more ambitious proponents of the globalization thesis (Peter Drucker, Reich, Ohmae and others), and then counterposes the critique of the concept of globalization that had by then sprung up across the disciplines. Dicken remained committed in 1998 to his earlier claims that the world economy is in the midst of a fundamental transformation, but by then he was beginning to hedge about its nature and consequences:

> The most significant development in the world economy during the past few decades has been the *increasing internationalization – and, arguably, the increasing globalization – of economic activities*. (Dicken, 1998, p. 1, original emphasis)

The fourth edition of the book appeared in 2003. Here we find important continuities with Dicken's earlier arguments, to be sure. Dicken continues to maintain that TNCs play a critical role in world economic transformation. But he is much more circumspect in assessing the extent and implications of this transformation. In making these arguments, Dicken purposely tilts against the globalization thesis literature, which he sees as exaggerating and even misunderstanding the nature of the trends in the global economy. He writes:

> My basic theme is that globalization is not some inevitable kind of end-state but, rather, a complex, indeterminate set of *processes* operating very unevenly in both time and place. (Dicken, 2003, p. xv, original emphasis)

> [The book's] underlying theme is that, while there are indeed *globalizing* processes at work in *transforming* the world economy into what might reasonably be called a new geo-economy, such processes – and their outcomes – are far more diverse than we are generally led to believe. (Ibid., p. 1, original emphasis)

The difference in thought in evidence here is rather striking. Dicken takes pains to emphasize that globalization should be thought of as a *set of processes or tendencies* in the world economy. Most importantly, in his view, the functional integration of economic activities that he cites as central to globalization is occurring unevenly – unevenly in terms of geography, but also in terms of sector. It is true, he claims, that TNCs are integrating and coordinating investment, trade and especially production in some regions and some industries, but he now emphasizes that global economic activity remains terribly concentrated and that (as a consequence) substantial parts of the globe are largely uninvolved in these processes. Indeed, even in those parts of the world where integration is deepest, many industries remain domestically oriented.

This relates to what is perhaps the most important distinction between the first and most recent editions. In the latter Dicken takes great pains to emphasize the continuing salience and power of the nation state in directing and shaping the global transformations that he tracks. Indeed, in this edition the nation state is placed on equal footing with the TNC as architects of the world economy, and as determining economic flows and outcomes.

One final point deserves mention. In the 2003 text, Dicken emphasizes that

> processes of globalization are not simply unidirectional, for example from the global to the local, but that globalization processes are deeply embedded, produced and reproduced in particular contexts. Hence, the specific assemblage of characteristics of individual nations and of local communities will not only influence *how* globalizing processes are experienced but also will influence the *nature* of those globalizing processes themselves. We must never forget that all 'global' processes originate in specific places. (Dicken, 2003, p. 1, original emphasis)

The critical ideas here are the embeddedness (territorial, institutional, etc.) of economic processes and the mutual effectivity of the local and the global, which together imply the continuing salience of local practices, institutions, and local political strategies and struggles. We also find an awareness of the reversibility of the processes to which Dicken draws our attention. Dicken separates himself from any teleological notion of history in which the world is being pulled toward some end-state called globalization.

Dicken's own evolution reflected (and indeed, contributed much to) a broader shift in the center of gravity in the globalization debate during the 1990s and since. By the mid-1990s many dissenters had begun to take exception to virtually all the claims of the globalization thesis. Notable in this connect are Hirst and Thompson, whose *Globalization in Question* contains a 200-page indictment of the globalization thesis. The first chapter of the second edition (1999) is entitled 'Globalization: A Necessary Myth?'; it includes the following:

> It is widely asserted that we live in an era in which the greater part of social life is determined by global processes, in which national cultures, national economies and national borders are dissolving. Central to this perception is the notion of a rapid and recent process of economic globalization. A truly global economy is claimed to have emerged or to be in the process of emerging, in which distinct national economies and, therefore, domestic strategies of national economic management are increasingly irrelevant. The world economy has internationalized in its basic dynamics, it is dominated by uncontrollable market forces, and it has as its principal economic actors and major agents of change truly transnational corporations that owe allegiance to no nation-state and locate wherever on the globe market advantage dictates. (Hirst and Thompson, 1999, p. 1)

Hirst and Thompson take issue with all these claims. Through extensive empirical work they drive home several important conclusions: that genuinely transnational corporations are the exception rather than the rule, since most international corporations operate in relatively few countries which tend to be regionally concentrated; similarly, that trade, investment and finance remain territorially concentrated (especially among the advanced industrialized countries); hence, that all these processes are amenable to control by the coordinated actions of the world's leading countries. Rather than recognize the global economy as an inexorable force driving political strategies and economic outcomes, they direct our attention to the thoroughly political nature of the global neoliberal (or indeed, any other) regime.

There is by now a vast literature that complements these criticisms of the globalization thesis. The unifying themes of much of this literature are social economic in nature, including a rejection of the severe essentialism–reductionism couplet that founds the strong globalization thesis. Rather than conceptualizing the global economy as a disembedded institution with a logic of its own (be it a *telos* or a set of laws of motion) that dictates economic, political, social and cultural outcomes, the economy appears in these critiques as entirely instituted by and dependent upon all the non-economic aspects of society. This implies that the political, social and cultural bear on economic practices, institutions and outcomes every bit as much as the reverse. Moreover, rather than standing over and against the local, the global economy is rooted there – in *this* place and *that*. Determinations, as Dicken reminds us, run both ways between the local and the global. In place of the view of autonomous economic practice (be it the drive of capital to accumulate or the human drive to act rationally) as an ontological essence that drives human history, the critique comprises accounts that highlight the mutual causality between (and even, for some, the overdetermination of) economic and non-economic processes.

A range of diverse literatures has emerged that draw on these insights. In development, there has been growing unease with the universalist (neoliberal) prescriptions of the IMF/World Bank of the 1980s and 1990s. Economists such as Joseph Stiglitz have famously excoriated these institutions for the resoluteness with which they have recognized and promoted just one development path for all countries, and for the related failure to be sensitive to institutional context in its prescriptions. In making these arguments Stiglitz is echoing the sentiments expressed by countless heterodox economists over the past two decades who have sought to rescue development policy from the neoclassical reductionism that forecloses on all sorts of viable alternatives (see Chang and Grabel, 2004). Similar themes have now emerged in studies of the advanced industrialized countries. For instance, rather than treating the elimination of capital controls during the 1980s as a natural outcome of economic and technological forces (see above), Eric Helleiner (1995) has offered a historically rich and nuanced account that emphasizes the political determinants of this transformation. For him, although important economic actors had an interest in capital account liberalization, political actors sought liberalization for other reasons (pertaining in part to the desire of the UK and the USA to retain hegemony during this period); moreover, the protection and insurance of emergent financial markets by states were critical to the expansion of international portfolio investment in the 1980s and 1990s. Without a dependable lender-of-last-resort, global financial market activity could not have expanded as it did. In these and related ways, Helleiner demonstrates the political construction of global financial markets that the globalization thesis advocates treated as a simple outcome of autonomous economic forces.

Insights such as Helleiner's are now found routinely within the emerging 'varieties of capitalism' literature that seeks to account for the failure of the convergence thesis. Much of this literature demonstrates the resilience of alternative models of economic organization (including institutions, practices, norms and outcomes) even in the face of global economic pressures (see Rhodes, 1997; Hall and Soskice, 2001; Mosher and Franzese, 2002). Instead, we find the continuing presence and success of alternative forms of market economy. A key lesson of this literature is that even if the global economy were to present similar challenges to all countries (which is indeed unlikely, owing to the diverse ways in which countries are positioned economically), it would not dictate the same response to these challenges. Instead, each country must (and can) find its own way as it navigates the waters of the world economy. Critically, the paths available and chosen are largely shaped by domestic political forces (influenced though they may be by international forces) rather than strictly determined by imperatives associated with the global economy.

3. Expanding the normative terrain

The globalization thesis entails an important normative implication. If the trajectory of the world economy is indeed governed by an authoritarian market that is insulated from ordinary politics, then the range of action that is available to political and economic actors is severely constrained. For those advocates of the globalization thesis who view globalization as both inevitable and benign, the normative imperative is simply to find ways to conform to the pressures emanating from the global economy so as to secure the benefits that this kind of economy promises. Friedman's 'golden straitjacket' is representative of this way of thinking, as is Reich's emphasis on the need to invest in the education of future 'symbolic analysts' who add value and hence secure high incomes even in the face of global market competition. Most of these accounts emphasize the need for the state to reform its practices so as to allow market forces to mediate economic flows and outcomes without undue interference. For the World Bank, for instance, states must orient their development strategies to the world market rather than take steps to insulate themselves from its opportunities and pressures.[4] To do otherwise would threaten to disrupt the altogether beneficial processes of market competition. In contrast, for many Marxists and other advocates of the globalization thesis who view globalization as inevitable but harmful, the normative imperative is to resist – to exploit the internal contradictions associated with globalization to seek its replacement by a more orderly and just economic system. The challenge is to identify these contradictions and the agents who stand to resist efficaciously under the conditions given by global capitalism (see Panitch and Leys, 2004 for important and powerful contributions to this tradition).

These are, of course, simplifications of rather complex sets of arguments. My intent here is to draw into sharp relief what is at stake in the debate over the globalization thesis. 'Ought' implies 'can' – and to the degree that globalization is theorized as dictating what can be done, it equally dictates what ought to be done. We find here in the shadows of the globalization thesis, then, a starkly impoverished normative landscape.

With this in view it becomes clear that this debate, which appears in the first instance as merely positive in its terms, is infused with normative content. Social economic (and other heterodox) accounts of the world economy that refuse adherence to ontological essentialism and explanatory reductionism confront ethical questions and challenges that the globalization thesis advocates ignore as simply beside the point.

One of the most powerful statements of this idea appears in the work of Gibson-Graham (1996, 2006), who offers a feminist post-structuralist critique of much radical political economy (although the critique would apply equally to mainstream neoclassical theory). Gibson-Graham argues that we should recognize theoretical accounts as 'scripts' that don't simply describe what is, as they may purport to do, but that instead enlist agents to take on roles that enable and disable action and thereby shape the world they inhabit. For instance, an orthodox Marxian conception of globalization that posits the capitalist TNC as powerful, impenetrable and unmovable by ordinary political practices may have the effect of imbuing workers (and the communities that host corporations) with a sense of defeatism and acquiescence in the face of demands for wage, tax and other concessions. To the degree that the discourse by which the world economy is theorized has this effect, it doesn't describe corporate power as it is in and of itself, but (discursively) constructs the corporation with powers and capacities that it would not otherwise enjoy (Gibson-Graham, 1996, p. 127). In this view, corporate hegemony is shaped powerfully by the knowledges, beliefs and consequent behaviors of those it confronts. In this sense, the discourses that we bring to bear in knowing globalization are 'performative', not simply descriptive; they interpellate subjects (*pace* Althusser), giving rise to their particular attributes, qualities and capacities. And if that is true, then we need to take much better care in advancing discourses that are structured around determining essences since those may have the effect of suppressing the space that otherwise exists for human agency. This is particularly true for those who advocate the achievement of economic justice: intemperate analyses of the barriers that obstruct genuine improvement may have the unintended effect of shoring up rather than weakening them.

To make this point, Gibson-Graham identifies in the Marxian globalization script a representation of global capitalism as 'unified', 'singular' and 'total'. It is unified in its systematicity and integration (1996, pp. 253–6). This unity implies that there is no space for amelioration: since it cannot be resisted or meaningfully reformed piecemeal, it must be confronted and overturned all at once, as a whole (no matter how remote might be this possibility). It is singular in that its inherent properties (its protean qualities, its internal laws of motion and so forth) are not shared by any alternative system. Hence it has no peer that can withstand competition with it (ibid., pp. 256–8). And it is total in the sense that it encompasses all social processes. There is no meaningful space beyond global capitalism – it infuses and saturates all that exists. In Gibson-Graham's words, 'Our lives are dripping with Capitalism. We cannot get outside Capitalism; it has no outside' (ibid., p. 258). Armed with these attributes, global capitalism appears as the master term in political economy discourse (not unlike the phallic in reductionist feminist theory) that defines the nature of all other terms and that, importantly, thoroughly defines the limits of meaningful political and ethical practice.

Gibson-Graham's emphasis on the social (in her case, discursive) construction of the global economy's attributes reveals new space for efficacious action. She argues for an 'ethic of the local', one that identifies the myriad spaces available at all levels (including the local) not to resist or overthrow capitalism (necessarily), but to build diverse economies based on alternative principles of sharing, cooperation, non-capitalist markets etc. (Gibson-Graham, 2003, 2006). Since capitalism does not infuse all moments and aspects of social (or even economic) existence, we ought not think of these initiatives as simply or necessarily oppositional or as struggles of resistance, since in fact in many sites there may not be anything there to resist. What there is, is the need to theorize alternative economic practices as both available and desirable, and to work to secure political, cultural, economic and social supports so that these alternatives can flourish.[5] I return to this theme below.

4. Social economics and global economic policy reform

These arguments suggest that we confront important practical questions about the kinds of reform that we might seek to ensure that international economic integration serves the needs of people across the globe. Here we confront questions traditionally raised in social ethics, such as what goals ought policy seek to achieve. In other work I have argued at length for the value of Amartya Sen's capabilities approach as a guide for engineering and as a standard for assessing the legitimacy of policies and strategies (see DeMartino, 2000). This framework entails a commitment to the promotion of the substantive freedoms of those most impoverished – in his words, it requires enhancement of people's capabilities to achieve functionings, where functionings refer to the states or conditions, the beings and doings, that people have reason to value (Sen, 1992). Since Sen's work in this area is by now well known, I shall not explicate it here but turn instead to what it might mean for global policy regimes.

The international neoliberal policy regime that is in process of construction is justified by its economic proponents on neoclassical welfarist grounds. This defense claims that the liberalized global market economy will generate greater efficiency than any imaginable alternative regime. But this normative perspective (and the policy prescriptions it yields) is universally rejected by heterodox approaches to political economy, and particularly within the social economic, institutionalist and Marxist traditions. All of the latter emphasize the normative salience of substantive freedom and equality. The idea is that people should enjoy relatively equal freedom to live valued lives. Sen's capabilities approach encapsulates this sentiment. Hence it is not surprising that the approach has been warmly received by so many heterodox economists.

To date, Sen's work has done much to reorient domestic-level development policy away from economic efficiency and growth toward a much wider conception of 'development as freedom' (Sen, 1999). His work has been fully embraced by agencies such as the UNDP, whose Human Development Index (which measures income, educational attainment, health, gender equality and other aspects of social existence) incorporates the capabilities approach. But it nevertheless remains the case that Sen's work has had very little impact on debates about global economic policy regimes (such as trade and investment regimes). In this domain, the welfarist emphasis on efficiency and growth remains hegemonic.

One interpretation of this circumstance is that the best that can be achieved at the global level are policies that increase economic efficiency and, thereby, promote economic growth. Hence, for instance, we may conclude that free trade and liberalized capital flows are desirable since they promote growth in developing countries, and thereby provide the material foundations to enact capabilities-enhancing development policies domestically (even if, by itself, free trade does not affect capabilities directly). Any interference with liberalized global economic flows, the argument continues, would reduce economic growth in the world's poorest countries, and thereby obstruct the expansion of capabilities there.

This view is deficient on several grounds. First, rejection of the reductionist logic of neoclassical theory implies that we cannot be at all sure that liberalized global flows will indeed promote rapid economic growth. Whether free trade promotes growth, for instance, will depend on the way in which the opportunities and challenges associated with trade are mediated by local institutions, resources and practices. Hence the effect of free trade is context-dependent and contingent rather than fully determined. This implies that in many cases free trade might be capabilities-reducing – and we might expect that this will be true particularly for those who are already capabilities-impoverished, since they would (by definition) have the fewest resources available to insulate themselves from economic disruption (Rodrik, 1997). Second, even if we reject the notion that the global fully determines the local, it is nevertheless true that the nature of the global regime will have effects on domestic processes and outcomes that reach beyond simple economic flows. Global economic changes may bias local political outcomes in one direction or another by empowering some agents and disempowering others. Hence it is not enough to promote growth by any means available first, and to attend to capabilities equality second – since the first move will have effects that may preclude the ultimate goal. The elimi-nation of capital controls is again instructive: even if these have political preconditions and require political supports (as Helleiner reminds us), once they are instituted they undoubtedly provide institutional investors with a degree of control over political processes and outcomes that might prevent, for instance, progressive taxation that would be required to enhance the capabilities of the poor (Grabel, 1996; Harmes, 1998).

I am suggesting here that the social economic rejection of the economic determinism that inheres in the strong globalization thesis is not to be taken to imply that global processes and regimes are irrelevant with respect to human development. Far from it. Instead, the mutual determination of the local and the global implies that both terrains matter deeply – and that a progressive economic politics that seeks genuine human development (and equality) must attend to the nature of policy regimes all the way up, and all the way down.

I have advanced and argued elsewhere for a new set of global economic policy regimes that would be apt to promote global equality of human capabilities (DeMartino, 2000). These entail a new trade regime that rewards countries for promoting human development, a new regime to reg-ulate the behavior of TNCs, and a new labor mobility regime. The hope is that such regimes will affect not only international economic flows, impor-tant as this goal may be, but that they will also alter domestic political forces in such ways as to promote the influence of those agents that are pushing for human development. In this conception, which accepts eco-nomic influence but rejects economic determinism, attention is and must be paid to the interpenetration of the economic and the political.

5.   Looking forward

To date the task implied by this project – of envisioning and establishing achievable global and local economic policy regimes that will serve the end of the development and equality of human capabilities – remains in its infancy. This stems in large part from the intellectual influence of the strong globalization thesis over the past several decades. As examined above, this thesis has suppressed awareness of the space that exists for alternative directions. But if the claim presented above concerning the waning influence of the strong globalization thesis is correct, then we might have reason for a degree of optimism about new opportunities for social economists to contribute much to new understandings of what is possible and desirable in the global and local policy arenas.

But what might these new understandings entail? Let me conclude with brief thoughts about just one possibility that is consistent with Sen's capabilities framework. Returning to the work of Gibson-Graham, one fruitful theoretical path forward might entail a rejection of the notion of economic development as involving any one kind of economic practice. We might come to view 'the economy' as an ensemble of diverse 'alternative economies' including (for instance) market and non-market practices, capitalist and non-capitalist commodities and firms, gifting, volunteering and many other non-exchange forms of provisioning, etc. We might pay more attention to the ways in which these economic practices and institutions interact, and explore the ways in which they provide conditions of existence for each other's vitality (and the vitality of the communities that engage in them). We might come to recognize that policy regimes that ignore the heterogeneity of any and all economies, and that seek to install and support what are taken to be the primary economic practices without due regard for other 'economic species' that cohabit the same space are apt to undermine the economic ecosystem in ways that deprive people of the means necessary to thrive. In this account, then, we would not simply identify the market (say) as the problem or the solution; we would instead look to theorize how a policy regime that single-mindedly promotes markets might actually interfere with their operation while threatening other economic forms that are vital to the achievement and advancement of human capabilities.

The language here purposely draws on conceptions from the field of ecology. There is much concern today about the deleterious consequences of the promotion of monoculture as a means to promote agricultural efficiency. We have learned that this strategy is unsustainable for many reasons. Not least, it requires increasing energy inputs and pesticides per calorie produced, it exacerbates the vulnerability of agricultural production to environmental and other shocks, it degrades agricultural land, etc. As a consequence, there is much greater appreciation today of the need to sustain agricultural/genetic diversity and to employ natural and complementary systems for managing yields, protecting against pests, ensuring soil quality, and maintaining the health of animal and plant life (Pollan, 2006).

Central principles of social economics, especially its commitment to holistic, non-reductionist social science, suggest the value of theorizing the economy in similar ways. From this perspective, economic development should promote economic 'polyculture' rather than 'monoculture' as a means to secure human development and protection against economic risk. And this implies that theoretical work might be fruitfully directed at exploring the manner in which policy regimes can achieve this diverse economy – not just a Keynesian 'mixed' economy with the correct balance between the private and public sectors, but an economy in which both the private and public sectors are themselves thoroughly heterogeneous and given to experimentation, alteration and reform.

In the global arena this way of thinking generates an argument against overspecialization of national economies based on comparative advantage, as Herman Daly has argued (Daly, 1993). Overspecialization leaves communities vulnerable to shocks and requires wastage of resources (and overdependence on fossil fuels) for transporting the goods that pass through global markets. But it also impoverishes the community by eliminating diversity of opportunities upon which a rich human and social existence depends. As a consequence of these insights, this way of thinking implies that global regimes must recognize the value of and protect national and local economic heterogeneity while at the same time allowing communities to enhance their capabilities through international economic integration. It implies that these global policy regimes must enhance national and local economic policy autonomy so that they can take the steps necessary to sustain their economic ecosystems in pursuit of human development and stability.

In all of this, social economics has a vital role to play. Once we reject the reductionism inherent in the strong globalization thesis, we may be emboldened to think out loud about the kinds of alternative regimes that are both available and desirable. And if the discourses we use not only describe the global regime's properties but actually inscribe them, if our discourses are not simply explanatory but performative, then the advocacy of social economic alternatives is nothing less than an ethical imperative for those seeking a more just global economy.

Acknowledgment

Thanks to Kate Watkins, who provided invaluable research assistance for this project.

Notes

1. Conversely, some argued that the period from 1870 to World War I was also an era of globalization, and that the late twentieth-century events therefore represented a return

2.   Two pages later Dicken writes, 'The most significant development in the world economy during the past few decades has been the *increasing globalization of economic activities*' (italics in the original; ibid., p. 3).
3.   See Berger and Dore (1996) – especially the editors' introduction – for a comprehensive but concise introduction to the academic debate over convergence as it stood in the early to mid-1990s.
4.   For instance, see its *World Development Report, 1995* for a particularly forceful and concise statement of the need for developing states to liberalize while opening up to the world economy.
5.   These supports are not to be read as an indication that these alternatives are peculiarly vulnerable: indeed, capitalist processes are every bit as dependent on these supports as would be any other economic practice. Over the past decade Gibson-Graham has co-founded the Community Economies Project, which has sought to discover, theorize and nurture alternative economic institutions and practices in the USA, Australia and other parts of the world. This work is predicated on the ideas presented in the text – that rather than being unified, singular and total, global capitalism is porous, disorganized and permissive of all sorts of alternative economic structures and practices. This implies the need to restore the 'ethic of the local' as a consequence of understanding the space available for the remaking of economic identities and practices. See www.communityeconomies.org/ for a full description of the Project.

The first paragraph top:
to this kind of regime following a long intervening period of state interference. Bairoch and Kozul-Wright (1996) examine this thesis carefully and ultimately reject it.

References

Bairoch, P. and R. Kozul-Wright (1996), 'Globalization myths: some historical reflections on integration, industrialization and growth in the world economy', *United Nations Conference on Trade and Development*, No. 113, March.
Berger, S. and R. Dore (eds) (1996), *National Diversity and Global Capitalism*, Ithaca, NY: Cornell University Press.
Chang, H.J. and I. Grabel (2004), *Reclaiming Development: An Alternative Economic Policy Manual*, London: Zed Books.
Daly, H. (1993), 'The Perils of Free Trade', *Scientific American*, November, 41–57.
DeMartino, G. (2000), *Global Economy, Global Justice: Theoretical Objections and Policy Alternatives to Neoliberalism*, London: Routledge.
Dicken, P. (1992), *Global Shift*, 2nd edn, New York: Guilford Press.
Dicken, P. (1998), *Global Shift*, 3rd edn, New York: Guilford Press.
Dicken, P. (2003), *Global Shift*, 4th edn, New York: Guilford Press.
Friedman, T.L. (2000), *The Lexus and the Olive Tree: Understanding Globalization*, New York: Farrar, Straus & Giroux.
Friedman, T.L. (2005), *The World is Flat: A Brief History of the 21st Century*, New York: Farrar, Straus and Giroux.
Fukuyama, F. (1989), 'The End of History?', *The National Interest*, **18**, Summer, 3–18.
Gereffi, G. and M. Korzeniewicz (eds) (1994), *Commodity Chains and Global Capitalism*, Westport, CT: Praeger.
Gibson-Graham, J.K. (1996), *The End of Capitalism (As We Knew It): A Feminist Critique of Political Economy*, Oxford: Blackwell Publishers.
Gibson-Graham, J.K. (2003), 'An ethics of the local', *Rethinking Marxism*, **15** (1), 49–74.
Gibson-Graham, J.K. (2006), *A Postcapitalist Politics*, Minneapolis, MN: University of Minnesota.
Goodman, J. and L. Pauly (1993), 'The obsolescence of capital controls? Economic management in an age of global markets', *World Politics*, **46**, 50–82.
Grabel, I. (1996), 'Marketing the Third World: the contradictions of portfolio investment in the global economy', *World Development*, **24** (11), 1761–76.
Hall, P. and D. Soskice (eds) (2001), *Varieties of Capitalism: The Institutional Foundations of Comparative Advantage*, Oxford: Oxford University Press.

Harmes, A. (1998), 'Institutional investors and the reproduction of neoliberalism', *Review of International Political Economy*, 5 (1), 92–121.

Helleiner, E. (1995), 'Explaining the globalization of financial markets: bringing states back in', *Review of International Political Economy*, 2 (2), 315–41.

Hirst, P. and G. Thompson (1999), *Globalization in Question*, 2nd edn, Cambridge: Polity Press.

Mosher, J.M. and R.J. Franzese, Jr (2002), 'Comparative institutional and policy advantage: the scope for divergence within European economic integration', *European Union Politics*, 3 (2), 177–203.

Ohmae, K. (1994), *The Borderless World: Power and Strategy in the Interlinked Economy*, New York: The Free Press.

Ohmae, K. (1995), *The End of the Nation State: The Rise of Regional Economies*, New York: The Free Press.

Panitch, L. and C. Leys (eds) (2004), *The Empire Reloaded*, London: Merlin Press.

Pollan, M. (2006), *The Omnivore's Dilemma: A Natural History of Four Meals*, New York: Penguin Press.

Reich, R.B. (1991), *The Work of Nations*, New York: Alfred A. Knopf.

Rhodes, M. (1997), 'Globalization, labour markets and welfare states: a future for "Competitive Corporatism"?', in M. Rhodes and Y. Meny (eds), *The Future of European Welfare*, London: Macmillan.

Rodrik, D. (1997), *Has Globalization Gone too Far?*, Washington, DC: Institute for International Economics.

Sen, A. (1992), *Inequality Reexamined*, Cambridge, MA: Harvard University Press.

Sen, A. (1999), *Development as Freedom*, New York: Alfred A. Knopf.

Strange, S. (1996), *The Retreat of the State: The Diffusion of Power in the World Economy*, Cambridge: Cambridge University Press.

Tilly, C. (1995), 'Globalization threatens labor's rights', *International Labor and Working-class History*, 47, 1–23.

Wilks, S. (1994), 'Class compromise and the international economy: the rise and fall of Swedish social democracy', *Capital and Class*, no. 58, 89–111.

World Bank (1995), *World Development Report, 1995: Workers in an Integrating World Economy*, New York: Oxford University Press.

PART II

THE SOCIALLY
EMBEDDED INDIVIDUAL

Chapter 5: 'Individual preferences and decision-making', by Shaun P. Hargreaves Heap

The dominant model of decision-making in economics identifies the individual with their preferences; and decisions are made so as best to satisfy these preferences. The concept of preference is thus the lynchpin on which instrumental reason works and it is largely untheorized because, paradigmatically, *de gustibus non est disputandum*. One way of understanding the contribution of socio-economics is that it does not accept that preferences are a given in this sense: they are, instead, socially and historically constituted. The social aspect of this naturally weakens the individualism of the dominant model. The historical dimension then creates the space for a different and dynamic conception of the individual as someone who in some degree chooses and becomes responsible for their preferences; and it is in this way that they gain a sense of identity.

Chapter 6: 'The conception of the socially embedded individual', by John B. Davis

The chapter describes the conception of the socially embedded individual, and compares it to the conception of the standard atomistic individual. The difference between these two conceptions is that the former explains individuals and their behaviour 'externally' in terms of their social relationships and the latter explains them 'internally' in terms of their private tastes and preferences. The two conceptions also support two different normative visions of individuals and society, with the conception of the embedded individual supporting a social justice view and the atomistic conception supporting a liberal society view. The chapter surveys recent contributions to the embedded individual conception, and then discusses two fundamental issues raised by these contributions: (a) the relation of social identity to personal identity, and (b) the problem of inequality. The chapter closes with comments on how thinking about individuals in economics may evolve in the future, particularly in connection with the current process of change in economics as a whole.

Chapter 7: 'The social dimension of internal conflict', by David George

This chapter considers the social implications of internal conflict while contrasting the second-order preference approach to such conflict with the two-selves and multiple-selves approaches. The initial focus is on second-order preferences. The chapter starts by reviewing how in the absence of property rights and social conventions, market forces would be inefficient in the creation of preferences, tending to produce too many preferences that agents would prefer not to have. Social considerations enter at two levels. First, consideration is given to whether preferred preferences are any more or less likely to be socially created than unpreferred preferences. Second, attention is given to whether the content of preferences that agents prefer having tend to be more or less concerned with the well-being of others than do unpreferred preferences. The chapter goes on to consider three problems with two-selves and multiple-selves approaches to internal conflict. Towards the conclusion, evidence is offered that suggests the problem of unpreferred preferences is growing.

Chapter 8: 'The socio-economics of consumption: solutions to the problems of interest, knowledge and identity', by Metin M. Coşgel

This chapter is a review of the socio-economic literature on consumption. Considering consumption as a social activity, it examines how consumption solves the problems of interest, knowledge and identity. It also discusses the main themes and important contributions in each category, and offers suggestions for further research.

5 Individual preferences and decision-making
Shaun P. Hargreaves Heap

1. Introduction

The dominant model of decision-making in economics identifies the individual with their preferences; and decisions are made so as best to satisfy these preferences. The concept of preference is thus the lynchpin on which instrumental reason works and it is largely untheorized because, paradigmatically, *de gustibus es non disputandum*.

One way of understanding the contribution of social economics is that it does not accept that preferences are a given in this sense: they are, instead, socially and historically constituted. The social aspect of this naturally weakens the individualism of the dominant model, but the historical dimension creates the space for a different and dynamic conception of the individual as someone who in some degree chooses and becomes responsible for their preferences.

Of course, there are several ways to elaborate this distinguishing observation about the individual in social economics. The virtue of using the language of preferences to cash out social and historical location in this context is that it preserves a point of connection with the dominant model. This both enables a form of dialogue and avoids the charge that 'making individuals social and historical' is no more than a slogan. It could, however, have two possible disadvantages. First, the traffic across the preference bridge may in practice blur the distinction between social economics and the dominant model. Since substance matters more than titles, I am not especially disturbed by such ambiguities regarding provenance. Second, although the concept of preference is famously elastic, this approach may place too much of a burden on it. If this proves to be the case, then this, too, is a useful inference.

I take up the social and historical aspects of the contribution of social economics respectively in the next two sections. In the final section, I consider in more detail how the idea of individual identity is understood when the individual is socially and historically located, and I discuss some of the key likely areas for future work.

2.   Social location

A person's preferences over outcomes may exhibit a social character in a variety of ways. The least problematic conceptually for the dominant model of individual agency is when a person's preference over outcomes takes account of how any state of affairs affects not only themselves but also others.

Various models of altruistic behaviour have a long history in this respect and have often been invoked to explain, for instance, why people cooperate in prisoner's dilemma games. A recent line of argument (see Fehr and Schmidt, 1999) in this vein posits more specifically that individuals dislike inequality. Thus individual i's utility function representation of their preferences in an interaction with 'j' takes the form of (5.1), where $\$_i$ refers to the financial return to 'i', and 'c' is a parameter capturing the weight attached to the dislike for inequality.

$$U_i = \$_i - c.\max(0, \$_i - \$_j) - c.\max(0, \$_j - \$_i) \qquad (5.1)$$

To see the effect of this type of social (or 'other-regarding') preference, consider the interaction given by Figure 5.1. This is a prisoner's dilemma when each individual's utility is assumed to depend (positively) *only* on his or her financial return because the dominant action for each person is 'defect' even though the ensuing outcome is Pareto-dominated by the strategy pair of mutual 'cooperation'. If, however, people playing this game dislike inequality and have preferences of the form given by (5.1), then the game is transformed. In particular, when 'c' has the value 0.5, Figure 5.2 now captures the interaction in terms of utility payoffs.

There are two Nash equilibria in the game of Figure 5.2: [cooperate, cooperate] and [defect, defect]. Hence if acting rationally on one's preferences (with common knowledge of this rationality and common priors) licenses actions that are in a Nash equilibrium, it will no longer be surprising to find that people sometimes choose to cooperate in the interaction depicted in Figure 5.1 (as they often do experimentally; see Dawes and Thaler, 1988).

		B	
		Cooperate	Defect
A	Cooperate	$3,$3	0,$4
	Defect	$4,0	$1,$1

Figure 5.1   Financial payoffs

		B	
		Cooperate	Defect
A	Cooperate	3,3	–2,2
	Defect	2,–2	1,1

Figure 5.2   Utility payoffs

This type of 'social' preference is benign in the sense that it can unlock the dilemma faced by those who seem to be in a free-rider or prisoner-dilemma type of interaction. In turn, this can materially affect some of the arguments around the need for institutions of collective action. The point is this. The existence of interactions that take the form of the prisoner's dilemma/free rider supply *prima facie* grounds for constraining individual freedom by substituting a mechanism of collective action for that of individual decision-making. This was, for example, famously Hobbes's argument for a sovereign and it has formed the basis for contractarian arguments in support of the state ever since. Hence, in so far as people do have social preferences of this kind, the need to constrain individual freedom in order to avoid the inefficient outcomes found in a state of nature is reduced because they will be avoided automatically, so to speak, through the good offices of individual sociality.

The same cannot be said of another kind of 'other-regarding' preference: relative comparison. The thought that people might specifically like to do better than others, so that how well they are doing relatively matters as well as how they are faring absolutely, has a long history of interest outside of economics (e.g. see Boudon, 1986) and at the margins of the discipline (e.g. in discussions of poverty and through the work of Veblen, 1889). It has, though, recently become a central consideration in the discussion of the so-called happiness paradox. This is the paradox that while we seem to pursue more wealth with great vigour and indeed enjoy much higher levels of it than our parents did, there is little evidence that we seem to be any happier than they were (e.g. see Frank, 1997; Oswald, 1997). If people are significantly concerned with their relative position, then it will be clear that an increase in everyone's income need not make people much happier. The effect is the same as when everyone stands in a sporting arena: no one gets a better view as compared with when everyone was sitting down.

The implication as far as government intervention is concerned is rather different for this kind of 'other-regarding' preference. Since the individual pursuit of more goods and services has a negative external effect here on others, there are grounds for intervention to discourage such effort (e.g. through taxes on consumption).

There is another broad category of social preference that is distinguished by its conditional nature: that is, a person is motivated by a concern for another when they expect this to be reciprocated. There is both experimental evidence of this conditional behaviour and examples from history, like the 'live and let live' norm at the beginning of World War I (see respectively Clark and Sefton, 2001; Axelrod, 1984). There are several formulations and I shall consider two that at first glance seem rather different but which plausibly belong to the same tradition, drawing on sociological and anthropological insights regarding the influence that the norms of a group have on intergroup behaviour. Within economics, these ideas have notably begun to receive more attention through the discussion of social capital. Here, it is often argued that people who belong to a group behave differently among themselves as compared with outsiders because their internal exchanges are guided by norms of trust that enable savings in transaction, monitoring costs, etc. (see Fukuyama, 1995; *Economic Journal* feature, 2002). The importance of group membership in this respect can be thought to arise because membership encodes an expectation of reciprocation that is important for triggering these shared 'other-regarding' preferences. In this way, these models of individual decision-making provide a way of making operational at the level of the individual some of the arguments that have been advanced in relation to how groups and their norms constitute a form of social capital.

The importance of reciprocation for the generation of new social payoffs has a much longer pedigree in economics. Adam Smith (1759 [1976]) famously argued that people obtained a very special pleasure from sharing judgements regarding what was appropriate behaviour. The origin of such shared judgements in Smith is the 'sympathy' that we feel for others which he treats as a psychological fact and which he suggests is the basis for our moral judgements. Such 'sympathy' is, in effect, no different from the kind of feeling that the altruist has. What distinguishes Smith is the further argument that people enjoy a special pleasure from mutual sympathy: 'nothing pleases us more than to observe in men a fellow feeling with all the emotions of our own breast'. So when Jill acts and Jack sympathizes or approves and Jill knows that Jack sympathizes in this way, she gets a very special pleasure. This is very different from the reflective effect among altruists because they take their character from the initial experience: if this is good then others feel it as good; if it is bad then others feel it as bad. With mutual sympathy, when Jill experiences something bad, Jack's initial sympathy will also experience the badness, but when Jill knows that Jack has sympathized, she derives a positive pleasure (see Sugden, 2002). Since moral ideas encode feelings of sympathy, the sharing of these ideas (so that they become norms) becomes a guide to the actions that will generate the special pleasure of mutual sympathy. Or to put this slightly differently, the shared rules of moral conduct create an expectation that one should act in a particular way, and acting in accord with this expectation creates the special pleasure of mutual sympathy.

The first formal 'modern' model of decision-making with this reciprocal quality comes originally from Geanakoplos et al. (1989), but is probably best known through Rabin (1993), which I set out in (5.2) and (5.3) below. Equation (5.2) has a similar form to (5.1) in the sense that it comprises of two parts. The first is the 'material' payoffs that 'i' receives from some outcome O: that is the utility value of whatever are the material aspects of the outcome for 'i' ($=M(O)$). So in the game of Figure 5.1, this would be the utility value of the $ outcome. The second part is the 'psychological' payoff associated with this outcome ($=P(O)$). This is akin to the element in (5.1) that comes from people valuing equality, but it now has a more complicated form, set out in (5.3).

$$U_i(O) = (1-v)\, M_i(O) + vP_i(O), \qquad (5.2)$$

where 'v' is a parameter that weights the 'material' and 'psychological' aspects of an outcome.

$$P_i(O) = f_i(O)[1 + f_j(O)], \qquad (5.3)$$

where 'f' is a function that identifies the fairness (i.e. $f > 0$) or unfairness (i.e. $f < 0$) of each person's action.

Here 'i' enjoys positive 'psychological' payoffs when the outcome involves either *both* people acting 'fairly' ($f > 0$) or *both* acting 'unfairly' ($f < 0$). In other words, it depends on reciprocation. The positive effect of both behaving badly is sometimes controversial but can account for why people punish each other when each expects the other to breach whatever is the reigning norm of fairness. It is not an essential part of this theory. Equally Rabin's original expression for how 'fairness' might be judged is controversial, but can easily be amended.

Such amendments may change some the character of the behaviour that is predicted but they are unlikely to change an important feature of this kind of modelling. It is worth bringing out. To judge the 'fairness' or 'rightness' of someone's action, you typically need to know what they were expecting you to do. Thus 'cooperate' may be the 'right' action in a prisoner's dilemma when the other person expects you to 'cooperate', but if they expect you to 'defect', then 'defect' might be the 'right' action in the sense that this is what the prevailing norm within that group dictates. This dependence of the psychological payoffs on expectations potentially complicates the usual chain of causation in game theory whereby beliefs about what others will do are to be derived from knowledge of the payoffs and the assumptions of rationality, common knowledge of rationality and common priors. Instead, in this case, one would need to fix beliefs before the payoffs could be determined. To place some restriction on the admissible beliefs for this purpose and so bring some determinacy to the analysis, it is natural to require that beliefs are equilibrium ones. But once this is done, there is a sense in which the whole apparatus of game theory becomes strangely irrelevant since once one knows equilibrium beliefs, one knows the actions that are to be undertaken, in which case there is no real need to calibrate payoffs in their light in order to show that the actions are, indeed, in equilibrium relative to these payoffs (see Hargreaves Heap and Varoufakis, 2005).

The second example of conditional social preferences comes from the work on 'we' or 'collective' intentionality (see Sugden, 2000; Tuomela, 1995; Davis, 2003). When a central defender in a soccer match tackles and wins the ball in the penalty area and decides to pass the ball promptly to a colleague in mid-field, there is a natural question. Why didn't he or she try to beat a few of the opposing players before passing or shooting at the opposition goal? Anyone who has played football will know that the 6m pass is humdrum, whereas the pleasure of taking the ball past an opponent is second only to scoring a goal. One explanation is that the defender discounts this pleasure by the risk of failure and the attendant threat of being dropped from the team, transferred, etc. Alternatively, when he or she puts on a number 5 shirt, it could be said that they become a member of a team and so now decides what to do with reference to the team's interests and not his or her own. This is the idea behind 'collective' or 'we' intentionality: when we belong to a team we reason using a different set of collective preferences. This reasoning is sometimes called 'team reasoning'.

Thus for example in the prisoner's dilemma of Figure 5.1, when A and B belong to the same team, the team's interests might be defined by the average payoff with the result that the payoffs become those of Figure 5.3.

A team thinker then considers what action each member of the team should take in order to maximize the average payoff, with the result that, in this case, each team member decides to cooperate. Reciprocation is crucial in this account because the transformation from Figure 5.1 to Figure 5.3 occurs only when team members play with each other (see Bacharach, 1999, where this is explicit). One team player interacting with a non-team player would have no reason to use 'team reasoning' because he or she is not in a team in these circumstances.

		B	
		Cooperate	Defect
A	Cooperate	3,3	2,2
	Defect	2,2	1,1

Figure 5.3   Team payoffs

These theories introduce two difficult and related issues concerning how particular norms arise and how groups or teams are formed. I shall say more about this in the final section. For now, these issues supply a useful backdrop for the discussion of the historical aspect of agency in social economics.

3.   Historical location
There are two broadly different but not necessarily mutually exclusive ways in which the historical dimension of individual decision-making arises in social economics. Both potentially supply parts of an answer to the question of where norms and groups come from by appealing to the history of social interaction, but they differ, at least on first inspection, over the way that individual decision-making occurs historically.

The first has history as something that, so to speak, exercises an influence behind the person's back. In one version of this, the individual is socialized through institutions such as the family, and this helps explain how they come to have their preferences (see Etzioni, 1988, 1993; Becker, 1992, for example).

In another version of history behind the back, the individual is thought to be boundedly rational in the sense that people have (some) preferences but rely on rules of thumb instead of calculations as to how best to satisfy them, and it plots how these rules might evolve through learning. When the rules apply to behaviour in social interactions that are repeated within a population, learning takes on a social character and can explain the emergence of conventions (shared rules) among that population (see Sugden, 1986).

A simple intuition for the evolutionary argument comes from imagining a population that interacts in ways that resemble two motorists converging from different roads on the same intersection. If some people start to use a rule that assigns priority to one of the parties when they meet, then those using the rule will achieve a mutually superior outcome, with one person speeding up and the other slowing down, as compared with the free-for-all without a rule when there will always be some crashes or delays as both stop. This advantage encourages others to use the same rule until it spreads within a population.

Since the shared rule is in effect a coordinating device, there is no reason to expect any particular rule to emerge. 'Give way to the right' works as well, in principle, as 'give way to the left' or 'give way to the major road' or any of a number so long as it is shared. This has the interesting effect of making the details of history matter because 'who' chose 'what' 'when' influences the actual selection of a rule and typically the character of the rule will affect the distribution of the gains from coordination in society. Thus, in the 'crossroads of life', one is as likely to find rules such as 'give way to the male/female' or 'give way to the old/young' emerging, with consequent interesting effects on social stratification.

It is sometimes suggested (e.g. in evolutionary accounts of morality and some versions of evolutionary psychology) that these historical processes can account for the emergence of shared moral views. The difficulty with this, however, is that the evolutionary learning model explains the emergence of a convention, a simple shared rule. It does not explain how such a rule comes to have normative appeal: that is, how it comes to be seen not just as the sensible thing to do, but also the 'right' thing. It is tempting to rely on some psychological mechanism that turns an 'is' into an 'ought' for this purpose, but this would seem in some minimal way to require some expanded sense of rationality or agency (even if it too can be given an evolutionary explanation), and in this way this approach seems likely to come to occupy much of the same terrain as the next that I discuss.

The second historical approach relies explicitly on psychological insights and makes individuals 'rational' in a different way at the outset. It is often argued that the concept of the individual *qua* individual in the dominant model of decision-making is surprisingly slight. He or she is no more than a set of preferences and yet there are richer models of individuality within the liberal political tradition: notably those that derive from Kant and involve the idea of autonomy. Autonomous individuals are those who consciously, rationally in Kant's case, select what ends to pursue; this is the motivating thought of the other historical approach.

Little headway has been made using Kant's particular understanding of rationality for this purpose (although see O'Neill, 1989), but many psychologists have worked with a looser sense of autonomy and studied how particular psychological processes might affect the choice of ends. In particular, they posit in one way or another that people like to be able to reflect on what they do and find that their actions are worthy. Not unsurprisingly, perhaps, and especially when the philosophical difficulties of such a project are taken seriously, people often fall short on this account and so develop psychological mechanisms of dissonance avoidance. The character of these mechanisms together with the history of individual behaviour can then help explain how (social) preferences change.

One of the influential theories in this regard is Deci's (1975) model of extrinsic and intrinsic reason.[1] On this account, there are two broad types of justification for an action: it either follows from the circumstances that an individual found themselves in (i.e. 'extrinsic' reason) and/or it was just the 'right' thing to do (i.e. 'intrinsic' reason). With some licence it is not difficult to translate this into the familiar rational choice distinction between the constraints on choice and the preferences which inform the evaluation of the options. Where the theory offers new purchase is by hypothesizing that people exercise economy in their justifications by appealing to one or other type of reason, and this provides a dynamic for the evolution of the type of reason over which the individual has some control: intrinsic reason. Thus, when a person finds that there are both extrinsic and intrinsic reasons for an action, they will shade their assessment of its intrinsic worth. Conversely, if a person finds themselves doing something that appears to have little extrinsic or intrinsic value, they will revise upwards their assessment of its intrinsic worth. In this way, there is a theory of how people's assessment of the intrinsic worth of an action can change, and when intrinsic worth turns on shared ideas of what actions are worthy, we have, in effect, a theory of how social preferences can change. It depends on actions and whether they can be justified by appeals to external reason.

It will be obvious how this might help with the issue of how conventions acquire normative force, and the idea has been used to explain a variety of phenomena in economics (see Frey, 1997). For example, an abiding puzzle for the dominant rational choice model concerns why the introduction of systems of payment by results frequently seems to have no good effect. It is puzzling because one would ordinarily, from the position of the rational choice model, expect that payment by results should overcome the agency problem that would otherwise exist within a firm. However, if there is a fairness norm within the firm (e.g. see Akerlof and Yellen, 1990), the introduction of a payment by results system suddenly supplies an additional 'extrinsic' reason for supplying high effort. Working with high effort then becomes, so to speak, overdetermined and workers adjust their perception of the intrinsic value of such action. In this way the fairness norm is undermined and so is any positive contribution it makes here and in any other areas where the goodwill of workers matters within the firm (see Hargreaves Heap, 2004, for an analysis of the reverse process, where participation helps create intrinsic reasons).

4.   Identity and future research

The presence of psychological processes of the kind just sketched is often taken as evidence that we are in some sense less than rational or at least less consciously in charge of ourselves than we ideally imagine. So it may at first sight seem strange to want to use the evidence of these psychological processes as testaments to our individual identities. The point is, however, that at least some of these psychological processes are precisely intelligible as pragmatic responses to what are known philosophical difficulties with questing for something like a sense of self-worth. So their operation illustrates something *more* rather than something less about the individual.

In much the same way, it is tempting to conclude that the dependence on group membership discussed earlier further weakens any claim that the individuals in social economics have an individual identity. Again that would be a mistake. Granted that people like to feel that their actions reflect well upon them and the associated desire to avoid senses of guilt, shame or embarrassment which can arise when they do not, people need some standard by which to judge the rightness of their actions. This cannot be a purely personal standard, otherwise it will be open to personal manipulation and so fail to perform the psychological role of validating action. It must be external to the individual, and this externality comes through such standards being shared with others. Adam Smith (1759 [1976]) provides an early example of this point and its connection with moral norms.

> When we are about to act, the eagerness of passion will seldom allow us to consider what we are doing, with the candour of an indifferent person . . .
>
> When the action is over, indeed, and the passions which prompted it have subsided, we can enter more coolly into the sentiments of the indifferent spectator . . . It is seldom, however, that they are quite candid even in this case . . . It is so disagreeable to think ill of ourselves, that we often purposely turn away our view from those circumstances which might render that judgement unfavourable. He is a bold surgeon, they say, whose hand does not tremble when he performs an operation on his own person; and he is often equally bold who does not hesitate to pull off the mysterious veil of self-delusion, which covers from his view the deformities of his own conduct. (Ibid., pp. 157–8)

It is in this context that Smith argues we come to rely on norms or rules of moral conduct.

> Nature, however, has not left this weakness . . . altogether without remedy; nor has she abandoned us entirely to the delusions of self love. Our continual observations upon the conduct of others, insensibly lead us to form to ourselves certain general rules concerning what is fit and proper either to be done or to be avoided.
>
> It is thus that the general rules of morality are formed. They are ultimately founded upon the experiences of what, in particular instances, our moral

faculties, our natural sense of merit and propriety, approve, or disapprove of. We do not originally approve or condemn particular actions; because upon examination, they appear to be agreeable or inconsistent with a certain general rule. The general rule, on the contrary, is formed by finding from experience, that all actions of a certain kind, or circumstanced in a certain manner, are approved or disapproved of. (Ibid., p. 159)

The last part of this argument is, of course, controversial and I shall return to it in a moment. For now what is important is that Smith supplies an early version of a philosophically famous (and in some forms contentious) argument (over the impossibility of private languages) which makes membership of groups unavoidable if individuals wish to reflect on the worth of their actions (as this is how standards become external, and so psychologically valuable, to the individual). Thus dependence on groups does not gesture to some lack of individuality; rather it marks a kind of individuality where identity comes from a sense of self-worth.

There are two things to say about this. The first is that the concept of 'preference' may well be stretched too much in this context. The social preferences that express a person's sense of self-worth are rather different to the symptomatic preferences for apples and oranges in the textbook. If the textbook usually deals with the physical properties of outcomes, these social preferences turn on their symbolic properties; and these in turn depend on shared ideas about what is worthy. Or to put this slightly differently, if behaviour is to be justified, then one cannot appeal to a 'preference' because a 'preference' is just that. The currency of justification is ideas, even if their influence can be redescribed using the concept of a social preference and so keep some formal faith with the dominant instrumental model. (The same point can be made in relation to the use of the concept of a 'metapreference' to describe how people come to value their preferences.)

One agenda for future research follows directly from this. Although we know that norms or belonging to a group can affect behaviour and we have some idea of the psychological mechanisms that affect the strength of these influences, we lack detailed, systematic knowledge of why groups sometimes exercise very strong influence over their members and sometimes not, or why people regard some groups as more relevant for their identities than others. In short, this is really a call to continue the research that I have been sketching in Sections 2 and 3 because the activation and influence of social preference is still inadequately understood (see Henrich et al., 2001, for a pioneering experiment on cross-country differences in the play of an ultimatum game).

Second, even if the individual outside of the group or groups is in some sense unimaginable when they hanker after self-worth, there remains a question as to whether self-worth quite equates with autonomy. Groups may be indispensable, but to what extent do people choose the ones to which they belong? Likewise the presence of psychological mechanisms such as those described in Section 3 may be a testament to the quest for a sense of self-worth, but surely people navigate this psychological world with varying degrees of personal control. Some people have greater resources for reflexivity and so come to have a stronger sense of identity than others. It is for this reason that some authors in the social economic tradition have gone beyond social and historical location and argued that individual identity comes, for instance, from being able to choose the groups/norms that one wishes to identify with. Identity comes through having 'capabilities' is one way of putting this point (see Sen, 1985; Davis, 2003).

This signals the second item on the agenda for future research that I shall mention. Although 'capabilities' are often associated with a variety of resources, there is an aspect of capabilities that has not received much attention: the resources for discussing and debating ideas about what is worthy in society. While the models of norm evolution sketched in Section 3 depend in some measure on processes that go on behind a person's back, it should not be forgotten that there are, of course, a variety of domains, such as those of politics and the pulpit, where the shared beliefs of a society are explicitly debated and discussed. The media is another. It would be good to know more about how the constitution of these discursive institutions affects the character of these discussions. There are some broad-brush generalities of the kind that associate the penetration of the market/capitalism into these institutions with the rise of a postmodern system of belief (e.g. Jameson, 1991), but there is little of a detailed and systematic kind that might form the basis for a thoroughgoing political economy of identity formation.

Note

1. There are various other well-known psychological biases that might also be associated with a broad concern to find that one's action reflects well upon one. The most obvious is the 'self-serving bias' which is found for example when a significant majority of any population thinks that their skills are above the average for that group. Likewise, the law of small numbers, which captures the way that we are often too quick to extrapolate from a small number of observations, might be thought to come from a perceived weakness in not knowing (or an intolerance of uncertainty).

References

Akerlof, George and Yellen, Janet (1990), 'The fair wage hypothesis and unemployment', *Quarterly Journal of Economics*, **105** (2), 255–83.
Axelrod, R. (1984), *The Evolution of Cooperation*, New York: Basic Books.
Bacharach, M. (1999), 'Interactive team reasoning: a contribution to the theory of cooperation', *Research in Economics*, **53**, 117–47.
Becker, G. (1992), 'The economic way of looking at life', *American Economic Review*, **101**, 385–409.

Boudon, R. (1986), 'The logic of relative frustration', in J. Elster (ed.), *Rational Choice*, Oxford: Basil Blackwell, pp. 171–96.

Clark, K. and M. Sefton (2001), 'The sequential prisoner's dilemma: evidence on reciprocation', *Economic Journal*, **111**, 51–68.

Davis, J. (2003), *The Theory of the Individual in Economics: Identity and Value*, London: Routledge.

Dawes R. and R. Thaler (1988), 'Anomalies: cooperation', *Journal of Economic Perspectives*, **2**, 187–97.

Deci, E. (1975), *Intrinsic Reason*, New York: Plenum Press.

Economic Journal feature (2002), 'Social capital', **112**, F417–F479.

Etzioni, A. (1988), *The Moral Dimension*, New York: Free Press.

Etzioni, A. (1993), *Parenting Deficit*, London: Demos.

Fehr, E. and K. Schmidt (1999), 'A theory of fairness, competition and cooperation', *Quarterly Journal of Economics*, **114**, 817–68.

Frank, R. (1997), 'The frame of reference as a public good', *Economic Journal*, **107**, 1832–47.

Frey, B. (1997), *Not Just for the Money: An Economic Theory of Personal Motivation*, Cheltenham, UK and Lyme, USA: Edward Elgar.

Fukuyama, F. (1995), *Trust*, Harmondsworth: Penguin Books.

Geanakoplos, J., D. Pearce and E. Stacchetti (1989), 'Psychological games and sequential rationality', *Games and Economic Behaviour*, **1**, 60–79.

Hargreaves Heap, S. (2004), 'A note on participatory decision making and rationality', *Cambridge Journal of Economics*, **28**, 457–67.

Hargreaves Heap, S. and Y. Varoufakis (2005), *Game Theory*, London: Routledge.

Henrich, J., R. Boyd, S. Bowles, C. Camerer, E. Fehr, H. Gintis and R. McElreath (2001), 'In search of Homo Economicus: behavioural experiments in 15 small scale societies', *American Economic Review*, **91**, 73–78.

Jameson, F. (1991), *Postmodernism or the Cultural Logic of Late Capitalism*, Durham, NC: Duke University Press.

O'Neill, O. (1989), *Construction of Reason*, Cambridge: Cambridge University Press.

Oswald, A. (1997), 'Happiness and economic performance', *Economic Journal*, **107**, 1815–31.

Rabin, M. (1993), 'Incorporating fairness into economics and game theory', *American Economic Review*, **83**, 1281–302.

Sen, A. (1985), *Commodities and Capabilities*, Amsterdam: North-Holland.

Smith, A. (1759 [1976]), *The Theory of Moral Sentiments*, Oxford: Clarendon Press.

Sugden, R. (1986), *The Economics of Rights, Cooperation and Welfare*, Oxford: Basil Blackwell.

Sugden, R. (2000), 'Team preferences', *Economics and Philosophy*, **16**, 175–204.

Sugden, R. (2002), 'Beyond sympathy and empathy: Adam Smith's concept of fellow feeling', *Economics and Philosophy*, **18**, 63–87.

Tuomela, R. (1995), *The Importance of Us: A Philosphical Study of Basic Social Notions*, Stanford, CA: Stanford University Press.

Veblen, T. (1899), *The Theory of the Leisure Class: An Economic Study of Institutions*, New York: Macmillan.

6 The conception of the socially embedded individual
John B. Davis

Social economics differs in many respects from standard mainstream economics, but one of the most fundamental differences is that it employs a conception of the human individual as socially embedded rather than as atomistic. Indeed, just as the atomistic individual conception is one of the defining characteristics of mainstream economics, so the socially embedded individual conception is one of the defining characteristics of social economics. Broadly speaking, the difference between these two conceptions rests on whether individuals and their behavior are explained 'externally' in terms of their social relationships or 'internally' in terms of their private tastes and preferences. The former perspective sees social life as intrinsic to our understanding of individuals as social beings; the latter perspective operates with a view of social life restricted to the market interaction of individuals understood as non-social beings. It follows that these two conceptions of the individual also support two different normative visions of individuals and society. The socially embedded individual conception is associated with normative principles that emphasize relationships between people, such as equality, fairness and the (positive) freedom to achieve, whereas the atomistic individual conception is associated with normative principles that emphasize the independence of individuals, such as autonomy, rights and (negative) freedom from social interference. We can characterize the former approach as a social justice view and the latter approach as a liberal society view. Each has strongly contrasting social economic policy recommendations associated with it, particularly with respect to the role given to the market in modern economies, and indeed much of modern history can be explained in terms of conflicting horizons laid out by these two views.

This chapter is devoted to explaining the socially embedded individual conception. Given that there are many ways in which social relationships can be discussed, there are also many ways in which individuals can be understood to be socially embedded. The first section of the chapter accordingly surveys a variety of recent contributions to this understanding, giving attention both to those that explicitly develop socially embedded individual conceptions and also to those that do so more indirectly by criticizing the standard atomistic individual conception. The second and third sections then discuss two fundamental issues raised by these contributions: (a) the relation of social identity to personal identity, and (b) the problem of inequality. The fourth section closes the chapter with comments on how thinking about individuals in economics may evolve in the future.

1. Recent contributions to the conception of the socially embedded individual

An important challenge to the conception of the socially embedded individual is to explain how individuals can still be individual when socially embedded. There has been a long debate in economics between proponents of methodological individualism – the idea that economic explanations should take individuals as entry points – and proponents of methodological holism – the idea that economic explanations should take social aggregates (such as classes, social groups etc.) as entry points. Critics of the atomistic individual conception who also reject methodological individualism thus often also adopt methodological holism as their perspective, and accordingly sometimes find themselves treating 'socially embedded individual' as an oxymoron. Their reasoning is that as social structures are primary, they must be determinative of individual behavior (just as methodological individualists argue that as individuals are primary, they must be determinative of social structures). But both perspectives are too narrow since it can be argued that social structures influence individuals and that individuals also influence social structures, and thus that each constitute independent agents. On this wider view, then, 'socially embedded individual' is a meaningful conception whose understanding requires the analysis of both types of influences.

This has been done by many in connection with a cross-disciplinary social science and philosophy investigation termed structure–agency theory, whose premise is that individuals and societies both need to be explained in terms of their mutual influences upon one another. Sociologist Mark Granovetter stated this in an especially influential way in arguing that socially embedded individuals are neither 'atoms outside a social context' nor beings who 'adhere slavishly to a script written for them by the particular intersection of social categories they happen to occupy' (Granovetter, 1985, p. 487). Sociologist Anthony Giddens advanced one particular view of structure–agent interactions he termed 'structuration theory', which treats individuals and social structures as interdependent and inseparable or as a duality of structure (Giddens, 1976). Economist Tony Lawson argues that 'social structure [is] dependent upon human agency . . . open to transformation through changing human practices' (Lawson, 1997, p. 158).

But how is it, we should ask, that individuals are indeed agents when social structures are said to affect them? Put differently, how can we invest individuals with a relative autonomy when we recognize they are acted upon by society? The answer lies in deepening the concept of the individual as an agent to include the idea of being a reflexive being. A long history of social psychology (cf. Davis, 2003, pp. 114ff.) treats individuals as reflexive beings in virtue of their ability to form self-concepts and engage in different kinds of self-referring behavior. Of course social factors influence how individuals form self-concepts, but the idea that they are able to reflexively take themselves as subjects as objects of their thinking and activity, or objectify themselves as subjects, implies that individuals can detach themselves in some degree from the determining effects of social factors influencing them. This relative detachment allows us to suppose that individuals also influence social structures, just as social structures influence individuals, and enables us to then treat the idea of the individual being socially embedded as a coherent and meaningful conception.

We can accordingly first distinguish explicit contributions to the socially embedded individual conception as those that employ some sort of structure–agent modeling of individual and society and which characterize individuals in some fashion as reflexive beings. Six different types of contributions fall within this description: social economic, institutionalist, critical realist, feminist, intersubjectivist and expressivist.

The social economic conception of the socially embedded individual is often referred to as *Homo socio-economicus* (O'Boyle, 1994). As Mark Lutz puts it, 'persons as *social individuals* are embedded in a web of constitutive social relations' (Lutz, 1999, p. 6) such as community, family, and a variety of wider social relationships, all of which support different sets of social values that individuals rely upon to guide their daily lives. Economic relationships, such as consumption, production and exchange, then, are framed by these constitutive social relations, so that social values always underlie economic values. Lutz accordingly explains the individual as a dual self in that individuals possess first-order preferences over goods and work and also second-order or social value preferences over these first-order preferences. David George uses this framework to argue that pro-market policies often promote first-order preferences at the expense of second-order ones, as for example when individuals are encouraged to consume products they believe they should avoid (George, 2001). Amartya Sen brings out the reflexivity inherent in this dual self-conception of the individual when he characterizes individuals as beings able to engage in rational self-scrutiny (Sen, 2002). One way in which individuals can be seen to exercise rational self-scrutiny in their interaction with others is captured by collective intentionality theory. When individuals express intentions using the 'we' pronoun, they need to ask themselves whether those to whom the 'we' applies would agree with what they express (Davis, 2003, ch. 7). In such settings, individuals are both influenced by social relationships and social structures, and influence them as well, with the latter depending upon their ability to place themselves in social contexts.

Thinking about the individual in institutionalist economics goes back to Charles Cooley's 'looking-glass self' that makes how individuals judge themselves a matter of how they believe they appear to others (Cooley, 1902, pp. 179ff.). George Mead's symbolic interactionism later expanded this view to include the idea that the mind and self are products of social processes (Mead, 1934), so that self-reflection is embedded in social life. Institutionalism originates in the evolutionary views of Thorstein Veblen and the idea that social processes evolve. In a structure–agent framework, the evolution of the economy as a social economic process involves 'both the dependence of institutions upon individuals and the molding of individuals by institutions' – both 'upward and downward causation' processes (Hodgson, 2000, p. 326). Upward causation, which occurs when individuals influence and create institutions, depends upon learning seen as a recursive social practice. Individuals develop habits around social rules and customs in their social environment, but modify those habits as they adjust them to their own circumstances. At the same time, individuals not only rely on social rules and customs and tailor them to their own cases, but they also do this as social rules and customs themselves evolve in response to the actions of individuals (Dolfsma, 2002). The institutionalist learning-based view of individuals, then, treats individuals as socially embedded, reflexive beings constantly adjusting to their own changing circumstances in a historical process that is itself dynamic.

Tony Lawson develops a critical realist understanding of the structure–agent model that makes 'social structure dependent upon human agency . . . open to transformation through changing human practices which in turn can be affected by *criticising* the conceptions and understandings on which people act' (Lawson, 1997, p. 158). Social structure changes because human practices change as a result of individuals' reflection upon them and their place within them. Lawson characterizes the rationality of individuals thus understood as a 'situated rationality' in which individuals occupy social positions structured by rules, obligations and the powers that accompany them, and act within this social space. Much of this activity is routinized and relies on tacit knowledge and skills that individuals exercise unconsciously. Yet that this activity can become conscious means that it can still be seen as intentional. The overall structure–agent model that Lawson employs, then, is one in which social structures and human agency co-evolve in social processes that reproduce and transform them both.

Individuals are reflexive beings, but the basis on which they are is continually changing. This arguably produces a need in individuals for an 'inner security' in the form of 'a significant degree of continuity, stability and sameness in daily affairs' (ibid., p. 180). Put in terms of the concept of the individual, socially embedded individuals exhibit a need for an 'ontological security' that preserves their status as individual agents in a social world that is constantly changing.

Feminist economists emphasize the social construction of individual life in terms of such social identities as gender, race or ethnicity, nationality, etc. As Nancy Folbre puts it, 'individuals are so embedded in a complex structure of individual and collective identities and competing interpretations of these that sometimes they do not even know whose interests they are acting on' (Folbre, 1994, p. 16). For example, women have quite different social identities associated with work and family, and often find their responsibilities to each domain in conflict. This shows, however, that individuals cannot be reduced to their social identities, since they must determine how they organize and negotiate these different domains. In this regard, they are reflexive beings who evaluate how they believe they fit into the social relationships they occupy. At the same time, how many individuals together respond to their many social relationships in turn influences the development of social structures themselves. One manifestation of this is social economic policy designed to improve the capacity of women to operate in multiple domains, such as legislation aimed at discriminatory practices in the workplace that penalize women for household caring responsibilities. Thus feminists also employ a socially embedded individual conception, and treat individuals and social structures as mutually influencing.

Two additional conceptions of individuals as socially embedded are intersubjectivist economics (or French conventions theory) and the expressivist individual view. Intersubjectivist economics (Dupuy, 1989; Orlean, 1992; Thévenot, 1989) draws on the phenomenon of speculation in financial markets to argue that 'what we think, desire and decide as economic actors depends a great deal on what other actors are seen to think, desire, and decide' (Fullbrook, 2002, p. 2). Individuals thus explained exhibit strategic rationality, whereby they take into account whether others will cooperate or compete, and also a communicational rationality, whereby they make shared commitments to various norms and social conventions. The expressivist individual view is developed by Shaun Hargreaves Heap (2001), who focuses on individuals' reflective capacities and sense of self-worth, and Philippe Fontaine (1997), who focuses on the differences and relationships between individuals' sympathetic and empathic identification with others. Both views are influenced by Adam

Smith's 'impartial spectator' perspective that individuals can adopt to judge their relations to others (Smith, 1976 [1759]).

In addition to these six socially embedded individual conceptions, there exist contributions to thinking about the individual in economics in recent mainstream economics that make more indirect contributions to thinking about individuals as socially embedded. Two are discussed here. Behavioral economics, whose origins lie in psychology, and complexity economics, whose sources are physics and biology, both make cases for seeing individuals as socially embedded by criticizing different aspects of the standard atomistic individual conception.

Behavioral economics emphasizes the need to replace the standard view of the individual as *Homo economicus* by a more realistic conception of the individual as *Homo sapiens*. Whereas the former is a hyperrational being, for the latter 'the degree of rationality bestowed to the agents depends on the context being studied' (Thaler, 2000, p. 134). Of course 'context' can mean many things, and indeed in much of behavioral economics research it is treated as a relatively abstract principle. For example, contrary to the standard view of choice, behavioralists argue that individual decision-making exhibits framing effects and reference-dependence reflecting the anchoring of choice in particular circumstances (Tversky and Kahneman, 1991). But many of the applications of these concepts give the principle of context important social content. Thus framing effects and the reference-dependence of choice have been shown to produce hyperbolic time discounting, which implies that people tend to ignore the future. Behavioralists have accordingly recommended social economic policies that correct for this bias (e.g. Madrian and Shea, 2001), thus translating an abstract principle of context into a social one. Context, then, socially embeds individuals, and the atomistic individual conception that ignores context fails to represent individuals adequately.

Complexity economics investigates economic systems that exhibit non-linear dynamics, and uses an approach termed agent-based modeling to represent individuals in such systems (Tesfatsion, 2006). In contrast to standard economics with its single conception of the individual as an abstract atomistic being, complexity economics assumes agents or individuals are interactive and heterogeneous, and then explains the non-linear dynamics of different economic systems in terms of the co-evolution of different kinds of agents' expectations of each other and the systems they jointly occupy. For example, Alan Kirman's fish market model distinguishes buyers who tend to be loyal to certain sellers from buyers who regularly visit many different sellers, and then investigates how one particular fish market (in Marseille, France) evolves patterns of prices and distribution that reflects specific social-historical circumstances (Kirman, 2001).

Another example is the Santa Fe stock market model (cf. Arthur, 1995), which looks at different populations of agents, and traces the movement of asset values that results from their interaction over time. As do the behavioralists, complexity theorists fault the atomistic individual conception as a key obstacle to more realistic explanations of economies, and although they do not base their arguments directly on a conception of the individual as socially embedded (as do the six approaches discussed above), they end up making a case for just such a conception.

All eight of the approaches discussed here, then, reject the dichotomy between methodological individualism and methodological holism, and employ some kind of structure–agent analysis in which causal influences operate in two directions. The section that follows addresses two sets of issues that arise in this framework.

2.   Social identity and personal identity

One particularly important problem that the socially embedded individual conception encounters is the problem of multiple selves. As a conception of the individual that is 'externally' based in social relationships, individuals' multiple selves can be understood to be their different social identities, or how they identify with others. As emphasized by Folbre (1994) and Sen (2006), however, our different social identities often conflict with one another, and this invites us to ask what the unity of the self consists in, and indeed raises the question whether the socially embedded individual is a single being at all. The multiple-selves problem also arises in connection with the atomistic individual conception (cf. Davis, 2003, ch. 4), but that this conception is 'internally' based in the private tastes of individuals arguably makes the problem irresolvable (cf. ibid.). In the case of the socially embedded individual conception, in contrast, it is reasonable to say that individuals have ties to others and also act independently. The question is how this can best be explained.

How, then, does the individual with many social identities still count as a single individual? Extending the identity concept, we can say that individuals with many social identities are single individuals when they are shown to have personal identities consistent with their many social identities. Let us begin to explain this idea by making two points about the concept of social identity. First, defining the concept of social identity as the idea of individuals identifying with others, others may be understood either as (a) social groups, such as are characterized by shared language, ethnicity, religion, work etc., or as (b) simply other individuals, such as friends, family members, neighbors etc. Second, whether social identity takes the social group form or the other individuals' form, the idea of individuals identifying with others can be interpreted in two different ways depending on who is responsible for the identification. Either (a) individuals themselves can identify with others, or (b) they can be identified with others by third parties.

These two distinctions allow us to set forth four types of social identity: (1) individuals themselves identify with other individuals; (2) individuals themselves identify with groups of individuals; (3) individuals are identified with other individuals by third parties; (4) individuals are identified with groups of individuals by third parties. These four types are shown in Figure 6.1. Examples of each are: (1) a person identifies with a sick friend; (2) an immigrant identifies with a native language group; (3) social service workers socially identify individuals according to their family dynamics; (4) statisticians socially identify individuals according to race and ethnicity.

Given that we are operating with a conception of the individual as socially embedded, let us then explain an individual's personal identity within this social identity framework. Doing so is consistent with the socially embedded individual conception set out in the last section if we suppose that individuals and social structures are mutually influencing. It is also consistent with seeing socially embedded individuals as reflexive beings if we define the personal identity of socially embedded individuals as an ability to organize and balance their many social identities by

	Identification with	
	individuals	groups
individuals themselves	(1) sick friend	(2) native language
third parties	(3) social service workers	(4) statisticians

Who determines (row label)

Figure 6.1   Types of social identity with examples

engaging in self-reflection regarding what their different social ties and social identities involve. We can see better what this involves by applying Figure 6.1.

Consider the two cells in the first row where the difference is between individuals themselves identifying with other individuals or identifying with social groups. Here the ability of individuals to organize and balance their different social identities, understood as maintaining personal identities, is a matter of how they themselves balance these two kinds of connections. For example, an immigrant may identify with a native language group (a social group identification), but put this aside to care for a sick friend (social identification with another individual), also from the same native language group, who does not maintain that social identity. Other combinations of course are also possible, and thus the point is that part of what is involved in individuals having personal identities is how they themselves organize these two types of social identity.

Consider next the second row as contrasted with the first row. The second row explains the social identities of individuals as society sees them, rather than as individuals see them. As a structure–agent framework treats individuals and social structures as mutually influencing, the relationship between personal identity and social identity also needs to capture the influence society has on this understanding. That is, not only do individuals organize and balance their different kinds of social identities (plus the different social identities within each category) in creating personal identities for themselves, but they must also contend with how society sees these balances as well.

For example, in cell (3) a family social worker may make judgments about family dynamics which family members must themselves appraise relative to their own social identifications with one another. Whether such judgments are accepted or rejected then involves individuals in balancing and organizing their personal identities in a way that goes beyond how they see these relations in the absence of third parties. Or, in cell (4), social statisticians classify individuals as members of social groups, which individuals themselves appraise in judging their sense of their social group social identities, since what social statisticians say may or may not be relevant from the individual's perspective. Again, how individuals see their social identities is influenced by how others see them.

The concept of personal identity used here is specific to the conception of individuals as socially embedded, and contrasts with personal identity concepts which ignore or de-emphasize sociality, and rather focus on individuals' psychological characteristics (e.g. Parfit, 1986). The concept here also specifically addresses the concerns of Folbre (1994) and Sen (2006), who recognize that our different social identities often conflict, raising the question whether the socially embedded individual is a single being at all. Key to this understanding is the idea of reflexivity, or the idea that individuals can take a position towards themselves. That this individualizes them is due to the fact that individuals can only take themselves as subjects as objects. No one can truly adopt the subject perspective for other individuals. That behaving reflexively also gives a unity to the individual is due to the singularity of this perspective. Yet that personal identity understood in this way is framed in terms of individuals' social identities makes it appropriate for thinking of individuals as socially embedded.

3. The problem of inequality

Inequality is an important problem for those concerned with social relationships, and who see individuals as socially embedded. Further, equality is defended as a value by those who derive their normative ideals from social justice views. But if individuals are all unique in having different personal identities in virtue of there being different ways in which they each organize and balance all their different social identities, how should the ideal of equality apply to them? One view of equality inscribed in many nations' laws and constitutions and also in many international covenants and doctrines is that equality is a matter of individuals having equal rights to certain freedoms, such as religion, speech, political participation, cultural commitments and other liberties generally regarded as civil rights. We might accordingly regard these freedoms as foundations for equality. But this understanding of equality only takes us so far toward realizing equality in that having equal civil rights is often compatible with considerable inequality when individuals are economically unequal. Unfortunately, expanding our understanding of equality to include economic equality, particularly as when understood as income inequality, encounters significant conceptual problems. Complete and comprehensive measures of income inequality appear to be unavailable, so that what we are left with at best is a loose 'quasi-orderings' framework whose application is inherently problematic (Sen, 1997).

Faced with these difficulties, Sen recommends asking what the appropriate conceptual 'space' should be in which we investigate inequality, and suggests that we 'concentrate on the individual's real opportunity to pursue her objectives' (ibid., p. 198). His reason is that it is not just income or the goods bought with income that determines how individuals stand relative to one another, but how individuals with their different personal characteristics are able to make use of income and the goods it allows them to buy. Focusing on 'the individual's real opportunity to pursue her objectives' captures this two-sided relation, and changes the 'space' in which we evaluate inequality. Following Aristotle, then, this 'space' can be understood to be 'the space of "functionings", the various things a person may value doing (or being)' (ibid., p. 199). The approach Sen then develops is the 'capability approach', which represents individuals' real opportunities to pursue their different objectives either in terms of their realized functionings or in terms of the options or alternatives they possess, also understood as their capabilities.

The capability approach thus makes a virtue out of the differences between people, and promises a new approach to the problem of explaining inequality. Basically equality is a matter of individuals being equally able to pursue their real opportunities or capabilities. But what does this involve? Since any given individual has many capabilities, they might be more or less successful in their pursuit of their capabilities according to how many of them they are able to pursue. Individuals might then achieve equality in some respects – for example, being well housed, having good nutrition, and having adequate health care – but not achieve equality in other respects – for example, education. This problem has led to arguments that there ought to be a list of basic or essential capabilities, all of which individuals should be able to achieve if equality is to be achieved (Nussbaum, 2003). Sen, however, believes there cannot be one single list of essential capabilities, because we cannot anticipate what capabilities people will wish to pursue in the future, because we cannot know what future individuals will understand about their world and wish to value, and because it would be a denial of democracy to determine a list for others (Sen, 2005).

Nonetheless, there seems to be one basis on which equality might still be understood in the capability framework. It is suggested by Sen in his Aristotelian rationale for making the 'space' in which we investigate inequality the real opportunities–capability space when he says we need to shift our focus to the 'various things a person may value doing' (Sen, 1997, p. 198). The idea that individuals are able to determine what they value is very close to the idea that they are able to reflexively evaluate themselves relative to their options. In order to determine what one values, one must ask how one's options fit into one's conception of oneself. This conception can of course be changing as one pursues various objectives and creates new ones. Indeed, there is an obvious dynamic involved in individuals pursuing the things they value doing over their lifetimes that is often framed in terms of the idea of personal development.

How does this, then, link up with the idea of equality as a normative ideal? The previous section defined the personal identity of socially embedded individuals in a reflexive way as individuals' ability to organize and balance their many social identities through engaging in a process of self-reflection regarding what their different social ties and identities involve. Although Sen's emphasis on the 'various things a person may value doing' is not immediately framed in terms of individuals' management of their different social identities, this latter emphasis is not inconsistent with his, and indeed Sen allows elsewhere that social identity plays a large role in life (Sen, 2006). Thus, if equality is to be determined in the space of capabilities, and what capabilities individuals pursue is determined by individuals themselves, then equality is a matter of individuals being equally able to pursue their personal identities, as they see them. Of course this is a very general view of equality, and it is hardly clear on the surface what would be required to make this ideal a basis for concrete social economic policy. Nonetheless, support for seeing individuals as being able to pursue personal identities as a foundation for equality links up with other normative notions arguably also connected to equality. That is, it can be argued in terms of the reflexivity idea that pursuing a personal identity is tied to such normative values as freedom, having self-respect, and individual dignity (Davis, 2006). Equality as a normative ideal, then, gains in clarity and credibility as it is integrated with and interpreted in terms of other accepted normative ideals.

4.   New directions

How will thinking about individuals in economics evolve in the future? There has been considerable change in the economics research frontier in recent decades, and all the new approaches that have emerged there in one way or another criticize the atomistic individual conception, and lend support for an understanding of individuals as socially embedded (Davis, forthcoming). In addition, it has long been argued in heterodox economic approaches that the atomistic individual conception does not stand up to critical evaluation, and that individuals are socially embedded. Thus it is worth asking what this apparent shift in thinking may entail, since in the postwar period economics has been strongly structured around the idea that individuals are essentially atomistic.

Consider, then, one influential result on the economics research frontier, a recent laboratory experiment called the public goods game (Fehr and Gächter, 2000). The game/experiment is organized around individuals repeatedly contributing to a public good. In initial rounds of the game contributions are high, but as the game proceeds some individuals free-ride on the contributions of others, ultimately leading most individuals to abandon their contributions, so that the public good is no longer provided. A variation of the game, however, allows individuals to punish free-riders at a cost to themselves, and this reduces free-ridership, and restores the public good. The conclusion that is drawn from this is that the way in which the game is played – with or without punishment – determines its outcome. Whether public goods are provided in real economies, it follows, is also determined according to whether punishment of free-riders is possible. Put more generally, how interaction between individuals in economic life plays out is a matter of the kind of institutional structure in which they are embedded.

The public goods game, of course, is a highly simplified experiment meant to illuminate one specific principle, namely, that institutional structure plays a role in determining economic behavior. In contrast, in real economies this kind of simplification tends to conceal rather than illuminate the complex ways in which institutions, social networks, values, habits, inherited beliefs and expectations all interact to create the larger context in which we observe individual behavior. Thus the logical strategy behind the new research in economics that builds on experimental results and sees individuals as non-atomistic is to incorporate increasingly complex institutional considerations into the analysis in an effort to incorporate the role complex social frameworks have in economic life. In effect, the goal is to begin to see the economy as a social economy, where this refers to the larger social space in which economic life occurs.

Thinking about individuals in economics in the future, then, may require considerably more attention to social structure than has been the case in the past, so that what it means for individuals to be socially embedded will depend on a greater understanding of how individuals interact in different and overlapping ways across social-institutional contexts. This would almost certainly constitute an improvement in the understanding of individual interaction in current economics built around atomistic individuals engaged at a distance with one another in markets. The argument of this chapter is that this path of development for economics would preserve the basic outlines of the socially embedded individual conception as set forth here that sees individuals as reflexive beings influenced by and influencing the social structures they occupy.

References

Arthur, B. (1995), 'Complexity in economic and financial markets', *Complexity*, **1**, 20–25.
Cooley, C. (1902), *Human Nature and the Social Order*, New York: Scribner.
Davis, J. (2003), *The Theory of the Individual in Economics: Identity and Value*, London: Routledge.
Davis, J. (2006), 'The normative significance of the individual in economics', in J. Clary, W. Dolfsma and D. Figart (eds), *Ethics and the Market: Insights from Social Economics*, London: Routledge, pp. 69–83.
Davis, J. (forthcoming), 'Competing conceptions of the individual in recent economics', in Harold Kincaid and Don Ross (eds), *Handbook on the Philosophy and Economics*, Oxford: Oxford University Press.
Dupuy, J.-P. (1989), 'Convention et common knowledge', *Revue économique*, **40** (2), 361–70.
Dolfsma, W. (2002), 'The mountain of experience: how people learn in a complex, evolving environment', *International Journal of Social Economics*, **29** (8), 675–84.
Fehr, Ernst and Simon Gächter (2000), 'Fairness and Reciprocity', *Journal of Economic Perspectives*, **14** (3), 159–81.

Folbre, N. (1994), *Who Pays for the Kids? Gender and the Structures of Constraint*, London: Routledge.

Fontaine, P. (1997), 'Identification and economic behavior: sympathy and empathy in historical perspective', *Economics and Philosophy*, **13** (2), 261–80.

Fullbrook, E. (2002), 'Introduction: why Intersubjectivity?', in E. Fullbrook (ed.), *Intersubjectivity in Economics: Agents and Structures*, London: Routledge, pp. 1–8.

George, D. (2001), *Preference Pollution: How Markets Create Desires We Dislike*, Ann Arbor, MI: University of Michigan Press.

Giddens, A. (1976), *Central Problems in Social Theory*, Berkeley, CA: University of California Press.

Granovetter, M. (1985), 'Economic action and social structure: the problem of embeddedness', *American Journal of Sociology*, **91** (3), 481–510.

Hargreaves Heap, S. (2001), 'Expressive rationality: is self-worth just another kind of preferences?', in U. Mäki (ed.), *The Economic World View*, Cambridge: Cambridge University Press, pp. 98–113.

Hodgson, G. (2000), 'What is the essence of institutional economics?', *Journal of Economic Issues*, **34** (2), 317–29.

Kirman, A. (2001), 'Market organization and individual behavior: evidence from fish markets', in J. Rauch and A. Casella (eds), *Networks and Markets*, New York: Russell Sage, pp. 155–95.

Lawson, T. (1997), *Economics and Reality*, London: Routledge.

Lutz, M. (1999), *Economics for the Common Good*, London: Routledge.

Madrian, B. and D. Shea (2001), 'The power of suggestion: inertia in 401(k) participation and savings behavior', *Quarterly Journal of Economics*, **116** (4), 1149–87.

Mead, G. (1934), *Mind, Self, and Society*, Chicago, IL: University of Chicago Press.

Nussbaum, M. (2003), 'Capabilities as fundamental entitlements: Sen and social justice', *Feminist Economics*, **9** (2–3), 33–59.

O'Boyle, E. (1994), 'Homo socio-economicus: foundational to social economics and social economy', *Review of Social Economy*, **52** (3), 286–313.

Orlean, A. (1989), 'Mimetic contagion and speculative bubbles', *Theory and Decision*, **27**, 63–92.

Parfit, D. (1986), *Reasons and Persons*, Oxford: Oxford University Press.

Sen, A. (1997), *On Economic Inequality*, enlarged edn, with James Foster, Oxford: Clarendon Press.

Sen, A. (2002), *Rationality and Freedom*, Cambridge, MA: The Belknap Press of Harvard University Press.

Sen, A. (2005), 'Human rights and capabilities', *Journal of Human Development*, **6** (2), 151–66.

Sen, A. (2006), *Identity and Violence: The Illusion of Destiny*, New York: W.W. Norton.

Smith, A. (1976 [1759]), *The Theory of Moral Sentiments*, eds D. Raphael and A. Macfie, Oxford: Clarendon Press.

Tesfatsion, L. (2006), 'Agent-based computational economics: a constructive approach to economic theory', in Leigh Tesfatsion and Kenneth L. Judd (eds), *Handbook of Computational Economics Vol. 2: Agent-Based Computational Economics*, Amsterdam: North-Holland, pp. 831–80.

Thaler, Richard (2000), 'From Homo economics to Homo sapiens', *Journal of Economic Perspectives*, **14** (1), 133–41.

Thévenot, L. (1989), 'Equilibre et rationalité dans un univers complexe', *Revue économique*, **40** (2), 147–97.

Tversky, Amos and Daniel Kahneman (1991), 'Loss aversion in riskless choice: a reference-dependent model', *Quarterly Journal of Economics*, **106** (4), 1039–61.

7 The social dimension of internal conflict
David George

When questions of justice are addressed by social economists, the usual focus is on *distributive* justice. While widening income and wealth disparities are making such distributive issues more urgent than ever, this chapter will focus on a question just as important to a society having complete economic equality as to a society with great inequality. Are the rules by which the actions of sellers influence the tastes of buyers to be regarded as just? Sections 1 and 2 will provide some background, defining second-order preferences and summarizing my previous conclusions about the market's failure in shaping preferences. The two sections that then follow will address social issues. Section 3 considers the impact that social forces other than the market have on our preferences while Section 4 explores how the social considerations of preferred preferences compare to the social considerations of preferences that are not preferred. Section 5 describes why 'two-selves' models of conflict have prevailed in mainstream theory and the limitations of these models, and Section 6 reflects on future trends and offers some policy suggestions.

1. Defining second-order preferences
A first step in distinguishing metapreferences (or 'second-order preferences') from 'regular' preferences (or 'first-order preferences') is to specify what a second-order preference is *not*. It is not, as sometimes suggested, simply a better preference. One believing that it is might say, for example, that a person unhappy with her eating habits likely has a first-order preference for a high-calorie meal but a second-order preference for a low-calorie meal. This definition of the second-order preference treats it as nothing more that a *superior* preference ranking over the very same set of possibilities. Let there be two possibilities facing this person: to have a high-calorie cheeseburger (H) or to have a low-calorie tuna sandwich (L). One employing such a definition would describe the first-order preference as 'H pref L' and the second-order preference as 'L pref H'.

I have argued elsewhere[1] that this is an unsuccessful characterization of internal conflict that basically assumes away conflict within the 'self' by asking us to treat what we have long known as a 'self' (you, the reader, for example) as really many selves.[2] Consider the problem with this. For me to announce that I prefer a beer to a glass of water must rule out the possibility that I also prefer a glass of water to a beer. To say that I can simultaneously experience both of these preferences signals a misunderstanding of what 'preference' means and might be compared with simultaneously alleging that Michelle is taller than Rebecca and that Rebecca is also taller than Michelle, or that Jason is older than Brad while Brad is also older than Jason. A rewarding feature of the use of a second-order preference in understanding internal conflict is that it requires no such contradictory claims about the conflicted person.

Keeping in mind what a second-order preference *is not*, the question now becomes, what is it? A person's second-order preference ranking is a ranking of the first-order preference rankings themselves. In the present example, suppose that the individual's second-order preference ranking 'a preference for L' is preferred to 'a preference for H'. If this agent were to experience a first-order preference for H, we would have an instance of a discontented agent, as shown in column 1 of Figure 7.1. The agent has the preference she would rather not have, but given that this is her preference, she acts upon it by choosing H. In contrast to this, the contented agent shown on the right happens to have the preference that she prefers having, and accordingly chooses the low-calorie meal.

The second-order preference, standing alone, cannot be said to be a 'superior preference'. To see why this is so, put yourself in the place of the contented agent just discussed. To say that you prefer to prefer a low-calorie meal only makes sense if it is assumed that you will have the ability to act upon the preference that you have. Imagine two scenarios. In the first scenario, every day for the next month the preference that you prefer prevails, such that if the low-calorie tuna sandwich were available, it would be your choice. But over the same period of time, no food at all is available, and you are thus unable to act on this preferred preference. In the second scenario, you have each day the preference that you do not wish to have but *are* able to act on this unpreferred preference. In other words, you prefer the high-calorie meal while at the same time preferring to prefer the low-calorie meal and find that the high-calorie meal is available for you to select and consume. Clearly, in this case, having the preferred preference but being

	Discontented agent	Contented agent
Second-order preference	(L pref H) pref (H pref L)	(L pref H) pref (H pref L)
First-order preference	H pref L	L pref H
Choice	H	L

Figure 7.1 Internal conflict and internal harmony

unable to act upon it paints a grim picture (starvation?) while having the unpreferred preference but being able to act upon it paints one that is less grim (being in the grip of a crummy preference but at least being able to act upon it and not starve).

Looking at this in terms of what appears in Figure 7.1, the situation on the right (the 'contented agent') is superior to what appears on the left only if that bottom line is included and L can indeed be chosen. Thus the second-order preference is not categorically 'better than' an unpreferred first-order preference. Rather, experiencing the preferred preference is only unequivocally a good thing if you are then able to act on it. Thus, if you prefer to have a preference for L, then having this preference will indeed be a good thing if you are able to act upon it and select L. A second-order preference is not inherently superior to a first-order preference. Rather, second-order preferences, the ranking of first-order preferences, allow us to speak of better and worse first-order preferences only if we assume the ranked items are available. And being thus able to evaluate first-order preferences will allow us to reach an important conclusion.

2.   Evaluating the market

Profit-maximizing firms, if unconstrained by laws or by social conventions, are unlikely to create the preferences that people would prefer having. It is on the first of these two important conditionals – the absence of laws – that my previous work has primarily focused, and I will begin with it here. For all the criticism directed at government by the strongest supporters of *laissez-faire*, none, to my knowledge, choose to downplay the importance of property rights. A sense of what belongs to whom is a prerequisite to market interactions and must remain salient to all participants as buying and selling occurs. Also uncontroversial is the enforcement of property rights after exchanges have occurred. For one person to take what is legally another's must permit the victim to draw upon the state to seek capture, prosecution and punishment.

While all of this is well known when it comes to the goods and services exchanged in the marketplace (the objects of our first-order preferences), it is largely ignored when objects of our second-order preferences are at issue. Returning to the earlier example, if this person were to prefer the low-calorie tuna sandwich over the high-calorie cheeseburger and were to thus select the tuna sandwich, it would become hers and not something that can be taken from her without her permission. The very thought of someone approaching this person as she is about to enjoy her sandwich and replacing it with a cheeseburger is, on the face of it, comical and transparently wrong. To have chosen what she did makes it hers and it cannot be taken from her. Contrast this with our disregard for each other's second-order preferences. If one prefers a 'preference for a low-calorie tuna sandwich' over a 'preference for a high-calorie cheeseburger' and happens to be experiencing this preference while preparing to order, this preference is very much hers. But if the description of the cheeseburger offered on the menu is sufficiently tempting, it is of course possible that this preference for the tuna sandwich will be, so to speak, taken from her and replaced by a preference that she would prefer not to have. Once this preference is imposed upon her, rational action consists of choosing the previously unpreferred, but now preferred, cheeseburger (moving, in other words, from the 'contented' state to the 'discontented' state in Figure 7.1). Most of us have gone through such experiences. And given our shared twenty-first-century cultural beliefs about what is our property and what is not, most of us do not blame anyone for replacing something that we had with something less desirable. To take a tangible 'thing' (such as the tuna sandwich) and replace it with another tangible 'thing' (such as the cheeseburger) is universally recognized as illegal and immoral. But to take a 'preference for a thing' (such as a preference for a low-calorie tuna sandwich) and replace it with a 'preference for another thing' (such as a preference for a high-calorie cheeseburger) is taken to be a legitimate action.

As conventional economists are quick to point out, the absence of property rights leads to inefficiencies. The commons will be overgrazed, the air will be overpolluted, and the roadway will be overused, all as a consequence of the absence of property rights in these commonly held assets. But by the same reasoning, preferences worse than what they replace will too often be created by actors within the marketplace. Since preference changers (acting through marketing and advertising) do not have to compensate those who are harmed (people whose preferences are affected for the worse), there is too much creation of worse preferences. By the same line of reasoning, these sellers will too seldom create preferences that are better than what they replace since those enjoying the improved preferences cannot be compelled to compensate the sellers who create this better state of affairs. The conclusion is straightforward: markets fail us in the creation of our preferences.

This failure would appear to be much like any other failure that follows from 'insufficiently defined property rights'. There is, however, one important difference. The philosopher Harry Frankfurt (1971) argues that the capability of having second-order preferences is what separates humans from other forms of life.[3] Animals certainly have preferences in the economic sense of the term. In cases where the cost – albeit non-monetary – is raised, animals of all types will 'demand less'. To take one well-known example, raise the number of pecks necessary for a pigeon to acquire additional food, and the pigeon will demand less (Kagel and Battalio, 1975).

But by Frankfurt's account, animals do not experience second-order preferences, only humans do.[4] Just how he reaches this conclusion is not of immediate importance. What is important is that 'preferences about our preferences' is the defining feature of personhood for Frankfurt. To conclude that markets are poorly suited to the creation of desired preferences becomes all the more serious a shortcoming, for this market failure involves precisely the types of preferences that, according to Frankfurt, are unique to humans.

Now it might be argued that any attempt to institute enforceable property rights in our preferences would be prohibitively costly. In such instances, however, it appears that societies typically adopt social conventions that serve as what might be called 'implicit property rights'. A pedestrian occupying public space at an intersection while waiting for the light to change has no formal property rights to the space that she occupies. But for someone to move her aside because he or she wants to occupy that particular space would be universally regarded as wrong and such action is avoided as a consequence. Although formal property rights are lacking, social conventions make it 'as if' one owned the space one occupied for the time that one occupied it. When it comes to our preferences for our preferences, contemporary society accords neither formal property rights nor informal moral claims stemming from social conventions. Quite simply, the preferences we happen to have can be 'taken' from us without legal recourse or social censure.[5]

3.   Social influence on tastes

Now to the main question: how does social economics fit into this picture? If social economics is to be regarded as primarily a challenge to the main normative conclusions of mainstream economics, what has been outlined to this point might be treated as sufficient. But surely there can be more than just that. While markets are deficient in the taste-shaping exercise when judged in the way offered by mainstream economics (insufficient property rights), does the existence of a richer social fabric than assumed by mainstream economic analysis complicate the story?

As a first consideration, are there notable differences between social influence on the creation of first-order preferences and social influence on the creation of second-order preferences? While John Kenneth Galbraith (1958) was critical of the market's influence on our first-order preferences, a close look at his argument suggests that he held socially created preferences in lower regard than preferences originating in the agent. The essence of Galbraith's criticism was that tastes 'created' by the market (a 'social creation') are of less importance than those originating with the individual. This conclusion followed from Galbraith's observation that our most important, 'original' preferences for food and shelter occur prior to and independent of socialization. These original preferences are treated as the most important in the sense that they are the first that a person would choose to satisfy. Galbraith went on to reason that affluence is accompanied by the rise of less urgent preferences and it is these preferences that are subject to manipulation by market forces.[6]

This observation by Galbraith was used to firm up a more basic point that he made, namely, that a system that creates the tastes that it proceeds to satisfy is worthy of less praise than one that satisfies existing tastes. While the tastes that were created by the sellers were worthy of some suspicion for that reason alone, the fact that such tastes were just icing on the cake for an agent whose more urgent, primary tastes had already been satisfied cast them in an even less flattering light. Galbraith essentially elevated the status of the 'pre-social' preferences relative to those that were socially created.

In what became an often-repeated response to Galbraith's argument by the classical, libertarian wing of the economics profession, Friedrich Hayek (1961) observed that preferences created by sellers are no more likely to be a cause of internal discontent than are those that arise *sui generis*. While we do not usually think of Hayek as a social economist, the point he made here did indeed appear to follow from a strong appreciation of the social dimension of the market. Just as he suggested, the preferences created in us by others are often those we most value. Preferences for Picasso, for French food, or for economics journals do not arise independently of society. And, just as surely, they do not tend to be less valued by those experiencing them than the more basic preferences for water or sleep.

More significant than society's role in determining an agent's second-order preferences is society's role in making the preferred preferences become a reality. As I argued in the second half of *Preference Pollution* (George, 2001, chs 5–9), there has been an erosion in the strength of non-market mechanisms that help to shape our tastes as we prefer to have them shaped. Social prohibitions against excessive debt, gambling and sexual indiscretions have become harder to defend in contemporary society. The possibility that shame may serve a useful role in the shaping of tastes fits poorly with the social libertarianism that we usually associate with contemporary liberals and fits equally poorly with the economic libertarianism that we associate with conservatives.[7] In the name of recognizing the power and maturity that each of us possesses, the dominant cultural message is that each of us should be radically free to decide for ourselves what to consume. With society backing away from providing guidelines to the taste-shaping project, advertisers and marketers are given a free hand in molding tastes, the possibility that one whose tastes are thus molded might be made worse off as a consequence by going from having a preference that he prefers having to one that he does not having fallen from the conversation. Liberation has a decidedly conservative, free market feel, as the paternalistic and maternalistic efforts of friends to shape us loses out to more impersonal market forces that shape us in the way allegedly dictated by market forces.

To summarize, the argument that markets fail in the shaping of tastes, while as valid as any other 'externalities' argument, is strengthened when the increasing legitimation of market persuasion is taken into account. The ability of the public to perceive air and water pollution has not been lessened as market forces have gained strength. The environmental damage that unconstrained markets would cause is no less obvious to our senses today than it would have been under a different sort of economic regime. The pollution of preferences is a more curious sort of development, as the legitimacy of an ethos that countered the market's taste-shaping dominance has lessened. We appear to be having a harder time supporting those social institutions that would override the market's influence on our tastes.

4.   Are preferred preferences more social?

My attention to the social dimensions of the preference-changing practices encountered in market societies has focused to this point on society as shaper of our tastes. There is another question worth taking up at this point. Do the preferences that people prefer having tend to reflect social embeddedness more than those that they would rather not have? Before attempting to answer this question, it is necessary to settle on some criteria for measuring how 'social' a preference is. As many textbooks point out, there is nothing in the standard economic assumption that agents maximize their utility that requires the assumption of selfishness. Altruists are said to maximize just as surely as are the narrowly selfish. But a careful look at what follows in most texts (and professional articles) will show that unless otherwise stated, narrow selfishness is assumed. Thus, for example, public choice theory has built its entire edifice on the unexamined assumption that government decision-makers are narrow maximizers, the possibility that well-being for the greater society might motivate political decisions seldom noted.

Accepting the existence of non-selfish preferences raises another question. Is it more likely that a preference that a person would like to see replace what he is currently experiencing would involve more or less concern for the well-being of others? One of the attractive features of the second-order preference structure is its abstractness and consistency with a wide range of empirical realities. There are likely some people who feel insufficiently assertive and too willing to do what is in the social interest but not their own narrow interest. An individual might, for example, prefer to take on the largest part of a joint project while preferring to prefer to insist that others carry more of the weight. Less understandably, one might prefer to be law-abiding, while preferring to prefer to be a thief.

While acknowledging such possibilities, it seems likely that much more often the preferences people would prefer having embody more rather than fewer positive connections with others. What is more common: someone making a resolution to give more to worthy causes or someone making a resolution to give less? Someone making a resolution to visit friends and family more often or someone making a resolution to care less? Both are of course possible, but my suspicions would be that the former resolutions to be more socially minded tend to beat out their opposites. If this is so, the implication is that the preferences people would prefer having would be more generous to others than those that they in fact experience. Approaching this issue from a slightly different angle, just consider the classic unpreferred preferences. They tend to involve habits that provide short-term gains but long-term pain. People who prefer to smoke, people who prefer to eat unhealthy food, people who prefer to drink heavily, people who prefer to be idle rather than active, are all people who prefer to rid themselves of preferences that are in no way productive of spillover benefits to the wider society.

5. The problem with multiple selves

It was earlier noted that a second-order preference is sometimes wrongly treated as simply a better first-order preference. I emphasized that simultaneously existing first-order preferences that contradicted one another were methodologically incoherent. There are several reasons why these models have maintained their resilience. First, it is common to confuse first-order preferences that are 'overall' in scope with those that are 'intrinsic'. Second, for the mainstream economists who have relied on the two-selves approach, the ability to predict is what matters, not the realism of assumptions. And third, unlike first-order preferences, second-order preferences are not obviously revealed by choice. I shall take these one at a time.

An overall first-order preference is an 'all things considered' preference. To say, for example, that I prefer a cheeseburger is to say that the future contingent on the act of having the cheeseburger is preferable to me than the future contingent on not having it. In contrast, an 'intrinsic' preference limits the scope and focuses only on the cheeseburger, independent of what it might cause to happen in the longer run.[8] It is not unusual to hear someone announce something like the following: 'Although I prefer a cheeseburger, since I am on a diet I shall exercise willpower and not have it.' This might be interpreted to mean that the person's preference for the cheeseburger is simply not being revealed or that this apparent 'individual' is in fact two people, the talking one who prefers the cheeseburger and the acting one who does not.

The 'intrinsic'–'overall' distinction provides a better explanation for what is going on. Give a moment's thought to the above fictitious quote (nearly all of us can relate to this in some way) and consider the following translation: 'I would prefer to have a cheeseburger if my having it could be a completely isolated event having no impact whatsoever on my weight or anything else in my future. But since I know my having the cheeseburger will have some future effects I instead have an overall preference not to have the cheeseburger.' This suggests that we should not think of two warring 'selves' within the person but rather two different definitions of a first-order preference. By one definition (the 'intrinsic') the agent prefers the cheeseburger. But by the other (the 'overall') he does not. And it is the 'overall' that is always revealed by the choice that is made.

This brings us to the second explanation for the relative popularity of the 'two-selves' model, namely, the mainstream belief that 'assumptions don't matter'. Despite having little support among philosophers of science, Milton Friedman's (1953) claim that simplicity and ability to predict should be the test of a theory rather than the realism of its assumptions has exerted enormous influence since first offered over 50 years ago. According to Friedman, a theory's ability to accurately predict was what mattered, not the accuracy of the assumptions on which the theory rests. Because it was observed that people would sometimes deliberately limit their range of choices by, for example, flushing cigarettes down the toilet, a way had to be found to 'explain' such behavior, and predict when it might occur in the future. Now *if* it were true that each of us was made up of two (or more) competing selves, then, yes, control exercised by one of these selves might indeed limit the choices that the 'other self' could in the future make. That this way of explaining the phenomenon is itself a metaphor in need of explanation simply did not matter to those raised in the Friedman methodological tradition. People behaved 'as if' they had two or more selves and accurate predictions could follow from the assumption that they in fact did.

Reliance on the existence of second-order preferences provides an explanation for the paradox that we sometimes feel 'as if' we are two selves, while the assumption of two selves literally assumes the problem away. There is, however, an even more significant disadvantage of relying on the two-selves explanation. Normative conclusions are impossible when one preference ranking gains power at the expense of another if it is assumed that these preference rankings belong to different selves within the person. This is acknowledged by those who have been reliant on the two-selves models. As Thomas Schelling (2006, pp. 77–8) states:

The simplicity with which we can analyze the strategy of self-command by recognizing the analogy with two selves comes at a price . . . Each self is a set of values: and though the selves share most of those values, on the particular issues on which they differ fundamentally there doesn't seem to be any way to compare their utility increments and to determine which behavior maximizes their collective utility.

For Schelling, this price was apparently worth paying, but for the sorts of normative questions that social economists naturally gravitate toward, this is clearly too great a price to pay. One self within me may prefer smoking and one self within me prefer abstaining. The distribution of utility is affected by who 'wins' but not overall well-being. In contrast, if I prefer to prefer to not smoke, then preferring to not smoke (and abstaining) leaves me unequivocally better off than would 'preferring to smoke and smoking'. At a less immediate level, the uncovering of a market failure is possible with second-order preferences but does not at all follow from the two-selves approach.

The third reason for the dominance of the two-selves models relative to the second-order preference models has to do with the discomfort many economists have with the very notion of a second-order preference. As John Davis (2003) has emphasized, the notion of an internal self is held in low regard by neoclassical economists, and appreciation of the internal self is a precondition for the acceptance of the second-order preference in ways that do not apply to the first-order preference.

While the philosophical contribution of Friedman consisted of the case for an instrumentalist view of the subject – theory justified by its ability to predict – this in turn was part of an older positivist tradition that defined people as agents of action, not subjectively lived lives. This positivism likely peaked in the 1930s when 'revealed preference' was introduced as a behavioral replacement for the amorphous, unobservable concept of utility. People's first-order preferences were revealed by what they chose. Since these first-order preferences were typically defined over bundles of things, the very act of behaving was the act of revealing one's first-order preferences.

In contrast to this, second-order preferences are not so readily revealed through action. It is true that some actions may indirectly suggest a second-order preference. Thus, for example, one might take action now to remove, say, fattening food, from tomorrow's choice set. These actions have become too prevalent to deny, and as discussed above, have usually simply been attributed to the existence of a second self within the person rather than the existence of a second-order preference. For the latter to be an acknowledged phenomenon, one must be willing to grant that we are more than our behaviors and to accept that what one chooses to do now might in a very

indirect way represent a manifestation of choosing what one's future preferences will be. While 'having' a preference does not entail being able to
'choose' with respect to the items over which the preference is defined, the
cases where choices can be observed have simply been granted a higher
status by economists. Thus second-order preferences are only very indirectly manifested in behaviors. For a discipline less than comfortable with
introspection, such preferences are easy to omit from the conversation.

6.   Predictions and policy prospects

The problem of unpreferred preferences is not something that an economy
can expect to overcome as prosperity spreads. If anything, we might anticipate the very opposite.[9] Those living at or near subsistence have preferences
to act in ways that keep them alive. It is safe to say that such people usually
have no regrets about having these preferences for life's basics. It is their
budget constraints, not their preferences, that they would like to see change.

Incomes have been growing unequally for the last 30 years as the relatively
affluent have enjoyed much greater relative income gains than those at and
near the bottom in the USA and throughout most of the world.[10] However
unfair this may seem, it remains true that in most countries there have been
real gains for all. And with these gains comes more discretionary spending
and greater danger of more unpreferred preferences. Added to this are two
other historical trends that suggest the problem has likely worsened.

Before describing these trends, it will be necessary to digress briefly.
There is ample casual empirical evidence that the greater the time lapse
between a decision to consume and the consumption act itself, the more
likely is the first-order preference to be preferred.[11] If a person could decide
today what to have for lunch tomorrow, she would be more likely to be
moved by a preferred preference than would be true if she decided just
minutes before tomorrow's lunch. Similarly, there is casual empirical evidence that the smaller the time lapse between a decision to consume and
the consumption act itself, the less likely is the first-order preference to be
preferred. A choice having a non-monetary cost provides the best example
of this. If any weight gain and damaging health effect from a particular
meal could be experienced by this individual at the very same time that a
meal is eaten, she would be more likely to be moved by a preference that she
prefers than would be true if these costs could be delayed. Summarizing,
other things being equal, the closer to the time of consumption decision are
the costs and the more distant are the benefits, the greater is the likelihood
that one will prefer the preference that moves one to act.

Over at least the last century, benefits have been brought close to the time
that a consumption decision is made and costs have been pushed further
away.[12] Rather different social trends appear to lie behind these trends: the

pulling forward of benefits mainly attributable to economic growth and specialization, the pushing away of costs mainly attributable to the erosion of customs and laws that stood in the way of certain marketing practices.

Starting with the pulling forward of benefits, when production-for-self was more common there was a natural delay between the consumption decision and the consumption act. As a consequence, what one chose to eat, for example, had to be determined by decisions made considerably earlier. With specialization, what one produces ceases to exactly dictate what one will ultimately consume. Rather than reaping what one sows, one who sows earns an income for doing so and can proceed to metaphorically 'reap' something else altogether, the act of consumption now contingent on the decision to consume itself.

The pushing away of costs is the result not of specialization but changed definitions of acceptable marketing practices. While 'buy now, pay later' is an expression going all the way back to the 1920s, the remarkable extension of credit just in the past 15 years has made clear the negative effects that this can have. The media tend to focus on the bankruptcies that will (and have) accompanied abuse of credit, but largely unconsidered is the harm done to a sizeable percentage of such borrowers who find themselves in the grip of unpreferred preferences when making their purchase decisions.[13]

As far as attempting to suggest what sort of public policy might be directed at improving our preferences, it is worth noting that becoming better informed is not much of a solution. Providing clear information about products undoubtedly has beneficial effects, but not because first-order preferences are brought into accord with second-order preferences. Better information instead has more to do with changing *both* the first-order and the second-order preference simultaneously than it does with simply changing the first to accord with the second. To illustrate, imagine being all set to take a drink of water when you are stopped and informed that the water has been poisoned. In this case, prior to the information it is likely that your second-order preference was in accord with your first. In other words, it is likely that you preferred the water and preferred having this preference. It is also likely that the news of the poisoning changed both your first- and second-order preferences. Not only did you not prefer to drink the water, but you preferred this preference.

While this is an extreme example, it captures the beneficial effect of receiving information and must be contrasted with information that changes the second-order preference but not the first. Imagine someone completely unaware of a cheeseburger's bad health effects who suddenly learns about the harm they can cause. This is more likely to change the second-order preference of the agent than the first. Information, in short, is clearly important for improving our preferences (both first- and second-order) but is not necessarily a very useful way to attempt to better align first-order preferences with second-order preferences.

Regarding public policy, it is significant that public support for actions to combat global warming had to be preceded by public awareness that there was even a problem. Policy actions to promote preferred preferences would similarly have to await a public awareness that there is indeed a problem with the market's effects on our tastes. At present, proposals for taste-changing policies by government are usually regarded as paternalistic meddling, with elected elites simply 'telling the people what they should like'. Were it to become common knowledge that humans have a special type of preference and that the market is deficient in its response to these preferences, creative calls for action would come forth. Until then, spreading the word that second-order preferences exist would appear to be the only sensible policy.

Notes

1. George (1993, 2001, pp. 32–4).
2. For examples of the two-selves literature, see Ainslie (2001), Elster (1986), Etzioni (1986) and Schelling (2006, chs 5–8). For an exchange on the advisability of relying on the two-selves model, see Brennan (1989) and Lutz (1993). A closer look at the two-selves model is offered in Section 5.
3. Frankfurt's article (1971) is generally credited with being the first on this subject. For Frankfurt, a 'free will' was manifested in having the preferences that one preferred having. Animals, not having the ability to reflect upon their preferences, could only have freedom to act upon their will, but not a 'free will'. Another philosopher, Richard Jeffrey (1974), followed a more formal development. Amartya Sen (1974, 1977) was the first economist to make use of second-order preferences. My writings (1984, 1993, 1998, 2001) remain the only ones by economists to emphasize the normative dimension of the subject. Use of the normative conclusions that I have reached (George, 1984, 1993, 1998, 2001) remain largely outside of economics. See, for example, normative considerations coming from within the legal profession (Anonymous, 2003) and from the perspective of political theorist Benjamin Barber (2007, p. 221).
4. With advances in the brain sciences, a number of characteristics previously thought to reside exclusively with humans have been found in other species as well. See, for example, Marino (2004). The self-reflective abilities of dolphins may indicate that they too can evaluate their preference. This would mean that second-order preferences are not 'uniquely human' but would otherwise not affect the analysis.
5. As I argue at some length (George, 2001, chs 6–9), moral and ethical considerations which historically have served as constraints on taste-changing behaviors have been weakening for at least a century. See Hodgson (2003) for an institutionalist perspective on the role of institutions in the shaping of tastes.
6. While discretionary spending and the possibility of unpreferred preferences may increase with affluence, a recent empirical study by Banerjee and Duflo (2007) indicates that the poor spend more on 'discretionary' goods than previously thought. This casts greater doubt on the soundness of Abraham Maslow's 'hierarchy of needs'. According to Maslow, 'If all the needs are unsatisfied, the organism is then dominated by the physiological needs, all other needs may become simply nonexistent or be pushed into the background. It is then fair to characterize the whole organism by saying simply it is hungry, for consciousness is almost completely preempted by hunger' (1954, p. 92).

7. 'Liberal' and 'conservative' are being defined here in the sense most common in the USA.
8. A second-order preference would almost always be 'overall' in nature. It would be possible, but very unusual, for one to prefer, for example, a preference to eat healthily just because having the preference isolated from what this may cause in the long run is seen as desirable. By their very nature, second-order preferences take the long view, rather than a short-run perspective.
9. For a collection of excerpted articles on the consumer culture, see Goodwin et al. (1997). For a deeply pessimistic analysis of consumerism's effect on affluent economies, see Barber (2007).
10. Jantti and Sandstrom (2005) conclude the following: '[O]ur results certainly suggest that in most countries, based on the available evidence, inequality has tended to increase. Moreover, the increase seems to have occurred mainly through a disproportionate increase in the income share of the richest fifth.'
11. The intemporal choice literature supports these conclusions without specifically bringing second-order preferences into the discussion. See, for example, Loewenstein and Thaler (1989) and Laibson (1997).
12. See George (2001, pp. 97–8).
13. For an extended discussion of the spread of consumer credit, see George (2001, ch. 9). For a recent institutionalist treatment of contemporary difficulties that consumer credit has created, see Dolfsma and McMaster (2007).

References

Ainslie, George (2001), *Breakdown of Will*, Cambridge: Cambridge University Press.
Anonymous (2003), 'Notes: the elephant in the room: evolution, behavioralism, and counter-advertising in the coming war against obesity', *Harvard Law Review*, **116** (4), 1161–84.
Banerjee, Abhijit V. and Esther Duflo (2007), 'The economic lives of the poor', *Journal of Economic Perspectives*, **21** (1), 141–67.
Barber, Benjamin R. (2007), *Consumed: How Markets Corrupt Children, Infantilize Adults, and Swallow Citizens Whole*, New York: W.W. Norton.
Brennan, Timothy J. (1989), 'A methodological assessment of multiple utility frameworks', *Economics and Philosophy*, **5**, 189–208.
Davis, John B. (2003), *The Theory of the Individual in Economics: Identity and Value*, New York: Routledge.
Dolfsma, Wilfred and Robert McMaster (2007), 'Revisiting institutionalist law and economics – the inadequacy of the Chicago School: the case of personal bankruptcy law', *Journal of Economic Issues*, **41** (2), 557–65.
Elster, Jon (1986), *The Multiple Self*, Cambridge: Cambridge University Press.
Etzioni, Amitai (1986), 'The case for a multiple-utility conception', *Economics and Philosophy*, **2**, 159–83.
Frankfurt, Harry G. (1971), 'Freedom of the will and the concept of a person', *Journal of Philosophy*, **68**, 5–20.
Friedman, Milton (1953), *Essays in Positive Economics*, Chicago, IL: Chicago University Press.
Galbraith, John Kenneth (1958), *The Affluent Society*, New York: New American Library.
George, David (1984), 'Metapreferences: reconsidering contemporary notions of free choice', *International Journal of Social Economics*, **11**, (3–4), 92–107.
George, David (1993), 'Does the market create preferred preferences?', *Review of Social Economy*, **51**, 323–46.
George, David (1998), 'Coping rationally with unpreferred preferences', *Eastern Economic Journal*, **24** (2), 181–94.
George, David (2001), *Preference Pollution: How Markets Create the Desires We Dislike*, Ann Arbor, MI: University of Michigan Press.
Goodwin, Neva R., Frank Ackerman and David Kiron (eds), (1997), *The Consumer Society*, Washington, DC: Island Press.
Hayek, Friedrich (1961), 'The non-sequitur of the "dependence" effect', *Southern Economic Journal*, **27**, 346–8.

Hodgson, Geoffrey M. (2003), 'The hidden persuaders: institutions and individuals in economic theory', *Cambridge Journal of Economics*, **27**, 159–75.
Jantti, Markus and Susanna Sandstrom (2005), 'Trends in income inequality: a critical examination of the evidence in WIID2', unpublished manuscript.
Jeffrey, Richard C. (1974), 'Preferences among preferences', *Journal of Philosophy*, **71**, 377–91.
Kagel, John H. and Raymond C. Battalio (1975), 'Experimental studies of consumer demand behavior using laboratory animals', *Economic Inquiry*, **13** (1), 22–38.
Laibson, David (1997), 'Golden eggs and hyperbolic discounting', *Quarterly Journal of Economics*, **112**, 443–77.
Loewenstein, George and Richard H. Thaler (1989), 'Intertemporal choice', *Journal of Economic Perspectives*, **3** (4), 181–93.
Lutz, Mark A. (1993), 'The utility of multiple utility: a comment on Brennan', *Economics and Philosophy*, **9**, 145–54.
Marino, Lori (2004), 'Dolphin cognition', *Current Biology*, **14**, R910–R911.
Maslow, Abraham H. (1954), *Motivation and Personality*, New York: Harper & Row.
Schelling, Thomas C. (2006), *Strategies of Commitment and Other Essays*, Cambridge, MA: Harvard University Press.
Sen, Amartya K. (1974), 'Choice, orderings and morality', in S. Korner (ed.), *Practical Reason*, Oxford: Blackwell, pp. 54–67.
Sen, Amartya K. (1977), 'Rational fools: a critique of the behavioural foundations of economic theory', *Philosophy and Public Affairs*, **6**, 317–44.

8 The socio-economics of consumption: solutions to the problems of interest, knowledge and identity
Metin M. Coşgel

Consumption is a social activity. Although economics textbooks typically portray the choice of a consumption bundle simply as the solution to a constrained maximization problem with given preferences, social economists have variously expanded the basic theory of choice and offered alternatives to it based on insights from heterodox approaches and other disciplines. They have shown that consumption choices not only maximize utility but also display wealth, express beliefs and maintain identity.

There are numerous comprehensive reviews of the enormous multidisciplinary literature on consumption.[1] Rather than aim at a similar standard review of this literature, it would be more appropriate for this volume to adopt a distinct approach in evaluating socio-economic contributions. An approach that has been useful in studying various economic phenomena, helping to shed new light on old problems and to discover new problems for further exploration, is to view the economy as conversation. To sustain a coherent line of thought throughout the review, I adopt this approach in studying consumption and interpret previous social economic studies of consumption as investigations of behavior and institutions that contribute to these conversations. I organize these studies into a coherent whole and distinguish between conversations according to the type of problem they aim to solve. Identifying three types of conversations relevant to the study of consumption – solving the problems of interest, knowledge and identity – I discuss the main themes and important contributions in each category and offer suggestions for further research.

Consumption as conversation

A productive line of research based on the rhetorical approach has been to adopt the metaphor of conversation in studying economists and the economy. This approach has been useful for understanding the literary character of economics and for showing how economists use metaphors, stories, analogies and various other rhetorical devices in scholarly discourse.[2] As a simple extension of this approach from the world of economists to the economy itself, the metaphor of conversation has also been adopted in studying various economic phenomena, including entrepreneurship, strategic communication, the domestic economy and herd behavior.[3] As McCloskey (1994, p. 367) has put it, 'the economy, like economics itself, is a conversation'.

The metaphor of conversation has also been used explicitly in studying consumption.[4] Just as individuals engage in verbal conversations in the economy while bargaining for a price or negotiating a contract, they engage in non-verbal conversations while consuming goods and services. They map colors with gender by purchasing blue clothes for boys and pink for girls, tell stories about themselves by their choices of music and books, and project characters based on the use of cigarettes, alcohol and drugs. Conversations in the economy and culture include both verbal and non-verbal forms of communication.

The metaphor of conversation is sufficiently broad to encompass the social economic literature on consumption. Contributions to this literature may be viewed as efforts to understand different aspects of this conversation, though they may not have been labeled as such. Although significant differences exist among the studies of consumption, these differences reflect the types of conversations they study. By identifying the categories of these conversations, we can construct a coherent analytical framework to examine the literature systematically.

To identify conversations in the economy that share distinct features, let us classify them according to their purpose, the type of problem they aim to solve. Although not all conversations aim to solve a problem, considering them as purposeful activities in solving problems helps to construct an analytical procedure to distinguish between different types of contributions to the literature on consumption.

Conversations involving consumption can be categorized into three types.[5] Those in the first type aim to solve the problem of interest: how to align the incentives of the participants. The problem arises because people have their own interests, which often conflict with the interests of others. Conversations may resolve the conflict by allowing participants to talk about their motivations, recognize mutual interests, or reach agreements that will ensure mutually beneficial behavior.

Conversations of the second type deal with the problem of knowledge; how to align localized, dispersed information.[6] Our actions often depend on information about the preferences, beliefs, plans and behavior of others, information about how they will act and what they know or care about. The problem of knowledge arises because this information may not be readily available to everyone. There are clear overlaps between the problems of interest and knowledge because they both deal with missing information.

Although the unavailability of information may be a problem in both types of conversations, the nature of the problem is categorically different between them. In the problem of interest the availability of information becomes a problem when individuals withhold it strategically or reveal inaccurate information because of conflicting interests. The focus in the problem of knowledge is not on the desire to withhold the information but on the inability to obtain it easily. The problem remains even if interests do not conflict and individuals are willing to share information voluntarily, because information is dispersed and needs to be acquired through conversation.

Conversations of the third type deal with the problem of identity: how to align discrepancies between commitment and behavior. These conversations are different from others in that they may also take place within one self. The problem arises because people may fail to deliver on their implicit or explicit commitments to various dimensions of their identity. A father may forget about his daughter's piano recital, a student may prepare insufficiently for an exam, or a religious person may miss the weekly service. Conversations with self or others may help to prevent these failures by reinforcing or reminding us of our commitments.

To see the difference between the three types of conversations, suppose you were able to hear some of the conversations taking place in a restaurant. At one table you might hear a conversation of the first type between a job candidate and the head of the search committee for an academic position discussing the qualifications of the candidate or the match between their interests. A second type of conversation could be taking place at the next table between a group of old friends catching up with each other by talking about their families, new hobbies, or changing worldviews. Yet another table might witness a conversation of the third type where a devout Muslim explains to a friend his choice of orange juice over wine based on his religious beliefs.

Consumption is clearly an integral part of these conversations. Just as an individual would say something to join one of these conversations, his or her clothing, food, drink, jewelry, ornaments, make-up, hairstyle and so on also contribute to the conversation. The job candidate may wear a suit and tie, shave or trim his beard, and refrain from heavy alcohol during dinner. In catching up with each other, old friends learn new things from each other not only from their jokes and stories but also from their clothing, hairstyle, make-up, and recent choices of books, music and movies. Similarly, given Islamic prohibitions on pork and alcohol and strict guidelines on some items of clothing, a Muslim's consumption patterns of food, alcohol and clothing would make clear statements about the level of his or her religious commitment.

How consumption solves the problems of incentives, knowledge and commitment

A common element of socio-economic studies of consumption is their desire to escape the narrow confines of the standard neoclassical theory of choice. A well-known criticism of this parsimonious theory is that it strips away any analysis of its social dimension (Hirschman, 1985; Sen, 1977). It focuses on the moment of choice, the final outcome of a sequence that follows the preference–utility–demand path. Unsatisfied by this approach, social economists have developed a significant body of research to broaden the standard theory by probing deeper into social influences on preferences and choice. Viewing the standard theory as void of social content, they have also developed alternatives informed by other disciplines and heterodox approaches.

The typology of conversations developed above can also be used to categorize the socio-economic approaches to consumption. These studies have variously contributed to our understanding of how consumption contributes to a conversation. Because they have emerged from a variety of concerns, approaches and disciplinary backgrounds, they have naturally focused on different types of conversations. By grouping them according to the types of conversations they study, we can examine their place in a coherent whole, view old ideas in a new light, and identify their strengths and weaknesses.

1.   The problem of interest

The first set of socio-economic approaches studies how consumption contributes to conversations solving the problem of interest. The basic problem here is that someone may possess private information that might be of interest to others, but there may be no easy way to reveal it to them. The most obvious case is when an individual has information which he has no incentive to share freely and truthfully with others. But the problem may persist even when the informed would gain from making the information known to others and the uninformed would gain from learning it. This would be the case when there is no cost to revealing incorrect, misleading information. In particular, verbal self-serving claims may not be credible (Farrell, 1995).

Although uttering words may be cheap, transitory and unverifiable, consuming goods is usually costly, lasting and directly observable. Social economists have identified various types of consumption behavior and institutions that provide solutions to the problem of interest by allowing individuals to find more credible ways to convey information. There are two general ways in which consumption can help to solve the problem of interest, depending on whether the speaker or the listener takes the lead for the revelation of private information. It can either help the informed party to talk credibly to the uninformed, or help the uninformed elicit verifiable statements from the informed. The former is called signaling in the general literature on incentives, and the latter is called screening.

In the signaling type of solution to the problem of interest, privately informed individuals take the lead by choosing observable consumption items that reveal information to others. A wealthy person may buy an expensive car, live in an outwardly expensive-looking home, and wear expensive clothing and jewelry, not necessarily because he has a preference for them but because these items credibly signal his wealth. In his classic analysis of the 'leisure class' in the late nineteenth century, Veblen (1899) introduced the term 'conspicuous consumption' to describe this type of behavior, insisting that 'an expenditure to be reputable it must be wasteful' (ibid., p. 97). Systematic analysis of this phenomenon has a long and distinguished history, including early contributions by Smith (1776 [1976]) and Rae (1834).[7] Extensions and implications of this behavior have also been discussed in formal models of status signaling (Spence, 1974, ch. 8; Ireland, 1994), consumption externalities (Leibenstein, 1950), and positional goods (Hirsch, 1976; Frank, 1985).

The second set of solutions to the problem of interest, called screening, refers to the activities taken by an uninformed individual to elicit reactions from informed individuals that will cause them to separate themselves into categories or reveal private information. A modest or socially conservative individual trying to decide whether to go out on a blind date may ask the potential date if he would rather meet in a bar or a coffee shop to determine his type from his consumption habits. Some of the consumption norms prescribed by religions may be interpreted as screening mechanisms. Viewing religion as providing various benefits subject to free-rider problems and noting the difficulty of separating devout believers from imitators, Iannaccone (1992) has argued that various dietary restrictions and consumption guidelines that might seem bizarre to an outsider actually serve the function of screening out imitators. Although there may be various other circumstances where consumption may cause individuals to separate themselves into groups along some revealing dimension, the nature and consequences of this type of phenomena have not been systematically studied to my knowledge.

2.   *The problem of knowledge*

Economists are generally familiar with the problem of knowledge through Hayek's pioneering work on the properties of the market system (Hayek, 1948). All economies face the basic problem of how to coordinate activities, how to determine who should use which resources and technology to produce what and for whom. A fundamental component of achieving effective coordination is that the required information on tastes, technology, resources and so on is not freely available to everyone. The cost varies according to the type of mechanism used to solve the problem. Whereas in a command economy dispersed information must somehow be transmitted to the central authority through a costly process, the market system can solve the coordination problem more effectively by economizing on information demands, because prices summarize all relevant information. In an ideal market system individuals need to know only their own tastes, skills and the prevailing prices.

The problem of knowledge exists in a broader sense than concerns the coordination of production because in a changing world various constraints on the human capacity to learn, reason and remember make it difficult for us to acquire the localized, dispersed knowledge that we need even for ordinary decisions. As a typical example, consider the problem of deciding which side of the road to drive on. To avoid a head-on collision, you need to know the lane preferences of the cars coming from the other direction. The problem in this type of a situation is not that individuals have an incentive to withhold the required information or state it inaccurately, but that it can be extremely costly for others to acquire.

The solution to the problem in the driving example is for everyone going in one direction to drive on the same side of the road and those going in the other direction to drive on the opposite side, a convention that cheaply substitutes for the required knowledge. One of the significant accomplishments of social scientists has been to show how various similar norms, conventions, and other formal and informal institutions, such as the law, money, the price system and property rights, provide solutions to the problem of knowledge.[8]

Consumption institutions also help solve the problem of knowledge. They do this by fulfilling a dual function. They provide knowledge not only to the consumer but also to the audience about the meanings of goods, knowledge they need to encode and decode messages. Consumption institutions regulate communication by constraining and facilitating consumption. As constraints, they restrict the range of choices for the consumer by encoding a message and the range of interpretations of the message by the audience. As facilitators, they substitute for extensive reasoning and deliberation, thus abbreviating the knowledge required for decisions and interpretations (Coşgel, 1997).

Clothing and grooming conventions, for example, provide knowledge. Males and females typically follow different patterns in most societies, reducing the difficulty of determining the gender of others. Mapping colors with gender (e.g. blue for boys and pink for girls) in children's clothing, for example, makes it easier to differentiate between boys and girls. Similar dress codes, such as to wear formal attire for certain occasions and casual for others, also solve the problem of knowledge by providing shared categories of communication. These norms and conventions work by constraining the range of choices available to consumers and economizing on their knowledge requirements, and by reducing the need for extensive information, reasoning and memory.

The problem of knowledge has been an important theme in consumer studies and in sociological and anthropological studies of consumption. A common starting point in these studies is to view goods as a system of communication. As Douglas and Isherwood (1979, p. 95) argue, 'Man needs goods for communicating with others and for making sense of what is going on around him.' Similar to words, items of personal consumption make statements. A consumer's emotions, personality, ideas, beliefs and so on find expression in a consumption bundle. Combining insights from a variety of disciplines, McCracken (1990) considers the mobile quality of meaning, and provides a theoretical account of the structure and movement of the cultural meaning of consumer goods. Applying some of these insights to economics, Coşgel and Minkler (2004b) discuss how religious consumption norms help solve the problem of knowledge.

3.   *The problem of identity*

Standard economic theory is an exception among the social sciences in its longstanding neglect of the concept of identity. Consistent with its central role in contemporary society, identity is a fundamental concept in sociology, psychology, anthropology and other social sciences. It has been shown to affect various social outcomes, such as ethnic conflicts, sports team loyalty, gender discrimination and religious behavior. Standard economic models of behavior, however, have generally ignored the influence of identity on behavior and outcomes. These models have typically considered individuals as represented by subjective preferences, assumed to be given, smooth, independent and unproblematic. The determinants of preferences and their relationship to identity are left outside of analysis.

Although standard economic models have historically failed to consider the influence of identity, some recent studies have sought to incorporate identity explicitly into economic models of behavior by using insights from other disciplines (Akerlof and Kranton, 2000, 2002). Identity has also been the focus of attention in methodological debates and heterodox approaches to economic behavior. These studies share a concern with the sources, dimensions and implications of identity, considering it in relation to conceptions of the individual, commitment and integrity. In philosophical discussions of integrity, for example, having integrity is typically conceptualized as having commitments that define an individual's identity, or sense of self (Coşgel and Minkler, 2004a).

The problem of identity arises when there is a discrepancy between the committed and displayed behavior. An individual may violate a commitment for a variety of reasons, including errors of judgment and weakness of will. One may be committed to a cause or person or a moral or religious principle, but find oneself doing things that conflict with that commitment and sense of self.

To solve the problem of identity, individuals engage in conversations with self and others that help prevent or remove the conflict. Consumption, of course, is an important part of these conversations, helping to maintain identity by telling others and reminding ourselves of our commitments. The consumption of ornaments and religious symbols, for example, serves this function. Patterns of consumption based on age, ethnicity, gender and other dimensions of identity also help align commitment and behavior. The problem of identity suggests that individuals choose items of consumption not just to align interests or to communicate dispersed information, but also to maintain a sense of self.

Consistent with the absence of the concept of identity from mainstream economics, the problem of identity is also typically ignored in standard theories of consumption, where the individual is represented by his or her subjective preferences and single utility function. Recognizing the limitations of the standard theory, a significant body of research has developed over time that has studied the concept of the individual and the relationship between identity and consumption choices from a variety of perspectives. Contributors to this literature can be divided into two groups: those maintaining the basic framework and revising conceptions of preferences and utility; and others going beyond the basic framework and considering the individual as socially embedded.[9]

Studies in the first group preserve the basic framework of the independent individual in standard theory of choice, but complicate the analysis by considering multiple selves. The starting point in this type of analysis is to consider identity as consisting of a collection of selves. The problem is formalized in terms of an internal structure of preferences and by asking how this collection can be treated as a single unity.

The relationship between the subsets of preferences has been formalized in various ways. Perhaps the oldest way of thinking about the problem of multiple selves, dating back at least to the ideas of Plato and Aristotle, is to formulate the problem as the weakness of will. This refers to a situation when an individual somehow chooses the less desired of the available options. More recently, the weakness of will has been explained by Elster

(1979) as the time inconsistency of preferences and by Davidson (2001) as having competing actions that the individual ought to perform.[10]

The problem has also been formalized in terms of a hierarchical organization of preferences. In a pioneering work that links identity with intentionality, Frankfurt (1971) has viewed the ability to form a ranking of intentions and being able to detachedly evaluate first-order intentions (e.g. beliefs and desires) as the distinguishing characteristic of individuals. Sen (1977) has similarly used the concept of metapreference to solve the problem, arguing that individuals have higher-order preferences (metapreferences) over their first-order preferences used in ranking bundles of goods. More recently, George (2001) has used the concept of second-order preference to examine preference pollution, the struggle against market influence on unpreferred preferences.

The literature on multiple selves is voluminous, including various other interesting, creative ways of dealing with the problem. These include Harsanyi's (1955) 'subjective' and 'ethical' preferences, Thaler and Shefrin's (1981) principal–agent view of the internal structure of the individual (based on an analogy with the internal structure of the firm), Schelling's (1984) concept of 'self-command', and Khalil's (2004) view of the self as a 'complex entity'.

There are, however, well-documented problems with the preference-based models of multiple selves as revisions of the standard theory of choice. The most important is that by preserving the basic framework, these studies leave open the question of how exactly one should aggregate choice across the collection of selves. The problem of a conflict within the self is essentially an intrapersonal choice problem, analogous to the problem of collective choice involving a collection of separate individuals. This, of course, makes this framework subject to the same type of problems identified in Arrow's impossibility theorem.[11]

The second group of studies dealing with the problem of identity rejects the atomistic view of individuals and considers their interdependence and the social relationships between them. Although mainstream economists have recently taken important steps in this direction, much of the literature on the socially embedded individual in economics has come from heterodox approaches. Various ideas have been proposed to explain how being in a society influences an individual's identity and consumption choices. Kuran (1995) has argued that individuals may display different behavior in public than in private because of reputational concerns faced in society. An influential perspective has been to add a social dimension to the hierarchical dual-self view by considering individuals as possessing first- and second-order preferences that can be reflexive and socially constructed. Etzioni (1988) has proposed an 'I&We' paradigm for the study of economic behavior based on the assumption that people have two sources of valuation: pleasure and morality. He assumes that humans are able to pass moral judgments on their urges, choosing primarily on the basis of emotions and value judgments, and rendering decisions not as independent individuals but as members of collectivities. Lutz and Lux (1988) have similarly developed a paradigm of humanistic economics based on the dual-self theory of human personality, aiming for a more complete image of the person that posits the presence of mutual interest in addition to self-interest. Institutional economists have long maintained a view of the individual as socially constituted, generally maintaining closer links with methodological holism in explaining behavior. There have been numerous other approaches to social embeddedness, variously showing how identity and choice are influenced by such phenomena as gender (Folbre, 1994), religiosity (Coşgel and Minkler, 2004a), socio-cultural values (Dolfsma, 2004), and reflexive capacities (Hargreaves Heap, 2001).

Although explanations based on the narrow, extreme variants of the atomistic and embedded views of individuals have been biased and unsatisfactory, the literature has evolved toward a more sophisticated view of individual identity by combining insights from both variants.[12] While trying to escape the limitations of the concept of the atomistic individual, some of the earlier studies of social embeddedness may make the mistake of going to the other extreme by committing the equally narrow and problematic perspective of social determinism and leaving out the individual altogether. More recent studies, however, have consciously sought to maintain a desirable balance between these views, examining individual actions within social constraints but without making those constraints the sole determinant of behavior. In parallel methodological terms, this has meant steering away from narrow variants of both holism and individualism. Consistent with other pluralistic developments recently observed in social sciences (e.g. the spread of new institutionalism in mainstream economics and also across other disciplines), successful explanations have been grounded not just in atomistic individuals and universal forces but also in politics, culture, history and society.

One way to formulate the plurality of identity dimensions has been to distinguish between personal and social identity. This is a well-known distinction in social psychology, originally developed to study the basis for intergroup discrimination (Tajfel and Turner, 1979). According to social identity theory, being a member of a group is based on the subjective perception of the self as a member of a specific category. Social identification is a powerful motive that influences people with group social identity to conform more in behavior, including consumption choices, with the group norm. Research has shown that people purchase products that enable the enactment of social identities (Kleine et al., 1993).

New directions

It will not have escaped the reader's attention that some of the leading contributions to the literature on consumption have an interdisciplinary flavor. Consumption is a subject that cuts across various disciplines, each bringing its own perspective and capabilities that have been developed over time through the division of labor. These contributions show how the benefits of specialization reach beyond a discipline, as new ideas and methods are cross-fertilized into other disciplines. Such cross-fertilizations have recently been the genesis of some of the most innovative recent developments in the social sciences. As Dogan and Pahre (1990, p. 1) argue, 'innovation in the social sciences occurs more often and with more important results at the intersections of disciplines'. Scholars have spread the benefits of specialization across disciplinary boundaries by exporting their own refined ideas, methods and perspectives to other disciplines and by importing useful developments from others. I believe successful developments in the study of consumption will also come increasingly from cross-fertilizations between economics, sociology, anthropology, social psychology, marketing and other disciplines.

Economists have variously borrowed the products and technologies of other disciplines for cross-fertilization. They have followed developments in mathematics and statistics closely, borrowing freely to improve their own techniques of mathematical proof and quantitative analysis. They have also borrowed from business and social sciences, developing such subfields as financial economics, demographic economics and political economy. Specialization has also led to various sorts of lending from economics to other disciplines, economists crossing disciplinary boundaries to contribute to developments in other disciplines or to create new subspecialties at the cross-sections of two or more disciplines (Dogan and Pahre, 1990). This type of cross-fertilization has allowed disciplines to extend their conventional boundaries by identifying fertile areas where narrow applications of the traditional tools and concepts of other disciplines have proven inadequate or incomplete. Economics has extended into law, history and sociology, leading to the establishment and development of various sub-disciplines, such as economics of law, economic history and rational choice sociology.

Although it is of course difficult to forecast the future of intellectual developments, the interdisciplinary nature of consumption studies and recent patterns in this and other fields of economics suggests that significant developments will be in the form of cross-fertilizations. This can happen in at least two ways. The first is by strengthening established trade links between disciplines that have proven particularly suitable for cross-fertilization. There are various established trade flows in the social economic studies of how consumption contributes to the three categories of conversations, as can be seen from the origins of the leading contributions to each literature. Based on their comparative advantage, economists have dominated the study of conversation of the first type. Specialized in the study of incentives, they have focused on the problem of interest, exporting their ever-improving products to other disciplines. Researchers in anthropology, sociology and consumer studies have excelled in studying conversation of the second type. Following the pioneering contribution of Mary Douglas and others, they have produced and exported various new theoretical insights and applied field research on how consumption contributes to solving the problem of knowledge. Leadership in studying the third type of conversations has come primarily from philosophy, sociology and social psychology. Traditionally specialized in studying how morality, commitment, community and similar phenomena affect behavior, they have exported various tools, concepts and ideas for the study of how consumption solves the problem of identity.

Analogous to importers and exporters of consumer goods and production technologies, economists would do well to invest in trade relationships to improve their own products and the well-being of their discipline. This means improving their own products not only for their own consumption but also for better marketability and applicability to the demands of other disciplines. Specialization, after all, makes sense only if it aims at trade, and specialization for its own sake without due regard for others' use risks losing market share. Investing in trade relationships also means keeping abreast of new developments in other disciplines in order to identify better imports. By identifying a new theoretical development or finding a more suitable technique in another discipline, an economist would be better able to improve existing social economic studies of consumption.

The second type of significant development in the social economic study of consumption takes the form of establishing new trade routes with other disciplines by identifying underdeveloped or entirely new areas for cross-fertilization. Insights from other disciplines can be used in numerous ways to push the boundaries of our knowledge of the economy as a whole. Possibilities include extension of the coverage of previous path-breaking studies to other topics and the use of new tools, concepts and theories recently developed in other disciplines. This may mean going beyond the old-fashioned ideas that have failed to sustain productive cross-fertilizations for the social economic study of consumption and looking for new developments in other disciplines for inspiration. Given continual changes in social sciences, emergence of new specializations and subdisciplines, and the growth and development of new research tools and techniques, opportunities for trade are always changing as well. Another possibility is to look for opportunities for interdisciplinary collaboration. Rather than import or export ideas (indirectly and through an intermediary), one way to gain the benefits of specialization and cross-fertilization more directly is for economists to collaborate with scholars in other disciplines.

The categorization used here in reviewing the literature should itself help to identify new lines of research or to provide novel perspectives on old questions. For example, viewing consumption as conversation suggests a new approach in studying preference change. Notwithstanding the well-known argument of Stigler and Becker (1977) urging economists to consider preferences as given and avoid preference-based explanations, economists have variously joined the effort to explain how and why preferences change. The recent literature on the subject includes the contributions of Dolfsma (2004), George (2001) and Karni and Schmeidler (1990). Viewing consumption as conversation, we can approach preference change in relation to changes in the topic, audience, or the setting of the conversation, forcing a change in statements and arguments.

Viewing consumption as conversation also provides a novel way to examine the relationships between disciplines and suggests new forms of interdisciplinary interaction. There are interesting parallels between some types of conversations, pointing toward potential areas of common research. Conversations dealing with the problems of knowledge and identity, for example, intersect when the conversation is about the communication of identities. By exploring such commonalities, it may be possible to identify areas for collaboration or cross-fertilization between disciplines.

Identifying commonalities and differences in the conversations of interest should also help us to understand the relationship between the mainstream and heterodox approaches to economics. These approaches need not be in conflict with each other if their primary focus is on different types of conversations. Heterodox approaches have historically shown a greater interest in studying conversations dealing with the problems of knowledge and identity than those dealing with the problem of interest. Austrian economists, for example, have been more interested in the problem of knowledge than others, while mainstream economists have shown little interest in the problem (either assuming it away based on the assumption of perfect information or restricting it to informational asymmetries related to the problem of interest). Differences between the orthodox and heterodox approaches to economics may have more to do with their ranking of the importance of conversations than different ways of studying these conversations. This can be seen in the recent success of new institutional economics, whose leading proponents have borrowed selectively from the tools and concepts of orthodox economics to study their own, often different, conversations and at the same time maintained a pluralistic attitude toward other approaches that have proven better suited to the study of some phenomena. Social economic studies of consumption might benefit more from approaches that seek out areas of potential complementarity and cross-fertilization between the orthodox and heterodox approaches to economics, rather than those that merely highlight areas of fierce competition. There is much here for future researchers to explore and expand.

Notes

1. See, for example, Aldridge (2003), Deaton and Muellbauer (1980), Fine (2002), Kasser and Kanner (2004), Roth (1989).
2. Klamer (1983), McCloskey (1985), Klamer et al. (1988).
3. Coşgel and Klamer (1990), Farrell (1995), Gudeman and Rivera (1990), McCloskey and Klamer (1995), Shiller (1995).
4. See, for example, Coşgel (1992, 1994, 1997), Douglas and Isherwood (1979), Fine (2002).
5. See Coşgel (2008) for a similar classification used to understand differences between economics and anthropology.
6. For the importance of the distinction between information and knowledge in the Austrian tradition, see Boettke (2002).
7. For the history of conspicuous consumption in economic and social thought, see Mason (1981, ch. 1).
8. For further discussion and examples in various disciplines, see Geertz (1983), Knudsen (2004), Langlois (1986, 1993), North (1990), Sowell (1980) and Sugden (1989).
9. This division parallels Davis's (2003) excellent review of the literature on the individual in economics.
10. See also Elster (1986) for a collection of different perspectives on the multiple self.
11. For details, see Davis (2003, ch. 4).
12. Davis (2003, pp. 189–90) argues that the ideas in the two traditions have evolved in different directions.

References

Akerlof, George A. and Rachel E. Kranton (2000), 'Economics and identity', *Quarterly Journal of Economics*, **105** (3), 715–53.
Akerlof, George A. and Rachel E. Kranton (2002), 'Identity and schooling: some lessons for the economics of education', *Journal of Economic Literature*, **40**, 1167–201.
Aldridge, Alan (2003), *Consumption*, Cambridge: Polity Press.
Boettke, Peter (2002), 'Information and knowledge: Austrian economics in search of its uniqueness', *The Review of Austrian Economics*, **15** (4), 263–74.
Coşgel, Metin M. (1992), 'Rhetoric in the economy: consumption and audience', *Journal of Socio-Economics*, **21**, 363–77.
Coşgel, Metin M. (1994), 'Audience effects in consumption', *Economics and Philosophy*, **10**, 19–30.
Coşgel, Metin M. (1997), 'Consumption institutions', *Review of Social Economy*, **55** (2), 153–71.
Coşgel, Metin M. (2008), 'Conversations between anthropologists and economists', in Stephen Gudeman (ed.), *Economic Persuasions*, New York: Berghahn Books.
Coşgel, Metin M. and Arjo Klamer (1990), 'Entrepreneurship as discourse', unpublished manuscript.
Coşgel, Metin M. and Lanse Minkler (2004a), 'Rationality, integrity, and religious behavior', *Journal of Socio-Economics*, **33**, 329–41.
Coşgel, Metin M. and Lanse Minkler (2004b), 'Religious identity and consumption', *Review of Social Economy*, **33** (3), 329–41.
Davidson, Donald (2001), *Essays on Actions and Events*, Oxford: Clarendon Press.

Davis, John (2003), *Theory of the Individual in Economics*, New York: Routledge.

Deaton, Angus and John Muellbauer (1980), *Economics and Consumer Behavior*, New York: Cambridge University Press.

Dogan, Mattei and Robert Pahre (1990), *Creative Marginality: Innovation at the Intersections of Social Sciences*, Boulder, CO: Westview Press.

Dolfsma, Wilfred (2004), *Institutional Economics and the Formation of Preferences*, Cheltenham, UK and Northampton, MA, USA: Edward Elgar.

Douglas, Mary and Baron Isherwood (1979), *The World of Goods*, New York: Basic Books.

Elster, Jon (1979), *Ulysses and the Sirens*, New York: Cambridge University Press.

Elster, Jon (ed.) (1986), *The Multiple Self*, New York: Cambridge University Press.

Etzioni, Amitai (1988), *The Moral Dimension*, New York: The Free Press.

Farrell, Joseph (1995), 'Talk is cheap', *The American Economic Review*, **85** (2), 186–90.

Fine, Ben (2002), *The World of Consumption*, 2nd edn, New York: Routledge.

Folbre, Nancy (1994), *Who Pays for the Kids?: Gender and the Structures of Constraint*, New York: Routledge.

Frank, Robert H. (1985), *Choosing the Right Pond: Human Behavior and the Quest for Status*, Oxford: Oxford University Press.

Frankfurt, Harry G. (1971), 'Freedom of the will and the concept of a person', *Journal of Philosophy*, **68**, 5–20.

Geertz, Clifford (1983), *Local Knowledge*, New York: Basic Books.

George, David (2001), *Preference Pollution*, Ann Arbor, MI: The University of Michigan Press.

Gudeman, Stephen and Alberto Rivera (1990), *Conversations in Colombia: The Domestic Economy in Life and Text*, New York: Cambridge University Press.

Hargreaves Heap, Shaun (2001), 'Expressive rationality: is self-worth just another kind of preference?', in Uskali Mäki (ed.), *The Economic World View*, Cambridge: Cambridge University Press, pp. 98–113.

Harsanyi, John C. (1955), 'Cardinal welfare, individualistic ethics, and interpersonal comparisons of utility', *Journal of Political Economy*, **63**, 309–21.

Hayek, Friedrich A. (1948), *Individualism and Economic Order*, Chicago, IL: University of Chicago Press.

Hirsch, Fred (1976), *Social Limits to Growth*, Cambridge, MA: Harvard University Press.

Hirschman, Albert O. (1985), 'Against parsimony', *Economics and Philosophy*, **1**, 7–21.

Iannaccone, Laurence R. (1992), 'Sacrifice and stigma: reducing free-riding in cults, communes, and other collectives', *Journal of Political Economy*, **100** (2), 271–92.

Ireland, N.J. (1994), 'On limiting the market for status signals', *Journal of Public Economics*, **53**, 91–110.

Karni, Edi and David Schmeidler (1990), 'Fixed preferences and changing tastes', *American Economic Review*, **80** (2), 262–7.

Kasser, Tim and Allen D. Kanner (eds) (2004), *Psychology and Consumer Culture*, Washington, DC: American Psychological Association.

Khalil, Elias (2004), 'The gift paradox: complex selves and symbolic good', *Review of Social Economy*, **33** (3), 379–92.

Klamer, Arjo (1983), *Conversations with Economists*, Totowa, NJ: Rowman & Allanheld.

Klamer, Arjo, Deirdre N. McCloskey and Robert Solow (eds) (1988), *The Consequences of Economic Rhetoric*, New York: Cambridge University Press.

Kleine, Robert E., Susan Schultz Kleine and Jerome B. Kernan (1993), 'Mundane consumption and the self: a social-identity perspective', *Journal of Consumer Psychology*, **2** (3), 209–35.

Knudsen, Christian (2004), 'Alfred Schutz, Austrian economists and the knowledge problem', *Rationality and Society*, **16** (1), 45–89.

Kuran, Timur (1995), *Private Truths, Public Lies*, Cambridge, MA: Harvard University Press.

Langlois, Richard N. (1986), *Economics as a Process*, New York: Cambridge University Press.

Langlois, Richard N. (1993), 'Orders and organizations: toward an Austrian theory of social institutions', in B. Caldwell and S. Böhm (eds), *Austrian Economics: Tensions and New Directions*, Dordrecht: Kluwer Academic Publishers.

Leibenstein, Harvey (1950), 'Bandwagon, snob, and Veblen effects in the theory of consumers' demand', *Quarterly Journal of Economics*, **64**, 183–207.

Lutz, Mark A. and Kenneth Lux (1988), *Humanistic Economics*, New York: The Bootstrap Press.

Mason, Roger S. (1981), *Conspicuous Consumption: A Study of Exceptional Consumption Behavior*, New York: St Martin's Press.

McCloskey, D.N. (1985), *The Rhetoric of Economics*, Madison, WI: The University of Wisconsin Press.

McCloskey, Deirdre N. (1994), *Knowledge and Persuasion in Economics*, Cambridge: Cambridge University Press.

McCloskey, Deirdre and Arjo Klamer (1995), 'One quarter of GDP is persuasion', *American Economic Review*, **85** (2), 191–5.

McCracken, Grant (1990), *Culture and Consumption*, Bloomington, IN: Indiana University Press.

North, Douglass C. (1990), *Institutions, Institutional Change and Economic Performance*, New York: Cambridge University Press.

Rae, John (1834), *Statement of Some New Principles on the Subject of Political Economy: Exposing the Fallacies of the System of Free Trade, and of Some Other Doctrines Maintained in the 'Wealth of Nations'*, Boston, MA: Hillard, Gray, & Co.

Roth, Timothy (1989), *The Present State of Consumer Theory*, New York: University Press of America.

Schelling, Thomas C. (1984), *Choice and Consequence*, Cambridge, MA: Harvard University Press.

Sen, Amartya (1977), 'Rational fools, a critique of the behavioral foundations of economic theory', *Philosophy and Public Affairs*, **6**, 317–44.

Shiller, Robert J. (1995), 'Conversation, information, and herd behavior', *The American Economic Review*, **85** (2), 181–5.

Smith, Adam (1976), *An Inquiry into the Nature and Causes of the Wealth of Nations*, originally published in 1776, Oxford: Oxford University Press.

Sowell, Thomas (1980), *Knowledge and Decisions*, New York: Basic Books.

Spence, A. Michael (1974), *Market Signaling, Information Transfer in Hiring and Related Processes*, Cambridge, MA: Harvard University Press.

Stigler, George J. and Gary S. Becker (1977), 'De gustibus non est disputandum', *The American Economic Review*, **67**, 76–90.

Sugden, Robert (1989), 'Spontaneous order', *The Journal of Economic Perspectives*, **3** (4), 85–97.

Tajfel, Henri and John C. Turner (1979), 'An integrative theory of intergroup conflict', in W.G. Austin and S. Worchel (eds), *The Social Psychology of Intergroup Relations*, Monterey, CA: Brooks/Cole, pp. 33–47.

Thaler, Richard and H.M. Shefrin (1981), 'An economic theory of self-control', *Journal of Political Economy*, **89**, 392–406.

Veblen, Thorstein (1899), *The Theory of The Leisure Class*, London: Allen & Unwin.

PART III

INDIVIDUALS IN CONTEXT

Chapter 9: 'Capabilities and well-being', by Irene van Staveren

The capability approach (CA) was initiated by Amartya Sen, as a critique of neoclassical economics. Most basically, the CA replaces utility with capabilities as the relevant informational space for analysis, and it substitutes a conception of rationality as utility maximization with the notion that people choose 'what they have reason to value' in order to lead a flourishing life. But the CA is also a response to needs-based theories, which give a central role to goods, rather than to what these can do for people. The CA has formed the basis for the human development paradigm and the annual *Human Development Reports* published by the UN. These reports present rich data on capabilities and functionings that are not expressed in money terms but as years of schooling and life expectancy, for example. The chapter discusses three issues that are central in CA debates: freedom, personhood and well-being.

Chapter 10: 'Culture, values and institutions', by Paul D. Bush

This discussion of culture, values and institutions is based on the analytical structure developed by US institutional economists writing in the theoretical tradition of the original institutional economics (OIE). The concept of culture is a fundamental principle in the OIE analysis of the nature of institutions and the process of institutional change. The incorporation of the concepts of culture, values and institutional change in economic analysis is a diagnostic feature of the OIE that differentiates it from mainstream, neoclassical economics which is bereft of the concept of culture. Among the essential features of the OIE analysis is the proposition that the individual is both conditioned by culture and a creator of culture. This notion is incompatible with the neoclassical formulation of the autonomous individual as an economic agent. The arguments presented in this discussion identify the critical role values play in the structure of institutions and the process of institutional change.

Chapter 11: 'Caste and diversity in India', by Ashwini Deshpande

Despite being nearly 2500 years old, the caste system, with several transformations over the centuries, continues to be one of the most important descriptors of intergroup disparity in India. It also forms one of the planks on which the Indian affirmative action programme is based. Caste hierarchies are not linear and are contested, but the position of the ex-untouchable castes at the bottom of the socio-economic ladder is unambiguous. This is one feature that has withstood all transformations of the caste system. In addition, these castes suffer the stigma of untouchability, which has been legally abolished for over 50 years. Caste and race are often compared for their similarities, but there are important differences between the two concepts and systems, as caste divisions are not based on phenotype. The economic literature on the caste system is limited and focuses, both theoretically and empirically, on identity, discrimination and economic outcomes, and on the degree of continuity and change in the caste system.

Chapter 12: 'Feminism and/in economics', by Edith Kuiper

Feminist historians have indicated six feminist waves throughout Western history, the last four of which developed alongside and together with economic science. This chapter provides a first account of the relation between feminism and economic science over the last three centuries, showing a long tradition of economic discussions on women's wages, employment, production and poverty. It addresses in more detail the recent development of feminist economics, and explores a few fields in economics in which feminist perspectives are expected to have a substantial impact, such as the history of economics, macroeconomics, public administration, finance and business.

9 Capabilities and well-being
Irene van Staveren

Introduction

The capability approach (CA) was initiated and guided by Amartya Sen, since the 1980s, as an alternative to neoclassical welfare economics. The approach emerged gradually out of his rich critique of mainstream economics, in particular his dissatisfaction with conventional notions of rationality (e.g. in 'Rational fools', 1977), efficiency (e.g. in 'The impossibility of a Paretian liberal', 1970), utility (e.g. in *On Ethics and Economics*, 1987), and well-being (e.g. in *Development as Freedom*, 1999). Arising out of this critique, the CA can be characterized as an alternative approach to the analysis of poverty and well-being, one that has tried to find a middle ground between purely subjective theories of well-being on the one hand, such as the preference-based neoclassical paradigm, and, on the other hand, purely objective theories focusing on goods or, a bit less objective, needs. In the CA, it is people's capabilities to function that is the central focus of well-being analysis, in other words, what people are able to be or do, rather than what they have in terms of income or commodities.

This chapter will show that, methodologically, the CA differs from neoclassical economics in some important ways. Most basically, the CA replaces utility with capabilities as the relevant informational space for analysis, and it substitutes a conception of rationality as utility maximization with the notion that people choose 'what they have reason to value' in order to lead a flourishing life. Hence the whole utilitarian basis of neoclassical analysis is replaced, which makes many neoclassical concepts and theorems redundant, from Edgeworth boxes to Pareto efficiency.

Obviously, commodities and incomes do play a role in the CA, but exclusively as means, not as part of the ends. This move away from the neoclassical concern with goods and incomes generated through markets also allows the CA to make space for goods that are not produced or transacted through markets, such as the goods and services produced with unpaid work. Hence goods acquired (through market exchange, own production, transfers or gifts) are the means for the development of capabilities, not the end, nor a proxy for measuring well-being. But the transformation of goods into capabilities does not occur in a social vacuum. Sen acknowledges how personal and social differences between agents may affect the transformation of commodities into capabilities. Here, his concern with inequality comes into the analysis of capabilities. He maintains that it is capabilities that should be made equal through policies addressing poverty and well-being, not marginal utilities as in welfare economics, or primary goods as in Rawls's (1971) *Theory of Justice* (Sen, 1987). His argument against Rawls's view is that an equal distribution of primary goods for people with different personal circumstances, for example in the case of a blind man or a breastfeeding mother, will result in different capabilities and, hence, inequalities in functionings.[1] He sought to compensate for such differences by focusing on capabilities instead, recognizing that people in disadvantaged situations would require more and/or different resources in order to attain the same level of capabilities as people situated in more fortunate circumstances. Comparable to Rawls, however, Sen favors the equalization of *basic* capabilities, not necessarily all capabilities. Finally, Sen recognizes that there may be biases in the transition from capabilities – what one is able to be or do – to functionings – one's actual beings and doings.

The CA, hence, can be situated somewhere in between neoclassical economics with its concern with subjective well-being, and Rawls's theory of justice and its concern with the achievement of primary goods for everyone. It develops such an intermediate theoretical position, however, not independent from heterodox economic traditions. In particular, we recognize a role for institutions, for example in a country's system of entitlements to food, and there is attention to social relations and values in the CA, for example in the analysis of how groups in society perceive their own functionings in relation to those of others.

Philosophers have been attracted to the CA partly because of the ethics that is clearly part of it. Sen rejects the positivist fact/value dichotomy that still finds so much support among economists, and argues that as soon as we want to understand, and do something about poverty, we can no longer take a neutral position (Walsh, 2003). Moreover, he denies that such a position is feasible at all, arguing that we, as scientists, always have a positional objectivity, never a view from nowhere (Sen, 1993). However, the ethics of the CA is not very clear-cut, as it does not fit squarely in either of the two major ethical alternatives to the consequentialist theory of utilitarianism, that is, Kantian deontology or Aristotelian virtue ethics. Rather, it incorporates elements of all three ethical theories, including consequentialism, although not of the utilitarian kind (Jackson, 2005). The CA therefore is sometimes referred to as a 'thick vague theory' of the good, clearly involving ethical evaluations but not including explicit normative guidelines that would hold independent of specific social contexts. Sen's concern with equality and human dignity clearly has Kantian roots (Pauer-Studer, 2006), while his concern with human flourishing and attention to individual context evidently derives from Aristotle (van Staveren, 2001). It is in particular the Aristotelian dimension of the CA that has brought it to the attention of the philosopher Martha Nussbaum. She has made some significant contributions to the approach, some together with Sen, and others alone, diverting from the path he has carved out starting from economics. The major differences between Nussbaum's CA and Sen's CA are threefold (Nussbaum, 2000, 2003; Nussbaum and Glover, 1995).

First, Nussbaum consistently speaks of capabilities, in the plural, emphasizing the incommensurability between different capabilities, as well as their interconnectedness. Sen does not at all disagree with the plurality of capabilities, but he does not want to go down the path of identifying a complete and universal list of capabilities, and therefore prefers to speak of capability, singular, while acknowledging that this may contain several capabilities as subsets, with different sets for different times and places. Nussbaum clearly acknowledges the contextuality of capabilities, but nevertheless formulates a tentative list of ten general capabilities. 'I consider the list as open-ended and subject to ongoing revision and rethinking . . . [and] that the items on the list ought to be specified in a somewhat abstract and general way, precisely in order to leave room for the activities specifying and deliberating by citizens and their legislatures and courts that all democratic nations contain' (Nussbaum, 2003, p. 42). Her list contains the following capabilities: (1) life, (2) bodily health, (3) bodily integrity, (4) senses, imagination and thought, (5) emotions, (6) practical reason (perception of the good and critical reflection about the planning of one's life), (7) affiliation (to others and from others to oneself), (8) other species, (9) play, and (10) control over one's environment (political and material). Sen, however, never wants to make a list, fearing that it may be used as a once-and-for-all policy tool. In a response to those who favor Nussbaum's approach, he states: 'I have nothing against the listing of capabilities but must stand up against a grand mausoleum to one fixed and final list of capabilities' (Sen, 2004, p. 80).

Second, Nussbaum recognizes that for the realization of equal capabilities for everyone, some rule is necessary about priorities. She finds such a rule in Rawls's maximin criterion of fairness. This criterion states that inequality can only be allowed when the activities driving the inequality benefit the most disadvantaged.[2] Applying this idea to the CA, Nussbaum proposes a minimum threshold for each capability, that should be derived from countries' constitutions. Policies for furthering capabilities should therefore prioritize to get everyone across the threshold level for each capability, before spending resources on further increases of capabilities. This is an important difference with Sen, as he leaves his CA more open to prioritizations through public debate, allowing for outcomes that do not support norms such as Rawls's maximin rule. In other words, Sen chooses not to set thresholds because he wants to leave that normative decision to political communities themselves.

Third, Nussbaum's CA is less liberalist, in the sense of heralding freedom, and more universalist than Sen's. Nussbaum recognizes the fallacies of an exclusive focus on the value of freedom, remarking that more freedom to increase their capabilities for some may reduce the freedom of others to enlarge their capabilities. Instead, she favors the Aristotelian idea of balancing values, such as freedom and justice. By staying closer to a more balanced concept of human flourishing, she is critical of Sen's conflation of capability with freedom, arguing that some capabilities are located in a different space, for example that of affiliation or the natural environment. 'In other words, all societies that pursue a reasonably just political conception have to evaluate human freedoms, saying that some are central and some trivial, some good and some actively bad' (Nussbaum, 2003, p. 45).

Nussbaum's approach has met, like Sen's, both with support and criticism. In particular, some feminist economists have found her CA helpful in analyzing and evaluating differences in the well-being of women and men (see, for example, a special issue of *Feminist Economics* that has been dedicated to Sen's work, while featuring Nussbaum's contributions to the CA quite favorably; Agarwal et al., 2003). At the same time, Nussbaum's approach has received criticisms, also from feminists. A major critique concerns her capabilities list, which is found to be too universalist. In a rich empirical study of capabilities of women in the UK, wherein Ingrid Robeyns (2003) has followed Sen's approach of finding out people's valued capabilities through discussions, Nussbaum's list was only partially confirmed. Whereas Nussbaum had developed her list on the basis of literary accounts of well-being (in particular from Greek tragedies, but also from Charles Dickens's novel *Hard Times*, for example), and drawing on interviews with poor women in India, Robeyns used UK household survey data and discussions with UK women on the capabilities that appeared to be important to them. Although the differences are not very large, there are a few significant differences between Nussbaum's list and Robeyns's findings, in particular relating to the value of time and the issue of child care.

Another critique of Nussbaum's CA concerns her Rawlsian threshold for capabilities. The threshold may imply, when followed strictly, that investment in human and physical resources for long-run economic development should be replaced by short-run focused capabilities investments that will lift everyone up above a certain threshold, even when constraining long-run development. For example, in the case of education in a least developed country, strict application of the threshold to the distribution of public resources to education may imply that there should be no expansion in secondary and tertiary schooling unless all boys and girls go to primary school. But wouldn't this deprive some bright boys and girls who cannot afford private education of the opportunity to further learning and contributing to the country's development as doctors, lawyers, or IT specialists? In other words, a threshold makes much sense from a fairness perspective, but from a more general well-being perspective, which addresses not only opportunities but also outcomes, the difficult question is where the threshold should be placed.

Besides Sen and Nussbaum, others have contributed to the development of the CA, in particular since the 1990s, when the approach gained more influence in policy debates. From the early 1990s onwards, the CA has informed the policy approach of human development, in which human development is regarded not only as the means but also the end of development. This policy application of the CA has found its way to the UNDP's annual *Human Development Reports*. In the reports, the CA has been concretized in the Human Development Index (HDI) as an alternative measure of human well-being to GDP.[3] The *Human Development Reports* have had important impacts on policy-makers, as they have made clear that income alone is an insufficient measure of well-being, and economic growth does not guarantee the improvement of human development for everyone. The commitments that the four major international development organizations (United Nations, World Bank, IMF and OECD) made in the year 2000 about poverty reduction for the year 2015 through the Millennium Development Goals (e.g. reducing poverty by 50 percent and universal primary and secondary education for boys and girls) reflect this influence of the human development paradigm on policy-makers.

The CA developed by Sen, Nussbaum and others is a valuable theoretical advance for the analysis of well-being, as well as a significant innovation for policy advice on poverty reduction. Sen's consistent critiques of the mainstream have shaken up at least some corners of the discipline, especially since he received the Nobel Prize in 1998. This clarity also characterizes his CA even though there remain substantial deliberate open ends, leading to major debates.

Freedom, personhood and well-being: three contested issues

Within the CA, there are some important debates, of which I will briefly discuss three: the debate whether capability should be regarded as freedom or more; the debate about the picture of personhood underlying the CA; and the debate about where the CA is located or should be located on a subjective–objective well-being continuum. Many debates have been informed by a gender perspective: Sen has always been open to the workings of gender, in both his theoretical and his empirical work (Sen, 1990, 1992, 1995). He has been part of the emergence of feminist economics from the beginning, and his work has been received well, although not uncritically, by feminists analyzing the gender dimensions of well-being (see, for example, the special issue of the journal *Feminist Economics* dedicated to Sen's work[4]). My discussion of the three issues below will be informed partially by work done from a gender perspective.

Capability as freedom
Since his 1999 book *Development as Freedom*, Sen has erased the distinction between capability and freedom: he has now chosen to conceptualize capability *as* freedom: the freedom to be or do what one has reason to value. His arguments are quite strong, referring both to freedom as a value in its own right and to freedom as instrumental for well-being, but also pointing to freedom as the route to debate and agree on values. In particular, Sen points out that democracy and free public discussion help to increase the public awareness of capability failures for groups of people, while freedom also allows an exchange of ideas and open public decision-making about a society's priorities. The intrinsic value of freedom is for Sen the freedom of opportunity, which provides individuals with choices, requiring a range of opportunities that includes a 'best' one, as he has clarified in his latest book, *Rationality and Freedom* (Sen, 2002, p. 509). The instrumental value of freedom is also referred to as the process view of freedom and provides scope for autonomy and immunity from interferences by others, but does not necessarily provide sufficient and relevant opportunities.

But are all capabilities about freedom? Doesn't the conflation of these two thick concepts represent a limitation of the CA instead of an elaboration? Several authors have doubts about this and question the tight connection of capability with freedom (Giri, 2002; van Staveren, 2001; Gasper, 2002; Deneulin, 2002; Gasper and van Staveren, 2003; Nussbaum, 2003; Nelson, 2004). Des Gasper has noted that it may become operationalized as a view of well-being that is simply favoring more choice. The risk of this simplification is that 'it never considers when choice can become oppressive', Gasper (2000, p. 999) remarks. In particular, the reduction of capabilities to opportunities ignores the bads of opulence, overwork or addiction to television or pornography. These freedoms to eat, work and watch to ever greater extents may reduce well-being for others whose access to resources may be constrained, or may affect others' well-being through externalities arising from overconsumption of such goods, for example rising healthcare costs. But such freedoms may also negatively affect the well-being of the overconsumers themselves, whose functioning may suffer from obesity, stress, addiction, and subsequent negative health effects (Gasper, 2002; Deneulin, 2002). This recognition, of course, brings in questions about weakness of will, paternalism and informed choice, which the CA addresses in the space it allows for public discussion on capabilities.

A different argument against reducing capabilities to freedom alone has been given by Gasper and van Staveren (2003). They remark that in a conflation of capability with freedom, 'there is no longer a highlighted distinction between the value of autonomous agency and all the opportunities to achieve other values that may be provided through such agency' (ibid., p. 144). In other words, while more freedom can be interpreted as having more options to choose from, without being constrained in one's choosing, this may not necessarily lead to more freedom as an outcome of one's choices, because some capabilities may entail other values than freedom. Such other values may, instead, refer to friendship, democracy, or respect. But also a whole value domain of women's economic activities remains out of sight by an exclusive focus on freedom: the values of caring, which tend to be both fulfilling for care givers and to care receivers. At the same time, caring is often a burden to care givers, limiting their freedoms, even when they choose to care. Should this be a reason to evaluate caring negatively, and favor freedom always over caring? Moreover, do we want to live in a world without caring, or would it even be possible to have human development in a world where caring is stripped to a bare minimum so as to prevent possible limitations on people's freedoms? This example suggests that capabilities may include freedom, but should not be reduced to it. Julie Nelson (2004) similarly criticizes Sen's exclusive focus on freedom as well as his degree of emphasis on pure reason. She argues that this focus ignores other dimensions of human well-being such as the human need for affiliation, a sense of belonging, capacity for emotion, the experience of feelings. Like Nussbaum (2001), Nelson argues that emotions have a cognitive dimension, they inform and motivate people, which is different from but complementary to the cognitive processes of pure reason.

Marc Fleurbaey (2002) therefore wonders why Sen ties freedom so closely to capabilities and not to functionings instead. He argues that functionings may include freedom as autonomy and the exercise of choice, which goes beyond a focus on mere access to functionings. In such a more detailed understanding of functionings, those poor who fail to seize the opportunities offered through capabilities will not be abandoned, Fleurbaey states. Therefore, he argues that 'it seems an unnecessary, and indeed dangerous, move to shift the ethical perspective altogether from a theory of achievement to a theory of opportunities' (Fleurbaey, 2002, p. 74). Séverine Deneulin (2002, p. 516) takes this point up in relation to the issue of paternalism, suggesting that policies that restrict people's freedom to live in unhealthy or otherwise undesirable ways represent a kind of paternalism that we should not fear, 'since that type of paternalism is nothing more than the refusal to see another person suffering from not being able to live a human life'.

It seems that Sen has put himself in a somewhat difficult position by trying, at the same time, to keep the doors wide open to economists and policy-makers (to whom his book *Development as Freedom* was largely addressed, arising out of a series of lectures for the World Bank) while also trying to do justice to the complex meanings of the value of freedom.

Personhood and capabilities

Whereas Sen acknowledges the role of certain psychological processes in the CA, such as adaptive preferences, his examples of capabilities mostly refer to physical situations of impaired capabilities, such as in the cases of hunger and illiteracy. Gasper (2000) rightly notes that personal but learned skills of reasoning and acting are thereby largely ignored, while Livet (2006) points at the process of path-dependency in which earlier acquired capabilities affect the range of later acquired capabilities and functionings. Sen does distinguish between the freedom of agents to choose (agency freedom) and the freedom to improve one's own well-being (well-being freedom). This distinction is not made in neoclassical economics where agents are assumed to act in their self-interest. Instead, Sen's split between agency freedom and well-being freedom allows for other-directed choices, that would support the well-being of others rather than that of the agent herself. But this distinction, although important, does not yet provide a rich picture of agency and the plurality of capabilities. If agents occasionally act to help others, under what circumstances, for what purposes, and driven by which motivations? This remains underdeveloped: Sen's picture of an agent appears to lack the moral capabilities that would be required for the development of plural capabilities of oneself and others (van Staveren, 2001).

Giri (2002) highlights that Sen's emphasis on freedom requires attention to the responsibility of a person, an insight that Sen has recognized but not incorporated in his CA. How can agents develop a plurality of capabilities and pursue their own and others' well-being without feeling, in some way, responsible for this? Moreover, Giri regrets that Sen remains with a rather dualistic view of human motivation, posing self-interest against altruism. Adam Smith, Giri says, was already dissatisfied with such dichotomous thinking about human agency, in his elaboration of the idea of the impartial spectator, and he suggests that the way out of the dichotomy lies in self-development. In order to address the rather thin view of personhood in Sen's CA, Benedetta Giovanola (2005) has pointed in the direction of anthropological richness as the starting point for developing a notion of personhood in the CA. This would allow a better balance between the subjective and objective extremes in which the CA is situated: 'human essence is something potential [to be realized], and can only be fulfilled in particular ways that vary from person to person. Therefore, anthropological richness is at the same time universal and particular, since every human being expresses – or at least should express – it through his or her particularity' (Giovanola, 2005, p. 262). In a feminist analysis of agency and interdependence, Fabienne Peter (2003) has directed attention to the need for such richness in order to develop an understanding of situated agency, not only in anthropological terms but also in moral terms. She agrees with Sen that in a context of strong gender inequality, women's agency may be severely restricted. 'But', she argues, 'limited effective agency does not imply impaired moral autonomy, absence of agency-capability, and thus absence of judgment' (Peter, 2003, p. 27).

Davis (2002) identifies part of the thinness of Sen's view of personhood in a lack of space for personal change in a person's capabilities, and shows how this may be addressed by looking at the social embeddedness of persons. In his book on the individual in economics, Davis (2003) pleads for an understanding of an agent as socially embedded and reflexive, two features that turn an agent into a person, going beyond the standard picture of an agent, characterized as merely a chooser.

In Sen's earlier work, there is quite a bit of attention to personhood, and he has made elaborate efforts to go beyond a simplistic image of agency, using concepts such as sympathy and commitment. But somehow these concepts have not been sufficiently taken on in the notion of personhood in the CA.

Subjective versus objective well-being

The CA is meant to represent an advance beyond, on the one hand, the subjective well-being measure of utility, and, on the other hand, the objective well-being measure of commodities. In the debates on this issue, two questions have emerged. First: does the CA represent an acceptable mean between these two extremes, or is it biased to one side? Second: how should the CA be related to a new variant of subjective well-being measures, namely happiness studies which rely on relative interpersonal comparisons of self-reported well-being? In the literature, these two questions tend to be discussed together, so I shall not try to separate them here as that would be rather artificial. I shall refer in particular to a recent volume of the *Review of Social Economy* (vol. 58, no. 2, 2005) dedicated to a discussion between the capability approach and happiness studies.

A starting point in the discussion on subjective and objective well-being is an enquiry about well-being. As Gasper (2005) has shown, there are quite a few nuances and overlaps between concepts of well-being. Moreover, one needs to recognize that agents may pursue their own well-being but may also choose to further the well-being of someone else – however defined. Happiness, as a subjective measure of well-being, does not easily connect to capability, which has a more objective status. Gasper warns that a connection may easily slide into the conventional hedonistic view of well-being of mainstream economics, and therefore calls for more attention in CA to objective measures of well-being. Taking this point further, Miriam Teschl and Flavio Comim (2005) refer to Kahneman's work in economic psychology on a more objective approach to happiness, which is a mix of hedonic and affective experiences reported by individuals for a 'representative moment', hence in real time rather than in the abstract, as is the case in many happiness surveys. But this solution may still suffer from the individualist focus of well-being in the CA. This tension points to the need to distinguish between types of capabilities: skills, attitudes and dispositions, next to opportunities (Gasper and van Staveren, 2003). Whereas opportunity capabilities are more subjective, reflecting 'what people have reason to value', the skill-type capabilities seem to be of a more objective, or at least a more structured and reflective, kind referring to concrete skills, attitudes and dispositions. Examples of capabilities as skills, attitudes and dispositions are: being able to appear in public without shame, to do a task demanding physical effort, or to make up one's personal human resources development plan. Whereas the opportunity capabilities are more individualistic, the others may be regarded as more social or structural, to use Jackson's (2005) words. Nussbaum's list contains a mix of the two types of capabilities – as opportunities and as skills/attitudes/dispositions – which may provide a good starting point for further balancing the CA between subjective and objective measures of well-being.

The next section will discuss briefly what might be expected from empirical applications (e.g. Robeyns, 2002; Alkire, 2002; Kuklys, 2005), in particular in relation to social economics.

Capabilities and well-being from a social economic perspective

Sen has made a great effort, throughout his career, to remain connected to the mainstream, to debate with welfare economics and engage in policy discussions on a variety of development issues, ranging from acceptable inflation rates to impacts of globalization. Because of his continuous engagement, several authors have concluded that Sen is more a reformist than a radical, more concerned with keeping the mainstream on board than with developing a more independent alternative to welfare economics. Peter Evans (2002), for example, argues that Sen has not taken his approach far enough to be able to function as an alternative to mainstream economics.

John Cameron (2000, p. 1043), like Evans, has praised Sen's continuous debate with the mainstream, but he also assesses that 'the analysis of capabilities, functionings and wellbeing as a foundation for a comprehensive re-thinking of inequality and development appears to have stalled by its failure to transcend the epistemological constraints of mainstream economics'. Indeed, many of the critiques discussed above seem to be rooted in the recognition of inconsistencies between the ambition of the CA, on the one hand, and its remaining ties with neoclassical economics, on the other.

It may therefore well be that connections between the CA and heterodox traditions could turn out more fruitful for the development of the CA, helping it to move further away from mainstream habits while supporting it with an already developed, though admittedly fallible, alternative methodology. For socio-economics, the methodological resources offered would be, among others, a socially structured view of behavior, an explicit concern with morality, and a critical stance on an exclusively liberalist political philosophy. At the same time, the CA presents to social economists an approach that focuses on capabilities and functionings, as concepts that may well fit a concern with social structure. Let me, very briefly, try to indicate how the CA and social economics may benefit from a stronger mutual engagement. I shall make use of work that has already been undertaken at the crossroads of these two traditions, in particular on households and gender, on the one hand, and on labor markets on the other hand.

Elizabeth Oughton and Jane Wheelock (2003) have applied the CA to their study of livelihoods of households with micro businesses. Their study has shown that what matters for the well-being of small-scale entrepreneurs is a variety of capabilities that can be used both in household tasks and for business purposes. They also show that there exists a set of gendered constraints on acquiring sufficient capabilities, and on the conversion of capabilities to adequate functionings for each member of the household. Their application of the CA illustrates that capabilities go beyond freedoms, but also involve affiliations, and that functionings need to be understood in terms of functionings of *what* and for *whom*. John Davis (2002) has elaborated the gender dimensions of the constraints on women's capabilities in and outside households, drawing on the work by feminist economist Nancy Folbre. He has elaborated the CA in order to allow for capability development over time, in relation to a concept of personhood that understands individuals as members of groups. On labor markets, the CA has been employed in order to further specify labor capabilities, in terms of skills, rather than opportunities. In such applications, the CA offers a wider understanding of skills than as human capital, or as specific job-related skills. For example, David Levine (2004) has redefined poverty as the absence of freedom to do skilled labor, pointing to problems of unemployment and exclusion. Rather than seeing capabilities only as opportunities, as in Sen's approach, he understands labor capabilities as labor-market-related skills that should not go to waste. Similarly, Jean-Michel Bonvin and Nicolas Farvaque (2005) have characterized job seekers in terms of their capabilities rather than in terms of preferences for income and leisure, providing a deeper understanding of the workings and wrongs of labor markets in relation to job seekers' skills. Finally, in a conceptual paper, tentatively linking capabilities to culture and social structure, William Jackson (2005) has further distinguished capabilities. He has suggested differentiating individual from social and structural capabilities, in order to move away from a too individualist focus of capabilities, and to better acknowledge the role of social structures and institutions.

In conclusion, there appears to be an exciting road ahead for the further development of a social economic capability approach – but a road not without pitfalls. There are some side-paths that may rather lead one into the bush – or back to the highway of mainstream economics. So the traveler may be advised to watch out for particularly two suspicious turns: first, the one that conflates capabilities with freedom, reducing the approach to opportunities; and second, a too individualistic understanding of capabilities that ignores various biases that prevent capabilities from being transformed into functionings.

Notes

1. So, with an equal amount of food for a breastfeeding mother and a woman who is not breastfeeding, the breastfeeding mother's functionings are likely to be less, because the nutritional value of the food intake is used partially for the production of milk.
2. For example, when medical doctors are paid higher salaries than nurses but they contribute more importantly to the curing of a substantial number of the most disadvantaged patients, such income inequality would be justified, in Rawls's view.
3. The HDI is a composite index, consisting of measures of inequality in income, education (school enrolment and literacy) and health (life expectancy). The measure has been critiqued, refined and expanded, so that today it is accompanied, for example, by a Gender Development Index (GDI), giving lower HDI rankings to countries that exhibit larger gender inequalities.
4. *Feminist Economics,* **9** (2–3); see also Agarwal et al. (2006).

References

Agarwal, Bina, Jane Humphries and Ingrid Robeyns (eds) (2003), Special Issue on Amartya Sen's Work and Ideas: A Gender Perspective, *Feminist Economics,* **9** (2/3).
Agarwal, Bina, Jane Humphries and Ingrid Robeyns (eds) (2006), *Capabilities, Freedom, and Equality: Amartya Sen's Work from a Gender Perspective,* Delhi: Oxford University Press.
Alkire, Sabina (2002), *Valuing Freedoms: Sen's Capability Approach and Poverty Reduction,* Oxford: Oxford University Press.
Bonvin, Jean-Michel and Nicolas Farvaque (2005), 'What informational basis for assessing job-seekers? capabilities vs preferences', *Review of Social Economy,* **63** (2), 269–89.

Cameron, John (2000), 'Amartya Sen on economic inequality: the need for an explicit critique of opulence', *Journal of International Development*, **12**, 1031–45.

Davis, John (2002), 'Capabilities and personal identity: using Sen to explain personal identity in Folbre's "structures of constraint" analysis', *Review of Political Economy*, **14** (1), 481–96.

Davis, John (2003), *The Theory of the Individual in Economics*, London: Routledge.

Deneulin, Séverine (2002), 'Perfectionism, paternalism and liberalism in Sen and Nussbaum's capability approach', *Review of Political Economy*, **14** (4), 497–518.

Evans, Peter (2002), 'Collective capabilities, culture, and Amartya Sen's *Development as Freedom*', *Studies in Comparative International Development*, **37** (2), 54–60.

Fleurbaey, Marc (2002), 'Development, capabilities, and freedom', *Studies in Comparative International Development*, **37** (2), 71–7.

Gasper, Des (2000), 'Development as freedom: taking economics beyond commodities – the cautious boldness of Amartya Sen', *Journal of International Development*, **12**, 989–1001.

Gasper, Des (2002), 'Is Sen's capability approach an adequate basis for considering human development?', *Review of Political Economy*, **14** (4), 435–61.

Gasper, Des (2005), 'Subjective and objective wellbeing in relation to economic inputs: puzzles and responses', *Review of Social Economy*, **63** (2), 177–206.

Gasper, Des and Irene van Staveren (2003), 'Development as freedom – and as what else?', *Feminist Economics*, **9** (1), 137–62.

Giovanola, Benedetta (2005), 'Personhood and human richness: good and wellbeing in the capability approach and beyond', *Review of Social Economy*, **63** (2), 249–67.

Giri, Ananta (2002), 'Rethinking human wellbeing: a dialogue with Amartya Sen', *Journal of International Development*, **12** (7), 1003–18.

Jackson, William (2005), 'Capabilities, culture, and social structure', *Review of Social Economy*, **63** (1), 101–24.

Kuklys, Wiebke (2005), *Amartya Sen's Capability Approach: Theoretical Insights and Empirical Applications*, Berlin: Springer.

Levine, David (2004), 'Poverty, capabilities and freedom', *Review of Political Economy*, **16** (1), 101–15.

Livet, Pierre (2006), 'Identities, capabilities, and revisions', *Journal of Economic Methodology*, **13** (3), 327–48.

Nelson, Julie (2004), 'Freedom, reason, and more: feminist economics and human development', *Journal of Human Development*, **5** (3), 309–33.

Nussbaum, Martha (2000), *Women and Human Development: The Capabilities Approach*, Cambridge: Cambridge University Press.

Nussbaum, Martha (2001), *Upheavals of Thought: The Intelligence of Emotions*, Cambridge: Cambridge University Press.

Nussbaum, Martha (2003), 'Capabilities as fundamental entitlements: Sen and social justice', *Feminist Economics*, **9** (2/3), 33–59.

Nussbaum, Martha and Jonathan Glover (eds) (1995), *Women, Culture and Development: A Study of Human Capabilities*, Oxford: Clarendon Press.

Oughton, Elizabeth and Jane Wheelock (2003), 'A capabilities approach to sustainable household livelihoods', *Review of Social Economy*, **61** (1), 1–22.

Pauer-Studer, Herlinde (2006), 'Identity, commitment and morality', *Journal of Economic Methodology*, **13** (3), 349–69.

Peter, Fabienne (2003), 'Gender and the foundations of social choice: the role of situated agency', *Feminist Economics*, **9** (2/3), 13–32.

Rawls, John (1971), *A Theory of Justice*, Cambridge, MA: Harvard University Press.

Robeyns, Ingrid (2002), *Gender Inequality: A Capability Perspective*, Cambridge: PhD dissertation.

Robeyns, Ingrid (2003), 'Sen's capability approach and gender inequality: selecting relevant capabilities', *Feminist Economics*, **9** (2/3), 61–92.

Sen, Amartya (1970), 'The impossibility of a Paretian liberal', *Journal of Political Economy*, **78**, 152–7.

Sen, Amartya (1977), 'Rational fools', *Philosophy and Public Affairs*, **6**, 317–44.

Sen, Amartya (1987), *On Ethics and Economics*, Oxford: Basil Blackwell.

Sen, Amartya (1990), 'Gender and cooperative conflicts', in Irene Tinker (ed.), *Persistent Inequalities*, Oxford: Oxford University Press, pp. 123–49.

Sen, Amartya (1992), 'Missing women', *British Medical Journal*, **304**, 586–7.

Sen, Amartya (1993), 'Positional objectivity', *Philosophy and Public Affairs*, **22** (2), 126–45.

Sen, Amartya (1995), 'Gender inequality and theories of justice', in Martha Nussbaum and Jonathan Glover (eds), *Women, Culture and Development*, Oxford: Clarendon Press, pp. 259–73.

Sen, Amartya (1999), *Development as Freedom*, New York: Oxford University Press.

Sen, Amartya (2002), *Rationality and Freedom*, Cambridge, MA: Belknap/Harvard University Press.

Sen, Amartya (2004), 'Capabilities, lists, and public reason: continuing the conversation', *Feminist Economics*, **10** (3), 77–80.

Staveren, Irene van (2001), *The Values of Economics: An Aristotelian Perspective*, London: Routledge.

Teschl, Miriam and Flavio Comim (2005), 'Adaptive preferences and capabilities: some preliminary conceptual explorations', *Review of Social Economy*, **63** (2), 229–47.

Walsh, Vivian (2003), 'Sen after Putnam', *Review of Political Economy*, **15**, 315–94.

10 Culture, values and institutions
Paul D. Bush

Introduction

The concept of culture is an idea that receives a variety of formulations across the broad reach of the humanities, fine arts and social sciences, defying all claims of exclusive use by any particular academic specialization. In the social sciences, cultural anthropology is perhaps the first discipline to embrace it as a fundamental principle of organized research. It has substantially influenced the other social sciences, providing both theoretical and empirical insights into the nature of culture. The first coherent treatment of the role of culture in economic affairs was presented by Thorstein B. Veblen in his classic study, *The Theory of the Leisure Class* (1899). Following Veblen and the evidence supplied by cultural anthropology, American institutional economists have incorporated the concept of culture both in their critique of mainstream (neoclassical) economics and in their formulation of institutional economic analysis. The culture concept is *the* diagnostic feature of institutional economics which sets it apart from the economic orthodoxy found in the mainstream economic literature (Junker, 1968, p. 201; Hamilton, 1970, pp. 71–2; Mayhew, 1994, p. 116; Hodgson, 2000, p. 327). It is for this reason that the present discussion of culture, values and institutions is couched in terms of the methodological and substantive arguments developed by economists writing in the tradition of American institutional economics, which will be referred to here as the 'original institutional economics' (OIE).[1]

The juxtaposition of the terms 'culture', 'values' and 'institutions' in the title of this chapter reflects the theoretical structure of the institutionalist treatment of the institutional structure of society and changes within it. The evolutionary analysis of institutional economics focuses on the process of institutional change, which is, at bottom, a change in the society's value structure. Since the value structure of society is a major component of a society's culture, institutional change necessarily entails cultural change. It is the purpose of this chapter to sketch some of the major features of this argument.

Culture

The culture concept
Culture is composed of the total social and physical environment of the individual. The social environment includes the language, values, religious beliefs, myths and rituals, and the arts and sciences that *condition* the individual's habits of thought and behavior, as he/she relates to others within his/her community and with the physical environment within which the community exists. The physical environment of the community is composed of the ecological processes of topography, climate, flora and fauna; that is, it is composed of any aspect of the geologic and biologic dimensions of human existence, whether or not they are fully apprehended by the community.

A critical feature of the concept of culture is the idea that human beings learn their culture from their elders and pass it on to the next generation (Linton, 1955, p. 3; Ayres, 1961, pp. 74–6). Human behavior is, therefore, learned behavior; it is not innate or impervious to change. The immediate implication of this line of reasoning for economics has been noted by Anne Mayhew. Citing a variety of terms institutionalists have used to convey the concept of culture, she writes: 'Whatever the phrase, the common idea has been that what economists describe are regularities of behavior and that those regularities are specific to time and place and persist because of enculturation rather than because of some innate and constant human characteristics' (Mayhew, 1987, p. 588). The notion that 'regularities of behavior' are 'specific to time and place' identifies the institutionalist belief that economic theories must incorporate the historical and cultural dimensions of economic behavior as endogenous variables. The notion that regularities in economic affairs manifest learned behavior, rather than inherent characteristics of human nature, sets institutional economics on an intellectual journey quite different from that of economic orthodoxy.

Mainstream economics is bereft of the culture concept
Mainstream economic theories present the behavior of the economic agent as independent of his/her cultural setting. According to mainstream economists, the extent to which culture may play a role in the formation of preferences need not concern the economist. They argue that it is, at best, exogenous to their models of economic behavior, and, in itself, it is not subject to 'scientific' inquiry. Thus the presumed human inclination to 'prefer more to less', which is a basic axiom of the modern mainstream theory of consumer choice, does not take into account the role that enculturation plays in the determination of consumer behavior; 'preferring more to less' may be a form of learned behavior found in some cultures, but not

in others. The culture concept rejects the view of the isolated individual whose behavior is driven by a set of unique preferences that are independent of the preferences of others.[2] As Veblen (1919, p. 324) notes, such an isolated individual is a cultural impossibility.

While few mainstream economists would contend that human beings can exist in social isolation, their conception of human interaction is entombed within the a-cultural, a-historical pecuniary logic of the theoretical marketplace. In consequence, 'society' itself amounts to little more than the algebraic summation of individual behaviors. As will be argued below, the culture concept entails a dynamic interaction between society and the individual that is beyond the intellectual reach of the notion of society as an algebraic summation of individual behaviors.

The individual as an agent of cultural change

The anthropological evidence suggests that 'all cultures, even the simplest, seem to be in a continuous state of change' (Linton, 1955, p. 41). But if it is true that individual habits of thought and behavior are culturally determined and passed down from generation to generation, how does culture change? The answer institutionalists give to this question constitutes perhaps their most important contribution to economic analysis in particular and social inquiry in general.

The institutionalist answer lies in the formulation of the relationship that exists between the culture and the individual. Marc Tool states the relationship succinctly: 'As a social organism, a person is both a conditioner of culture and is conditioned by the culture, inescapably so' (Tool, 1979, p. 52).[3] He elaborates on this theme as follows:

A person becomes 'socialized' – in the anthropological sense – as he or she is indoctrinated into the mores and folkways of the group. But these same habits of mind and habits of action do, on occasion, come under examination. They are, after all, the fruits of initiative behavior in an earlier day. Hence, as every individual finds himself or herself conforming to the settled conventions of the society, he or she nevertheless is potentially a nonconformist whenever he or she seeks to review and revise any of the cultural 'givens.' An individual participating as a member of a community is obviously a culture-building animal. Within culturally defined limits – and the limits themselves are subject to progressive redetermination – an individual is a free agent; that is, he or she has *discretion*. (Ibid., italics in the original)[4]

Although enculturation results in the individual's internalization and habituation of cultural values, institutionalists from Veblen to Tool have held the view that habits can be broken and that the traditional way of doing things can, and does, come under the critical scrutiny of human beings exercising their capacity for critical thinking.

Both Thorstein Veblen and John Dewey commented on the consequences faced by the individual who, in Veblen's words, seeks 'release from
the dead hand of conventional finality' by attempting to initiate social
innovations in thought and behavior. Veblen notes that if the individual is
'an effectual factor in the increase and diffusion of knowledge . . . [he]
becomes a disturber of the intellectual peace' (Veblen, 1934, p. 227). He is,
Veblen says, 'an intellectual wayfaring man, a wanderer in the intellectual
no-man's-land'. Such individuals are 'aliens of the uneasy feet . . .' (ibid.).
Dewey, whose philosophy informs so much of contemporary American
institutionalist methodology, sets forth an argument that is almost identical to Veblen's. 'Every *new* idea,' he says, 'every conception of things
differing from that authorized by current belief, must have its origin in an
individual' (Dewey, 1916, p. 346, italics in the original). 'But a society governed by custom' does not encourage the development of new ideas; on the
contrary, it attempts to suppress them, 'just because they are deviations
from what is current' (ibid.). Dewey concludes by noting that '[t]he man
who looks at things differently form others in such a community is a suspect
character . . .' (ibid.).

Thus Veblen's 'alien of the uneasy feet', who becomes 'a suspect character' in Dewey's comment, is subject to social sanctions for disturbing 'the
intellectual peace' of the community. It is clear from these passages that
both Veblen and Dewey viewed the exercise of creative intelligence in the
problem-solving processes of the community to be a complex undertaking
at best, with the individual as an agent of cultural change becoming
embroiled immediately in social processes that entail conflict and resistance. The history of ideas certainly confirms these observations. As will be
seen below, they are also highly pertinent to the concept called 'ceremonial
encapsulation'.

Values

The value system of culture
Perhaps the most critical element of any culture is its value system which,
among other things, prescribes the following: the range of acceptable
behavior (i.e. *mores*); the sanctions for unacceptable behavior; the obligations of the individual to the group and vice versa; the elites who may legitimately exercise discretion over the behavior of others (i.e. the use of power
in human relations); the system of invidious distinctions among individuals and groups with respect to their inherent worth as human beings; and
the appropriate objects of human desire, along with the standards for the
prizing of them. Most importantly for the purpose of this discussion, the
value system of the culture *prescribes the standards of judgment by which*

behavior is correlated in the daily problem-solving activities of the community. This is by no means an exhaustive list of the ways in which cultural values affect the life processes of the community, but it will suffice for our purposes.

Valuation as 'prizing'

It should be noted in passing that valuation as 'prizing' is the preoccupation of neoclassical economics analysis. It was the neoclassical formulation of 'economic man' as engaged in a single-minded prizing of goods and services to satisfy human wants, specified only by the individual's unique utility (preference) function, that led Veblen to make his classic observation: 'The hedonistic conception of man is that of a lightning calculator of pleasures and pains . . .' (Veblen, 1919, p. 73). Following the orthodox conception of social causality, since production is only the *means* to the *end* of consumption, valuation in the form of 'prizing' is the ultimate incentive for all economic activity. Indeed, the 'prizing' of goods and the means of their production through the pecuniary logic of the price system is the diagnostic characteristic of the neoclassical view of the meaning and significance of economics. But what is missing in the neoclassical view of prizing behavior is the possibility that both the object(s) of 'prizing' and the acceptable mode of 'prizing' are forms of learned behavior that are culturally determined.

Veblen attacked this static, a-cultural conception of human nature on the grounds that it blocked any possible development of economics as an evolutionary science. In effect, he argued that the essence of economic behavior does not lie in the capacity of human beings to engage in 'prizing'; he believed, rather, that their capacity for valuation on a much broader scale of human events was their most important economic attribute.

The capacity of the individual (and communities) to generate and adapt to changes in the culture (both social and physical) involves far more than the mere business of 'prizing' goods and services. A more sophisticated capacity to evaluate the *status quo*, and determine whether or not it is suitable to meet the contemporary needs of the community, comes into play when individuals and communities sense that what *is* the case *ought not be* the case. This form of valuation requires the capacity to evaluate the appropriateness of current social practices, not in terms of individual preferences, but in terms of the well-being of the community taken impersonally. Veblen referred to this evaluative capacity as the 'parental bent', which he described as 'an unselfish solicitude for the well-being of the incoming generation'. It also entails, he said, 'a bias for the highest efficiency and fullest volume of life in the group' (Veblen, 1914, p. 46). It is this evaluative capacity that plays a major role in the process of institutional change.

Values as standards of judgment

In the prior discussion of 'prizing', the term 'valuation' was employed. The reason for this usage is that a normative 'valuation' is a judgment that something is either good or bad, better or worse, desirable or undesirable, and so forth. A 'valuation' always presumes a standard of judgment. In the orthodox formulation of the theory of consumer choice, the 'valuation' is the 'prizing' of one bundle of goods over another; 'the standard of judgment' is the maximization of utility (in the cardinal utility version) or the optimization of the preference function (in the ordinal utility version). For purposes of clarity in the following discussion, a 'standard of judgment' will be called a 'value', and the application of a standard of judgment to a normative choice will be called a 'valuation'.

Value judgments

An additional terminological clarification is required by the distinction between a 'value' and a 'valuation'. The selection of a value as a standard of judgment will be called a 'value judgment'. Note that this is a far more restrictive use of the term 'value judgment' than is found in the general economic literature. In discussions of economic methodology, the term 'value judgment' usually refers to any form of normative proposition. But this conventional usage blurs the distinction between a 'valuation', which employs a *given* standard of judgment, and a 'value judgment', which involves the *selection* of a standard of judgment. Both are expressed in the form of normative propositions, but they involve different kinds of normative considerations (Bush, 1993, p. 89).

The cultural significance of a 'value judgment' lies in the fact that it is a deliberative undertaking, whereas a 'valuation' need not be. One of the most important notions associated with the culture concept is the proposition that learned behavior is habituated, not in the initial learning, but over time as the individual incorporates the learned behavior into his/her behavioral patterns. 'Valuations' are prime examples of habituated behavior. What this means is that individuals are seldom consciously aware of the standard of judgment (i.e. the 'value') that justifies or validates any given 'valuation' they may make. As habits of thought, 'valuations' are deeply embedded in the traditions of the community, and it is the force of tradition that most members of the community will take as sufficient justification for any given 'valuation'. A 'value judgment', on the other hand, is not a mode of habituated behavior; it is at the core of behavioral innovation. As will be argued below in the discussion of institutional change, consciously made 'value judgments', not habituated 'valuations', are at the heart of institutional change.

Culture contains both ceremonial and instrumental modes of valuation
Institutionalists argue that all cultures contain both ceremonial and instrumental modes of valuation (Ayres, 1961, pp. 77–8; Hamilton, 1970, p. 111; Junker, 1968; Mayhew, 1981, p. 515; Tool, 1979, pp. 166–7). These two modes of valuation reflect the efforts of mankind to cope with the most profound issues of human existence. John Dewey describes the situation as follows:

> Man who lives in a world of hazards is compelled to seek for security. He has sought to attain it in two ways. One of them began with an attempt to propitiate the powers which environ him and determine his destiny. It expressed itself in supplication, sacrifice, ceremonial rite and magical cult . . . The other course is to invent arts and by their means turn the powers of nature to account; man constructs a fortress out of the very conditions and forces which threaten him. (Dewey, 1929, p. 3)

Dewey called the first mode of coping 'the quest for certainty'; the second he described in terms of the rise of science (which depends upon instrumental valuation, defined below; see also Bronowski, 1965, pp. 45–6).

Consistent with Dewey's observations, institutionalists treat ceremonial valuations as being grounded in absolutistic dogma, which is impervious to modification through inquiry. On the other hand, they argue that instrumental valuations (which are most consistently applied in science) are free of absolutisms and tested by their consequences. Thus they are subject to modification (and even rejection) through inquiry.

The first suggestion of these two modes of valuation in the institutionalist literature is found in Veblen's distinction between 'invidious' and 'non-invidious' habits of thought and behavior (Veblen, 1899). Invidious habits of thought and behavior are concerned with status and power. They have their origins in invidious distinctions among individuals and groups of individuals with respect to their inherent worth as human beings (ibid., p. 34). Valuations based on invidious distinctions are self-serving, justifying the superiority of one individual or group of individuals over others. Non-invidious habits of thought and behavior arise in the arts and sciences of a culture. Non-invidious valuations take into account the well-being of the community as a whole without reference to status, power, or privilege, as in the case of the 'parental bent'.

With respect to the behavior of the consumer, Veblen offers 'conspicuous consumption' as an example of invidious behavior which involves the waste of the community's resources as individuals attempt to display their social status through the purchase of goods and services.[5] In contrast, non-invidious consumption of goods and services is consumption consistent with the need of the community to sustain its capacity to provision itself.

It involves the acquisition of the means of life for individuals and households without regard to their status and without the wasteful diversion of the community's resources to create differential advantages for a few at the expense of the many. In his analysis of the business enterprise, Veblen draws a distinction between (invidious) 'pecuniary' employments and (non-invidious) 'industrial' employments, the former being occupied with *acquisition* (i.e. 'making money'), and the latter being occupied with *production* (i.e. 'making goods') (Veblen, 1899, pp. 208 and 239). The pecuniary employments generate 'exploitation', whereas the industrial employments render 'serviceability' (ibid., p. 209).

The Veblenian dichotomy
The two modes of valuation in culture are manifest in Veblen's distinction between the invidious and non-invidious habits of thought and behavior. The 'ceremonial' aspect reflects the invidious and the 'technological' (instrumental) aspect reflects the non-invidious. The juxtaposition of these aspects of culture has come to be known in the OIE literature as the 'Veblenian dichotomy'.

It was Clarence E. Ayres who argued that the Veblenian dichotomy ultimately points to two different modes of valuation within a culture (Ayres, 1944). Ayres perceived deep-seated similarities in Veblen's theory of society and John Dewey's theory of valuation, which he combined to produce a theory of institutions and institutional change that has had an enormous influence in the OIE literature.[6]

Neoinstitutional thought
Ayers argued that the essence of technology did not lie in its physical manifestations such as laboratories, electronics, skyscrapers and aeronautics; it lay, instead, in its mode of valuation, which Ayres, following Dewey, called 'instrumental' valuation. As indicated in the previous remarks, instrumental valuation is tested by its consequences. In contrast, ceremonial standards of judgment are not tested by their consequences (irrespective of rhetorical claims to the contrary); they are tested instead by their 'authenticity' established through their conformance with myths, tradition, holy writs and ideology. Since instrumental values are subject to open-ended inquiry, they may be modified or completely rejected on the basis of their perceived consequences.[7] As such, instrumental valuation is a self-correcting mode of valuation. Ceremonial valuation, on the other hand, is subject to 'legitimate' inquiry only by an elite (e.g. priesthood, party leadership etc.) entrusted with the sacred responsibility of preserving the ceremonial practices of the community. Such inquiry is not open-ended; it is ultimately truncated by the absolutistic characteristics of ceremonially

warranted values, leaving their justification shrouded in myths and ideological rhetoric. Ayres's explicit introduction of value theory into institutional analysis launched a new era in the OIE literature, which Marc Tool
dubbed 'neoinstitutional' thought (Bush, 1995, pp. 10–11).

Institutions

Ayres's student, J. Fagg Foster, significantly advanced the neoinstitutionalist
research program by formulating what he called the 'theory of institutional
adjustment'. His contribution begins with his definition of an institution as
'socially prescribed patterns of correlated behavior' (Foster, 1981, pp. 908
and 940; Tool, 2000, p. 25). According to Foster, all institutions perform *both*
ceremonial and instrumental functions, which is his crucial insight.[8] In
Foster's treatment, the ceremonial/instrumental dichotomy refers not to an
analytical distinction *between* institutions and technology, as Ayres often
seemed to argue; it refers to a distinction between ceremonial and instrumental modes of valuation that exist *within* any given institution.

Several crucial ideas are clarified by this definition. First, 'the social prescriptions' alluded to refer to the cultural sanction of given patterns of
behavior that comprise an institution. Second, the notion of a 'correlated
pattern of behavior' brings directly into view the role of values in the institutional structure: they serve as standards of judgment by which behaviors
are correlated. Third, the 'correlation of behavior' can be achieved either
by ceremonially warranted values or instrumentally warranted values.
Finally, institutional change is, at bottom, a change in the value structure
of the institution; that is, an institutional change occurs when there is a
change in the mode of valuation in the correlation of some of the behavioral patterns of the institution. If instrumental values displace ceremonial
values in the correlation of behavior within the institution, a 'progressive'
institutional change is said to have occurred. If, on the other hand, ceremonial values displace instrumental values in the correlation of behavior
within the institution, a 'regressive' institutional change is said to have
occurred (Bush, 1987, pp. 1100–103).

The individual fits into this analytical schema as an agent who performs
any specific behavior (or role) within a given behavioral pattern.
Individuals obviously participate in many different institutions and may
play many different roles in a given institution. However, it is the 'behavior'
or 'role' performed by the individual, not the individual him/herself, that is
the most elementary component of an institution. In other words, *an institution is not composed of individuals; it is composed of behavioral patterns.*
Institutions cannot be reduced to individual behavior; and, conversely, as
argued above, institutions, let alone society, cannot be derived from an algebraic summation of individual behaviors. This last proposition, if accepted

as a principle of economic analysis, eliminates methodological individualism as a meaningful intellectual blueprint for the study of institutions or society.

The theory of institutional adjustment

The technological dynamic   According to the neoinstitutional analysis, technological innovation is the driving force in institutional change. Foster has referred to this as the 'Principle of Technological Determination' (Foster, 1981, pp. 932–3). 'Technology' for Foster (and all neoinstitutionalists, including Ayres) encompasses the exercise of human creativity across all of the arts and sciences of a culture (Ayres, 1944, pp. 105–24). Thus the neoinstitutionalist conception of technological innovation, in addition to innovations in science and technology, includes innovations in the fine arts – the case of Impressionism, among others, is discussed by Ayres (1944, pp. 105–6) – and popular culture – the case of pop music is discussed by Dolfsma, 2002). As Ayres put it, '[s]o defined, technology includes mathematical journals and symphonic scores no less than skyscrapers and assembly lines, since all these are equally the product of human hands as well as brains' (Ayres, 1961, p. 27). Neoinstitutionalists attempt to trace technological innovation through a complex process of cumulative and circular causation.

All kinds of social changes may be observed in most cultures, even within relatively short periods of time. Human existence is everywhere a matter of flux and change. This is no less true of the ceremonial practices of the community as it is true of instrumental practices.

In the ceremonial realm, heads of state change, political elites rise and fall, hemlines go up or go down, wars are won or lost, hermeneutical readings of sacred texts change, but all of these things can happen without any change in a culture's value system or institutional structure.[9] As long as there is no change an institution's value structure, there is no institutional change.

In the instrumental realm of culture, technological innovations always entail changes in the standards by which behavior is correlated. This involves the use of value judgments which supplant old standards of judgment with new standards of judgment, and, thus, carries the potential for institutional change (as described below).

Progressive institutional change   When a technological innovation occurs, it expands the community's fund of knowledge. But whether or not the technological innovation will be incorporated into the problem-solving processes of the community is determined by ceremonial practices prevailing at the time. As Veblen observed, innovation has the potential for disturbing the 'intellectual peace' of the community. The intellectual peace of the community is to a large extent bound up in its ceremonial practices. In consequence, the innovation is evaluated for its potential to upset the status patterns, power relationships, privileges and obligations, and other considerations that are endemic to the ceremonial habits of thought and practice of the community. While such concerns understandably come under the watchful eyes of the ruling elites of the community, it is also the case that the 'common folk' may perceive that they have a stake in maintaining the *status quo* (Veblen, 1899, p. 204). Even if one is of humble origins, 'knowing one's place', as defined by the ceremonially warranted invidious distinctions of the community, is widely regarded in many societies as a source of psychological comfort and security; thus class and caste systems find support from the bottom up as well as from the top down. Accordingly, a technological innovation might meet with ceremonially warranted resistance from *any* sector of the community.

Ceremonial resistance is, of course, based on perceptions that might be incorrect. The potential impact of the innovation on the *status quo* may not be correctly anticipated, and actions taken to resist it may have unintended consequences.

Ceremonial encapsulation A technological innovation requires an instrumentally warranted change in the way in which behavior is correlated in a given area of human activity. Depending on what Ayres called the 'permissiveness' of ceremonial practices in that area of human activity, the introduction of new instrumentally warranted patterns of behavior may be either resisted or accommodated (Ayres, 1944, pp. 177–8). The concept of 'ceremonial dominance' has been developed to give analytical effect to Ayres's notion of 'pemissiveness' (Bush, 1987, pp. 1085–6). Ceremonial dominance refers to the apparent tendency of ceremonially warranted patterns of behavior to dominate instrumentally warranted patterns of behavior in institutional structures. Thus the higher the degree of ceremonial dominance, the greater the resistance to technological innovations.

Even if a technological innovation is permitted to enter the problem-solving processes of the community, it is permitted to do so only to the extent that it does not significantly upset the *status quo*. This process has been called 'ceremonial encapsulation' (Bush, 1987, pp. 1092–9). It involves the clustering of new ceremonially warranted patterns of behavior to encapsulate the new instrumentally warranted patterns of behavior entailed in the innovation. In other words, technological innovations, in order to be absorbed into the problem-solving processes of the community, must meet the standard of 'ceremonial adequacy'.

Examples of ceremonial encapsulation are not hard to find. Technological innovations on the factory floor by assembly-line workers are seldom approved unless, in doing so, management can protect its superior status in the decision-making hierarchy of the firm. This is a form of 'past-binding' ceremonial encapsulation (Bush, 1987, pp. 1094–5), which preoccupied Ayres in his discussion of institutional resistance to change. Technological innovations in an industry seldom occur without an effort by dominant firms in the industry to gain control of the technology in order to maintain or enhance their market position and to exercise discretion over alternative technological futures. This has been referred to as 'future-binding' ceremonial encapsulation (Bush, 1987, p. 1095). The oil industry is a case in point.

With the exception of the 'Lysenko effect' discussed below, ceremonial encapsulation is a process that, in spite of the constraints it places on innovation, does permit innovation to occur to some extent or another. This means that some new instrumentally warranted patterns of behavior enter the problem-solving processes of the community. To the extent that this happens, the practice of instrumental valuation inches its way forward into the institutional structure. As old, ceremonially warranted habits of thought and behavior are displaced by new instrumentally warranted patterns of behavior, progressive institutional change occurs. The introduction of instrumental valuation in the one aspect of the community's life may well have a demonstration effect that encourages the expansion of instrumental valuation in other aspects of culture not envisioned in the original innovation. For example, the adoption of household recycling practices might induce the adoption of recycling in the workplace, or vice versa (Santopietro, 1995, p. 521). The gradual spread of progressive institutional change, which results ultimately from the ceremonially encapsulated technological innovation, is an unintended consequence of the imperfect effort to control the impact of the innovation.

The rate at which instrumental valuation is diffused throughout the institutional structure of the culture is a function of (1) the degree of ceremonial dominance in affected institutions; (2) the intellectual capacity of the members of the culture to perceive the necessity of adopting of this mode of valuation – this is Foster's 'Principal of Recognized Interdependence' (Foster, 1981, p. 933); and (3) the amount of dislocation it will cause in the institutional structure. It should be noted that items (2) and (3) are non-ceremonial constraints on the diffusion of instrumental valuation throughout the culture.

Minimal dislocation   'Minimal dislocation' is the last of Foster's principles of institutional adjustment (Foster, 1981, p. 933; Tool, 1979, pp. 172–5;

2000, pp. 94–5). Tool characterizes this idea as follows: 'This principle affirms that all institutional adjustments [involving 'progressive' institutional change] must be capable of being incorporated into the remainder of the institutional structure without significantly disrupting instrumental functions of nonproblematic structure' (2000, pp. 94–5).

It will be recalled that the theory of institutional change contemplates the 'ceremonial encapsulation' of instrumentally warranted patterns of behavior. This means that ceremonially encapsulated instrumental patterns of behavior, which play a beneficial role in the community's life processes, could be dislodged by technological innovations elsewhere in the institutional structure. While this kind of dislocation probably cannot be avoided, it needs to be minimized if the technological innovation is to successfully enter the problem-solving processes of the community.

The apparent ignorance of the principle of minimal dislocation played havoc with many of the efforts made by the USA and its cold war allies in the aftermath of the collapse of the Soviet Union. 'Shock therapy' and other 'throw-the-baby-out-with-the-bathwater' strategies designed to convert the communist system of Eastern Europe to capitalism entailed maximum dislocation of institutional structures that had many instrumentally efficient practices embedded in them. The loss of economic security and the disruption of the supply of necessary goods and services were the immediate results, and the political repercussions of these short-sighted policies continue to plague former Soviet bloc countries (Tool, 1995, pp. 210–11).

Examples of 'progressive' institutional change Based on the foregoing analysis, the following three historical cases are offered as examples of 'progressive' institutional change.

Over the centuries, a shift occurred in the legal foundations of Anglo-Saxon jurisprudence from status to contract (Maine, 1861, p. 100). The old system of status was founded on ceremonially warranted invidious distinctions (based on blood lineage and regal edict) that awarded superior status before the bar of one class of citizenry over another. It was displaced by the instrumentally warranted notion of a contract negotiated by equals, irrespective of their social status.

The elimination of anti-miscegenation laws in the USA after World War II is another example of progressive institutional change. The anti-miscegenation laws, which prohibited interracial marriages, were based on the ceremonially warranted invidious distinctions engendered by racism; their elimination increased the instrumentally warranted freedom of members of all races to choose whom they wished to marry.

Lastly, the GI Bill at the end of World War II in the USA changed the criteria of eligibility to pursue a degree in higher education from the ceremonially warranted ability-to-pay (privilege based on family income) to the instrumentally warranted criterion of ability-to-learn.[10] The benefit to society as a whole of this piece of legislation can be measured by the contribution a highly educated workforce made to the economic growth the USA enjoyed in the two decades following the war.

In two of the examples above, ceremonial encapsulation in the initial phase of the process is readily evident. In the case of the shift from status to contract in Anglo-Saxon jurisprudence, a new form of invidious distinction emerges with the improved legal status of the common man; it is the 'ability-to-pay' brought about by the pecuniary logic of the ideology of 'free markets'. In the case of the GI Bill, the instrumentally warranted eligibility based on the ability-to-learn was ceremonially encapsulated by the status of 'veteran'. In the case of the elimination of the anti-miscegenation laws, there would appear to be no discernible ceremonial encapsulation directly associated with it.

These examples are taken from the formal structure of society, legal opinions and legislation, because they are easily traced in the historical record. But it is probably true that the greater incidence of progressive institutional change takes place in the informal institutional structure of society as members of the community go about the business of life. A minimally adequate discussion of examples of informal institutional changes cannot be undertaken in the space available here.

Regressive institutional change   Regressive institutional change is characterized by a form of ceremonial encapsulation that is so overpowering that it nullifies some existing instrumentally warranted patterns of behavior as well as any contemplated increase in them. It displaces instrumentally warranted patterns of behavior with ceremonially warranted patterns of behavior, causing a loss in instrumental efficiency in the community's problem-solving processes. This form of ceremonial encapsulation has been called the 'Lysenko effect'. It is named after Tyrofim D. Lysenko, the Russian 'agrobiologist' who convinced Stalin that genetic changes in wheat (and other organisms) could be engineered through environmental conditioning (Bush, 1987, pp. 1098–101). Stalin embraced Lysenko's theories as the only biological theories consistent with Marxist–Stalinist doctrines. Lysenko's theories, although they contradicted the evidentially warranted hypotheses developed over a century in the biological sciences in Russia and the rest of the world, became the official dogma of the Soviet Union. Genuine scientific inquiry ceased in the biological sciences as Lysenkoism reigned supreme. This episode is offered as the definitive case of the displacement of instrumentally warranted scientific hypotheses by ceremonially warranted dogma. Incredibly, 'Lysenkoism' was not officially abandoned in the Soviet Union until the Premiership of Nikita Khrushchev in the late 1950s.

Another example of the 'Lysenko effect' is found in the racial theories of the Nazi party in Germany. The Holocaust was rationalized by the ceremonially warranted ersatz 'science' that taught the superiority of the Aryan 'race'. This instance of the corruption of science by ideology resulted directly in the murder of millions of Jews and other *Untermenschen* during the Third Reich. Standing at the pond of the Auschwitz death camp into which the ashes from the crematorium were flushed, Jacob Bronowski remarked: 'When people believe that they have absolute knowledge, with no test in reality, this is how they behave' (Bronowski, 1973, p. 374).

A Lysenko-type phenomenon is presently gathering momentum in the USA. As in the previous two examples of regressive institutional change, it also involves the promotion of ersatz science. This is the effort to promote the 'science' of 'intelligent design' as a legitimate scientific alternative to the theory of evolution. Under this guise, creationists and other leaders of the Christian right hope to persuade school boards around the country to require that 'intelligent design theory' be taught in biology classes as a 'scientific' alternative to the theory of evolution. This campaign has received support from President Bush and other social-conservative Republicans. Some local school boards in various states have already succumbed to the political pressure that the anti-evolution forces have mounted, and they have mandated the teaching of 'intelligent design' as an alternative to evolution. Such mandates clearly fall within the category of regressive institutional change and lay the foundation for further regressive changes elsewhere in the culture.

Conclusion

The concept of culture is the diagnostic characteristic of OIE analysis that sets it apart from mainstream, orthodox economics in the USA and abroad. Thorstein Veblen introduced cultural considerations to the institutionalist literature in *The Theory of the Leisure Class*. Research in cultural anthropology during the twentieth century provided the evidence needed to justify the incorporation of the culture concept in the institutionalist research program.

Among the most important features of the use of the culture concept in institutional economics are the propositions that (1) human behavior is enculturated, not a manifestation of an invariant human nature and (2) the individual is not only a product of culture but also a creator of it. The pursuit of these ideas leads to a rejection of the methodological individualism of mainstream economic literature. It also provides a foundation for a study of the role of institutions in the economic affairs of the community.

The cultural value system becomes a focal point in the study of institutions and institutional change. Culturally prescribed values function as standards of judgment by which behavior is correlated within an institutional structure. Institutionalists believe that there are two modes of valuation within any given institution: the ceremonial and the instrumental. Ceremonial values correlate behavior in, among other things, the display of status and the use of power in human affairs; they rationalize the *status quo*. Instrumental values correlate behavior in those problem-solving activities of the community that sustain its life processes and that depend upon the use of the arts and sciences.

Institutional change is, at bottom, a change in the value structure of the institution. The dynamic force for institutional change is technological innovation in the arts and sciences (broadly defined). Technological innovation induces the adoption of new, instrumentally warranted patterns of behavior, which are resisted by the ceremonial practices of the community. 'Progressive' institutional change occurs when instrumentally warranted patterns of behavior displace ceremonially warranted patterns of behavior in the institutional structure. 'Regressive' institutional change occurs when ceremonially warranted patterns of behavior displace instrumentally warranted patterns of behavior.

Thus the relationship of culture to values and values to institutions becomes the key to an understanding of the nature of institutional change and its impact on human, particularly economic, affairs.

Notes

1. This usage is employed to distinguish it from the neoclassical-oriented new institutional economics (NIE). These two forms of economic analysis are, in the present writer's view, basically incompatible, but some commentators see compelling similarities in the two approaches (Hodgson, 1994b).
2. It is fairly well accepted by mainstream economists that the preferences of others can be introduced as arguments in the utility function of a given individual. But this mathematical amendment to an ordinal utility function does not in itself address the questions raised by the cultural isolation of the individual otherwise presumed in the theory of consumer choice.
3. Apparently unaware of Tool's contribution, Tony Lawson uses language almost identical to Tool's in describing what he calls the 'transformational model of social activity' (2003, p. 40).
4. See also Tool (1995, p. 183), Jensen (1988, p. 119), Jennings and Waller (1995, p. 407), Hodgson (1998, pp. 118 ff., 1994a, 2004, p. 179), Samuels (1991, pp. 519–20) and Dopfer (1994).
5. Veblen (1899, p. 100) believed that all goods (consumer and producer) contained both invidious and non-invidious characteristics in varying proportions, paralleling the mix of ceremonial and instrumental aspects of culture generally.
6. Hodgson (1998) is highly critical of the notion of the 'Veblenian dichotomy' and disputes the value of Ayres's contributions.
7. This reflects the pragmatic instrumentalist belief that no proposition is so settled as to be beyond inquiry (Dewey, 1938, p. 16).

8. The discussion from this point forward reflects not only Foster's views, but also the elaboration on his views by his students (e.g. Bush, 1987; Junker, 1968; and Tool, 1979, 1995).
9. There is, of course, the possibility that war will lead to acculturation (i.e. cultural borrowing resulting from the contact of members of different cultures). Cultural borrowing was a subject that Veblen (1915) dwelt upon in his *Imperial Germany*.
10. While state universities and scholarships for the poor existed in the USA before World War II, the GI Bill was the first federal sanction of this new, instrumentally warranted standard of judgment applied uniformly across all institutions of higher learning, both public and private.

References

Ayres, Clarence E. (1944), *The Theory of Economic Progress*, Chapel Hill, NC: The University of North Carolina Press.
Ayres, Clarence E. (1961), *Toward a Reasonable Society*, Austin, TX: University of Texas Press.
Bronowski, Jacob (1965), *Science and Human Values*, New York: Harper & Row.
Bronowski, Jacob (1973), *The Ascent of Man*, Boston, MA: Little, Brown & Company.
Bush, Paul D. (1987), 'The theory of institutional change', *Journal of Economic Issues*, **21** (3), 1075–116.
Bush, Paul D. (1993), 'The methodology of institutional economics: a pragmatic instrumentalist perspective', in Marc R. Tool (ed.), *Institutional Economics: Theory, Method, Policy*, Boston, MA: Kluwer Academic Publishers, pp. 59–107.
Bush, Paul D. (1995), 'Marc R. Tool's contributions to institutional economics', in Charles M.A. Clark (ed.), *Institutional Economics and the Theory of Social Value: Essays in Honor of Marc R. Tool*, Boston, MA: Kluwer Academic Publishers, pp. 1–28.
Dewey, John (1916), *Democracy and Education*, New York: The Macmillan Co.
Dewey, John (1929), *The Quest for Certainty*, in Jo Ann Boydston (ed.), *John Dewey, The Later Works, 1925–1953, Volume 4: 1929*, Carbondale, IL: Southern Illinois University Press, 1984.
Dewey, John (1938), *Logic: The Theory of Inquiry*, in Jo Ann Boydston (ed.), *John Dewey, The Later Works, 1925–1953, Volume 12: 1938*, Carbondale, IL: Southern Illinois University Press, 1986.
Dolfsma, Wilfred (2002), 'Mediated preferences – how institutions affect consumption', *Journal of Economic Issues*, **36** (2), 449–57.
Dopfer, Kurt (1994), 'How economics institutions emerge: institutional entrepreneurs and behavioral seeds', in Yuichi Shionoya and Marc Perlman (eds), *Innovation in Technology, Industries, and Institutions*, Ann Arbor, MI: The University of Michigan Press, pp. 299–329.
Foster, J. Fagg (1981), 'The papers of J. Fagg Foster', edited by Baldwin Ranson, *Journal of Economic Issues*, **15** (4), 657–1012.
Hamilton, David (1970), *Evolutionary Economics*, Albuquerque, NM: University of New Mexico Press.
Hodgson, Geoffrey M. (1994a), 'Cultural and institutional influences on cognition', in Geoffrey M. Hodgson, Warren J. Samuels and Marc R. Tool (eds), *The Elgar Companion to Institutional and Evolutionary Economics, Vol. A–K*, Aldershot, UK and Brookfield, USA: Edward Elgar, pp. 58–63.
Hodgson, Geoffrey (1994b), 'Institutionalism, "old" and "new"', in Geoffrey M. Hodgson, Warren J. Samuels and Marc R. Tool (eds), *The Elgar Companion to Institutional and Evolutionary Economics, Vol. A–K*, Aldershot, UK and Brookfield, USA: Edward Elgar, pp. 397–402.
Hodgson, Geoffrey (1998), 'Dichotomizing the dichotomy: Veblen versus Ayres', in Sasan Fayazmanesh and Marc R. Tool (eds), *Institutionalist Method and Value: Essays in Honour of Paul Dale Bush, Volume 1*, Cheltenham, UK and Northampton, MA, USA: Edward Elgar, pp. 48–73.
Hodgson, Geoffrey (2000), 'What is the essence of institutional economics?', *Journal of Economic Issues*, **34** (2), 317–29.

Hodgson, Geoffrey (2004), *The Evolution of Institutional Economics*, London: Routledge.
Jennings, Ann and William Waller (1995), 'Culture: core concept reaffirmed', *Journal of Economic Issues*, **29** (2), 407–18.
Jensen, Hans E. (1988), 'The theory of human nature', in Marc R. Tool (ed.), *Evolutionary Economics, Volume I: Foundations of Institutional Thought*, Armonk, NY: M.E. Sharpe, pp. 89–123.
Junker, Louis J. (1968), 'Theoretical foundations of neo-institutionalism', *The American Journal of Economics and Sociology*, **27** (20), 197–213.
Lawson, Tony (2003), *Reorienting Economics*, London: Routledge.
Linton, Ralph (1955), *The Tree of Culture*, New York: Alfred A. Knopf.
Maine, Henry J.S. (1861 [1972]), *Ancient Law*, London: J.M. Dent.
Mayhew, Anne (1981), 'Ayresian technology, technological reasoning, and Doomsday', *Journal of Economic Issues*, **15** (2), 513–20.
Mayhew, Anne (1987), 'Culture: core concept under attack', *Journal of Economic Issues*, **21** (2), 587–603.
Mayhew, Anne (1994), 'Culture', in Geoffrey M. Hodgson, Warren J. Samuels and Marc R. Tool (eds), *The Elgar Companion to Institutional and Evolutionary Economics, Vol. A–K*, Aldershot, UK and Brookfield, USA: Edward Elgar, pp. 115–19.
Samuels, Warren J. (1991), ' "Truth" and "discourse" in the social construction of economic reality: an essay on the relation of knowledge to socioeconomic policy', *Journal of Post Keynesian Economics*, **13** (4), 511–24.
Santopietro, George D. (1995), 'Raising environmental consciousness versus creating economic incentives as alternative policies for environmental protection', *Journal of Economic Issues*, **29** (2), 517–24.
Tool, Marc R. (1979), *The Discretionary Economy*, Santa Monica, CA: Goodyear Publishing Company.
Tool, Marc R. (1995), *Pricing, Valuation and Systems: Essays in Neoinstitutional Economics*, Aldershot, UK and Brookfield, USA: Edward Elgar.
Tool, Marc R. (2000), *Value Theory and Economic Progress: The Institutional Economics of J. Fagg Foster*, Boston/Dordrecht/London: Kluwer Academic Publishers.
Veblen, Thorstein (1899 [1975]), *The Theory of the Leisure Class*, New York: Augustus M. Kelley.
Veblen, Thorstein (1914 [1964]), *The Instinct of Workmanship*, New York: Augustus M. Kelley.
Veblen, Thorstein (1915 [1964]), *Imperial Germany and the Industrial Revolution*, New York: Augustus M. Kelley.
Veblen, Thorstein (1919), 'Why is economics not an evolutionary science?', in Thorstein Veblen, *The Place of Science in Modern Civilisation*, New York: B.W. Huebsch, pp. 56–81.
Veblen, Thorstein (1934), 'The intellectual pre-eminence of Jews in modern Europe', in Leon Ardzrooni (ed.) *Essays in Our Changing Order*, New York: Augustus M. Kelley, 1964, pp. 219–31.

11 Caste and diversity in India
Ashwini Deshpande

Introduction

Insights into the Indian caste system, in its changing manifestations from the ancient through the colonial to the contemporary, come primarily from the vast pool of research that has been undertaken by sociologists, historians, political scientists – almost all social scientists except economists. Faced with analyzing persistent underdevelopment in India, the primary focus of economic research on inequality and poverty has been on the overall trends. Intergroup disparity is only recently coming to the fore in shaping the contours of research on inequality to gain deeper insights into the pattern of stratification.

Intergroup disparity in India is multifaceted: religion, region/language, gender and class are all very important descriptors of intergroup disparity. I focus on caste because of the enduring relevance of caste categories in contemporary India, and due to the presence of caste-based affirmative action policies enshrined in the constitution of independent India. Also, while caste is conventionally associated with Hinduism, all major religions in India exhibit features of caste divisions.

Caste in English translates two distinct concepts – the varna and the jati. Briefly, the varna system divided the ancient Hindu society into initially four, later five, distinct varna (castes), that are mutually exclusive, hereditary, endogamous and occupation-specific: Brahmins (priests and teachers), Kshatriya (warriors and royalty), Vaisya (traders, merchants, moneylenders) and Sudras (those engaged in menial, lowly jobs), that later split into those doing the most despicable menial jobs, the *Ati Sudra* or the former 'untouchables'.

The operative category that determines the contemporary social code, however, is the jati. There exist 2000–3000 jatis that are regional categories (they share the basic characteristics of varnas), and it is tempting to think of jatis as mere subsets of varna. However, jatis follow a much more complex system of hierarchy and rules of conduct towards each other. A one-to-one correspondence between jati and varna (note the uncertainty in the number of jatis in contrast to the certainty in the number of varnas) does not always exist and thus it is not unusual for a given jati to claim a coveted varna status nor for this claim to be disputed by other jatis. It is useful to think of varnas as a fluid scale over which jatis try to align themselves.

The traditional characteristic of the caste system is the link between caste and occupation. The economic and hence the occupational structure over several centuries has changed fundamentally, while caste divisions have changed from the varna to the jati. Additionally, the post-independence constitution guarantees each Indian the freedom of choice of occupations. Thus, *prima facie*, the link between caste and occupation seems to be severed. For instance, the erstwhile warrior castes will not necessarily choose the military as a career, and conversely, the military is no longer the preserve of certain castes. It is also true that any kind of skill acquisition (for example, admission to a management or a computer course, or to a dental school) is not contingent upon one's caste. Indeed, independent India is supposed to be a casteless society.

This begs the obvious question about the the overlap of caste and class in contemporary India, as well as historically. Defining hierarchy in this system is more complex that appears at first blush. A critical idiom was (and continues to be) ritual purity/pollution through which hierarchy expressed itself in this system. This would place the Brahmins very firmly at the top of the hierarchy. However, along with this, another pervasive principle was the jatis' relationship to land, where landowners occupied the top of the pyramid and the landless the bottom. Given that the ritually the most pure jatis necessarily were not big landowners, this intermeshing of hierarchies based on ritual criteria and the nature of the group's access to arable land renders the hierarchy more complex (and is also why caste does not collapse into class, even though the overlap is large).

For a contemporary examination of the overlap of caste and class, we require an investigation into ancient occupations that have survived changes in economic structure (i.e. priests in temples, scavengers, traditional moneylenders, and the whole spectrum of agricultural jobs). Are these jobs still performed by castes to whom they were traditionally allocated, or is the reshuffling of the deck total; that is, is the modern occupational structure randomly distributed across castes? It is likely that we may find more continuity than change.

What happens to those who are released from traditional jobs, because those occupations themselves are vanishing? If it is the case that lower castes tend to get absorbed into lower-paying and less prestigious modern occupations and higher castes get concentrated at the upper end of the modern spectrum, then we would be witnessing the result of what can be termed cumulation of advantage or privilege over the years (or its reverse, disadvantage or denial of privilege). The link between caste and occupation could technically be broken, yet the overlap can be very strong.[1] This issue is additionally complicated by the gender angle. In

Deshpande (2001b) I discuss how the responsibility of preserving traditional occupations often falls on women while men seek alternative employment.

Thus the contemporary situation could be regarded as a permutation of an earlier caste structure where the link between caste and occupation may be strong for some castes, weak for others, but the association between caste and status or, more correctly, between caste and privilege persists. It can be argued that the cumulative advantage of the upper castes has been so strong that they no longer need an institutional structure of hereditary reservations in order to perpetuate their privilege.

Additionally, caste is much more than just an economic relationship, its social facets well researched by sociologists. For instance, the ati-sudras were historically considered untouchable (below the line of ritual purity), in that even their presence was considered 'polluting' to the upper castes. Urban settings may witness far fewer overt instances of untouchability than more traditional rural settings; however, in a society in which untouchability has been formally abolished for half a century, this should be the least of the outcomes expected. In rural areas, the social and political manifestations of caste are much more obvious. Caste shapes interactions in the political arena crucially although the exact links between jati and politics are debated by political scientists. Thus caste remains a powerful and potent force in Indian society decisively shaping the contours of social and political development.

Defining caste inequality

Since caste divisions are not dichotomous, the meaning of caste inequality is not obvious analytically. In principle, this means the Herculean task of unraveling the complexity of the web of relationships between individual jatis and their varna counterparts, assuming it is possible at all. National-level data sets 'solve' this problem by collecting data on three broad divisions (four for data collected after the mid-1990s): the Scheduled Castes (SCs), Scheduled Tribes (STs) and Others (everyone else).[2] The fourth category after the mid-1990s is OBCs (Other Backward Castes), although the national census continues with the older three-way division.

While it is analytically simple, this three- or four-way division *underestimates* the relative disadvantage of the SCs, since the 'Others' is a very large, heterogeneous category containing a whole range of castes, including castes that are socially and economically not necessarily very distinct from the SCs. If empirical studies establish intercaste disparity between SCs and Others, it is reasonable to infer an even greater disparity between castes at two polar ends.

Race and caste

In Western Europe and in the Americas, particularly North America, skin color (and phenotype), or what is popularly known as 'race', forms the basis of group disparities. Even though it is established that there is greater variation in phenotype and appearance within races than between them, the concept of race has proved to be a powerful tool that is used to keep the minorities in these societies segregated, discriminated against and oppressed. In a country that celebrates its multiculturalism, Canada's use of the term 'visible minorities' makes this distinction explicit. Visible are those whose skin color is not white; the 1986 Employment Equity Act designated the visible minorities and other groups such as women and disabled persons as facing discrimination in the labor market. As it turns out, the racial/ethnic differentiation picture in Canada is complex and the single umbrella term of 'visible minorities' does not capture the multifaceted nature of discrimination in the labor market. However, the fact remains that skin color or phenotype forms a crucial group marker.

However, not all ethnic disparities and conflicts in the world are based on skin color. Take, for instance, conflicts that have been particularly bloody and violent, such as those in Rwanda, Sri Lanka or Israel, or the Ethiopian conflict that led to the formation of Eritrea. In fact, conflicts in all African countries where ethnic conflict does not involve a group of European descent are between groups whose identities are not based on skin color. Indeed, even inside Europe, the Balkan crisis does not originate in race-based conflicts. In both Singapore and Malaysia, intergroup disparity is based on national origins. Thus, in non-color-based societies, the conflicting groups are not defined on the basis of skin color or race but are based upon other social categories – religion, nationality or other ethnic groupings. In such societies skin color is considered more an individual attribute than a group characteristic. Thus it is entirely possible in these societies that individual distinctions in skin color are noticed or that they might be considered an attribute of beauty, but the 'defining' character of social groups is not their common skin color.

India is an interesting country in that the definitions of group identity are multifaceted, as mentioned before. Thus, to talk in terms of a single majority or a dominant group that is in conflict with one or several subaltern groups is not very meaningful in understanding the totality of group divisions in the country. To go back to the two examples referred to earlier, within Hinduism, caste is an important group identifier. Viewed this way, the subaltern groups would be the low castes. However, at the time of independence from British rule, the country was divided on religious lines, with religious schisms defining the socio-political fabric. Thus, in present-day India, the majority comprises all Hindus (including low castes) pitted against the subaltern Muslim community. In addition, linguistic groups, regional groups and women all add layers of complexity to the meaning of intergroup disparity that makes straightforward generalizations confounding.

There is another reason that makes India of special interest. The caste system has fascinated Western scholarship, which often sees direct parallels between racial divisions in color-segregated societies and the caste divisions in India. While several of the manifestations of racism and casteism are identical, especially towards those at the receiving end, we would like to suggest that there are fundamental differences between race and caste as social categories.[3] To begin with, the histories of the two systems differ vastly. Racism is a direct product of slavery under colonialism: the ascriptive differences between the slaves and their masters were extended to defining group characteristics. It is important to note that the negative stereotyping of blacks truly begins with capitalism and is consolidated during colonialism.

Caste, on the other hand, represents a system of social stratification that pre-dates colonialism by centuries. Therefore, for caste to be color-coded, there would have to be a strong historical basis. As it turns out, the history of present-day India does not offer straightforward answers to why the caste system ought to be color-coded. The racial theory of the Indian civilization is a formation of the late nineteenth century, when 'in the wake of slave emancipation, white–black relations in the Anglo-Saxon world were being restructured with ideological support from a rush of racial essentialism' (Trautmann, 1997, p. 208). Another reason that the theory is erroneous is that the Indus valley civilization pre-dates the arrival of the Aryan-speaking people, so to argue that the Indian (*sic*) civilization is the product of the conflict between lighter-skinned Aryans and darker-skinned aborigines is misleading. This racial theory was extended to the formulation of the racial theory of caste.[4] One important basis of the racial theory of caste is that 'varna' can be interpreted as skin color. However, there is no evidence to suggest that the 'varnas' are racially different among themselves. Trautmann (1997, p. 211) analyzes the British colonial quest:

In this fantastic back-projection of systems of racial segregation in the American South and in South Africa onto early Indian history, the relations of the British 'new invader from Europe' with the peoples of India is prefigured thousands of years before by the invading Aryans. But what the British encountered was not their Aryan brethren, as Max Mueller wanted to have it, but a 'mingled population' toward whom a supposed perduring prejudice of whites against interracial sexual relations (or rather a perduring mixture of repulsion and desire) structured those relations in a certain hypergamous way.

Given the ongoing controversy around the origins of the caste system, a detailed assessment is outside the scope of this brief account; however, a few comments are in order. First, the historical origins of the caste system are fuzzy and it is *not* conclusively established that a system of social stratification did not exist before the Aryan invasion. The implication is that if something akin to the caste system existed among the generally dark-skinned aborigines, then skin color would have not been the basis for the various social distinctions. It also helps to remember that Aryans were, truly speaking, a linguistic group and not a 'race' in the current sense of the term.[5] The racial theory of caste advocates that the Brahmin might have descended from the Aryan, thus explaining his superiority in the caste hierarchy. However, it is noteworthy that the Brahmin was a professional priest without parallel in Aryan tradition elsewhere; in later India, he acquired virtual monopoly of almost all ritual (Kosambi, 1985). Also, given centuries of migration and intermarriage, there is absolutely no evidence of one particular group being descendants of the Aryan-speaking people. The word 'arya' or 'arya putra' is sometimes found in the literature to refer to the royalty, who are not Brahmins, but are typically Kshatriya (though not always; there have been important Sudra kings as well). To make the picture more complicated, Kosambi (1985) traces the pre-Aryan features of Brahminism and also non-Aryan descent of several Brahmin castes. He suggests that the Brahmin priest was an unsupported individual, often on the tribal fringe. It is with his alliance with the warrior classes that the reorganization of the caste system begins. Kosambi links this to a 'higher level of production, regular settlements, the inevitable decay of tribal organization with the rise of a new type of property' (ibid., p. 107).

Second, the presumed skin colors of the four varnas that are found in the nineteenth-century discourse are difficult to justify: white for Brahmins, red for Kshatriya, yellow for Vaisyas and black for Sudras. Klass (1980) suggests that varna may not refer to complexion or supposed skin color, but rather to some kind of spiritual coloration or aura (ibid., p. 40). It is interesting to note that the Manusmriti, a text dated between the fourth century BC and the second century AD that outlines the basic differences between castes and sets forth a highly detailed caste code, has no reference to skin color as being the basis of the ranking of castes.[6] Given that today there are close to 3000 jatis in existence, a jati–color link is close to impossible to establish.

Third, the geographical variations in skin-shade differences in India seem to dominate the caste differences.[7] India is a virtual ethnographic museum, as all the major racial types can be seen in different regions of the country: the Caucasian type, the Negroid type, the Mongoloid type and so forth. Klass (1980) also points out how skin color and hair color lighten as one moves from the south-east to the north-west of the country and finds no reason to believe that this would have been otherwise 3000 years ago.

In its attempt to 'prove' the racial theory of the Indian civilization, the British administration had commissioned investigations into the distinctions in skin shade and phenotypical features (such as length of the nose, cephalic index etc.). Herbert Hope Risley (1851–1911), a member of the Indian Civil Service, who served in India from 1873 to 1910, was instrumental in concretizing the racial theory of caste – see the 1901 census report (*The People of India*, Risley, 1999) and a journal article 'The study of ethnology in India' (Risley, 1891). One of the best-known statements of Risley is 'the social position of a caste varies inversely as its nasal index'. Trautmann (1997), after a detailed review of contending theories and evidence, concludes that 'both Risley and Max Mueller show a tendency to exaggerate the significance of noses in ancient Indian evidence' (Aryans presumably with long, leptorhine noses in conflict with a 'black snub nosed – platyrhine – race'). Klass (1980) points to the near impossibility of determining with certainty the skin color and phenotype a given group might have had 3000 to 5000 years ago. Ghurye (1932) summarizes the conclusions of Risley's studies and reports that a systematic relationship between jati affiliation, skin color and phenotypical features cannot be drawn. He finds, for instance, that a Brahmin in Uttar Pradesh has more in common with a 'chamar' (a Dalit caste) in Uttar Pradesh than with a Brahmin in Kerala.

Thus jati is not ascriptive in that it is not possible to identify the jati simply by looking at the individual. Often, though not always, jati is indicated by the last name (surname) of the person. However, naming conventions differ across the country: for instance, in the four southern states, traditionally the first name is written last. Even when jati is indicated by the last name, since jatis are regional categories, it is impossible to remember the exact placement of close to 3000 categories. However, people have a way of ascertaining the jati of an individual if they want to – either directly or by discreet inquiry. But this requires some effort and the corresponding inclination, which is typically not made with respect to *each* person that one interacts with. Thus one important difference that emerges between caste and race is that it is not just the body that is the source of the understanding of the self.

In conclusion, one can say that skin shade does not form the basis for social stratification in Indian society, whereas caste does. Having said that, it is equally true that, as in several other societies, a lighter skin (the word used in India is 'fair' rather than 'white') is considered an attribute of beauty, but there is no socially recognized group of fair-skinned individuals in opposition to another group of darker individuals.

The economic literature on caste inequality
A comprehensive review of the economic literature on caste inequality can be found in Deshpande (2003). However, restatement of some of the issues that the literature covers is useful.

Identity, discrimination and economic outcomes
The theoretical models that exist represent an eclectic mix, ranging from statistical discrimination to Leontief-style input–output modeling. The field called the 'economics of rural organization' that emerged as the new neoclassical paradigm in the 1960s highlighted the role of institutions when faced with transaction costs and imperfect information. The paper by Akerlof (1984) falls into this tradition. Meanwhile, Hoff et al. (1993) suggest that changes in the field of development economics over the last four decades can be summed up as broadly constituting three traditions – planning, the Institutionalist tradition, and the Chicago School. The 'economics of rural organization' can be seen filling the gap between the latter two competing traditions, *within* the overall neoclassical tradition. Becker's work on discrimination is a legendary representative of the Chicago School, although he does not focus on the caste system in particular.

Akerlof (1984) provides, within a modified Arrow–Debreu framework, an explanation of segregated or caste economy which may be self-perpetuating. It falls in the class of models that focus on identity and economic outcomes, that is, statistical discrimination through use of indicators. The paper discusses distortions to the Arrow–Debreu framework by the use of indicators that owe their existence to social convention. This can be contrasted with the Chicago School, which explains discrimination by a 'taste for discrimination' (Becker, 1971, p. 14). An individual X will discriminate against Y simply because he has a taste for it and he 'must act *as if* he were willing to pay something, either directly or in the form of a reduced income, to be associated with some person instead of others' (ibid.).[8]

In the Akerlofian statistical discrimination, all members of a given group (race or caste) are perceived as having equal ability, so that in a caste economy 'the behavior of one member of society toward another is predicted by their respective caste statuses' (Akerlof, 1984, p. 24). The identity of the agent, *perceived by other agents*, is seen as an indicator of merit and in turn determines outcomes. In a system where there are social costs (for instance, sanctions in the form of being declared an outcaste) associated with breaking traditional norms and practices, his model demonstrates the tendency to thwart change to the social code of a segregated society.[9] This model is closer to the 'disadvantage model' that is used to explain racial disparity – identity is seen as a set of characteristics attributed to an individual that either explains how others would behave towards the individual (Akerlof, 1984) or how this individual would behave in society (Akerlof and Kranton, 1998).

These models do not address the fundamental question of how these assessments are formed. Are they based on averages that the group is presumed to possess? Assuming, temporarily, that the averages are 'accurately' estimated, this means that the outliers in the group, specifically those with attributes much higher than average, will suffer. However, *beliefs* about the group frequency distribution and the true group frequency distribution may differ widely. This difference would be driven by prejudice, but the theoretical apparatus of imperfect information does not allow an evaluation of the process by which indicators are formed, left as they are to 'social convention'.

Turning to these models and the Indian caste system, one finds a whole range of questions left unanswered. For instance, why are the attitudes of the upper castes towards the Dalits derogatory? Are they due to the fact that the Dalits are genuinely 'inferior'? If Dalits acquired superior human capital indicators over time, would these attitudes change accordingly? Why are the upper castes 'superior' anyway? Is it due to their inherent characteristics, or due to a social institution that was created by the privileged to maintain their privilege? If it is the latter, then the existence of discrimination would have very little to do with either presumed or actual characteristics of the Dalits.

By focusing on a given individual (Akerlof and Kranton, 1998), we overlook conflicting social prescriptions. Social prescriptions are defined by the authors as 'what actions are . . . appropriate' and function as 'powerful motivations to behavior' (ibid., p. 1). Are social prescriptions an aggregate of individual prescriptions? Are there dominant prescriptions of privilege that determine what social codes or norms ought to be? This is the classic problem of interpersonal comparisons.

Then comes the question of the identity 'A' would like to possess, versus the identity that society bestows upon 'A' – in the contemporary context of caste, excellently summarized by the juxtaposition of the terms Dalit and Harijan (the former a term of pride for untouchables, the latter term, coined by Gandhi, considered patronizing). Further, if A chooses to be nonconformist, an issue that Akerlof and Kranton (1998) address, adopting a deviant behavior in terms of the prevalent social code might simply mean that he or she may be acting true to their self-perceived identity. Here we are entering a gray area. Rebellion and protest take a myriad forms – almost all forms are 'socially' unacceptable, although the degrees of unacceptability vary with the particular form.

Continuity and change
In the Akerlof (1984) model, while there is a theoretical possibility of an anti-caste coalition succeeding in breaking free of the code, this possibility falls victim to the free-rider problem. Akerlof writes 'usually the greatest returns go to those who do not break social customs . . . the models of statistical discrimination and caste explain why economic rewards may follow those who follow prevailing social customs' (ibid., p. 44). Lal (1988), in developing an economic rationale for the Hindu social system, uses essentially the Akerlofian argument (indeed, his model is a variant of the Akerlof model) to explain the relative stability in the caste system.[10]

One can see other more powerful disincentives to the formation of such a coalition: prejudice and the desire to perpetuate their domination and the power to prevent such a coalition on the part of the upper castes, coupled with fear of a backlash on the part of the lower castes. In this context, Kuran (1987) argues that the system continues because the most oppressed are in fact its supporters. This support could either be forced because of fear of reprisal, or genuine, due to a mistaken fatalism. This formulation ignores huge chapters out of India's history, which is replete with social reform and religious protest against the caste system (see Deshpande, 2000b, for details of the Bhakti movement that started in the eighth to ninth century AD). The Sikh revolt against Hinduism was initially anti-caste, but with the formation of castes within the new religion, Sikhism, ended up with a situation no different from before. It is also argued that a strong caste consciousness prevents the formation of a class consciousness.

In general, if construction of identity flows from a set of presumed characteristics, can social change come if subjects of discrimination acquire the socially desirable characteristics (assuming, of course, the highly unlikely possibility that a well-formulated consensus exists on this)? Or would victims of discrimination have to resort to protest (perhaps violent)? Can either legal reform or external force (or both) be agents of change? We would like to know how the Akerlof (1984) equilibrium would change if the indicators for the Dalits improved over time.

Caste and patronage
Platteau (1992) attempts to tread a completely different path by exploring caste relationships as a system of 'aristocratic patronage', where relations between upper and lower castes have elements of patronage.[11] He realizes and admits that the jajmani system (the system of reciprocal obligations between jatis) cannot be equated with patron–client relationships, but feels it contains such elements. An untouchable dependent may have hereditary relationships with several members of upper castes (meaning that several generations of a given untouchable family work for corresponding

generations of one or more upper-caste families and receive remuneration), implying the presence of non-exclusive, non-dyadic clientelist relationships.

Contrary to the interlinked rural market models that assume competition, Platteau's (1992) system assumes very stable relationships, blocking the development of competition and formalizing a scheme of stable, hierarchical relationships based on servitude and coerced labor. The instrument of patronage in the models is the provision of land plots to the untouchable clients to ensure compliance and docility.

While social insurance to the clients does exist, it could take a variety of forms other than provision of land. In view of the antagonism and tension in upper- and lower-caste relations there exists a very high degree of landlessness among the SCs that this model does not treat. Platteau's paper models caste relationships as an informal system of indentured servitude. The jajmani system is far more complex. In addition to the land-based work, Dalits under the traditional jajmani system performed jobs that were completely divorced from land – especially the most menial ones, such as working with dead animals (removal and leather making), lifting human feces, cremating the dead, sweeping and so on.

Despite these serious limitations, Platteau's paper does address *the link between land ownership and caste status*. This is an important facet of caste inequality. His models suggest that radical land reform would destroy the root of the untouchables' dependence on their upper-caste landowning masters. The long-unfinished agenda of land reform in India could provide a clue to one of the important causes of the perpetuation of caste inequality in the rural areas.[12]

This still leaves open the issue of low caste status and consequent discrimination that stems from traditional menial jobs. In Platteau's (1992) dynamic models, the jajmani system does not turn out to be robust in the face of a number of changes. A weakening or even the end of jajmani may not mean the end of casteism. To understand this, note the continuation of inequality and discrimination towards those seen as descendants of slaves in the USA, where slavery has been abolished for over 130 years.[13] These models confirm the traditional positive association between caste hierarchy and economic status.

Social mobility

At the time of India's independence in 1947, the belief was that modern industrial development and urbanization would gradually loosen the web of caste stratification and eventually lead to its demise.[14] Have the most deprived been able to move into the uppermost echelons of the economy? Nafziger (1975), in an investigation into caste origins of industrialists in certain regions of South India, rejects the Horatio Alger model and finds a low degree of both caste and class mobility. He finds overlap in feudal dominance and prestige with capitalist control of business, hence a continuation of the privilege and social prestige of the high-income upper-caste families (fitting in with the trend of low-class mobility historically and internationally).

Mayoux (1993, pp. 563, 556), in a case study of the silk-reeling industry in Karnataka – small-scale industry, supported and promoted by the government targeting the disadvantaged groups – finds limited evidence of upward mobility (though 'not for the poorest of the poor') and finds 'structural disadvantages for those with little capital persist in the industry'. Those at the bottom attributed their lack of success not only to fate but also to their inability to get credit. And 'in some cases, reluctance to lend . . . based on prejudice . . . is certainly an element in the lower levels of lending to Scheduled Castes' (ibid., p. 557). The significance of this finding cannot be overemphasized. Lanjouw and Stern (1998, p. 37) discuss the poor access to credit for the lowest castes (Jatabs) in Palanpur and suggest that this may be the reason why 'Jatabs sometimes lease out their land on cash rent, despite the unattractive terms of cash rent contracts'.

Chandra (1997), examining the migration patterns of the Kanbis (a low cultivator caste) from Gujarat to Kenya between 1911 and 1939, argues that the caste acquired wealth abroad and, coupled with the adoption of Brahminical practices upon their return to India, managed to advance in the caste hierarchy to the middle range with the new name Patidar. This could be a case illustrating the validity of the specific process of 'Sanskritization' or a more general one of wealth leading to a higher caste status.[15] It challenges the notion of the Indian society as rigid and inflexible. Jayaraman and Lanjouw (1998, p. 38) report that 'several village studies find that the turbulence surrounding caste relations at the middle and upper levels of the social distribution is less marked among the lowest castes'. Also, they raise the larger question of whether '*Sanskritisation* should be seen as contributing to the breakdown of the caste based patterns of behavior, or rather the opposite . . .' (ibid., p. 46).

Discrimination as an obstacle to mobility?
If successful self-employment is seen as a tall order, what about recruitment as wage labor, where presumably the classic capitalist incentives of profit maximization would override all other non-economic considerations, such as the caste identity of the worker? Bhattacherjee (1985) tries to assess caste discrimination, over and above 'institutional factors' such as unequal access to education and industrial training, and finds evidence of discrimination in the form of unequal pay for equal work in the modern urban labor market. It could be argued that human capital characteristics (such

as education) could explain earning differences and that discrimination against SCs begins earlier – in unequal access to education. This is the so-called 'pre-market' discrimination, which even the most ardent supporters of the market will acknowledge. Dhesi and Singh (1988), in a sample study of Delhi, find evidence pointing to differential access to education among different religion caste categories, as well as evidence of wage discrimination. The high incidence of illiteracy among SCs explains a significant portion of their lower earnings.

Banerjee and Knight (1985) examine the crucial issue of whether discrimination in the labor market takes the form of wage discrimination or job discrimination.[16] They find evidence of differences in the earning functions for SCs and non-SCs that cannot be explained by characteristics, and this they take as a measure of wage discrimination. Their data also suggest that caste discrimination may be a formal-sector phenomenon since formal-sector jobs are prized jobs and hence resistance to hiring scheduled castes is greater. They find that 'it is in the allocation of workers to jobs that discrimination is most likely to be practiced. An employer would have no aversion to employing an untouchable provided that he worked in an untouchable's job' (Banerjee and Knight, 1985, p. 301).

Lakshmanasamy and Madheswaran (1995) examine data on technical and scientific manpower in the four southern states of India. The paper looks at evidence of discrimination in a sample of 67 927 workers. What they fail to point out is the fact that the SCs were only 5.3 percent of the sample – much below their proportion in the population – which indicates discriminatory exclusion. They find a statistically significant difference in earnings between the SCs and the others. They also suggest that the level of earnings of the SCs may be due to the reservation policy, implying that without this policy the earnings disadvantage would be even greater.

The odd note in the paper comes in the authors' uncritical acceptance of statistical discrimination: 'it is possible that profit maximizing employers use caste as a screening device for differences in productivity in the absence of perfect information' (Lakshmanasamy and Madheswaran, 1995, p. 75). Here all the questions that we raised about the Akerlof model become relevant. What needs to be asked is why this imperfection of information becomes critical only *vis-à-vis* an SC employee. What if, due to the same imperfect information, an upper-caste employee turns out to be less productive than expected? What insurance do the employees seek to acquire against this risk?

Discrimination could take other forms, too. Banerjee and Bucci (1994), in an analysis of on-the-job search, find that, after entering urban employment, scheduled caste migrants displayed a greater propensity than non-scheduled castes for on-the-job search in the informal sector but not in the formal sector. This seems surprising in view of the fact that the government policy of reserving jobs for the SCs applies in the public sector establishments of the formal sector.

But they interpret this as evidence of discrimination, based on the results of an earnings function analysis (another paper) of the same sample that found that, in the formal sector, earnings were lower for the SCs. They point out that 'the continuation of the search efforts shows that the SCs did not necessarily have lower expectations and were not prepared meekly to accept their economic lot' (ibid., p. 42).

Jayaraj and Subramanian (1994) propose a number of real-valued indices of discrimination and link them with measures of inequality. They also provide estimates for caste-based disparity in the distribution of consumption expenditures in rural India, based on NSS data 'perhaps constitut[ing] not so much "findings", properly speaking, as a confirmation of one's worst suspicions – namely, that in the matter of caste discrimination in India, there is much cause for disquiet' (ibid., p. 19). They find evidence of 'systematically inferior status experienced by the Scheduled Castes and Tribes' (ibid., p. 14).

The bulk of the literature on affirmative action comes from sociologists and political scientists. For instance, Pai Panandiker (1997) and Chopra (1997) make comments on the nature of the affirmative action program in India that are thought-provoking, but do not provide any data to help us assess the validity of their claims. Chitnis (1997) suggests that 'SCs and STs [are] not uniformly as backward as they were . . .' (ibid., p. 91). How does one establish the validity of this, if not by all-India quantitative analysis? In fact, the Jayaraj and Subramanian (1994) study, mentioned above, suggests that Chitnis's argument may not be borne out by the facts.

Nesiah (1997) outlines the poor track record of SC–ST recruitment in public employment. Galanter (1997) outlines the larger problem of discrimination: 'preferential treatment has kept the beneficiary groups and their problems visible to the educated public, it has not stimulated widespread concern to provide for their inclusion, apart from what is mandated by government policy . . . [T]his lack of concern is manifest in the record of private sector employment [where the reservation system does not apply in India]' (Galanter, 1997, p. 191). He discusses the broader (and in a sense more crucial) question of whether affirmative action in India has succeeded in integrating the most marginalized groups into the mainstream or if beneficiaries of affirmative action still face rejection in the set-up to which they are admitted.

Thus available evidence and literature confirm the enduring relevance of caste as not only a social but also an economic category, while it is equally true that intergroup disparity in India is multifaceted.

Notes

1. The issue of the overlap between caste and class is complex and is not discussed here in detail. For instance, while untouchable castes have often turned to 'jobs which could be done without coming into close physical contact with caste Hindus' (Mencher, 1974, p. 473) and thus form a large proportion of landless labor, not all landless labourers are untouchables (as Mencher discusses). There are issues about the growing proletarianization and the role of economic policy that are fascinating, but are beyond the scope of this chapter.

2. More than 50 million Indians belong to tribal communities which are distinct from Hindu caste society. These are the Adivasis, who have origins that precede the Aryans and even the Dravidians of the South. Many have lifestyles and languages that are distinct from any of the known religions in India. At the time of formulating the affirmative action policy, jatis and tribes that were economically the weakest and historically subjected to discrimination and deprivation were identified in a government schedule as the target group of the reservation policy. These were called the Scheduled Castes (SCs) and Scheduled Tribes (STs). The former untouchable castes often identify themselves by the original Sanskrit, but now Marathi word Dalit (meaning 'the oppressed'), employed as a term of pride. While the SC/ST nomenclature has grown out of government policy, Dalit is a more loosely defined social category. I use both the words in the chapter, and the context makes their usage clear.

3. See Beteille (1971) for a concise and lucid review of the differences as well as the similarities between the two systems.

4. See Klass (1980) for an excellent critical review of the theories of the origins of the caste system.

5. The notion of the 'Aryan race' was created by the German Sanskritist Friedrich Max Mueller in the nineteenth century. While he consistently advocated the brotherhood of the Aryan peoples, the kinship between Indians and Europeans, interestingly, he never visited India. For a critical account of his two race theory of India, see Trautmann (1997), ch. 6.

6. See Mueller (1964).

7. See the introduction to NFHS (1995) for broad geographical patterns.

8. Both the Chicago School (Becker) and the economics of rural organization (Akerlof) have been criticized for an excessive focus on questions of efficiency at the expense of distribution. See Hoff et al. (1993) for a more detailed discussion.

9. An objection to this from a sociological perspective could be that the contemporary meaning of 'belonging to a caste' is not clear – for instance, to what extent caste affiliation determines the behavior of its members. Or, what exactly is the contemporary nature of sanctions – do they apply only to marriage or to other social behaviors? All these questions are important but outside the purview of economic inquiry.

10. Lal's (1988, p. 72) argument is that given a set of problems that the ancient Indians were facing, such as political instability, the need for a secure labor supply for labor-intensive settled agriculture in the Indo-Gangetic plains, uncertainty concerning outputs and so forth, the caste system was a 'second best optimal response'. An analysis of this argument necessitates forays into ancient history that are well beyond the brief of this chapter.

11. He argues that patronage relationships display four main characteristics, which very briefly can be stated as follows: (a) they are highly asymmetrical; (b) they contain a strong element of affection; (c) they are comparatively stable; and (d) they involve multiple facets of the actors concerned and imply a set of reciprocal obligations that stretches over a wide and loosely defined domain, including some degree of social security to the client, which could be important to poor villagers deprived of significant access to land. The rationale of patronage from the point of view of the patron for this point is made explicit later – basically they are assured of a pool of readily available trustworthy and compliant labor for agricultural tasks and for ritual, social and political activities or duties.

12. Struggles for greater equality in land holdings were a part of the independence movement, and their strength varied across regions. Land reform after independence has been

under the purview of state governments, thus depending entirely on the political will of a given state government. These two factors together have contributed to the lop-sided nature of land reforms. This is discussed in some detail in Deshpande (2001a).

13. For a comprehensive examination of the economic consequences of contemporary racism in the USA, see Darity and Myers (1998).
14. Parallel claims have been made by Brazilian scholars about the impact of industrialization on racial attitudes in their country. For a discussion of some of the theories and the 'dissonance between theory and data' see Lovell (1994).
15. This term is due to Srinivas (1962), who believed that 'Sanskritisation is both a part of the process of social mobility as well as the idiom in which mobility expresses itself . . . [it] can also occur independently of the acquisition of political and economic power (p. 9). This is how he describes the process: 'A low caste was able, in a generation or two, to rise to a higher position in the hierarchy by adopting vegetarianism and teetotalism, and by Sanskritising its ritual and pantheon. In short, it took over, as far as possible, the customs, rites, and beliefs of the Brahmins, and the adoption of the Brahminic way of life by a low caste seems to have been frequent, although theoretically forbidden' (Srinivas, 1962, p. 42).
16. Wage discrimination is defined as 'unequal pay for workers with the same economic characteristics even within the same job' and job discrimination is defined as 'unequal pay for workers with the same economic characteristics which results from their being employed in different jobs' (Banerjee and Knight, 1985, p. 278).

References

Akerlof, George (1984), 'The economics of caste and of the rat race and other woeful tales', in *An Economic Theorist's Book of Tales*, Cambridge: Cambridge University Press, pp. 23–44.

Akerlof, George and Rachel Kranton (1998), 'Economics and identity', unpublished manuscript.

Banerjee, Biswajit and Gabriella A. Bucci (1994), 'On-the-job search after entering urban employment: an analysis based on Indian migrants', *Oxford Bulletin of Economics and Statistics*, **56** (1), 33–47.

Banerjee, Biswajit and J.B. Knight (1985), 'Caste discrimination in the Indian urban labour market', *Journal of Development Economics*, **17**, 277–307.

Becker, Gary S. (1971), *The Economics of Discrimination*, Chicago, IL: The University of Chicago Press.

Beteille, Andre (1971), 'Race, caste and ethnic identity', *International Social Science Journal*, **23** (4), 519–35.

Bhattacherjee, Debashish (1985), 'A note on caste discrimination in a Bombay automobile firm', *Industrial Relations*, **24** (1), 155–9.

Chandra, Vibha P. (1997), 'Remigration: return of the Prodigals – an analysis of the impact of the cycles of migration and remigration on caste mobility', *International Migration Review*, **31** (1), 162–70.

Chitnis, Suma (1997), 'Definitions of the terms scheduled castes and scheduled tribes: a crisis of ambivalence', in V.A. Pai Panandiker (ed.), *The Politics of Backwardness: Reservation Policy in India*, Delhi: Konark Publishers, pp. 88–107.

Chopra, Pran (1997), 'An overview' in V.A. Pai Panandiker (ed.), *The Politics of Backwardness: Reservation Policy in India*, Delhi: Konark Publishers, pp. 13–28.

Darity, William A. Jr and Samuel L. Myers Jr (1998), *Persistent Disparity: Race and Economic Inequality in the United States since 1945*, Cheltenham, UK and Northampton, MA, USA: Edward Elgar.

Deshpande, Ashwini (2001a), 'Caste at birth? Redefining disparity in India', *Review of Development Economics*, **5** (1), 130–44.

Deshpande, Ashwini (2001b), 'Casting off servitude: assessing caste and gender disparity in India', in Kathleen Blee and France Winddance Twine (eds), *Feminism and Antiracism: International Struggles for Justice*, New York and London: New York University Press, pp. 328–48.

Deshpande, Ashwini (2003), 'Recasting economic inequality', in William Darity Jr and Ashwini Deshpande (eds), *Boundaries of Clan and Color: Transnational Comparisons or Inter-group Disparity*, London: Routledge, pp. 112–29.

Dhesi, Autar S. and Harbhajan Singh (1988), 'Education, labour market distortions and relative earnings of different religion-caste categories in India (a case study of Delhi)', *Canadian Journal of Development Studies*, **X** (1), 75–89.

Galanter, Marc (1997), 'Pursuing equality: an assessment of India's policy of compensatory discrimination for disadvantaged groups', in Sudipta Kaviraj (ed.), *Politics in India*, Delhi: Oxford University Press, pp. 187–99.

Ghurye, G.S. (1932), 'Caste and race in India', Mumbai: Popular Prakashan (reprint, 2000).

Hoff, K., A. Braverman and J. Stiglitz (1993), *The Economics of Rural Organisation: Theory, Practice and Policy*, Oxford: Oxford University Press.

Jayaraj, D. and S. Subramanian (1994), 'Caste discrimination in the distribution of consumption expenditure in India: theory and evidence', Working Paper No. 18, August, Centre for Development Economics, Delhi School of Economics.

Jayaraman, Raji and Peter Lanjouw (1998), 'The evolution of poverty and inequality in Indian villages', Policy Research Working Paper No. 1870, The World Bank.

Klass, Morton (1980), *Caste: The Emergence of the South Asian Social System*, Philadelphia, PA: Institute for the Study of Human Issues.

Kosambi, Damodar Dharmanand (1985), *An Introduction to the Study of Indian History*, Bombay: Popular Prakashan.

Kuran, Timur (1987), 'Preference falsification, policy continuity and collective conservatism', *The Economic Journal*, **97**, 642–65.

Lakshmanasamy, T. and S. Madheswaran (1995), 'Discrimination by community: evidence from Indian scientific and technical labour market', *Indian Journal of Social Sciences*, **8** (1), 59–77.

Lal, Deepak (1988), *Hindu Equilibrium, vol. 1: Cultural Stability and Economic Stagnation: India, c. 1500 BC–AD 1980*, Oxford: Clarendon Press/New York: Oxford University Press.

Lanjouw, Peter and Stern Nicholas (1998), *Economic Development in Palanpur over Five Decades*, Oxford: Clarendon Press.

Lovell, Peggy A. (1994), 'Race, Gender, and Development in Brazil', *Latin American Research Review*, **29** (3), 1–36.

Mayoux, Linda (1993), 'A development success story? Low caste entrepreneurship and inequality: an Indian case study', *Development and Change*, **24** (3), 541–68.

Mencher, Joan (1974), 'The caste system upside down, or the not-so-mysterious East', *Current Authropology*, **15** (4), December, 469–93.

Mueller, F. Max (ed.) (1964), 'The laws of Manu', trans. G. Buehler, in *Sacred Books of the East, Vol. XXV*, Delhi: Motilal Banarsidass.

Nafziger, E.W. (1975), 'Class, caste and community of South Indian industrialists: an examination of the Horatio Alger model', *Journal of Development Studies*, **11** (2), 131–48.

Nesiah, Devanesan (1997), *Discrimination With Reason? The Policy of Reservations in the United States, India and Malaysia*, Delhi: Oxford University Press.

NFHS (1995), *National Family Health Survey* (India and various states in India), Bombay: International Institute for Population Sciences.

Pai Panandiker, V.A. (1997), 'Introduction', in V.A. Pai Panandiker (ed.), *The Politics of Backwardness: Reservation Policy in India*, Delhi: Konark Publishers, pp. 1–12.

Platteau, J.-P. (1992), 'Aristocratic patronage as an ingredient of the caste system: formal analysis and dynamic considerations', STICERD Discussion Paper, No. 36, London School of Economics.

Risley, H.H. (1891), 'The study of ethnology in India', *The Journal of the Anthropological Institute of Great Britain and Ireland*, **20**, 235–63.

Risley, H.H. (1999), *The People of India*, 2nd edn, edited by W. Crooke, New Delhi: Asian Educational Services.

Srinivas, M.N. (1962), *Caste in Modern India and Other Essays*, New York: Asia Publishing House.

Trautmann, T.R. (1997), *Aryans and British India*, Berkeley/Los Angeles/London: University of California Press.

12 Feminism and/in economics
Edith Kuiper

1. Introduction

Feminism is as old as humanity. Women have been standing up to defend their equality with men and their rights as women over the centuries, using all possible means of publication available. The first feminist texts and publications emerged in the late Middle Ages and their number increased in the seventeenth and eighteenth centuries. Organized feminism is a phenomenon of a more recent date: the first women's organizations were founded around 1850. We, contemporary readers, are used to perceiving the most recent feminist wave as 'the second wave of feminism'. Historians, however, have identified many more feminist waves, up to six or more in Western history (see, e.g., Akkerman and Stuurman, 1998; Offen, 2000).

Since the early Enlightenment, the dawn of economic science, four feminist waves have occurred and had an impact on economics as a science. Feminist historians of economics claim that (anti-)feminism and economic science developed not separately, but that, instead, these developments were closely linked (Pujol, 1992; Seiz, 1993; Nelson, 1995). Images around the roles of women and men in the reproductive process are reflected in the use of metaphors in science and importantly have structured the conceptualization of objectivity and rationality (see, e.g., Keller, 1987; Harding, 1986; Bordo, 1987). In economic science notions of sex and gender have had an impact on the way concepts such as 'skills', 'labour', 'productivity' and 'value' were given content (Seiz, 1992; Nelson, 1995). In her book *Feminism and Anti-Feminism in Early Economic Thought*, Michèle Pujol (1992) indicates how feminism and especially anti-feminism reflected on neoclassical economists' perceptions of women as non-rational agents, their explanations of wage differences between women and men, and the conceptualization and valuation of women's work (see also Pujol, 1995).

Although more research on this is required to come to more final conclusions, from what is known so far it appears that throughout the history of economics, economists showed little interest in the economic experiences and problems of women, tended to rationalize rather than challenge unequal gender relations, and developed a focus and language that made it difficult for women to get their concerns on the agenda (see also Seiz, 1995, p. 111). There are some interesting counter-examples (see, e.g., Dimand

and Nyland, 2003; Bodkin, 1999; Forget, 2001), but these publications on economic differences between women and men did not make it to the mainstream of economic theorizing.

On the other hand, the tradition of feminist economic authors appears to have been much richer than recorded in the history of economic thought. This chapter briefly outlines the various feminist waves through recent history and their impact on economics as a science. The emergence of feminist economics in the 1990s meant the introduction of the gender concept in economics. Feminist economists argue that gender is a structuring element in both the economy and in economic science, thus challenging mainstream economics and elaborating a gender-aware approach to economics (see Kuiper and Sap, 1995; Ferber and Nelson, 1993, 2003). The second section of this chapter discusses in more detail current topics in feminist economics, and explores some future directions.

2.   Feminist waves and economic science

To make the claim that feminism developed in waves – in upheavals and then backlashes or restorations, and then upheavals again[1] – assumes a definition of what feminism contains.[2] In her book *The Creation of Feminist Consciousness* (1993), Gerda Lerner (1993) characterizes feminist consciousness as consisting of the awareness of women (1) that they belong to a subordinate group and they have suffered wrongs as a group; (2) that their condition of subordination is not natural, but is societally determined; (3) that they must join with other women to remedy these wrongs; and (4) that they must and can provide an alternative vision of societal organization in which women as well as men will enjoy autonomy and self-determination (ibid., p. 14).[3]

European Feminisms 1700–1950 by Karen Offen identifies several 'challenges to male hegemony' throughout Western history. She judges that these feminist waves achieved a large part of their pre-1950 objectives, though not without a great deal of resistance and struggle (Offen, 2000, p. 13). Akkerman and Stuurman (1998) distinguish six feminist waves. The first wave is characterized as 'late-medieval and Renaissance feminism' (1400–1600), the start of which is generally timed as the publication of Christine de Pisan's *The Book of the City of Ladies* (1406). The second wave is referred to as 'rationalist feminism' (1600–1700). During the emergence of political economy, the third wave of feminist writing occurs, referred to as 'Enlightenment feminism' (1700–1800). Then follows the fourth wave, 'Utopian feminism' (1820–50), the fifth wave that is referred to as 'liberal feminism' (1860–1920), and since the 1960s the sixth wave, 'contemporary feminism'. Our interest here is in those waves that coincide with the development of economic science.

Enlightenment feminism
In the seventeenth up to the late eighteenth century, when science emerged together with its academic institutions as we know them today, girls did not have access to universities, and the debating clubs and scientific societies that were newly founded in those days did not admit women in their meetings either.[4] In the salons in Paris women did have access, participated in and in many cases organized the discussions, but had no access to the Académie Française.[5] In England feminists such as Elizabeth Montagu, Catharine Macaulay and Hannah More met over dinner with Samuel Johnson, James Boswell, Horace Walpole and the like, but they did not have access to the meetings in coffee houses or societies such as the Literary Society of Glasgow and the Select Society in Edinburgh (see, e.g., Habermas, 1962; Ellis, 2001). It was in these societies that Adam Smith and David Hume had their discussions on political and economic issues, in which women hardly figured (see, e.g., Pujol, 1992; Kuiper, 2001; Shah, 2006).

The early feminist texts that address economic issues and stem from this period (e.g. Astell, 1694, 1700; Collier, 1739; de Lambert, 1748) stressed women's status as rational and moral beings, argued for improvement of their education and criticized women's legal, moral and economic position in marriage. In the second half of the century, feminist economic texts addressed women's education, their low wages and access to decent work (see, e.g., the work of Hannah More, Sarah Trimmer, Maria Edgeworth and Mary Hays). In the last decade, just before and during the French Revolution, the discussion about women's natural and political rights reaches a height in the work by Mary Wollstonecraft (1792) in England and Etta Palm (1790) and Olympe de Gouges (1791) in France. Soon, however, women were explicitly excluded from full political rights in France and later in England and the Netherlands as well. The conservative responses to the French Revolution increasingly set the tone, and in the following years the ideology of women's domestication got the upper hand (Offen, 2000).

At the end of the century, there are some women economic authors who aim more directly at an academic audience intending to contribute to the political economic discussions (see, e.g., Sophie de Grouchy Condorcet, 1798; Priscilla Wakefield, 1798). Political economists, however, did not see the need to translate these texts or refer to them, and political economy develops without acknowledging women as agents (Bodkin, 1999).

Utopian feminism (1820–50)
The rise of feminist waves in the nineteenth century was importantly supported by increasing literacy and improved education for women, development of nation-state formation, and mass emergence of women on the

urban labour markets (Offen, 2000, pp. 79–83). Women had always worked, for pay or not for pay: they contributed to the family income by working on the farm, in domestic industries, shops, workshops, industries, as teachers and so on.[6] The shift in women's productive work from home production such as dairy, spinning and weaving, subsistence farming to industrial production, which took place in England at the end of the eighteenth century, went with a period of poverty and high unemployment for middle- and working-class women. Pinchbeck (1930) reports that these changes eventually went with, on the one hand, an overall improvement of wealth and working conditions and, on the other hand, a deterioration of women's economic independence. This worked out differently for different classes. Aristocratic women depended strongly on their father, brothers, husbands and/or their sons, who represented them in legal matters. When her 'protector' lost his fortune, the woman concerned, with no other professions open to her than governess or taking up needlework, often faced poverty or ended up in prostitution (see also Pinchbeck, 1930, p. 315). For the working classes, women's wages were very low, which made it hard if not impossible to run a family on their own.

The response to the French Revolution turned out badly for the feminist case and it wasn't until the 1820s that feminist voices picked up again (see, e.g., Thompson and Wheeler, 1825). Ideas about equality of women and men, in particular women's equal political rights as propagated by Mary Wollstonecraft and others, had shifted to the background, but feminists such as Flora Tristan argued for the improvement of women's education, working conditions and pay (Tristan, 1843). Utopian socialists such as Fourier and Saint-Simon supported these demands and requests (Forget, 2001, 2003; see also Poldervaart, 1993). Like most liberal economists of their time, Simon, Michelet and Comte argued for economic chivalry: the rise of men's wages to the level of a family wage so they could provide for the family on their own (Offen, 2000, p. 136). The family model in which the father had the authority, and the wife was economically dependent on the husband, while her main task was seen as raising and morally educating the children, was, although highly disputed at the time, further articulated and perceived basic to a stable economy by Jean-Baptiste Say. It was not the utopian socialist, but rather Say's, vision of gender relations that became naturalized in nineteenth-century economics (Forget, 2003, p. 206; see also Scott, 1989).

Liberal feminism (1860–1920)
In the eighteenth and nineteenth centuries the nuclear family model emerged with industrialization, together with a sex-segregated labour market in which women were 'protected' from specific jobs and labour

conditions by the Factory Acts of 1842, 1844 and 1848 (Holcombe, 1983; Groenewegen, 1994, p. 4). This legislation developed alongside the patriarchal ideal of the dependent housewife and the domestication of women, which resulted in the late nineteenth century in the Victorian cult around motherhood, and the imagination of women as fragile, dependent, irrational and a-sexual. This ideology was supported by Darwin's and Spencer's ideas about the English family male-headed household as the height of evolutionary development. Nevertheless, and against the ideology of the day, women were engaged in paid work and constituted about 30 per cent of the total labour force over the years 1841–1911 (Groenewegen, 1994, p. 6).

Due to sustained feminist pressure, marriage laws concerning divorce and women's rights to property were changed in the 1870s–1890s in England (Holcombe, 1983; Offen, 2000). Women gained access to the higher education in the 1860–80s in most European countries and in the USA (Pott-Buter, 1992). Feminists renewed the debates on women's wages, access to professions and the detrimental effects of the Factory Acts in the 1870 and 1880s. Women's access to political power was a topic of heated discussion, debates and political struggle by the suffragettes, resulting in women's right to vote in the early twentieth century.

In the 1890s economists entered these discussions and conducted economic research on women in industry, women's wages and poverty (see Groenewegen and King, 1994). Charlotte Perkins Gilman published her *Women & Economics* (1898). Millicent Fawcett, Ada Heather-Bigg, Beatrice Webb-Potter and others debated the differences in pay between women and men, women's lack of access to professions and training, and investigated women's work and their working conditions. Edward Cadbury, M. Cecile Matheson and George Shann (Cadbury et al., 1907) for instance, conducted a large-scale systematic study on working-class women, *Women's Work and Wages: A Phase of Life in an Industrial City*, in which they attack women's economic dependence and give it as a major cause of early marriages and prostitution (Pujol, 1992, p. 68).

In political economy feminism was represented, articulated and made visible by Harriet Taylor and John Stuart Mill, who argued for gender equality and access to all professions for women and men (Mill, 1869; see also Bodkin, 1999; Forget, 2003). Socialist authors such as August Bebel (1879) and Friedrich Engels (1884) discussed the Woman Question, but perceived it secondary to socialist aims and strategy. Economists such as Edgeworth, Marshall and Jevons did address women's issues but placed married women outside the realm of the economy, supported lower wages for women, and argued that men had to provide for their families, while women needed only to provide for themselves (Pujol, 1992).

During the nineteenth century the women's movement became organized. As part of the centennial of the French Revolution, international congresses were organized on women's rights in Paris, and the Union Universelle des Femmes was founded in 1890 as one of the first in a number of international women's organizations (Offen, 2000; Pietilä, 2002). At the World Exhibition of Vienna in 1873 a Pavilion of Women's Work was erected, and more would follow at the exhibitions in Philadelphia, Chicago, Paris and The Hague, which became important events for the national women's movements. These pavilions presented women's work, art, living and working conditions, and showed new ideals and practices around women's lives and work (Pepchinksi, 2000). The image that women were not rational, did not work or should only work 'as long as she retains her tender and unselfish instincts, and has not been hardened by the strain and stress of unfeminine work' (Marshall, 1890, p. 564) had by then, however, taken firm root in the minds of economists and had become part of the implicit assumptions of mainstream economics (see Bodkin, 1999; Pujol, 1995).

Contemporary feminism (1960–present)
After World War II, the exclusion of women from the work they had been doing during the war in the USA and Western Europe went with the promotion of the male-headed household ideology. The work of women economists gathered dust, as the mathematization and the development of general theory took off in economics.

In the 1960s, the dominant gender ideology of the homemaking housewife became increasingly unsatisfactory and untenable for women, new forms of contraception became available and economic growth produced an increase in demand for labour. This gave rise to a new feminist wave that had economic independence and reproductive freedom high on the agenda. In the 1970s and 1980s a re-emerging international women's movement found support with the United Nations.[7] At UN conferences human rights issues took centre stage, next to reproductive rights and economic issues. The progress made on the Beijing Platform for Action (1995) has been closely monitored, the results of which have been presented at various later UN conferences.

In economic science the increase of women in the labour market was initially treated as an anomaly: a deviation from the normal situation that required an explanation (see, e.g., Mincer, 1962). Gary Becker (1981) describes 'the altruistic family' – a family ruled by a male altruist and a wife, 'the beneficiary, who is economically dependent on him' – as the most efficient organization of the family, thus reproducing the patriarchal reasoning of Marshall, Edgeworth and Pigou (Pujol, 1992; Kuiper, 2001).

Human capital theory, home economics and mainstream labour market theory shielded – in Lakatosian terms – the hard core of the neoclassical research programme from empirical testing; the basic assumptions of economic behaviour, efficiency and rationality were now beyond question and increasingly defined the field of economics as such (see, e.g., Hausman, 1992).

In the 1980s, the rise in number of women economists, supported by the Committee on the Status of Women in the Economics Profession (CSWEP), brought about research on women's issues from a feminist perspective. In 1992 the International Association for Feminist Economics (IAFFE) was founded with the aim to develop, support and disseminate feminist economic research (see Ferber and Nelson, 2003). One way in which this was done was through the journal *Feminist Economics*, which started in 1995. Feminist economics as a field was strongly international from the start. This was partly due to the fact that neoclassical economics had by then achieved the summit of its influence in academic education and as a base for international economic policy programmes of international financial institutions such as the IMF and the World Bank. The consequences of the use of these models that did not take women into account were felt by women worldwide, inside and outside academia (Beneria, 1995). Feminist economics gave voice to these concerns and provided a framework of analysis.

3. Feminist economics as a field
Feminist economists recognize gender as fundamental to the economy and economic science. As a field of study, feminist economics differs from other subfields in economics, as most feminist economists tend to vary widely in their theoretical and political perspectives in their research. In addition, it is not a women's-only endeavour: there are a substantial number of men working in the field as well.[8] Because feminist economics came about later than women's studies in other fields, such as philosophy, sociology, biology and physics, feminist economists could build on women's and gender studies research already done in other fields.

Attempts to define feminist economics vary. Julie Nelson, for instance, perceives feminist economics as a field that studies how societies organize and take care of their provisioning (Nelson, 1993). Myra Strober (1994), on the other hand, describes feminist economics as a field of study that is directed towards the improvement of the economic position of women. In whatever manner the field is defined, feminist economics is in the first place a community of feminist economists that investigates economic behaviour and institutions taking women as well as men into account, adjusting and transforming available economic research methods and policy tools, and providing new ones if necessary. Thus by taking into account women's economic behaviour and gender – next to race and class – as a structuring principle in the economy and in economics, it aims at explaining better than other contemporary economic approaches.

The concept of 'gender' was coined in the early 1980s in women's studies and involved a major conceptual innovation in many scientific fields.[9] Conceptualizing differences between women and men as socially and culturally constructed rather than as biologically given made it possible – instead of assuming that the behaviour and characteristics of women and men are identical and/or static and unchangeable – to investigate and theorize these differences. Where before social, economic and other differences between women and men were mostly explained by their biology or by referring to their perceived role in the reproductive process, notions of femininity and masculinity could now be analysed in their historical context (see, e.g., Harding, 1986; Scott, 1986). For feminist economists this meant that they could investigate and theorize about the impact of the economy – trade, policies, investments, business cycles etc. – on social, economic and power differences between women and men, and vice versa, the impact of changing gender relations on the economy.

Feminist economists found gender also to be fundamental to economic science. Julie Nelson (1992, 1995) shows that the dominant value system in economics values masculinity over femininity; terms such as 'rationality' had become linked with masculinity, and in opposition to that, 'irrationality' to 'femininity' (see Ferber and Nelson, 1993). Others, such as Pujol (1992), Folbre (1992) and Seiz (1993), point to the long and predominant tradition of economists taking a masculine perspective on the economy – the perspective from the social position generally taken by men in our society – which means that most economic theories do not address, include or explain women's economic behaviour (Nelson, 1992; Ferber and Nelson, 2003; Kuiper and Sap, 1995). Labour theory, for instance, was developed on the basis of the traditional male-headed family (see, e.g., Pencavel, 1986). The individual in these theories is a man whose behaviour is analysed as the result of a free choice between money, leisure and hours worked. The standard model in this field is built on the implicit assumption that this individual is married with a wife who stays at home and takes care of the children (see Kuiper, 2001). These basic assumptions mean that theories like this are of little use for the analysis of gender inequality and other women's issues in economics.

Feminist economists have brought new questions to the table. They ask, for instance, why the occupational distributions and earnings of women differ so much from those of men. What have been the effects of economic transition in former socialist countries on women's employment and entrepreneurship, and on gender relations? What explains the rapid rise in the incidence of poverty among women and children? What is the content and value of the unpaid work in the household, and what are the effects of government spending on women's productivity and income? What is the impact of gender inequality on economic growth? Addressing these and similar questions requires new or an adjustment of data, methods, theories and sometimes even entire new methodologies (Seiz, 1995; see also Kuiper and Sap, 1995; Ferber and Nelson, 2003; Barker and Kuiper, 2003).

Where before data on women's economic position, work in the household and in care activities were lacking (see, e.g., Goldschmidt-Clermont, 1982, 1987; Waring, 1988), substantial improvements have been made since. The UN Statistical Office and the UN Development Report (see, e.g., UNDP, 1995) now produce time-use research and other gender-sensitive data. Gender-indicators have been developed. Examples are the Gender-related Development Index and Gender Empowerment Measure, developed and reported on in the UN *Human Development Reports*, and others such as the Relative Status of Women Index (Dijkstra and Hanmer, 2000). Nationally and internationally important steps have been made in engendering statistics to make it possible to assess gender equality and the gender effects of various policies (see World Bank, 2001; UNRISD, 2005; UNDESA, 2006).

As quantitative approaches were often limited in addressing gender issues, many feminist economists have also turned to using more qualitative data, sometimes in combination with quantitative approaches. This enables them to address issues that are otherwise hard to solve, such as measuring poverty and the distribution of income in the household (Seiz, 1992; Pujol, 1997; see, e.g., Kim, 1997; Olmsted, 1997; Cantillion and Nolan, 2001).

In analysing, conceptualizing and explaining gender economic issues, such as the value and division of unpaid work, women's labour participation, care and policy issues, feminist economists make use of various economic theoretical approaches. Post-Keynesian theory (see, e.g., Danby, 2004), Amartya Sen's capability approach (special issue of *Feminist Economics*, 2003), Kaleckian models (see, e.g., Seguino, 2006), game and bargaining theory (see, e.g., Ott, 1992; Agarwal, 1997) and evolutionary models (see, e.g., Himmelweit, 2003) are all applied and adjusted to accommodate the inclusion of women and their concerns.

Feminist philosophers of economic science developed critiques of orthodox, modernist perceptions of objectivity as applied in economics arguing that the positivist perception of science in a sexist or male-biased context does not guarantee value-neutral results (see, e.g., *Feminist Economics*, volume 9, numbers 2/3, 2003; Barker and Kuiper, 2003; Zein-Elabdin and Charusheela, 2004). On the contrary, the claim of value-neutrality may very well shield research and theory from the investigation of male bias and other values inherent in current research practice (Harding, 1995). Overall, feminist economists emphasize the influence of male bias and race and class prejudices on economic science, its ontology and epistemology (see, e.g., Longino, 1990; Ferber and Nelson, 1993). Instead of acknowledging the dominance of one paradigm or theory as proof of an achieved objectivity and maturity of the discipline, or taking a relativist position, feminist economists in general value critical discussions highly, guaranteeing that various theoretical approaches are able to present their results to contribute to these discussions (Seiz, 1995; Kim, 1997; Peter, 2003).

Assessing the practice of feminist economic research, Harding (1987) distinguished three methodologies: (1) feminist empiricism, which urges social scientists to address women's issues and to follow existing research norms more rigorously; (2) feminist standpoint theory, which claims a difference in basic experiences between women and men as basis for knowledge development; and (3) post-modernist feminism, which raises questions about science as an epistemological project (ibid., pp. 182–9). Gillian Hewitson (1999) describes the field of feminist economics as still predominantly based on biological differences instead of on gender as a socially constructed concept, and argues for the deconstruction of the main economic concepts, metaphors and texts.

Harding (1987, p. 186) speaks of transitional methodologies, but feminist economics can perhaps best be called transformative, as taken as a whole it addresses economic science as a social and historical institution that needs adjustment at various levels to integrate women and considerations of gender, as well as race and class.

4. Recent topics and issues in feminist economics

Over the last 15 years feminist economics has evolved substantially (see Ferber and Nelson, 2003). The focus in the field has shifted from a critique of neoclassical economics towards the elaboration of a gender-aware understanding of the economy. In addition, the women's movement is no longer the exclusive social recourse and target group of feminist economics; there are now also women and men, working in national and international institutions such as banks, donor organizations, research institutes and governments, who bring in their ideas, questions and concerns, and thus contribute to feminist economics. Finally, where historically feminist economists were focused on explaining women's wages, employment, labour market participation and unpaid work (see, e.g., Bergmann, 1986; Blau et al., 2002; Jacobsen, 2003), there are now new fields in economics in which feminist economists are increasingly becoming productive. In the rest of this chapter, I discuss a few of these fields.

History of economics
Historians of economics are recovering the work of women economic authors and analysing texts addressing women's and gender issues throughout the history of economic thought. Biographies of individual women economists had already been produced earlier on in the twentieth century (see, e.g., Cole, 1946). Collections of women economic authors came about from the 1970s onward (see, e.g., Thomson, 1978; Groenewegen, 1994; Dimand et al., 1995). More recently, Dimand et al. (2000) have provided biographies and bibliographies of more than 100 women economists throughout the history of economics, and Madden et al. (2004) assembled a bibliography of hundreds of publications by women in the nineteenth and twentieth centuries. Overall these publications by women authors have a somewhat different focus from what we now know as historical economic texts (see Groenewegen and King, 1994; Nyland, 2006). There is still much work to do on the analysis of the content of these publications of women authors, and how they differ and contribute to the current account of the history of economics. A start has been made with assessing the impact and role of gender in these and mainstream texts (see, e.g., Dimand and Nyland, 2003), which sheds important new light on the development of economic theories over the centuries. Last but not least, such research provides a more substantial historical background for feminist economics.

Macroeconomics
In the 1970s the first articles and books were published that pointed to the lack of attention to and knowledge about women's position in development countries and the gender effects of macroeconomics policies (see, e.g., Boserup, 1970). Over the past few decades, feminist economists have critically assessed the standardized policies of cuts in government spending, deregulation, trade liberalization and shifts from import substitution to export promotion policies by the World Bank, the IMF and national governments (see, e.g., Beneria, 1995, 2003; Elson, 1991, 1995). Over the past decades the World Bank has come to acknowledge the role of gender in development, and *Engendering Development* (2001) provides an important overview of the research and theoretical approaches to gender and poverty. These results however, are still far from integrated in the 'general' macroeconomic modelling that is done elsewhere in the Bank (Bergeron, 2006).[10]

Diane Elson, Caren Grown and Nilifur Cagatay have made a start with integrating gender concerns in macroeconomic modelling (see Cagatay et al., 1995; Elson and Cagatay, 2000). Including women's unpaid work in the household and their work in subsistence agriculture, for instance, produces different outcomes and explanations from orthodox macroeconomic models. More work in this direction is promising and now possible, due to research and data that are becoming available from time-use research and policy assessment programmes.

Public administration

Acknowledging the budget as an important policy tool at the national and local level, and as a way to obtain important information on policy-making and economic behaviour, feminist economists have been involved in discussions on gender-sensitive budgeting from the start. Gender-sensitive budgeting aims to (1) mainstream gender issues within government policies; (2) promote greater accountability for governments' commitment to gender equality; (3) change budgets and policies (Sharp and Broomhill, 2002; UNIFEM, 2006).[11] The endeavour to obtain insights into the effects of public spending on women and men to improve its effectivity links up with an international shift in public administration and accounting towards programme budgeting that is target-based. To date the UNDP and the UNIFEM as well as many regional and local initiatives are active in about 70 countries worldwide to screen economic and social policies on its gender impact (gender impact analysis), often in cooperation with the local Ministry of Finance. These initiatives are backed up by the UN Gender Statistics that works with national bureaux of statistics to integrate gender considerations in their data production and where relevant to obtaining more sex-disaggregated data (UNDESA, 2006). The outcomes and data produced in this process can be expected to produce new insights and theoretical innovations in public administration, as well as in other fields such as policy-making and welfare economics.

Finance

The world of finance has remained untouched by feminist analysis for quite a while, although this has recently been changing. There is, for instance, an increase of interest in the impact of international capital flows on women (see, e.g., Singh and Zammit, 2000). It also becomes clear that women and men's behaviour differs where it concerns savings and investments, which has important implications for local and national policy-making (MacLennan, 2001). In addition, gender has been shown to play a considerable role in the organization and on the effects of micro-financing and micro-credits.[12] These and other issues concerning finance have now become topic of feminist analysis and theorizing.

Business

Partly due to unemployment and discrimination – and more than men invoked by push rather than by pull factors – women have turned to starting their own businesses. Especially in Central and Eastern Europe the percentage of women starting their own businesses is high; it is higher than that of men (Rumnska-Zimny, 2003; Aidis et al., 2007). Over the last decades an increasing amount of research has been done on women's experience and problems in starting their own businesses, the glass ceiling in women's careers, diversity in human resources management and on the differences in management styles between women and men. This kind of research is now presented and discussed in the international feminist economics fora, such as conferences, journals etc., and feeds into feminist economics theorizing (see, e.g., Nelson, 2003).

5.   Concluding remarks

In this chapter, we followed, in large steps, the feminist waves through history and their impact on economic science. We had a closer look at the emergence and content of feminist economics, and its impact on other fields in economics. Where worldwide progress has been made toward gender equality, feminist approaches to economics – taking women and gender into account – have made an inroad into economic science. It is still, however, far from being fully incorporated in general economic theorizing.

Concerning feminism and/in economics, the discipline seems to stand at a cross-roads: to integrate women and 'women's issues' as part and topic of economic science, or to continue explaining gender as static, context-free and biologically based, thus pushing the analysis of 'women's issues' over the boundary of the discipline. There are, of course, many interests at work to retain old assumptions, and to keep the basic images and metaphors intact. When these are very strong, external pressure and funds will be required for breaking through the established notions and paradigms that reproduce male bias. The scientific method, on the other hand, claims to be sufficient to make sure that facts are faced. Feminist economists work to bring these facts to the table and to make sure they have a seat themselves and join the discussions.

Acknowledgement

This chapter has been made possible by support of the Netherlands Organization for Scientific Research.

Notes

1.   Other metaphors are also being used. Karen Offen (2000) applies the imagery of volcanos, using terms such as eruptions, etc.
2.   For a history of the term feminism and its first usage, see Offen (2000, pp. 19–26).
3.   There are various definitions that largely overlap. See, e.g., Akkerman and Stuurman (1998); Kelley (1984); Offen (2000).
4.   Women did have their own organizations, as, for example, het Natuurkundig Genootschap der Dames (the Ladies' Scientific Society in the Netherlands) (Sturkenboom, 2004).

5. It was not, however, until far into the twentieth century that women gained access to the Royal Society and to the Académie Française (Noble, 1992).
6. Pinchbeck (1930) provides an overview of the occupations in which women worked in 1842, showing a strong concentration of women in jobs as domestic servants, factory operatives, needlewomen, agricultural workers and those employed in domestic industries (ibid., p. 315). Harriet Martineau reports in 1859 that two out of six million British women worked for pay and earned enough to be economically independent (Yates, 1985). For the sex segregation of the English labour market in the nineteenth century, see also Groenewegen (1994, p. 8).
7. Four international UN women's conferences would take place: in Mexico City (1975), Copenhagen (1980), Nairobi (1985) and Beijing (1995) (see, e.g., Pietilä, 2002).
8. The most common misunderstandings about feminist economics are that it consists of a group of economists with a shared political agenda, or a group of economists with a shared economic theory like Marxists or institutionalists, or a women's-only group that analyses the economy from a woman's perspective. There are groups of feminist economists who can be characterized as such, but the field as such cannot be defined in this way.
9. 'Gender can be defined as an *asymmetrical* category of human thought, social organization, and individual identity and behavior' (Harding, 1986, p. 55, emphasis as in original). Gender is also an important means to reproducing power relations (see, e.g., Scott, 1986, p. 1067).
10. See Kuiper and Barker (2006) for an extensive discussion of this report.
11. The first Gender Budget Initiative was conducted by the Government of Australia, which produced a Women's Budget Statement in 1984, and annually from 1987 (Elson, 2006; see also Sharp and Broomhill, 2002). In 1994 civil society in South Africa worked with Parliamentarians investigating the allocation of resources over (programmes for) women and men and their effectivity (Budlender and Sharp, 1998).
12. In 1997 the UN reported on *The Role of Microcredit in the Eradication of Poverty* that 'by providing opportunities for self-employment, many studies have concluded that these programmes have significantly increased women's security, autonomy, self-confidence and status within the household' (UN, 1997, p. 19). Whereas the successes for the extremely poor are more ambiguous, there is a widespread agreement about their success in helping the poor improve their situation, although some are more critical (see, e.g., Rankin, 2002).

References

Agarwal, Bina (1997), ' "Bargaining" and gender relations: within and beyond the household', *Feminist Economics*, **3** (1), 1–51.
Aidis, Ruta, Friederieke Welter, David Smallbone and Nina Isakove (2007), 'Female entrepreneurship in transition economics: the case of Lithuania and Ukraine', *Feminist Economics*, **13** (2), 157–83.
Akkerman, Tjitske and Siep Stuurman (eds) (1998), *Perspectives on Feminist Political Thought in European History: From the Middle Ages to the Present*, London and New York: Routledge.
Astell, Mary (1694) *A Serious Proposal to the Ladies, for the Advancement of their True and Greatest Interest*, Part I, 4th edn, London: R. Wilkin.
Astell, Mary (1700), *Some Reflections Upon Marriage, Occasion'd by the Duke and Dutchess of Mazarine's Case; Which is also considered*, London.
Barker, Drucilla K. and Edith Kuiper (eds) (2003), *Toward a Feminist Philosophy of Economics*, London and New York: Routledge.
Bebel, August (1879), *Woman in the Past, Present & Future*, London: Zwan Publications.
Becker, Gary (1981), *A Treatise on the Family*, Cambridge, MA: Harvard University Press.
Beneria, Lourdes (1995), 'Towards a greater integration of gender in economics', *World Development*, **23** (11), 1839–50.
Beneria, Lourdes (2003), 'Economic rationality and globalization: a feminist perspective', in M.A. Ferber and J.A. Nelson (eds), *Feminist Economics Today: Beyond Economic Man*, Chicago, IL: University of Chicago Press, pp. 115–33.

Bergeron, Suzanne (2006), 'Colonizing knowledge: economics and interdisciplinarity in engendering development', in Edith Kuiper and Drucilla K. Barker (eds), *Feminist Economics and the World Bank*, London and New York: Routledge, pp. 127–41.

Bergmann, Barbara (1986), *The Economic Emergence of Women*, New York: Basic Books.

Blau, Francine, Marianne A. Ferber and Anne E. Winkler (2002), *The Economics of Women, Men and Work*, 4th edn, Englewood Cliffs, NJ: Prentice-Hall.

Bodkin, Ronald G. (1999), 'Women's agency in classical economic thought: Adam Smith, Harriet Taylor Mill, and J.S. Mill', *Feminist Economics*, **5** (1), 45–60.

Bordo, Susan (1987), *The Flight to Objectivity: Essays on Cartesianism and Culture*, Albany, NY: State University of New York Press.

Boserup, Esther (1970), *Women's Role in Economic Development*, London: Gower.

Budlender, Debbie and Rhonda Sharp (1998), *How to do a Gender-sensitive Budget Analysis: Contemporary Research and Practice*, London: Commonwealth Secretariat.

Cadbury, Edward, M. Cecile Matheson and George Shann (1907), *Women's Work and Wages: A Phase of Life in an Industrial City*, Chicago: University of Chicago Press.

Cantillon, Sara and Brian Nolan (2001), 'Poverty within households: measuring gender differences using nonmonetary indicators', *Feminist Economics*, **7** (1), 5–23.

Cagatay, Nilufer, Diane Elson and Caren Grown (1995), 'Introduction', *World Development*, **23** (11), 1827–36.

Cole, Margaret (1946), *Beatrice Webb 1858–1943*, New York: Harcourt Brace.

Collier, Mary (1739), *The Woman's Labour*, available on Internet: http://duke.usask.ca/~vargo/barbauld/related_texts/collier.html (accessed 31 January 2007).

Danby, Colin (2004), 'Toward a gendered Post Keynesianism: subjectivity and time in a non-modernist framework', *Feminist Economics*, **10** (3), 55–75.

Dijkstra, A. Geske and Lucia C. Hanmer (2000), 'Measuring socio-economic gender inequality: toward an alternative to the UNDP Gender-Related Development Index', *Feminist Economics*, **6** (2), 41–75.

Dimand, Mary Ann, Robert Dimand and Evelyn L. Forget (eds) (1995), *Women of Value: Feminist Essays on the History of Women in Economics*, Aldershot, UK and Brookfield, USA: Edward Elgar.

Dimand, Robert and Chris Nyland (eds) (2003), *The Status of Women in Classical Economic Thought*, Cheltenham, UK and Northampton, MA, USA: Edward Elgar.

Dimand, Robert, Mary Ann Dimand and Evelyn L. Forget (2000), *A Biographical Dictionary of Women Economists*, Cheltenham, UK and Northampton, MA, USA: Edward Elgar.

Ellis, Markman (2001), 'Coffee-women, "The Spectator" and the public sphere in the early eighteenth century', in E. Eger, C. Grant, C.Ó. Gallchoir and P. Warburton (eds), *Women, Writing and the Public Sphere 1700–1830*, Cambridge: Cambridge University Press, pp. 27–52.

Elson, Diane (1991), *Male Bias in the Development Process*, Manchester: Manchester University Press.

Elson, Diane (1995), 'Gender awareness in modelling structural adjustment', *World Development*, **23** (11), 1851–68.

Elson, Diane (2006), *Budgeting for Women's Rights*, New York: United Nations Development Fund for Women (UNIFEM).

Elson, Diane and Nilifur Cagatay (2000), 'The social content of macroeconomic policies', *World Development*, **28** (7), 1347–64.

Engels, Friedrich (1884 [1985]), *The Origin of the Family, Private Property and the State*, London: Penguin.

Ferber, Marianne A. and Julie A. Nelson (1993), *Beyond Rational Man*, Chicago, IL: University of Chicago Press.

Ferber, Marianne A. and Julie A. Nelson (2003), *Feminist Economics Today: Beyond Economic Man*, Chicago, IL: University of Chicago Press.

Folbre, Nancy (1992), ' "The Improper Arts": Sex in Classical Political Economy', *Population and Development Review*, **18** (1), 105–21.

Folbre, Nancy (1994), *Who Pays for the Kids?*, London New York: Routledge.

Forget, Evelyn (1999), *The Social Economics of Jean-Baptiste Say: Markets and Virtue*, London and New York: Routledge.

Forget, Evelyn (2001), 'Saint-Simonian Feminism', *Feminist Economics*, **7** (1), 79–96.

Forget, Evelyn (2003), 'The market of virtue: Jean-Baptiste Say on women in the economy and society', in Robert Dimand and Chris Nyland (eds) (2003), *The Status of Women in Classical Economic Thought*, Cheltenham, UK and Northampton, MA, USA: Edward Elgar, pp. 206–23.

Goldschmidt-Clermont, Louise (1982), *Unpaid Work in the Household*, Geneva: International Labour Organization.

Goldschmidt-Clermont, Louise (1987), *Economic Evaluations of Unpaid Household Work: Africa, Asia, Latin America and Oceania*, Geneva: International Labour Organization.

Gouges, Olympe de (1791[1989]), *Verklaring van de Rechten van de Vrouw en Burgeress* (Declaration of the Rights of Woman and Citizenship), Kampen: Kok Agora.

Groenewegen, Peter (ed.) (1994), 'Introduction', in Peter Groenewegen (ed.), *Feminism and Political Economy in Victorian England*, Aldershot, UK and Brookfield, USA: Edward Elgar.

Groenewegen, Peter and Susan King (1994), 'Women as producers of economics articles: a statistical assessment of the nature and the extent of female participation in five British and North American journals 1900–39', University of Sydney Working Papers in Economics, No. 201.

Grouchy, Sophie de, Marquise de Condorcet (1798), 'Lettres à C[abanis], sur la Théorie des sentiments moraux', in Adam Smith, *Théorie des sentiments moraux*, translated from the 7th edn [1792] by Sophie de Grouchy, Marquise de Condorcet, Paris: F. Buisson.

Habermas, Jürgen (1962), *Strukturwandel der Öffentlicheit*, Darmstadt and Neuwied: Herman Luchterhand Verlag; *The Structural Transformation of the Public Sphere: An Inquiry into a Category of Bourgeois Society*, trans. Thomas Burger, Cambridge: Polity Press, 1989.

Harding, Sandra (1986), *The Science Question in Feminism*, Ithaca, NY: Cornell University Press.

Harding, Sandra (1987), 'Conclusion: epistemological questions', in S. Harding (ed.), *Feminism and Methodology*, Bloomington, IN: Indiana University Press.

Harding, Sandra (1995), 'Can feminist thought make economics more objective?', *Feminist Economics*, **1** (1), 17–32.

Hausman, Daniel M. (1992), *The Inexact and Separate Science of Economics*, Cambridge: Cambridge University Press.

Hewitson, Gilian (1999), *Feminist Economics: Interrogating the Masculinity of Rational Economic Man*, Cheltenham, UK and Northampton, MA, USA: Edward Elgar.

Himmelweit, Susan (2003), 'An evolutionary approach to feminist economics: two different models of caring', in Drucilla K. Barker and Edith Kuiper (eds) (2003), *Toward a Feminist Philosophy of Economics*, London and New York: Routledge, pp. 247–65.

Holcombe, Lee (1983), *Wives & Property. Reform of the Married Women's Property Law in Nineteenth-Century England*, Toronto and Buffalo: University of Toronto Press.

Jacobsen, Joyce (1998), *The Economics of Gender*, 2nd edn, Malden, MA: Blackwell.

Jacobsen, Joyce (2003), 'Some implications of the feminist project in economics for empirical methodology', in Drucilla K. Barker and Edith Kuiper (eds), *Toward a Feminist Philosophy of Economics*, London and New York: Routledge, pp. 89–104.

Kelley, Joan (1984), *Women, History and Theory: The Essays of Joan Kelly*, Chicago, IL and London: The University of Chicago Press.

Keller, Evelyn Fox (1987), *Reflections on Gender and Science*, New Haven, CT: Yale University Press.

Kim, Marlene (1997), 'Poor women survey poor women: feminist perspectives in survey research', *Feminist Economics*, **3** (2), 99–117.

Kuiper, Edith (2001), *The Most Valuable of All Capital: A Gender Reading of Economic Texts*, Amsterdam: Thela Thesis.

Kuiper, Edith and Drucilla K. Barker (eds) (2006), *Feminist Economics and the World Bank*, London and New York: Routledge.

Kuiper, Edith and Jolande Sap with Notburga Ott, Susan F. Feiner and Zafiris Tzannatos (eds) (1995), *Out of the Margin: Feminist Perspectives on Economics*, New York and London: Routledge.

Lambert, Anne Thérèse de (1748), *Oeuvres de Madame la marquise de Lambert*, Amsterdam.
Lerner, Gerda (1993), *The Creation of Feminist Consciousness: From the Middle Ages to Eighteen-seventy*, New York and Oxford: Oxford University Press.
Longino, Helen (1990), *Science as Social Knowledge*, Princeton, NJ: Princeton University Press.
MacLennan, Barbara (2001), 'Finance, gender and structural change in the European union', in Lars Magnusson and Bo Strath (eds), *From the Werner Plan to the EMU: In Search of a Political Economy for Europe*, Brussels: P.I.E.–Peter Lang.
Madden, Kristen K., Janet A. Seiz and Michèle Pujol (2004), *A Bibliography of Female Economic Thought to 1940*, London and New York: Routledge.
Marshall, Alfred (1890 [1930]) *Principles of Economics*, 8th edn, London: Macmillan.
Mill, John Stuart (1869 [1970]) *The Subjection of Women*, London: MIT Press.
Mincer, Jacob (1962), 'The labor participation of married women', in H.G. Lewis (ed.), *Aspects of Labor Economics*, Princeton, NJ: Princeton University Press, pp. 63–97.
Nelson, Julie A. (1992), 'Gender, metaphor, and the definition of economics', *Economics & Philosophy*, **8** (1), 103–25.
Nelson, Julie A. (1993), 'The study of choice or the study of provisioning? Gender and the definition of economics', in Marianne A. Ferber and Julie A. Nelson (eds), *Beyond Economic Man*, Chicago, IL: University of Chicago Press, pp. 23–36.
Nelson, Julie A. (1995), 'Feminism and economics', *Journal of Economic Perspectives*, **9** (2), 131–48.
Nelson, Julie A. (2003), 'Separative and soluble firms: androcentric bias and business ethics', in M.A. Ferber and J.A. Nelson (eds) (2003), *Feminist Economics Today: Beyond Economic Man*, Chicago, IL: University of Chicago Press, pp. 81–99.
Noble, David F. (1992), *A World Without Women: The Christian Clerical Culture of Western Science*, New York and Oxford: Oxford University Press.
Nyland, Chris (2006), 'Women and the history of labour economics', paper presented at the IAFFE conference, 7 July, Sydney, Australia.
Offen, Karen (2000), *European Feminisms 1700–1950: A Political History*, Stanford, CA: Stanford University Press.
Olmsted, Jennifer (1997), 'Telling Palestinian women's economic stories', *Feminist Economics*, **3** (2), 141–51.
Ott, N. (1992), *Intrafamily Bargaining and Household Decisions*, New York: Springer.
Palm, Etta (1790), *Discourse on the Injustice of the Laws in Favour of Men, at the Expense of Women*, Paris.
Pencavel, John (1986), 'The labor supply of men. A survey', in O. Ashenfelter and R. Layard (eds), *Handbook of Labor Economics*, Amsterdam and New York: North-Holland, pp. 3–102.
Pepchinski, Mary (2000), 'The women's building and the world exhibitions: exhibition architecture and conflicting feminine ideals at European and American world exhibitions 1873–1915', accessed 9 August 2007, available at www.tu-cottbus.de/BTU/Fak2/TheoArch/wolke/eng/Subjects/001/Pepchinski/.
Peter, Fabienne (2003), 'Is critical realism a useful ontology for feminist economics?', *Feminist Economics*, **9** (1), 93–101.
Perkins Gilman, Charlotte (1898), *Women & Economics: A Study of the Economic Relation between Men and Women as a Factor in Social Evolution*, Boston, MA: Small, Maynard & Co. Reprinted with an introduction by Carl N. Degler, New York: Harper & Row, 1962.
Pietilä, Hilkka (2002), *Engendering the Global Agenda: The Story of Women and the United Nations*, Geneva: NGLS.
Pinchbeck, Ivy (1930 [1969]), *Women Workers and the Industrial Revolution 1750–1850*, London: Frank Cass & Co.
Poldervaart, Saskia (1993), *Tegen conventioneel fatsoen en zekerheid: Het uitdagende Feminisme van de utopisch socialisten (Against Conventional Prudence and Security: The Challenging Feminism of the Utopian Socialists)*, Amsterdam.
Pott-Buter, Hettie A. (1992), Facts and Fairy Tales about Female Labor, Family and *Fertility: A Seven Country Comparison 1850–1990*, Amsterdam: Amsterdam University Press.

Pujol, Michèle (1992), *Feminism and Anti-Feminism in Early Economic Thought*, Aldershot, UK and Brookfield, USA: Edward Elgar.

Pujol, Michèle (1995), 'Into the margin!', in E. Kuiper and J. Sap with N. Ott, S.F. Feiner and Z. Tzannatos (eds) (1995), *Out of the Margin: Feminist Perspectives on Economics*, New York and London: Routledge, pp. 17–34.

Pujol, Michèle (1997), 'Introduction. Broadening economic data and methods', *Feminist Economics*, **3** (2), 119–20.

Rankin, Katharine N. (2002), 'Social capital, microfinance, and the politics of development', *Feminist Economics*, **8** (1), 1–24.

Rumnska-Zimny, Ewa (2003), 'Women's entrepreneurship and labour market trends in transition countries', in United Nations, *Women's Entrepreneurship in Eastern Europe and CIS Countries*, New York and Geneva: UNECE.

Scott, Joan (1986), 'Gender: a useful category of historical analysis', *The American Historical Review*, **91** (5), 1053–75.

Scott, Joan (1989), *Gender and the Politics of History*, New York: Columbia University Press.

Seguino, Stephanie (2006), 'Taking gender differences in bargaining power seriously: equity, labor standard, and living wages', in Edith Kuiper and Drucilla K. Barker (eds) (2006), *Feminist Economics and the World Bank*, London and New York: Routledge, pp. 94–116.

Singh, Ajit and Ann Zammit (2000), 'International capital flows: identifying the gender dimension', *World Development*, **28** (7), 1249–68.

Seiz, Janet (1992), 'Gender and economic research', in Neil de Marchi (ed.), *Post-Popperian Methodology of Economics: Recovering Practice*, Boston, MA: Kluwer, pp. 273–319.

Seiz, Janet (1993), 'Feminism and the history of economic thought', *History of Political Economy*, **25** (1), 185–201.

Seiz, Janet (1995), 'Epistemology and the tasks of feminist economics', *Feminist Economics*, **1** (3), 110–18.

Shah, Sumitra (2006), 'Sexual division of labour in Adam Smith's work', *Journal of the History of Economic Thought*, **28** (2), 221–41.

Sharp, Rhonda and Ray Broomhill (2002), 'Budgeting for equality: the Australian experience', *Feminist Economics*, **8** (1), 25–47

Strober, Mary (1994), 'Rethinking economics through a feminist lens', *American Economic Review*, **84** (2), 143–7.

Sturkenboom, Dorothee (2004), *De elektrieke kus: Over vrouwen, fysica en vriendschap in de 18e en 19e eeuw (The Electric Kiss: On Women, Physics and Friendship in the 18th and 19th Century)*, Amsterdam: Augustus.

Thompson, William and Anna Doyle Wheeler (1825), Appeal of *one half* the *human race, women, against* the *pretensions* of the *other half, men* to *retain them* in *political* and *thence* in *civil* and *domestic slavery*, London: Longman.

Thomson, Dorothy L. (1978), *Adam Smith's Daughters*, New York: Exposition Press.

Tristan, Flora (1843), *Union ouvrière*, Paris: Prévot, translation with introduction by Beverly Livingston, The Workers' Union, Urbana, IL and London: University of Illinois Press, 1989.

United Nations Development Programme (1995), *Human Development Report 1995. Gender and Human Development*, New York: Oxford University Press.

UNIFEM (2006) *Gender Responsive Budgeting in Practice: A Manual*, New York: UNIFEM.

United Nations (UN) (1997), *The Role of Microcredit in the Eradication of Poverty*, Washington, DC: Oxford University Press.

United Nations Department of Economics and Social Affairs (2006), *The World's Women 2005: Progress in Statistics*, New York: UNDESA.

UN Research Institute for Social Development (2005), *Gender Equality: Striving for Justice in an Unequal World*, Geneva, Switzerland.

Wakefield, Priscilla (1798), *Reflections on the Present Condition of the Female Sex, with Suggestions for Its Improvement*, London: J. Johnson and Darton & Harvey.

Waring, Marilyn (1988), *If Women Counted: A New Feminist Economics*, with an introduction by Gloria Steinem, New York: HarperCollins.

Wollstonecraft, Mary (1792), *A Vindication of the Rights of Women*, London: J. Johnson.

World Bank (2001), *Engendering Development: Through Gender Equality in Rights, Resources, and Voice*, New York: Oxford University Press.
Yates, Gayle Graham (ed.) (1985), *Harriet Martineau on Women*, New Brunswick, NJ: Rutgers University Press.
Zein-Elabdin, Eiman O. and S. Charusheela (2004), *Postcolonialism meets Economics*, New York and London: Routledge.

PART IV

GROWTH AND (IN-)EQUALITY

Chapter 13: 'Income distribution and inequality', by Frank A. Cowell
What are the principal issues on which research on income distribution and inequality focus? How might that focus shift in the immediate future? We examine the standard market-based approaches to theorizing on the income distribution and the challenges to this analysis posed by the economics of information and various types of market failure. We also consider the problems of representing the income distribution in a way that has economic meaning and of comparing distributions in terms of inequality and social welfare. There is also a snapshot view of some of the remarkable empirical developments concerning the income distribution in advanced countries in the late twentieth and early twenty-first centuries.

Chapter 14: 'The social economics of growth and income inequality', by Morris Altman
Ethical behaviour and an economic growth theory are integrated into an analytical framework building upon conventional economic theory and the insights of Adam Smith, Richard Ely and John Ryan. The social economics of growth requires a rigorous theory of growth framed in a fashion that allows one to address and evaluate the impact of ethical behaviour upon the economy and socio-economic well-being. Of vital importance is the end-game of the growth process in terms of how growth affects all members of society and whether it constitutes consistent ethical behaviour, and whether such behaviour is by necessity of the market exceptional or inevitable. The modelling framework discussed suggests that ethical behaviours are both consistent with and contribute to vigorous economic growth. However, for ethical behaviours to dominate requires a conducive institutional environment, and a high level of democratic governance in the context of a competitive economic environment, one where, as Adam Smith recognized, there is balance in the power relationship between servant and master.

13 Income distribution and inequality
Frank A. Cowell

The produce of the earth – all that is derived from its surface by the united application of labour, machinery, and capital, is divided among three classes of the
community; namely, the proprietor of the land, the owner of the stock or
capital necessary for its cultivation, and the labourers by whose industry it is cul-
tivated. . . . To determine the laws which regulate this distribution, is the principal problem in Political Economy. (David Ricardo, *On The Principles of Political
Economy and Taxation*. London: John Murray, 1817 (3rd edn 1821))

1. Introduction

The central place that Ricardo accorded the subject of income distribution
in nineteenth century political economy is appropriate also in twenty-
first-century socio-economics. Although the field was relatively neglected
by economists for several decades, in the last 15 years there has been a resurgence of interest driven partly by developments in economic theory and
partly by major developments in the interpersonal income distributions
within many developed countries (Atkinson, 1997).

In recent years the subject of economic inequality has developed in such
a way as to have a life of its own separate from the obvious connection with
the distribution of income, the distribution of wealth, the structure of
wages and other related empirical topics. This distinct area of study has
been built upon new insights in welfare economics and on the relationship
to information theory (Cowell, 2000; Sen and Foster, 1997).

Our treatment of this pair of subjects is organized as follows. Section 3
examines the ways in which economic analysis has attempted to explain what
drives income distribution; in Section 4 we look at ways of analysing the personal income distribution as a prelude to a more thorough consideration of
inequality (Section 5); Section 6 looks at new directions in which the analysis
may proceed. But first let us briefly think about the main focus of our subject.

2. Income

Why the focus on *income* rather than some other measurable quantity? In
many treatments of the subject income plays one of two roles, sometimes
both:

- *Income as a proxy for economic welfare.* If one adopts an individualistic, welfarist approach to social economics, then it is reasonable to

be concerned with individual well-being or utility. In some respects the flow of income captures this, but it has been argued that consumption expenditure may be a more appropriate economic indicator (Blundell and Preston, 1998).[1] It should also be acknowledged that individual well-being may be determined not only by the level of one's own income but also by its relation to the incomes of others (Ferrer-i-Carbonell, 2005).

- *Income as command over resources.* This role of income can be interpreted in more than one way. If one has in mind spending power, then perhaps disposable income (income after taxes and compulsory deductions?) may be an appropriate concept. But if 'inequality' is associated with economic power and status, then a measure of wealth may be more appropriate.

The focus on income as conventionally defined clearly has shortcomings. An uncritical use of income in either of the above roles may neglect questions of time (people's incomes often change systematically over their lifetime) and of risk (people's incomes often change erratically in the short run): more sophisticated income concepts can be used that take account of these factors, but it is harder to get reliable data to estimate them. Also left open are important theoretical and practical questions: for each type of income one needs to be clear about who or what the 'income receiver' is (a single person? a family or household? a firm? a taxpayer?); particular care must be taken when using standard data sources to make international comparisons (Atkinson and Brandolini, 2001).

3.   Economics and income distribution

In economic analysis 'income distribution' is interpreted in two principal ways: the functional distribution of income (i.e. the distribution of income among factors) and the size distribution of income (or distribution of income among persons).

We briefly deal with the way each of these is conventionally handled in economics, focusing on the forces that determine the shape of the income distribution (Section 3.1). Then, in Section 3.2, we look at challenges to the orthodoxy and the way these challenges have enhanced our understanding of the analysis of income distribution in recent years.

3.1   *The standard approach*

Functional distribution   The functional distribution of income is an integral part of the economic analysis of relative prices, output and employment. In this sense there are several theories of income distribution corresponding to different theoretical and ideological stances on these central issues. However, these various analyses usually focus on the same basic economic concepts: employment of the factors of production – land, labour and capital – and the rates of remuneration of their services – rent, wages and profit.

The conventional approach is to treat questions of distribution as part of the neoclassical analysis of prices and resource allocation in a story such as the following. A competitive firm takes the price it can get for its output and the prices it must pay for inputs as given in the market: it selects its level of output and adjusts its demand for inputs so as to maximize profits at those prices; each household takes as given the prices paid to it for the labour services supplied by members of the household just as it takes as given the prices to be paid for goods and services it needs. It adjusts the quantities of the goods and services demanded or supplied in the market so as to maximize satisfaction within the limitations imposed by its budget. In this story prices adjust so as to ensure equilibrium in all markets: equilibrium means that aggregate supply of each commodity is at least as great as aggregate demand. In particular factor income, the reward for each type of labour, each natural resource and capital asset is determined by its market-clearing price. So the functional distribution of income – the issue referred to directly by Ricardo in the epigraph – is in this way automatically determined by the market mechanism. Shocks to the system – for example changes in the stock of natural resources, or a shift in the preference patterns of consumers – will change the income distribution through this mechanism as prices adjust to new equilibrium levels.

Personal distribution   The distribution of income between persons or between households can be fitted into the above scenario. Key decisions that determine incomes in the long run can each be analysed as particular cases of the household's optimization problem: household saving, self-investment in human capital or the purchase of education for children are determined by price signals. To complete the theory of income distribution within this framework one also needs a description of the system of property rights that prevails within the community. The question of who owns the natural resources, the capital equipment and the profits of the firms is central to the determination of household incomes: household budgets are jointly determined by market prices and property rights, and will be affected by a change in the pattern or system of ownership.

However, more is required to complete the personal income distribution story. In order to draw conclusions about the distribution of income in the long run one also needs to consider the evolution of property rights across the generations (Piketty, 2000). This will depend, among other things, on how families are formed (do the rich predominantly marry the rich?[2] do the poor have more children?), on the motives for bequeathing wealth to the next generation (do parents compensate disadvantaged children? is the amount bequeathed the outcome of dynastic optimization or largely a matter of chance?[3]) and the role of the state through taxation (Cremer and Pestieau, 2006).

3.2   Challenges and developments

The orthodox neoclassical story outlined in Section 3.1 has been called into question on account of its restrictive assumptions concerning the economic processes involved. Because these assumptions are central to the theory rather than being merely convenient simplifications, many economists have questioned the relevance of various aspects of the standard account of income distribution. We briefly mention three points of focus.

The role of prices   The predominant interest of the neoclassical orthodox theory of income distribution in smooth adjustments to market-clearing equilibria may be inappropriate to a theory of the functional distribution of income. As a response to this, economists who are strongly influenced by Keynes's approach to macroeconomics have developed a number of alternative theories of the functional distribution of income using components of the Keynesian system, for example the work of Kaldor (1955) and Pasinetti (1962). Key features of such alternative theories are rule-of-thumb savings decisions by capitalists and workers, and a rigid technique by which labour and capital are combined to produce output; they play a role in some of the modern theory of growth and its relationship to factor incomes (Bertola, 1993).

Monopoly power   The standard theory neglects barriers to competition and monopoly power as of secondary importance in the competitive market story. Restraints on competition – in the form of segmentation of the labour market and outright discrimination – are of major importance in analysing the lower tail of the size distribution of earnings; and monopoly power may be particularly important in the upper tail, for example in the determination of earnings in professions with restricted entry. Monopolistic pricing by firms has also been seen as of prime importance in the functional distribution of income (Kalecki, 1939): such power plays an important part in the Marxian concept of exploitation and in distribution theories based on struggle between classes representing different factors of production. The assumption of competition is also likely to be inadequate in analysing economics that have a substantial public sector.

Modern treatments of the labour market take seriously the problem of monopsony by powerful firms in determining labour incomes and the potential role for a minimum wage (Manning, 2003).

Information   The standard story in Section 3.1 assumes effectively perfect information on the part of economic agents. However, uncertainty is itself a potent force generating inequality in both labour income and income from assets, in that the rich not only are better able to bear risk but also may have superior information which can be exploited in the stock market and the labour market. Moreover, some of the barriers to competition may have been erected by firms in response to uncertainty. Hence considerable interest has developed in the distributional implications of theories of output, employment and the structure of wages that explicitly incorporate imperfect information, in particular screening and signalling, phenomena that may result in equilibrium income inequality (Salanié, 1997). Because of imperfect information it is in the interest of economic agents to make use of social networks formed from social contacts which may also buttress equilibrium (Ioannides and Loury, 2004; Manski, 2000).

4.   The personal distribution

4.1   *Representations of income distribution*
We first examine the problems of depicting and interpreting the personal income distribution; then we briefly consider the merits of formal modelling.

Statistical tools   To present the bald facts about income inequality one could just draw an empirical frequency distribution (histogram). But it is worth considering two other presentations of the data that have become familiar in the literature; we shall illustrate the techniques using readily available tax data from the USA.

The background story for the first presentation is eloquently set out in Pen (1974).[4] Imagine that each person's height were in proportion to his income and that the entire population were to file past in a parade that lasted exactly one hour. If we do this thought experiment for the USA, then the picture that emerges is that shown in Figure 13.1.[5] It is clear that this is just the inverse of the conventional distribution function F: if x is income, then $p = F(x)$ gives the proportion of the population with incomes less than or equal to x and Figure 13.1 just plots x against p. One standard feature of empirical income distributions emerges clearly from the diagram: the dotted line depicts the position of the person with average income ($48 889) and it is clear that this is more than two-thirds along in the parade (so that the mean is substantially greater than the median).

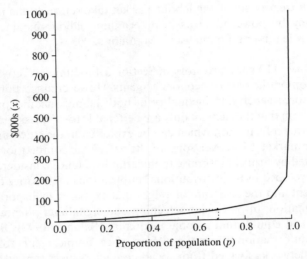

Figure 13.1   Parade diagram: US income before tax, 2003

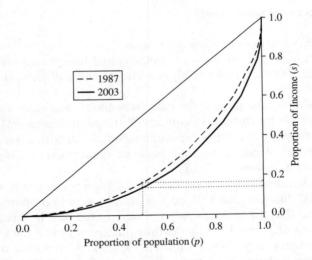

Figure 13.2   Lorenz diagram: US income before tax, 1987 and 2003

The second standard presentation is shown (using the same data source) in Figure 13.2. The horizontal axis is just as for Figure 13.1: on the vertical axis is plotted s, the income shares of the population. The Lorenz curve (Lorenz, 1905) is a graph of income shares against population shares for a

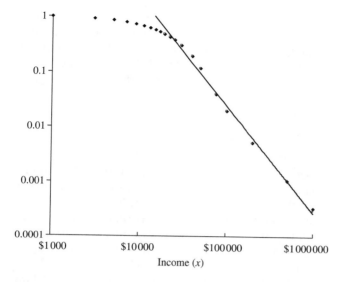

Figure 13.3   Pareto diagram: US pre-tax income, 2003 (α = 1.95)

particular distribution so that a particular (p, s) point can be read as 'the bottom $100p$ per cent of the population receive $100s$ per cent of total income'.[6] It is clear that this graph captures an intuitive concept of inequality comparison: to see this, Figure 13.2 also includes the corresponding graph for 1987; note that the share of the bottom 50 per cent of the population $(p = 0.5)$ in 2003 is unambiguously less than in 1987 and that the same conclusion would have been obtained if we had chosen any other p-value; so according to this 'shares ranking' income seems to be more unequally distributed in 2003 than in 1987. One might wonder whether the intuition could or should be formalized: this point is taken up in Section 5 below.

Modelling the distribution   Once one considers anything beyond the simplest example of interpersonal income distribution there is a strong temptation to find some way of simplifying the representation of the distribution and its associated inequality. One way of doing this is to use a parametric model – in other words a suitable *functional form*, where 'suitability' is interpreted as meaning that the salient features of the empirical distribution are captured. There are several candidate functional forms borrowed from statistics including the log-normal, beta and gamma distributions (Cowell, 2008; Kleiber and Kotz, 2003), but of particular interest is Pareto's (1965) insight, all the more remarkable since it was based on the limited data available at the end of the nineteenth century. Figure 13.3

presents the same information as that presented in Figure 13.1 but now it plots $1 - F(x)$ against income x, each on a logarithmic scale. A naked-eye inspection suggests that the points where x is at least \$50 000 lie almost on a straight line, as shown.[7] If one accepts the straight-line representation on this diagram for $x \geq x_0$ where $x_0 := \$50\,000$, then in this income range we have

$$F(x) = 1 - \left[\frac{x}{x_0}\right]^\alpha$$

where the parameter α is the slope of the fitted line in Figure 13.3.

Clearly the advantage of this is that the complexity of the distribution is reduced to a single parameter α – the lower is the value of this parameter, the 'fatter' is the tail of the associated frequency distribution and, in some sense, the higher is the inequality displayed by the distribution. Some of the disadvantages are obvious: no attempt is made to capture information from the bottom end of the income distribution, the estimate of α may be quite sensitive to the statistical method employed (Cowell and Victoria-Feser, 2007) and the use of α as an indicator of 'equality' is based on nothing stronger than an informal impressionistic argument.

From the time of Pareto's discovery of this relationship (1896) there has been interest in whether it somehow characterizes a 'law' of income distribution – whether the straight-line approximation described above is generally a good one (it is) and whether it is reasonable to assume that across countries there is a natural tendency for α to approach one particular value (it isn't) (Persky, 1992).

4.2 Income distribution: recent developments

A renewed interest in income distribution has developed because of the recent history of the personal income distribution. After several decades of apparent stasis from the late 1970s onwards there has been a remarkable increase in the dispersion of incomes in many countries. Figure 13.4 (taken from Piketty and Saez, 2003) demonstrates one aspect of the situation for the case of the USA:[8] this charts the shares of the topmost income receivers over the twentieth century.

The apparent secular increase in inequality is in both income derived from assets (note the role played by capital gains in this) and in labour income. This latter component has been driven by a recent increased dispersion of wage rates in industrialized countries (Gottschalk and Smeeding, 1997, 2000); explanations for this remarkable phenomenon have been sought in the effects of technological advances on wage dispersion via productivity growth (Acemoglu, 2002; Blau and Kahn, 1996; Goldin and Katz, 1996; Krueger, 1993; DiNardo and Pischke, 1997) and in the effects

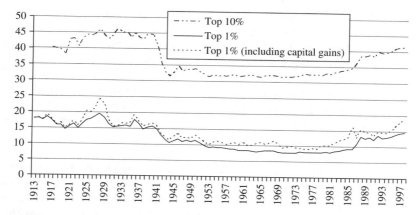

Figure 13.4   Top income shares in the USA, 1913–97

of international trade (Burtless, 1995; Krugman and Venables, 1995; Marjit and Acharyya, 2003; Richardson, 1995).

5.   Inequality

To pass from the description and analysis of income distribution to a systematic consideration of inequality one needs to address a number of questions about the value judgments implicit in inequality comparisons and a number of ethical and practical questions associated with the use of an inequality measure.

5.1   Connections with income distribution

Values   Perhaps the overriding question is, why one should be concerned with inequality? The standard answer is that it is rooted in an ethical approach to distributional questions (Sen and Foster, 1997). Further, social values are in turn related to individual concerns and views: people care about distributional fairness and they reveal a concern for fairness through their behaviour in experimental settings (Charness and Rabin, 2002; Fehr and Fischbacher, 2002, 2003); to some extent a concern for fairness is also revealed in surveys (Inglehart et al., 2004).

A fundamental concept that is usually applied in inequality comparisons captures an element of this fairness-in-distribution point. The *transfer principle* (Dalton, 1920) states the following: take an *n*-person income distribution $(x_1, x_2, \ldots, x_n)$ where x_i is the income of person *i*; for any *i* and *j* among these *n* persons consider the distribution formed by transferring a small amount of income δ from *i* to *j* (so x_i is replaced by $x_i - δ$ and x_j is replaced by $x_j + \delta$); then, if $x_i < x_j$, the income distribution must become more unequal, if $x_i > x_j$, the income distribution must become less unequal. We have seen a glimpse of this principle in the representation of the income distribution using the Lorenz curve (Figure 13.2): one can imagine the 2003 distribution being 'created' from the 1987 distribution by a series of poorer-to-richer transfers that successively reduce the income shares of the poorer members of the community; this implies that the 2003 distribution (outer Lorenz curve) must exhibit greater inequality than the 1987 distribution (inner Lorenz curve) (Atkinson, 1970).

Measurement   Why should one be interested in inequality *measurement*? One good answer is that the 'shares ranking' outlined in Section 4.1 is limited as a practical tool: the type of clear-cut conclusion drawn from Figure 13.2 ('2003 is more unequal than 1987') is not always possible because in many instances the relevant Lorenz curves intersect; to resolve the apparent ambiguity in the Lorenz comparison a summary numerical value for each Lorenz curve is sought. An appealing intuitive way of doing this is to take the area trapped between the Lorenz curve and the equality line in Figure 13.2: the normalized value of this area[9] yields the *Gini coefficient*. Formally the Gini is defined as

$$\frac{1}{2n^2 \bar{x}} \sum_{i=1}^{n} \sum_{j=1}^{n} |x_i - x_j|, \qquad (13.1)$$

where $\bar{x} := \frac{1}{n}\sum_{i=1}^{n} x_i$ denotes mean income. The formula (13.1) provides another simple and natural interpretation: take all the possible pairs of income-receivers in society (i, j) and compute the absolute difference between their incomes – the Gini is a normalized average of those differences.

In view of this attractive solution to the measurement problem, the question arises, why not just use the Gini coefficient to quantify inequality and leave the matter there? There are two main points in reply. First, there are other perfectly good summary statistics that combine intuitive appeal with familiarity and simplicity of computation; for example, one could use the *coefficient of variation*

$$\sqrt{\frac{1}{n}\sum_{i=1}^{n}\left[\frac{x_i}{\bar{x}} - 1\right]^2}, \qquad (13.2)$$

which is obviously related to the variance; this and other intuitively reasonable measures may deserve to be considered alongside the Gini coefficient.[10] Second, it may be more appropriate to base inequality measurement on some sort of social evaluation of income distribution rather than just on personal intuition.

5.2 *Welfare economics and distribution*

In the context of income-distribution analysis social welfare can be represented as a value $W(x_1, x_2, \ldots, x_n)$, where W is a function with 'suitable' properties. It is commonly, though not universally, assumed that social welfare function W can be written in additive form so that the social welfare associated with a particular income distribution is given by

$$\sum_{i=1}^{n} u(x_i), \qquad (13.3)$$

where u is a 'social-evaluation function' that is increasing (so that more income for person i means higher social welfare) and strictly concave (so that a poorer-to-richer transfer will reduce W – the transfer principle again). An example of this type of function is given in Figure 13.5. Let us look at two important ways in which this apparatus is used.

Welfare dominance For the above special type of W-function there is a nice relationship with the Lorenz concept. For any distribution, construct the *Generalized Lorenz Curve* (GLC) by multiplying each income share by the mean of the distribution; then if the GLC for distribution A lies somewhere above and nowhere below the GLC for distribution B social welfare

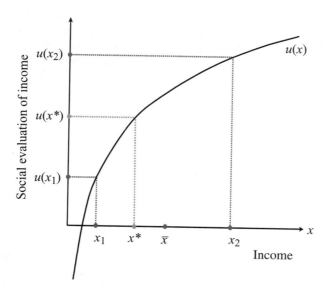

Figure 13.5   Social evaluation function u, *equally-distributed-equivalent income* x* *and mean income* x̄

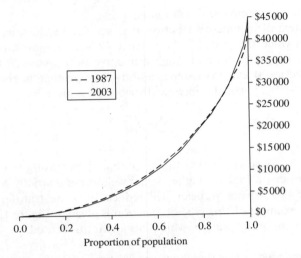

Figure 13.6   Generalized Lorenz diagram: US income before tax, 1987 and 2003 (in 2003 $)

must be higher in *A* than in *B* for *every* possible *W* of the above type (Shorrocks, 1983).

Figure 13.6 draws the GLCs for the US data that we used earlier: it is clear that the two curves intersect, but what does this mean? Both average income and inequality increased over 1987–2003; social welfare increased because of the first effect and decreased because of the second, but neither of the two effects dominates; different *W*s, corresponding to different specifications of *u* in (13.3), will yield different conclusions as to whether welfare rose (because of the growth in total income) or fell (because of the more unequal shares in total income).

Welfare-based inequality measurement   Find the income level which, if received by everyone, would yield the same level of social welfare. From (13.3) this is a number *x** such that

$$u(x^*) = \frac{1}{n}\sum_{i=1}^{n} u(x_i). \tag{13.4}$$

*x** is a effectively a dollar measure of social welfare and is illustrated in Figure 13.5, for a two-person income distribution (x_1, x_2). If x_1 and x_2 are moved further apart from each other, then clearly the gap between *x** and the mean $\bar{x}$ increases; so we could use the proportionate size of this gap, $1 - x^*/\bar{x}$, as an index of inequality. In the special case where *u* (*x*) takes the form $\frac{1}{1-\varepsilon}[x^{1-\varepsilon} - 1]$, this concept yields the class of *Atkinson indices* (Atkinson, 1970):

$$1 - \left[\frac{1}{n} \sum_{i=1}^{n} \left[\frac{x_i}{\bar{x}} \right]^{1-\varepsilon} \right]^{\frac{1}{1-\varepsilon}}$$

(13.5)

The number ε, the degree of relative inequality aversion, is a parameter that characterizes individual members of the class of inequality and may take any positive value.[11] It encapsulates the imputed social values regarding inequality: at the limiting value of zero one is imputing complete indifference to inequality, so that social welfare is measured by mean income ($x^* = \bar{x}$); as successively higher values of ε are considered, we are imputing a higher premium on inequality and, for any given income distribution, the gap between x^* and $\bar{x}$ will increase.

To illustrate, suppose we calculate social welfare for the 1987 and 2003 income distribution data, taking this specific form of the social evaluation function u. We can do this using the equally distributed equivalent income x^*: for successively higher values of inequality aversion ε we will get lower values of x^* in each of the two years. The results are depicted in Figure 13.7: for low values of ε (close to indifference to inequality) welfare is clearly higher in 2003, reflecting the higher mean income in that year; but for higher values of ε (above about 0.76, where the curves cross) the premium being put on inequality is so high that welfare is counted as higher in 1987 than in 2003.

6. New directions?
Two broad channels show considerable promise for the immediate future of research on income distribution and inequality.

6.1 Data developments
The availability of new, reliable data sources almost inevitably has a stimulating effect on research. The development of micro-data on incomes in developing economies has facilitated not only the analysis of income distribution within each country concerned but the tricky question of meaningful international comparisons. It enables one to better address questions such as whether inequality is good for growth (Aghion et al., 1999) and the directions that the world distribution of income is taking (Sala-i-Martin, 2006).

However, as Figure 13.4 shows, significant improvements in data availability are not confined to developing countries. A renewed interest in the fine detail of the income distribution among the seriously rich has led to the synthesis of data from tax authorities that has added a new perspective

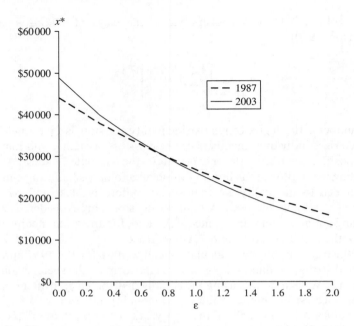

Figure 13.7   Social welfare for different degrees of inequality aversion: US income before tax, 1987 and 2003 (in 2003 $)

to international comparisons (Piketty, 2007); new work making available micro-data on wealth will also enhance understanding of what is going on in the upper tail of the income distribution (Sierminska et al., 2006).

6.2   Inequality and the basis for social intervention
The idea of inequality has long been associated with public policy prescriptions, addressing questions of whether more resources should be devoted to redistributive programmes, the meaning of tax progression and so on. For the last 35 years or so this literature has largely been based on essentially a welfarist approach to social judgements (Sen, 1979). Moreover, the particular form of welfarism has typically been rather narrow: the nature of inequality and of inequality aversion has been sought in a kind of social analogy with risk and risk aversion.

Recent years have seen a reappraisal of this theoretical underpinning. The analysis of preferences under uncertainty and of preferences has been developed to richer models than simple expected utility and to encompass broader concepts of risk aversion (Chateauneuf et al., 2004); this is leading to parallel developments in the treatment of the concept of inequality aversion (Chateauneuf and Moyes, 2000). Furthermore, the growing appreciation of the contribution of 'behavioural public economics' (Bernheim and Rangel, 2005) has led to a search for an understanding of social welfare criteria that are not based on simplistic models of individual rationality. Along with this a strong interest has developed in non-welfarist policy prescriptions that are based on broader criteria of fairness and that show appropriate concern for individual responsibility (Fleurbaey, 2008; Kanbur et al., 2006). This reappraisal has influenced thinking about the ethical basis of inequality analysis: Devooght (2008) has examined a responsibility-sensitive approach to income inequality and Cowell and Ebert (2004) have shown how alternative philosophical approaches to welfarism can be encapsulated in inequality measures that are related to concepts of deprivation.

These developments are likely to ensure that concerns with inequality will remain high on the socio-economics research agenda for some time to come.

Notes

1. Among other things, use of consumption data can avoid a number of difficult technical problems that arise from the presence in practice of zero and negative incomes.
2. See for example Fernández et al. (2005); Liu and Lu (2006).
3. See for example Arrondel and Laferrère (2001); Kopczuk and Lupton (2007).
4. Pen's story was originally told for the UK and for income distribution data from the 1960s. Nevertheless the central message is still valid for the twenty-first century and for other countries' data.
5. Source: http://www.irs.gov/taxstats/indtaxstats/article/0,,id=134951,00.html. Table 1.1–2003, Individual Income Tax Returns, Selected Income and Tax Items, by Size and Accumulated Size of Adjusted Gross Income. These data do not embody the ideal definition of income and income-receiver for welfare analysis (below) but they can be conveniently used to illustrate all the techniques presented here. The data have been truncated below to eliminate negative and zero incomes to provide a consistent distribution that can be used in all the presentation techniques covered below – Pen (1974) did not truncate his data, but used only the parade presentation.
6. Two points to note. (1) Because the population is implicitly arranged in ascending order of income, the graph must be increasing and convex and start from (0, 0). (2) If there were perfect equality, then everywhere we would have $p = s$ and the Lorenz curve would be a straight line; following convention this has been drawn in Figure 13.2.
7. For demonstration purposes this has been fitted using ordinary least squares (OLS) to the top 11 observations.
8. The increase in inequality shown by the shares ranking (Figure 13.2) is consistent with this: in contrast to Figure 13.2, which plots the income share s of the bottom p of the population, Figure 13.4 plots $1 - s$ (corresponding to the top $1 - p$ of the population) against time.
9. Normalization involves dividing this area by the area of the whole triangle, namely $\frac{1}{2}$. This is exactly the same as the formula given in 1.
10. Because different inequality measures encode different information about the income distribution, thay can give qualitatively different answers in cases where Lorenz curves intersect: it is not hard to find cases where the Gini indicates that distribution A is more unequal than distribution B, but that the coefficient of variation indicates the opposite.
11. The limiting form of u as $\varepsilon \to 1$ is $\log(x)$ and the limiting form of (13.5) as $\varepsilon \to 1$ is $1 - \exp((1/n)\Sigma_{i=1}^{n}\log(x/\mu))$.

References

Acemoglu, D. (2002), 'Technical change, inequality, and the labor market', *Journal of Economic Literature*, **40**, 7–72.

Aghion, P., E. Caroli and C. Garcia-Penalosa (1999), 'Inequality and economic growth: the perspectives of the new growth theories', *Journal of Economic Literature*, **37**, 1615–60.

Arrondel, L. and A. Laferrère (2001), 'Taxation and wealth transmission in France', *Journal of Public Economics*, **79**, 3–33.

Atkinson, A.B. (1970), 'On the measurement of inequality', *Journal of Economic Theory*, **2**, 244–63.

Atkinson, A.B. (1997), 'Bringing income distribution in from the cold', *The Economic Journal*, **107**, 297–321.

Atkinson, A.B. and A. Brandolini (2001), 'Promise and pitfalls in the use of secondary data-sets: income inequality in OECD countries as a case study', *Journal of Economic Literature*, **39**, 771–99.

Bernheim, B.D. and A. Rangel (2005), 'Behavioral public economics: welfare and policy analysis with non-standard decision makers', Working Paper 11518, National Bureau of Economic Research, http://www.nber.org/papers/w11518.

Bertola, G. (1993), 'Factor shares and savings in endogenous growth', *The American Economic Review*, **83**, 1184–98.

Blau, F.D. and L.M. Kahn (1996), 'International differences in male wage inequality: institutions versus market forces', *Journal of Political Economy*, **104** (4), 791–837.

Blundell, R. and I. Preston (1998), 'Consumption inequality and income uncertainty', *The Quarterly Journal of Economics*, **113**, 603–40.

Burtless, G. (1995), 'International trade and the rise in earnings inequality', *Journal of Economic Literature*, **33** (2), 800–816.

Charness, G. and M. Rabin (2002), 'Understanding social preferences with simple tests', *Quarterly Journal of Economics*, **117**, 817–69.

Chateauneuf, A., M. Cohen and I. Meilijson (2004), 'Four notions of mean-preserving increase in risk, risk attitudes and applications to the rank-dependent expected utility model', *Journal of Mathematical Economics*, **40**, 547–71.

Chateauneuf, A. and P. Moyes (2000), 'Inequality measurement and the weakening of the transfer principle', Technical Report, GRAPE.

Cowell, F.A. (2000), 'Measurement of inequality', in A.B. Atkinson and F. Bourguignon (eds), *Handbook of Income Distribution*, Amsterdam: North-Holland, pp. 87–166.

Cowell, F.A. (2008), *Measuring Inequality*, 3rd edn, Oxford: Oxford University Press.

Cowell, F.A. and U. Ebert (2004), 'Complaints and inequality', *Social Choice and Welfare*, **23**, 71–89.

Cowell, F.A. and M.-P. Victoria-Feser (2007), 'Robust stochastic dominance: a semi-parametric approach', *Journal of Economic Inequality*, **5**, 21–37.

Cremer, H. and P. Pestieau (2006), 'Wealth transfer taxation: a survey of the theoretical literature', in L.-A. Gérard-Varet, S.-C. Kolm and J. Mercier-Ythier (eds), *Handbook of the Economics of Giving, Reciprocity and Altruism*, Vol. 1, Amsterdam: North-Holland, pp. 1107–34.

Dalton, H. (1920), 'Measurement of the inequality of incomes', *The Economic Journal*, **30**, 348–61.

Devooght, K. (2008), 'To each the same and to each his own: a proposal to measure responsibility-sensitive income inequality', *Economica*, **74** (298), 280–95.

DiNardo, J. and J.-S. Pischke (1997), 'The returns to computer use revisited: have pencils changed the wage structure too?', *Quarterly Journal of Economics*, **112**, 291–303.

Fehr, E. and U. Fischbacher (2002), 'Why social preferences matter – the impact of non-selfish motives on competition, cooperation and incentives', *The Economic Journal*, **112**, C1–C33.

Fehr, E. and U. Fischbacher (2003), 'The nature of human altruism', *Nature*, **425**, 785–91.

Fernández, R., N. Guner and J. Knowles (2005), 'Love and money: a theoretical and empirical analysis of household sorting and inequality', *Quarterly Journal of Economics*, **120**, 273–344.

Ferrer-i-Carbonell, A. (2005), 'Income and well-being: an empirical analysis of the comparison income effect', *Journal of Public Economics*, **89**, 997–1019.

Fleurbaey, M. (2008), *Fairness, Responsibility and Welfare*, Oxford: Oxford University Press.

Goldin, C. and L.F. Katz (1996), 'Technology, skill, and the wage structure: insights from the past', *American Economic Review*, **86**, 252–7.

Gottschalk, P. and T.M. Smeeding (1997), 'Cross-national comparisons of earnings and income inequality', *Journal of Economic Literature*, **35**, 633–87.

Gottschalk, P. and T.M. Smeeding (2000), 'Empirical evidence on income inequality in industrialized countries', in A.B. Atkinson and F. Bourguignon (eds), *Handbook of Income Distribution*, Amsterdam: North-Holland, pp. 261–307.

Inglehart, R., M. Basáñez, J. Díez-Medrano, L. Halman and L. Luijkx (eds) (2004), *Human Beliefs and Values: A Cross-cultural Sourcebook based on the 1999–2002 Values Surveys*, Mexico: Siglo Veinteiuno.

Ioannides, Y.M. and L.D. Loury (2004), 'Job information networks, neighborhood effects, and inequality', *Journal of Economic Literature*, **42**, 1056–93.

Kaldor, N. (1955), 'Alternative theories of distribution', *The Review of Economic Studies*, **23**, 83–100.

Kalecki, M. (1939), *Essays in the Theory of Economic Fluctuations*, London: Allen & Unwin.

Kanbur, R., J. Pirttilä and M. Tuomala (2006), 'Non-welfarist optimal taxation and behavioural public economics', *Journal of Economic Surveys*, **20**, 849–68.

Kleiber, C. and S. Kotz (2003), *Statistical Size Distributions in Economics and Actuarial Sciences*, Hoboken, NJ: John Wiley.

Kopczuk, W. and J.P. Lupton (2007), 'To leave or not to leave: the distribution of bequest motives', *Review of Economic Studies*, **74**, 207–35.

Krueger, A.B. (1993), 'How computers have changed the wage structure: evidence from microdata', *Quarterly Journal of Economics*, **108**, 33–60.

Krugman, P. and A.J. Venables (1995), 'Globalization and the inequality of nations', *The Quarterly Journal of Economics*, **110**, 857–80.

Liu, H. and J. Lu (2006). 'Measuring the degree of assortative mating', *Economics Letters*, **92**, 317–22.

Lorenz, M.O. (1905), 'Methods for measuring concentration of wealth', *Journal of the American Statistical Association*, **9**, 209–19.

Manning, A. (2003), *Monopsony in Motion: Imperfect Competition in Labor Markets*, Princeton, NJ: Princeton University Press.

Manski, C.F. (2000), 'Economic analysis of social interactions', *The Journal of Economic Perspectives*, **14**, 115–36.

Marjit, S. and R. Acharyya (2003), *International Trade, Wage Inequality and the Developing Economy: A General Equilibrium Approach*, New York: Springer.

Pareto, V. (1965), *Écrits sur la Courbe de la Repartition de la Richesse*, Vol. 3 of *Oeuvres Complètes*, Geneva: Librairie Droz.

Pasinetti, L.L. (1962), 'Rate of profit and income distribution in relation to the rate of economic growth', *The Review of Economic Studies*, **29**, 267–79.

Pen, J. (1974), *Income Distribution*, 2nd edn, London: Allen Lane, The Penguin Press, pp. 48–59.

Persky, J. (1992), 'Retrospectives: Pareto's law', *The Journal of Economic Perspectives*, **6** (2), 181–92.

Piketty, T. (2000), 'Theories of persistent inequalities', in A.B. Atkinson and F. Bourguignon (eds), *Handbook of Income Distribution*, Amsterdam: North-Holland, pp. 429–76.

Piketty, T. (2007), 'Top incomes over the twentieth century: a summary of the main findings', in A.B. Atkinson and T. Piketty (eds), *Top Incomes Over the Twentieth Century: A Contrast Between Continental European and English-speaking Countries*, Oxford: Oxford University Press.

Piketty, T. and E. Saez (2003), 'Income inequality in the United States, 1913–1998', *Quarterly Journal of Economics*, **118**, 1–39.

Richardson, J.D. (1995), 'Income inequality and trade: how to think, what to conclude', *The Journal of Economic Perspectives*, **9**, 33–55.

Sala-i-Martin, X. (2006), 'The world distribution of income: falling poverty and . . . convergence, period', *Quarterly Journal of Economics*, **121**, 351–97.

Salanié, B. (1997), *The Economics of Contracts: A Primer*, Cambridge, MA: MIT Press.

Sen, A.K. (1979), 'Personal utilities and public judgements: or what's wrong with welfare economics?', *The Economic Journal*, **89**, 537–58.

Sen, A.K. and J.E. Foster (1997), *On Economic Inequality*, 2nd edn, Oxford: Clarendon Press.

Shorrocks, A.F. (1983), 'Ranking income distributions', *Economica*, **50**, 3–17.

Sierminska, E., A. Brandolini and T. Smeeding (2006), 'The Luxembourg Wealth Study – a cross-country comparable database for household wealth research', *Journal of Economic Inequality*, **4**, 375–83.

14 The social economics of growth and income inequality
Morris Altman

Introduction

Economic growth is of fundamental importance to social and material well-being, and it is therefore of fundamental importance to identify the determinants of growth and those conditions by which most individuals benefit from the growth process. By tradition, social economics has been particularly concerned with the social justice implications of economic theory and policy. It has also paid special attention to the nature and extent of the social embeddedness of individual decision-making. I focus on the determinants of growth, which touch upon social context, and how these determinants relate to social justice concerns. With regard to the latter, special attention is paid to the level of material well-being as well as the well-being derived from rights which enable individuals to construct and realize their true preferences. True preferences are the choices that an individual would choose to make under ideal choice conditions, such as individual freedom (absence of coercion), and full information, given their social context (Altman, 2006a; Nussbaum, 2000). Traditional and current discourse on the determinants of growth pay little heed to social context and social justice concerns, apart from the embedded assumption that sustained growth should, as a rule, improve the material well-being of the population at large – a trickle-down effect. Given a free market, inclusive of free trade and capital flows, plus the rule of law, with minimal government intervention, economic growth should be maximized, as should the material welfare of society at large. Moreover, critical determinants of growth such as technological change are assumed to be largely exogenously determined – a largely random phenomenon which can be optimally tapped into by free markets in the context of a well-governed private property institutional setting.

Based on previous research (Altman, 2000, 2001b, 2003, 2006b), I make the case for the importance of institutions and, related to this, power relationships in determining the extent and the distribution of beneficiaries of the growth process (see Rothschild, 2002, on the importance of power in economic theory). Conventional economics, which downplays the role of institutions as a causal determinant of growth and development, as well as the new institutional economics, pioneered by Douglass North (1990), Mancur Olson (2000) and Oliver Williamson (1975), which focuses on private property rights, free markets and transaction costs, pay little analytical heed to bargaining power as a core independent variable in modeling growth and development (Hodgson, 1988; Schmid, 2004). I argue that the actual bargaining power of workers, peasants and women, for example, in the market and household domain affect the growth process and help explain growth over historical time. Moreover, understanding power relationships allows one to predict the direction and extent of growth and economic development. But, just as significantly, a modeling framework where power is an explicit independent variable helps explain and predict who the beneficiaries of growth are most likely to be. A key point made in this chapter is that improvements in the bargaining power of workers, peasants and women (in the market and in the household) serve to encourage both economic efficiency and technological change, *ceteris paribus*. Key to their bargaining power are labor and gender rights. With regard to labor (the main focus of this chapter), free labor in and of itself goes some way to enhance labor power, especially when labor markets are tight. Tight labor markets, given free labor, yield higher levels of growth wherein the majority of the population garner significant benefits. Both weak labor markets and a weak labor rights regime yield lower rates of growth. However, even low-wage regimes can sustain high rates of growth up to a certain threshold point, under certain conditions, especially when they are economically far behind in terms of the use of dominant technologies. But relatively backward economies can grow even faster and in a more sustained fashion if contextualized in a relatively high-wage institutional framework. In this case, many more people would benefit from growth. But this model does not specify inevitability to high-wage, high-growth economic regimes; there exists no Marxian or Hegelian imperative to what some might refer to as the 'good society'. This would be the case with many free market economists and more recently with a school of behavioral experimental economists where it is argued that reciprocal altruism and altruistic punishment in the context of effort variability results in employers paying workers a fair wage (Fehr and Gächter, 2000, 2002). Whether economies move in this direction is highly contingent upon the power relationships among economic agents and their preferences, and the institutional framework of decision-making. If the dominant players prefer a low-wage, low-growth regime – such as holds in many authoritarian rent-seeking societies – such a regime dominates.

Another important point that emanates from this modeling framework is that economic growth is consistent with high wages and a relatively egalitarian (not equal) distribution of income within the framework of a market economy. The model presented here also suggests a positive causal relationship between ethical behavior, inclusive of environmentally friendly behaviors, and economic growth. Conventional economic theories' standard prediction that improvements in the material and social well-being of the majority are causally and negatively related to economic growth and development is highly misleading, predicated upon a static analytical framework, one that pays no heed to the dynamic positive relationship between improvements in the material well-being of the people writ large and both economic efficiency and growth. The conventional wisdom still largely predicts a negative relationship between income equality, levels of labor compensation, ethical behaviors and growth.

An ethical dimension to growth

The economics literature currently highlights the importance of high growth rates, low levels of inflation, low government budget deficits and debt to gross domestic product (GDP) ratios, low levels of government investment and high stock prices. Positive (objective–scientific) economics attempts to determine how these and related economic targets can be realized in an optimal fashion. The ethical dimension here is implicit, for there is a presumption that achieving such targets represents that which is good. Sometimes explicitly and often implicitly it is assumed that if such targets are met, society at large, rich, poor and middle class alike, will benefit. Failure in this domain will result in economic hardship for all. But the improvement in the level of socio-economic well-being of the people is rarely situated at the forefront of the growth discourse. However, this was not always the case. One can of course legitimately introduce normative considerations into the conventional growth discourse. But here one often speaks to the issue of the extent of negative economic trade-offs which need to be determined when one interjects ethical considerations into the growth narrative. There should be higher wages, more income equality, labor rights, gender rights, human rights, a greener economy – but what are the costs of the realization of such ethical considerations?

To avoid accusations of misrepresenting the scientific core of economic reasoning it is best to refer briefly to Adam Smith's understanding of the fundamentals of economics and growth, especially with regard to introducing ethical considerations. Smith well recognized that markets and capitalism were nothing new. Of vital concern to Smith was how to reconfigure capitalist society so that it best benefited the common people – not largely the elites, as in days gone by. Smith makes the case that inquiring about the wealth of nations is very much about improving the welfare of the people. This is a critical ethical imperative of his studies into the workings, growth and development of market economies. Smith ([1776] 1937, p. 78) argues:

Is this improvement in the circumstances of the lower ranks of the people to be regarded as an advantage or as an inconveniency to the society? The answer seems at first sight abundantly plain. Servants, labourers and workmen of different kinds, make up the far greater part of every great political society. But what improves the circumstances of the greater part can never be regarded as an inconveniency to the whole. No society can surely be flourishing and happy, of which the far greater part of the members are poor and miserable. It is but equity, besides, that they who feed, cloath and lodge the whole body of the people, should have such a share of the produce of their own labour as to be themselves tolerably well fed, cloathed and lodged.

Also, unlike many conventional economists, Smith makes the case that there need not be a trade-off between significant ethical labor market considerations and the health of the market economy. Indeed, his thoughts have been resurrected in different forms as part and parcel of contemporary x-efficiency (Altman, 1992, 1996, 2006c; Leibenstein, 1966, 1979) and efficiency wage theories (Akerlof, 1984; Akerlof and Yellen, 1986) where the latter still remain somewhat outside of the mainstream. Smith ([1776] 1937, p. 81) makes the case that

The liberal reward of labour, as it encourages the propagation, so it increases the industry of the common people. The wages of labour are the encouragement of industry, which, like every other human quality, improves in proportion to the encouragement it receives. A plentiful subsistence increases the bodily strength of the labourer, and the comfortable hope of bettering his condition, and of ending his days perhaps in ease and plenty, animates him to exert that strength to the utmost. Where wages are high, accordingly, we shall always find the workmen more active, diligent, and expeditious, than where they are low . . .

For Adam Smith, ethical considerations are introduced from the word go. Studying growth and markets is all about figuring out how to improve the welfare of the people, people who ideally are relatively free from coercion by their neighbors and the state. Smith concludes that free markets embedded in a world of moral sentiment are the best means to realize his ethical considerations. But he also recognizes the importance of power relationships in the real world of servants and masters. Smith ([1776] 1937, p. 66) acknowledges the natural unequal advantage that masters have over servants, and that even so masters combine with the sanction of the state to further increase their bargaining power. Workers combine, or attempt to do so, often in face of state opposition, to countervail their natural disadvantage. The resulting bargaining relationships affect the income that labor earns. For Smith, writing in the eighteenth century, the interests of servants are best served when markets are tight, contributing to enhancing the bargaining power of labor. Vibrant growth contributes significantly to this, and the realization of Smith's ethical ideal of improving the well-being of the people at large. Smith's modeling narrative informs the growth frame-work presented in this chapter.

One of the founders of the American Economic Association and the *American Economic Review*, Richard T. Ely (1886), was also a great advo-cate of including ethical considerations in the economist's tool box. Writing in the late 1880s, he argued that such a linkage was finally being established. Ely maintains that economists should ask about the purpose of economic life and then seek and propose the means to achieve one's proposed ethical ideal. This task is best achieved by understanding how economies evolved over time and the role played by human agency. Ely (1886, pp. 531–2) writes:

> The ethical school of economics aims, then, to direct in a certain definite manner, so far as may be, this economic, social growth of mankind. Economists who adhere to this school wish to ascertain the laws of progress, and to show men how to make use of them . . . It is desired in future so to guide and direct the forces which control production and distribution of economic goods, that they may in the highest degree subserve the ends of humanity.

A similar position has been recently articulated by Schmid (2004). More specifically, Ely argues (1886, p. 531):

> It is well to describe somewhat more in detail the ethical ideal which animates the new political economy. It is the most perfect development of all human fac-ulties in each individual, which can be attained. There are powers in every human being capable of cultivation; and each person, it may be said, accomplishes his end when these powers have attained the largest growth which is possible to them. This means anything rather than equality. It means the rich diversity for differentiation accompanies development . . . What the political economist desires, then, is such a production and such a distribution of economic goods as must in the highest practicable degree subserve the end and purpose of human existence for all members of society.

Ely's ethical stance is very similar to the capabilities and functionings (Aristotelian) ethic more recently developed and modeled by Sen (1987, 2000) and Nussbaum (2000, 2003). The main point for Ely is that econo-mists should place their ethical perspective at the forefront of the analyti-cal questions they address and, as for Smith, this perspective is linked to economic science as a means towards improving the well-being of human-ity. The ethical ideal for both Smith and Ely is situated in the market economy and a rigorous understanding of its workings.

My final point of reference is John Ryan (1906, 1935), intellectual father of the living wage movement. He too approaches his work quite explicitly underlying the ethical dimension of his projects: to improve the level of material well-being of society at large, providing each individual with the capacity to be the best that they desire to be. This is best achieved by giving each individual the minimum required to realize this objective. Ryan (1935, p. 319) argues:

> there is a certain minimum of goods to which every worker is entitled by reason of his inherent right of access to the earth. He has a right to at least a decent livelihood. The elements of a decent livelihood may be summarily described as: food, clothing, and housing sufficient in quantity and quality to maintain the worker in normal health, in elementary comfort, and in an environment suitable to the protection of morality and religion; sufficient provision for the future to bring elementary contentment, and security against sickness, accident, and invalidity; and sufficient opportunities of recreation, social intercourse, education, and church membership to conserve health and strength and to render possible in some degree the exercise of the higher faculties.

Ryan maintains that a living wage should not be achieved at the expense of undermining the sustainability of the economy. It must be consistent with the profitability of the firm in a market economy – something for economists to help determine. Otherwise, the weakened economy would yield a lower standard of well-being to the poorest members of society. Ryan also rejects the conventional wisdom (of his time and indeed of ours) that a living wage would cause economic harm. He maintains that a living wage would have a productivity-enhancing effect for workers and management. Although a living wage should not undermine economic viability, Ryan charges that conventional wisdom is too quick to condemn a living wage as producing negative economic effects. Thus Ryan argues that ethical behavior (a living wage) is consistent with a vibrant market economy and is best achieved by enhancing the bargaining power of labor where workers tend to be at a natural disadvantage – this echoes the insights of Adam Smith.

In terms of the social economics' rendering of economic growth presented in this chapter, the *raison d'être* of modeling growth is to determine the manner in which particular ethical considerations impact positively or negatively upon the growth process. In other words, what are the opportunity costs of behaving morally or ethically? Or, is it the case that ethical behavior yields economic benefits that countervail or even outweigh the costs? A model is set up that allows for the testing of ethical propositions especially with regard to the potential impact on growth of improvements in the material well-being of laborers and in environmental well-being. The critical ethical consideration here is that growth should be about bettering the human condition. But this cannot be achieved without some understanding of the growth process.

Some relevant stylized facts about growth

Before discussing an alternative theory of growth, it is important to establish some basic facts related to contemporary economic growth and per capita income. First, although the world population has increased by over 2 billion people from the 1970s to the new millennium, average real per capita income increased by almost 40 percent in less developed economies, while infant mortality and adult illiteracy were cut in half (World Bank, 2003, pp. 1–3). In addition, there has been a dramatic decline in the absolute number of people living in acute poverty (less than $1 per day), perhaps by as many as 400 million, albeit over 1 billion people still suffer from such poverty (World Bank, 2006, p. 66). China, India, Bangladesh and Pakistan have taken the lead in this domain. Sub-Saharan African, plagued by civil wars, AIDS and rent-seeking, has witnessed an increase in the number of absolute poor from over 150 million to 160 million. Economic growth appears to have been statistically responsible for half of the total variation in poverty reduction in the last two decades of the twentieth century, and more specifically a 1 percent increase in the per capita growth rate for one year (or a 1 percent increase in per capita income) is associated with a 2.4 percent reduction in the mean poverty rate. However, poverty reduction as well as related and socially significant variables such as mortality, morbidity and life expectancy are highly and positively correlated with the distribution of income and changes to the distribution of income. *Ceteris paribus*, the more equal the distribution of income, the more severe is the reduction of poverty and related social ills for every measured increase in economic growth (World Bank, 2006, p. 88). There has been growth and, for many, life has became better. But improvements could have been even more impressive under different institutional parameters – for example, where more income equality prevails. As discussed below, more income equality in a growing economy need not imply a shift of income from one individual to another, but rather income should increase at a faster rate among the lower income groups.

Increasing reference is made to the UN's Human Development Index (HDI) since the HDI is a broader measure of well-being. The HDI is an unweighted index comprising index numbers for real per capita GDP, life expectancy and education. It is possible for countries' HDI ranking to be below or above their per capita GDP ranking depending on the manner in which income is used. Figure 14.1, constructed from UN data (United Nations, 2006), plots the relationship between the HDI ranking and per capita GDP for 2004. Obviously the two are closely related. Indeed, I find a correlation coefficient between per capita GDP and the HDI of 0.75 and between the rankings of these variables of 0.94. The higher the average income, the higher the HDI ranking. There is some variation about the mean, especially among the poorest nations. However, to achieve high levels of socio-economic well-being requires high levels of per capita GDP, which can only be achieved by high rates of growth among the poorer

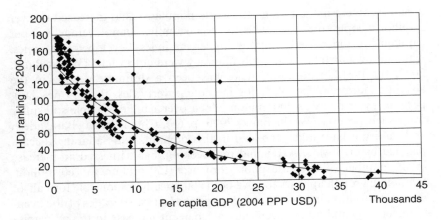

Figure 14.1   HDI and per capita GDP

countries. A social economist would address the possible causal linkages between social variables and high levels of per capita income, and ask to what extent democratic governance contributes to the tight relationship between high levels of income and high HDI rankings – a hypothesis ventured and defended by Sen (2000).

Figure 14.2, derived from the same UN data (United Nations, 2006), examines the statistical relationship between infant mortality rates per 1000 and per capita GDP, a very practical measure of well-being which affects measured life expectancy at birth. The correlation coefficient here is −0.60 – not as overwhelming as the previous correlation between income and the HDI. However, clearly high per capita income is strongly related to diminutions in infant mortality. What is also clear is that the lowest levels of infant mortality are only realized at higher levels of per capita GDP and that the highest-income economies are all characterized by low levels of infant mortality. It is also true that low-income economies can achieve fairly low levels of infant mortality – there is a huge variation in infant mortality rates at low levels of income, from fewer than 20 per thousand to over 160. In other words, most low-income economies sustain much higher levels of infant mortality than is necessary given their income. Per capita income is not everything, but once per capita GDP rises above $5000 a fall in infant mortality becomes realizable. In terms of the HDI and related measures of well-being, per capita income level and therefore growth is of some significant consequence. But it is important to determine the extent to which socio-economic variables, especially those related to ethical considerations, positively affect per capita income, growth and levels of well-being.

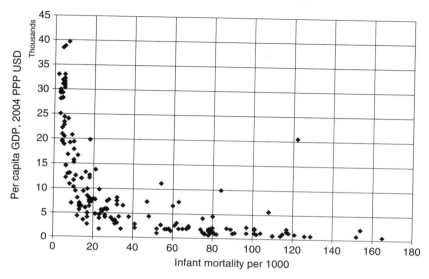

Figure 14.2   Infant mortality and GDP per capita

This brings me to a brief discussion of the relationship between income inequality, levels of per capita income and economic growth. For those concerned about the socio-economic well-being of the population at large, it would be somewhat distressing if the facts clearly indicated that high levels of income and high levels of growth required high levels of income inequality. The latter is suggested by the highly influential Kuznets curve (Kuznets, 1955), specifying a positive relationship between income per capita and income inequality among less developed economies. But Figure 14.3 and 14.4, derived from UN data (2006), strongly suggest that this is not the case. Indeed, the opposite statistical relationship holds, albeit not a strong one. Both increases in per capita income and per capita growth rates are negatively related to levels of income inequality, which is proxied here by the ratio of the income held by the top to the bottom 20 percent of the income cohort. From the data plotted on these charts, there is a correlation coefficient between income inequality and per capita GDP of −0.25 and between income inequality and per capita income growth of −0.12. From Figure 14.3, the highest levels of income inequality are associated with the lowest levels of per capita income. Moreover, a wide array of income distribution, largely between a ratio of 10 and below, is associated with almost the entire range of per capita GDP recorded here. High levels of income inequality do not appear to be either necessary or sufficient to generate high levels of real per capita income. Figure 14.4

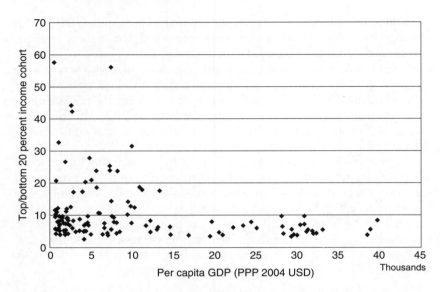

Figure 14.3   Income inequality and per capita GDP

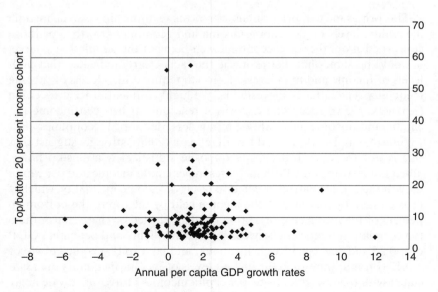

Figure 14.4   Growth and income inequality

illustrates the relationship between per annum real per capita GDP growth (in the 1990–2004 period) and income inequality. The highest levels of income inequality are associated with the lowest growth rates. It is also the case that low levels of income inequality are associated with a very wide range of growth rates, ranging from high negative to high positive rates. Income inequality does not appear to be necessary for the realization of high levels of per capita income and growth (see also Altman, 2003; Atkinson, 1994; Helpman, 2004, p. 93; Schmidt-Hebbel and Serven, 1996).

On theoretical grounds it was traditionally maintained that high rates of inequality are required to generate the savings needed to support the investments necessary to generate high growth rates and technological change. The assumption here is that individuals with higher incomes are characterized by a higher average and marginal propensity to save, and that these savings are translated into productive investment expenditure inclusive of plant and equipment embodying best-practice technology. But to the extent that poorer and middle-income individuals save and that the marginal propensity to save is small to zero after a certain threshold of high income (affected by the level of income inequality), increasing levels of income inequality need not have any positive causal relationship with growth. Also, to the extent that higher levels of income generated by very high levels of income inequality yield 'unproductive' investments, the export of savings, or simply conspicuous consumption, one would not expect increasing levels of income inequality to yield higher rates of growth. Moreover, as per capita income increases even without any increase in income inequality, *ceteris paribus*, saving rates can be expected to increase to the extent that as income rises this increases the capacity of individuals to save. Low-savings economies can also borrow from high-savings economies. This possibility further weakens any expected linkage between economic growth and income inequality. Finally, to the extent that the determination of growth rates is dominated by changes in levels of economic efficiency and induced technological change, this further weakens the ties that might otherwise bind income inequality and economic growth. The evidence clearly suggests that such a positive relationship does not exist; but it is also the case that any positive rate of growth is statistically associated with at least low levels of income inequality: a minimum ratio of between 3 and 4.

One other bit of empirical evidence is useful to contemplate: the relationship between economic freedom and per capita income. Much of the contemporary literature, when it opens the door to institutional variables, focuses on private property rights and more generally on economic freedom, as necessary and even sufficient for sustained economic development. The new institutional economics is representative of this view.

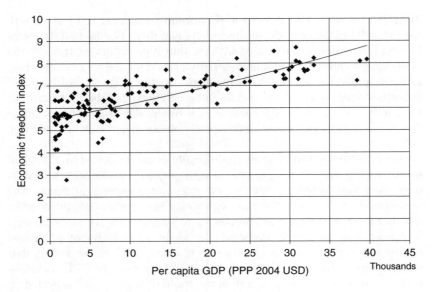

Figure 14.5   GDP per capita and economic freedom

Figure 14.5, derived from UN (2006) and Fraser Institute (2007) data, suggests a strong positive relationship between the two variables, with a correlation coefficient of 0.76 between economic freedom and per capita GDP. The measure of economic freedom used here includes private property rights as well as the extent of government intervention in the economy. But it is most interesting that among the poorer countries the economic freedom index ranges from its very lowest to about 7. Increasing economic freedom along this range in itself does not correlate with increasing per capita income. On the other hand, a relatively high economic freedom index of between 5 and 7 is consistent with per capita income ranging from the lowest levels to the mid-20 000-dollar range. A relatively high level of economic freedom is no guarantee of a high level of income. Indeed, as one moves into yet higher levels of economic freedom, these too are consistent with a wide range of income levels, albeit per capita income is now higher than when the economic freedom index is below 7. The data suggest that a certain threshold level of economic freedom is necessary for high levels of per capita income to be realized, but this is certainly far from being sufficient. Other variables must be at play. Moreover, the hypothesis that simply increasing economic freedom will generate economic growth and development is not supported by the data.

Modeling economic growth and social economics

The modeling framework introduced here explicitly begins with the basic Solow (1956) model. In this model the equilibrium aggregate growth rate is given by the rate of growth in employment plus the rate of exogenously given technological change, and the growth in per worker output is largely determined by the rate of technological change (see Gylfason, 1999; Helpman, 2004; Jones, 1988; Lucas, 1988; Romer, 1994) on this and alternative modeling frameworks such as endogenous growth theory). At any given point in time output per worker is given by the capital to labor ratio plus the prior injection of technological change. *Ceteris paribus*, the labor productivity yields output per person. Of course, if employment increases relative to population, output per person increases and vice versa. This latter point, rarely mentioned in the contemporary literature, underlines one important implication of demand- and supply-side employment policy. The Solow model gives short shrift to the long-run importance of increasing the capital to labor ratio to augmenting output per capita, independent of technological change, since it is assumed that there are limits to which increases in factor inputs per worker, such as capital and land, and even human capital can increase labor productivity – there are diminishing returns to factor inputs. Output per worker is a function of both capital per worker (the former is a proxy for non-human inputs) and technological change. Output per worker can be increased by raising the capital stock per worker, which, in turn, requires increasing the savings rate. But increasing the savings rate can have a positive but limiting effect upon output per worker given diminishing returns to capital. Nevertheless, if the savings rate is increased, output per worker is increased.

These points and more are illustrated in Figure 14.6. We begin with a rather low labor productivity (Q/L) ratio at a. This is given by the capital to labor ratio K/L^*. In equilibrium this, in turn, is given by the savings rate and labor productivity (Q/L). This savings curve is a scaled-down version of the production function (YW_0), scaled down by the savings rate. *Ceteris paribus*, increases in the savings rate pivots upward the savings curve. Also coming into play is the required investment curve $[(n+d)^*(K/L)]$, where n is the rate of employment growth, d is the rate of depreciation of capital stock, and (K/L) is the capital to labor ratio. This curve (of a constant slope equivalent to the (Q/K) output to capital ratio) represents the amount of new investment per worker required to cover depreciation and the growth in employment. Given savings curve $s(Q/L)$, this required investment curve yields an equilibrium capital to labor ratio at a'. At this point K/L^* is the level of capital per worker which is sustainable in equilibrium given n and d. In terms of the Solow model, that which increases K/L yields increases in Q/L along the production function, YW_0, for example – there are limits to

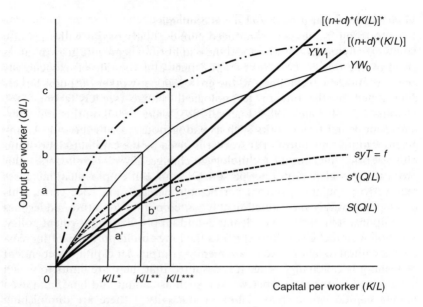

Figure 14.6   Determinants of output per worker

which increasing K/L will generate more output per worker and therefore
per capita. Increasing the savings rate to $s^*(Q/L)$ serves to increase the equilibrium K/L to K/L^{**}. This increases labor productivity from a to b.
Growth takes place as the economy is transitioning between a and b –
between one equilibrium state and another. Increasing the capital to labor
ratio holds most promise in the relatively poor economies with low
capital to labor ratios. Increasing depreciation or employment (such as to
$[(n + d)^*(K/L)]^*$, *ceteris paribus*, serves to increase the demand on a given
amount of savings yielding a lower equilibrium level of K/L to $K/L/^*$ and
therefore a lower equilibrium level of labor productivity (*d*).

But what holds most promise in the Solow model, but goes largely unexplained, is technological change, which shifts outward the production function – more output per unit of capital. Without continuous technological
change, *ceteris paribus*, output per worker and therefore per capita output
will not increase over time. Technological change is illustrated by an
outward shift in the production function to YW_1. This shifts also causes an
outward shift in the savings curve to $syT=f$ from $s^*(Q/L)$, as aggregate
savings increase with increasing labor productivity even holding the savings
rate (the propensity to save) constant. This allows for an increase in the
capital to labor ratio to K/L^{***}. At the end of the day, Q/L increases from
b to c as a consequence of technological change. To the extent that *n* or *d*

have increased to $[(n + d)*(K/L)]*$, technological change serves to neutralize the negative impact which this might otherwise have had on the economy – the capital to labor ratio is kept at $K/L**$ and output at b. Unlike increases in capital stock, which are a positive function of savings and a negative function of employment growth and the depreciation rate and are thereby constrained by these variables, technological change faces no such constraints. What can also shift the production function outward are increases in efficiency and increases in productive human capital investment, inclusive of job training. The impact of these increases, including technological, on per capita output is mitigated somewhat to the extent that they are capital biased, causing the required investment curve to pivot upwards.

The revised model introduces labor market and governance variables as determinants of the level of material well-being. Both these variables affect the level of economic efficiency and the rate of technological change, providing some explanation for what is assumed to be exogenous in the Solow model. In the conventional modeling, firms and individuals within firms are assumed to be behaving efficiently in the realm of production. All agents are assumed to be working as well and as hard as they can irrespective of market structure and incentives. I assume, based on the evidence, that the quality and quantity of effort inputs are variable and can be affected by working conditions (see Altman, 1992, 1996, 1998, 2001b, 2002, 2004, 2005b, 2006c; Frantz, 1997; Leibenstein, 1966, 1979). Leibenstein refers to a scenario where firms are not performing as efficiently as possible as x-inefficiency. Therefore improved working conditions, inclusive of wages and fairness considerations, yield higher productivity, whereas deterioration in such conditions causes productivity to fall. Under these assumptions high-wage regimes need not be more costly than lower-wage regimes and the latter need not be more cost-competitive than their higher-wage counterparts.

However, firms' capacity to respond to increasing wages and improved working conditions by improving efficiency might be limited – hitting the wall of eventually diminishing returns – inducing firms to search for other means to remain competitive. One such means is technological change. Traditionally increasing labor costs serve to move the firm along the production isoquant (along which an identical level of output is produced by alternative combinations of capital and labor) as firms reallocate resources away from labor to capital in an effort to minimize the extent to which unit costs increase. But this is not technological change. I argue that one can model the impact of increasing labor, and indeed of other factor input costs, as inducing the firms to shift inward the production isoquant where the new and old isoquants are characterized by the same level of output.

This is technological change, since factor productivity is increased and productivity is higher as a consequence of labor costs and overall improvements in working conditions. In this model, induced technological change might just be sufficient to offset expected or actual increases in unit costs. Moreover, the new technology (or old but previously unadopted technology) might not be viable for low-wage firms to the extent that they are less efficient than the high-wage firms and may not be profitable enough to adopt. It is the high-wage-induced increased efficiency which makes such technological change profitable. Technology which is of a dominant type would be adopted irrespective the wage rate (Altman, 1998, 2001b).

A key point made in the alternative modeling is that increasing wages can both benefit labor as well as induce more efficiency and technological change, thereby increasing the size of the economic pie. Increasing labor income is not a zero-sum game as it would be in the conventional-type modeling. Increasing wages has the effect of shifting outward the production function as in Figure 14.6. Movements from YW_0 to YW_1 can be in part endogenously explained by labor market events. In additional, increasing wages can help explain the extent and rate of investment in research and development and the adoption and the extent of adoption of resulting new technologies – which go largely unexplained in the endogenous growth models. Also, investment in human capital becomes more profitable and therefore more likely if high wages or returns can be expected. Moreover, cross-country differences in working conditions and rates of change therein can help explain persistent cross-country differences in per capita output and in levels of material well-being and associated well-being indicators, such as life expectancy and child mortality. And, to the extent that changes in labor costs are simply offset by changes in efficiency and technical change, firm owners and managers have no immediate material incentives to develop more productive firms. They are no better off materially in a low- or high-wage environment.

Some of these thoughts are illustrated in equation (14.1) and Figure 14.7.

$$\left[AC = \frac{w}{\left(\frac{Q}{L}\right)} \right] \tag{14.1}$$

In a simple model of the firm with one factor input, labor (L), average cost (AC) equals the wage rate (w), a proxy for all labor costs, divided by labor productivity (Q/L). In the conventional model, given no effort variability, increasing labor costs results in increasing average costs. And, if firms are able to diminish wages, average costs fall, making the firm relatively more competitive. However, if effort is variable, increases in labor costs can be

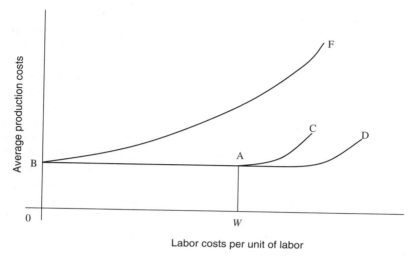

Figure 14.7   Average costs and alternative costs of labor

offset by increasing labor productivity by increases to the quality and quantity of effort inputs. Moreover, cuts to labor costs can result in offsetting cuts to labor productivity following from a drop in the quality and quantity of effort inputs. If one introduces a more realistic model, with more than one factor input, labor productivity need increase only by the percentage increase in labor costs scaled down by the share of labor to total costs. So if labor costs rise by 10 percent and labor represents only 20 percent of total costs, labor productivity need increase by only 20 percent of 10 percent or by 2 percent.

Figure 14.7 maps the relationship between average costs and labor costs in a one-factor input model of the firm. Curve BF represents the conventional wisdom, where increasing wages (labor costs) yields higher average costs and vice versa. BA represents the alternative modeling where changes in labor costs have no effect on average costs. Relatively low- and high-wage firms are equally cost-competitive up to point A and wage rate *W*. Thereafter (past point A to C), given technology, increasing labor costs yields higher average costs as effort inputs cannot be increased sufficiently to generate adequate productivity offsets. Past point A, the alternative model collapses into the conventional rendering. Technological change, induced by increasing labor costs, is illustrated by leftward shifts in this cost function, from BAC to BAD. Induced technological change provides firms with an additional degree of freedom with regard to increasing wage and other labor costs.

Ethical implications of the alternative growth model

There are important institutional hypotheses that follow from this model (see also Altman, 2005a, 2005b). Given that tight labor markets can be productivity-enhancing, that which tightens labor markets such as labor benefits, institutions which protect labor rights (such as the right to bargain collectively) and protect and facilitate the mobility of labor, can be productivity-enhancing. Institutions which prevent employers from circumventing increasing labor market power can have the same productivity-enhancing effect. Moreover, in the tradition of Adam Smith, increasing trade, inclusive of international trade, can be expected to enhance labor productivity by tightening labor markets (Altman, 2007). Such policies might involve minimalist (safety net) interventions suggested such as minimum wages, social security, unemployment insurance, job retraining, and public healthcare, all which tend to increase the reservation wage. On another note, market-oriented minimalist interventions to address the externalities caused by pollution need not have the negative economic effects predicted by the standard model where such interventions generate efficiencies, technological change and new cost-competitive product offsets (Altman, 2001a). Institutions that foster civic rights such as free and effective speech on the market and in the political realm (Hirschman's 'voice'), accountability and transparency can also serve to strengthen the bargaining power of labor, but also serve to reduce the transaction cost of doing business. The latter can reduce the cost of capital and increase economic efficiency, enhancing the growth in per capita output.

Gender rights, which provide women with the capacity to be who they choose to be and have a voice in decision-making processes in the household and firm, can affect the growth process and thereby the level of per capita output. For example, giving women information and rights over pro-creation, *ceteris paribus*, tends to reduce the number of live births per family. Reducing the population growth rate reduces n in Figure 14.6, increasing the level of per capita output. The empowerment of women also tends to create a more efficient healthy household environment, improving the household human capital stock and human capital formation. This too serves to increase the rate of per capita output by shifting outward the production function (Altman, 1999; Altman and Lamontagne, 2004; Folbre, 2001; Nussbaum, 2000; Sen, 2000). Given the importance of population growth and human capital formation to the growth process, the empowerment of women in terms of equality of opportunity and voice can be predicted to continue to play a critical role in enhancing society's level of material well-being.

In the alternative model of growth labor rights, civic rights and gender rights, many of which can be grouped as negative liberties – the freedom from coercion – can play a fundamentally important role in determining the level of per capita output and the potential level of material well-being. These particular rights also serve to realize important ethical objectives for those most concerned with the market-serving social and material interest of Smith's servants, not largely those of the master. Property rights, in this case, would not suffice to generate 'optimal' growth or levels of per capita output. A certain critical level of property rights is critical for successful economic development to take place, but the alternative model suggests the importance of particular ethical imperatives which might also prove vital. A case can also be made that where tight labor markets prevail in conjunction with free labor, incentives abound to develop the institutional foundations necessary to make tight labor markets with resultant high-priced labor (characterized by higher levels of material well-being) economically viable. On the other hand, if the powers that be are able to neutralize market-generated increases in the bargaining power of labor, this alternative set of institutional parameters can maintain the *status quo ante* of economic inefficiency, laggard technological change and economic backwardness. The last might be consistent with preferences of members of the economic elite if their overall utility is enhanced in a relatively low-wage rent-seeking environment. In the alternative model there is no imperative given by market forces that yield high-wage (and more ethical from a Smithian perspective) economic regimes.

Last but not least, the alternative model suggests that a more equal distribution of income is quite consistent with higher growth rates and higher levels of per capita income. In the dynamic model discussed here (Altman, 2003), high wage growth tends not to be distribution-neutral. It is rather biased towards labor, yet it need not shift income away from any one group. Income becomes more equally distributed as the less well off gain proportionally more than the most well off. In this model, dynamic growth yields a more equal distribution of income up to a point, consistent with persistent growth and the maximization of socio-economic welfare of society at large. Consistent with the evidence, severe inequalities of income are not necessary for rapid growth and high levels of per capita income. Indeed, the opposite appears to be the case.

Conclusion

In line with Adam Smith's ethical considerations and more recently Deirdre McCloskey's discourse on bourgeois virtues (2006), market economies and bourgeois society are quite consistent with ethical behavior and social justice considerations. Moreover, such behavior positively contributes to dynamic growth and the realization of higher levels of material well-being. Nevertheless, unethical behavior is also quite consistent with a competitive

market economy. Bourgeois virtues, moral sentiments and ethical behaviors
need not drive out of existence in either the short or long run (through some
evolutionary process) their unethical counterparts. Rather, institutional
arrangements with particular emphasis on power relationship among
economic agents and democratic institutional forms are necessary for
ethical behaviors, consistent with market economies and their flourishing,
to dominate.

References
Akerlof, George. A. (1984), 'Gift exchange and efficiency-wage theory: four views', *American Economic Review, Papers and Proceedings*, **74**, 79–83.
Akerlof, George A. and Janet L. Yellen (eds) (1986), *Efficiency Wage Models of the Labor Market*, Cambridge and New York: Cambridge University Press.
Altman, Morris (1992), 'The economics of exogenous increases in wage rates in a behavioral/x-efficiency model of the firm', *Review of Social Economy*, **50**, 163–92.
Altman, Morris (1996), *Human Agency and Material Welfare: Revisions in Microeconomics and their Implications for Public Policy*, Boston, MA: Kluwer Academic Publishers.
Altman, Morris (1998), 'High path to economic growth and development', *Challenge: The Magazine of Economic Affairs*, **41**, 91–104.
Altman, Morris (1999), 'A theory of population growth when women really count', *Kyklos*, **52**, 27–43.
Altman, Morris (2000), 'Labor rights and labor power and welfare maximization in a market economy: revising the conventional wisdom', *International Journal of Social Economics*, **27**, 1252–69.
Altman, Morris (2001a), 'When green isn't mean: economic theory and the heuristics of the impact of environmental regulations on competitiveness and opportunity cost', *Ecological Economics*, **36**, 31–44.
Altman, Morris (2001b), *Worker Satisfaction and Economic Performance*, Armonk, NY: M.E. Sharpe.
Altman, Morris (2002), 'Economic theory, public policy and the challenge of innovative work practices', *Economic and Industrial Democracy: An International Journal*, **23**, 271–90.
Altman, Morris (2003), 'Economic growth and income equality: implications of a behavioral model of economic growth for public policy', *Canadian Public Policy*, **24**, S87–S118.
Altman, Morris (2004), 'Why unemployment insurance might not only be good for the soul, it might also be good for the economy', *Review of Social Economy*, **62**, 517–41.
Altman, Morris (2005a), 'Reconciling altruistic, moralistic, and ethical behavior with the rational economic agent and competitive markets', *Journal of Economic Psychology*, **26**, 232–57.
Altman, Morris (2005b), 'Behavioral economics, rational inefficiencies, fuzzy sets, and public policy', *Journal of Economic Issues*, **34**, 683–706.
Altman, Morris (2006a), 'Human agency and free will: choice and determinism in economics', *International Journal of Social Economics*, **33**, 677–97.
Altman, Morris (2006b), 'The state and economic efficiency: a behavioral approach', in Steven Pressman (ed.), *Alternative Theories of the State*, New York: Palgrave Macmillan, pp. 164–90.
Altman, Morris (2006c), 'What a difference an assumption makes: effort discretion, economic theory, and public policy', in Morris Altman (ed.), *Handbook of Contemporary Behavioral Economics: Foundations and Developments*, Armonk, NY: M.E. Sharpe, pp. 125–64.
Altman, Morris (2007), 'Economic growth, "globalisation" and labour power', *Global Business and Economics Review*, **9**, 297–318.
Altman, Morris and Lamontagne, Louise (2004), 'Gender, human capabilities and culture within the household economy: different path to socio-economic well-being?', *International Journal of Social Economics*, **31**, 325–64.

Atkinson, Anthony B. (1994), 'Seeking to explain the distribution of income', Discussion Paper WSP 106, London School of Economics.

Ely, Richard T. (1886), 'Ethics and economics', *Science*, **7** (175), 529–33.

Fehr, Ernst and Simon Gähter (2000), 'Fairness and retaliation: the economics of reciprocity', *Journal of Economic Perspectives*, **14**, 159–81.

Fehr, Ernst and Simon Gächter (2002), 'Altruistic punishment in humans', *Nature*, **415**, 137–40.

Folbre, Nancy (2001), *The Invisible Heart: Economics and Family Values*, New York: New Press.

Frantz, Roger S. (1997), *X-Efficiency Theory, Evidence and Applications* (Topics in Regulatory Economics and Policy, 23), Boston/Dordrecht/London: Kluwer Academic Publishers.

Fraser Institute (2007), *Economic Freedom of the World 2007 Annual Report*, http://www.freetheworld.com/release.html.

Gylfason, Thorvaldur (1999), *Principle of Economic Growth*, Oxford: Oxford University Press.

Helpman, Elhanan (2004), *The Mystery of Economic Growth*, Cambridge, MA: Belknap, Harvard University Press.

Hirschman, Albert O. (1970), *Exit, Voice, and Loyalty: Responses to Decline in Firms, Organizations, and States*, Cambridge, MA: Harvard University Press.

Hodgson, Geoffrey M. (1988), *Economics and Institutions: A Manifesto for a Modern Institutional Economics*, Cambridge: Polity Press.

Jones, Charles I. (1998), *Introduction to Economic Growth*, New York and London: W.W. Norton & Co.

Kuznets, Simon (1955), 'Economic growth and income inequality', *American Economic Review*, **45**, 1–28.

Leibenstein, Harvey (1966), 'Allocative efficiency vs. "X-efficiency"', *American Economic Review*, **56**, 392–415.

Leibenstein, Harvey (1979), 'A branch of economics is missing: micro-micro theory', *Journal of Economic Literature*, **17**, 477–502.

Lucas, Robert E. Jr (1988), 'On the mechanics of economic development', *Journal of Monetary Economics*, **22**, 3–42.

McCloskey, Deirdre N. (2006), *The Bourgeois Virtues: Ethics for an Age of Commerce*, Chicago, IL and London: University of Chicago Press.

North, Douglass C. (1990), *Institutions, Institutional Change and Economic Performance*, New York: Cambridge University Press.

Nussbaum, Martha (2000), *Women and Human Development: The Capabilities Approach*, New York: Cambridge University Press.

Nussbaum, Martha (2003), 'Capabilities as fundamental entitlements: Sen and social justice', *Feminist Economics*, **9**, 33–59.

Olson, Mancur (2000), *Power and Prosperity: Outgrowing Communist and Capitalist Dictatorships*, New York: Basic Books.

Romer, Paul M. (1994), 'The origins of endogenous growth', *Journal of Economic Perspectives*, **8**, 3–22.

Rothschild, Kurt W. (2002), 'The absence of power in contemporary economic theory', *Journal of Socio-Economics*, **31**, 433–42.

Ryan, John A. (1906), *A Living Wage: Its Ethical and Economic Aspects*, New York: Macmillan.

Ryan, John A. (1935), *Distributive Justice: The Right and Wrong of Our Present Distribution of Wealth*, rev. edn, New York: Macmillan.

Schmid, Allan. A. (2004), *Conflict and Cooperation: Institutional and Behavioral Economics*, Oxford: Blackwell.

Schmidt-Hebbel, Klaus and Luis Serven (1996), 'Income inequality and aggregate saving: the cross-country evidence', World Bank Policy Research Paper 1561, http://www-wds.worldbank.org/servlet/WDSContentServer/WDSP/IB/1996/01/01/000009265_3961019172012/Rendered/PDF/multi0page.pdf.

Sen, Amartya (1987), *Commodities and Capabilities*, Oxford: Oxford University Press.

Sen, Amartya (2000), *Development as Freedom*, New York: Anchor Books.

Smith, Adam ([1776] 1937), *An Inquiry into the Nature and Causes of the Wealth of Nations*, New York: Modern Library.

Solow, Robert M. (1956), 'A contribution to the theory of economic growth', *Quarterly Journal of Economics*, **70**, 65–94.

UN (2006), *Human Development Report 2006: Beyond Scarcity: Power, Poverty and the Global Water Crisis*, New York: Palgrave Macmillan, http://hdr.undp.org/hdr 2006/statistics/data/.

Williamson, Oliver E. (1975), *Markets and Hierarchies: Analysis and Antitrust implications*, New York: Free Press.

World Bank (2003), *World Development Report 2003: Sustainable Development in a Dynamic World Transforming Institutions, Growth, and Quality of Life*, Oxford: Oxford University Press.

World Bank (2006), *World Development Report 2006: Equity and Development*, Oxford: Oxford University Press.

PART V

SOCIALLY EMBEDDED EXCHANGE: MARKETS

Chapter 15: 'Markets', by Geoffrey M. Hodgson

Despite strong interest in market outcomes, economists have previously paid relatively little attention to the institutional structure of markets. By contrast, sociologists have often regarded the study of markets as the job of the economist. Consequently, both economists and sociologists have neglected the institutional character of markets. This chapter considers the historical evolution of markets and offers several alternative definitions, involving different degrees of historical specificity. It is argued that recent developments in economics and sociology point to a more nuanced view of markets, involving a recognition of different types of market mechanisms and institutions. These developments include work in experimental economics and auction theory, and from socio-economics and economic sociology. Accordingly, social scientists have rediscovered the institutional texture of market systems. A definition of markets is offered that is consistent with these developments.

Chapter 16: 'Are markets everywhere? Understanding contemporary processes of commodification', by Luís Francisco Carvalho and João Rodrigues

Commodification, that is the expansion of markets and of market rhetoric, is increasingly shaping the socio-economic dynamics of our societies. However, this concept remains conspicuously absent from mainstream economics. Economic imperialism, neoliberal policies and the so-called 'commodification debate' are explored in order to reveal how, despite this absence, dominant economic discourses and social processes of commodification are part of an interconnected and mutually reinforcing movement. Given the importance of these trends, the chapter intends to show the fruitfulness of an interdisciplinary research agenda built around this problematic. Social economics can give important contributions to push this agenda forward.

Chapter 17: 'Work: its social meanings and role in provisioning', by Deborah M. Figart and Ellen Mutari

Work, rather than simply a means to material ends, is part of a complex process of social provisioning. Since social economics is concerned with economic well-being broadly defined, including the just and ethical organization of social institutions and norms, it is well situated to advance our understanding of the social meanings that work can provide. Work is defined by sets of social relations and institutions that are themselves embedded in other social relations and institutions. The task, therefore, for social economists, has been to analyse the conditions under which paid and unpaid work are currently performed and to recommend managerial and public policies, as well as other social institutions and customs, that would enable work to meet expanded criteria of job quality. Identity, along with the non-material aspects of social provisioning, are emerging areas in which social economics can also continue to affect the study of work.

15 Markets
Geoffrey M. Hodgson

Economists have long been concerned with market prices and quantities. However, despite this ongoing preoccupation, they have until recently paid relatively little attention to the institutional structure of markets and the details of market rules and mechanisms. It is odd that for a period of time more discussion of such structures was carried on by those describing themselves as sociologists.

Markets dominate the modern world economy, yet economists have had little to say about market institutions. Why? In part this is explained by a reluctance of many post-1945 economists to adopt historically specific definitions (Hodgson, 2001), especially with a concept so central as the market. Yet an adequate recognition of markets as institutions must also acknowledge that they are historically specific phenomena.

This chapter first considers the historical evolution of markets and several alternative definitions of them, involving different degrees of historical specificity. It is proposed that developments since the 1980s point to a more nuanced view of markets, recognizing different types of market mechanisms and institutions. These developments include work in economic sociology, experimental economics and auction theory. A definition of markets is offered that is consistent with these developments.

The astonishing lacuna
No fewer than three Nobel Laureates have noted the paradoxical omission of discussion of markets institutions in the literature in economics. George Stigler (1967, p. 291) wrote: 'The efficacy of markets should be of great interest to the economist: Economic theory is concerned with markets much more than with factories or kitchens. It is, therefore, a source of embarrassment that so little attention has been paid to the theory of markets and that little chiefly to speculation.' Stigler's highly appropriate plea for the theoretical study of markets went unheard for a long time.

However, matters had not been rectified when Douglass North (1977, p. 710) similarly remarked: 'It is a peculiar fact that the literature on economics and economic history contains so little discussion of the central institution that underlies neo-classical economics – the market.' Even in the 1980s Ronald Coase (1988, p. 7) could still observe that 'in modern economic theory the market itself has an even more shadowy role than the firm'. Economists are interested only in 'the determination of market prices' whereas 'discussion of the market place itself has entirely disappeared'.

Of course, while economics textbooks have little to say about the structure of markets, the m-word is commonplace, and markets are classified by their degrees of competition or their numbers of buyers and sellers. By contrast, it is the institutional aspects and detailed mechanisms of markets that have been widely neglected. For much of the twentieth century there has been little discussion of how specific markets are structured to select and authenticate information, and of how specific prices are actually formed. Economists refer to the 'forces' of supply and demand, and locate market equilibria at the intersection of their curves in price–commodity space, but until recently they have offered little discussion of the mechanisms through which these forces operate. Instead, 'the market' has been treated as a relatively homogeneous and undifferentiated entity, with little consideration of different market mechanisms and structures. While market outcomes such as prices are always central to the discussion, there is generally comparative neglect of the detailed rules and mechanisms through which prices are formed, and the concept of the market itself often goes undefined. Remarkably, there is no entry on markets in either the massive 1968 edition of the *Encyclopaedia of the Social Sciences* or the otherwise comprehensive 1987 edition of *The New Palgrave: A Dictionary of Economics*.

Our task is to try to identify the nature of market phenomena. A brief historical sketch of the evolution of the market follows, including a review of various meanings of the term. This is followed by a discussion of why the specific anatomy of markets has been neglected by economists, what recent developments in economics and elsewhere have helped to remedy the deficiency, and the contribution of economic sociologists and social economists. A definition of the market is offered.

A very brief history
Within prehistorical tribes there were frequent transfers of goods from one individual or family to another. Such gifts and transfers have occurred within human societies for hundreds of thousands of years. However, the available anthropological evidence suggests that much of this internal circulation was powered by custom and tradition. It often involved ceremony and personal, reciprocal actions. These personal, familial and kin-based exchanges are very different from modern contracts in the highly organized and money-driven competitive markets of today. By contrast, such ceremonial transfers involved 'the continuous definition, maintenance and fulfilment of mutual roles within an elaborate machinery of status and privilege' (Clarke, 1987, p. 4). This internal circulation of goods had little to do with voluntary, contractual transfer of ownership or property rights

in the modern sense. It was more to do with the validation of custom and social rank.

Nevertheless there were developed systems of trade between tribes, at least as far back as the last Ice Age. This trade occurred at the meeting of different tribal groups. As Max Weber (1927, p. 195) wrote, commerce did 'not take place between members of the same tribe or of the same community' but was 'in the oldest social communities an external phenomenon, being directed only towards foreign tribes'. The proposition that trade developed first externally and between communities – rather than within them – has withstood scholarly re-examination.

With the rise of more complex societies, particularly the ancient civilizations, both external and internal trade increased substantially. The development of money and coinage facilitated its expansion. Our first evidence of organized markets, in the sense of a place involving multiple buyers and sellers where goods are bought and sold, appears in classical antiquity. In Athens in the sixth century BC there was a marketplace (or *agora*) where goods were regularly traded according to defined rules (Polanyi, 1971; North, 1977). At around the same time there was an annual auction market in Babylonia where young women were put on display and male bidders competed for marriage rights (Cassady, 1967).

There has been some debate on whether these ancient civilizations were predominantly market economies. Karl Polanyi and a number of scholars have denied this (Finley, 1962; Polanyi et al., 1957). By contrast, Peter Temin (2006) has argued that the Roman Empire contained developed and interlocking markets with variable prices, albeit without a highly developed banking system and with a relatively limited market for capital. Clearly, the resolution of this debate depends largely on both the definition of the market and the extent to which the defined phenomena dominated production and distribution.

After the fall of the Western Roman Empire in AD 476, European and Mediterranean trade contracted dramatically. Trade internal to social economic systems also declined, with feudal institutions governing much of economic activity.

Markets for slaves existed in classical antiquity and persisted in some regions until the modern era. By contrast, feudal serfs were not owned as chattels, but they did not enjoy the right to choose their masters. Feudal institutions, driven by traditional obligations rather than voluntary contract, meant that the hiring of labourers was marginalized and markets for wage labourers were rare.

In several countries, the principal organized markets were chartered by the king. However, systematic evidence of the king enforcing his right to license all markets and fairs does not appear until the thirteenth century.

As in previous history, the most important driving force behind the general expansion of trade in the medieval period, including in Italy, was mercantile activity, often over long distances. 'Strange though it may seem,' wrote the historian Henri Pirenne (1937, p. 140), 'medieval commerce developed from the beginning not of local but of export trade.'

With the decline of bonded labour, which began as early as the fourteenth century in England, employment contracts were limited largely to casual labourers, alongside a large number of self-employed producers and others in peasant family units. In England it was not until about the eighteenth century that a class of potentially mobile wage labourers emerged who constituted the most important source of labour power. Organized markets for employees, involving labour exchanges or employment agents, did not become prominent until the nineteenth century.

Turning to capital markets, an early market for debts was the French *courratier de change* in the twelfth century. After the development of a banking system in Venice in the thirteenth century, trade began in government securities in several Italian cities. In 1309 a 'Beurse' was organized in Bruges in Flanders, named after the Van der Beurse family, who had previously hosted regular commodity exchanges. Soon after, similar 'Beurzen' opened in Ghent and Amsterdam. In 1602 the Dutch East India Company issued the first shares on the Amsterdam Bourse or Stock Exchange. The London Stock Exchange, founded in 1801, traces its origins to 1697 when commodity and stock prices began to be published in a London coffee house. The origins of the New York Stock Exchange go back to 1792, when 24 stockbrokers organized a regular market for stocks in Wall Street.

Clearly, in the last four centuries markets have expanded enormously in scope, volume, sophistication and economic importance. Today, markets pervade internal as well as external trade and dominate the global economic system. Financial markets are particularly extensive and important. The modern era of globalization is often identified with the growth of global commodity and financial markets since the middle of the nineteenth century.

Against this historical background, at least three different ways of defining markets emerge, involving different degrees of historical specificity. The broadest definition of 'market' refers to all forms of transfer of goods or services, including customary or ceremonial transfers within tribes and households, exchanges of property between tribes, and modern organized markets with multiple buyers and sellers. An intermediate option would be to identify markets with all forms of voluntary trade involving discernible property rights. The third and most restrictive option is to define the market more narrowly as a sphere of organized, competitive exchange. These options are now addressed.

What is a market?

Ludwig von Mises, a leading member of the Austrian School, is one of the few economists to address the concept of the market at some length. In his 1949 book *Human Action* he devotes an extensive chapter to 'the market', where he sees the market economy as 'the social system of the division of labour under private ownership of the means of production' (1949, p. 257). He explicitly excludes from this category economies under social or state ownership of the means of production, but nevertheless regards such systems as strictly 'not realizable'. Crucially, the historical and territorial boundaries of his concept of the market depend very much on what is meant by 'private ownership'. Von Mises associates private ownership with the rise of civilization, and defines ownership in terms of full control of the services that derive from a good, rather than in legal terms. These specifications amount to a definition of the market that embraces all forms of trade or exchange that involve private property, defined loosely as assets under private control.

Von Mises associates private property and exchange with the rise of civilization. Nevertheless, he defines these terms in a manner that could apply to earlier periods of human history. It then becomes unclear whether or not ceremonial transfers and ritualistic gift-giving are regarded as 'exchanges' of 'property', and whether or not these activities come within the sphere of 'the market'. The historical compass of market institutions then critically depends on what we mean by exchange and property.

Because von Mises downplays the legal aspects of property and exchange, he also fails to probe the nature of the rights that form part of the exchange. Instead he upholds that uncoerced and informed consent by the parties to the transaction is sufficient to constitute the contractual and property rights involved. A problem with this idea is that contracts involving mutual individual consent itself require a legislative and institutional framework to legitimize, scrutinize and protect individual property rights. Several historical cases of the spontaneous evolution of systems of enforced property rights do exist, but they generally rely on reputational and other monitoring mechanisms that are more difficult to sustain in large-scale, complex societies (Sened, 1997).

Another intellectual tradition places more emphasis on the legal and statutory basis of individual rights. I refer to the nineteenth-century German Historical School, their predecessors such as Karl Heinrich Rau, and successors in the twentieth century among the original American institutionalists, particularly John Rogers Commons. Both Rau and Commons (1924) argued that exchange is more than a voluntary and reciprocal transfer of resources: it also involves the contractual interchange of statutory property rights. They argued that exchange had to be understood and analysed in terms of the key institutions that are required to sustain it.

This narrower and more legalistic understanding of private property and contractual exchange confines them both in longevity and scale. Statutorily endorsed property rights, applied to moveable goods and services, were not codified until the ancient civilizations. In feudal times, much of the transfer of goods and services was achieved by custom or coercion rather than by contract and consent. Indeed, economic historians such as North (1981), who attempt to explore the origins of modern markets and commodity exchange, generally focus on the late medieval or early modern period as the era in which well-defined individual property rights began to spread widely from specific parts of the world.

A second important dilemma emerges: whether the market is regarded as coextensive with the exchange of private property *per se*, or whether it is given an even narrower meaning and used to refer to forms of *organized* exchange activity. At least two factors argue in favour of the narrower definition of the term.

The first consideration is the commonplace use of the word 'market' and its equivalent in other languages. A 'market' originally referred to a specific place where people gathered and exchanges of a particular kind occurred. This clearly applies to the first market in Athens in the sixth century BC. Medieval markets permitted by royal charters were located in specific towns. In Europe and elsewhere in the last 300 years organized town and village markets have become commonplace. There are also permanent buildings that function as 'markets' or 'exchanges' for agricultural products, minerals, financial stocks and so on. Although it has acquired additional meanings, the term 'market' still refers to a place where trade is organized.

Second, there is a well-researched form of exchange that takes place in different contexts and involves different considerations. In three seminal and influential works, George B. Richardson (1972), Victor P. Goldberg (1980) and Ronald Dore (1983) point out that many real-world commercial transactions do not take place in the competitive arena of a market. Instead they involve firms in ongoing contact, in which they exchange relevant information before, during and after the contract itself. The relationship is durable and the contract is often renewed. This is often described as 'relational exchange'. Why do such partners choose an ongoing exchange relationship, rather than the more competitive institution of the market? Among the explanations in the literature is the importance of establishing ongoing trust in circumstances of uncertainty where product characteristics are complex, unusual or involve continuous potential improvements. Whatever the reason for its existence, such relational contracting is very different from the more anonymous and competitive exchanges in organized markets. Relational exchanges are nevertheless still contractual exchanges of property rights, in their fullest and most meaningful sense. If they are distinguished by definition from market exchanges, then not all exchanges take place in markets. Furthermore, the exchange of goods or services that are strictly unique may be regarded as a non-market phenomenon, even if the exchange is not relational. The term 'market' is thus reserved for forms of exchange activity with many similar exchanges involving multiple buyers or sellers.

In part, it is the degree of organization of exchange activity that differentiates markets from relational exchange. In financial markets, for example, there are typically strict rules concerning who can trade and how trading should be conducted. Specific institutions sift information and present it to traders to help the formation of price expectations and norms. Market institutions in other contexts monitor the quality of goods and the instruments of weight and measure. Within these structures, trading networks emerge on the basis of business connections and reputations.

Modern telecommunications have made it possible to organize a market unconfined by any specific physical location. Bidders can communicate with other traders and the market organizers over long distances, as with many financial markets. The market*place* can itself disappear, as in the case of Internet-based markets, such as eBay. The latter case nevertheless remains a market, because it is subject to codified procedures and rules.

Taking on board the above arguments, the market may be defined in the following terms. Markets involve multiple exchanges, with multiple buyers or multiple sellers, and thereby a degree of competition. A market is an institution through which multiple buyers or multiple sellers recurrently exchange a substantial number of similar commodities of a particular type. Exchanges themselves take place in a framework of law and contract enforceability. Markets involve legal and other rules that help to structure, organize and legitimize exchange transactions. They involve pricing and trading routines that help to establish a consensus over prices, and often help by communicating information regarding products, prices, quantities, potential buyers or possible sellers. Markets, in short, are organized and institutionalized recurrent exchange.

Nevertheless, it is often difficult to draw the line between organized and relational exchange, with many possible intermediate cases. However, such definitional difficulties are typical when dealing with highly varied phenomena and are commonplace in some other sciences, notably biology. Nevertheless, such distinctions are important. The difficulty of defining a species does not mean that species should not be defined.

The operation of the law of one price is often taken as an indication of the existence of a market. Of course, imperfect information and quality

258   *The Elgar companion to social economics*

variations can explain variations within a market from a single price. Nevertheless, the organized competition of the market and its associated information facilities are necessary institutional conditions for any gravitation by similar commodities to a single price level.

We may contrast the narrower definition of the market given above – as an institution with multiple buyers or multiple sellers, and recurrent exchanges of a specific type of commodity – with the much broader definitions raised earlier. These differences in definition do not simply affect the degree of historical specificity of 'market' phenomena; they also sustain different theoretical frameworks and promote different questions for research. Some explanations for this divergence arise in the next section.

Past neglect of the institutional character of markets
On the whole, the institutional character of markets has been neglected when institutions have been neglected. Exceptions consist of economists who placed a special emphasis on institutions. The institutional character of markets was emphasized by German Historical School economists such as Gustav Schmoller and Werner Sombart in the nineteenth century (Hodgson, 2001). The British dissident economist John A. Hobson (1902, p. 144) wrote: 'A market, however crudely formed, is a social institution.' Likewise, for the American institutionalist John Maurice Clark (1957, p. 53), 'the mechanism of the market, which dominates the values that purport to be economic, is not a mere mechanism for neutral recording of people's preferences, but a social institution with biases of its own.' Coase, North and others have helped to revive an interest in the institutional structure of markets that was eclipsed by developments in mainstream economics during much of the twentieth century.

Another reason why social scientists have neglected the institutional character of markets lies in the use of looser definitions of key concepts such as property, exchange and market, as discussed in the preceding section. Many economists have upheld that the principles of their subject should be as universal as possible – like physics – to the extent that substantial consideration of historically or nationally specific institutional structures is lost. The idea that economics should be defined as a general 'science of choice' (Robbins, 1932) is part of this tradition. Consequently, terms such as property, exchange and market are given a wide meaning. Accordingly, many forms of human interaction have been regarded as 'exchange' and summations of such 'exchanges' are loosely described as a 'markets'. These loose definitions seemingly apply to many different types of system, from tribal societies through classical antiquity to the modern capitalist world.

Accordingly, the market assumes a de-institutionalized form, as if it was the primeval and universal ether of all human interactions. Whenever people gather together in the name of self-interest, then a market somehow emerges in their midst. The market springs up spontaneously. It results neither from a protracted process of multiple institution-building nor from the full development of a historically specific commercial culture. Moral and ethical considerations become secondary, as everyone is simply assumed to be maximizing their utility rather than otherwise taking account of ethical imperatives.

Many sociologists have also assumed a de-institutionalized concept of the market. This is partly the result of the influence of a notion, promoted by Talcott Parsons and others, that sociology should also aspire to a high degree of historical generality (Holmwood, 1996; Hodgson, 2001). Accordingly, sociologists such as Peter Blau (1964) developed an 'exchange theory' where the concept of exchange was even broader than that used by many economists, including the 'exchange' of greetings and smiles and having no necessary relationship to exchanges of property rights.

Within sociology, the existence of a general and de-institutionalized concept of the market also results from the influence of Marxism. Despite its emphasis on historical specificity, Marxism also treats markets as uniform entities, ultimately permeated by just one specific set of pecuniary imperatives and cultural norms. Marxists stress the supposed universal logic of the market system, rather than specific institutional market structures or rules.

Reflecting similar defects in neoclassical economics, exponents of the 'rational choice' approach within sociology have also defined markets in ahistorical terms. Characteristically, James Coleman (1990, pp. 35–6) sees markets as simply 'transfers of rights or resources' within 'systems of relations' or a 'system of exchange'. For Coleman, markets cover a wide range of phenomena including taxation and gift-giving, as well as agreed legal contracts between two parties.

From the 1940s to the 1970s, economists attempted to understand the universal functioning of markets within the framework of general equilibrium theory. However, even here significant attention had to be paid to institutional mechanisms and structures. Something special like the 'Walrasian auctioneer' had to be assumed in order to make the model work. Some elemental institutional structures had to be assumed to make the model function on its own terms. The limits to this project of theoretical generalization became more apparent in the 1970s, when it was shown that few general conclusions could be derived. Hugo Sonnenschein and others demonstrated that within general equilibrium theory the aggregated excess demand functions can take almost any form (Kirman, 1989; Rizvi, 1994).

Within the general equilibrium approach a complete set of markets for all present and future commodities in all possible states of the world is typically assumed. The existence of 'missing markets' poses a challenge for this approach (Magill and Quinzii, 1996). Crucially, if market institutions are themselves scarce and costly to establish, then some may be missing for that reason. Furthermore, while capitalism has historically promoted market institutions, modern developed capitalism prohibits several types of market, such as markets for slaves, votes, drugs, or futures markets for labour. In particular, the development of markets for children or slaves within capitalism would undermine the egalitarian legal principles that modern capitalism has championed. For such reasons, 'missing markets' are inevitable, even within modern global capitalism.

The revived understanding by economists of markets as institutions

After technical problems with general equilibrium theory were exposed by Sonnenschein and others, economists shifted their attention to game theory. By its nature, game theory tends to lead to less general propositions and points instead to more specific rules and institutions. As game theory became fashionable in the 1980s, it became a theoretical tool in the 'new institutionalist' revival in economic theory.

Several further developments helped to promote the study of markets as social institutions, in both economics and sociology. In economics the basic theory of auctions emerged in the 1970s and 1980s (McAfee and McMillan, 1987). It was assumed that participants in an exchange did not have complete information and it was shown that choices concerning auction forms and rules could significantly affect market outcomes. These ideas assumed centre stage in the 1990s with the use by governments of auction mechanisms in electricity and telecommunications deregulation, most notably in the selling of the electromagnetic spectrum for telecommunications services, and subsequently with the growth of auctions on the Internet.

A closely related development was the rise of experimental economics in the 1980s. By simulating markets in the laboratory, modern experimental economists have found that they have had also to face the unavoidable problem of setting up its specific institutional structure. Simply calling it a market is not enough to provide the experimenter with institutionally specific structures and procedural rules. As leading experimental economist and Nobel Laureate Vernon Smith (1982, p. 923) wrote, 'it is not possible to design a laboratory resource allocation experiment without designing an institution in all its detail'. Experimental economics has underlined the importance of these specific rules, by showing that market outcomes are sometimes relatively insensitive to the information-processing capacities of the agents involved, because particular constraints govern the results.

In the real world, each particular market is entwined with other institutions and a particular social culture. Accordingly, there is not just one type of market but many different markets, each depending on its inherent routines, cultural norms and institutional make-up. Differentiating markets by market structure according to textbook typology – from perfect competition through oligopoly to monopoly – is far from the whole story. Institutions, routines and culture have to be brought into the picture. Experimental economists have discovered an equivalent truth in laboratory settings, and have learned that experimental outcomes often depend on the tacit assumptions and cultural settings of participants. Different types of market institution are possible, involving different routines, pricing procedures and so on. This has been acknowledged by a growing number of economists, as the notion of a single universal type of market has lost credibility (McMillan, 2002).

Events also helped to remind social scientists of the importance of market institutions. Following the collapse of the Eastern bloc in 1989–91, a number of advisers presumed that many markets would emerge spontaneously in the vacuum left after central planning. This view turned out to be mistaken, as capital and other markets were slow to develop and their growth was thwarted by the lack of an appropriate institutional infrastructure. Several formerly planned economics slipped back into severe recessions. Critics such as Coase (1992, p. 718) drew attention to the necessary institutional foundations of the market system: 'The ex-communist countries are advised to move to a market economy . . . but without the appropriate institutions, no market of any significance is possible.'

Recent contributions by economic sociologists and social economists
Sociologists, like economists, had previously paid relatively little attention to market institutions. However, when 'economic sociology' was revitalized in the 1980s, its mission was to address the social structures and institutions of economic life, which had been long neglected even by economists. The breakdown of the Parsonian hegemony in the discipline, under which sociology was largely conceived in general and ahistorical terms, also created an opportunity for the historically and institutionally specific discourse of the economic sociologists.

Leading economic sociologists such as Mark Granovetter (1985) addressed the arguments of Polanyi (1944) concerning the degree of 'embeddedness' of markets in social relations. However, this discourse was encumbered by inadequate definitions of the 'social', the 'economic' and what 'embedded' meant. The lack of consensus on the meaning of these crucial words, and consequently whether institutions such as the family are 'economic' or 'social', has undermined the key concept of 'embeddedness'. Consequently, Neil Fligstein (1996, p. 656) reports that the 'empirical literature has failed to clarify the precise nature of social embeddedness'.

Later Granovetter wrote: 'I rarely use "embeddedness" any more, because it has become almost meaningless, stretched to mean almost anything, so that it therefore means nothing' (Krippner et al., 2004, p. 113).

While the discourse on embeddness reached a dead end, economic sociologists have nevertheless made a huge contribution to our understanding of the operation of financial and other markets (Abolafia, 1996; Baker, 1984; Burt, 1992; Fligstein, 2001; Lie, 1997; Swedberg, 1994; White, 1981, 1988, 2002). These works show how specific networks and social relationships between actors structure exchanges, and how cultural norms govern market operations and outcomes. Amitai Etzioni (1988) has accordingly emphasized that such considerations mean that ethical issues impinge on human behaviour, even in a market context.

Remarkably, however, several of these considerations have emerged in empirical and simulation work by economists, which stresses the importance of learning and previous experience in trading partner selection and in the decision to accept a transaction (Kirman and Vignes, 1991; Härdle and Kirman, 1995). The general equilibrium approach has been overshadowed by an array of theoretical and empirical methodologies, including game theory, agent-based modelling, laboratory experimentation and real-world observation. A milestone paper by Alvin Roth (2002) challenges the view of a single universal theory of market behaviour. While those economists who had paid attention to different market mechanisms had typically been preoccupied with a search for 'optimal' rules and institutional forms, gradually this has become a will-o'-the-wisp with the realization that typical assumptions in the emerging literature concerning cognitive and information impairments have made this search difficult or impossible (Lee, 1998; Mirowski, 2007). Generally, economists have begun to adopt an much more nuanced and institution-rich concept of the market (McMillan, 2002). These developments have gone so far as to challenge the meaning and legitimacy of the boundaries between economics and sociology.

In this context, markets reappear as varied and historically specific phenomena. Both economists and sociologists are now paying detailed attention to the nature of specific market rules and mechanisms. An outcome is to challenge the former widespread notion – shared by many theorists from Marxists to the Austrian School – that 'the market' is a singular type of entity entirely understandable in terms of the same principles or laws. While Friedrich Hayek (1948) and his Austrian followers should be given inspirational credit for their emphasis on the informational limitations inherent in all complex economic systems, they stressed that markets are the most effective processors of information while downplaying or ignoring the differences between their various types.

Conclusions

There is no methodological golden rule that unfailingly points to the superiority of one definition over another. Indeed, a number of options for defining a market exist. The broadest option is to regard the market as the universal ether of human interaction, depending on little more than the division of labour. A second option is to regard the market as synonymous with commodity exchange, in which case it dates at least as far back as the dawn of civilization.

However, several considerations militate in favour of a narrower definition, and recent developments in economic theory and economic sociology point in this direction. In the narrower sense, markets are organized recurrent exchange. Where they exist, markets help to structure, organize and legitimize numerous exchange transactions. Pricing and trading procedures within markets help to establish a consensus over prices, and communicate information regarding products, prices, quantities, potential buyers or possible sellers.

Variation in market rules and procedures means that markets differ substantially, especially when we consider markets in different cultures. The markets of 2000 years ago were very different from the electronic financial markets of today. In the real world, and even in a single country, we may come across many different examples of the market. The market itself is neither a natural datum nor an ubiquitous ether, but a social institution, governed by sets of rules restricting some and legitimizing other behaviours. Furthermore, the market is necessarily entwined with other social institutions, such as in many cases the local or national state. It can emerge spontaneously, but it is often promoted or guided by conscious design.

Given the arguments outlined here, the unnuanced but familiar pro- and anti-market policy stances are both insensitive to the possibility of different types of market institution. Instead of recognizing the important role of different possible cultures and trading customs, both the opponents and the advocates of the market have focused exclusively on its general features. Marxists for instance have inferred that the mere existence of private property and markets will encourage acquisitive, greedy behaviour, with no further reference in their analysis to the role of ideas and culture in helping to form the aspirations of social actors. This is the source of their 'agoraphobia', or fear of markets. Obversely, over-enthusiastic advocates of the market claim that its benefits stem simply and unambiguously from the existence of private property and exchange, without regard to possible variations in detailed market mechanism or cultural context. In a strange alliance, Marxists and many market advocates underestimate the degree to which all market economies are unavoidably made up of densely layered and interconnected social institutions.

Such complex institutional arrangements mean that markets can take a variety of forms with important differences in outcomes. Because markets involve institutional and cultural, as well as monetary, factors, their analysis can usefully draw insights from several disciplines. Indeed, both economists and sociologists have made indispensable contributions to our understanding of how markets work.

References

Abolafia, Mitchel Y. (1996), *Making Markets: Opportunism and Restraint on Wall Street*, Cambridge, MA: Harvard University Press.
Baker, Wayne E. (1984), 'The social structure of a national securities market', *American Journal of Sociology*, **89** (4), 775–811.
Blau, Peter (1964), *Exchange and Power in Social Life*, New York: Wiley.
Burt, Ronald S. (1992), *Structural Holes: The Social Structure of Competition*, Cambridge, MA: Harvard University Press.
Cassady, Ralph (1967), *Auctions and Auctioneering*, Berkeley and Los Angeles: University of California Press.
Clark, John Maurice (1957), *Economic Institutions and Human Welfare*, New York: Alfred Knopf.
Clarke, David L. (1987), 'Trade and industry in Barbarian Europe till Roman times', in Michael M. Postan and Edward Miller (eds) (1987), *The Cambridge Economic History of Europe, Vol II, Trade and Industry in the Middle Ages*, 2nd edn, Cambridge: Cambridge University Press, pp. 1–70.
Coase, Ronald H. (1988), *The Firm, the Market, and the Law*, Chicago, IL: University of Chicago Press.
Coase, Ronald H. (1992), 'The institutional structure of production', *American Economic Review*, **82** (4), 713–19.
Coleman, James S. (1990), *Foundations of Social Theory*, Cambridge, MA: Harvard University Press.
Commons, John R. (1924), *Legal Foundations of Capitalism*, New York: Macmillan.
Dore, Ronald (1983), 'Goodwill and the spirit of market capitalism', *British Journal of Sociology*, **34** (4), 459–82.
Etzioni, Amitai (1988), *The Moral Dimension: Toward a New Economics*, New York: Free Press.
Finley, Moses I. (ed.) (1962), *Second International Conference of Economic History, Vol. I: Trade and Politics in the Ancient World*, New York: Arno.
Fligstein, Neil (1996), 'Markets as politics: a political-cultural approach to market institutions', *American Sociological Review*, **61** (4), 656–73.
Fligstein, Neil (2001), *The Architecture of Markets: An Economic Sociology of Twenty-first Century Capitalist Societies*, Princeton, NJ: Princeton University Press.
Goldberg, Victor P. (1980), 'Relational exchange: economics and complex contracts', *American Behavioral Scientist*, **23** (3), 337–52.
Granovetter, Mark (1985); 'Economic action and social structure: the problem of embeddedness', *American Journal of Sociology*, **91** (3), 481–510.
Härdle, Wolfgang K. and Alan P. Kirman (1995), 'Nonclassical demand: a model-free examination of price quantity relations in the Marseille fish market', *Journal of Econometrics*, **67** (1), 227–57.
Hayek, Friedrich A. (1948), *Individualism and Economic Order*, London and Chicago, IL: George Routledge/University of Chicago Press.
Hobson, John A. (1902), *The Social Problem: Life and Work*, London: James Nisbet.
Hodgson, Geoffrey M. (2001), *How Economics Forgot History: The Problem of Historical Specificity in Social Science*, London and New York: Routledge.
Holmwood, John (1996), *Founding Sociology? Talcott Parsons and the Idea of General Theory*, London and New York: Longman.

Kirman, Alan P. (1989), 'The intrinsic limits of modern economic theory: the emperor has no clothes', *Economic Journal (Conference Papers)*, **99**, 126–39.

Kirman, Alan P. and A. Vignes (1991), 'Price dispersion: theoretical considerations and empirical evidence from the Marseilles fish market', in Kenneth J. Arrow (ed.) (1991), *Issues in Contemporary Economics: Proceedings of the Ninth World Congress of the International Economic Association*, New York: New York University Press.

Krippner, Greta, Mark Granovetter, Fred Block, Nicole Biggart, Tom Beamish, Youtien Hsing, Gillian Hart, Giovanni Arrighi, Margie Mendell, John Hall, Michael Burawoy, Steve Vogel and Sean O'Riain (2004), 'Polanyi Symposium: a conversation on embeddedness', *Socio-Economic Review*, **2** (1), 109–35.

Lee, Ruben (1998), *What Is an Exchange? The Automation, Management, and Regulation of Financial Markets*, Oxford: Oxford University Press.

Lie, John (1997), 'Sociology of markets', *Annual Review of Sociology*, **23**, 341–60.

Magill, Michael and Martine Quinzii (1996), *Theory of Incomplete Markets*, 2 vols, Cambridge, MA: MIT Press.

McAfee, R. Preston and John McMillan (1987), 'Auctions and bidding', *Journal of Economic Literature*, **25** (2), 699–738.

McMillan, John (2002), *Reinventing the Bazaar: A Natural History of Markets*, New York and London: Norton.

Mirowski, Philip (2007), 'Markets come to bits: evolution, computation and markomata in economic science', *Journal of Economic Behavior and Organization*, **63** (2), June, 209–42.

Mises, Ludwig von (1949), *Human Action: A Treatise on Economics*, London and New Haven, CT: William Hodge and Yale University Press.

North, Douglass C. (1977), 'Markets and other allocation systems in history: the challenge of Karl Polanyi', *Journal of European Economic History*, **6** (3), 703–16.

North, Douglass C. (1981), *Structure and Change in Economic History*, New York: W.W. Norton.

Pirenne, Henri (1937), *Economic and Social History of Medieval Europe*, New York: Harcourt Brace.

Polanyi, Karl (1944), *The Great Transformation: The Political and Economic Origins of Our Time*, New York: Rinehart.

Polanyi, Karl (1971), *Primitive and Modern Economics: Essays of Karl Polanyi*, edited with an introduction by George Dalton, Boston, MA: Beacon Press.

Polanyi, Karl, Conrad M. Arensberg and Harry W. Pearson (eds) (1957), *Trade and Market in the Early Empires*, Chicago, IL: Henry Regnery.

Richardson, George B. (1972), 'The organisation of industry', *Economic Journal*, **82**, 883–96.

Rizvi, S. Abu Turab (1994), 'The microfoundations project in general equilibrium theory', *Cambridge Journal of Economics*, **18** (4), 357–77.

Robbins, Lionel (1932), *An Essay on the Nature and Significance of Economic Science*, London: Macmillan.

Roth, Alvin E. (2002), 'The economist as engineer: game theory, experimentation, and computation as tools for design economics', *Econometrica*, **70** (4), 1341–78.

Sened, Itai (1997), *The Political Institution of Private Property*, Cambridge: Cambridge University Press.

Smith, Vernon L. (1982), 'Microeconomic systems as an experimental science', *American Economic Review*, **72** (5), 923–55.

Stigler, George J. (1967), 'Imperfections in the capital market', *Journal of Political Economy*, **75** (3), 287–92.

Swedberg, Richard (1994), 'Markets as social structures', in Neil J. Smelser and Richard Swedberg (eds) (1994), *Handbook of Economic Sociology*, Princeton, NJ: Princeton University Press, pp. 255–82.

Temin, Peter (2006), 'The economy of the early Roman Empire', *Journal of Economic Perspectives*, **20** (1), Spring, 133–51.

Weber, Max (1927), *General Economic History*, trans. Frank H. Knight from the German edition of 1923, London: Allen & Unwin.

White, Harrison C. (1981), 'Where do markets come from?', *American Journal of Sociology*, **87** (3), 517–47.

White, Harrison C. (1988), 'Varieties of markets', in Barry Wellman and S.D. Berkowitz (eds)
(1988), *Social Structure: A Network Approach*, Cambridge, MA: Harvard University Press.
White, Harrison C. (2002), *Markets from Networks: Socioeconomic Models of Production*,
Princeton, NJ: Princeton University Press.

16 Are markets everywhere? Understanding contemporary processes of commodification
Luís Francisco Carvalho and João Rodrigues

1. Introduction

The expansion of markets and of market rhetoric is one of the defining signs of our age. In this chapter, we explore the sense by which dominant economic discourses and social processes of commodification are part of an interconnected movement. By so doing, we show how economics relates with the way the economy is structured. Economic theory influences the way individuals perceive themselves and their motivations, how they perceive others with whom they interact, and the type of institutional context where this interaction takes place. We contend that the so-called 'economic imperialism' is an extreme version of a tendency, carried out most expressively in mainstream economics, to universalize and naturalize a contentious version of a particular economic institution – the market – and the egoistic motivations that individuals supposedly exhibit within it. In fact, economists who subscribe to economic imperialism end up favouring the idea that everything can be seen as reducible to a market transaction, leaving 'no other nexus between man and man than naked self-interest, than callous "cash payment"' (Marx and Engels, 1998 [1848], p. 242).

These imperialistic discourses, by creating a series of metaphors through which all sorts of human interactions are perceived, should not be seen as innocuous exercises, because the way we look at the world influences how we act upon it. Commodification, moreover, implies a shared understanding of what is involved in social relations, so that as commodification of goods and services proceeds, supported by the discourses that promote it, there will certainly be, as Fred Hirsch (1976) argued, an increased risk of eroding prevalent social norms and values.

In order to deepen this line of enquiry, we shall first try to clarify the meaning(s) of commodification. In the third section, we shall critically describe the origins and major themes of the 'economic imperialism' movement in economics, showing how this way of thinking about economic and social problems cannot be disconnected from the policies of commodification in neoliberal times, to which we shall allude in Section 4. In Section 5, the so-called 'commodification debate', a growing controversy that trespasses various disciplinary traditions, will be scrutinized. Finally, some remarks on the relevance of a social economic approach to commodification will be sketched in Section 6.

2.   Defining commodification

The concept of commodification has a wide currency outside economics, most notably in areas such as moral and political philosophy, law, anthropology, economic sociology or human geography. In economics, it has virtually been monopolized by heterodox economists from various quadrants including Marxist, feminist, institutionalist or social economists.

In this chapter, we put forward a definition of commodification that attempts to capture the various understandings that can be found both in heterodox economics (Folbre and Nelson, 2000; Fine, 2002a) and in other fields of enquiry (Anderson, 1993; O'Neill, 1998; Radin, 1996; Castree, 2003; Williams, 2005).

We define commodification as the process whereby an object (in the widest sense of the term, meaning a thing, an idea, a creature, etc.) comes to be provided through, and/or represented in terms of, a market transaction.

Commodification may take place when an object is brought to the market to be transacted in exchange of money. The generalization of this process presupposes a historically rooted socio-economic system – capitalism – whose provision process is organized around markets and money-mediated exchanges. In markets, objects become commodities when their property, or temporary control, is transferred between individual or collective actors, and their value is crystallized in a price (Hodgson, 1988). However, as Castree (2003, p. 277) remarks, the 'commodity status of a thing, object, idea, creature, person or what-have-you is not intrinsic to it, but rather assigned'. This assignment is supported by an institutional process that ensures a critical condition for the functioning of the market: the definition and guarantee of property rights. Property rights sustain the alienability of the object, i.e. the physical and/or moral separation from its owner, the seller, on a formally volunteer basis, as when the buyer and the seller agree on its monetary value.

The process of commodification may also take place at the level of discourse when the object (a thing, an idea, a creature, etc.) is depicted *as if* being part of a market transaction. Its social value is then exhausted by the price tag metaphorically attached to it, thereby eroding the plurality of human values and generalizing a private-gain, money-minded, mentality. By force of repetition, this discourse may transform individual perceptions and modes of action, favouring the kind of instrumental and calculative behaviour presupposed by it. Because it does not face the same constraints that might hamper the expansion of actual markets, the process of commodification by discourse might have a wider range of application.

The above discussion on the meanings of commodification raises the question of the boundaries between market and non-market modes of provision. In fact, even in capitalism, there is always a variety of non-market institutions – the state, the family or the community – which might ensure the provision of goods and services by invoking patterns of interaction and individual motivations differing from those that are said to be prevalent in markets. Redistribution or reciprocity, as Polanyi (1991) has argued, can guarantee that fundamental human needs are met without organizing the provision process around market transactions. This does not mean, as we shall see, that non-market modes of provision cannot be infused by processes of 'market mimicry' (Marquand, 2004).

It is important to notice that this division, between market and non-market arenas, can be difficult to establish in practice given the contested and complex nature of markets themselves. The creation of markets is a political process requiring the intervention of an organized power that is capable of imposing a set of rules defining who can participate, what are the legitimate objects of exchange (i.e. what entities can actually be considered as commodities), and the 'rights–obligations' structure that each agent faces when exchanging those commodities (Chang, 2002). The recognition of the 'legal–institutional nexus' is therefore crucial:

> Emphasizing the institutional nature of the market requires that we have to bring politics explicitly into the analysis of the market, not just into the analysis of the state and stop pretending – as the neoliberals do – that markets need to be, and can be, 'depoliticised'. Markets are in the end political constructs, in the sense that they are defined by a range of formal and informal institutions that embody certain rights and obligations, whose legitimacy (and therefore contestability) is ultimately determined in the realm of politics. (Chang, 2003, p. 54)

Markets are institutions that depend on and are intermingled with other institutions. They are also structured by certain social norms that ensure their viability. Therefore markets cannot be separated from the state or from the wider society. The crucial concept of embeddedness, developed by Karl Polanyi (1957), captures this idea that the market cannot be properly conceived without the constituent non-market political, social and moral elements that shape and constrain it.

3. Commodification by discourse: economic imperialism

In this section, we focus on one of the most salient instances of commodification in discourse, the so-called 'economic imperialism',[1] that is, the extension in the use of neoclassical microeconomic theory to subjects outside the conventional realm of the 'economic', thereby 'invading' or 'colonizing' domains that were previously occupied by other social sciences. It is interesting to note that this expansionist strategy is in marked contrast to the approach developed by the pioneers of microeconomics, the marginalists of the last quarter of the nineteenth century. In fact, Jevons, Edgeworth or Marshall were careful to ascribe a well-delimited space of applicability to their proposed new kind of economic theory, thus establishing a contrast with the classical political economy it was meant to supersede.[2]

The methodological work of Lionel Robbins (1935 [1932]) marks a significant turning point that somehow paved the way and legitimated the subsequent imperialistic developments. The unifying attribute of economics' subject-matter ceased to be a specific type of phenomenon; economics would now be defined by the study of a particular behavioural pattern. Hence the well-known claim that 'economics is the science which studies human behaviour as a relationship between ends and scarce means which have alternative uses' (Robbins, 1935 [1932], p. 15). Thus defined, economics could considerably expand the issues it dealt with, far beyond the conventional disciplinary boundaries, as Robbins himself admitted: 'Everywhere we turn, if we choose one thing we must relinquish others which, in different circumstances, we would wish not to have relinquished. *Scarcity of means to satisfy ends of varying importance is an almost ubiquitous condition of human behaviour*' (ibid., p. 15, emphasis added).

The end of the 1950s and the following decade saw the emergence of a series of deliberate attempts to expand the use of neoclassical microeconomic analysis beyond the conventional economic territory. A particularly telling example of this move is the domain of political action, where the works of Anthony Downs (1957), James Buchanan and Gordon Tullock (1962) or Mancur Olson (1965) were very influential in laying the foundations for the public choice school, which, by extending to political behaviour the same self-interested logic of the 'economic man', would prove instrumental in the critique of public activism, and hence in the ascendance of neoliberalism. The analysis of legal norms was another important domain subjected to a process of 'colonization' by mainstream economics, with significant political implications. The law and economics movement, where Richard Posner (2002 [1981]) figures prominently, has been a highly influential approach, which tends to promote legal arrangements conducive to the extension of the reach of markets, even in highly contested fields, such as the proposal to institute a market for baby adoption (Landes and Posner, 1978).

It was Gary Becker, himself a major contributor to the law and economics movement, who would be most strongly identified with economic imperialism, or, to use his own formulations, 'the economic approach to human behavior' (Becker, 1976) or 'the economic way of looking at behavior' (Becker, 1993). Starting from the strong claim that 'the economic approach is a comprehensive one that is applicable to all human behavior' (1976, p. 8), Becker makes the central assumption that 'tastes' are stable and universal, so that the observed differences in behaviours across individuals, or over time for the same individual, cannot be explained by changing tastes (Stigler and Becker, 1977). Becker's explanatory strategy takes a different view of consumer/household behaviour – households should be viewed not merely in the light of conventional consumer theory, but also as producers, using market goods, time, skills and other inputs, to produce what he significantly calls 'commodities' (children, status, sex, leisure activities etc.). This framework has been extensively used by Becker to deal with a wide array of subjects. According to the systematization he himself provided in his Nobel Lecture, one could mention discrimination against minorities, criminal activity, education/human capital and issues of formation, dissolution and structuration of families (Becker, 1993).

The importance of Becker's contribution to economic imperialism should not be underestimated, but it must be acknowledged that imperialistic efforts change over time. If we refer to the contemporary situation, we may observe a sensible transformation in the way concepts and analytical tools that originated in neoclassical economics are being subjected to an expansionist use, to the point where it is legitimate to speak of a new variety of economic imperialism. This point has been articulated by Fine (2002a), who notes the 'revolutionary' nature (in the Kuhnian sense) of the work based on market imperfections, most significantly asymmetries of information, and the individual rational/optimizing responses to those 'imperfections'.[3] This perspective greatly increases the scope of the issues potentially falling under economic analysis: 'the new approach purports to be able to explain the presence and impact of economic and social structures, institutions, customs and culture, and even apparent violation of "rational" behaviour as their consequence' (Fine, 2002a, p. 13). For Fine (ibid., p. 12), a significant departure from old-styled, Becker-like, imperialism is implied, since the idea that 'all economic and social phenomena are reduced to a world as if a perfect market' is abandoned. We should note, however, the fundamental continuity at the methodological level, with the reliance on methodological individualism and on rational/optimizing behaviour.

In the celebratory account of economic imperialism offered by Lazear (2000),[4] three 'themes' are identified as the fundamental attributes of economic theory, and as those characterizing its expansionist use: individual rational maximizing behaviour; depiction of the outcome of individual interactions as equilibrium; and emphasis on the concept of efficiency. In a similar vein, Becker (1976, p. 4) had already stated that 'the combined assumptions of maximizing behavior, market equilibrium, and stable preferences . . . form the heart of the economic approach'. The economic approach so defined can be potentially extended to an infinite number of human interactions since it considers that individuals respond to explicit or implicit prices in all situations, be it in the political realm, within the family, or in the definition of the legal norms that rule their behaviour. Prices give individuals all the information they need in their pursuits, and market incentives seem sufficient to signal the avenues through which the maximizer should follow. When they don't, individuals rationally devise institutional arrangements that functionally allow exceptional market failures to be superseded.

Economic imperialism has its roots in what Polanyi (1991) calls the formalistic perspective of the economy. The formalistic perspective presupposes that economics can be defined as the science of individual autonomous rational choice among different alternatives in a context of scarcity. Associated with this notion of rationality is the idea of the inevitable trade-offs that every individual decision presupposes. These trade-offs can be successfully faced only if there is a careful computation of the implicit or explicit relative prices involved. Isolated individuals, concentrated on the prosecution of their self-interest, are permanently evaluating the different courses of action available through the computation of their prospective costs and benefits. This conception of individual choice contributes to the idea that markets and their price signals can be seen as if they were indeed everywhere: 'the dominant model of human choice, rationality and value . . . seems tailor-made to represent the norms of the market as universally appropriate for nearly all human interactions' (Anderson, 1993, pp. xi–xii).

The capacity to extend the reach of markets is related to the way we conceive them. The lack of institutional structure of markets, in mainstream economics accounts, is responsible for the ease with which markets tend to be seen as unproblematically emerging from spontaneous interactions between individuals.[5] It is therefore not surprising that 'all the distinctions involved are erased, and everything is reduced to "goods"' exchanged in markets (Fine, 2002a, p. 34). We are in the presence of what Chang (2003) aptly designates by 'the market primacy assumption', leading to the incapacity of the formalistic perspective to grasp the specificities and the problematic nature of commodification processes.

4.   Neoliberalism and the policies of commodification

Economic imperialism has been concomitant with the regaining of the hegemony of the market in public discourse that has legitimized the progressive emergence of a 'global neoliberal regime', which took root in the 1970s and was consolidated in the 1980s and 1990s (Crotty, 2000). Economic imperialism is then part of a wider set of neoliberal economic theories. These theories do not emerge in a historical vacuum and cannot be analysed without taking into account their obvious political role: 'their political role is, first, to reduce capitalism to the interplay of supply and demand, secondly (subject to some specific qualifications), to reduce markets to prices and thirdly to naturalize markets' (Harriss-White, 2003, p. 484).

Neoliberal economic theories, according to Chang (2002), emerged as an alliance between neoclassical economics and the Austrian–libertarian tradition, based on a more or less clear division of labour: the former provided the analytical tools with a universalistic ambition, encompassing in its analysis all kinds of human behaviours and social interactions; the latter supplied a robust moral and political philosophy, able to create what Birchfield (1999) names a 'gramscian common sense discourse' about the desirability of a 'new free-market capitalism'. One can therefore conceive neoliberalism as a renewed theoretical effort to justify and argue for the universalization of market-based social relations, with the corresponding penetration in almost every single aspect of our lives of the discourse and/or practice of commodification, capital accumulation and profit making (Wood, 1997).

It is the ideological facet of this process that Carrier (1997) has tried to analyse by making reference to the hegemony of the 'market model', conceived as the dominant public language, which 'shapes what can be debated and how it can be debated' and promotes a motivational structure favouring certain behavioural patterns (Carrier, 1997, pp. 50–51). Therefore, if commodification is partially a matter of social understandings, it is important to recognize the influence mainstream economic discourse may have in shaping those understandings. This influence may be exercised through two channels: (1) the direct role that the popularized versions of neoliberal economic theory have in the creation of a new common sense; and (2) the influence that neoliberal theory has in the conduction of public policy and institutional design.

In fact, if, through the influence of certain economists, public discourses and policies adhere to commodified understandings and promote commodification processes, then a 'common frame' is created with an impact on the way individuals interpret the situations that they are facing, and also on the type of motivations that will be nurtured. As behavioural economists and legal scholars have emphasized, individuals do interpret behaviour within a framework of social norms that define how the relevant goods should be valued and how people should behave. Furthermore, people do value expressive meanings because they provide information about what is expected from them in a certain context and about what they can expect from others (Kahan, 1998). In this sense, neoliberalism can be conceived as a way to create a frame in which the choices in all areas of social life come to be conceived as if they were private choices among different commodities in a market context. One is perhaps confronted here with a kind of 'cognitive simplifier' which, among other things, facilitates the commensurability among different goods, thereby generating a market evaluation that simply ignores the value dimensions that cannot be translated into monetary terms (Radin, 1987; Bowles, 1998).

This market frame has become dominant in part through the policies of commodification inspired by neoliberal economic theory. Even acknowledging the complex nature of commodification processes, one can discern a common trend. This trend can be apprehended by noticing the tremendous transformations in the structure of most economies induced by policy choices which include the liberalization of financial and commercial flows (Helleiner, 1995); massive processes of privatization of state-owned enterprises accompanied by a state-sponsored submission of a number of sectors to competition (Pitelis and Clarke, 1993); efforts to deregulate 'labour markets', i.e. to change the 'rights–obligations' structure in favour of employers (Chang, 2003); or efforts to scale down the welfare-state regimes which previously ensured a non-commodified provision of a vast array of social services (Esping-Andersen, 1994).

The transformations mentioned have been notorious in realms of social life where markets and market norms have previously not played a significant role. Indeed, the reforms witnessed, in several countries, in education or healthcare provision, can be seen as instances of a process where market norms progressively become the reference point in the conduction of public policies. The recent accounts of reforms and tendencies in healthcare provision and in education reveal some major trends in public policies' agenda, promoted by national governments and by international institutions. Healthcare and education – especially higher education – have been increasingly treated as if they were commodities by market-oriented reformers, and state and other public organizations are generally adopting commercial practices typical of private firms (McMaster, 2002). The synthesis provided by Dolfsma et al. (2005, p. 351) for the case of healthcare provision can then be seen to have a wider application:

> The value of the activity is concentrated on exchange-value as opposed to use-value, hence the requirements of measurement, encouraging a focus on outcomes, through such indices as performance indicators. A consequencialist tendency and attitude is thus promoted. In essence this involves 'the market', and references to the market, adopting greater prominence than other organizational mechanisms.

The promotion of individualized monetary incentives for the professionals involved in these activities, combined with the fostering of a competitive environment, are also central to this market-oriented reform process.[6] Encouraging organizations to ensure, by their own means, the financial resources needed for their own functioning is one of the mechanisms used to achieve the desired transformations. As Pellegrino (1999) and Dolfsma et al. (2005) have argued for the case of the commodification of healthcare, and Noble (2002) and Levidow (2005) for the case of higher education, one important part of the process involves recasting the relation among providers and recipients involved in these areas as a commercial relation. This can be attempted not only by changing institutional arrangements that structure the interaction, but also by changing the language used to depict it. In healthcare, the patient is represented as a consumer, who, as in any market, should be free to choose among different alternatives according to its preferences. These preferences tend to be backed by money, as the 'consumer' is increasingly called to support a greater part of the costs of healthcare provision. In higher education, teaching and research activities are increasingly seen as 'products' that must attract the 'demand' of students, in the case of teaching, and of private firms, in the case of research. Even when institutions remain formally within the public sector, their financial resources tend to be linked with success in the competitive struggle with similar institutions in the 'market', and their performance is increasingly assessed in terms of narrow cost-efficiency.

Despite its apparent strength, the trend towards the increasing commodification of social life is empirically contested. One of the recent attempts to do so was made by Williams (2005), who tries to present empirical evidence to argue against what he calls the 'commodification thesis', i.e. against the idea of an unstoppable and inexorable increase in recent decades of the proportion of services and goods that are 'produced for monetized exchange by capitalist firms for the purpose of profit, rather than by the state or community' (Williams, 2005, p. 2). Using, among other indicators, the results of time-use surveys or the percentage of employment generated by the non-profit sector, Williams's study seems to attest the resilience, even in the most affluent societies, of non-paid work, non-monetized exchange or monetized exchange which is not for profit. Together, non-commodified forms of work seem to account for a significant proportion of the economic practices in those economies. If Williams provides a correct picture of the tendencies of our times, the institutional plurality and the diversity of economic practices are here to stay, and commodification, very strictly defined, does not exhibit any tendency to grow.

Nevertheless, as we have shown, there has been, since the 1970s, a neoliberal reassertion of commodification not only in discourse but also in a diverse set of practices promoted by specific policies. Even Williams, otherwise sceptical about the strength of commodification, recognizes the pervasiveness of this trend when he declares: 'wherever one looks, public policy is actively engaged in supporting the development of a commodified economy as the path to progress' (Williams, 2005, p. 187).[7]

The robustness of the neoliberal trend can also be seen in the nature of the instruments that are increasingly applied to assess the impact of public policies themselves. For example, in environmental policies, one of the most powerful mechanisms to treat nature as a commodity is the generalization of the use of cost–benefit analysis (CBA) to evaluate the impact of different public policies in the area of environmental protection (Heinzerling and Ackerman, 2004). CBA emerges generally as a set of methods to identify and balance systematically the monetary impacts of a certain public decision, implying an identification of the overall monetary costs and benefits and determining the liquid benefits of a public policy when compared with the *status quo ante*. While recognizing that in the areas of social regulation it is extremely difficulty to assess the impacts of a decision through the computation of its monetary costs and benefits, the defenders of CBA nevertheless argue that this is the only way to clarify and rationally solve the trade-offs that are inherent to any public decision (Arrow et al., 1996). This notion of trade-off is concomitant with the notion of rational choice in contexts of scarcity – the only way, or so the argument goes, to approach areas of potential social conflict (Paavola and Bromley, 2002).

CBA can then be seen as another effort to replicate, within public policy, the image that neoclassical economic theory has created of individual behaviour. In the area of public policy, individual welfare becomes the sole criterion of evaluation by scrutinizing individual preferences as revealed in real or simulated market-mediated choices (Anderson, 1993). The inevitable trade-offs are rationally approached through an idealized market institution – considered to be the sole institutional source of efficiency. CBA is therefore a deliberate and sophisticated attempt to mimic markets through the public estimation of prices, constituting, according to Sen (2000), one of the most powerful ways of drawing 'market analogies' by assigning a monetary value to nature, precisely as if it were a commodity. It is not fortuitous that the most articulated defenders of CBA, such as Arrow et al. (1996), are at the same time enthusiastic promoters of the actual use of the market for the resolution of environmental problems. This process can then be captured by the concept of proxy commodification 'which can be a precursor of real commodification or coexist with it' and involves 'treating uncommodified entities as commodities by way of manufactured markets via cost–benefit analysis and other techniques' (Castree, 2003, p. 288).

A new line of theoretical and empirical research has recently captured the influence of economics on the dynamics of market creation, which is at the core of neoliberalism. The works of Callon (1998) and MacKenzie and Millo (2003), among others, have stressed the performative dimension of economic discourse, i.e. the ways and means by which it can shape the world in its own image, thereby creating an empirical reality conforming to its own theoretical dispositions. The seemingly unstoppable expansion of the boundaries of markets and of market understandings, i.e. commodification, promises to offer still more avenues to attest the fruitfulness of the 'performative approach' to the articulations between economics and the economy.

Having provided some elements that may serve to identify the tendencies for commodification at an ideological and policy level, one should be careful not to overemphasize their capacity to structure the world in their own image. In fact, and as we have already mentioned, this is a much-contested process.

5. The 'commodification debate': a critical overview

The processes of commodification in discourse and practice gave rise to a very interesting discussion, involving scholars from various disciplinary backgrounds, about the proper place of markets – the so-called 'commodification debate'. One can perceive two major positions in this debate: (1) the idea of 'separate spheres', market and non-market, with their own distinctive sets of practices and meanings, which should remain autonomous; and (2) an opposing view which refuses to subscribe to this supposed dichotomy and insists on the complex and hybrid nature of market (and non-market) arenas of human interaction.

The 'separate spheres thesis' argues for the appropriateness of drawing a line between those things that can properly be conceived as commodities, and those things that cannot, at least not without disturbing consequences, be thought of and transformed into mere commodities exchanged in markets. Among the most influential proponents of this view are Michael Walzer (1983), Elizabeth Anderson (1993) and Michael Sandel (1998).

We think that Sandel's (1998) analysis is representative of the main issues involved in this position. He argues that commodification can be critically assessed by a discourse centred on 'the moral limitations of markets', primarily justified by their corrosive effects on the plurality of values in society. Therefore, certain things and social relations should be insulated from the market.

A point emphasized by Sandel (1998, p. 104), typical of separate spheres theorists, is the association between the moral corrosion induced by market expansion and commensurability (i.e. the idea 'that all goods can be translated without loss into a single measure or unit of value'). Since commensurability is rejected because there is an irreducible plurality of values, the door is opened for Walzer's concept of 'blocked exchanges', i.e. for the careful definition of areas of social life that should not be governed by market norms:

> often enough money fails to represent value; the translations are made, but as with good poetry, something is lost in the process. Hence we can buy and sell universally only if we disregard real values; while if we attend to values, there are things that cannot be bought and sold . . . the abstract universality of money is undercut and circumscribed by the creation of values that can't be easily priced or that we don't want priced. (Walzer, 1983, p. 97)

Walzer (1983) presents a list of disparate items that fall under the heading of 'blocked exchanges', ranging from votes to marriage and friendship. Indeed, it is possible to conceive that certain goods should be insulated from the 'cash nexus', due to their intrinsic characteristics.[8] Additionally, the moral limits of markets can also be apprehended from a perspective that stresses the type of relations involved in markets and the self-interested behaviours favored by them (Cohen, 2003).

The main problem, according to this perspective, is that there are certain values that cannot flourish in the private realm of commodity production and consumption, presupposing instead shared public understandings that the market by itself does not favour. Anderson's (1993) distinction between commodity values, gift values and shared values tries to capture the essential difference in social relations when goods are provided through market and non-market institutions. Gift values find their worth in being given for reasons other than self-interest. Therefore they have an expressive dimension, associated with the intrinsic value of certain social bonds.[9] For goods to be conceived as the expression of gift relationships they must be provided through non-market institutions, the only way to preserve a space for the acknowledgement of individual motivations not reducible to self-interest. Shared values, on the other hand, imply that goods can be valued only when held in common by the members of a certain group, signalling the existence of goals to which its members are jointly committed. This also presupposes non-market institutions nurturing the idea that the fruition of the shared good expresses the participation in a collective endeavour. Anderson's main point is that shared and gift values are shattered when certain goods previously delivered by non-market means are brought under the market. Therefore, according to separate spheres theorists, individual motivations and social expectations, like trust and mutual obligation, themselves the product of non-market institutional arrangements, can be threatened if the market becomes the central institution.

Margaret Radin has been a central figure in the commodification debate, particularly among law scholars. Her contributions directly confronted economic imperialism, as expressed in the law and economics movement inspired by Richard Posner – the quintessential commodified view of the world (Radin, 1987, 1996). By doing this, she exposed the gap between the self-portrayed axiological neutrality of economic imperialism and its inescapable adherence to and promotion of certain values.

Simultaneously, Radin (1989, 1996) criticized the compartmentalization of social life proposed by separate spheres theorists, arguing against a strict association between spheres of life, values and motivations. According to Radin (1996, p. 30), the 'separate spheres' perspective 'prevents us from appreciating the non-market aspects of many of our market relations; it prevents us from seeing fragments of a non-market social order embedded or latent' in market interactions. Therefore the contested nature of market relations is not taken into account. The coexistence of many understandings of what is involved in markets, and of how these different understandings can give rise to several forms of 'incomplete commodification' (i.e. forms of defining the rights–obligations structure of the market transaction to protect certain social interests), is not grasped by separate spheres theorists. For Radin (1989), it would be more realistic to fight over the meaning of social interactions within the market than simply to try to erect barriers walling off certain transactions, thus leaving an important part of human interactions non-scrutinized.[10]

Finally, the separate spheres theory is equated with a 'domino theory', since it favours the idea that, for certain social goods, market expansion necessarily entails the corrosion of non-commodified representations, thus opening the road to 'a slippery slope leading to market domination' (Radin, 1987, p. 1912). Markets are therefore naturalized and viewed as a more resilient domain against which only a few artificial and fragile barriers can be opposed.

By refusing the dichotomous logic of 'separate spheres', Margaret Radin sets the stage for the second major view on the commodification debate: a 'postmodern' turn that insists on the complex and hybrid nature of market (and non-market) arenas of human interaction. In this perspective, the 'separate spheres' critique of commodification is dismissed as too unilateral a view. As Williams and Zelizer (2005, p. 368) claim, 'a more useful approach is to recognise that many market transactions have elements of emotion and sociability, and that many intimate transactions have economic dimensions – so much so that the Hamlet question of whether to "commodify or not to commodify" only serves to confuse us'.[11] Three implications are drawn from this position: (1) the market does not entail the erosion of the plurality of values since it is permeated by them; (2) the process of market expansion contains a potential for emancipation from oppressive non-market structures; and (3) the interesting research question ceases to be whether to 'commodify or not to commodify', becoming one of grasping 'who controls the process and the proceeds' of market transactions (Williams and Zelizer, 2005, p. 373).

Some feminist economists have been important in bringing this position of the debate into economics (e.g. Nelson, 1999; Folbre and Nelson, 2000; Van Staveren, 2001). They argue that the conception of the market (and, more generally, of the economic realm) implicit in the separate spheres thesis is, paradoxically, close to mainstream economics accounts. The economy and economics are thus equated with the 'market sphere', while politics or morality are seen as belonging to exterior 'spheres'; therefore the provision processes that ensure material reproduction, and the science that studies them, end up dissociated from moral and political concerns (Nelson, 2004). These economists favour instead an alternative theoretical approach to 'real' markets, as arenas of human interaction which are richly textured with different social meanings:

> In hypothetical idealized markets, in which purely self-interested autonomous agents interact mechanically, commodification is a given. In contrast, real world markets are often domains of rich and complex social relationships, including aspects of reward, appreciation, reparation, gift and so on. (Folbre and Nelson, 2000, pp. 11–12)

Real markets are of course full of contradictory elements. This means that commodified understandings do not deterministically follow commodified modes of provision. Nevertheless, as commodification of social life is institutionally promoted, one may expect that the multifarious meanings and qualitative distinctions associated with social values can become increasingly narrow. In fact, some particular understandings are, in market contexts, more powerful than others. Their power is rooted in the capacity that the social groups who control the commodified mode of provision have to produce and reproduce structural inequalities and the ideological apparatus which legitimates them. By doing so they ensure a provisional, and always contested, hegemony over social meaning, favouring a 'rhetoric of economic correctness' (Aune, 2001).

The issue of power is related to the social relations that form the background conditions of individuals who participate in markets, thus engendering a potential asymmetric capacity to structure the terms of market exchanges, and conditioning the degree of autonomy possessed by individuals (Nussbaum, 1998). Fabienne Peter has recently argued that the tendency of mainstream economics to adhere to a very narrow conception of individual choice in markets obscures one critical issue: 'the fact that one makes a choice between given alternatives does not mean that one has consented to the constraints that shape the set of alternatives, nor, for that matter, that one has the possibility to express one's consent and dissent in the first place' (Peter, 2004, p. 6). Therefore one should look carefully into the context of the transaction, asking if the seemingly voluntary agreement to sell and buy a commodity does not arise, for example, from the material destitution of one of the parts of the relation (Lutz, 1995). Radin and Sunder (2005, p. 16), in their discussion about the limits of market exchange, have put the matter bluntly but clearly by using the most extreme examples of commodification:

> Markets affect the rich and poor differently. The poor are more likely to be the sellers, and the rich, the buyers, of questionable commodities such as sexual services and body parts. Unequal distributions of wealth make the poorest in society, with little to offer in the marketplace, more likely to commodify themselves – their bodies for sex, their reproductive capabilities, their babies and parental rights.

In sum, commodification involves power relations within a market institution that is unavoidably an 'arena in which some have freedom and some are exposed to that freedom' (Schmid, 2002, p. 135). The enquiry into why and how the parties involved in a market relation can become, due to the structural asymmetry of their conditions of departure, 'object and subject of commodification' (Radin and Sunder, 2005) is therefore crucial. One should then recognize and give an analytically proper place to the potential moral agency of those who are the 'objects' of commodification, which may explain the multiple expressions of 'social resistance' to these processes. Socially embedded groups and individuals[12] may tend to look to certain goods, to the practices associated with their provision, and to the values expressed by those practices, in ways that are totally or at least partially incompatible with market modes of provision. This kind of analytical framework could account for the continuing efforts to block market exchange, or at least to structure markets in ways that prevent full commodification.

6. Final remarks: social economics and commodification

In this chapter we have looked at the increasing relevance of commodification processes within the context of neoliberalism. Following a brief discussion of the concept of commodification, we have explored one of its most significant instances in terms of economic discourse: economic imperialism, or the expansion of neoclassical analytical tools to encompass a vast range of issues conventionally outside the realm of economics. The trend towards commodification was also considered as a set of transformative practices at the core of the rise of neoliberalism. Finally, the stimulating interdisciplinary debate prompted by these developments was critically assessed.

Our overarching goal was to bring the concept of commodification and some of the debates that surround it into economics. We think social economics is in a privileged position to undertake this endeavour. Although the precise meaning of a social economic approach may be the subject of several interpretations, we retain as crucial the presence of the following dimensions: (1) a recognition of the inescapable social nature of economic action and phenomena; (2) a rejection of the fact/value split, meaning that social research has an inherently normative element that must be underlined from the beginning; (3) a commitment to a critical perspective, informed by normative choices, that refuses the naturalization of social reality so often present in economics; and (4) a willingness to incorporate insights from outside economics. Each of these four dimensions can translate themselves into relevant research issues.

Bringing the 'social' within the 'economic' means, first of all, that some degree of autonomy of the social *vis-à-vis* the economic must be recognized, so that it is not possible to express all the domains of social life in the language of the categories associated with the market discourse. Furthermore, and following Polanyi's insights, economic action and phenomena are themselves embedded in society, and any endeavours to disembed them, both in theory and in social practice, are ultimately self-defeating.

The normative elements are particularly relevant to the research on commodification, since, as we have noted, the expansion of markets and of market rhetoric can have adverse consequences on the plurality of moral values that structure and give meaning to human interactions. If we hold a normative perspective that favours the preservation, and even nurturing, of what Anderson (1993) calls 'shared' and 'gift' values, the assessment of these moral consequences, and the search for alternatives capable of avoiding them, are important focal points for future research.

A critical view of the trend towards increasing commodification should be keen to emphasize that these processes are not 'natural' or 'inevitable', but the result of specific political choices, which, like all human choices, are placed in history and can be reversed. The ability to historicize contemporary realities can place them in a long-term perspective, as a process of re-commodification, after the commodification which marked the nineteenth-century liberal order, and the de-commodification of the twentieth-century welfare states.

Finally, given the vitality of the discussion on commodification outside economics, in contrast with its revealing quasi-absence within the discipline, the need for a thoroughly interdisciplinary dialogue is a crucial feature of any meaningful research agenda from a social economics perspective.

Acknowledgements

João Rodrigues acknowledges the support of a scholarship from the Portuguese Science Foundation (SFRH/BD/17973/2004). We would particularly like to thank Ana C. Santos for the detailed criticisms and suggestions she offered us. We also want to thank José Castro Caldas, Ana Costa, Fátima Ferreiro, Helena Lopes, Julie Nelson, Tiago Mata and Nuno Teles for having read and commented on drafts of this chapter at several stages. We also thank Ioana Negru for discussing a previous version presented at the Association for Heterodox Economics Annual Conference 2006. The editors of this volume also gave us precious suggestions. All errors and omissions are our own.

Notes

1. Or 'economics imperialism', to mark a clear distinction from the more canonical use of the expression in the theories of Hobson, Lenin, Luxembourg, and the like. In the sense retained in our analysis, it seems to have originated with Boulding (1969).
2. As the opening paragraph of Marshall's (1920, p. 1) *Principles* stated: 'Political Economy or Economics is a study of mankind in the ordinary business of life; it examines that part of individual and social action which is most closely connected with the attainment and with the use of the material requisites of wellbeing.'
3. For a general overview of the economics of information approach, by one of its leading proponents, accounting for its origins and impacts on economics, see Stiglitz (2000).
4. Fine (2002b) provides a critical appraisal of Lazear's article, from a heterodox, or 'political economy', perspective.
5. For instance, a standard microeconomics textbook puts forward the following definition: 'a market exists whenever two or more individuals are prepared to enter into an exchange transaction' (Gravelle and Rees, quoted in Rosenbaum, 2000, p. 459).
6. Hodgson (1997) and Le Grand (2003), among others, have identified a general tendency for public policies to redesign institutions so that they become similar to a certain vision of the market with its emphasis on monetary incentives and disincentives, ensuring that presumed self-interested individuals pursue the ends best favoured by policy-makers.
7. This should perhaps have made him aware of the limits of his highly empiricist methodology of time-use surveys in assessing the reach of commodification processes.
8. Friendship and trust are cases in point. In fact a plausible understanding of friendship and trust makes them logically contradictory with commodification: when we buy them we cease to have them (Arrow, 1974).
9. This point was voiced by Titmuss (1970) in his influential study on blood donation.
10. 'Blocked exchanges' are conceived only as an extreme case within a continuum, ranging from total market inalienability to unfettered commodification (Radin, 1987).
11. This article is inserted in a recent edited volume – Ertman and Williams (2005a) – that not only maps the contested terrain of the commodification debate, but also signals an apparent predominance of theoretical views that refuse 'a world bifurcated into separate hostile spheres whose boundary is policed by commodification anxiety' (Ertman and Williams, 2005b, p. 4).
12. These embedded individuals, as defined by Davis (2003), have multiple attachments and social relations, market and non-market.

References

Anderson, Elizabeth (1993), *Values and Ethics in Economics*, Cambridge, MA: Harvard University Press.

Arrow, Kenneth (1974), *The Limits of Organisation*, New York: W.W. Norton.

Arrow, Kenneth et al. (1996), *Benefit–Cost Analysis in Environmental, Health and Safety Regulation*, Washington, DC: American Enterprise Institute.

Aune, James A. (2001), *Selling the Free Market: The Rhetoric of Economic Correctness*, New York: Guilford Press.

Becker, Gary S. (1976), *The Economic Approach to Human Behavior*, Chicago, IL: University of Chicago Press.

Becker, Gary S. (1993), 'Nobel Lecture: the economic way of looking at behavior', *Journal of Political Economy*, **101** (3), 385–409.

Birchfield, Vichi (1999), 'Contesting the hegemony of market ideology: Gramsci's common sense and Polanyi's double movement', *Review of International Political Economy*, **6** (1), 27–54.

Boulding, Kenneth (1969), 'Economics as moral science', *American Economic Review*, **59** (1), 1–12.

Bowles, Samuel (1998), 'Endogenous preferences: the cultural consequences of markets and other economic institutions', *Journal of Economic Literature*, **36**, 75–111.

Buchanan, James and Gordon Tullock (1962), *The Calculus of Consent*, Ann Arbor, MI: University of Michigan Press.

Callon, Michel (1998), 'Introduction: the embeddedness of economic markets in economics', in Michel Callon (ed.), *The Laws of the Markets*, New York: Blackwell Publishers, pp. 1–57.

Carrier, James (1997), 'Introduction', in James Carrier (ed.), *The Meaning of the Market: The Free Market in Western Culture*, Oxford: Berg, pp. 1–67.

Castree, Noel (2003), 'Commodifying what nature?', *Progress in Human Geography*, **27** (3), 273–97.

Chang, Ha-Joon (2002), 'Breaking the mould: an institutionalist political economy alternative to the neo-liberal theory of the market and the state', *Cambridge Journal of Economics*, **26**, 539–59.

Chang, Ha-Joon (2003), 'The market, the state and institutions in economic development', in Ha-Joon Chang (ed.), *Rethinking Development Economics*, London: Anthem Press, pp. 41–60.

Cohen, I. Glenn (2003), 'The price of every thing, the value of nothing: reframing the commodification debate', *Harvard Law Review*, **117** (689), 689–709.

Crotty, James (2000), 'The structural contradictions of the global neoliberal regime', *Review of Radical Political Economics*, **32** (3), 361–8.

Davis, John B. (2003), *The Theory of the Individual in Economics*, London: Routledge.

Dolfsma, Wilfred, John Finch and Robert McMaster (2005), 'Market and society: how do they relate, and how do they contribute to welfare?', *Journal of Economic Issues*, **39** (2), 347–56.

Downs, Anthony (1957), *An Economic Theory of Democracy*, New York: Harper & Row.

Ertman, Martha A. and Joan C. Williams (eds) (2005a), *Rethinking Commodification: Cases and Readings in Law and Culture*, New York: New York University Press.

Ertman, Martha A. and Joan C. Williams (2005b), 'Preface: freedom, equality, and the many futures of commodification', in Martha M. Ertman and Joan C. Williams (eds), *Rethinking Commodification: Cases and Readings in Law and Culture*, New York: New York University Press, pp. 1–7.

Esping-Andersen, G. (1994), 'Welfare states and the economy', in N. Smelser and R. Swedberg (eds), *Handbook of Economic Sociology*, Princeton, NJ: Princeton University Press, pp. 711–32.

Fine, Ben (2002a), *The World of Consumption: The Material and Cultural Revisited*, 2nd edn, London: Routledge.

Fine, Ben (2002b), ' "Economic imperialism": a view from the periphery', *Review of Radical Political Economics*, **34** (2), 187–201.

Folbre, Nancy and Julie Nelson (2000), 'For love or money – or both?', *Journal of Economic Perspectives*, **14** (4), 123–40.

Harriss-White, Barbara (2003), 'On understanding markets as social and political institutions', in Ha-Joon Chang (ed.), *Rethinking Development Economics*, London: Anthem Press, pp. 481–9.

Helleiner, Eric (1995), 'Explaining the globalization of financial markets: bringing states back in', *Review of International Political Economy*, **2** (2), 315–41.

Heinzerling, Lisa and Frank Ackerman (2004), *Priceless: On Knowing the Price of Everything and the Value of Nothing*, New York: The New Press.

Hirsch, Fred (1976), *Social Limits to Growth*, Cambridge, MA: Harvard University Press.

Hodgson, Geoffrey (1988), *Economics and Institutions*, Cambridge: Polity Press.

Hodgson, Geoffrey (1997), 'Economics, environmental policy and the transcendence of utilitarianism', in J. Foster (ed.), *Valuing Nature?*, London: Routledge, pp. 48–63.

Kahan, Dan (1998), 'Social meaning and the economic analysis of crime', *Journal of Legal Studies*, **27**, 609–22.

Landes, Elizabeth and Richard Posner (1978), 'The economics of the baby shortage', *Journal of Legal Studies*, **7** (2), 323–48.

Lazear, Edward P. (2000), 'Economic imperialism', *Quarterly Journal of Economics*, **115** (1), 99–146.

Le Grand, Julian (2003), *Motivation, Agency and Public Policy*, Oxford: Oxford University Press.

Levidow, L. (2005), 'Neoliberal agendas for higher education', in Alfredo Saad-Filho and Deborah Johnston (eds), *Neoliberalism: A Critical Reader*, London: Pluto Press, pp. 156–62.

Lutz, Mark (1995), 'Centering social economics on human dignity', *Review of Social Economy*, **53** (2), 171–94.

MacKenzie, Donald and Yuval Millo (2003), 'Constructing a market, performing theory: the historical sociology of a financial derivatives exchange', *American Journal of Sociology*, **109** (1), 107–45.

Marquand, David (2004), *Decline of the Public*, Cambridge: Polity Press.

Marshall, Alfred (1920), *Principles of Economics*, London: Macmillan.

Marx, Karl and F. Engels (1998 [1848]), 'The Communist Manifesto', in Leo Panitch and Colin Leys (eds), *The Communist Manifesto Now*, New York: Monthly Review Press, pp. 240–302.

McMaster, Robert (2002), 'A socio-institutionalist critique of the 1990's reforms of the United Kingdom's National Health Service', *Review of Social Economy*, **60** (3), 403–33.

Nelson, Julie (1999), 'Of markets and martyrs: is it OK to pay well for care?', *Feminist Economics*, **5** (3), 43–59.

Nelson, Julie (2004), 'Clocks, creation and clarity: insights on ethics and economics from a feminist perspective', *Ethical Theory and Moral Practice*, **7**, 381–98.

Noble, David F. (2002), 'Technology and the commodification of higher education', *Monthly Review*, March, 26–40.

Nussbaum, Martha (1998), 'Whether from reason or prejudice: taking money for bodily services', *Journal of Legal Studies*, **27**, 693–724.

Olson, Mancur (1965), *The Logic of Collective Action: Public Goods and the Theory of Groups*, Cambridge, MA: Harvard University Press.

O'Neill, John (1998), *The Market: Ethics, Knowledge and Politics*, London: Routledge.

Paavola, Jouni and Daniel Bromley (2002), 'Contested choices', in Daniel W. Bromley and Jouni Paavola (eds), *Economics, Ethics and Environmental Policies*, Oxford: Blackwell, pp. 3–14.

Pellegrino, Edmund D. (1999), 'The commodification of medical and health care: the moral consequences of a paradigm shift from a professional to a market ethic', *Journal of Medicine and Philosophy*, **24** (3), 243–66.

Peter, Fabienne (2004), 'Choice, consent and the legitimacy of market transactions', *Economics and Philosophy*, **20**, 1–18.

Pitelis, Christos and Thomas Clarke (1993), 'Introduction: the political economy of privatization', in Thomas Clarke and Christos Pitelis (eds), *The Political Economy of Privatization*, London: Routledge, pp. 1–28.

Polanyi, Karl (1957), *The Great Transformation*, Boston, MA: Beacon Press.
Polanyi, Karl (1991), 'The economy as instituted process', in Mark Granovetter and Richard Swedberg (eds), *The Sociology of Economic Life*, New York: Westview Press, pp. 31–50.
Posner, Richard (2002 [1981]), *The Economic Analysis of Law*, New York: Aspen Publishers.
Radin, Margaret (1987), 'Market inalienability', *Harvard Law Review*, **100** (8), 1849–937.
Radin, Margaret (1989), 'Justice and the market domain', in J. Pennock and J. Chapman (eds), *Markets and Justice (NOMOS XXXI)*, New York: New York University Press, pp. 165–97.
Radin, Margaret (1996), *Contested Commodities*, Cambridge: Cambridge University Press.
Radin, Margaret and Madhavi Sunder (2005), 'The subject and object of commodification', in Martha M. Ertman and Joan C. Williams (eds), *Rethinking Commodification: Cases and Readings in Law and Culture*, New York: New York University Press, pp. 8–33.
Robbins, Lionel (1935 [1932]), *An Essay on The Nature and Significance of Economic Science*, London: Macmillan.
Rosenbaum, Eckehard (2000), 'What is a market? On the methodology of a contested concept', *Review of Social Economy*, **58** (4), 455–82.
Sandel, Michael (1998), 'What money cannot buy. The moral limits of markets', *The Tanner Lectures on Human Values*, Oxford, available at http://www.tannerlectures.utah.edu/lectures/documents/sandel00.pdf.
Schmid, Allan (2002), 'All environmental policy instruments require a moral choice as to whose interests count', in Daniel W. Bromley and Jouni Paavola (eds), *Economics, Ethics and Environmental Policies*, Oxford: Blackwell, pp. 133–47.
Sen, Amartya (2000), 'The discipline of cost–benefit analysis', *Journal of Legal Studies*, **29** (2), 873–912.
Stigler, George J. and Gary S. Becker (1977), 'De gustibus non est disputandum', *American Economic Review*, **67** (2), 76–90.
Stiglitz, Joseph E. (2000), 'The contributions of the economics of information to twentieth century economics', *Quarterly Journal of Economics*, **115** (4), 1441–78.
Titmuss, Richard M. (1970), *The Gift Relationship: From Human Blood to Social Policy*, London: Allen & Unwin.
Van Staveren, Irene (2001), *The Values of Economics: An Aristotelian Perspective*, London: Routledge.
Walzer, Michael (1983), *Spheres of Justice*, New York: Basic Books.
Williams, Colin (2005), *A Commodified World? Mapping the Limits of Capitalism*, London: Zed Books.
Williams, Joan C. and Viviana Zelizer (2005), 'To commodify or not to commodify – that is not the question', in Martha M. Ertman and Joan C. Williams (eds), *Rethinking Commodification: Cases and Readings in Law and Culture*, New York: New York University Press, pp. 362–82.
Wood, Ellen (1997), 'Modernity, postmodernity or capitalism?', *Review of International Political Economy*, **4** (3), 539–60.

17 Work: its social meanings and role in provisioning

Deborah M. Figart and Ellen Mutari

The work life of human actors plays a significantly different role within social economics than within mainstream economics. In the textbook model of the labor market, paid employment generates disutility compensated by monetary remuneration. The remuneration is then used to purchase market goods and services to satisfy human wants. Neoclassical labor market theory thus reflects the implicit purpose of economic life in the mainstream (neoclassical) definition of economics articulated by Lionel Robbins in 1935: 'the science which studies human behavior as a relationship between ends and scarce means which have alternative uses' (quoted in Dugger, 1996, p. 31). This definition is one manifestation of what Jon Wisman (2003) has termed 'the material progress vision' in which economic growth is a primary goal of economic life. According to Wisman, 'In some expressions of this vision, material abundance is viewed not only as the prerequisite, but also as the guarantor, of freedom, equality, and justice' (ibid., p. 427).

Social economists challenge the prioritization of material goods and services as the end of economic life. Instead, work itself can be a source of satisfaction. Wisman, for example, suggests that meaningful and challenging work can enhance cognitive development, self-esteem and a sense of community.[1] It is the social relations organizing how work is performed that largely determine whether work is meaningful or alienating (Edwards and Wajcman, 2005). Paid work, of course, is not the only life activity that provides opportunities for meaning. Social economists are therefore concerned with both unemployment (since it limits an individual's access to the material, social and psychological benefits of work) and overemployment (which limits an individual's access to time for other life endeavors). While some social economists emphasize one problem over the other (Mitchell and Wray, 2005) – either the goal of 'full employment' or the goal of reductions in consumption and work hours (George, 2000) – both too little work and too much work can be viewed as inhibiting human flourishing.

Work, rather than simply a means to material ends, is part of a complex process of *social provisioning*. Social provisioning has been advanced as an alternative to Robbins's definition of the terrain of economics

(Figart, 2007). Marilyn Power notes that the term emphasizes 'economic activities as interdependent social processes' (2004, p. 6). Social provisioning indicates that the object of study is how society organizes economic activities, mediated by culture, ideology and institutions (ibid., p. 7). The processes involved in social provisioning, according to William Dugger, 'produce goods and services, but they also produce people' (1996, p. 36). Social provisioning provides an alternative framework for understanding work, one that is consonant with the principles of social economics.

After a brief survey of recent empirical and theoretical research by social economists and others sharing similar perspectives, we shift to the broad theme of job quality, contending that specific issues such as access to steady work, adequate wages, time autonomy and the ability to reconcile paid employment with other life pursuits are all dimensions of the quality of one's work life. Job quality has been an important topic among various schools of heterodox economics, but is largely ignored by mainstream economists. In the final section, we explore the insights gained from a social provisioning approach to the study of job quality, arguing that this is an important area for future studies of work. In particular, social economists have much to contribute on the relationship between work (paid and unpaid) and identity. While most of this chapter focuses on past research on the realm of paid employment, the importance of the interaction between paid and unpaid work activity is a recurring theme.[2] Paid employment, the unpaid work of social reproduction and 'volunteer' work to maintain communities are all socially necessary aspects of provisioning. However, because provisioning is a social process, they are also activities fraught with meaning – both positive and negative. Since social economics is concerned with economic well-being broadly defined, including the just and ethical organization of social institutions and norms, it is well situated to advance our understanding of the complex meanings that work can provide.

Social economists on work: state of the literature
Social economists approach the study of paid employment as they do other realms of economic life. Work is defined by sets of social relations and institutions that are themselves embedded in other social relations and institutions. This broad lens contrasts with mainstream labor economics' more narrow focus on labor market behavior and outcomes that are principally guided by the rational choices of individuals, households and firms (Golden, 1996). According to the neoclassical model, each individual worker makes subjective judgments about the so-called 'labor–leisure trade-off' in offering their labor services.[3] Wage differentials are explained in terms of the equality between remuneration and an employee's contribution to

production, ensured by the workings of supply and demand in the market-place. As the price of an input to the production process, wages are a cost that must be offset by an at least equal benefit to the individual employer purchasing labor services – the equality of exchange. This benefit is the revenue gained by selling labor's product. Market mechanisms, specifically adjustments in the quantity of labor supplied and demanded, are hypothe-sized to regulate wages until costs and benefits are equalized. Compensating differentials theory maintains that workers will trade off poor working con-ditions for higher wages, implying that these job characteristics are inde-pendently determined.

For social economists, economic behavior, even within a market economy, has multiple motivations (including morality, altruism and col-lective intentions) and modes (including cooperation and commitment) (see Beckert, 2006; Davis, 2006). While social economists differ on the foun-dations for ethical economic behavior (Aristotelian, Kantian etc.), one principle that consistently reappears is human dignity. John B. Davis, for example, asserts that social economics rests on 'the idea of a decent society as one which does not undermine human dignity through the existence of institutions that humiliate individuals' (2006, p. 70). Social economists thus interrogate employment and other economic activities by examining whether or not they foster human dignity. Again, this contrasts with main-stream approaches in which efficiency as an alleged means of utility maxi-mization is the primary criterion for normative judgments. The task for social economists, therefore, has been to analyze the conditions under which paid and unpaid work are currently performed and to recommend managerial and public policies, as well as other social institutions and customs, that would enable work to meet these expanded criteria.

The study of work is a distinct project, however, because social econo-mists recognize that labor markets are fundamentally different than markets for typical commodities. Robert Prasch (2004), in an essay com-bining both institutional and social economics perspectives, suggests three distinguishing characteristics of labor:

1. Labor cannot be separated from its providers.
2. Labor cannot be stored.
3. Labor embodies the quality of self-consciousness.

As Prasch notes (2004, p. 155, n. 1), the concept of labor as 'different in form and ethical status from a bag of concrete' was first articulated by Karl Polanyi ([1944] 1957), who termed labor a 'fictitious commodity'. Also following the legacy of Polanyi, social economists have docu-mented the processes by which globalization and economic liberalization have attempted to commodify work (see, e.g., Hodgson, 2005; Williams, 2006).

Social and structural factors affecting work time have been a particular focus. For example, Lonnie Golden (1996) provides an alternative way of modeling outcomes related to the mean, duration, variability and flexibility of work. Asserting that neoclassical models cannot explain the 'simultaneous growth of the twin labor market failures of underemployment and overemployment' (ibid., p. 3), Golden argues that the current distribution of hours is neither efficient nor socially productive. His model incorporates elements of post-Keynesianism (market adjustments via quantities rather than prices) and structural approaches (institutionalist and segmented labor market theories' emphasis on historical time, social customs and feedback effects). One implication of his 'holistic framework' is that public policy interventions are necessary to improve social welfare (see also Golden, 1998; Sousa-Poza and Henneberger, 2002).

Wage-setting is another area where social economists have long distinguished themselves from mainstream approaches. Much of this work is grounded in the legacy of Catholic social thought advocating the need for a 'living wage' (Figart, 2001). Over a century ago, Monsignor John A. Ryan, for example, argued that human dignity is only possible if one has 'decent livelihood', the ability to live in 'a reasonable degree of comfort' (Ryan, 1906, p. 73). In a society in which wage-earning is the primary means of provisioning, the right to dignity thus leads to a right to a living wage. Social reformers of the early twentieth century were themselves forging 'a kind of "social" economics that allowed sentiment, morality, and ethics to intrude on discussions of appropriate wages' (Robinson, 2004, p. 249). Contemporary social economists have continued to base the claim to a living wage (implemented through minimum wage and other regulations) on its relationship to human dignity. Adequate wages are viewed as a means to 'self-sufficiency' and an antidote to poverty among the working poor (Ciscel, 2004; Nissen, 2004). They are also postulated to boost effective demand (thereby raising employment) and to pressure employers to invest in productivity-enhancing technologies (thereby reducing either employment or work hours). More than simply changing economic outcomes, however, minimum wage laws and other employment policies serve as institutional markers of procedural fairness (Davis, 1999, p. 501).

Oren Levin-Waldman (2003) treats dignity, however, not simply as an end in itself but as a means of ensuring democracy. Democracy, he argues, requires autonomous citizens, and 'autonomy depends on access to and control over economic resources' (ibid., p. 499). Robert Prasch and Falguni Sheth (1999) also link adequate wages and a defense of the minimum wage to citizenship. But they enlarge the traditional (Lockean) definition of the ideal 'autonomous' citizen to account for the contributions of those with family obligations and who do unpaid work in the home.

Wage-setting figures prominently in social economists' work on discrimination. Much of this work consists of empirical studies documenting labor market discrimination against women and various racial–ethnic groups (see, e.g., Lovell, 2000; Srinivas, 2007). In particular, several studies examine persistence and change in the degree and form of earnings inequality as economic and social institutions evolve (Mason, 2000; Deshpande, 2000). Traditional methodologies for measuring discrimination, and the definition of discrimination itself, have come under scrutiny, however, for focusing exclusively on outcomes rather than economic processes (Figart, 2000; Figart and Mutari, 2004).

Social economists have only recently begun addressing issues of unpaid work and caring labor, drawing upon insights from feminist economics (see, e.g., van Staveren, 2005). Inequality in allocation of paid and unpaid labor, coupled with women's increased participation in paid labor, has had economic consequences, including the reduction of social capital and pressures on social reproduction processes while maintaining women's diminished bargaining power (Heath et al., 1998). Other studies addressing the role of households in economic well-being have utilized capabilities theory to argue that social economists must move beyond traditional indicators of material opulence as an evaluative criterion (Oughton and Wheelock, 2003; Altman and Lamontagne, 2004). As noted by Stephanie Seguino and Sandra Butler, 'The assumption that well-being (or utility) can be reduced to material goods and leisure time ignores the importance of psychological well-being induced by a variety of factors such as stability, safety, nurturing, and belongingness and the means by which parents attempt to provide these to children' (1998, pp. 208–9). This need to move beyond material opulence (or material provisioning) is an important emerging theme, one that we will explore further in the next two sections.

Main issues and implications

The various dimensions of work studied by social economists reflect an overarching concern with job quality. Adequate and fair wages, timing and duration of work hours that reflect individual and social needs, and working conditions that foster dignity, autonomy and citizen engagement are all characteristics of what have been termed 'good jobs'. What social economists are contributing to the job quality literature, however, is not simply a critique of neoclassical models rooted in labor supply and demand. Social economics, with its emphasis on social, and not simply material, provisioning, enriches our understanding of meaningful work.

Much of the early literature about 'good jobs' versus 'bad jobs' within economics and sociology relied upon a definition of economics as concerned with *material provisioning*.[4] Defining economics as the study of how human beings materially provision for themselves dates back to the work of eighteenth-century classical economists such as Adam Smith, but fell out of favor with the rise of neoclassical economics during the twentieth century. Heterodox economists, especially institutional economists writing in the tradition of Thorstein Veblen and John Commons, continued to utilize the concept of 'provisioning' as central to what economic actors do, but such work was increasingly marginalized within the discipline (Boulding, 1986; Forstater, 2004; Nelson, 2006). The definition of economics as material provisioning, although better than the neoclassical study of constrained choice, was limited in other ways. Specifically, as noted by Julie Nelson, material provisioning excludes 'the non-physical sources of human satisfaction' (1993, p. 32). The limits of the material provisioning framework, as opposed to social provisioning, is reflected in the economic literature on job quality.

Scholarship in the 1950s through the 1970s sought to catalog the hierarchical rankings of jobs in the economy in order to explain poverty and unemployment among disadvantaged workers. Bad jobs were jobs that did not facilitate a socially recognized material standard of living, in other words, a living wage. In contrast with neoclassical economists, institutional and radical economists viewed wage differentials and differences in employment status as resulting from structural barriers rather than the market value of an individual's attributes. Dual labor market theory, for example, posited a distinction between a primary sector and a secondary sector (Doeringer and Piore, 1971). In this framework, 'Good jobs were well-paid, secure, and connected to paths of upward mobility. Bad jobs were low-paid, unstable, and dead-end' (Tilly, 1997, p. 269). An individual's pay and promotion prospects were determined largely by the industrial sector in which s/he worked. Economic restructuring, specifically the declining share of employment in the manufacturing sector and the increase in service sector employment, was interpreted as a declining primary sector and expanding secondary sector (Levy and Murnane, 1992; Gittleman and Howell, 1995).

Wages, the primary means of provisioning in a market economy, were the principal basis for categorizing jobs and industries in early research. Further examination, however, led scholars to conclude that service industries include both a high-wage and a low-wage sector. According to a study by economist Joseph Meisenheimer (1998, p. 28), the best-compensated workers in some service industries earn considerably more than the best-compensated in other industries; but the lowest-paid workers in services also fare worse than lower-paid workers elsewhere. Even within industries, job quality varies substantially. Hunter's (2000) study of nursing homes found substantial variation in the quality of entry-level jobs for nursing assistants; in his study, as in most, job quality was determined by wages, benefits, and opportunities for training and advancement. As a result of such research, labor economists in the institutional and Marxian traditions noted that both the primary and secondary sectors had, in fact, primary and subordinate jobs within them (Gordon et al., 1982; Craig et al., 1985; Albelda et al., 2004). These structural divisions were often differentiated by race-ethnicity, gender and nation within an increasingly global economy.

Heterodox economists have also argued that good jobs and bad jobs are often allocated on the basis of the gender and race-ethnicity of the worker (see, e.g., Gittleman and Howell, 1995; Cherry, 2001). This leads to discrimination against individuals, but also differences in remuneration, status, working conditions and access to job ladders on the basis of the gender-typing and sometimes the racial-ethnic typing of particular occupations or jobs. The characteristics of good jobs are generally associated with occupations held by white males, while working women and men of color are concentrated in subordinate sectors. The problem with such analyses, however, is that they presume that occupational structures are fixed; gender and race-ethnicity determine placement but not the quality of the jobs themselves (Figart and Mutari, 2004).

Studies of job quality have also been influenced by recent trends increasing labor market flexibility. In a comparative study based on data collected by the International Labour Organization, Joseph Ritter and Richard Anker (2002) found that job satisfaction was largely a factor of several qualities identified by Guy Standing (1999) as declining with global flexibilization. These included work security (on-the-job safety), employment security (job stability), security of occupational skills (meaning transferability of skills) and voice representation security (especially unionization and employer attitudes). Similarly, Kalleberg et al. (2000) note the expansion of non-standard employment relations (part-time employment, temporary and contingent work, day labor and contract work) as a reason to reassess job quality. They found that non-standard employment was consistently associated with the characteristics of bad jobs – which they defined in terms of wages and the provision of material benefits of health insurance and pensions. In contrast, the positive forms of flexibility – those that provide workers with control over their schedules – seem to be concentrated in well-paid jobs with substantial authority, according to Elaine McCrate (2005). Her findings also suggest that women do not have greater access to flexible jobs than men, and black workers actually have more rigid schedules.

Research on job quality has moved beyond a narrow focus on material provisioning to explore other job characteristics. Though pay is 'the single most important element of job quality in the view of most workers' (Meisenheimer, 1998, p. 24), non-monetary characteristics also matter. Jencks et al. (1988), for example, culled 48 job characteristics from a national telephone survey in the USA, the 1980 Survey of Job Characteristics. Of these, 14 (earnings plus 13 non-monetary variables) had statistically significant effects on the way workers evaluated their jobs. The non-monetary factors included: hours, vacation time, on-the-job training, risk of job loss, educational requirements, proportion of repetitive work and relative position ('Does your boss have a boss?'). Also important were organizational factors such as union coverage, state/local employee, federal employee, and working conditions such as whether and to what extent workers get dirty, decide their own hours and are subjected to frequent supervision (see Jencks et al., 1988). Using multiple regression analysis, a weighted index of job desirability (IJD) was constructed. While the index was highly correlated with pay, the 13 non-monetary job characteristics, taken together, were twice as important as earnings in determining a job's desirability.

As a result of these and similar studies, researchers acknowledged that people themselves place more value on job aspects such as autonomy, fulfillment and ability to balance work and family. The comparative study by Ritter and Anker (2002), for example, confirmed that job characteristics providing satisfaction tend to cluster; jobs that are good in one dimension such as pay tend to be rated highly by incumbents on other factors as well.

Tracing changes in the conceptualization of good and bad jobs, Chris Tilly (1997) praised the index of job desirability developed by Jencks et al. as an important landmark in integrating a variety of job characteristics. Nevertheless, he noted that there continue to be conceptual difficulties in characterizing job quality. For example, it is empirically unclear whether 'bad' and 'good' characteristics cluster together (as assumed by dual labor market and segmentation theories) or whether they are independently determined. It *is* clear that job characteristics are shaped by employers' expectations about the job-holders – that some jobs are created as breadwinner jobs while others are designed for workers with family responsibilities, for example.

Most importantly, Tilly asserted that 'the term good job implies that certain jobs are good regardless of who holds them' (1997, p. 269). This assumption is increasingly problematic if we pay attention to the diversity of workers and their needs, dreams and desires. Different workers may hold different values, and social values may themselves change over time. Social context matters, as the definition of social provisioning declares.

Attention to the diversity of economic actors is also a hallmark of capabilities theory as articulated by Amartya Sen, Martha Nussbaum and others (Nussbaum and Sen, 1993). In his book *Inequality Reexamined*, Sen posed the dilemma of how to create ethical social arrangements in light of human diversity. Most ethical judgments are based on the assertion of some fundamental equality. For Sen, diverse humans should be equally capable of achieving 'functionings that he or she has reason to value' (1995, pp. 4–5). Well-being, according to Sen (1999), is dependent upon both meeting basic needs and having meaningful choices about how to live. Access to resources is a prerequisite. One way of envisioning good jobs, therefore, is as a means of providing access to resources that enable people to achieve well-being as they define it.

Steven Pressman and Gale Summerfield (2000) have described ways in which Sen applied his framework to work. Employment, they note, 'yields many benefits besides economic goods and services; it provides social contacts, skills and psychological well-being or self-esteem' (ibid., p. 93). In fact, Sen critiqued the behavioral foundations of neoclassical theory by stressing that work effort is motivated by a sense of commitment and a belief in shared goals more than simple remuneration: 'Every economic system has, therefore, tended to rely on the existence of attitudes toward work which supersedes the calculation of net gain from each unit of exertion' (1977, p. 334). In a study of Canadian social policies, Andrew Jackson of the Caledon Institute draws upon a capabilities framework, arguing that ' "Good jobs in good workplaces" are needed if individuals are to be able to develop their talents and capacities to actively participate in society, and to enjoy a broad equality of life-chances' (2003, p. 1). He further notes that:

> Inclusion in the labour market means more than having a job which provides an income and a modicum of 'human capital.' It also means being able to derive some meaning and fulfillment from work. Jobs are valued by workers not only for purely economic reasons, but also to the extent that they provide interesting work, self-dignity and respect, and good relations with co-workers and supervisors. (Ibid., p. 8)

The capabilities framework has influenced a stream of research and policy analysis on 'decent work'. The concept of 'decent work' originated from the policy agenda of the International Labour Organization (ILO), set forth in a 1999 Report of the Director-General (Ghai, 2003). The four components of decent work, according to the ILO, are (1) opportunities for safe and remunerated employment (both formal and informal); (2) social protection (including many of the traditional elements of social welfare policies); (3) workers' rights (incorporating the ability to associate and organize, as well as the absence of discrimination, forced labor, and child labor); and (4) social dialogue (collective bargaining rights, but also a voice for workers in civil society). In this framework, process and voice are as important as outcomes in defining job quality. While many studies deriving from the decent work paradigm have focused on macroeconomic indicators comparing countries (Ghai, 2003; Ahmed, 2003; Anker et al., 2003), the framework can be applied to analyzing the quality of specific jobs within an industrial relations system.

In a recent study of the impact of information and communication technologies on job quality, Jill Rubery and Damian Grimshaw (2001) utilize the ILO's conception of decent work to provide an expanded definition of job quality. They note, however, that job quality in individual places of employment requires a social and political context in which the macroeconomic indicators of decent work are already in place. Rubery and Grimshaw's nine dimensions of job quality include: (1) the opportunity to exercise skills for personal fulfillment and productive or social service; (2) autonomy and control on the job; (3) fairness of the system of managerial control and discipline; (4) opportunities for freedom of association and collective bargaining; (5) job security, including opportunities to use skills acquired with another employer; (6) job responsibilities, noting that these provide opportunities for both job satisfaction and stress; (7) work intensity, focusing on its implications for physical and mental health and for opportunities to have a satisfying personal and family life; (8) opportunities to develop and enhance one's skills or to move into more satisfying, more secure, or better-paid employment over a life cycle; and (9) opportunities for creative activities, problem solving, incremental innovation and personal initiative in the interest of improving quality or service. This broad conceptualization of job quality is consonant with the social provisioning approach.

New directions for studying work within social economics

Recent work on identity within social economics suggests fruitful avenues for further research. Social economists have emphasized the concept of human dignity as a basis for personal identity of socially embedded individuals, positing the promotion of human dignity as a social value and a normative standard for policy.[5] Dignity requires personal integrity and internal coherence. Humiliation, in contrast, represents the violation of human dignity. Humiliating social institutions, according to John Davis, 'undermine individuals' personal integrity or their sense of identity' (2006, p. 80).[6] Systematic humiliation, including institutional discrimination, denies people self-respect.

Economic activity is essential to the construction of identity. Provisioning is a gendered and racialized process. Masculinity, under the male-breadwinner family model, is, in part, based on the ability to provide for a family. The good jobs held by white males were created as jobs for primary breadwinners. Employer policies, labor activism and negotiations, and labor market regulations were constructed to reinforce gendered social practices such as the male-breadwinner family and married women's domestic labor (Figart et al., 2002; Mutari, 2004). At the same time, the male-breadwinner family, though hegemonic, was never universal. Regional economies historically relied upon the labor force participation of both men and women of color, especially African-American men and women. Minority-concentrated jobs were structured for co-breadwinners, thus diminishing individual salaries and opportunities for advancement. Further, working conditions based on relations of subservience continued long after slavery. The male-breadwinner family and public policies designed to foster it became one means of defining a commonality of whiteness.

Members of privileged groups develop property rights in their racial and gender identities, according to a game-theoretic model developed by William Darity, Patrick Mason and James Stewart (Darity et al., 2006). 'Whiteness' or 'maleness' are not simply descriptive characteristics, according to these authors, but may actually constitute 'productive property'. Being white, or male, or both, pays. For example, by asserting his identity as a white male (and thereby a 'breadwinner'), a worker might claim a priority position in discriminatory hiring queues. Such identities garner income and wealth for group members, making them intransigent over time. Identity, therefore, is constructed around issues of power and access to resources (see also Mason, 2000).

The construction and maintenance of identity, however, can also provide an important motivation for economic activity beyond power, access to resources and daily and intergenerational survival. This assertion is supported by empirical studies from outside the discipline of economics on people's experiences on what they themselves consider good jobs or good work (see, e.g., Gardner et al., 2001; Stebbins, 2004). When balanced against the large number of studies of bad jobs and declining working conditions, our understanding of what workers themselves view as good work is fairly limited. In a study of professionals who do 'good work', defined as vocations involving expertise and a social purpose, Gardner et al. maintained that such work contributes to a holistic sense of identity: 'a person's deeply felt convictions about who she is, and what matters most to her existence as a worker, a citizen, and a human being' (2001, p. 11). Minimally, one must be able to reconcile what one does with a 'mirror test'. That is, one must be able to be proud of what one does.

Unfortunately, these empirical studies of good work focus on a narrow selection of professional occupations. In contrast, Joanne Ciulla, in her book

The Working Life, contended that too often 'Academics who write about work . . . mistakenly assume that everyone wants a job like theirs' (2000, p. xiii). Focusing on the diversity of human situations, she observed that a variety of activities provide individuals with meaning. We need to recognize this diversity (not everyone wants to be a college professor), while also recognizing that these diverse meanings are formed within a social context (a culture where intellectuals are perceived as snobbish, self-absorbed and unproductive). As a further example, the stay-at-home mother may be doing work that is in fact important and fulfilling, but her choice to forego paid employment is also shaped by prevailing gender relations. How do we value caring labor while enlarging women's opportunites? In response to this tension between diversity and universality, Ciulla emphasizes the importance of values such as justice, mutual respect, honesty and dignity in improving the experience of diverse forms of work. These are job characteristics that foster a positive sense of personal identity.

Work is not simply a commodity and it is not subject to natural laws governing its allocation. Paid and unpaid work are human activities that contribute to a process of social provisioning. Therefore the ethical treatment of workers and the just organization of employment institutions are intrinsic areas of study for social economists. Identity, along with the non-material aspects of social provisioning, are emerging areas in which social economics can also continue to impact the study of work.

Notes

1. See also Kelloway et al. (2004). For a history of the concept of the disutility of work within mainstream economics, see Spencer (2003).
2. Further, this chapter emphasizes employment issues at the micro and meso level, rather than the macroeconomics of job creation and unemployment.
3. As feminists have long noted, the assumption that all unpaid time is 'leisure' is gender biased.
4. In contrast, the quality of workers, measured in terms of their human capital attainment, is of greater concern than job quality for mainstream policy approaches. See Rima (2000) for a critique of this position.
5. The social economics view of individual identity contrasts with the neoclassical rational economic actor who is unreflective about his or her preferences, concerned only with outcomes, not processes, and lacks internal coherence (Teschl, 2006).
6. Ciulla also found that workers she interviewed contrasted humiliation and dignity as central criteria in evaluating their jobs.

References

Ahmed, Iftikhar (2003), 'Decent work and human development', *International Labour Review*, **142** (2), 263–71.
Albelda, Randy, Robert Drago and Steven Shulman (2004), *Unlevel Playing Fields: Understanding Wage Inequality and Discrimination*, 2nd edn, Boston, MA: Economic Affairs Bureau.
Altman, Morris and Louise Lamontagne (2004), 'Gender, human capabilities and culture within the household economy: different paths to socio-economic well-being?', *International Journal of Social Economics*, **31** (3/4), 325–64.

Anker, Richard, Igor Chernyshev, Phillippe Egger, Farhad Mehran and Joseph A. Ritter (2003), 'Measuring decent work with statistical indicators', *International Labour Review*, **142** (2), 147–77.

Beckert, Jens (2006), 'The moral embeddedness of markets', in Betsy Jane Clary, Wilfred Dolfsma and Deborah M. Figart (eds), *Ethics and the Market: Insights from Social Economics*, London: Routledge, pp. 12–25.

Boulding, Kenneth E. (1986), 'What went wrong with economics?', *American Economist*, **30** (1), 5–12.

Cherry, Robert (2001), *Who Gets the Good Jobs? Combating Race and Gender Disparities*, New Brunswick, NJ: Rutgers University Press.

Ciscel, David (2004), 'The determination of living wages', in Deborah M. Figart (ed.), *Living Wage Movements: Global Perspectives*, London: Routledge, pp. 51–66.

Ciulla, Joanne B. (2000), *The Working Life: The Promise and Betrayal of Modern Work*, New York: Three Rivers Press.

Craig, Christine, Elizabeth Garnsey and Jill Rubery (1985), 'Labour market segmentation and women's employment: a case study from the United Kingdom', *International Labour Review*, **124** (3), 267–80.

Darity, William A., Jr, Patrick L. Mason and James B. Stewart (2006), 'The economics of identity: the origin and persistence of racial identity norms', *Journal of Economic Behavior & Organization*, **60** (3), 283–305.

Davis, John (1999), 'Is trade liberalization an important cause of increasing U.S. wage inequality? The interaction of theory and policy', *Review of Social Economy*, **57** (4), 487–506.

Davis, John (2006), 'The normative significance of the individual in economics: freedom, dignity, and human rights', in Betsy Jane Clary, Wilfred Dolfsma and Deborah M. Figart (eds), *Ethics and the Market: Insights from Social Economics*, London: Routledge, pp. 69–83.

Deshpande, Ashwini (2000), 'Recasting economic inequality', *Review of Social Economy*, **58** (3), 381–99.

Doeringer, Peter B. and Michael J. Piore (1971), *Internal Labor Markets and Manpower Analysis*, Lexington, MA: D.C. Heath & Co.

Dugger, William M. (1996), 'Redefining economics: from market allocation to social provisioning', in Charles J. Whalen (ed.), *Political Economy for the 21st Century: Contemporary Views on the Trend of Economics*, Armonk, NY: M.E. Sharpe, pp. 31–43.

Edwards, Paul and Judy Wajcman (2005), *The Politics of Working Life*, Oxford: Oxford University Press.

Figart, Deborah M. (2000 [1997]), 'Gender as more than a dummy variable: feminist approaches to discrimination', *Review of Social Economy*, **63** (3), 509–36.

Figart, Deborah M. (2001), 'Ethical foundations of the contemporary living wage movement', *International Journal of Social Economics*, **28** (10/11/12), 800–814.

Figart, Deborah M. (2007), 'Social responsibility for living standards: presidential address, Association for Social Economics, 2007', *Review of Social Economy*, **65** (4), 391–405.

Figart, Deborah M. and Ellen Mutari (2004), 'Wage discrimination in context: enlarging the field of view', in Dell P. Champlin and Janet T. Knoedler (eds), *The Institutionalist Tradition in Labor Economics*, Armonk, NY: M.E. Sharpe, pp. 179–89.

Figart, Deborah M., Ellen Mutari and Marilyn Power (2002), *Living Wages, Equal Wages: Gender and Labor Market Policies in the United States*, London and New York: Routledge.

Forstater, Mathew (2004), 'Envisioning provisioning: Adolph Lowe and Heilbroner's worldly philosophy', *Social Research*, **71** (2), 399–418.

Gardner, Howard, Mihaly Csikszentmihalyi and William Damon (2001), *Good Work: When Excellence and Ethics Meet*, New York: Basic Books.

George, David (2000), 'Driven to spend: longer work hours as a byproduct of market forces', in Lonnie Golden and Deborah M. Figart (eds), *Working Time: International Trends, Theory and Policy Perspectives*, London: Routledge, pp. 127–42.

Ghai, Dharam (2003), 'Decent work: concept and indicators', *International Labour Review*, **142** (2), 113–45.

Gittleman, Maury B. and David R. Howell (1995), 'Changes in the structure and quality of jobs in the United States: effects by race and gender, 1973–1990', *Industrial and Labor Relations Review*, **48** (3), 420–40.

Golden, Lonnie (1996), 'The economics of worktime length, adjustment, and flexibility', *Review of Social Economy*, **54** (1), 1–45.

Golden, Lonnie (1998), 'Working time and the impact of policy institutions: reforming the overtime hours law and regulation', *Review of Social Economy*, **56** (4), 522–41.

Gordon, David M., Richard Edwards and Michael Reich (1982), *Segmented Work, Divided Workers: The Historical Transformation of Labor in the United States*, Cambridge: Cambridge University Press.

Heath, Julia A., David H. Ciscel and David C. Sharp (1998), 'The work of families: the provision of market and household labor and the role of public policy', *Review of Social Economy*, **56** (4), 501–21.

Hodgson, Geoffrey M. (2005), 'Knowledge at work: some neoliberal anachronisms', *Review of Social Economy*, **63** (4), 547–65.

Hunter, Larry W. (2000), 'What determines job quality in nursing homes?', *Industrial and Labor Relations Review*, **53** (3), 463–81.

Jackson, Andrew (2003), *'Good Jobs in Good Workplaces': Reflections on Medium-term Labour Market Challenges*, Ottawa, Ontario: Caledon Institute of Social Policy.

Jencks, Christopher, Lauri Perman and Lee Rainwater (1988), 'What is a good job?: a new measure of labor-market success', *American Journal of Sociology*, **93** (6), 1322–57.

Kalleberg, Arne L., Barbara F. Reskin and Ken Hudson (2000), 'Bad jobs in America: standard and nonstandard employment relations and job quality in the United States', *American Sociological Review*, **65** (2), 256–78.

Kelloway, E. Kevin, Daniel G. Gallagher and Julian Barling (2004), 'Work, employment, and the individual', in Bruce E. Kaufman (ed.), *Theoretical Perspectives on Work and the Employment Relationship*, Urbana-Champaign, IL: Industrial Relations Research Association, pp. 105–31.

Levin-Waldman, Oren (2003), 'The minimum wage and the cause of democracy', *Review of Social Economy*, **61** (4), 487–510.

Levy, Frank and Richard J. Murnane (1992), 'U.S. earnings levels and earnings inequality: a review of recent trends and proposed explanations', *Journal of Economic Literature*, **30** (3), 1333–81.

Lovell, Peggy A. (2000), 'Race, gender and regional labor market inequalities in Brazil', *Review of Social Economy*, **58** (3), 277–93.

Mason, Patrick L. (2000), 'Understanding recent empirical evidence on race and labor market outcomes in the USA', *Review of Social Economy*, **58** (3), 319–38.

McCrate, Elaine (2005), 'Flexible hours, workplace authority, and compensating wage differentials in the U.S.', *Feminist Economics*, **11** (1), 11–39.

Meisenheimer, Joseph R. II (1998), 'The services industry in the "good" versus "bad" jobs debate', *Monthly Labor Review*, **121** (2), 22–47.

Mitchell, William and L. Randall Wray (2005), 'Full employment through job guarantee: a response to critics', Working Paper No. 39, Kansas City, MO: Center for Full Employment and Price Stability.

Mutari, Ellen (2004), 'Brothers and breadwinners: legislating living wages in the Fair Labor Standards Act of 1938', *Review of Social Economy*, **62** (2), 129–48.

Nelson, Julie A. (1993), 'The study of choice or the study of provisioning? Gender and the definition of economics', in Marianne A. Ferber and Julie A. Nelson (eds), *Beyond Economic Man: Feminist Theory and Economics*, Chicago, IL: University of Chicago Press, pp. 23–36.

Nelson, Julie A. (2006), *Economics for Humans*, Chicago, IL: University of Chicago Press.

Nissen, Bruce (2004), 'The Miami living wage ordinance', in Deborah M. Figart (ed), *Living Wage Movements: Global Perspectives*, London: Routledge, pp. 157–70.

Nussbaum, Martha C. and Amartya Sen (eds) (1993), *The Quality of Life*, Oxford: Oxford University Press.

Oughton, Elizabeth and Jane Wheelock (2003), 'A capabilities approach to sustainable household livelihoods', *Review of Social Economy*, **61** (1), 1–22.

Polanyi, Karl ([1944] 1957), *The Great Transformation: The Political and Economic Origins of Our Time*, Boston, MA: Beacon Press.

Power, Marilyn (2004), 'Social provisioning as a starting point for feminist economics', *Feminist Economics*, **10** (3), 3–19.

Prasch, Robert E. (2004), 'How is labor distinct from broccoli? Unique characteristics of labor and their importance for economic analysis and policy', in Dell P. Champlin and Janet T. Knoedler (eds), *The Institutionalist Tradition in Labor Economics*, Armonk, NY: M.E. Sharpe, pp. 146–58.

Prasch, Robert E. and Falguni Sheth (1999), 'The economics and ethics of minimum wage legislation', *Review of Social Economy*, **47** (4), 466–87.

Pressman, Steven and Gail Summerfield (2000), 'The economic contributions of Amartya Sen', *Review of Political Economy*, **12** (1), 89–113.

Rima, Ingrid H. (2000), 'Sectoral changes in employment: an eclectic perspective on "good" jobs and "poor" jobs', *Review of Political Economy*, **12** (2), 171–90.

Ritter, Joseph A. and Richard Anker (2002), 'Good jobs, bad jobs: workers' evaluations in five countries', *International Labour Review*, **141** (4), 331–58.

Robinson, Tony (2004), 'Hunger discipline and social parasites: the political economy of the living wage', *Urban Affairs Review*, **40** (2), 246–68.

Rubery, Jill and Damian Grimshaw (2001), 'ICTs and employment: the problem of job quality', *International Labour Review*, **140** (2), 165–92.

Ryan, John A. (1906), *A Living Wage: Its Ethical and Economic Aspects*, London: Macmillan.

Seguino, Stephanie and Sandra S. Butler (1998), 'To work or not to work: is that the right question?', *Review of Social Economy*, **56** (2), 190–219.

Sen, Amartya K. (1977), 'Rational fools: a critique of the behavioral foundations of economic theory', *Philosophy and Public Affairs*, **6** (4), 317–44.

Sen, Amartya (1995 [1992]), *Inequality Reexamined*, Cambridge, MA: Harvard University Press.

Sen, Amartya (1999), *Development as Freedom*, New York: Anchor Books.

Sousa-Poza, Alfonso and Fred Henneberger (2002), 'An empirical analysis of working-hours constraints in twenty-one countries', *Review of Social Economy*, **60** (2), 209–40.

Spencer, David A. (2003), 'Love's labor's lost? The disutility of work and work avoidance in the economic analysis of labor supply', *Review of Social Economy*, **61** (2), 235–50.

Srinivas, Sumati (2007), 'Social attitudes and the gender pay gap in the USA in recent years', *International Journal of Social Economics*, **34** (4), 268–75.

Standing, Guy (1999), *Global Labour Flexibility: Seeking Distributive Justice*, London: Macmillan.

Stebbins, Robert A. (2004), *Between Work & Leisure: The Common Ground of Two Separate Worlds*, New Brunswick, NJ: Transaction Publishers.

Teschl, Miriam (2006), 'The impact of identity on economics', in Betsy Jane Clary, Wilfred Dolfsma and Deborah M. Figart (eds), *Ethics and the Market: Insights from Social Economics*, London: Routledge, pp. 84–97.

Tilly, Chris (1997), 'Arresting the decline of good jobs in the USA?', *Industrial Relations Journal*, **28** (4), 269–74.

Van Staveren, Irene (2005), 'Modelling care', *Review of Social Economy*, **63** (4), 567–86.

Williams, Colin C. (2006), 'Beyond the market: representing work in advanced economies', *International Journal of Social Economics*, **33** (3/4), 284–330.

Wisman, Jon D. (2003), 'The scope and promising future of social economics', *Review of Social Economy*, **41** (4), 425–45.

PART VI

SOCIALLY EMBEDDED EXCHANGE: FIRMS

Chapter 18: 'Firms: collective action and its supportive values', by Helena Lopes and José Castro Caldas

Mainstream theories of the firm tend to rely only on two ideal-type principles of order – *separation* (the market mechanism) and *command* (the surrender of individual autonomy to an 'external' agent) – thus marginalizing a third one – *association* (the adoption of collective goals by individuals and the corresponding collective action). This is the case both with Coase and with Alchian and Demsetz, from whom all the present-day multiple and conflictive mainstream theories descend. The chapter surveys and analyses these 'classic' approaches and some of their developments, and argues that multiple principles of order, including association, will have to be mobilized in order to explain firms. It further recalls Chester Barnard's as an instance of such a pluralistic view. Barnard's intuitions, when combined and integrated with more recent contributions from different social disciplines that account for the values that support collective action within firms, may provide a sound foundation for a socio-economic understanding of the firm.

Chapter 19: 'Knowledge spillover entrepreneurship and innovation in large and small firms', by David B. Audretsch and Max Keilbach

The strikingly high observed rates of innovative activity for small and new firms has generated the Schumpeterian paradox. How is it possible that new and small firms are able to generate innovations in the absence of their own knowledge resources? The purpose of this chapter is to suggest a reconciliation of this paradox. The knowledge spillover theory of entrepreneurship posits that entrepreneurship is an endogenous response to knowledge generated but not entirely commercialized by incumbent firms and other organizations. Entrepreneurship serves as a conduit of knowledge spillovers by providing the mechanism by which knowledge created within one organizational context becomes commercialized through the creation of a new firm.

Chapter 20: 'Firms, managers and restructuring: implications of a social economics view', by Hans Schenk

This contribution recalls that most mergers undertaken by large firms fail economically, and subsequently argues that this is to be expected in an economy that is dominated by the few. This expectation follows if one is prepared to drop maximization-of-rationality presumptions, and instead adopts a view that allows firms to behave strategically. In particular, the author argues that firms tend to imitate their peers for a mixture of reasons, especially in order to reduce the risk of falling behind. This phenomenon is able to account for the fact that mergers and acquisitions always appear in waves. After the peak, and because of the high failure rates, many mergers must be broken up again, which is something that currently belongs to the expertise of private-equity-leveraged buyout firms. This is not without its own problems, however. Rather than accepting the costs of such restructuring carousels, it is suggested to reintroduce the public purpose standard in merger control so that inefficient mergers will become less normal.

18 Firms: collective action and its supportive values
Helena Lopes and José Castro Caldas

1. Introduction

Firms have always been a source of embarrassment to mainstream economics. In the past the problem was that an explanation for their existence was missing. In fact, Adam Smith had identified the division of labour as the key to the wealth of nations, and noted that it could be achieved either in the market or within the pin factory. But while he elaborated extensively on why the division of labour was dependent on markets, he did not feel the need to explain why specialization, rather than market mediated, was sometimes effected within the pin factory. Two centuries later Coase (1937) identified this blind spot in Smith's legacy. He perceptively noted that for a theoretical account that depicted the 'normal economic system' as one that 'works itself' in the absence of any type of central control, firms would remain abnormal facts unless an explanation were provided for their very existence.

Coase did indeed advance such an explanation. However, instead of just filling a gap in Smith's legacy, thus helping economics to move forward, he opened a Pandora's box. In fact, what came after Coase was not just the elaboration of his approach, but multiple and conflictive theories. For mainstream economics, today, what is perceived as a deficiency is not the lack of a theory of the firm but the absence of a unified approach (Garrouste and Saussier, 2005).

In this chapter we recall and briefly analyse some of the most influential theories of the firm[1] in economics, with a focus on the competing explanations provided for the problem of aligning individual behaviour and organizational goals – the problem of order. We argue in favour of a broader view, which acknowledges the social dilemmatic nature of collective action within firms and the unavoidable moral dimension of all attempts to overcome it.

Accounts of order in mainstream economics, as elaborated in Section 2, tend to rely on two pure principles of order – *separation* (the market mechanism) and *command* (the surrender of individual autonomy to an 'external' agent) – or rather, on specific combinations of those principles. A third pure principle – *association* (the adoption of collective goals by individuals

305

and the corresponding collective action) – is usually either excluded or casually referred to in passing.

Sections 3 and 4 present a survey of the received theories of the firm, which all descend from two seemingly contradictory seminal contributions – Coase's (1937) and Alchian and Demsetz's (1972). While Coase's approach, which inaugurated the transaction cost lineage, draws mostly on direction, a form of *command*, Alchian and Demsetz's (1972), which preceded agency and new property rights theories, claims to be a theory of *separation*. Common in those views is the underrating of *association*.

In Section 5, it is argued that multiple principles, including association, will have to be mobilized in order to explain firms. An instance of such a pluralistic view is Chester Barnard's (1938). By recalling Barnard's *The Functions of the Executive*, in Section 6, we intend to suggest that it may provide a sound foundation for future advances in the understanding of the firm. In Section 7 we show that Barnard's intuitions can be combined with and integrate recent contributions from different social disciplines that account for the values that support collective action within firms. Section 8 concludes.

2.   Principles of order: separation, command and association

Separation and *command* are the ideal-type principles under which different 'solutions' to the problem of social order have been advanced in mainstream economics. Although differing in every other respect, those principles hold in common the behavioural assumptions of self-interest and opportunism. Under those assumptions individuals are supposed to ignore the consequences of their actions for others except when the welfare of others has an impact on their own self-satisfaction. They are opportunistic in the sense that their conformance to moral or social norms of conduct is conditional on a cost–benefit analysis and they act only for the achievement of common goals when no opportunity exists that might yield a larger payoff.

Separation as a solution to the problem of social order is well illustrated by Mandeville's *Fable of the Bees* according to which individuals, or rather, bees, which mind only their own business, successfully achieve the best possible social outcome.

Separation is not a Robinson Crusoe world. Although confined within protected property divides, separated individuals interact. They recognize the benefits of specialization, and, as Mandeville's bees did, they exchange productive services and products, thus capturing the gains of commerce.

With time *The Fable of the Bees* became the metaphor behind mainstream accounts of the economy, and separation the 'natural' principle of order. Since it clearly seems fitter to describe markets, one could hardly expect to re-encounter it in respect of firms. But, as we shall see, Alchian and Demsetz's intention has been precisely to unveil organization, exposing the surrogate market within, thus dissolving the puzzle of the existence of islands of command in the market ocean.

In mainstream accounts separation seldom stands alone. As a principle of social order it collapses whenever the trivial fact is acknowledged that self-serving individuals may conflict. In that case, separation (the market) fails and some other (artificial) principle has to be called for in order to avoid 'the war of all against all'. That principle is command.

Command, in its pure form, involves the surrender of individual autonomy and resulting coercion. Its two poles are power and obedience – the attribution of the prerogative of making decisions to some individuals, and of the duty to obey to others. Under command, individuals are constrained to obey simply because the cost of exit is untenable. Such is Hayek's picture of central planning or Marx's description of the capitalist firm.

The employment relationship, which is at the core of the capitalist firm, may be conceived from the point of view of separation – as a market exchange of the productive services of labour or, as in Marx, but also in Simon (1957), Coase (1937) and Arrow (1974, p. 25), as 'different in many ways from an ordinary commodity contract', in that the 'employee is selling willingness to obey to *authority*'.

In fact, the relationship can also be conceived under both principles: as long as entry and exit at low cost in the labour relationship are guaranteed, there is separation; but to the extent that liquidity may depend on the general conditions of society, the possibility of exit may be more or less constrained. Also depending on the general conditions of society, namely unemployment and property assignments, the constraints imposed on the freedom of the parties may be asymmetrical. It makes sense to relate the asymmetric assignment of rights and duties between employers and employees, and the acceptance of subordination by employees, to coercion. But the possibility of someone *preferring* obedience even when she could exercise direction exists and must be considered.[2]

Association, the third principle of order underrated in mainstream accounts of order, is voluntary action of individuals towards a common goal. It involves a balanced assignment of rights and duties among all concerned, namely decision rights, which may nevertheless be delegated. It presupposes the capacity of individuals to communicate, to identify common goals, to frame the action context in *we* terms, to conceive themselves as part of a team and to commit themselves to act accordingly. Association may only be made sense of once a moral capacity of individuals is acknowledged. To associate is always to engage in mutual trust relations. For self-serving, opportunistic individuals association breaks down in free-riding. In economics, therefore, association is either taken as infeasible (Olson, 1971) or postponed to an uncertain future.

3.   Setting the stage
Coase's questions are still the starting point for all mainstream discussions on the firm. Having in mind the background that presents coordination through market transactions directed by price movements as a superior mechanism in respect to efficiency, Coase enquired why, 'within the firm, these market transactions are eliminated and in place of the complicated market structure with exchange transactions is substituted the entrepreneur co-ordinator, who directs production'. Or, even more bluntly: 'why is there any organization?' (Coase, 1937, pp. 35–6).

His answer, we recall, is that 'there is a cost of using the price mechanism' (ibid., p. 38): costs in discovering the relevant prices, and costs of negotiating separate contracts to each transaction. Conversely, within the firm, 'a factor of production (or the owner thereof) [meaning capital] does not have to make a series of contracts with the factor with whom he is cooperating [meaning labour] . . . for this series of contracts is substituted by one' (ibid., p. 39). Therefore, from Coase's perspective the firm would emerge to economize on the costs of market contracting.

Coase clearly understood the nature of the labour contract as one in which one party 'agrees to obey the directions of [another] within certain limits' (ibid.), and which involves a set of rights and obligations that are substantively and normatively different from those of a pure market transaction of commodities:

> (1) The servant must be under the duty of rendering personal services to the master or to others on behalf of the master, otherwise the contract is a contract for sale of goods or the like.
> (2) The master must have the right to control the servant's work . . . It is this right of control and interference . . . which is the dominant characteristic in this relation and marks off the servant from an independent contractor . . .
> We thus see that it is the fact of direction which is the essence of the legal concept of 'employer and employee'. (Ibid., p. 54)

The puzzling question in respect to Coase's paper is, of course, the assumption of obedience. Contracts are negotiated and celebrated among human beings, not among factors of production, and obedience in social relations is highly problematic. However, Coase takes obedience for granted – once a contract is celebrated, both parties will comply. Issues related to incompleteness, opportunism and the difficulties of monitoring and of measuring performance are left unexamined.

More than three decades later, Alchian and Demsetz (1972) took up once again Coase's question – why is there any organization? – advancing this time an answer that did not take obedience for granted.

Their rationale for the existence of firms was clearly stated: (a) 'resource owners increase productivity through cooperative specialization' (Alchian and Demsetz, 1972, p. 777); (b) gains from specialization can be obtained either within an organization such as the firm, or across markets; (c) an 'economic organization', be it the market or the firm, will be efficient to the extent that it will apportion 'rewards in accord with productivity' (ibid., p. 778); (d) team production, that is, production that uses several resources, owned by different people, may yield an output that is larger than the sum of separable outputs; (d) in face of team production any decentralized market mechanism will fail in aligning productivity and rewards due to 'metering problems', that is, the difficulty of measuring individual productivity and apportioning proportional rewards; (e) if 'there is a net increase in productivity available by team production, net of metering cost . . . , then team production will be relied upon rather than a multitude of bilateral exchange of separable individual outputs' (ibid., p. 780); but (f) the efficient solution of the metering problem in team production requires a 'centralized contractual agent' (ibid., p. 778).

In this account 'resource owners' are caught in a social dilemma – a collective action problem. They all recognize the advantage of team work but since in 'team production, marginal products of cooperative team members are not so directly and separably (i.e. cheaply) observable' (ibid., p. 780), the alignment of rewards and input contribution cannot be taken for granted, and, in the absence of such an alignment, they all have an incentive to shirk on their productive efforts. The incentive to shirk would be absent if there were a cost to shirking. However, such a cost could not be imposed on each other in a decentralized way. Given that metering, monitoring and punishing are costly, a second-order collective action problem would arise since every 'owner of resources' would have once again an incentive for shirking in those tasks. In sum, in face of this double collective action problem any decentralized mechanism that might align productivity and rewards would fail.

While decentralized methods would fail, a centralized one might work: 'One method of reducing shirking is for someone to specialize as a monitor to check the input performance of team members' (Alchian and Demsetz, 1972, p. 781). As pointed out by the authors, this will immediately lead to the vexed question of who will monitor the monitor. The solution, however, is straightforward:

to give him [the monitor] title to the net earnings of the team, net of payments to other inputs. If owners of inputs agree with the monitor that he is to receive any residual product above prescribed amounts (hopefully, the marginal value products of the other inputs), the monitor will have an added incentive not to shirk as a monitor. (Ibid., p. 782)

Although dependent on the strong assumption of the possibility of meter-ing individual productivity and the corresponding alignment of rewards, we have here a coherent explanation not only of the firm but of the privately owned firm. The 'owners of resources' have an incentive to cooperate – they are entitled to rewards which are in accord with productivity – and the monitor, as a residual claimant, also has an incentive not to shirk as a monitor. The alignment of individual action and organizational goals acquires a Hobbesian flavour – the surrender of autonomy, the subordina-tion of 'owners of resources', is justified on the grounds that rational and free individuals voluntarily submit to monitoring for the sake of efficiency:

> hence, team members who seek to increase their productivity will assign to the monitor not only the residual claimant right but also the right to alter individ-ual membership and performance on the team . . . [O]nly the monitor may uni-laterally terminate the membership of any of the other members. (Alchian and Demsetz, 1972, p. 782)

It might therefore be argued that in Alchian and Demsetz's view of the firm there is command after all. Nevertheless the authors themselves insist on denying it:

> The firm . . . has no disciplinary power of fiat, no authority, no disciplinary action any different in the slightest degree from ordinary market contracting between any two people. I can 'punish' you by withholding future business or by seeking redress in the courts for any failure to honor our exchange agreement. That is exactly what the employer can do. (Ibid., p. 777)

Instead, they present the firm as a surrogate market: 'the firm takes on the characteristics of an efficient market in that information about the charac-teristics of a large set of inputs is now more cheaply available' (ibid., p. 795). As long as the monitor is supposed to perform only the market's function of aligning performance and rewards,[3] the authors may be justified in asserting that 'the firm can be considered a privately owned market', and that 'the firm and the ordinary market' are only 'competing types of markets' (ibid.). To that extent, but only to that extent, Alchian and Demsetz's is a theory of the firm based on *separation*.

4.   Developments in the theory of the firm: new clothes for command and separation

Building on Coase's, and on Alchian and Demsetz's seminal works, three distinctive but interrelated approaches have emerged: transaction cost, agency and property rights theories.[4] Contrary to Walrasian orthodoxy, these approaches hold that most contracting is unavoidably incomplete due to uncertainty and information asymmetries. Another central common feature is the main behavioural assumption of self-interest seeking with allowance for guile.[5]

Transaction cost theories

Transaction cost theory shares with Coase a predominant focus on transaction costs and organizational issues. Bounded rationality, time, uncertainty, privately held information, opportunism and asset specificity[6] are all elements introduced into the theory by Williamson and his followers, which contribute to substantially enhance both *ex ante* and *ex post* (re)negotiation costs. Transaction cost theory then focuses on the formal and informal institutional arrangements that may minimize these transaction costs as time goes by. To make it simple, bounded rationality, uncertainty and asymmetries of information make it difficult (*ex ante*) to write complete contracts, and opportunism and asset specificity make it difficult (*ex post*) to enforce previous agreements. The costs of constant negotiation and adaptation to contingencies may make it worth organizing the transaction so that all the relevant assets are commanded by a single economic entity. Managed coordination is thus substituted for price-guided coordination.

Within the firm, the existence of firm-specific human assets, that is, the specific human capital of employees, leaves both the workers and the firm vulnerable to being held up: the firm may attempt to take advantage of the loss incurred by the worker if he leaves, and the worker may threaten to leave the firm and take with him his valuable know-how. How is this dilemma – made explicit by the adoption of opportunism as the relevant behavioural assumption – to be solved within this theoretical framework?

Part of the solution put forward involves the acknowledgement of non-pecuniary individual motives such as reciprocity, trust and reputation. However, the crafting of credible commitments requires fiat and complex contracting. As it is assumed that both firms and employees have interest in a long-term relationship, workers may voluntarily agree to carry out the employer's commands as long as they are fairly treated by the firm; the firm has in turn no incentive to take advantage of workers as long as they perform satisfactorily. In this sense, it is in each party's interest to build a good reputation, be trustworthy and cooperate.[7]

Trust and reciprocity are here conceived as instrumental behavioural norms that emerge from sustained interaction in organizations but that cannot alone account for order: 'Because the efficacy of a reputation effect varies with the nature of transactions and with the conditions of embeddedness (local sanctions and the like), this and other theories of spontaneous order often need to be augmented by providing transaction-specific intentional order of an ex post governance kind' (Williamson, 2005, p. 11). Hence transaction cost theory ultimately relies on the hierarchical mode of governance. Contracts are supposed to be enforced and authority made effective mainly by administrative control and by various sanctioning devices. Wlliamson's as much as Coase's is a hierarchical theory of the firm.

Agency theories
Agency theories represent a new attempt to free the theory of the firm from the element of command. They stress the limitations of hierarchies in ensuring obedience. Relying instead on the apportioning of rewards in accordance with productivity to achieve efficiency, they leave aside organizational features and concentrate on incentive devices that may promote the alignment of the employees' and the employers' conflicting interests.

Contrary to Alchian and Demsetz, whose theorization is confined to the analysis of team work, agency theories intend to generalize their argument to all contractual relationships involving the firm.

> We are sympathetic with the importance [Alchian and Demsetz] attach to monitoring, but we believe the emphasis that [they] place on joint production is too narrow and therefore misleading. Contractual relations are the essence of the firm, not only with employees but with suppliers, customers, creditors and so on. The problem of agency costs and monitoring exists for all of these contracts, independent of whether there is joint production in their sense; ie, joint production can explain only a small fraction of the behaviour of individuals associated with a firm.
> It is important to recognize that most organizations are simply legal fictions which serve as a nexus for a set of contracting relationships among individuals. (Jensen and Meckling, 1976, p. 8)

In agency theories, Alchian and Demsetz's 'contractual centralised agent' that monitors employees' performance no longer exists. The firm is formally reducible to a nexus of bilateral agency relations, defined as contracts under which the *principal* hires the *agent* to perform services on his/her behalf and monitors him on a bilateral basis.[8] Agency models then concentrate on the problem of metering, monitoring and rewarding workers' effort. As information is asymmetric and the optimal strategy of opportunistic agents does not optimize the utility function of the principal, a system of incentives has to be established to ensure that agents provide the expected level of effort.

The earlier models posit that pecuniary compensation is the sole motivator, and a multitude of models exist that propose sophisticated ways of tying compensation levels to absolute or comparative input or output measures. If agency relations are of a contractual nature and do not differ from other market relations, monetary signals alone are supposed to regulate employee/employer relations. Authority is eliminated as a variable of interest in the theory of the firm and substituted by autonomous parties contracting; markets are now everywhere.

However, as recognized by the prominent authors of the theory, the design of incentive-compatible devices does not empirically eliminate the issue of the enforcement of irreducibly incomplete contracts.[9] To make the argument more realistic, more recent models integrate non-pecuniary motives such as intrinsic motivations, preference for power, the ability to remain employed, co-workers' esteem or justice concerns, and enlarge the type of incentives accordingly. No mention is made of the possible conflict between those motives and pecuniary ones.[10]

Only when it comes to analysing group incentive schemes is the collective action nature of organizational life acknowledged. The free-riding problem and the associated threat of underperformance are then explicitly stated in a collective and productive setting, and the usual dyadic and exchange frame is dropped down. Peer pressure, multilateral monitoring, reputation and the internalization of the welfare of the group (Baron and Kreps, 1999) are then called for to align individual behaviour and collective goals.

In sum, separation, as the source of order within firms, is the driving principle in agency theory. However, when joint production is concerned, agency theory furtively departs from it.

The new property rights approach of firms
This approach focuses on what are viewed as ill-resolved problems in contractual theories: what are the benefits of organizing the transactions within the firm? How should the difficulties that arise from writing or enforcing incomplete contracts be handled?

Alchian and Demsetz's 'residual claimant' idea is here developed and the firm is defined as being composed of the assets that it owns or over which it has control (Grossman and Hart, 1986). Ownership is defined as the power to exercise control. Control rights are purchased (that is, firms come into existence) because they confer residual rights of control, that is, the right to control all aspects that are not *ex ante* specified or contractible (in particular, it is impossible *ex ante* to contractually specify a clear division of the surplus to be generated). Firms exist because the control of several assets by a single ownership unit may be more efficient than separate ownership, depending on the relative costs and benefits of such control. The central focus of the theory is the study of the optimal property assignment of assets.

In the seminal papers, employees are not substantively distinguished from outside independent contractors (Grossman and Hart, 1986, pp. 694, 717).

The specificity of the employment relationship resides in the fact that the employer purchases the residual rights of control over employees' *actions* instead of *assets*. Authority rights are but one type of property right that derives from the property of non-human assets. Employees have the obligation to obey as they have contracted with the non-human assets owners that the latter have the right to specify and decide what actions they have to undertake. Such a contract is assumed to be enforceable because of competition between employees: 'since there are many subordinates, none is in a position to refuse to carry out the owners' wishes or to argue about terms' (Grossman and Hart, 1986, p. 699). Therefore no special governance skills are required from managers to command the productive activity of employees.

> An important idea underlying the analysis is that a key right provided by ownership is the ability to exclude people from the use of assets. We have argued that this authority over assets translates into authority over people: an employee will tend to act in the interest of his boss. Although we have emphasized the role of tangible assets such as machines, location, or clients' lists, we suspect that the ideas may generalize to intangible assets such as goodwill. Some nonhuman assets are essential for the argument, however, and in fact we suspect that they are an important ingredient of any theory of the firm. The reason is that in the absence of any nonhuman assets, it is unclear what authority means. Authority over what? Control over what? Surely integration does not give a boss direct control over workers' human capital, in the absence of slavery. (Hart and Moore, 1990, p. 1150)

New property rights theory follows Alchian and Demsetz in not distinguishing the employment relationship from any other mercantile contract (in both cases the sanctions are the same; disruption of the relationship can take the particular form of firing), but it captures Coase's insight by assuming that one agent is more likely to do what another agent wants if they are in an employment relationship.

As explicitly recognized by the authors, ownership rights 'shift the incentives for opportunistic and distortionary behaviour, but [they] do not remove these incentives' (Grossman and Hart, 1986, p. 716). Command is clearly the solution advanced for the social dilemma within the firm: obedience is granted because the 'future livelihood [of employees] depends on [the owners of productive assets]' (Hart and Moore, 1990, p. 1150).

5.   The missing link: association
In mainstream theories of the firm, there are always elements of separation – relations are of a contractual nature – and command – the employment relationship involves subordination. In transaction cost and new property rights theories the element of command is salient; in Alchian and Demsetz's it is disguised under the clothes of separation.

In fact, Alchian and Demsetz's (1972) contention that the 'the firm and the ordinary market' are only 'competing types of markets' (ibid., p. 795) and that the power to manage is in no way different from the consumer's little power to 'assign his grocer to various tasks' (ibid., p. 777) is untenable. While the grocer can use the resources he owns as best suits him, the employee – such are the terms of the employment relationship – must use hers according to the directions of the monitor. The 'owner of resources' must accept the instructions of the monitor, as the grocer must accept orders, but while the 'owner of resources' has agreed to transfer the control over the use of inputs she owns, the grocer has not. This amounts to a fundamental difference between the division of labour in the market and its counterpart in the firm. While the first is supposed to be driven by free choice of autonomous individuals, the second is led by the discretion of a monitor who holds 'the right to alter individual membership and performance in the team'.

Alchian and Demestz's firm may indeed be viewed as the result of a Hobbesian social contract, in which the Leviathan's role is assigned to the residual claimant. In the same vein, the principal–agent employment relationship, which, in agency theories, is presented as a trivial contractual exchange, is in fact specific to the firm since it necessarily involves, as Coase noted, the direction by the principal over the agent.

Command, in its pure form, is a dual relation involving power and obedience. If the firm is to be ultimately explained by the unavoidable element of command, an account must be provided for both power and obedience. Understanding obedience, in particular, is crucial. As shown by the mainstream debates on the nature of the firm, assuming it at the outset won't do. Similarly, explaining it by evoking the structure of rewards and punishments internal to the firm is, to say the least, incomplete. As was clearly understood by Arrow (1974, p. 72), these structures 'account only in part for the extent to which authority is in fact exercised'. As also pointed out by Arrow (ibid.), if authority relied solely on rewards and punishments, 'authority would not be viable. Control mechanisms are, after all, costly. If the obedience to authority were solely due to potential control, the control apparatus would be so expensive in terms of resources used as to offset the advantages of authority.'

The third principle of order, *association*, or voluntary action of individuals towards a common goal, is marginalized in mainstream accounts of order, appearing as a footnote in the new institutional theories of the firm.[11] It is argued that the condition for an order based exclusively on this principle would be a capacity for commitment without limits – a moral imperative of some sort. Since such a commitment is in fact too demanding, the possibility of a pure associational order is at least highly problematic. Even when the capacity for commitment is acknowledged,[12] it is generally conceived as bounded by the weakness of the will, and conditional on the behaviour of others. Conditional commitment gives rise to a behavioural pattern that is usually described as reciprocity. The implication is that association cannot be taken for granted. The same reciprocity that on some occasions may sustain cooperation on other occasions may backfire, triggering a spiral of retaliations.

However, excluding the possibility of a purely associational order does not equate to the dismissal of the importance of association in any sustainable order. In noting the importance of direction and authority, the new institutional theories of the firm were pointing to one of the key elements in organization. However, in marginalizing association, they were missing another one.[13]

Every order may indeed require an element of command.[14] However, to be viable that element must be *authority* – one form of command that is not grounded on coercion and that is perceived as legitimate, eliciting consent. Consent in turn is always grounded in justice attributions, mutual commitments and trust, as discussed below.

Consented authority may thus be viewed as an associative relationship, involving reciprocity and presupposing not the self-centred opportunists of mainstream theories but individuals endowed with a moral capacity.

The bottom line is thus the need for an account of the firm that acknowledges the complementarity of multiple principles of order, including association. Such an account must take on board the moral capacity of individuals: as consent may account for authority, it is indeed morality that may explain the commitment and trust that sustain consented authority.[15]

6.   Revisiting Barnard: the moral element in the firm

Contractual theories, in keeping with their vision of economics as the analysis of *exchange*, view firms as devices that coordinate allocation of resources more efficiently than markets through sophisticated bilateral contracting. Agency problems, predominantly framed in a bilateral impersonal way, are to be solved by separation or command. However, the primary purpose of firms is the coordination of *production* rather than exchange, and production is most of the time a collective endeavour that requires cooperation between several individuals. Here, Williamson's famous 'in the beginning there were markets' is to be replaced by 'in the beginning there was joint production', and in place of a series of parallel bilateral contracts between potentially opportunistic individuals stands a collective action venture facing the risk of collapse. As stated by Demsetz (1995), incomplete information and opportunism generate a productive function for managers: that of reducing shirking behaviour.

It is precisely the complex *Functions of the Executives* that Barnard (1938) elaborates upon. At the time when Coase was formulating his transaction cost explanation of firms, Barnard was elaborating on the complementarity of principles of order to provide one of the most remarkable understandings of the firm.

Barnard (1938) conceives organizations as 'systems of cooperative services of persons' rather than as 'the sum of services of individuals' (a formula that accurately anticipates the contractual approach). A formal system of cooperation requires an objective, a purpose, and Barnard rightly points to the distinction to be made between collective and individual purposes or motives. Gregariousness calls for cooperative activity and 'social satisfactions' may be derived from the pursuit of collective purposes. However, adherence to the norms and values that sustain collective action should not be taken for granted. For Barnard, the viability of the cooperative effort, that is, the reconciliation of the 'opposite poles of the system',[16] with common purpose as one pole and the person's desires at the other, involves two dimensions:

> The persistence of cooperation depends on a) its effectiveness, and b) its efficiency. Effectiveness relates to the accomplishment of the cooperative purpose, which is social and non-personal in character. Efficiency relates to the satisfaction of individual motives, and is personal in character. The test of effectiveness is the accomplishment of a common purpose; effectiveness can be measured. The test of efficiency is the eliciting of sufficient individual wills to cooperate. (Barnard, 1938, p. 60)

Although persons are agents of the action, the action is not personal; it is collective, its character determined by the requirements of the system:

> An organisation comes into being when (1) there are persons able to communicate with each other (2) who are willing to contribute action (3) to accomplish a common purpose . . . These elements are necessary and sufficient conditions initially and they are found in all organizations.
>
> Willingness [to cooperate] . . . means self-abnegation, the surrender of control of personal conduct, the depersonalisation of personal action. Its effect is cohesion of effort, a sticking together. Its immediate cause is the disposition to 'sticking together'. (Ibid., pp. 82, 84)

How does Barnard explain the willingness to cooperate? If he dedicates lengthy developments to the issue of incentives,[17] the affording of which he recognizes to be one of the more important and difficult tasks of organizations, he also repeatedly warns against the abuse of monetary inducements. For him, the running of the system of cooperative effort involves, apart from incentives, two other closely integrated elements: authority and the 'moral element'.

> Authority is the character of a communication (order) in a formal organization by virtue of which it is accepted by a contributor or 'member' of the organization as governing the action he contributes; that is, as governing or determining what he does or he is not to do . . . According to this definition, authority involves two aspects: first, the subjective, the personal, the *accepting* of a communication as authoritative; and, second, the objective aspect . . . the 'system of coordination'. (Ibid., p. 163, italics added)

On this definition, authority is of both personal and institutional origin: it rests on the acceptance or consent of individuals as much as on institutionalized rules. The voluntary deference to organizational authorities depends on an efficient system of communication – that is, intelligible and consistent orders, efficient channels of communication, among others conditions – a system mainly understood by Barnard as 'lines of authority'.[18] The objective of communication is to define the common purpose and prescribe action; its challenge is to induce people to cooperate.

The *moral element* is defined as the ideal purpose or ends of organizations; it always refers to the future and implies foresight in terms of some norm of desirability (Barnard, 1938, p. 201).[19] Morality is defined by Barnard as the willingness to subordinate immediate self-interest to both ultimate personal interest and the general good, with the cautious qualification that, at the organization level, the 'general good' is also subject to moral justification. The uncertainty of the outcome, the delicacy of communication, the complexity and instability of motives call for the moral element because only a moral element may inspire cooperative attitudes by creating faith in the superiority of the common purpose and in the ultimate satisfaction of personal motives. The resolution of moral conflicts represents a major challenge to managers. Because every organization has many different and unavoidably divergent purposes, activities and orders may be seen by different members – or even by the same member – as *right* from one point of view but *wrong* from another. That is why Barnard considers the moral element as the most important factor for cooperation and 'moral creativeness' as the main function of executives.

As the sources of morals are diverse (practice and experience, religious beliefs, social environment, biological properties and phylogenetic history), a person most probably possesses several different codes of morals which may enter into conflict in some situations. Such conflict of codes is a serious personal issue and may result in moral deterioration, frustration, diminution of the sense of responsibility, or withdrawal. 'Moral creativeness' is the invention of a moral basis for the solution of moral conflicts by substituting a new action that avoids the conflict or by providing a moral justification for exception or compromise. The change of purpose proposed must be 'just', that is, consonant with the morality of the whole, as well as acceptable, that is, consonant with the morality of the individual. Without the moral element, organizations die because the moral element is indispensable in creating the desire for adherence – for which no incentive is a substitute.

Barnard's conception of order in organizations thus clearly relies on the complementarity between separation (incentives), command (hierarchy and authority) and association (morally grounded consent and trust). His insights have been confirmed by recent studies on trust and justice which throw light on the high correlation between trustworthiness attributions, justice perceptions and organizational commitment.

7.   Trust and justice as supportive values for collective action

The fact that cooperation depends on people *voluntarily* engaging in collective aims led organizational scholars to focus on trust and justice as key elements in the operation of organizations and networks. Departing from opportunism as the grounding assumption on which to devise institutional arrangements, social scientists have been looking for the motivational foundations of what we have called association.

Paradoxically, many of the theories advanced to give an account of trust and justice-driven behaviour rely on self-interest-seeking explanations; that is, they try to give an account of trust and justice motives in light of the separation principle. Axelrod (1984) argued that cooperation, of which trust is a basic requirement, is sustained by the 'shadow of the future'. Trust would result from a subjective probability calculation of the potential costs and benefits of future interactions. 'When we say we trust someone or that someone is trustworthy, we implicitly mean that the probability that s/he will perform an action that is beneficial or at least not detrimental to us is high enough to consider engaging in some form of cooperation with him/her' (Williamson, 1993, p. 463).

Trust, thus conceived, is in the process of being internalized by mainstream economics, where it plays the function of a social lubricant. The existence of trust in long-term relationships reduces transaction costs and promotes the self-enforcement of contracts, hence lessening the need for costly control and sanctioning mechanisms to protect people and organizations from opportunism and betrayal. In repeated games, trustworthiness is at the basis of reputation, and this often renders it an optimal strategy. Trust therefore appears as an efficient device at both personal and institutional levels if there is the expectation that enough others will reciprocate trusting behaviour, as will indeed happen between enlightened utility maximizers.

From this perspective trust has been conceptualized as a psychological state of perceived vulnerability or risk that is derived from individuals' uncertainty regarding the motives, intentions or prospective actions of others on whom they depend. If this vulnerability is assimilated to any other situation of uncertainty and seen as resulting from the respective calculation of risks and benefits, as seems to be the case, then there is no substantial difference at all between trust and any other risky economic exchange. But one may, on the contrary, consider that this vulnerability is deliberate and results from an orientation towards others that characterizes humans as social beings rather than from direct or indirect calculation of outcomes. If not, what would explain cooperation in one-shot experiments and real-life situations?

Social rather than calculative conceptions of trust are advanced that focus on perceived others' intentions and group identity (Tyler and Kramer, 1996). When positive intentions are attributed to a person or an authority, people tend to trust the person/authority and cooperate quite independently of the consequences of the person/authority's actions. In turn, the members of a group are more concerned about trustworthiness when they identify with the group; trust is viewed as being linked to the sense of identity people derive from their relationships within the group or with an authority. This sense of identity will in turn lead people to commit to certain behaviours and to comply with commitments and obligations.

Studies of moral development show that individuals acquire a capacity for commitment towards others that makes them comply with their obligations not because they may benefit from it but because it is the *morally* appropriate action. Moral definitions of trust can be found in the literature: trust is 'the expectation . . . of ethically justifiable behaviour – that is, morally correct decisions and actions based upon ethical principles of analysis' (Hosmer, 1995, cited by Kramer, 1999, p. 571).

The role of trust in authority relations has been widely emphasized by social psychologists (Tyler and Degoey, 1996, p. 332), who present empirical data showing that 'people's evaluations of the trustworthiness of organizational authorities shape their willingness to accept the decisions of authorities as well as influencing feelings of obligation to follow organizational rules and laws'. On the one hand, the ability to secure compliance with decisions without resorting to reward or coercion depends on trustworthiness attribution. On the other hand, trust has a crucial role in instilling feelings of obligation towards the organization, which ultimately constitute the effective solution to social dilemmas. In Barnard's language: 'The confidence engendered may even make compliance an inducement in itself' (Barnard, 1938, p. 174).

Social psychologists propose a long list of the conditions under which people are likely to attribute trustworthiness to authority (be it organizational entities or people in charge of authority): perceived integrity, consistency, openness, fairness, loyalty, promise fulfilment, etc. (Kramer, 1999). We find it remarkable that all these aspects are in some way captured by Barnard's concept of authority and its required moral element.

As for justice, the research in psychology began in the 1960s[20] by focusing on distributive justice (the perceived fairness of outcomes) but, in face of the inability of equity theory to completely explain and predict how people react to justice and injustice, attention shifted to procedural justice, that is, the perceived fairness of the process by which outcomes are arrived at. More recent and empirically robust theories try to account for the interactive relationship between procedural and distributive justice.

Here again, in psychology as in economics, attempts at explaining justice effects in 'separation' terms abound. In the enlightened self-interest models, the effect of procedural justice is to shape people's expectations of the outcomes they will receive in the long term: people prefer procedures that are fair rather than unfair because it makes them believe that the relationship will yield long-term benefits and they are hence willing to forego immediate benefits and behave fairly. In the same vein, the 'social preferences' economic models explain justice-driven behaviour by supposing that agents derive satisfaction from others' welfare. Interactions with others are subject to the same cost–benefit analysis as material payoffs in the form of psychological or emotional pains and benefits. The logic of the fairness equilibrium, for example, is quite simple: if i thinks that j is going to act fairly toward him, i is more likely to act fairly in return (Rabin, 1993). When both act fairly, both derive positive (non-material) utility from the exchange, in addition to any material utility.

Adopting a different perspective, the social psychology relational model provides an explanation of justice-driven behaviour based on self-identity and self-esteem concerns. Members play two different roles in organizations: they are both agents and receivers of the collective action (Brockner and Siegel, 1996). As agents, organizational members may feel responsible for collective outcomes and/or procedures. The perceived fairness of their own behaviour may affect their esteem and/or identity. As recipients of the collective action, members may infer from the fairness of others' behaviour the regard in which they are held by the collective. Through the process of reflected appraisal, in which people evaluate themselves as they believe that they are evaluated by significant others, their self-esteem and self-identity may be affected (Mead, 1934, cited in Brockner and Siegel, 1996). When people are fairly treated, their needs for self-esteem are satisfied, and their self-esteem also depends on the perceived rightness of their own behaviour.

One of the most important predictors of trustworthiness appears to be relational justice,[21] that is, the way in which people are personally treated: people trust authorities that treat them with respect and dignity. Procedural and relational justice relates to what Barnard calls the efficiency of the communication system as it may influence the attribution of legitimacy to authorities or rules. Organizational practices such as allowing participants to have voice or conscientiously explaining organizational purposes strongly affect justice perceptions, which affect in turn work performance and organizational citizenship behaviour (Cohen-Charash and Spector, 2001).

It is to be noted that if trust and justice are important in influencing civic engagement, they are obviously not self-sufficient. Other conditions must be met, such as perceptions of technical and functional competence on the part of organizational authorities, attributions of caring and benevolent concerns and, obviously, an adequate system of incentives.

8.   Final remarks

Theories of the firm in mainstream economics rely solely on separation and command. Association, another principle of order that is crucial in explaining the going concern of the firm, is either ignored or downplayed. The received theories collapse at the point of commitment with shared goals – the moral element that may sustain collective action within the firm.

We have argued for a pluralistic view of the firm, one that incorporates and takes into consideration the complementarity of different principles of order.

Pluralistic views of order within the firm have long been available, but their influence in economics has been limited. Although the new institutional economics tradition sometimes claims the influence of Barnard, its reluctance in respect of morality as an appropriate subject of scientific enquiry has crowded out the most interesting intuitions from this classical contribution. This is not surprising since it would involve a major departure from the ontological foundations of 'economic theory'.

Meanwhile, in the teaching of economics, Barnard's and other non-contractual accounts of the firm were forgotten, and the contractual perspective advanced to the point of having become the most influential rationale for institutional design in real-world organizations.

To the extent that the contractual approaches may be incomplete and biased, there is the possibility that they are presently misguiding management. In fact, evidence on unintended outcomes of an overreliance on incentives in institutional design is available and should be seriously considered.

Research leading to a broad and pluralistic understanding of the firm is a relevant and urgent endeavour calling for the contribution of all social sciences. By recalling Barnard's seminal contribution, and by showing how it fits into and may be complemented by recent findings, our purpose has been to sketch the map of the road ahead.

Notes

1. We concentrate on seminal New Institutional contributions; recent developments in this tradition, and other important alternative accounts of the firm, such as knowledge-based theories, are not discussed.

2. Commons believed that 'Labour, as such, is made up of young labourers and new labourers continually coming in, without experience or discipline. It is even immoral to hold to this miscellaneous labour, as a class, the hope that it can even manage industry . . . What we find that labour wants, as a class, is wages, hours, and security, without financial responsibility, but with power enough to command respect' (Commons, 1921, p. 284).

3. Without having to 'tell the servant when to work . . . and when not to work, and what work to do and how to do it . . .' (Coase, 1937, p. 54).

4. The analysis presented below tries to capture the prevailing features of each approach concerning the way in which the social dilemma within the firm is conceived; it will thus not do justice to the most sophisticated contributions.

5. 'Specifically, economic agents are permitted to disclose information in a selective and distorted manner. Calculated efforts to mislead, disguise, obfuscate and confuse are thus admitted. This self-interest seeking attribute is variously described as opportunism, moral hazard and agency' (Williamson, 1990, pp. 11–12).

6. An asset is considered to be specific when its value depends on the continuation in time of a particular relationship, or, differently stated, when its value is smaller outside than within the relationship.

7. Formal models of bilateral reciprocity and multilateral trust–reputation construction that show that spontaneous cooperative equilibria are (under restrictive assumptions) rationally sustainable have been developed within a very different strand of literature related to game theory (see Baron and Kreps, 1999, Appendix B, for an overview).

8. If the first agency models pictured firms as generalized one principal–many agent structures, more recent models picture them as webs of contracts. Employees then have implicit or explicit contractual relationships with the stockholders but also with their supervisor, their subordinates and some of their co-workers. All these contracts interrelate through incentives. 'A complete analysis of this phenomenon requires the development of a concept of "general equilibrium in contracts", that is of a set of contracts such that no pair of contracting parties has any incentives to resign their contract' (Cremer, 1990, pp. 54–5). Thus the equilibrium theoretical frame is the same for the firm and for the market.

9. See Gibbons (1998) and Prendergast (1999) for a review of the literature.

10. Baron and Kreps (1999, p. 279) summarize pay-for-performance shortcomings in five points: 'they misalign incentives, they put too much risk on employees, they have legitimacy problems, they are inflexible and they can kill intrinsic motivations'.

11. Alchian and Demsetz (1972) briefly refer to 'team spirit and loyalty' as a mechanism for enhancing team efficiency, and Coase and Williamson acknowledge the importance of trust in different passages.

12. Different explanations have been put forward for this capacity for commitment, ranging from moral sentiments, to social identity and collective intentions (Sugden, 2002; Davis, 2003).

13. Recently, however, a shift in perspective is under way, and attempts to incorporate trust in economics are numerous either in or outside the frame of the traditional ontology of individuals. Akerlof and Kranton (2005), in a recent but influential paper on (social) identity, assert that 'inculcating in employees a sense of identity and attachment to an organization is critical to well-functioning enterprises' (ibid., p. 10).

14. Command is an ideal type that may in practice take different forms, namely hierarchy and authority. A formal distinction may be useful: 'There is hierarchy among two subsets of participants A and B, when the subset B refers to the goals of subset A, rather than to its own, when making a decision, and it subordinates its decision to the decision of A in case of conflict' (Ménard, 1993, pp. 30–31). 'Authority may be understood as an implicit or explicit transfer of decision power from an agent or class of agents to others . . .' (ibid., p. 28).

15. The source of morality is obviously an open question. When and if a rational choice account is given for morality, an explanation for order among separate individuals will be available. Until then we are entitled to take it as a capacity of individuals on the same ground as self-love.
16. In present-day language, it can be rephrased as the intention to solve the social dilemma.
17. Barnard proposes an impressive list of possible incentives, from material inducements to the condition of communion, through conditions of work, ideal benefactions, opportunity of enlarged participation, etc. He also stresses the importance of complementing the 'method of incentives' with 'the method of persuasion', which consists in the process of changing attitudes.
18. Note that Barnard's *lines of authority* most probably means *hierarchy*, a term that never appears in his book. Barnard, like many other authors (Arrow, Williamson, among others), does not clearly distinguish between the two notions, even if he carefully differentiates *objective authority*, assimilated to *authority of position* from *authority of leadership*, assimilated to a personal ability (Barnard, 1938, p. 173).
19. The moral element is considered by Barnard as the antithesis of the *opportunistic* element, which relates to the means and conditions of attaining ends and always refers to the present.
20. See Cohen-Charash and Spector's (2001) review of literature on the role of justice in organizations.
21. Relational justice is closely related to – but distinguished by some psychologists from – procedural justice (Tyler and Kramer, 1996).

References

Akerlof, George and R. Kranton (2005), 'Identity and the economics of organizations', *Journal of Economic Perspectives*, **19** (1), 9–32.
Alchian, Armen and H. Demsetz (1972), 'Production, information costs and economic organization', *American Economic Review*, **62** (5), 777–95.
Arrow, Kenneth (1974), *The Limits of Organization*, New York: W.W. Norton & Co.
Axelrod, R. (1984), *The Evolution of Cooperation*, New York: Basic Books.
Barnard, Chester (1938), *The Functions of the Executive*, Cambridge, MA: Harvard University Press.
Baron, James and D. Kreps (1999), *Strategic Human Resources*, Hoboken, NJ: John Wiley & Sons.
Brockner, Joel and Phyllis Siegel (1996), 'Understanding the interaction between procedural and distributive justice – the role of trust', in Tom Tyler and Roderick Kramer (eds), *Trust in Organizations: Frontiers of Theory and Research*, London: Sage Publications, pp. 390–413.
Coase, Ronald (1937), 'The nature of the firm', reprinted in *The Firm and the Market*, Chicago, IL: University of Chicago Press, 1990.
Cohen-Charash, Yochi and Paul Spector (2001), 'The role of justice in organizations: a meta-analysis', *Organizational Behavior and Human Decision Processes*, **86** (2), 278–321.
Commons, John (1921), 'Industrial government', originally in *International Labour Review*, **1** (1), reprinted in *International Labour Review*, **135** (3–4), 1996, pp. 281–6.
Cremer, Jacques (1990), 'Common knowledge and the co-ordination of economic activities', in Aoki Masahoki, B. Gustafsson and Oliver Williamson (eds), *The Firm as a Nexus of Treaties*, London: Sage Publications, pp. 53–77.
Davis, John (2003), *The Theory of the Individual in Economics: Identity and Values*, London: Routledge.
Demsetz, Harold (1995), *The Economics of the Business Firm: Seven Critical Commentaries*, Cambridge: Cambridge University Press.
Garrouste, Pierre and S. Saussier (2005), 'Looking for a theory of the firm: future challenges', *Journal of Economic Behavior & Organization*, **58**, 178–99.
Gibbons, Robert (1998), 'Incentives in organizations', *Journal of Economic Perspectives*, **12** (4), 115–32.

Grossman, Sanford and O. Hart (1986), 'The costs and benefits of ownership: a theory of vertical and lateral integration', *Journal of Political Economy*, **94** (4), 691–719.

Hart, Oliver and J. Moore (1990), 'Property rights and the nature of the firm', *Journal of Political Economy*, **98** (6), 119–58.

Jensen, Michael and W.H. Meckling (1976), 'Theory of the firm: managerial behavior, agency costs and ownership structure', *Journal of Financial Economics*, **3** (4), 305–60.

Kramer, Roderick (1999), 'Trust and distrust in organizations: emerging perspectives, enduring questions', *Annual Review of Psychology*, **50**, 569–98.

Ménard, Claude (1993), *L'économie des organisations*, Paris: La Découverte.

Olson, Mancur (1971), *The Logic of Collective Action*, Cambridge, MA: Harvard University Press.

Prendergast, Canice (1999), 'The provision of incentives in firms', *Journal of Economic Literature*, **37** (1), 7–63.

Rabin, Matthew (1993), 'Incorporating fairness into game theory and economics', *American Economic Review*, **83** (5), 1281–1302.

Simon, Herbert (1957), *Models of Man: Social and Rational*, New York: John Wiley & Sons.

Sugden, Robert (2002), 'Fellow feeling', mimeo.

Tyler Tom and Peter Degoey (1996), 'Trust in organizational authorities – the influence of motive attributions on willingness to accept decisions', in Tom Tyler and Roderick Kramer (eds), *Trust in Organizations: Frontiers of Theory and Research*, London: Sage Publications, pp. 331–56.

Tyler Tom and Roderick Kramer (eds) (1996), *Trust in Organizations: Frontiers of Theory and Research*, London: Sage Publications.

Williamson, Oliver (1990), 'The firm as a nexus of treaties', in Aoki Masahoki, B. Gustafsson and Oliver Williamson (eds), *The Firm as a Nexus of Treaties*, London: Sage Publications, pp. 1–25.

Williamson, Oliver (1993), 'Calculativeness, trust and economic organization', *Journal of Law and Economics*, **34**, 453–500.

Williamson, Oliver (2005), 'The economics of governance', *AEA Papers and Proceedings*, **95** (2), 1–18.

19 Knowledge spillover entrepreneurship and innovation in large and small firms
David B. Audretsch and Max Keilbach

1. Introduction

Where do new opportunities come from and what is the response of decision-makers when confronted by such new opportunities? The disparate approaches pursued to answer these questions distinguish the literature on entrepreneurship from that on firm innovation. The model of the knowledge production function of the firm has assumed the firm to be exogenous, while opportunities are endogenously created through purposeful investments in the creation of new knowledge, such as expenditures on research and development and augmentation of human capital.

By contrast, in the entrepreneurship literature the opportunities are generally viewed as exogenous but the start-up of the new firm is endogenous to characteristics specific to the individual. The focus of the entrepreneurship literature in general, and entrepreneurship theory in particular, has been on the cognitive process by which individuals recognize entrepreneurial opportunities and then decide to attempt to actualize them through the process of starting a new business or organization. This approach has typically taken the opportunities as given and focused instead on differences across individual-specific characteristics, traits and conditions to explain variations in entrepreneurial behavior.

The purpose of this chapter is to reconcile these two disparate literatures on entrepreneurship and firm strategy. We do this by considering entrepreneurship to be endogenous – not just to differences in individual characteristics, but rather to differences in the context in which a given individual, with an endowment of personal characteristics, propensities and capabilities, finds herself.

We do not contest the validity of the pervasive entrepreneurship literature identifying individual-specific characteristics as shaping the decision to become an entrepreneur. What we do propose, however, is that such differences in the context in which any given individual finds herself, might also influence the entrepreneurial decision.

Rather than taking entrepreneurial opportunity as exogenous, this chapter places it at the center of attention by making it endogenous. Entrepreneurial opportunity is posited to be greater in contexts that are rich in knowledge but limited in those contexts with impoverished knowledge. According to the endogenous entrepreneurship hypothesis, entrepreneurship is an endogenous response to investments in knowledge made by firms and non-private organizations that do not fully commercialize those new ideas, thus generating opportunities for entrepreneurs. Thus, while most of the literature typically takes entrepreneurial opportunities to be exogenous, this chapter suggests that they are, in fact, endogenous, and systematically created by investments in knowledge.

A summary and conclusions are provided in the last section. In contrast to the prevalent approach in entrepreneurship theory, this chapter concludes that entrepreneurial opportunities are not exogenous but rather systematically generated by investments in ideas and knowledge that cannot be fully appropriated and commercialized by those incumbent firms and organizations creating the new knowledge.

2. Where does opportunity come from?

2.1 The entrepreneurial firm

Why do (some) people start firms? This question has been at the heart of considerable research, not just in economics, but throughout the social sciences. Herbert and Link (1989) have identified three distinct intellectual traditions in the development of the entrepreneurship literature. These three traditions can be characterized as the German tradition, based on von Thuenen and Schumpeter, the Chicago tradition, based on Knight and Schultz, and the Austrian tradition, based on von Mises, Kirzner and Shackle.

Stevenson and Jarillo (1990) assume that entrepreneurship is an orientation towards opportunity recognition. Central to this research agenda are the questions 'How do entrepreneurs perceive opportunities and how do these opportunities manifest themselves as being credible versus being an illusion?' Krueger (2003) examines the nature of entrepreneurial thinking and the cognitive process associated with opportunity identification, and the decision to undertake entrepreneurial action. The focal point of this research is the cognitive process identifying the entrepreneurial opportunity along with the decision to start a new firm. Thus a perceived opportunity and intent to pursue that opportunity are the necessary and sufficient conditions for entrepreneurial activity to take place. The perception of an opportunity is shaped by a sense of the anticipated rewards accruing from and costs of becoming an entrepreneur. Some of the research focuses on the role of personal attitudes and characteristics, such as self-efficacy (the individual's sense of competence), collective efficacy and social norms. Shane (2000) has identified how prior experience and the ability to apply specific skills influence the perception of future opportunities. The concept of the entrepreneurial decision resulting from the cognitive processes of opportunity recognition and ensuing action is introduced by Shane and Eckhardt (2003) and Shane and Venkataraman (2001). They suggest that an equilibrium view of entrepreneurship stems from the assumption of perfect information. By contrast, imperfect information generates divergences in perceived opportunities among different people. The sources of heterogeneity among individuals include different access to information, as well cognitive abilities, psychological differences, and access to financial and social capital.

It is a virtual consensus that entrepreneurship revolves around the recognition of opportunities and the pursuit of those opportunities (Venkataraman, 1997). Much of the more contemporary thinking about entrepreneurship has focused on the cognitive process by which individuals reach the decision to start a new firm. According to Sarasvathy et al. (2003, p. 142), 'An entrepreurial opportunity consists of a set of ideas, beliefs and actions that enable the creation of future goods and services in the absence of current markets for them.' These authors provide a typology of entrepreneurial opportunities as consisting of opportunity recognition, opportunity discovery and opportunity creation.

In asking why some do it, while others don't, scholars have focused on differences among individuals (Stevenson and Jarillo, 1990). As Krueger (2003, p. 105) observes, 'The heart of entrepreneurship is an orientation toward seeing opportunities', which frames the research questions, 'What is the nature of entrepreneurial thinking and what cognitive phenomena are associated with seeing and acting on opportunities?' The traditional approach to entrepreneurship essentially holds the context constant and then asks how the cognitive process inherent in the entrepreneurial decision varies among different individual characteristics and attributes (Shaver, 2003; McClelland, 1961). As Shane and Eckhardt (2003, p. 187) summarize this literature in introducing the individual–opportunity nexus, 'We discussed the process of opportunity discovery and explained why some actors are more likely to discover a given opportunity than others.' Some of these differences involve the willingness to incur risk, others involve the preference for autonomy and self-direction, while still others involve differential access to scarce and expensive resources, such as financial capital, human capital, social capital and experiential capital. This approach, focusing on individual cognition in the entrepreneurial process, has generated a number of important and valuable insights, such as the contribution made by social networks, education and training, and familial influence. The literature certainly leaves the impression that entrepreneurship is a personal matter largely determined by DNA, familial status and access to crucial resources.

2.2   The incumbent large firm

In contrast to the prevalent thinking concerning entrepreneurial start-ups, the predominant theory of firm innovation does not assume that opportunities are exogenous to the firm. Rather, innovative opportunities are the result of systematic effort by firms and the result of purposeful efforts to create knowledge and new ideas, and subsequently to appropriate the returns of those investments through their commercialization. Thus, while the entrepreneurship literature has taken entrepreneurial opportunities to be exogenous, the literature on firm innovation and technological change has taken the creation of such innovative opportunities to be endogenous.

The traditional starting point in the literature on innovation and technological change for most theories of innovation has been the firm (Cohen and Levin, 1989; Griliches, 1979; Venkataraman, 1997). In such theories firms are exogenous and their performance in generating technological change is endogenous (Cohen and Klepper, 1991, 1992).

The most prevalent model of technological change is the model of the knowledge production function, formalized by Zvi Griliches in 1979. According to the model of the knowledge production function, incumbent firms engage in the pursuit of new economic knowledge as an input into the process of generating the output of innovative activity. The most important input in this model is new economic knowledge. As Cohen and Klepper (1991, 1992) point out, the greatest source generating new economic knowledge is generally considered to be R&D. Other inputs in the knowledge production function have included measures of human capital, skilled labor and educational levels. Thus the model of the knowledge production function from the literature on innovation and technological change can be represented as

$$I_i = \alpha RD_i^\beta HK_i^\gamma \varepsilon_i, \qquad (19.1)$$

where I stands for the degree of innovative activity, RD represents R&D inputs, and HK represents human capital inputs. The unit of observation for estimating the model of the knowledge production function, reflected by the subscript i, has been at the level of countries, industries and enterprises.

Thus, in this view of firm innovation, the firm exists exogenously. It undertakes purposeful investments to create knowledge endogenously, which results in the output of innovative activity. Opportunities are not exogenous, but rather the result of purposeful and dedicated investments and efforts by firms to create new (knowledge) opportunities and then to appropriate them through commercializing their innovations.

3. The innovation paradox

When it came to empirical validation of the model of the knowledge production function, it became clear that measurement issues played a major role. The state of knowledge regarding innovation and technological change has generally been shaped by the nature of the data available to scholars for analysis. Such data have always been incomplete and, at best, represented only a proxy measure reflecting some aspect of the process of technological change. Simon Kuznets observed in 1962 that the greatest obstacle to understanding the economic role of technological change was a clear inability of scholars to measure it. More recently, Cohen and Levin (1989, p. 146) warned, 'A fundamental problem in the study of innovation and technical change in industry is the absence of satisfactory measures of new knowledge and its contribution to technological progress. There exists no measure of innovation that permits readily interpretable cross-industry comparisons.'

Measures of technological change have typically involved one of the three major aspects of the innovative process: (1) a measure of the inputs into the innovative process, such as R&D expenditures, or else the share of the labor force accounted for by employees involved in R&D activities; (2) an intermediate output, such as the number of inventions patented; or (3) a direct measure of innovative output.

These three levels of measuring technological change have not been developed and analyzed simultaneously, but have evolved over time, roughly in the order of their presentation. That is, the first attempts to quantify technological change at all generally involved measuring some aspects of inputs into the innovative process (Scherer, 1965, 1967; Grabowski, 1968; Mueller, 1967; Mansfield, 1968). Measures of R&D inputs – first in terms of employment and later in terms of expenditures – were only introduced on a meaningful basis enabling inter-industry and interfirm comparisons in the late 1950s and early 1960s.

A clear limitation in using R&D activity as a proxy measure for technological change is that R&D reflects only the resources devoted to producing innovative output, but not the amount of innovative activity actually realized. That is, R&D is an input and not an output in the innovation process. In addition, Kleinknecht (1987, 1991), Kleinknecht and Verspagen (1989) and Kleinknecht et al. (1991) have systematically shown that R&D measures incorporate only efforts made to generate innovative activity that are undertaken within formal R&D budgets and within formal R&D laboratories. They find that the extent of informal R&D is considerable, particularly in smaller enterprises. And, as Mansfield (1984) points out, not all efforts within a formal R&D laboratory are directed towards generating innovative output in any case. Rather, other types of output, such as imitation and technology transfer, are also common goals.

As systematic data measuring the number of inventions patented were made publicly available in the mid-1960s, many scholars interpreted this new measure not only as being superior to R&D but also as reflecting innovative output. In fact, the use of patented inventions is not a measure of innovative output, but is rather a type of intermediate output measure. A patent reflects new technical knowledge, but it does not indicate whether this knowledge has a positive economic value. Only those inventions that have been successfully introduced in the market can claim that they are innovations as well.

Empirical estimation of the model of the knowledge production function, represented by Equation (19.1), was found to be stronger at broader levels of aggregation such as countries or industries. For example, at the unit of observation of countries, the empirical evidence (Griliches, 1984) clearly supported the existence of the knowledge production function. This is intuitively understandable, because the most innovative countries are those with the greatest investments in R&D. Less innovative output is associated with developing countries, which are characterized by a paucity of new economic knowledge.

Similarly, the model of the knowledge production function was found to be empirically corroborated at the level of the industry (Scherer, 1983; Griliches, 1984). Again, this seems obvious as the most innovative industries also tend to be characterized by considerable investments in R&D and new economic knowledge. Not only are industries such as computers, pharmaceuticals and instruments high in R&D inputs that generate new economic knowledge, but also in terms of innovative outputs (Scherer, 1983; Acs and Audretsch, 1990; Dolfsma and van der Panne, 2005). By contrast, industries with little R&D, such as wood products, textiles and paper, also tend to produce only a negligible amount of innovative output.

Where the relationship became less robust was at the disaggregated microeconomic level of the enterprise, establishment, or even line of business: there is no direct deterministic relationship between knowledge inputs and innovative output. While innovations and inventions are related, they are not identical. The distinction is that an innovation is a new product, process, service, or organizational form that is introduced into the market. By contract, an invention may or may not be introduced into the market.

Besides the fact that many, if not most, patented inventions do not result in an innovation, a second important limitation of patent measures as an indicator of innovative activity is that they do not capture all of the innovations actually made. In fact, many inventions that result in innovations are not patented. The tendency of patented inventions to result in innovations and of innovations to be the result of inventions which were patented combine into what F.M. Scherer (1983) has termed the propensity to patent. It is the uncertainty about the stability of the propensity to patent across enterprises and across industries that casts doubt upon the reliability of patent measures. According to Scherer (1983, pp. 107–8), 'The quantity and quality of industry patenting may depend upon chance, how readily a technology lends itself to patent protection, and business decision-makers' varying perceptions of how much advantage they will derive from patent rights. Not much of a systematic nature is known about these phenomena, which can be characterized as differences in the propensity to patent.'

Mansfield (1984, p. 462) has explained why the propensity to patent may vary so much across markets: 'The value and cost of individual patents vary enormously within and across industries . . . Many inventions are not patented. And in some industries, like electronics, there is considerable speculation that the patent system is being bypassed to a greater extent than in the past. Some types of technologies are more likely to be patented than others.' The implications are that comparisons between enterprises and across industries may be misleading. According to Cohen and Levin (1989), 'There are significant problems with patent counts as a measure of innovation, some of which affect both within-industry and between-industry comparisons.'

Thus, even as superior sources of patent data were introduced, such as the new measure of patented inventions from the computerization by the US Patent Office, the reliability of these data as measures of innovative activity has been severely challenged. For example, Pakes and Griliches (1980, p. 378) warn that 'patents are a flawed measure (of innovative output); particularly since not all new innovations are patented and since patents differ greatly in their economic impact'. And in addressing the question 'Patents as indicators of what?', Griliches (1990, p. 1669) concludes that 'Ideally, we might hope that patent statistics would provide a measure of the (innovative) output. . . The reality, however, is very far from it. The dream of getting hold of an output indicator of inventive activity is one of the strong motivating forces for economic research in this area.'

It was well into the 1970s that systematic attempts were made to provide a direct measure of the innovative output. Thus it should be emphasized that the conventional wisdom regarding innovation and technological change was based primarily upon the evidence derived from analyzing R&D data, which essentially measure inputs into the process of technological change, and patented inventions, which are a measure of intermediate output at best.

The most ambitious major database providing a direct measure of innovative activity is the US Small Business Administration's Innovation Data Base (SBIDB). The database consists of 8074 innovations commercially introduced in the USA in 1982. These data were analyzed by Acs and Audretsch (1988, 1990) to analyze the relationships between firm size and technological change, and market structure and technological change, where a direct rather than indirect measure of innovative activity is used. Dolfsma and van der Panne (2005) analyze similar data but find no evidence at all that large firms are more innovative.

The knowledge production function has been found to hold most strongly at broader levels of aggregation. The most innovative countries are those with the greatest investments in R&D. Little innovative output is associated with less developed countries, which are characterized by a paucity of production of new economic knowledge. Similarly, the most innovative industries also tend to be characterized by considerable investments in R&D and new economic knowledge. Not only are industries such as computers, pharmaceuticals and instruments high in R&D inputs that generate new economic knowledge, but also in terms of innovative outputs (Audretsch, 1995). By contrast, industries with little R&D, such as wood products, textiles and paper, also tend to produce only a negligible amount of innovative output. Thus the knowledge production model linking knowledge-generating inputs to outputs certainly holds at the more aggregated levels of economic activity.

Where the relationship becomes less compelling is at the disaggregated microeconomic level of the enterprise, establishment, or even line of business. For example, while Acs and Audretsch (1990) found that the simple correlation between R&D inputs and innovative output was 0.84 for four-digit standard industrial classification (SIC) manufacturing industries in the USA, it was only about half, 0.40, among the largest US corporations.

At the heart of the conventional wisdom has been the widely accepted hypothesis that large enterprises able to exploit at least some market power are the engine of technological change. This view dates back at least to Schumpeter, who, in *Capitalism, Socialism and Democracy* (1942, p. 101) argued that 'The monopolist firm will generate a larger supply of innovations because there are advantages which, though not strictly unattainable on the competitive level of enterprise, are as a matter of fact secured only on the monopoly level.' The Schumpeterian thesis, then, is that large enterprises are uniquely endowed to exploit innovative opportunities. That is, market dominance is a prerequisite to undertaking the risks and uncertainties associated with innovation. It is the possibility of acquiring quasirents that serves as the catalyst for large-firm innovation.

In one of the most important studies, Scherer (1983) used the US Federal Trade Commission's Line of Business Data to estimate the elasticity of R&D spending with respect to firm sales for 196 industries. He found evidence of increasing returns to scale (an elasticity exceeding unity) for about

20 percent of the industries, constant returns to scale for a little less than three-quarters of the industries, and diminishing returns (an elasticity less than unity) in less than 10 percent of the industries.

While the Scherer (1983) and Soete (1979) studies were restricted to relatively large enterprises, Bound et al. (1984) included a much wider spectrum of firm sizes in their sample of 1492 firms from the 1976 COMPUSTAT data. They found that R&D increases more than proportionately along with firm size for the smaller firms, but that a fairly linear relationship exists for larger firms. Despite the somewhat more ambiguous findings in still other studies (Mansfield, 1981, 1983; Mansfield et al., 1982), the empirical evidence seems to generally support the Schumpeterian hypothesis that research effort is positively associated with firm size.

The studies relating patents to firm size are considerably less ambiguous. Here the findings unequivocally suggest that 'the evidence leans weakly against the Schumpeterian conjecture that the largest sellers are especially fecund sources of patented inventions' (Scherer, 1982, p. 235). In one of the most important studies, Scherer (1965) used the Fortune annual survey of the 500 largest US industrial corporations. He related the 1955 firm sales to the number of patents in 1959 for 448 firms. Scherer found that the number of patented inventions increases less than proportionately along with firm size. Scherer's results were later confirmed by Bound et al. (1984) in the study mentioned above. Basing their study on 2852 companies and 4553 patenting entities, they determined that the small firms (with less than $10 million in sales) accounted for 4.3 percent of the sales from the entire sample, but 5.7 percent of the patents.

Thus, just as there are persuasive theories defending the original Schumpeterian hypothesis that large corporations are a prerequisite for technological change, there are also substantial theories predicting that small enterprises should have the innovative advantage, at least in certain industries. As described above, the empirical evidence based on the input measure of technological change, R&D, tilts decidedly in favor of the Schumpeterian hypothesis. However, as also described above, the empirical results are somewhat more ambiguous for the measure of intermediate output – the number of patented inventions. It was not until direct measures of innovative output became available that the full picture of the process of technological change could be obtained.

Using the measure of innovative output from the US Small Business Administration's Innovation Data Base, Acs and Audretsch (1990) shows that, in fact, the most innovative US firms are large corporations. Further, the most innovative US corporations also tended to have large R&D laboratories and be R&D-intensive. At first glance, these findings based on direct measures of innovative activity seem to confirm the conventional wisdom. However, in the most innovative four-digit standard industrial classification (SIC) industries, large firms, defined as enterprises with at least 500 employees, contributed more innovations in some instances, while in other industries small firms produced more innovations. For example, in computers and process control instruments small firms contributed the bulk of the innovations. By contrast, in the pharmaceutical preparation and aircraft industries the large firms were much more innovative.

Probably their best measure of innovative activity is the total innovation rate, which is defined as the total number of innovations per thousand employees in each industry. The large-firm innovation rate is defined as the number of innovations made by firms with at least 500 employees, divided by the number of employees (thousands) in large firms. The small-firm innovation rate is analogously defined as the number of innovations contributed by firms with fewer than 500 employees, divided by the number of employees (thousands) in small firms.

The innovation rates, or the number of innovations per thousand employees, have the advantage in that they measure large- and small-firm innovative activity relative to the presence of large and small firms in any given industry. That is, in making a direct comparison between large- and small-firm innovative activity, the absolute number of innovations contributed by large firms and small enterprises is somewhat misleading, since these measures are not standardized by the relative presence of large and small firms in each industry. When a direct comparison is made between the innovative activity of large and small firms, the innovation rates are presumably a more reliable measure of innovative intensity because they are weighted by the relative presence of small and large enterprises in any given industry. Thus, while large firms in manufacturing introduced 2445 innovations in 1982, and small firms contributed slightly fewer, 1954, small-firm employment was only half as great as large-firm employment, yielding an average small-firm innovation rate in manufacturing of 0.309, compared to a large-firm innovation rate of 0.202 (Acs and Audretsch, 1988, 1990).

Thus there is considerable evidence suggesting that, in contrast to the findings for R&D inputs and patented inventions, small enterprises apparently play an important innovation-generating activity, at least in certain industries. By relating the innovative output of each firm to its size, it is also possible to shed new light on the Schumpeterian hypothesis. In their 1991 study, Acs and Audretsch find that there is no evidence that increasing returns to R&D expenditures exist in producing innovative output. In fact, with just several exceptions, diminishing returns to R&D are the rule. This study made it possible to resolve the apparent paradox in the literature that R&D inputs increase at more than a proportional rate along with firm size, while the generation of patented inventions does not. That is, while larger firms are observed to undertake a greater effort towards R&D, each additional dollar of R&D is found to yield less in terms of innovative output.

The model of the knowledge production function therefore became less compelling in view of a wave of studies that found that small enterprises were an engine of innovative activity in certain industries. The apparent contradiction between the organizational context of knowledge inputs, principally R&D, and the organizational context of small-firm innovative output resulted in the emergence of what has become known as the innovation paradox: either the model of knowledge production did not hold, at least at the level of the enterprise (for a broad spectrum across the firm-size distribution), or else the appropriate unit of observation had to be reconsidered. In searching for a solution, scholars chose the second interpretation, leading them to look beyond the boundaries of the firm for sources of innovative inputs.

4.   The Knowledge Spillover Theory of Entrepreneurship

4.1   The endogenous entrepreneurship hypothesis
Resolution to the innovation paradox came after rethinking not the validity of the model of the knowledge production function, but rather the implicit assumptions of independence and separability underlying the decision-making analytical units of observation – the established incumbent firm and the new entrepreneurial firm. Just as the prevailing theories of entrepreneurship have generally focused on the cognitive process of individuals in making the decision to start a new firm, so that the decision-making criterion is essentially internal to the decision-making unit – in this case the individual – the model of the knowledge production function generally limited the impact of the firm's investments in creating new knowledge to that decision-making unit – in this case the firm.

That these decision-making units – the firm and the individual – might actually not be totally separable and independent, particularly with respect to assessing the outcome of knowledge investments, was first considered by Audretsch (1995), who introduced 'the Knowledge Spillover Theory of Entrepreneurship'.

The reason for challenging the assumptions of independence and separability between (potential) entrepreneurs and firms emanates from a fundamental characteristic of knowledge that differentiates it from the more traditional firm resources of physical capital and (unskilled) labor. Arrow (1962) pointed out that knowledge differs from these traditional firm resources due to the greater degree of uncertainty, higher extent of asymmetries, and greater cost of transacting new ideas.

The expected value of any new idea is highly uncertain, and as Arrow pointed out, has a much greater variance than would be associated with the deployment of traditional factors of production. After all, there is relative certainty about what a standard piece of capital equipment can do, or what an (unskilled) worker can contribute to a mass-production assembly line. By contrast, Arrow emphasized that when it comes to innovation, there is uncertainty about whether the new product can be produced, how it can be produced, and whether sufficient demand for that visualized new product might actually materialize.

In addition, new ideas are typically associated with considerable asymmetries. In order to evaluate a proposed new idea concerning a new biotechnology product, the decision maker might not only need to have a PhD in biotechnology, but also a specialization in the exact scientific area. Such divergences in education, background and experience can result in a divergence in the expected value of a new project or the variance in outcomes anticipated from pursuing that new idea, both of which can lead to divergences in the recognition and evaluation of opportunities across economic agents and decision-making hierarchies. Such divergences in the valuation of new ideas will become greater if the new idea is not consistent with the core competence and technological trajectory of the incumbent firm.

Thus, because of the conditions inherent in knowledge – high uncertainty, asymmetries and transactions costs – decision-making hierarchies can reach the decision not to pursue and try to commercialize new ideas that individual economic agents, or groups or teams of economic agents, think are potentially valuable and should be pursued. The basic conditions characterizing new knowledge, combined with a broad spectrum of institutions, rules and regulations, impose what could be termed 'the knowledge filter'. The knowledge filter is the gap between new knowledge and what Arrow (1962) referred to as economic knowledge or commercialized knowledge. The greater the knowledge filter, the more pronounced the gap between new knowledge and new economic, or commercialized, knowledge.

The knowledge filter is a consequence of the basic conditions inherent in new knowledge. It also creates the opportunity for entrepreneurship in the Knowledge Spillover Theory of Entrepreneurship. According to this theory, opportunities for entrepreneurship are the duality of the knowledge filter. The higher the knowledge filter, the greater are the divergences in the valuation of new ideas across economic agents and the decision-making hierarchies of incumbent firms. Entrepreneurial opportunities are generated not just by investments in new knowledge and ideas, but in the propensity for only a distinct subset of those opportunities to be fully pursued by incumbent firms.

Thus, as Audretsch pointed out in 1995, the Knowledge Spillover Theory of Entrepreneurship shifts the fundamental decision-making unit of observation in the model of the knowledge production function away from exogenously assumed firms to individuals, such as scientists, engineers or other knowledge workers – agents with endowments of new economic knowledge. When the lens is shifted away from the firm to the individual as the relevant unit of observation, the appropriability issue remains, but the question becomes 'How can economic agents with a given endowment of new knowledge best appropriate the returns from that knowledge?' If the scientist or engineer can pursue the new idea within the organizational structure of the firm developing the knowledge, and appropriate roughly the expected value of that knowledge, she has no reason to leave the firm. On the other hand, if she places a greater value on his ideas than does the decision-making bureaucracy of the incumbent firm, he may choose to start a new firm to appropriate the value of his knowledge.

In the Knowledge Spillover Theory of Entrepreneurship the knowledge production function is actually reversed. The knowledge is exogenous and embodied in a worker. The firm is created endogenously in the worker's effort to appropriate the value of his knowledge through innovative activity. Typically an employee from an established large corporation, often a scientist or engineer working in a research laboratory, will have an idea for an invention and ultimately for an innovation. Accompanying this potential innovation is an expected net return from the new product. The knowledge worker would expect to be compensated for her potential innovation accordingly. If the company has a different, presumably lower, valuation of the potential innovation, it may decide either not to pursue its development, or that it merits a lower level of compensation than that expected by the employee.

In either case, the knowledge worker will weigh the alternative of starting her own firm. If the gap in the expected return accruing from the potential innovation between the inventor and the corporate decision maker is sufficiently large, and if the cost of starting a new firm is sufficiently low, the employee may decide to leave the large corporation and establish a new enterprise. Since the knowledge was generated in the established corporation, the new start-up is considered to be a spin-off from the existing firm. Such start-ups typically do not have direct access to a large R&D laboratory. Rather, the entrepreneurial opportunity emanates from the knowledge and experience accrued in the R&D laboratories with their previous employers. Thus the knowledge spillover view of entrepreneurship is actually a theory of endogenous entrepreneurship, where entrepreneurship is an endogenous response to opportunities created by investments in new knowledge in a given context that are not commercialized because of the knowledge filter.

The endogenous entrepreneurship hypothesis posits that entrepreneurship is a response to investments in knowledge and ideas by incumbent organizations that are not fully commercialized by those organizations. Thus those contexts that are richer in knowledge will offer more entrepreneurial opportunities and therefore should also endogenously induce more entrepreneurial activity, *ceteris paribus*. By contrast, those contexts that are impoverished in knowledge will offer only meager entrepreneurial opportunities generated by knowledge spillovers, and therefore will endogenously induce less entrepreneurial activity.

But what is the appropriate unit of observation to be used to frame the context and observe the entrepreneurial response to knowledge investments made by incumbent organizations? In his 1995 book, Audretsch proposed using the industry as the context in which knowledge is created, developed, organized and commercialized. The context of an industry was used to resolve the paradox concerning the high innovative output of small enterprises given their low level of knowledge inputs that seemingly contradicted the Griliches model of the firm knowledge production:

> The findings in this book challenge an assumption implicit to the knowledge production function – that firms exist exogenously and then endogenously seek out and apply knowledge inputs to generate innovative output . . . It is the knowledge in the possession of economic agents that is exogenous, and in an effort to appropriate the returns from that knowledge, the spillover of knowledge from its producing entity involves endogenously creating a new firm. (Audretsch, 1995, pp. 179–80)

What is the source of this entrepreneurial knowledge that endogenously generated the start-up of new firms? The answer seemed to be through the spillover of knowledge from the source creating it to commercialization via the start-up of a new firm: 'How are these small and frequently new firms able to generate innovative output when undertaking a generally negligible amount of investment into knowledge-generating inputs, such as R&D? One answer is apparently through exploiting knowledge created by expenditures on research in universities and on R&D in large corporations' (ibid., p. 179).

The empirical evidence supporting the Knowledge Spillover Theory of Entrepreneurship was provided by analyzing variations in start-up rates across different industries reflecting different underlying knowledge contexts (Audretsch, 1995). In particular, those industries with a greater investment in new knowledge also exhibited higher start-up rates while those industries with less investment in new knowledge exhibited lower start-up rates, which was interpreted as the mechanism by which knowledge spillovers are transmitted.

In subsequent research, Klepper and Sleeper (2000) showed how spin-offs in the automobile industry exhibited a superior performance when the founder came from a high-performing incumbent firm, as compared to a low-performing incumbent firm, or even from outside of the industry. The authors interpreted this result as indicating that the experience and ability to absorb human capital within the context of the incumbent firm influenced the subsequent entrepreneurial performance. Similar results were found by Agarwal et al. (2004).

Thus compelling evidence was provided, suggesting that entrepreneurship is an endogenous response to the potential for commercializing knowledge that has not been adequately commercialized by the incumbent firms. This involved an organizational dimension involving the mechanism transmitting knowledge spillovers – the start-up of new firms.

4.2   The localization hypothesis

The endogeneous entrepreneurship hypothesis involves the organizational interdependence between entrepreneurial start-ups and incumbent organizations investing in the creation of new knowledge (Audretsch et al., 2006; Audretsch, 2005). A second hypothesis emerging from the Knowledge Spillover Theory of Entrepreneurship, the localizational hypothesis, has to do with the location of the entrepreneurial activity.

An important theoretical development is that geography may provide a relevant unit of observation within which knowledge spillovers occur. The theory of localization suggests that because geographic proximity is needed to transmit knowledge, and especially tacit knowledge, knowledge spillovers tend to be localized within a geographic region. The importance of geographic proximity for knowledge spillovers has been supported in a wave of recent empirical studies by Jaffe (1989), Jaffe et al. (1993), Acs et al. (1992, 1994), Audretsch and Feldman (1996) and Audretsch and Stephan (1996).

As it became apparent that the firm was not completely adequate as a unit of analysis for estimating the model of the knowledge production function, scholars began to look for externalities. In refocusing the model of knowledge production to a spatial unit of observation, scholars confronted two challenges. The first was theoretical. What was the theoretical basis for knowledge to spill over, yet, at the same time, be spatially within some geographic unit of observation? The second challenge involved measurement. How could knowledge spillovers be measured and identified? More than a few scholars heeded Krugman's warning (1991, p. 53) that empirical measurement of knowledge spillovers would prove to be impossible because 'knowledge flows are invisible, they leave no paper trail by which they may be measured and tracked'.[1]

In confronting the first challenge, which involved developing a theoretical basis for geographically bounded knowledge spillovers, scholars turned to the emerging literature of the new growth theory. In explaining the increased divergence in the distribution of economic activity between countries and regions, Krugman (1991) and Romer (1986) relied on models based on increasing returns to scale in production. By increasing returns, however, Krugman and Romer did not necessarily mean at the level of observation most familiar in the industrial organization literature – the plant, or at least the firm – but rather at the level of a spatially distinguishable unit. In fact, it was assumed that the externalities across firms and even industries yield convexities in production. In particular, Krugman (1991), invoking Marshall (1920), focused on convexities arising from spillovers from (1) a pooled labor market; (2) pecuniary externalities enabling the provision of non-traded inputs to an industry in a greater variety and at lower cost; and (3) information or technological spillovers.

That knowledge spills over was barely disputed. Some 30 years earlier, Arrow (1962) had identified externalities associated with knowledge due to its non-exclusive and non-rival use. However, what has been contested is the geographic range of knowledge spillovers: knowledge externalities are so important and forceful that there is no reason that knowledge should stop spilling over just because of borders, such as a city limit, state line, or national boundary. Krugman (1991) and others did not question the existence or importance of such knowledge spillovers. In fact, they argue that such knowledge externalities are so important and forceful that there is no reason for a political boundary to limit the spatial extent of the spillover.

In applying the model of the knowledge production function to spatial units of observation, theories of why knowledge externalities are spatially bounded were needed. Thus it took the development of localization theories explaining not only that knowledge spills over, but also why those spillovers decay as they move across geographic space.

Studies identifying the extent of knowledge spillovers are based on the model of the knowledge production function applied at spatial units of observation. In what is generally to be considered to be the first important study refocusing the knowledge production function, Jaffe (1989) modified the traditional approach to estimate a model specified for both spatial and product dimensions. Empirical estimation of Equation (19.1) essentially shifted the knowledge production function from the unit of observation of a firm to that of a geographic unit. Implicitly contained within the knowledge production function model is the assumption that innovative activity should take place in those regions where the direct knowledge-generating inputs are the greatest, and where knowledge spillovers are the most prevalent. Jaffe (1989) dealt with the measurement problem raised by Krugman

(1991) by linking the patent activity within technologies located within states to knowledge inputs located within the same spatial jurisdiction.

Jaffe (1989) found empirical evidence supporting the notion that knowledge spills over for third-party use from university research laboratories as well as industry R&D laboratories. Acs et al. (1992) confirmed that the knowledge production function represented by Equation (19.1) held at a spatial unit of observation using a direct measure of innovative activity: new product introductions in the market. Feldman (1994) extended the model to consider other knowledge inputs to the commercialization of new products. The results confirmed that the knowledge production function was robust at the geographic level of analysis: the output of innovation is a function of the innovative inputs in that location.

While this literature has identified the important role that knowledge spillovers play, it provides little insight into the questions of why and how knowledge spills over. What happens within the black box of the knowledge production function is vague and ambiguous at best. The exact links between knowledge sources and the resulting innovative output remain invisible and unknown. None of the above studies suggesting that knowledge spillovers are geographically bounded and localized within spatial proximity to the knowledge source identified the mechanisms which transmit the knowledge spillover; rather, the spillovers were implicitly assumed to automatically exist, or fall like 'manna from heaven', but only within a geographically bounded spatial area.

One explanation was provided by the Knowledge Spillover Theory of Entrepreneurship, which suggests that the start-up of a new firm is a response to investments in knowledge and ideas by incumbent organizations that are not fully commercialized by those organizations.

Access to knowledge spillovers requires spatial proximity. While Jaffe (1989) and Audretsch and Feldman (1996) made it clear that spatial proximity is a prerequisite to accessing such knowledge spillovers, they provided no insight into the actual mechanism transmitting them. As for the Romer and Lucas models, investment in new knowledge automatically generates knowledge spillovers. Their only additional insight involves the spatial dimension – knowledge spills over but the spillovers are spatially bounded. Since we have just identified one such mechanism by which knowledge spillovers are transmitted – the start-up of a new firm – it follows that knowledge spillover entrepreneurship is also spatially bounded in that local access is required to access the knowledge facilitating the entrepreneurial start-up.

Localization hypothesis: Knowledge spillover entrepreneurship will tend to be spatially located within close geographic proximity to the source of knowledge actually producing that knowledge. Thus, in order to access spillovers, new firm start-ups will tend to locate close to knowledge sources, such as universities.

Systematic empirical support for both the localization hypothesis and the endogeneous entrepreneurship hypothesis is provided by Audretsch et al. (2005), who show that the start-up of new knowledge-based and technology firms is geographically constrained within close geographic proximity to knowledge sources. Based on data from Germany in the 1990s, their evidence shows that start-up activity tends to cluster geographically around sources of new knowledge, such as R&D investments by firms and research undertaken at universities. Their findings provide compelling support for the Knowledge Spillover Theory of Entrepreneurship in that entrepreneurial activity is systematically greater in locations with a greater investment in knowledge and new ideas.

Similarly, the research laboratories of universities provide a source of innovation-generating knowledge that is available to private enterprises for commercial exploitation. Jaffe (1989) and Acs et al. (1992), for example, found that the knowledge created in university laboratories 'spills over' to contribute to the generation of commercial innovations by private enterprises. Acs et al. (1994) found persuasive evidence that spillovers from university research contribute more to the innovative activity of small firms than to the innovative activity of large corporations. Similarly, Link and Rees (1990) surveyed 209 innovating firms to examine the relationship between firm size and university research. They found that large firms are more active in university-based research. However, small- and medium-sized enterprises apparently are better able to exploit their university-based associations and generate innovations. Link and Rees (1990) conclude that, contrary to the conventional wisdom, diseconomies of scale in producing innovations exist in large firms. They attribute these diseconomies of scale to the 'inherent bureaucratization process which inhibits both innovative activity and the speed with which new inventions move through the corporate system towards the market' (ibid., p. 25).

5. Conclusions

Something of a dichotomy has emerged between the literatures on entrepreneurial opportunities, and firm innovation and technology management. On the one hand, in the entrepreneurship literature, opportunities are taken to be exogenous to the fundamental decision-making unit – the individual confronted with an entrepreneurial decision. On the other hand, in the model of the knowledge production function opportunities are decidedly endogenous and the result of purposeful investments in the creation of new knowledge and ideas through expenditures on R&D and augmentation of human capital. This dichotomy reflects implicit assumptions about the independence and separability of the two essential decision-making units – the incumbent organization and the (potential) entrepreneur.

This chapter has drawn on emerging theories of entrepreneurship that challenge the assumption that opportunities are exogenous. The Knowledge Spillover Theory of Entrepreneurship inverts the assumptions inherent in the model of the knowledge production function for the firm. Rather than assuming that the firm is exogenous and then endogenously creates new knowledge and innovative output through purposeful investments in R&D and human capital, this view instead starts with an individual exogenously endowed with a stock of knowledge and ideas. The new firm is then endogenously created in an effort to commercialize and appropriate the value of that knowledge.

The prevalent and traditional theories of entrepreneurship have typically held the context constant and then examined how characteristics specific to the individual impact the cognitive process inherent in the model of entrepreneurial choice. This often leads to a view that is remarkably analogous to that concerning technical change in the Solow (1956) model – given a distribution of personality characteristics, proclivities, preferences and tastes, entrepreneurship is exogenous. One of the great conventional wisdoms in entrepreneurship is 'Entrepreneurs are born not made'. Either you have it or you don't. This leaves virtually no room for policy or for altering what nature has created.

This chapter has presented an alternative view. We hold the individual attributes constant and instead focus on variations in context. In particular, we consider how the knowledge context will impact the cognitive process underlying the entrepreneurial choice model. The result is a theory of endogenous entrepreneurship, where (knowledge) workers respond to opportunities generated by new knowledge by starting a new firm. In this view entrepreneurship is a rational choice made by economic agents to appropriate the expected value of their endowment of knowledge. Thus the creation of a new firm is the endogenous response to investments in knowledge that have not been entirely or exhaustively appropriated by the incumbent firm.

In the endogenous theory of entrepreneurship, the spillover of knowledge and the creation of a new, knowledge-based firm are virtually synonymous. Of course, there are many other important mechanisms facilitating the spillover of knowledge that have nothing to do with entrepreneurship, such as the mobility of scientists and workers, and informal networks, linkages and interactions. Similarly, there are certainly new firm start-ups that have nothing to do with the spillover of knowledge. Still, the spillover theory of entrepreneurship suggests that there will be additional entrepreneurial activity as a rational and cognitive response to the creation of new knowledge.

Those contexts with greater investment in knowledge should also experience a higher degree of entrepreneurship, *ceteris paribus*. Perhaps it is true that entrepreneurs are made. But more of them will discover what they are made of in a high-knowledge context than in an impoverished-knowledge context. Thus we are inclined to restate the conventional wisdom and instead propose that entrepreneurs are not necessarily made, bur are rather a response to high-knowledge contexts that are especially fertile in spawning entrepreneurial opportunities.

Note

1. Lucas (2001) and Lucas and Rossi-Hansberg (2002) impose a spatial structure on production externalities in order to model the spatial structure of cities. The logic is that spatial gradients capture some of the externalities associated with localized human capital accumulation.

References

Acs, Zoltan J. and David B. Audretsch (1988), 'Innovation in large and small firms: an empirical analysis', *American Economic Review*, **78** (4), 678–90.

Acs, Zoltan J. and David B. Audretsch (1990), *Innovation and Small Firms*, Cambridge, MA: MIT Press.

Acs, Zoltan J. and David B. Audretsch (eds) (1991), *Innovation and Technological Change: An International Comparison*, Ann Arbor, MI: University of Michigan Press.

Acs, Zoltan J., David B. Audretsch and Maryann P. Feldman (1992), 'Real effects of academic research', *American Economic Review*, **82** (1), 363–7.

Acs, Zoltan J., David B. Audretsch and Maryann P. Feldman (1994), 'R&D spillovers and recipient firm size', *Review of Economics and Statistics*, **100** (2), 336–67.

Agarwal, R., R. Echambadi, A.M. Franco and M.B. Sarker (2004), 'Knowledge transfer through inheritance: spin-out generation, development and survival', *Academy of Management Journal*, **47**, 501–22.

Arrow, Kenneth J. (1962), 'Economic welfare and the allocation of resources for invention', in R.R. Nelson (ed.), *The Rate and Direction of Inventive Activity*, Princeton, NJ: Princeton University Press, pp. 609–26.

Audretsch, David B. (1995), *Innovation and Industry Evolution*, Cambridge, MA: MIT Press.

Audretsch, David B. (2007), *The Entrepreneurial Society*, New York: Oxford University Press.

Audretsch, David B. and Maryann P. Feldman (1996), 'R&D spillovers and the geography of innovation and production', *American Economic Review*, **86** (3), 630–40.

Audretsch, David B. and Paula E. Stephan (1996), 'Company–scientist locational links: the case of biotechnology', *American Economic Review*, **86** (3), 641–52.

Audretsch, David B., Max Keilbach and Erik Lehmann (2006), *Entrepreneurship and Economic Growth*, New York: Oxford University Press.

Bound, John, Clint Cummins, Zvi Griliches, Bronwyn H. Hall and Adam Jaffe (1984), 'Who does R&D and who patents?', in Z. Griliches (ed.), *R&D, Patents, and Productivity*, Chicago, IL: University of Chicago Press, pp. 21–54.

Cohen, Wesley M. and Steven Klepper (1991), 'Firm size versus diversity in the achievement of technological advance', in Z.J. Acs and D.B. Audretsch (eds), *Innovation and Technological Change: An International Comparison*, Ann Arbor, MI: University of Michigan Press, pp. 183–203.

Cohen, Wesley M. and Steven Klepper (1992), 'The tradeoff between firm size and diversity in the pursuit of technological progress', *Small Business Economics*, **4** (1), 1–14.

Cohen, W. and D. Levinthal (1989), 'Innovation and learning: the two faces of R&D', *Economic Journal*, **99** (3), 569–96.

Cohen, Wesley M. and Richard C. Levin (1989), 'Empirical studies of innovation and market structure', in Richard Schmalensee and Robert Willig (eds), *Handbook of Industrial Organization*, Vol. II, Amsterdam: North-Holland, pp. 1059–107.

Dolfsma, Wilfred and Geren van der Panne (2005), 'Currents and sub-currents in the river of innovations – explaining innovativeness using new product announcements', unpublished manuscript.

Feldman, M.P. (1994), *The Geography of Innovation*, Economics of Science, Technology, and Innovation, vol. 2. Dordrecht: Kluwer Academic.

Grabowski, Henry G. (1968), 'The determinants of industrial research and development: a study of the chemical, drug, and petroleum industries', *Journal of Political Economy*, 76 (4), 292–306.

Griliches, Zvi (1979), 'Issues in assessing the contribution of R&D to productivity growth', *Bell Journal of Economics*, 10, 92–116.

Griliches, Z. (1984), *R&D, Patents, and Productivity*, Chicago, IL: University of Chicago Press.

Griliches, Zvi (1990), 'Patent statistics as economic indicators: a survey', *Journal of Economic Literature*, 28 (4), 1661–707.

Hebert, R.F. and Albert N. Link (1989), 'In search of the meaning of entrepreneurship', *Small Business Economics*, 1 (1), 39–49.

Jaffe, A., M. Trajtenberg and R. Henderson (1993), 'Geographic localization of knowledge spillovers as evidenced by patent citations', *Quarterly Journal of Economics*, 63, 577–98.

Jaffe, Adam B. (1989), 'Real effects of academic research', *American Economic Review*, 79 (5), 957–70.

Kleinknecht, Alfred (1987), 'Measuring R&D in small firms: how much are we missing?', *Journal of Industrial Economics*, 36 (2), 253–6.

Kleinknecht, Alfred (1991), 'Firm size and innovation: reply to Scherer', *Small Business Economics*, 3 (2), 157–8.

Kleinknecht, Alfred and Bart Verspagen (1989), 'R&D and market structure: the impact of measurement and aggregation problems', *Small Business Economics*, 1 (4), 297–302.

Kleinknecht, Alfred, Tom P. Poot and Jeroen O.N. Reiljnen (1991), 'Technical performance and firm size: survey results from the Netherlands', in Zoltan J. Acs and David B. Audretsch (eds), *Innovation and Technological Change: An International Comparison*, Ann Arbor, MI: University of Michigan Press, pp. 84–108.

Klepper, Steven and S. Sleeper (2000), 'Entry by spinoffs', unpublished manuscript, Carnegie Mellon University.

Krueger, Norris F. Jr (2003), 'The cognitive psychology of entrepreneurship', in Zoltan J. Acs and David B. Audretsch (eds), *Handbook of Entrepreneurship Research*, New York: Springer Publishers, pp. 105–40.

Krugman, Paul (1991), *Geography and Trade*, Cambridge, MA: MIT Press.

Link, Albert N. and John Rees (1990), 'Firm size, university based research, and the returns to R&D', *Small Business Economics*, 2 (1), 25–32.

Lucas, Robert E. (2001), 'Externalities and cities', *Review of Economic Dynamics*, 4, 245–74.

Lucas, Robert E. and Esteban Rossi-Hansberg (2002), 'On the internal structure of cities', *Econometrica*, 70 (4), 1445–76.

Mansfield, Edwin (1968), *Industrial Research and Technological Change*, New York, W.W. Norton, for the Cowles Foundation for Research Economics at Yale University, pp. 83–108.

Mansfield, Edwin (1981), 'Composition of R&D expenditures: relationship to size of firm, concentration, and innovative output', *Review of Economics and Statistics*, 63, 610–15.

Mansfield, Edwin (1983), 'Industrial organization and technological change: recent empirical findings', in John V. Craven (ed.), *Industrial Organization, Antitrust, and Public Policy*, The Hague: Kluwer–Nijhoff, pp. 129–43.

Mansfield, Edwin (1984), 'Comment on using linked patent and R&D data to measure interindustry technology flows', in Z. Griliches (ed.), *R&D, Patents, and Productivity*, Chicago, IL: University of Chicago Press, pp. 462–4.

Mansfield, Edwin (1995), 'Academic research underlying industrial innovations: sources, characteristics, and financing', *The Review of Economics and Statistics*, 77, 55–65.

Mansfield, Edwin, A. Romeo, M. Schwartz, D. Teece, S. Wagner and P. Brach (1982), *Technology Transfer, Productivity, and Economic Policy*, New York: W.W. Norton.

Marshall, A. (1920), *Principles of Economics: An Introductory Volume*, London: Macmillan.

McClelland, David (1961), *The Achieving Society*, New York: Free Press.

Mueller, Dennis C. (1967), 'The firm decision process: an econometric investigation', *Journal of Political Economy*, **81** (1), 58–87.

Pakes, Ariel and Zvi Griliches (1980), 'Patents and R&D at the firm level: a first look', NBER Working Paper No. 0561, Cambridge, MA: National Bureau of Economic Research, Inc.

Romer, Paul M. (1986), 'Increasing returns and long-run growth', *Journal of Political Economy*, **94** (5), 1002–37.

Sarasvathy, Saras D., Nocholas Dew, S. Ramakrishna Velamuri and Sankaran Venkataraman (2003), 'Three views of entrepreneurial opportunity', in Zoltan J. Acs and David B. Audretsch (eds), *Handbook of Entrepreneurship Research*, New York: Springer Publishers, pp. 141–60.

Scherer, Frederic M. (1965), 'Firm size, market structure, opportunity, and the output of patented inventions', *American Economic Review*, **55**, 1097–125.

Scherer, Frederic M. (1967), 'Market structure and the employment of scientists and engineers', *American Economic Review*, **57**, 524–30.

Scherer, Frederic M. (1982), 'Inter-industry technology flows in the United States', *Research Policy*, **11**, 227–45.

Scherer, Frederic M. (1983), 'The propensity to patent', *International Journal of Industrial Organization*, **1**, 107–28.

Schumpeter, Joseph A. (1942), *Capitalism, Socialism and Democracy*, New York: Harper & Row.

Shane, S. (2000), 'Prior knowledge and the discover of entrepreneurial opportunities', *Organization Science*, **11**, 448–71.

Shane, Scott and Jonathan Eckhardt (2003), 'The individual–opportunity nexus', in Zoltan J. Acs and David B. Audretsch (eds), *Handbook of Entrepreneurship Research*, New York: Springer Publishers, pp. 161–94.

Shane, S. and S. Venkataraman (2001), 'Entrepreneurship as a field of research: a response to Zahra and Dess, Singh, and Erickson', *Academy of Management Review*, **26**, 13–17.

Shaver, Kelly G. (2003), 'The social psychology of entrepreneurial behviour', in Zoltan J. Acs and David B. Audretsch (eds), *Handbook of Entrepreneurship Research*, New York: Springer Publishers, pp. 331–58.

Soete, Luc L.G. (1979), 'Firm size and inventive activity: the evidence reconsidered', *European Economic Review*, **12** (4), October, 319–40.

Solow, Robert (1956), 'A contribution to the theory of economic growth', *Quarterly Journal of Economics*, **70**, 65–94.

Stevenson, H. and J. Jarillo (1990), 'A paradigm of entrepreneurship: entrepreneurial management', *Strategic Management Journal*, **11**, 17–27.

Venkataraman, S. (1997), 'The distinctive domain of entrepreneurship research', in *Advances in Entrepreneurship, Firm Emergence and Growth*, Vol. 3, Greenwich, CT: JAI Press, pp. 119–38.

20 Firms, managers and restructuring: implications of a social economics view
Hans Schenk

Introduction

Since the early 1900s there have been five merger waves – three of which occurred after World War II – while at the time of writing Western economies are experiencing their sixth. The fifth, which had its rising tide from 1995 to 2000, required worldwide investments of no less than about US$12 000 billion. With about US$9000 billion, US and West European firms took the lion's share (for more details, see Schenk, 2006). At the time, by way of comparison, acquisition expenditures by US and European firms were about seven times larger than the UK's annual gross domestic product. On average, they amounted annually to about one-fifth of US GDP.

Put differently, US and West European investments in mergers and acquisitions were equal to approximately 60 per cent of their gross investments in machinery and equipment (gross fixed capital formation) and they easily outpaced those in research and development (R&D). Business enterprise investments in acquisitions were no less than about eight times higher than business enterprise expenditures on R&D.

The sixth wave, while aspiring to similar numbers as the fifth, has different characteristics, however. Similar to the fourth wave (taking place during the 1980s), a disproportionately large number of its acquisitions are leveraged buy-outs (LBOs), or in more modern parlance, private equity leveraged buy-outs (PELBOs). Many, if not most, of such buy-outs do – or are supposed to – create value from demerging previously formed concentrations, indicating a sort of continuous stop–go process, or as I would suggest and will elucidate in this chapter: indicating a *restructuring wave*.

If buy-outs are directed at undoing earlier mergers, this suggests that those mergers were inefficient. The importance of this should be immediately clear. Given the sheer size of merger waves, this inefficiency might have a crucial effect on the fate of the economies in which these mergers are undertaken. If they improve the way in which society generates wealth, economies will noticeably benefit, even apart from the question of to which parties the benefits will accrue. If, on the other hand, they do not generate wealth, or even destroy it, then economies will noticeably suffer.

Evidently, the way in which economies appreciate mergers – i.e. deal with potential benefits and disadvantages – may be of crucial macroeconomic importance.[1]

Therefore the present chapter will review the evidence on the performance of mergers. This review, together with the intertemporal clustering of mergers, raises questions with respect to the determinants of merger. Normally, mergers are regarded as a purely economic phenomenon. According to mainstream neoclassical thinking they take place as the result of firms' profit-maximizing behaviour. I shall demonstrate, however, that such a framework is inadequate in this respect. Instead, it will be argued that a social economics framework or an institutional economics framework is necessary. For the sake of transparency, the chapter starts with a small digression on what such a framework implies.

The chapter concludes with a discussion of current merger control regimes and asks whether these can be expected to further beneficial mergers and block mergers that are a threat to economic welfare.

Theoretical perspective

This chapter's title refers to the implications of a social economics view. What these implications are, of course, will be apparent only towards the end. Yet, in order to put the chapter into perspective, and in order to make clear what I mean by such a view, it is useful to make some introductory methodological remarks.

Without wishing to neglect the sometimes delicate differences between social economics, socio-economics, behavioural economics, political economy, heterodox economics, multidisciplinary economics and so on, my approach in this chapter will bear characteristics of each. I shall borrow from the corporate finance as well as corporate strategy literatures, from organizational sociology and psychology as well as game theory. But most clearly, my approach can be associated with institutional economics in the sense explained below.

Following the *Oxford Dictionary of Economics* (Black, 2002), institutional economics is 'the view of economics which stresses the importance of institutions in determining how economies really work'. This definition is not explicit on the sometimes very large differences between 'new'-style and 'old'-style institutional economics. New-style institutional economics – or simply neo-institutional economics – as this has developed following the works of, especially, Coase and Williamson, focuses on the ways in which individuals *create* institutions, intentionally or unintentionally – though as a result of rational behaviour. In contrast to neo-institutional economics stands what has been called the 'old' institutionalism. This describes how institutions mould individuals, how individuals are born into existing institutions instead of creating them. The differences are quite significant as old institutionalism abandons the supremacy of individualistic normative criteria while recognizing that voluntarism can be curbed by an individual's or an organization's environment.

According to Hodgson (1998), old institutionalism suggests that individuals are socialized within specific institutional settings and so institutions are logically privileged over a general historical model of the individual agent, whereas the new institutionalism preserves the neoclassical understanding of the individual with autonomously determined preferences (having adopted a paradigm in which methodological individualism reigns). One of Hodgson's key arguments is that the old institutionalism offers a perspective on the nature of human agency that is based on the concept of habit: 'The core ideas of institutionalism concern . . . habits, rules, and their evolution' (Hodgson, 1998, p. 168). Though not denying that rational action may occur, according to Hodgson, we should expect to find a great deal of imitation, inertia, lock-in and cumulative causation.

From now on, any reference in this chapter to institutional economics, or to an institutional approach, will be to this old-style institutionalism – for me this is clearly to be preferred, as I hope will become evident from what follows. Institutional economics touches on central tenets of behavioural economics despite the fact that the latter is rooted in methodological individualism. Behavioural economics uses the insights of (experimental) psychology to shed light on individual decision making. By far the majority of these insights have led it away from rational *homo economicus*, both in cases of judgement and in those of choice (see, e.g., Camerer and Loewenstein, 2004). In terms of choice behaviour, humans appear to be more sensitive to differences between a current situation and a 'reference level' than to the absolute characteristics of that situation, thus violating standard preference theory's assumption that preferences are not affected by an individual's transient asset position (recall, e.g., Kahneman and Tversky's finding that people are significantly more averse to losses than they are attracted to same-sized gains; see, e.g., Tversky and Kahneman, 1981). More generally, work in behavioural economics has shown that preferences are often ill defined and highly malleable. They are context-dependent rather than predefined in terms of indifference curves.

While behavioural economics focuses on charting a decision maker's non-rational behaviour from the impact it has, institutional economics asks which psychological as well as non-psychological factors cause decision makers to adopt such non-rational behaviour. It gives more attention to socialization processes that determine the actual characteristics of behaviour, and to processes of coercion, deprivation and exploitation, thus issues of power. The two, therefore, connect in opening up economic analysis for non-rational behaviour. In this way, they go considerably beyond just substituting bounded rationality for rationality. Even the managerial theory's mainstay of bounded rationality in the end simply assumes that players are *intentionally* rational, but only limited by human and organizational properties in achieving rationality.

As a consequence, a useful institutional approach should be one that transforms theories of rational action into theories of rule-based action, emphasizing not the efficiency of history but its inefficiencies. Firm behaviour should be interpreted as an expression of applying rules that adapt through conscious intent, learning, selection and imitation. In terms of Augier et al. (2000), the assumption of rational action, confounded by uncertainty, human limitations and conflicts (such as those between agents and principals), should be supplemented with the assumption of identity-based, rule-based action. In this view, actions may be related less to their absolute consequences than to their consistency with the demands of identity and the rules of appropriate behaviour.

In conclusion, the social economics view aspired to in this chapter must take into account that mergers may have to do less with rational, profit-maximizing behaviour than is usually assumed. Instead, an adequate approach should allow rule-based behaviour as much as it should allow for the possibility that mergers are not voluntary acts but are simply forced upon management decision makers by institutions in their environment, such as the stock market. Under the profit-maximizing assumption, mergers are normally studied as static, time-invariant phenomena whereas one should include the possibility of significant intertemporal variation. Most importantly, however, it implies that the assumption of *prevailing* rationality – implying that deviations from rationality will be punished, that rational players will eventually prevail – should not be held upright at any cost. In financial economics, this assumption is most poignantly present in the so-called theory of the market for corporate control, to which I shall return further below.

Merger performance

By now, the performance of mergers and acquisitions has been the subject of many dozens of studies, both in terms of real-value effects and in terms of shareholder-value effects (for a synopsis of the most important studies, see Schenk, 2006). By far the majority of studies have estimated shareholder-value effects, mostly using readily available stock market data, and using predicted normal returns as controls. Those studies that estimated real-value effects, however, have used more sophisticated data – usually drawn from firm statements – as well as more sophisticated methodologies. They have commonly used size- and industry-matched control groups of non-merging firms and/or *ceteris paribus* extrapolations of pre-merger performance. Although the findings of the various studies are not completely consistent, the general tendencies are clear. Besides, since both shareholder-value and real-value studies – under certain restrictions – share similar conclusions, the various findings must be regarded as convincing.

Real-value effects
The most common result of merger performance studies is that profitability and productivity, variously measured, do not improve as a result of merger. In many cases efficiency does not improve or in fact declines, while in other cases it improves, though not faster than would have been expected in the absence of merger. Since it is unlikely that the market power of merging firms *declines* after merger, any decline in profitability can be taken to indicate a decline in efficiency. Mergers and acquisitions appear to lead to less product variety while increases in the rate of technological progressiveness appear to remain forthcoming. Acquisition variables, after size, leverage, return on assets and liquidity are controlled for, appear statistically significant negative predictors of R&D intensity adjusted for industry. Market share growth seems to slow down after a merger as well, while acquired firms lose market share against control groups of firms that remain independent (Mueller, 1986). For instance, among the world's 18 largest pharmaceutical firms, 11 out of 12 that participated in mergers lost combined market share between 1990 and 1998 whereas all six of those that had not merged gained market share (*The Economist*, 22 January 2000).

Overall, several methodological criticisms may be brought against some of the established types of merger performance studies (see, e.g., Calomiris, 1999). However, the evidence appears consistent across studies of financial as well as non-financial mergers and across time periods.

In fact, the only substantial exception to the findings reported above is a study by Healy et al. (1992), who investigate post-merger cash flow for the 50 largest non-financial US mergers consummated between 1979 and 1984. By adopting the same index as Ravenscraft and Scherer (1987) did in the most revealing study to appear before the fifth merger wave (and arguably the best ever), Healy and co-authors purported to have refuted the Ravenscraft and Scherer findings. Their results showed that around two-thirds of these mergers had cash flow improvements *ex post*. However, Healy et al. deflated this index of performance by a market-based asset variable which can imply cash flow/asset performance indicator gains relative to the market even when cash flows are deteriorating relative to those of peer companies, namely if acquiring company market value falls relative to the general market – which, indeed, appeared to be the case. Indeed, when the authors in a later (substantially less well-known) study added acquisition premiums to the deflator, results deteriorated significantly (see Healy et al., 1997). On average, the mergers studied now appeared to be unprofitable and/or insignificantly different from sector indicators.

Shareholder-value effects

Similar results are obtained when the focus is on shareholder instead of real wealth. A review of 33 earlier studies by Mueller (2003) finds that while target shareholders usually gain from acquisitions, acquirer shareholders almost always lose, especially in the long run. Generally, the longer the post-merger assessment period, the more negative shareholder returns appear. Usually, positive abnormal returns are evident for only a few days around the event (and even then, only when pre-event build-ups of share prices are underestimated), but taking this as evidence requires a strong belief in the efficient market hypothesis. Another review confirmed Mueller's findings before testing it for a sample of 110 very large acquisitions – among them the most prolific of the century – undertaken during 1993–2001, thus including years that preceded the beginning of the fifth merger wave and followed its demise (Schenk, 2002). It found that for several different models – varying only in terms of event windows – the outcomes were all negative in terms of cumulative abnormal returns on the acquirer's side, running from minus 3.4 per cent to minus 8.5 per cent.

Interestingly, when taken together the data suggest the possibility of intertemporal (rather than intersector) variations in merger performance. One of our own studies, focusing on European mergers, divided a sample into five year cohorts (the first one starting in 1995, and the last one starting in 1999). For 400 post-merger days each, the study revealed that 'earlier' acquisitions perform better (or less badly) than 'later' acquisitions. As is shown in Figure 20.1, the 1995 cohort reached positive results but all others were in the negative, the 1999 cohort performing worst of all; it saddled its shareholders with an average cumulative loss of almost 25 per cent. Similarly, in a study of about 12 000 (US) acquisitions from 1980 to 2001, Moeller et al. (2003) found that while shareholders lost throughout the sample period, losses associated with acquisitions after 1997 were 'dramatic'.

The periodicity found in these studies is consistent with findings reported in Carow et al. (2004) in which stockholder returns for 520 acquisitions over 14 industry-defined merger waves during 1979–98 were investigated. They find that the combined returns for target and acquiring shareholders were higher for mergers that took place during the early stages of these waves. Well-performing acquirers all made their acquisitions during these same stages.

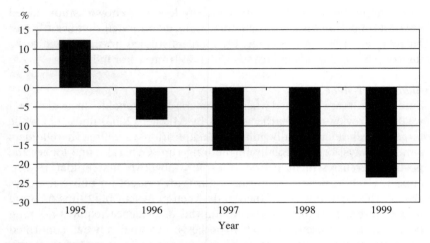

Source: Schenk (2005).

Figure 20.1   Shareholder returns of European mergers, 1995–99 (annual cohorts)

Finally, and although one might have justified doubts with respect to the specifics of meta-analyses, it is worthwhile to refer to a recent study that assessed the added effects of 93 studies with 852 effect sizes (i.e. germane bivariate correlations) with a combined *n* size of 206 910, where *n* was derived from adding the number of companies on which each of the 93 studies relied (King et al., 2004). Observed zero-order correlations between the variables of interest were weighted by the sample size of the study in order to calculate a mean weighted correlation across all of the studies involved. The sample included both shareholder- and real-value studies (with the latter limited to studies of the effects on return on assets, return on equity and return on sales). Abnormal (shareholder) returns for acquiring firms appeared to be only positive and significant at day 0. Except for an insignificant positive effect for an event window of 1–5 days, all others were negative and significant (i.e. for event windows of 6–21 days; 22–180 days; 181 days–3 years; and over 3 years). Similarly, all results for acquiring firm's return on assets, return on equity and return on sales were either insignificant or negative.

Summary and implications
Borrowing from an earlier conclusion by Scherer and Ross (1990, p. 173), we can conclude that 'the picture that emerges is a pessimistic one: widespread failure, considerable mediocrity, and occasional successes'. Taking

into account that most merger performance studies concern quoted firms – at least as acquirers – and that most quoted firms are large to very large firms, and generalizing over a great many studies, the verdict would be that, depending on the industry, between 65 and 85 per cent of large mergers and acquisitions fail to create wealth. I call such mergers 'uneconomic mergers'.

The most robust discriminator of success and failure seems to be intertemporality: the further down the merger wave, the more disappointing the economic results become. Private, mostly small, firms appear to be able to escape from this regularity (Moeller et al., 2003). The evidence must be seen as confidently suggesting that large firms are not good at creating efficiencies of whatever kind through merger. Interestingly, they are not good at creating monopoly rents through merger either – because in that case one would expect to find some superior profitability performance at the least.

It is important to notice that the results found are not just a coincidence, not just a feature of mergers in a particular era, or a particular industry. Rather, these results are common and recurring whenever a merger wave develops (for earlier merger waves, see Dewing, 1921; and Borg et al., 1989).

The performance findings also raise more fundamental questions. Assuming that executives are aware of the extremely small chances of success – which cannot be doubted since consultants' studies mostly take over the conclusions from academic research or come up with their own, very similar, conclusions; see, e.g., KPMG (1999) – we must, first, ask why they nevertheless go for it. Especially the fact that failure appears endemic makes it necessary to conclude that going for mergers cannot be an economically rational act. This is not just a case of aberrations; widespread merger failure appears to be a 'normal' fact of business life. It is therefore necessary to search for alternative explanations for this phenomenon.

A second fundamental question concerns the efficiency of the system in which merger firms are functioning. The neoclassical idea of an economy is built upon the disciplinary force of the market mechanism, more specifically the market for corporate control mechanism. Underperforming firms will become targets of more efficient firms that through a takeover will bring them back to efficiency optimization. It now appears, however, that this system is incapable of preventing uneconomic mergers. This suggests that it should either be reinforced or replaced.

Towards a social economics theory of merger

Having been confronted with what seems to be a merger paradox when viewed from within a neoclassical framework, mainstream financial economics has suggested that the problem is caused by inadequate *internal* control mechanisms. Given that shareholders (so-called principals) are not able to adequately control their managers (or agents) as a result of the enormous spread of ownership, executives would be encouraged to undertake uneconomic mergers in order simply to maximize their own goals, such as personal wealth, status and power. It is true that executive income, for example, has been found time and again to be positively correlated with firm size (Schmidt and Fowler, 1990). Since mergers are the quickest and easiest route to larger size, executives would be willing to sacrifice efficiency in return for a boost of their private wealth.

It is somehow hard to believe, however, that managers are structurally able to disguise and distort information and to mislead or cheat their principals on a scale large enough to explain the huge number of uneconomic mergers. On the contrary, managers may on average be just like ordinary people, i.e. they may enjoy performing responsibly in the interest of the owners because of a personal need for achievement, while interpreting responsibility as something that is defined in relation to others' perceptions (such as has been put forward in the 'stewardship theory'; see Davis et al., 1997).

If the principal–agent relationship is conceived in terms of enlightened self-interest, it may be difficult to decouple an agent's goals from those of her principal (see Wright et al., 2001). Also, there is not much evidence that managers would only cheat their principals when faced (or expecting to be faced) with rising profits that should be kept away from them. In fact, many of the most proliferate cases of cheating occurred when profits were decreasing rather than increasing (see Brenner, 2002). More generally, it is unclear how the inadequacy of internal controls would relate to the dynamics of merger waves.

Similarly, it would seem implausible that hubris is to blame for uneconomic mergers, as has been argued in a classic paper by Roll (1986). Hubris, indeed, is positively correlated to the height of bid premiums, which is a reliable predictor of merger failure (see, e.g., Raj and Forsyth, 2003), but intertemporal variations in the merger rate cannot be accounted for.

An adequate theory would need to be able to address the dynamics of mergers as well as their extremely high failure rate. I shall argue below that such a theory requires elements from the behavioural theory of the firm (particularly as developed by Cyert and March, 1963), from information theory (as developed by especially Scharfstein and Stein, 1990; Banerjee, 1992; and Bikhchandani et al., 1992), as well as from the theory of regret. More in particular, rather than requiring a logic of consequence, it requires a logic of appropriateness, the latter offering a perspective that sees human action as driven by rules of appropriate or exemplary behaviour, organized into institutions (see Olsen and March, 2004). Rules are then followed because they are seen as natural, rightful, expected and legitimate. An adequate theory must include a mechanism of diffusion that is able to cope with sudden multiplications of a phenomenon and a sense of counterfactuality, that is an idea about how one would have felt if another option than the actual one had been chosen. The following is an effort to develop such a theory.[2]

According to behavioural theory, uncertainty or lack of understanding with respect to goals, technologies, strategies, payoffs and so on – all of them typical of modern industries – are powerful forces that encourage imitation. Following Cyert and March (1963), DiMaggio and Powell (1983) suggest that when firms have to cope with problems with ambiguous causes or unclear solutions they will rely on problemistic search aimed at finding a viable solution with little expense. Instead of making decisions on the basis of systematic analyses of goals and means, organizations may well find it easier to mimic other organizations. Most eye-catching mergers are undertaken by large firms. These firms normally operate in concentrated industries and are usually active in several of those industries at the same time. In the typical situation of single-market or multi-market oligopoly, which involves both interdependence of outcomes and strategic uncertainty, adopting mimetic routines is therefore a likely way for solving strategic decision-making problems. Moreover, organizations with ambiguous or (potentially) disputable goals will be likely to be highly dependent upon appearances for legitimacy.

Reputation

This latter point is implied in one of the more interesting models of recent decision theory in which Scharfstein and Stein (1990) assume that there are two types of managers: 'smart' ones who receive informative signals about the value of an investment (e.g. a merger), and 'dumb' ones who receive purely noisy signals. Initially, neither these managers nor other persons (i.e. stakeholders) can identify the types, but after an investment decision has been made, stakeholders can update their beliefs on the basis of the following two pieces of evidence:

- whether their agent has made a profitable investment; and
- whether their agent's behaviour was similar to or different from that of other managers.

Given the quite reasonable assumption that there are systematically unpredictable components of investment value, and that whereas 'dumb' managers will simply observe uncorrelated noise, 'smart' managers tend to get correlated signals since they are all observing a piece of the same 'truth', it is likely that the second piece of evidence will get precedence over the first.

Since these signals might be 'bad' just as well as 'good', 'smart' managers may, however, all have received misleading signals. Since stakeholders will not be able to assess or even perceive these signals they will refer to the second piece of evidence in assessing the ability of 'their' managers. Now, if a manager is concerned with her reputation among stakeholders, then it will be natural for her to mimic a first-mover as this suggests to stakeholders that she has observed a signal that is correlated with the signal observed by the first-mover – which will make it more likely that she is a 'smart' manager.

The more managers adopt this behaviour, the more likely it will be that 'bad' decisions will be seen as a result of a common unpredictable negative component of investment value. The fact that many, perhaps even all, players committed the error will suggest that all were victims of a 'bad' signal. Erring managers will subsequently be able to share the blame of stakeholders with their peers. In contrast, a manager who takes a contrary position will *ex ante* be perceived as 'dumb'. She will therefore be likely to pursue an investment opportunity if peers are pursuing that – even if her private information suggests that it has a negative expected value. Thus Scharfstein and Stein's model explains why conventional wisdom teaches that it is better for reputation to fail conventionally than to succeed unconventionally – as was already proposed by Keynes (1936).

Rational herding
This result, however, is not generally dependent on reputational considerations. Whereas Scharfstein and Stein's model is essentially an agency model in which agents try to fool their principals and get rewarded if they succeed, Banerjee (1992) and Bikhchandani et al. (1992) have addressed the imitation phenomenon as a consequence of informational externalities. In these models each decision maker looks at the decisions made by previous decision makers in taking her own decision and opts for imitating those previous decisions because the earlier decision makers may have learned some information that is important for her. The result is herd behaviour, that is, a behavioural pattern in which everyone is doing what everyone else is doing.

These models are essentially those that explain why some person may choose not to go by her own information, but instead will imitate the choice made by a previous decision maker. Following Banerjee (1992), suppose that – for some reason – the prior probability that an investment alternative is successful is 51 per cent (call this alternative i_1), and that the prior probability that alternative i_2 is successful is 49 per cent. These prior probabilities are common knowledge. Suppose further that of ten firms – i.e. firms A, B, . . ., J – nine firms have received a signal that i_2 is better (of course, this signal may be wrong) but that the one firm that has received a signal that i_1 is better happens to choose first. The signals are of equal quality, and firms can only observe predecessors' choices but not their signals. The first firm (firm A) will clearly opt for alternative i_1. Firm B will now know that the first firm had a signal that favoured i_1 while her own signal favours i_2. If the signals are of equal quality, then these conflicting signals effectively cancel out, and the rational choice for firm B is to go by the prior probabilities, i.e. choose i_1. Her choice provides no new information to firm C, so that firm C's situation is not different from that of firm B. Firm C will then imitate firm B for the same reason that prompted firm B to imitate firm A, and so on: all nine follower firms will eventually adopt alternative i_1. Clearly, if firm B had fully relied on her own signal, then her decision would have provided information to the other eight firms. This would have encouraged these other firms to use their own information.

Thus, from a broader perspective, it is of crucial importance whether firm A's decision is the correct decision. If it is, then all firms will choose for the 'right' alternative, but if it is not, all firms will end up with a 'wrong' decision. Also, the result of this game is dependent on chance: were firm B, . . ., J to have had the opportunity to choose first, things would have come out entirely differently. However, when translated into our merger problem, if alternative i_2 is set equal to 'do not undertake a merger', then A's action ('merger') will always be the first to be observed as a deviation from actual practice, thus prompting firms B, . . ., J to respond. The mechanism is especially clear when a first and a second firm have both chosen the same $i \neq 0$ (where the point 0 has no special meaning but is merely defined as a point that is known, i.e. observable, to the other firms). That is, the third firm (firm C) knows that firm A must have a signal since otherwise it would have chosen $i = 0$. Firm A's choice is therefore at least as good as firm C's signal. Moreover, the fact that B has followed A lends extra support to A's choice (which may be the 'wrong' choice nevertheless). It is therefore always better for C to follow A.

The main virtues of Banerjee's model are (a) that some aspects of herd behaviour can be explained without invoking network externalities, i.e. without requiring that a decision maker will actually benefit from imitating earlier decision makers (which would be the case if undertaking some action is more worthwhile when others are doing related things); and (b) that it is possible that decision makers will neglect their private information and instead will go by the information provided by the actions of earlier decision makers (or the prior probabilities).

Cascades

Bikhchandani et al. (1992) use the metaphor of a cascade to stress essentially the same point. The process is depicted as a cascade since with increasing numbers of decision makers adopting a particular action, it becomes increasingly, that is more than proportionally, likely that the next decision maker will follow suit. According to Bikhchandani et al., a cascade will start if 'enough' predecessors have all acted in contradistinction to a subsequent decision maker's own information and if there is no *a priori* reason to expect that the signals received by the earlier decision makers are less valuable than the signal received by the subsequent decision maker. The first condition is dependent on the specification of the model. The latter condition is an assumption of the model (but can be adapted by introducing variations in signal strength). Ultimately, the reason that a decision maker will tend to disregard her own information is that she is sufficiently uncertain about the value of her signal to act upon it when faced by the decisions of others. Alternatively, it could be argued that she is simply economizing on the costs involved in gathering and processing information. Observing the choices of others and imitating these may be a cheap and helpful alternative in the light of the many uncertainties involved with strategic decision making.

Regret
Thus far we have shown that the intricacies of information diffusion in sequential games can cause imitation despite the fact that a follower's private information would indicate a deviation from the trajectory that seems to have been started. Notice, however, that they are couched in a positive payoff framework. Furthermore, they make use of binary action sets implying that only correct and incorrect decisions are possible and that a small mistake incurs the same loss as a large mistake. The introduction of a regret framework relaxes these conditions and increases the plausibility of models of herding behaviour. In their well-known series of experiments, Kahneman and Tversky (1979) found that people systematically violate two major conditions of the expected utility model's conception of rationality when confronted with risk: the requirements of consistency of and coherence among choices. They traced this to the psychological principles that govern the perception of decision problems and the evaluation of options. Apart from the fact that it appears to matter substantially in which frame a *given* decision problem is couched, even to the extent that preferences are reversed when that frame is changed, choices involving gains are often risk-averse and choices involving losses risk-taking. Thus it appears that the response to losses is more extreme than the response to gains. Kahneman and Tversky's 'prospect theory', of course, is consistent with common experience that the displeasure associated with losing a sum of money is greater than the pleasure associated with gaining the same amount.

Consequently, it is likely that the contents of decision rules and standard practices will be 'biased' in such a way that they favour the prevention of losses rather than the realization of gains. Thus behavioural norms that carry this property are more likely to be 'chosen' as Schelling's so-called focal points (Schelling, 1960). In practice, this will mean that firms are likely to adopt routines that imply a substantial degree of circumspection. A similar degree of circumspection is likely to develop if the decision maker is concerned with the regret that she may have upon discovering the difference between the actual payoff as the result of her choice and 'what might have been' the payoff were she to have opted for a different course of action. Regret in this case may be defined as the loss of pleasure due to the knowledge that a better outcome might have been attained if a different choice had been made. Under conditions of uncertainty a decision maker will modify the expected value of a particular action according to the level of this regret.

Minimax regret
Dietrich and Schenk (1995), building on Savage (1951) and Loomes and Sugden (1982), have suggested that one way of expressing this is by adopting a minimax-regret routine. Let us assume that a decision maker knows the payoffs for each decision alternative but that she is completely ignorant as to which state of nature prevails. The minimax-regret routine then prescribes that she should select the strategy that minimizes the highest possible regret assuming that the level of regret is linearly related to the differences in payoff. The minimax-regret criterion thus puts a floor under how bad the decision maker would feel if things went wrong. Moreover, doing so will protect her against the highest possible reproach that can be made by those stakeholders who assess the decision's utility on the basis of the true state of nature.

When put into a framework of competitive interdependence, this develops as follows. Given that firm A announces the acquisition of firm B, and that this acquisition for some reason attracts attention of its peers (rivals), then firm C will have to contemplate what the repercussions of this initiative for its own position might be. Suppose that there is no way that C can tell whether A's move will be successful or not. A's move could be genuinely motivated by a realistic expectation that its cost position will improve, or by a realistic expectation that its move will increase its rating with stakeholders or its earnings. That is, A's competitiveness position *vis-à-vis* its peers might be improved as a result of that move, say in terms of a first-mover advantage. But then again, it might not. For example, A's move might be purely motivated by the pursuit of managerial goals, or it might simply be a miscalculation caused by hubris. What is firm C to do?

Suppose that A's move will be successful, but that C has not reacted by imitating that move itself (which we will call scenario α). To what extent will C regret not having reacted? Alternatively, suppose that A's move will not be successful but that C has imitated it, solely inspired by the possible prospect of A's move being a success (scenario β). To what extent will C regret this when the failure of A's move becomes apparent? Within a minimax-regret framework, it is likely that C's regret attached to scenario α will be higher than the regret attached to scenario β. For in scenario α, C will experience a loss of competitiveness, while in scenario β its competitive position *vis-à-vis* A will not have been harmed. Of course, C could have realized a competitive *gain* in scenario β had it refrained from imitation, but in terms of the minimax-regret model C's regret of having lost this potential gain is likely to be relatively small. The implication is that under conditions of uncertainty a strategic move by firm A will elicit an imitative countermove by its rivals – even if the economic payoffs are unknown.

We conclude that a decision maker who is using a minimax-regret routine will imitate actions of earlier decision makers that are regarded as significant. Thus if – for some reason – a first decision maker within a strategic group has decided to undertake a merger, a second decision maker may follow suit even if her own information suggests otherwise. Evidently, such imitation may lead to cascades that will last a very long time. In a sense, mergers and acquisitions have then become 'taken-for-granted' solutions to competitive interdependence. This implies that firms may have become locked into a solution in which all players implicitly prefer a non-optimal strategy without having ready possibilities for breaking away from it.

Even if some firms do not adopt minimax-regret behaviour, it will be sensible for them to jump on a merger bandwagon too. For cascading numbers of mergers and acquisitions imply that the likelihood of becoming an acquisition target increases. Thus, given the finding that relative size is a more effective barrier against takeover than relative profitability (Dickerson et al., 2003), firms may enter the merger and acquisition game for no other reason than to defend themselves against takeover. It is needless to say that such defensive mergers will amplify the prevailing rate of mergers and acquisitions. The cascade will inevitably stop as soon as (a) the number of potential targets diminishes, which is a function of the intensity of the cascade, and (b) the disappointing merger returns reduce the chances for obtaining the financial means necessary for further merger investments.

Mergers that have been undertaken for minimax-regret or defensive reasons can be designated as *purely strategic mergers*. These are mergers that are intended to create strategic comfort for firms when faced with the uncertain effects of a competitor's moves, rather than economic wealth (or, for that matter, monopoly rents). It is precisely for this reason that it would be futile to wait on the so-called learning capacities of organizations to improve economic merger performance. In a system that is dominated by the few, such purely strategic mergers are simply part of the game – and since these mergers on average may turn out to be wealth-creating only by chance, uneconomic mergers will also be of the order of the day, more precisely: whenever firms are baiting each other into a merger wave.

The restructuring wave

It is now possible to derive the different stages of the restructuring wave, of which the merger wave is an integral part, see Figure 20.2. We have a logic of appropriateness (reputation), a diffusion mechanism (imitation) and a sense of counterfactuality (regret). The existence of strategic interdependence under uncertainty, under certain conditions such as concerning the availability of funds, will compel managements to undertake mergers even if these will not increase economic performance. Inertia may prevail, possibly for long periods, but as soon as an initial, clearly observable move has

Stage 1	*Preconditional* A booming economy provides the necessary means (cash; stock appreciations; borrowing facilities), but is not sufficient
Stage 2	*Event* A single (random) merger ignites the game
Stage 3	*Response* Minimax-regret and defensive routines lead to bursts of merger activity
Stage 4	*Depletion* The merger boom levels off as a result of lacking and/or lagging productivity/profitability gains, and price rises for targets
Stage 5	*Recovery* Reconstitution management sets in (sell-offs, divestitures, demergers; lay-offs); private equity setting in
Stage 6	*Normalization* The pool with targets is refilled

Source: Adapted from Schenk (2006).

Figure 20.2   The restructuring wave

been made by one or a few of the major players, it is likely that other players will rapidly follow with similar moves. With multi-market oligopoly omnipresent, and given the increasing weight assigned to stock market performance appraisals, the ultimate result can be an economy-wide merger boom.

Eventually, many firms will find themselves replete with acquisitions that were neither meant nor able to create wealth. As a consequence, after the strategic imperatives have receded, firms will start undertaking repair work. In the short run, they are likely to look for cheap and easy alternatives, such as economizing on all sorts of expenses (e.g. labour, R&D). In the medium run they will spin off many of the acquisitions made during the boom – sometimes at great cost. Indeed, it has been estimated that as much as half of all mergers and acquisitions will be undone within a period of ten post-merger years (Porter, 1987).

Thus the booming merger years now turn into a period in which mergers are relatively rare. In fact, it is likely that mergers that still happen during these depressed years have a relatively high chance of success (see Figure 20.1). First, the strategy pressure is relatively low so that the economic pros and cons of a merger or acquisition can be thought through carefully. Second, prices on the stock market are less inflated, and premiums need not have deterrence quality so that they can be relatively low. Meanwhile, beginning during the fourth merger wave in the 1980s, a complete new industry has grown that has specialized in facilitating spin-offs of previously acquired subsidiaries or divisions. Sometimes labelled locusts, these private equity companies (PECs) help acquisitive firms to get rid of their uneconomic acquisitions or make a profit from dissolving unsuccessful amalgamations altogether. Firms, or parts of them, are taken private so that they are no longer subject to the same rules of the game that have been adopted by quoted firms. It is only natural that these PECs have been able to flourish especially during 2003–7, for, apart from low interest rates until mid-2007, the fifth merger wave created many economically unsuccessful mergers, thus many opportunities for restructurings at low cost.

Not everything that glisters is gold, however. Recent calculations have shown that leveraged buy-outs appear to have a 3.5 higher bankruptcy chance than 'regular' takeovers (Schenk, 2007). Although it is difficult to ascertain the causes of this, it is remarkable that leveraged buy-outs appear to economize on capital investments, particularly investments in R&D (for earlier corroborations, see Long and Ravenscraft, 1993). It therefore seems possible that a mechanism that, according to mainstream finance, should pressure firms to focus on efficiency only, in fact also pressures them to economize on investment projects necessary for survival.

Implications

From the analysis above, it appears that uneconomic mergers are inevitable in a free market system in which (some) firms are quoted on the stock market (and protections against takeovers are not allowed or have been eliminated). The pressure to conform can be so strong that excessively risky behaviour – excessive from the viewpoint of the system as a whole – becomes the norm, at least for a while. Mergers and acquisitions have become the taken-for-granted solutions to strategic uncertainty. Under such circumstances the market for corporate control mechanisms is unavoidably perverted. While, in theory, it is meant to facilitate the eviction of underperforming firms, it now encourages underperforming firms to use it to their advantage: as a protection against takeover. Notice that this is a possibility that would be denied under the logic of consequence (mentioned in the beginning of this chapter). As soon as this logic is dropped, and as soon as firms are no longer regarded as unresisting instruments in the economy's drive for wealth, it becomes possible to accept that the normal behaviour of businesses may sometimes run counter to the public interest.

Internal controls would not be a solution either. During the last decade and a half, it has been increasingly suggested to reinforce the shareholders' grip on management. Seen from the current problematic, this would make sense only if shareholders could more easily pull themselves away from the strategic imperatives that are putting pressure on management than management itself. Since these shareholders in most cases happen to be other firms in the guise of investors or institutional investors who are caught in the same web, this is quite unlikely (see Berglöf, 1997).

Current competition and antitrust policies, though ultimately designed to prevent or punish corporate behaviour that is eating into society's wealth generation processes, are currently unable to protect the economy from uneconomic mergers. In a market economy there is a presumption that private agents should be free to pursue their own interests as they see fit up to the point at which this pursuit has (significantly) adverse consequences for economic welfare. Following this idea, most countries, indeed, have introduced laws or regulations that require certain (usually large) firms to submit certain (usually large) mergers for approval to the competition authorities. However, the tests used to assess welfare consequences have been designed around the idea that it is consumer welfare that counts – not the public interest, or at least not any more. Thus merger control normally amounts to an assessment of a merger's effect on allocative efficiency rather than productive or dynamic efficiency – which are the areas where the real problems of mergers tend to lie.

Apart from the fact that establishing allocative effects is not an easy task as a result of both conceptual and measurement problems (some would say an impossible one; see Dewey, 1996), these procedures implicitly assume that firms will never be allowed by their owners or the market for corporate control mechanism to undertake mergers that are not able to increase profits as a result of an increase in monopoly power or an increase in productive or dynamic efficiency. As we have seen, this presumption cannot be sustained.

Looking at the problem from a different angle, it could be argued that the occurrence of uneconomic mergers in itself is proof of pre-existing market power. Whatever the precise definition of the case, it is obvious that if society wanted to get rid of uneconomic mergers it would have to refocus its concentration regulations in such a manner that the public purpose would be re-established as a legitimate policy criterion. Despite the fact that political scientists have not been able to clearly identify the public interest – which may have contributed to its demise in competition policy – it is clear that public interest considerations can and are to be distinguished from private or sectional interests and that they make claims to underlying 'common' social values as the basis for justification of action (Hess and Adams, 1999).

Summary and conclusions
This chapter has suggested that the periodic omnipresence of failed mergers is not surprising since uneconomic mergers seem a natural result of competition among the few. Such competition encourages strategic rather than economic behaviour, that is, behaviour that is not primarily driven by the wish to create wealth but by the behavioural peculiarities of strategic interdependence.

Even if only some firms adopt a minimax-regret rationale, others will be forced to jump on merger bandwagons for defensive reasons. Once it becomes evident that this results in high costs to the firms themselves (or rather their shareholders and employees), they need to take corrective actions. As a consequence, such merger waves are followed by periods of restructuring, large-scale divestment and lay-offs. In the 1980s, financial technology has developed in such a way that leveraged buy-outs, especially by private equity companies, in principle can help facilitate this repair work. Unfortunately, it appears likely that this is not without its own problems. It is likely that the excessive use of leverage puts so much pressure on the firms to focus on cash flow that they will run a significantly higher bankruptcy risk.

In any case, it would seem much more efficient to avoid this carousel of detours, that is the merry-go-round of allowing many uneconomic mergers which subsequently have to be repaired by leveraged buy-outs.

Whereas the observed merger effects are rooted in the high levels of economic concentration that have become typical of modern economies, therefore a matter of competition policy, current merger regulations may not be the preferred means of control. Merger regulations have been designed to prevent as many harmful mergers as possible while preserving economically efficient mergers. As long as the consumer's interest remains the main vehicle for defining the wealth of nations, however, competition economists as well as authorities will be led away from the most pervasive problematic effect of mergers. Rather, one would want to see competition policy return to its roots by putting the public interest at centre stage.

Notes

1. In this chapter, I use the terms merger and acquisition interchangeably, unless noted otherwise.
2. The next few sections are largely adopted from Schenk (2006).

References

Augier, M., K. Kreiner and J.G. March (2000), 'Introduction: some roots and branches of organizational economics', *Industrial and Corporate Change*, 9 (4), 555–65.

Banerjee, A.V. (1992), 'A simple model of herd behavior', *Quarterly Journal of Economics*, 107 (3), 797–817.

Berglöf, E. (1997), 'Reforming corporate governance: redirecting the European agenda', *Economic Policy*, 24, 93–123.

Bikhchandani, S., D. Hirschleifer and I. Welch (1992), 'A theory of fads, fashions, custom and cultural change as informational cascades', *Journal of Political Economy*, 100 (5), 992–1026.

Black, J. (2002), *Oxford Dictionary of Economics*, Oxford: Oxford University Press.

Borg, J.R., M.O. Borg and J.D. Leeth (1989), 'The success of mergers in the 1920s. A stock market appraisal of the second merger wave', *International Journal of Industrial Organization*, 7 (1), 117–31.

Brenner, R. (2002), *The Boom and the Bubble. The US and the World Economy*, London and New York: Verso.

Calomiris, C.W. (1999), 'Gauging the efficiency of bank consolidation during a merger wave', *Journal of Banking & Finance*, 23, 615–21.

Camerer, C.F. and G. Loewenstein (2004), 'Behavioral economics: past, present, future', in C.F. Camerer, G. Loewenstein and M. Rabin (eds), *Advances in Behavioral Economics*, Princeton, NJ: Princeton University Press, pp. 3–51.

Carow, K., R. Heron and T. Saxton (2004), 'Do early birds get the returns? An empirical investigation of early-mover advantages in acquisitions', *Strategic Management Journal*, 25, 563–85.

Cyert, R.M., and J.G. March (1963), *A Behavioral Theory of the Firm*, 2nd edn 1992, Cambridge, MA: Blackwell.

Davis, J.H., F.D. Schoorman and L. Donaldson (1997), 'Toward a stewardship theory of management', *Academy of Management Review*, 22 (1), 20–47.

Dewey, D. (1996), 'Merger policy greatly simplified: building on Keyes', *Review of Industrial Organization*, 11, 395–400.

Dewing, A.S. (1921), 'A statistical test of the success of consolidations', *Quarterly Journal of Economics*, 36, 84–101.

Dickerson, A.P., H.D. Gibson and E. Tsakalotos (2003), 'Is attack the best form of defence? A competing risk analysis of acquisition activity in the UK', *Cambridge Journal of Economics*, 27, 337–57.

Dietrich, M. and H. Schenk (1995), 'Co-ordination benefits, lock-in, and strategy bias', Management Report 220, Rotterdam: Rotterdam School of Management, Erasmus University.

DiMaggio, P.J. and W.W. Powell (1983), 'The iron cage revisited: institutional isomorphism and collective rationality in organizational fields', *American Sociological Review*, **48**, 147–60.

Healy, P.M., K.G. Palepu and R.S. Ruback (1992), 'Does corporate performance improve after mergers?', *Journal of Financial Economics*, **31**, 135–75.

Healy, P.M., K.G. Palepu and R.S. Ruback (1997), 'Which takeovers are profitable? Strategic or financial?', *Sloan Management Review*, Summer, 45–57.

Hess, M. and D. Adams (1999), 'National Competition Policy and (the) public interest', NCDS Briefing Paper 3, Canberra: National Centre for Development Studies, Australian National University.

Hodgson, G.M. (1998), 'The approach of institutional economics', *Journal of Economic Literature*, **36**, 166–92.

Kahneman, D. and A. Tversky (1979), 'Prospect theory: an analysis of decision making under risk', *Econometrica*, **47** (2), 263–91.

Keynes, J.M. (1936), *The General Theory of Employment, Interest, and Money*, London: Macmillan.

King, D.R., D.A. Dalton, C.M. Daily and J.G. Covin (2004), 'Meta-analyses of post-acquisition performance: indicators of unidentified moderators', *Strategic Management Journal*, **25**, 187–200.

KPMG (1999), *Unlocking Shareholder Value: The Keys to Success. Mergers & Acquisitions, A Global Research Report*, London: KPMG.

Long, W.F. and D.J. Ravenscraft (1993), 'Decade of debt: lessons from LBOs in the 1980s', in M.M. Blair (ed.), *The Deal Decade*, Washington: Brookings Institution, pp. 205–38.

Loomes, G. and R. Sugden (1982), 'Regret theory: an alternative theory of rational choice under uncertainty', *Economic Journal*, **92**, 805–24.

Moeller, S.B., F.P. Schlingemann and R.M. Stulz (2003), 'Do shareholders of acquiring firms gain from acquisitions?', Working Paper 9523, Washington: National Bureau for Economic Research.

Mueller, D.C. (1986), *Profits in the Long Run*, Cambridge/New York: Cambridge University Press.

Mueller, D.C. (2003), 'The finance literature on mergers: a critical survey', in M. Waterson (ed.), *Competition, Monopoly and Corporate Governance. Essays in Honour of Keith Cowling*, Cheltenham, UK and Northampton, MA, USA: Edward Elgar, pp. 161–205.

Olsen, J.P. and J.G. March (2004), 'The logic of appropriateness', Discussion Paper 04/09, Centre for European Studies, University of Oslo.

Porter, M.E. (1987), 'From competitive advantage to corporate strategy', *Harvard Business Review*, **65** (May–June), 43–59.

Raj, M. and M. Forsyth (2003), 'Hubris amongst U.K. bidders and losses to shareholders', *International Journal of Business*, **8**, 1–16.

Ravenscraft, D.J. and F.M. Scherer (1987), *Mergers, Selloffs, and Economic Efficiency*, Washington, DC: Brookings Institution.

Roll, R. (1986), 'The hubris hypothesis of corporate takeovers', *Journal of Business*, **59** (2), 197–216.

Savage, L.J. (1951), 'The theory of statistical decision', *Journal of the American Statistical Association*, **46**, 55–67.

Scharfstein, D.S. and J.C. Stein (1990), 'Herd behavior and investment', *American Economic Review*, **80** (3), 465–79.

Schelling, T. (1960), *The Strategy of Conflict*, Cambridge, MA: Harvard University Press.

Schenk, H. (2002), 'Economics and strategy of the merger paradox' (in Dutch), in J.-C. Bartel, R.F. Van Frederikslust and H. Schenk (eds), *Mergers and Acquisitions: Fundamental Aspects* (in Dutch), Amsterdam: Elsevier, pp. 62–133.

Schenk, H. (2005), 'Organisational economics in an age of restructuring, or: how corporate strategies can harm your economy', in P. De Gijsel and H. Schenk (eds), *Multidisciplinary Economics*, Dordrecht: Springer, pp. 333–65.

Schenk, H. (2006), 'Mergers and concentration policy', in P. Bianchi and S. Labory (eds), *International Handbook of Industrial Policy*, Cheltenham, UK and Northampton, MA, USA: Edward Elgar, pp. 153–79.

Schenk, H. (2007), 'Private equity buy outs and bankruptcy risk', paper presented at the Annual Conference of EUNIP, Università di Firenze (I), 12–14 September.

Scherer, F.M. and D. Ross (1990), *Industrial Market Structure and Economic Performance*, 3rd edn, Boston, MA: Houghton Mifflin.

Schmidt, D.R. and K.L. Fowler (1990), 'Post-acquisition financial performance and executive compensation', *Strategic Management Journal*, 11 (7), 559–69.

Tversky, A. and D. Kahneman (1981), 'The framing of decisions and the psychology of choice', *Science*, 211 (30 January), 453–8.

Wright, P., A. Mukherji and M.J. Kroll (2001), 'A re-examination of agency theory assumptions: extensions and extrapolations', *Journal of Socio-Economics*, 30, 413–29.

PART VII

SOCIAL RELATIONS IN THE ECONOMY

Chapter 21: 'Social capital: a critique and extension', by Nicolas Sirven
This chapter highlights how the mainstream conception of social capital has been purposefully developed by the World Bank in order to rehabilitate the endogenous growth theory through a neoinstitutional approach. We assert that this methodology fails to legitimate institutions as a form of capital – namely social capital. As an alternative to the problems raised by this (mis)conception, we suggest a rights-based definition of social capital inspired by Bourdieu's seminal work. Social capital thus becomes an accountable form of capital that may lead to an alternative approach to the analysis of social features in economics.

Chapter 22: 'Social networks: structure and content', by Wilfred Dolfsma and Rick Aalbers
Social networks analysis is at the cutting edge of recent development in interdisciplinary social science. A broad range of social phenomena is analysed in terms of the social network structures that are at their roots, one example being the way in which people in an organization exchange knowledge. Networks allow for a qualitative analysis, but also for more quantitative analysis. Individuals can be seen as embedded in a number of different networks. Social network analysis has developed a number of different characterizations for network structure, each of which is argued and shown to have an influence on individuals' behaviour. Social network analysis is, however, a structural analysis of social reality and thus has little or no role for agency. The notion of gift exchange will offer a fuller, 'thicker' analysis of social reality and embeddedness, it is argued here, but is in need of further development.

Chapter 23: 'Communication in the economy: the example of innovation', by Stefan Kesting
Starting from Schumpeter's classical approach to innovation, this chapter argues that the creation, development and implementation of new ideas

are based on communication. From the pioneering work of Hirschman, Boulding, and Denzau and North, a model of communicative behaviour is generated and further elaborated with the help of Habermas's discourse ethics and Galbraith's theory of power. This approach distinguishes basically two modes of communication: a dialogical one and a persuasive one. That these modes are relevant as a foundation for innovation is shown in a review of the literature on networks, routines and scripts. The dialogical mode is used mainly to create *the new* while the persuasive mode is employed to put innovation into practice. In conclusion, it is argued that such a communicative foundation is needed to understand how creativity and power are used in innovative processes.

Chapter 24: 'Methodological approaches in economics and anthropology', by Pranab Bardhan and Isha Ray
In this chapter we argue that one of the key barriers to interdisciplinary work between economists and anthropologists is differences in methodology and epistemology – in what the two disciplines consider important to explain, and how they evaluate the criteria for a good explanation. We highlight three dichotomies that are emblematic of some of these differences: autonomy versus embeddedness, outcomes versus processes, and parsimony versus complexity. We show that whether individuals are conceptualized as autonomous agents within social structures or as products of the structures that bound their agency generates legitimate (but not insurmountable) differences between economists and anthropologists. We show that seeking to simplify social reality versus seeking to complicate dominant simplifications results in both intellectual and political divisions between the disciplines. Through this discussion we seek to understand what is important to each discipline, and to see the divides in the light of that understanding.

21 Social capital: a critique and extension
Nicolas Sirven

The concept of social capital has been widely used in the economic literature to assess issues on economic development (Isham et al., 2002; Grootaert and Van Bastelaer, 2002), health promotion (Hawe and Shiell, 2000; Almedom, 2005), or sustainable environmental governance (Pretty and Ward, 2001). Economists generally use 'social capital' to address a wide range of social phenomena that are believed to have an economic payoff. The hybrid nature of this concept raises interest, especially in social economics where the term 'social capital' seems to be used to mean anything one wants it to mean.

However, comments in the economic literature are rather ambivalent about the usefulness of 'social capital'. At least three main different opinions can be underlined. First, 'social capital' is thought to be an oxymoron, i.e. an awkward metaphor developed to gain conviction from a bad analogy (Solow, 1999; Arrow, 1999). The analysis of social phenomena in economics should thus be made without any reference to 'capital', a term that should be restricted to concepts as tangible as bricks and mortar (see, e.g., Dolfsma, 2001). Second, 'social capital' is seen as a Trojan horse that economists have built to colonize social science under the assumption of rationality (Fine and Green, 2000). Once again, the use of 'social capital' is contested because the undersocialized conception of *homo economicus* may introduce a distortion into the analysis of social behaviours (Granovetter, 1985). Third, a more optimistic view of 'social capital' makes it play the role of a 'missing link' (Grootaert, 1997) in the economic analysis of development and growth. This stresses the opportunity to bring the social back into the field of economics.

Notice that the last position could prefigure the dawn of a new approach to social sciences. However, such a project has been set aside by mainstream economists. Their analysis of social capital focuses on three usual economics topics. First, 'social capital' is defined as the social component of human capital (Becker and Murphy, 2000). It helps us understand how social forces (i.e. norms of behaviour due to belonging to a group) influence individual consumption choices through a social multiplier phenomenon (Glaeser et al., 2000). The purpose of this approach is to extend the arguments of the aggregated demand function. Second, 'social capital' is described as a social insurance that households develop when markets and the state are unable to give them social protection (Fafchamps and Lund, 2003). This theory is quite close to the analysis of gift exchange and allows us to consider social capital as an informal contract between two parties. Third, 'social capital' is analysed as the characteristics of social organization such as norms and values that help reduce the free-rider problem and lower transaction costs. This view of 'social capital' – as closely associated with the idea of mutual trust – has been revived by the World Bank (see Grootaert and Van Bastelaer, 2002) in a neoinstitutionalist perspective.

This chapter focuses on this last approach, which is certainly the one most discussed in recent economic debates. One reason for such popularity comes from the use of 'social capital' by the World Bank as a concept encompassing most of the theoretical and empirical work dealing with social phenomena (Grootaert and Van Bastelaer, 2002). My purpose is to retrace the different steps made by the mainstream approach to 'social capital' in order to show how the amalgamation of heterogeneous work on institutional and social fields as a form of capital leads to a dead end. Following a social economics perspective, I suggest an alternative definition of 'social capital' based on prior studies by Bourdieu (1980, 1986) and Coleman (1988). This 'return to the roots' allows us to propose the analysis of 'social capital' as a legitimate form of capital with expected capital-like properties.

The chapter is structured as follows. Section 1 reviews the World Bank approach to recover the analysis of social phenomena within a neoinstitutional approach. My aim is to prove that the term 'social capital' is used as a synonym for 'institutions'. In Section 2, I try to show why it is so important for endogenous growth theorists that institutions are considered as a form of capital. I also suggest that this approach fails. An alternative definition of social capital is then developed in Section 3 through a rights-based approach. Finally, I discuss the empirical and theoretical perspectives for this rights-based definition of social capital in economics.

1.   Looking at social capital with neoinstitutional goggles

Although the concept of social capital had previously been developed by social scientists such as Pierre Bourdieu (1980, 1986) and James Coleman (1988), it is widely acknowledged that Robert Putnam is the author who introduced this concept in the economic literature. In his seminal book, Putnam (1993) brings into play the concept of social capital so as to show how civic traditions affect the efficiency of regional governments in Italy. Social capital is assumed to create social trust, which in turns leads to strong, responsive, effective representative institutions that improve political outcomes. Social capital is defined as 'the features of social organization, such as trust, norms, and networks that can improve the efficiency of society by facilitating coordinated actions' (Putnam, 1993, p. 167). One can note that Putnam's work is closely related to Ostrom's (1990) thesis, which shows how some institutions succeeded in overcoming the problem of collective action (see Olson, 1971) through strong norms and sanctions within communities. From a theoretical perspective, this follows from a neoinstitutional approach that seeks to explain how and why some 'good' institutions make possible the achievement of certain goals that would have not been reached either by individuals acting alone or by markets and governments. Social capital is thus seen as 'the missing link' (Grootaert, 1997) for economic analysis and economic policies.

Subsequent studies by Putnam (1995) and Fukuyama (1995) popularized the idea that social capital is a cornerstone of development. The mid-1990s saw widespread use of the term 'social capital' in the economic literature. For instance, the number of new articles associated with the keyword 'social capital' in the Repec electronic database rose from ten in 1995 to 430 in 2001. During this period, the concept covered a wide range of social phenomena so that Dasgupta and Serageldin (1999, p. x) recognized that 'social capital means different things to different people'. As there was a need for clarification of this concept, in 1996 the World Bank launched the Social Capital Initiative (SCI), with the aim to unify under one banner the different views on social capital. At first sight, such an approach is of crucial interest, but the way the SCI has been carried out suggested that the concept is purposefully handled so as to become a synonym for 'institutions' in a neoinstitutionalist framework. Let us highlight the key stages of the reinterpretation of social capital by the World Bank.

The first step was made by Collier (1998), who suggests dividing the term into government social capital and civil social capital. The former concept deals with institutions set up by the government in order to realize benefits that would not be achieved through the market. It is assumed that the broadest definition of social capital includes government because it is a hierarchical non-market organization. The concept of civil social capital refers to non-government institutions that help to achieve collective goals without direct recourse to government powers of coercion. Collier asserts that those two forms of social capital can be both substitute and complement, but he remains somewhat elusive on that point.

Narayan (1999) extends Collier's analysis by means of the concept of governance (Berg and Whitaker, 1986). She stresses that government social capital is efficient when the overall governance environment leads to institutional performance, that is, when the criteria for 'good governance' are fulfilled. In a different way, civil social capital is efficient for the collective good of citizens if there are cross-cutting ties between networks, associations and other social groups, whereas social groups without cross-cutting ties lead only to the improvement of those groups. The state of well-being is reached when both of these forms of social capital are efficient: '[u]nder conditions of good governance, the functioning of the state complements the functions of the informal social groups' (Narayan, 1999, p. 15). In other words, a close collaboration between formal and informal institutions is a key for a better society. Problems within the society arise when – at least – one of the forms of social capital is inefficient. More precisely, '[a]s governance deteriorates, and government efficacy deteriorates, the informal social groups become substitutes for the state' (ibid., pp. 15–16). The author stresses that such a situation may lead to the development of coping strategies or conflict that would be harmful for the society.

At this stage, it must be emphasized that the World Bank implicitly assumes that social capital may play a negative role if the society is composed of insular social groups. This analysis is coherent with the work of Rubio (1997), who shows how some powerful criminal organizations in Colombia run an illegal economy in parallel with government institutions. These groups develop rent seeking and provide their members with higher outcomes than those they would earn through a regular career. Rubio (1997) calls 'perverse social capital' these kinds of institutions that promote opportunistic behaviours and lead to inefficient situations. In so far as social capital is two-sided, the analogy with the mainstream definition of institution is made much more easily since North (1990, p. 63) established that 'institutions everywhere are a mixed bag composed of those that lower [transaction] costs and those that raise them'.

As a consequence, the concept of social capital recovers the same range of dual effects that good and bad institutions are assumed to have on economic performance. Moreover, Knack (1999) uses the distinction between civil and government social capital so as to propose a survey of empirical studies on the effects of institutions on countries' economic performance. The concept of 'government social capital' encompasses studies dealing with civil liberties and political freedom (Kormendi and Meguire, 1985), frequency of political violence (Alesina et al., 1996), subjective political risk ratings (Mauro, 1995; Knack and Keefer, 1995) and so on. Studies focusing on civic community (Helliwell and Putnam, 1995), generalized trust (LaPorta et al., 1997; Knack and Keefer, 1997; Zack and Knack, 2001), social polarization (Easterly and Levine, 1997) or cultural explanations (Granato et al., 1996) are labelled under 'civic social capital'. As a synthesis, high levels of – good – social capital are found to be associated with economy-wide measures of performance such as growth, rates of investment, and with subsequent improvements in the distribution of income.

Collier's distinction has been especially useful in assigning the effects of institutions on economic performance to the concept of social capital.

Nevertheless, such a definition remains somewhat functional in that we can hardly separate what social capital actually is from what it does (Edwards and Foley, 1999). In order to clarify this concept, Pantoja (1999, p. 16) defines social capital as 'a social relational resource inherent to social networks and social organizations'. He then identifies six forms of social capital including different types of social interactions such as family and kinship connections, associational life, institutional and policy framework, and social norms and values. This work is interesting because it describes different forms of social capital; however, Pantoja (ibid., p. 26) acknowledges that '[t]hese forms do not exist in isolation, and many do not have clear or real boundaries either. In fact, many of them are embedded in other forms of social capital, or are necessary inputs for or outputs of other forms of social capital.' From a conceptual point of view, this analysis brings out many causal mechanisms (inputs/outputs) that remain somewhat fuzzy because no clear explanation is provided. Put differently, this approach for defining, monitoring and measuring social capital is potentially misleading.

Krishna and Uphoff (1999) suggested another approach to social capital that helps to refine the definition. They dichotomized social capital in two dimensions accounting for structural and cultural (or cognitive) forms of social relationships. Structural social capital is understood as the various social organizations that compose the society, such as families, social networks, associations and so on. Cultural social capital refers to shared norms, values, attitudes and beliefs. 'These two forms of social capital are interactive and mutually reinforcing, but they are distinguishable from one another in the following ways . . . The first form of social capital is external in that it can be observed and can be modified directly, while the second is internal, residing within people's heads, not easily changed' (Krishna and Uphoff, 1999, p. 7). This approach to social capital uses a distinction that can also be applied to institutions, as far as one can account for structural institutions – such as families, associations and so on, up to the state – and cultural (or cognitive) institutions such as norms, values and law. In a synthesis of findings from the SCI, Grootaert and Van Bastelaer (2002) adapted Uphoff's distinction from a micro scale to a macro one. As shown in Figure 21.1, social capital is defined by researchers from the World Bank as a multiform (cultural and structural) and multidimensional (from micro to macro) concept. The SCI gave rise to an inclusive definition of the concept, encompassing heterogeneous views from economics, sociology and political science (Fine, 2001). The concept of social capital deals with different social phenomena – from the creation of social networks to good governance criteria – that would otherwise be regrouped under the general term 'institutions'. In other words, both the catch-all definition of social

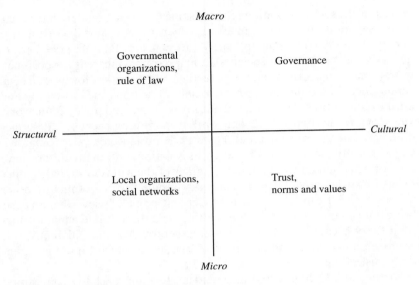

Source: Grootaert and Van Bastelaer (2002).

Figure 21.1   The World Bank conception of social capital

capital and its wide range of effects on economic performance make feasible the substitution of 'social capital' for 'institutions'.

2.   Cause and consequence of the use of 'social capital' as 'institutions'

The use of social capital as a synonym for institutions may result from recent advances in growth theory. A brief overview of these developments will help us to shed light on one of the most plausibles causes of the widespread use of 'social capital' in economics. To begin with, remember that the international debt crisis in the early 1980s saw the neglect of Keynesian and structural approaches for development, and hence the resurgence of neoclassical-based policies. For instance, structural adjustment programmes were set up in developing countries with the aim to reduce government spending through good governance and growth-oriented policies. From a theoretical point of view, the Solow (1956) growth model was found unable to explain long-run growth (see Romer, 1994), so alternative models of 'endogenous growth' (see Aghion and Howitt, 1999) were developed to overcome the limitations of neoclassical growth theory (NCGT). Romer (1994, p. 3) underlined that new growth theory (NGT) '. . . distinguishes itself from neoclassical growth by emphasizing that economic growth is an endogenous outcome of an economic system, not the result of forces that impinge from outside. For this reason, the theoretical work does not invoke exogenous technological change to explain why income per capital has increased by an order of magnitude since the industrial revolution.'

The most striking difference with the Solow model rests in the fact that the NGT model does not imply any conditional convergence (see Islam, 2003) because the rate of return on capital is constant. As a consequence, it was believed that by testing for convergence, one could test for the validity of alternative growth theories. From that perspective, most empirical studies on that topic point to the prevalence of diminishing returns on capital, which means that the convergence hypothesis seems to be true. However, some authors, such as Durlauf and Quah (1999) or Temple (1999), warn us that the NGT model should not therefore be entirely set aside. They assert that convergence is only one of the different growth topics covered by recent research. Advances in growth theory are indeed much larger than the convergence debate. For example, the NGT model helped to achieve a consensus on the idea that the growth process is an endogenous outcome of an economic system. Therefore recent research turned to the identification of the sources of growth, with special attention to the structural components of the economy. More precisely, particular focus was drawn to the role that institutions play as an input for economic growth (World Bank, 2003; see Aron, 2000 for a review of the evidence). Note that this approach to growth became very popular due to the prevalence of the neo-institutionalist thesis in the 1990s (e.g. North, 1990).

It is now taken for granted that institutions play a fundamental role in the growth process. But their place in theoretical models is debatable: some authors think institutions produce externalities (e.g. Hayami and Aoki, 1998), whereas Arrow (1998, p. 45) explicitly asserts that 'institutions are a form of capital'. The World Bank helped to develop the latter idea so that institutions could be seen as another form of capital, namely social capital. This breakthrough in growth analysis is the opportunity for NGT adherents to reopen the convergence debate. The reason is that each additional form of capital is logically associated with a new scale factor that may influence the rate of return of the overall stock of capital. From an empirical point of view, each new form of capital in the endogenous growth model requires the inclusion of new variables in regressions and may therefore change the general conclusion on convergence. To sum up, one can think that the use of social capital as a synonym for institutions is purposefully designed to uphold the endogenous growth model because alternative development models are missing – or undesirable.

Because of the reference to the endogenous growth model, the concept of social capital developed by the World Bank has to be deemed a proper form of capital, and one can no longer be satisfied with a metaphor. My feeling on that point is close to that of Solow (1999, p. 6), who thinks '[social capital] is an attempt to gain conviction from a bad analogy'. The main problem is to justify how different things such as the number of members in an association, mutual trust, good governance, social networks and so on can be added up to form a homogeneous stock of capital. Are these items fungible one with another or can one find a (shadow?) price for each of them? 'Any stock of capital is a cumulation of past flows of invest-ment, with past flows of depreciation netted out. What are those past investments in social capital? How could an accountant measure them and cumulate them in principle?' (Solow, 1999, p. 7). The literature remains quite vague on that fundamental point. The inability to account for social capital as a homogeneous form of capital comes undoubtedly from its width, and the consequence is to disable this concept from being a form of capital.

Moreover, three properties are usually associated with any stock of capital: it is expected to be accumulative, rentable and fungible. The last property seems to be achieved since Coleman's (1988) prior work on edu-cation. The author shows how family care helps children to succeed at school. Social capital is thus fungible in human capital. However, to our knowledge, the literature remains silent on the rates of substitution of social capital into the different forms of capital, especially physical capital. In brief, there is no satisfactory evidence that social capital is fungible into other forms of capital. Let us turn now to the first two properties. Their achievement requires a clear distinction between the causes and the conse-quences of social capital. Yet the definition of social capital developed by the World Bank regroups under the same banner – for example – the con-cepts of 'trust' and 'social networks' without any causal mechanism linking them, whereas it seems possible that social interactions within networks of relatives create mutual trust (Krackhardt, 1992). Are 'trust' and 'social net-works' both social capital? Are 'social networks' a cause of social capital? Is 'trust' a consequence of social capital? Etc. Once again, the conception of social capital appears to be fuzzy according to the definition chosen. Durlauf (2002, p. 460) stressed that '[o]ne important feature of these general definitions . . . is how they mix a number of disparate ideas. One such combination is the mixing of functional and causal conceptions of social capital.' This fuzziness may be tautological (Lin, 2001) in that it just shows how some aspects of the social structure affect some other aspects of the social structure.

From an empirical perspective, most studies on social capital 'typically do not incorporate a separate theory of the determinants of social capital formation, although they do often employ instrumental variables to account for the endogeneity of social capital' (Durlauf, 2002, p. 464). It will thus be very difficult – if not impossible – to explain the mechanism of social capital accumulation (and its depreciation rate) for as long as it is seen as an exogenous factor. In addition, the multidimensional scale of the concept gives rise to some problems of aggregation that may lower the returns on capital. Durlauf and Fafchamps (2003) give two examples. First, when an agent gets job information from his social network, he will be employed much more easily than someone who has no network to provide him with such information. One may conclude that social capital increases the probability of getting a job. However, at an aggregated level, having recourse to social capital produces inequality of opportunities among agents, rather than creating new jobs for everyone. Second, when a rural community develops strong norms of behaviour for the protection of natural resources, the agents that act as free-riders (e.g. by overexploiting the resources) have better welfare than the others. As a consequence, those who invest in social capital do not necessarily benefit from the returns on capital. It is thus possible (without any reference to 'perverse social capital') to show that the concept developed by the World Bank may not be profitable.

As a consequence, social capital as defined by the World Bank can hardly be deemed a form of capital because of the heterogeneous items it encompasses, and because of the lack of capital-like properties. These critiques join together with prior pessimistic views on the effectiveness of social capital (e.g. Portes and Landholt, 1996; Edwards and Foley, 1999; Baron et al., 2000; Durlauf, 2002; Sobel, 2001; Fine, 2001; Durlauf and Fafchamps, 2003; Dolsfma and Dannreuther, 2003). At this stage, we should wonder what to do with the term 'social capital'. Arrow's (1999, p. 4) position indicates a radical way: 'I would urge abandonment of the metaphor of capital and the term "social capital".' On the other hand, some authors support an alternative conception of social capital. For instance, Robison et al. (2002) suggest reducing the width of 'social capital' and purging it of functional considerations. Their point is to refer to the theory of altruism to award social capital (i.e. sympathy) some capital-like properties. Nevertheless, their study deals only with the properties inherent to a form of capital, and gives little attention to the concept of capital itself. Our purpose is to provide an alternative definition of social capital as an asset, that is, as a genuine form of capital.

3. A rights-based definition of social capital
Researchers from the World Bank draw on Putnam's (1993) neoinstitutional approach of social capital to develop an inclusive definition of the concept which leads unfortunately to a dead end. Part of the explanation

for such a failure is due to the expansion of the original meaning of social capital. Initially developed by sociologist Pierre Bourdieu (1979, 1980, 1986), the concept of social capital referred to 'a set of effective or potential resources associated with the possession of a network of more or less institutionalized durable relationships . . .; or, in other words, to the belonging to a group' (Bourdieu, 1980, p. 2). This definition introduces the fundamental idea that social capital is a resource for individual actors in a social environment. As a consequence, the social network is no longer seen as social capital, but rather as the social structure in which some social resources are embedded (Lin, 2001). Bourdieu (1980) points out that social networks are not given, but are the product of investment strategies consciously or unconsciously aimed at establishing or reproducing social relationships that are directly usable in the short or long term. The author also stresses that people transform contingent relationships into durable and useful relationships by means of 'exchange'.

The analysis of gift-giving covers this notion of 'exchange' and helps explain the creation of social capital. While not all gifts are motivated by self-interest (e.g. love and sympathy are alternative motives), creating and maintaining useful social links necessitates recourse to different kinds of gifts (information, time, money, food etc.). As Eijk et al. (2005, p. 7) state: 'gift exchange is a form of instrumental behavior . . ., but can also be an unintentional by-product'. The anthropological literature indicates that a 'gift' from an individual to another member of his network is not necessarily rational, but may follow from a set of normative obligations. According to prior work by Marcel Mauss (1924), individuals within a community are subject to three kinds of obligations: the gift has to be given, accepted and 'repaid'. The last obligation is consistent with the principle of reciprocity, which means that each giver is entitled (through norms, values and informal institutions of the community) to a gift that the given has to make in turn. To sum up this idea: 'one gives because one is constrained to, because the given has a kind of property right over everything the giver owns' (Mauss, 1924, p. 19; my translation).

The notions of rights and obligations are central to understanding the process of creation of social capital. 'If A does something for B and trusts B to reciprocate in the future, this establishes an expectation in A and an obligation on the part of B. This obligation can be conceived as a credit slip held by A for performance by B. If A holds a large number of these credit slips, for a number of persons with whom A has relation, then the analogy to financial capital is direct' (Coleman, 1988, p. 102). In other words, social capital is the set of 'credit slips' an agent has over the members of his own social network. However, this conception of social capital is somewhat static and, as a consequence, only partial. It is widely acknowledged that significant time may pass between the gift and the counter-gift, and so gift exchange is generally unbalanced when viewed at one particular point in time (Eijk et al., 2005). One could thus conclude that the reimbursement of the 'social debt' in the future will destroy the stock of social capital. The result is the same when the gift exchange remains unbalanced because the creditor aimed at maintaining a certain social status *vis-à-vis* the debtor. Social status may therefore be analysed as the effective counterpart of a social debt.

From a dynamic perspective, the stock of social capital does not necessarily diminish after a gift exchange. Gift-giving can be analysed as a social contract between two individuals. Note that such a contract is often enforced by the community through strong norms of reciprocity and sanction (Mauss, 1924) which guarantee the achievement of the 'transaction'. The contract is honoured when A gives something to B, and B reimburses his debt from A. This mutually beneficial social interaction between the two agents sets up a *precedent* which creates mutual trust (Zucker, 1986). This gives them both the right to establish another social contract with a high degree of confidence, as far as they remember the precedent. Agent A is willing to transfer his resources to agent B because A believes in being refunded by B – the debtor. Consequently, both A and B presume to be entitled to the other's resources, so that each of them can use his social relationships to get social support in the event of need.

Put differently, an agent feels he has a right over the resources of any other member of his social network with whom he shares a favourable precedent. This 'right over the resources' can be analysed as an *entitlement* (Bertin and Sirven, 2006), that is, as a legitimate (though non-legal) right. Because this particular right arises when a social transaction (gift-giving) is concluded, that is, when no credit slip is awaited, one may consider it as an '*ex nihilo*' right. Social capital is hence made up of both the 'credit slips' an agent can call in if necessary, and these '*ex nihilo*' rights coming from past successful social interactions. Social capital can thus be defined as the set of rights an agent can exercise over the members of his social network so as to access – partially or entirely – their personal resources. Social capital is a set of socially legitimated entitlements.

From an accountability point of view, the stock of social capital should be recorded on the left side of the balance sheet because it is made up of a set of 'rights over resources', which makes it play the role of an asset. This is a fundamental feature that social capital shares with other items (assets) on the left side of the capital account, especially with physical capital. A rights-based definition of social capital now makes the analogy with other forms of capital undeniable. While physical capital is made up of investments in one thing, and human capital comes from investments in oneself, social capital can be accumulated through investments in others. The main difference is that whereas other forms of capital can be obtained on the market (capital markets for financial capital, goods markets for physical capital, the labour market for human capital), it appears that social capital is only accumulated within the network of an agent's durable relationships.

The stock of social capital first depends on the amount of resources possessed by members of the same social network (Bourdieu, 1986): the richer they are, the more social support they can provide to each other. Second, social capital increases logically with the number of members (Bourdieu, 1980), as well as with the form of the network. This latter idea is brought into play by the structural approach of social capital in sociology (see Lin et al., 2001). It shows how weak ties may provide new information (Granovetter, 1973), whereas strong ties may lead to mutual trust and effective collective actions (Krackhardt, 1992). Third, the accumulation of social capital also derives from the lexicographical position of an individual within his network or community. This means each agent is defined by a set of rights and obligations defined by the norms and values of his social environment (Mahieu, 2001). For example, in most African societies, the youngsters have to take care of the elders. The new generation thus has more obligations than rights, but they will get more rights and fewer obligations as they become older. This situation can be analysed as a social contract described earlier, where the giver is young and the given is older. The stock of social capital of an agent in such a situation depends on his lexicographical position – due to his age. Notice that this last factor introduces the idea of availability of social resources within the network, whereas the first two factors just deal with the volume and the nature of these resources.

The properties of social capital as a rights-based form of capital have not yet been studied. Nevertheless, one can anticipate that such a conception will see social capital as accumulative, rentable and fungible. To sum up my position, gifts (made of time, money, efforts etc.) can be seen as a deliberate sacrifice in the present (i.e. the reduction of an agent's consumption) for future benefit (i.e. a social insurance in the event of need). Gift-giving is hence analysed as a social investment because the agents accumulate rights over the resources of their social network. Social capital is thus fungible in the sense that an agent can transform his rights in different resources owned by other members of his social network. This fungible characteristic makes social capital rentable in a micro perspective in that it allows some people to reach goals that they would not have reached otherwise.

4.   Discussion: which perspective for social capital in economics?

The rights-based definition of social capital is a means of (re)introducing Bourdieu's seminal work on the influence of social networks into the field of economics. Bourdieu (1979) uses social capital together with other different types of capital to analyse the distribution of powers[1] and its consequence among and between different social structures. Nevertheless, the various notions of capital he introduces are obviously metaphorical. Dolfsma (2001, p. 88) acknowledges on the one hand that '[t]he [capital] metaphor can be illuminating, especially when one discusses cultural or social capital in the political arena', but on the other hand, he insists on being cautious and explicit in academic discourse about the use of 'capital'. Taking this into account, the rights-based definition of social capital becomes very useful because it transforms social capital as a metaphor into a genuine form of capital with capital-like properties. Hence the rights-based approach of social capital can be seen as a first step to incorporate the role of social powers in economic analysis. This could lead to new advances in the analysis of non market behavior in economics like migration, discrimination or identity.

From an empirical point of view, a rights-based definition of social capital raises important issues. Indeed, it is difficult, if not impossible, to evaluate the set of rights an individual has over the resources of his social network. However, looking at gift-giving as a fundamental investment in social capital, it is possible to develop a proxy for investment in social capital. In most budget-consumption statistical surveys, households are asked about the gifts and remittances they give to and receive from other households. Paradoxically, such informal social transfers give monetary information on non-monetary behaviour. But they may also introduce a bias in that households having no transfers with others will be assimilated to those whose transfers cannot be accounted for (e.g. time, words etc.). Moreover, this methodology omits the analysis of the form of ties within social networks. To solve this, some specific statistical surveys taking account of these problems have already been done (timetable analysis, closed versus open networks analysis, etc.). Economists will certainly find several ideas to overcome a great many empirical problems in the structural approach of social networks developed in the field of sociology (see Wasserman and Faust, 1994).

From a theoretical point of view, the key question is: which model is appropriate for a rights-based approach of social capital? At first sight, one may think such a definition of social capital helps to rehabilitate the endogenous growth model because social capital can legitimately be considered as a form of capital. This is partially true. The endogenous growth model relies on the aggregation of individual production functions. However, from that perspective, social capital is a 'distributive' asset rather than a 'productive' one. For instance, the mobilization of an agent's social capital helps him to *access* the resources of other people, but does not increase the overall stock of resources available within the society (e.g. Durlauf and Fafchamps, 2003). Basically, the efficiency of social capital resides in that it is an exclusive resource (Bourdieu, 1980). In other words, social capital is effective at an individual level but it may generate inequality instead of efficiency at an aggregate level. The question of a general theory for social capital remains.

One opportunity could be to link the rights-based definition of social capital to the work of the United Nations Development Programme (UNDP) on human rights for development. The theoretical framework of the UNDP approach has mainly been influenced by Amartya Sen's *capability* approach (for a survey see Robeyns, 2005). It thus may be possible to connect a rights-based approach of social capital to Sen's concept of 'social capability', which deals with 'the ability to take part in the life of the community, to participate in social activities, to have a sense of belonging in the larger groups' (Sen, 1997, quoted in Narayan, 1999, p. 4). Such an approach could be facilitated with reference to Sen's (1981) concept of *entitlement* to involve a rights-based definition of social capital (see Bertin and Sirven, 2006). This theoretical field seems to be an interesting perspective from which to analyse how social forces influence – positively or negatively – freedom. In other words, a rights-based definition of social capital may offer a new way to investigate development issues.

Note

1. 'These fundamental social powers are, . . . firstly, *economic* capital [resources], in various kinds; secondly, *cultural* capital [social qualifications and attainment] or better, informational capital, again in various kinds; and thirdly, two forms of capital that are strongly correlated, *social* capital which consists of resources based on connections and group membership, and symbolic capital [prestige], which is the form the different types of capital take once they are perceived and recognized as legitimate' (Bourdieu, 1987, p. 4).

References

Aghion, P. and P. Howitt (1999), *Endogenous Growth Theory*, Cambridge, MA: MIT Press.
Alesina, A., S. Ozler, N. Roubini and P. Swagel (1996), 'Political instability and economic growth', *Journal of Economic Growth*, 1 (2), 189–211.
Almedom, A.M. (2005), 'Social capital and mental health: an interdisciplinary review of the evidence', *Social Science and Medicine*, 61, 943–64.
Aron, J. (2000), 'Growth and institutions: a review of the evidence', *World Bank Research Observer*, 15 (1), 99–135.
Arrow, K.J. (1998), 'The place for institutions in the economy: a theoretical perspective', in Y. Hayami and M. Aoki (eds), *The Institutional Foundations of East Asian Economic Development*, London: Macmillan, pp. 39–47.
Arrow, K.J. (1999), 'Observations on social capital', in P. Dasgupta and I. Serageldin (eds), *Social Capital: A Multifaceted Perspective*, Washington, DC: The World Bank, pp. 3–5.
Baron, S., J. Field and T. Schuller (eds) (2000), *Social Capital: Critical Perspectives*, New York: Oxford University Press.
Becker, G.S. and K.M. Murphy (2000), *Social Economics: Market Behavior in a Social Environment*, Cambridge, MA: Belknap Press.

Berg, R. and J.S. Whitaker (eds) (1986), *Strategies for African Development: A Study for the Committee on African Development*, Berkeley, CA: University of California Press.

Bertin, A. and N. Sirven (2006), 'Social capital and the capability approach: a social economic theory', in B.J. Clary, W. Dolfsma and D.M. Figart (eds), *Ethics and the Market: Insights from Social Economics*, Amsterdam: Routledge, pp. 191–203.

Bourdieu, P. (1979), *La Distinction: Critique Sociale du Jugement*, Paris: Editions de Minuit.

Bourdieu, P. (1980), 'Le capital social', *Actes de la Recherche en Sciences Sociales*, **31**, 2–3.

Bourdieu, P. (1986), 'The forms of capital', in J. Ridchardson (ed.), *Handbook of Theory and Research for the Sociology of Education*, Westport, CT: Greenwood Press.

Bourdieu, P. (1987), 'What makes a social class? On the theoretical and practical existence of groups', *Berkeley Journal of Sociology*, **32**, 1–17.

Coleman, J.S. (1988), 'Social capital in the creation of human capital', *American Journal of Sociology*, **94** (supplement).

Collier, P. (1998), 'Social capital and poverty', Social Capital Initiative, Working Paper No. 4, Washington, DC: The World Bank, mimeo.

Dasgupta, P. and I. Serageldin (eds) (1999), *Social Capital: A Multifaceted Perspective*, Washington, DC: The World Bank.

Dolfsma, W. (2001), 'Metaphors of knowledge in economics', *Review of Social Economy*, **59** (1), 71–91.

Dolfsma, W. and C. Dannreuther (2003), 'Subject and boundaries: contesting social capital-based policies', *Journal of Economic Issues*, **37** (2), 405–13.

Durlauf, S. (2002), 'On the empirics of social capital', *Economic Journal*, **112**, 459–79.

Durlauf, S. and M. Fafchamps (2003), 'Empirical studies of social capital: a critical survey', mimeo.

Durlauf, S.N. and D.T. Quah (1999), 'The new empirics of economic growth', in J. Taylor and M. Woodford (eds), *Handbook of Macroeconomics*, Volume 1A, Amsterdam/New York/Oxford: Elsevier Science/North-Holland, pp. 235–308.

Easterly, W. and R. Levine (1997), 'Africa's growth tragedy: policies and ethnic divisions', *Quarterly Journal of Economics*, **112** (4), 1203–50.

Edwards, B. and M.W. Foley (1999), 'Is it time to disinvest in social capital?', *Journal of Public Policy*, **19**, 141–73.

Eijk, R. van der, W. Dolfsma and A. Jolink (2005), 'No black box and no black hole: from social capital to gift exchange', ERIM Report Series in Management, Amsterdam: Erasmus University, mimeo.

Fafchamps, M. and S. Lund (2003), 'Risk-sharing networks in rural Philippines', *Journal of Development Economics*, **71**, 261–87.

Fine, B. (2001), *Social Capital versus Social Theory*, New York: Routledge.

Fine, B. and F. Green (2000), 'Economic, social capital, and the colonization of the social sciences', in S. Baron, J. Field and T. Schuller (eds), *Social Capital: Critical Perspectives*, New York: Oxford University Press, pp. 78–93.

Fukuyama, F. (1995), *Trust: The Social Virtues and the Creation of Prosperity*, New York: Free Press.

Glaeser, E.L., D. Laibson and B. Sacerdote (2000), 'The economic approach to social capital', *The Economic Journal*, **112**, 437–58.

Granato, J., R. Ingelhart and D. Leblang (1996), 'The effect of cultural values on economic development: theory, hypotheses, and some empirical tests', *American Journal of Political Science*, **40**, 607–31.

Granovetter, M. (1973), 'The strength of weak ties', *American Journal of Sociology*, **78** (6), 1360–80.

Granovetter, M. (1985), 'Economic action and social structure: the problem of embeddedness', *American Journal of Sociology*, **91** (3), 481–510.

Grootaert, C. (1997), 'Social capital: the missing link?', Social Capital Initiative, Working Paper No. 3, Washington, DC: The World Bank, mimeo.

Grootaert, C. and T. Van Bastelaer (2002), *The Role of Social Capital in Development*, Cambridge: Cambridge University Press.

Hayami, Y. and M. Aoki (eds) (1998), *The Institutional Foundations of East Asian Economic Development*, London: Macmillan.

Hawe, P. and A. Shiell (2000), 'Social capital and health promotion: a review', *Social Science and Medicine*, **51**, 871–85.

Helliwell, J. and R.D. Putnam (1995), 'Economic growth and social capital in Italy', *Eastern Economic Journal*, **21**, 295–307.

Isham, J., T. Kelly and S. Ramaswamy (eds) (2002), *Social Capital and Economic Development*, Cheltenham, UK and Northampton, MA, USA: Edward Elgar.

Islam, N. (2003), 'What have we learnt from the convergence debate?', *Journal of Economic Survey*, **17** (3), 309–62.

Knack, S. (1999), 'Social capital, growth and poverty: a survey of cross-country evidence', Social Capital Initiative, Working Paper No. 7, Washington, DC: The World Bank, mimeo.

Knack, S. and P. Keefer (1995), 'Institutions and economic performance: cross-country test using alternative institutional measures', *Economics and Politics*, **7**, 207–27.

Knack, S. and P. Keefer (1997), 'Does social capital have an economic payoff? A cross-country investigation', *Quarterly Journal of Economics*, **112** (4), 1251–88.

Kormendi, R. and P. Meguire (1985), 'Macroeconomic determinants of growth', *Journal of Monetary Economics*, **16** (2), 141–63.

Krackhardt, D. (1992), 'The strength of strong ties: the importance of philos in organizations', in N. Nohria and R.G. Eccles (eds), *Networks and Organizations: Structure, Form, and Action*, Boston, MA: Harvard Business School Press, pp. 216–39.

Krishna, A. and N. Uphoff (1999), 'Mapping and measuring social capital: a conceptual and empirical study of collective action for conserving and developing watersheds in Rajasthan, India', Social Capital Initiative, Working Paper No. 13, Washington, DC: The World Bank.

LaPorta, R., F. Lopez-de-Salinez, A. Shleifer and R.W. Vishny (1997), 'Trust in large organizations', *American Economic Review: Papers and Proceedings*, **87**, 333–8.

Lin, N. (2001), 'Building a network theory of social capital', in N. Lin, K. Cook and R.S. Burt (eds), *Social Capital: Theory and Research*, New York: De Gruyter, pp. 3–30.

Lin, N., K. Cook and R.S. Burt (eds) (2001), *Social Capital: Theory and Research*, New York: De Gruyter.

Mahieu, F.-R. (2001), *Éthique Économique: Fondements Anthropologiques*, Paris: L'Harmattan.

Mauro, P. (1995), 'Corruption and growth', *Quarterly Journal of Economics*, **110**, 681–712.

Mauss, M. (1924), 'Essai sur le don: forme et raison de l'échange dans les sociétés primitives', *L'année sociologique*, seconde série, 1923–1924, tome 1.

Narayan, D. (1999), 'Bonds and bridges: social capital and poverty', Washington, DC: The World Bank, Research Paper.

North, D.C. (1990), *Institutions, Institutional Change, and Economic Performance*, Cambridge, MA: Cambridge University Press.

Olson, M. (1971), *The Logic of Collective Action*, Cambridge, MA: Harvard University Press.

Ostrom, E. (1990), *Governing the Commons: The Evolution of Institutions for Collective Action*, New York: Cambridge University Press

Pantoja, E. (1999), 'Exploring the concept of social capital and its relevance for community-based development', Social Capital Initiative, Working Paper No.18, Washington, DC: The World Bank, mimeo.

Portes, A. and P. Landholt (1996), 'The downside of social capital', *The American Prospect*, **26** (May–June), 18–21.

Pretty, J. and H. Ward (2001), 'Social capital and the environment', *World Development*, **29** (2), 209–27.

Putnam, R.D. (1993), *Making Democracy Work*, Princeton, NJ: Princeton University Press.

Putnam, R.D. (1995), 'Bowling alone: America's declining social capital', *Journal of Democracy*, **6**, 65–87.

Robeyns, I. (2005), 'The capability approach: a theoretical survey', *Journal of Human Development*, **6** (1), 93–114.

Robison, L.J., A.A. Schmid and M.E. Siles (2002), 'Is social capital really capital?', *Review of Social Economy*, **60** (1), 1–21.

Romer, P.M. (1994), 'The origins of endogenous growth', *Journal of Economic Perspectives*, **8** (1), 3–22.

Rubio, M. (1997), 'Perverse social capital: some evidence from Colombia', *Journal of Economic Issues*, **31** (3), 805–16.

Sen, A.K. (1981), *Poverty and Famines: An Essay on Entitlement and Deprivation*, Oxford: Clarendon Press.

Sobel, J. (2001), 'Can we trust social capital?', *Journal of Economic Literature*, **40**, 139–54.

Solow, R.M. (1956), 'A contribution to the theory of economic growth', *Quarterly Journal of Economics*, **70**, 65–94.

Solow, R.M (1999), 'Notes on social capital and economic performance', in P. Dasgupta and I. Serageldin (eds), *Social Capital: A Multifaceted Perspective*, Washington, DC: The World Bank, pp. 6–10.

Temple, J. (1999), 'The new growth evidence', *Journal of Economic Literature*, **37** (1), 112–56.

Wasserman, S. and K. Faust (1994), *Social Network Analysis: Methods and Applications*, Cambridge: Cambridge University Press.

World Bank (2003), *World Development Report: Sustainable Development in a Dynamic World*, Washington, DC: The World Bank.

Zack, P. and S. Knack (2001), 'Trust and growth', *Economic Journal*, **111** (1), 295–321.

Zucker, L.G. (1986), 'Production of trust: institutional sources of economic structure, 1840–1920', *Research in Organizational Behavior*, **8**, 53–111.

22 Social networks: structure and content
Wilfred Dolfsma and Rick Aalbers

1. Introduction

Prominent economic sociologist Richard Swedberg (2005) has argued that social networks and the theory that has emerged from their study form the cutting edge of economic sociology. They also offer a promising avenue for future, interdisciplinary research. In addition to this, social networks are implicated in the full range of activities related to economic growth, from technological innovation to investment in physical, human and social capital, and to trade.

The term 'network' is, however, used in a number of different ways. Some use it metaphorically, indicating that a number of actors have some kind of relations giving rise to some kind of effect. Actor–network theory can be seen in this way. While this line of research has led to important insights, for instance in the development of technological knowledge (Latour, 1987), the workings of the network itself are taken into consideration only haphazardly. Some have used the term 'network' to point to structures that are in between market and hierarchy, hybrid forms not easily conceptualized by existing organizational theory or by mainstream economics (Powell, 1990; Ouchi, 1980). Still others have used characteristics of networks studied to include these in analyses and accounts that do not place the study of networks at the center of their attention. Finally, there is an increasing number of scholars, stretching across the disciplinary fields of sociology, psychology, management, mathematics and even economics, that devote their attention primarily to the networks themselves, their workings and their nature. These scholars are loosely networked in their own 'network'; they have conferences and journals.[1] We shall be discussing primarily the latter two approaches.

It is important to realize that when discussing social networks, persons or other entities active in a network can simultaneously be nested in other non-related networks. This point of view is referred to as Granovetter's (1985, 1992) concept of social embeddedness. ' "Embeddedness" is a multidimensional construct relating generally to the importance of social networks for action. Embeddedness indicates that actors who are integrated in dense clusters or multiplex relations of social networks face different sets of resources and constraints than those who are not embedded in such networks' (Moody and White, 2003, p. 105). Thornton and Flynn (2003) provide an overview of the embeddedness of relational networks (social networks). In line with Granovetter (1985), their notion of embeddedness rests in social structure as well as culture (Thornton, 2001) within and between hierarchies (Dacin et al., 1999; Burt, 2000). In the latter case embeddedness refers to the matrix structures, strategic alliances and transnational hierarchies in which actors operate. It is this entanglement of social networks with traditional economic concepts such as organization structures and transnational hierarchies that makes social network analysis (SNA) interesting from a social economic point of view.

2. Social networks

Social networks have been found by scholars in the social sciences to play a role in a number of different contexts and for a number of different reasons. Innovation patterns within and between firms (alliances) depend on the way in which networks are shaped. Entrepreneurs who are properly networked are more likely to succeed. Venture capitalists rely heavily on their networks when making investment decisions. Even in quite mature markets, where changes are rare and incremental, and so actors are well aware of their circumstances, one's network of contacts determines how successful one will be. If one has friends in one's network of friends who are obese, one is more likely to be obese too. This focus extends not just to studies in the social sciences (plural) but in the natural sciences as well (Strogatz, 2001), and so one can understand why the study of social networks has grown tremendously since the early 1970s.

The main benefits of social networks are derived from its capacity to generate, disperse, screen and enhance information (Campbell et al., 1986; Coleman, 1990; Granovetter, 1973). Burt elaborates on this benefit by stating that a network provides an actor with access to valuable information well beyond what the actor could process on its own (Burt, 1997). The network surrounding an actor essentially acts as additional processing capacity (Kijkuit and van den Ende, 2007). But with information technology increasingly catering for information gathering, it is especially the screening and enhancement of information that is the added value of today's social networks (ibid.).

One reason for the growth of this literature is, of course, the instantaneous appeal of social network analysis (SNA). The kind of visualization SNA allows for helps win converts. Figure 22.1, for instance, presents a characteristic pattern of knowledge transfer within a high-tech firm between people at the nodes, working in divisions (the circles). SNA, however, also allows for very sophisticated analyses, statistically and mathematically. Another reason for the growth of SNA in academia is that one need not think of people connected in a network. Instead of thinking of

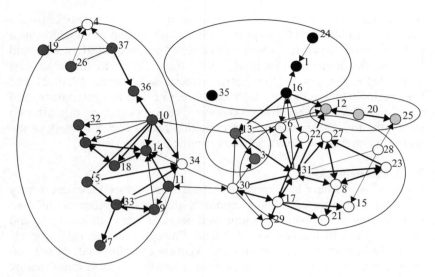

Source: Aalbers et al. (2006).

Figure 22.1   Innovation network at a high-tech firm (Siemens Netherlands)

people as the nodes in a network, one may think of firms and other organizations, groups, computers, scholarly journals, patents, industries, geographic regions and even nation-states (Thornton and Flynn, 2003). This brings together people with a diverse set of interests who share a single methodology. Rather than talking in terms of social networks existing 'out there', one may have to think of social networks as conceived by the scholar. In addition to the knowledge transfer or innovation network presented in Figure 22.1, for this same firm one could try to find the 'smokers' network' of people who stand outside smoking cigarettes together, the 'high-speed-train network' of people who are brought together to further campaign for local needs and sell a high-speed-train connection between Amsterdam and Paris, or a 'day-care-center network' of people who meet each other on early mornings and late afternoons where their children stay, possibly exchanging information. Social networks are, thus, not informal *per se*, and need to be brought out carefully by the scholar using the proper means. Some of this is discussed below.

A network can be defined as a set of entities (nodes) that interact in a specific way. Interactions have a specific structure that can be discerned and analyzed. If the nodes are in fact social entities, such as human beings or firms, one talks about social networks. In the economics literature different definitions of (interorganizational) networks exist as authors have studied different phenomena at different aggregation levels. Economic sociologists Podolny and Page (1998, p. 3) have defined relational networks at the organizational level as any collection of actors ($n \geq 2$) that pursues repeated enduring exchange relations with any other and, at the same time, lacks a legitimate organizational authority to arbitrate and resolve disputes that may arise during exchange. When elaborating on networks it is therefore important to realize that multiple levels of analysis can be chosen.

3. Networks and their building blocks: elements in SNA

To investigate networks in more detail a number of building blocks are commonly used to analyze the network structure. *Ties* indicate that during the time period defined, *nodes* one wants to study have interacted. These nodes, and the relations (ties) between them, form the key building blocks of a network and are usually taken to be the individual actors within the networks, and ties are the relationships between the actors.

The more nodes interact in a network, the larger the *network size*. If one thinks of nodes as individuals, one may consider a network in which a person operates as a resource on which to draw. Within a network the intensity of interaction between the different nodes may vary. In case of close interaction between two nodes one speaks of strong ties; whereas *ad hoc* interaction is referred to as a weak tie. The measurement of tie strength varies depending of the kind of network under investigation and the choice of the scholar studying the network. A frequently used measure is the frequency of interaction.

Granovetter (1973) has argued that a large network of ties, which are thus necessarily 'weak', is beneficial in terms of dispersing and obtaining new information, and in terms of mobilizing others in the network. In his examples, such a network where the number of ties is large but *tie strength* is weak will help a neighborhood stave off unwanted reconstruction by mobilizing enough others who can make a difference in their support. Such a network will also allow an individual to more easily 'get a job' (Granovetter, 1995). Granovetter thus famously stresses the importance of weak ties: 'The importance of weak ties is asserted to be that they are disproportionately likely to be bridges as compared to strong ties, which should be underrepresented in that role. This does not preclude the possibility that most weak ties have no such function' (Granovetter, 1982, p. 130).

Related to Granovetter's frequently referred to 'strength of weak ties' argument is the position developed by Ronald Burt. He has looked at the role of people who connect two or more otherwise unconnected networks (Burt, 1992). Such 'structural holes', as he calls them, will be able to exert control over the information flow between these networks in each of which knowledge may be available that is relevant for the other. Burt (2004) has shown, too, that people thus placed will also be in a better position to develop new ideas themselves. This linking-pin principle is referred to as brokerage in the SNA literature. The benefit of approaching knowledge transfer from a brokerage point of view is that brokerage includes information regarding the direct interaction with other persons, but contrary to centrality, which is discussed below, takes group membership into account (Granovetter, 1973; Nonaka and Teece, 2001; Schulz, 2003).

Regarding the different ways in which an individual can broker between any two other individuals in a network (Gould and Fernandez 1989; see Figure 22.2 and Table 22.1), a structural hole may be more or less involved in either of the two networks she connects. The connection of type 1, the coordinator, seems to be excluded, however. To some degree this weak ties argument of people being able purposefully to mobilize the network they have for a particular purpose depends on the extent to which they are able to fathom it: can they look beyond the connections that they themselves have to more indirect connections that may be mobilized? What *network horizon* do people have?

Too often an argument drawing on social network conceptions suggests that weak ties are favorable in all possible circumstances. For some purposes, however, weak ties with others one does not regularly entertain will

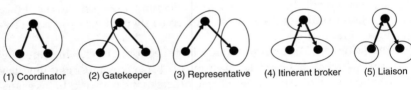

(1) Coordinator   (2) Gatekeeper   (3) Representative   (4) Itinerant broker   (5) Liaison

Source: Gould and Fernandez (1989).

Figure 22.2   *Five possible network roles*

Table 22.1   *Brokerage roles and group membership*

	Sender	Broker	Recipient
Coordinator	A	A	A
Gatekeeper	A	B	B
Representative	A	A	B
Consultant/itinerant broker	A	B	A
Liaison	A	B	C

Note: A, B, C denote different groups/affiliations/divisions.

not do. Hansen (1999), for instance, has shown that when 'complex' knowledge is to be transferred within a firm one needs strong ties. Strength of ties tends to be defined in terms of frequency of interaction. Other definitions of tie strength may be used as well. What is important, however, is that when a tie is strong, the people thus related will know each other better. There is likely to be more trust too, necessary for exchanging tacit knowledge or knowledge that could make either of the parties involved vulnerable (Bouty, 2000). In any case, it will be more likely that what the other communicates is understood. This argument is in line with that of Coleman (1988), who argues that there should be redundancy in a network for it to work properly.

A network that is fully connected is one where all nodes are tied to other nodes: *network density* is maximal here. Few networks are like this, however, if only because redundancy is costly.

Looking at the low-redundancy network (Figure 22.3a), it soon becomes clear that the position of person A will be most influential when exchanging information, because A has the opportunity to draw from alternative channels when the requested or sought-after information is not provided by one of the other persons in the network. In the case that B decides not to provide A with information, A can easily turn to C or D as an alternative. B does not have that option. In the high-redundancy network (Figure 22.3b), the contrary is the case: each person has access to the same

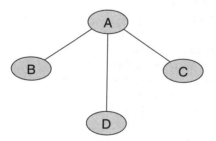

Figure 22.3a   Low-redundancy network

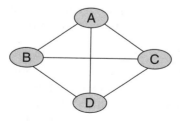

Figure 22.3b   High-redundancy network

information sources, requiring the maintenance of a significantly higher number of ties in the case of a larger network.

Parts within a network may interact more closely than other parts: *clustering* may be seen. In economic geography this phenomenon is much studied: what are the effects of clustering firms that interact regionally? One effect is that they may be more likely to be successful, for instance in terms of innovativeness (Giuliani and Bell, 2005). Silicon Valley is an example of this (Saxenian, 1994), one that many other regions and countries would like to emulate. In the entrepreneurship literature it is argued that the spatial location in a network affects an individual's and an organization's chances for discovering and exploiting entrepreneurial opportunities (Thornton and Flynn, 2003; Burt, 1992; Warren, 1967). To understand more fully what the structure of a social network means, several ideas have been developed in addition to that of tie strength. SNA allows one, for instance, to be clearer on what the Matthew effect actually might mean. 'For unto every one that hath shall be given, and he shall have abundance: but from him that hath not shall be taken away even that which he hath' (the Holy Bible, Matthew 25: 29). Sociologist Robert Merton (1968) has found that eminent scientists will often get more credit (citations, co-authorships, invitations) than a comparatively unknown researcher, even if their work is similar. Eminence may thus be measured in terms of how central a node is. As one of the most important measures in SNA research, centrality gives an indication of the influence of an individual within a network with regard to all other individuals within that network (Brass and Burckhardt, 1992). Centrality provides an evaluation of the locations of individuals within the network in terms of how close they are to the 'centre' of the action in a network. Centrality is, however, a notion that has several interpretations, leading to different conclusions as to which node is central in a network (cf. Freeman, 1978/9). Centrality can be analyzed in terms of

1.   degree: number of incoming and/or outgoing ties from a node;
2.   closeness: the 'distance' of a node from all other nodes in a network;
3.   betweenness: the extent to which agent is positioned on the shortest path between any other pair of agents in the network; and
4.   centrality in terms of the projection on the first eigenvector of the matrix.

Looking at Figure 22.3c, one can see how, according to degree centrality, all but node A and node G are equally central. Node D, however, is most central when measured in terms of betweenness centrality. Betweenness centrality is likely to be the best measure of centrality if control over the interaction processes (information exchange) is important. Needless to say,

Figure 22.3c   Network with seven nodes and six ties

some of these measures are sensitive to network size and cannot simply be compared between networks.

Regardless of which measure is chosen, centrality helps to identify persons (or any other entity, for that matter) with a high profile within the network they operate in. Highly central persons are highly involved in transferring information and are therefore highly aware of what is going on within the organization. Centrality is therefore an indication of the degree to which individuals have access to resources such as knowledge (Hoang and Antoncic, 2003). Centrality is therefore a useful approach in studying the diffusion of innovation within a company (Ibarra and Andrews, 1993).

Instead of lines between nodes, one may have arrows, thus distinguishing between incoming and outgoing connections. There need not be *reciprocity* between nodes, as some may receive more than they give. Figure 22.4 shows the citations that the *Journal of Evolutionary Economics* receives from other journals listed in Thomson's (Social) Science Citation Index. A similar picture can be drawn for citations from articles published in this journal to other journals. Comparing such figures may give rise to certain observations. In this particular case, this journal imports from hardcore game theory journals but does not export to them.

One can compare and analyze the development of networks through time, compare local clusters within a network with others, or compare different networks as a whole. Some have 'translated' competing theories in the social sciences as network structures that would be conducive to some purpose, subsequently testing which theory or combination of theories explains a phenomenon (Contractor et al., 2006). Based on graph theory, a field within mathematics, one can also simulate what will happen if a particular node from a network were to disappear. Such exercises are interesting scientifically, but pragmatically as well. Just consider what will happen to the firm if person 30 disappears from the network is represented in Figure 22.1.

4.   Grapevine or formal network: Siemens Netherlands

Very often networks of individuals are equated with informal relations between them. Indeed, focusing now on relations between individuals within a specific organization, it is claimed that informal ties between friends are most helpful, following Granovetter's (1973) argument (Freeman, 1991; Hansen, 1999; Powell et al., 1996). Nevertheless, informal networks of friends do not need to exist *per se*, and often emerge when formal governance structures for a particular task are lacking or are

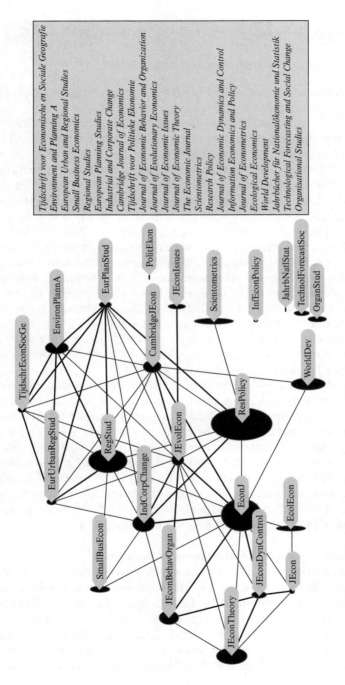

Tijdschrift voor Economische en Sociale Geografie
Environment and Planning A
European Urban and Regional Studies
Small Business Economics
Regional Studies
European Planning Studies
Industrial and Corporate Change
Cambridge Journal of Economics
Tijdschrift voor Politieke Ekonomie
Journal of Economic Behavior and Organization
Journal of Evolutionary Economics
Journal of Economic Issues
Journal of Economic Theory
The Economic Journal
Scientometrics
Research Policy
Journal of Economic Dynamics and Control
Information Economics and Policy
Journal of Econometrics
Ecological Economics
World Development
Jahrbücher für Nationalökonomie und Statistik
Technological Forecasting and Social Change
Organisational Studies

Source: Leydesdorff and Dolfsma (2007).

Figure 22.4   Citations to the Journal of Evolutionary Economics (JEvolEcon)

398

inadequate. Still, a formal (workflow) network will exist in an organization in addition to an informal (communication) network (Madhaven and Grover, 1998).

The formal network is the pattern of formal relations within an organization (cf. Simon, 1976). This communication network is used to exchange information, documents, schedules and other resources to get the job done. It is based on communication patterns derived from formal procedures and company manuals, and is reflected to some extent in the organization chart. People in formal structures may be held to account in a better way than in informal structures, actions and decisions are more likely to be recorded, and decisions to commit resources tend to have to be made here. The informal network, also called the 'grapevine', is the communication network that is used to discuss what is going on within the organization and who is doing what next in the formal circuit. Social relations here are based largely on friendship. Benefits of the informal network arise from its flexibility, both in using the network and in allowing it to be changed by the individuals themselves. The formal and the informal networks may be correlated, of course, in the sense that in part the same people are involved in each. Still, people relate differently with each other if they interact in contexts that they perceive as different. The informal network can supplement the formal network such that information flows between units that are not formally connected with each other. Informal relations may also undermine formal ones. When altering the formal structure of an organization it can be useful to draw on existing relations from the informal network.

Networks at Siemens

Siemens Netherlands offers an interesting example to illustrate the value of SNA, in this case to understand innovation processes (Aalbers et al., 2006). Siemens AG, a world leader in electrical engineering and electronics employing 417 000 employees in over 190 countries, is the world's largest and Europe's strongest conglomerate, according to the business press. Each of its business units (BU) makes its own decisions; BUs thus report both to the CEO in each daughter company and to the head of the BU at headquarters. At the same time, cooperation between BU units is critical for Siemens to develop and ship new products and services its customers need. Internal borders between divisions must be bridged so that knowledge can be combined and innovation will occur at Siemens.

It may, for instance, be asked whether the innovation network in which knowledge is transferred between individuals (Figure 22.1) can be accounted for by either the formal structures that exist within this company or by the informal relationships that people entertain. Network figures similar to that of Figure 22.1 represent the formal and the informal networks. Visualization shows how some divisions that have a clear possibility of contributing to Siemens Netherlands as a whole were in fact quite isolated. In line with Homans's (1951) argument, divisional membership is an important reason for employees to interact. Although not totally unexpected, this observation still came as something of a shock as people central in a network or people constituting a structural hole need not be highly ranked. What is more, key individuals left after this picture was drawn.

Skipping immediately to the conclusions, some obvious and some less obvious findings emerge. What seems obvious, but what had not been noted before, is that both the formal and the informal network contribute to knowledge transfer. What is less obvious, but a consolation for managers, is that the formal network contributes more to knowledge transfer than the informal one. Indeed, hardly any relation that is informal-only existed in this setting. Either formal relations breed trust and a kind of friendship or personal understanding, or informal relations are formalized by the people involved. Homans (1951) of course has emphasized the former. What is more, given that allegiance can be expected to play a bigger role in informal settings as it cannot be ordained, it is surprising to see that taking a central position in the formal network is more important for knowledge transfer than taking a central position in the informal network.

BOX 22.1   SOME CONSIDERATIONS OF METHOD

Information gathering for SNA is both easy and problematic (Marsden, 1990; Wasserman and Faust, 1984). It is easy as only a very few questions need to be asked. To ensure comparability with other studies, it is essential that the question respondents answer so that their network can be determined – the 'name generator' – is the same. As potentially $n-1$ data points go missing when a single individual does not respond, it is both essential to obtain a high response rate and be clear about one's target population. Obtaining a response rate close to 100 percent is more important than having a large population. If one starts with a clear view of the population one wants to target, a socio-centric approach to SNA can be used (Marsden, 2002). If, however, from the start the boundaries of a population are unclear, one has no other option but to use the egocentric approach. In the latter case, one starts gathering information by approaching an individual or some egos, and works one's way outward. This approach is often referred to as snowball sampling (Wasserman and Faust, 1984). It is important to use key informers to make sure that loosely connected clusters of nodes that do fit a definition of the population one holds are not left out.

Having collected such data, one can use freely available software programs such as Pajek (De Nooy et al., 2005) or UCINET (Borgatti et al., 2002) to prepare figures and do statistical analyses. In doing so, many of the prior discussed concepts such as centrality, reciprocity and density can be taken as a point of departure to increase one's understanding of a particular interaction pattern in a network.

A trend that is currently taking hold is the analysis of networks through time. It becomes possible to investigate the effect of policies, advisory or other external disruptions on a network and its performance. This can be beneficial for organizations aiming to improve their innovative capacity, but also to measure the effectiveness of logistical or financial transaction networks and their possible bottlenecks, or, for example entrepreneurial economical cluster analysis on a meso level.

5. The 'action problem' and gifts

With these latter observations, it becomes clear that what SNA does not primarily do is look at the contents of the relations it studies. SNA takes a structuralist view of social reality. How relations start, when they may discontinue, and how their nature may change is left underexplored. But an analysis of the structural component of relations, certainly over time, does allow one to achieve some understanding of their contents. Also, however, even when looking at an informal network it cannot be assumed that the individuals involved will trust one another. Agency plays no role in SNA. The reasons for people's behavior are sometimes explicitly not addressed (Hansen, 1999). To put it differently, SNA has an 'action problem' (Obstfeld, 2005). As such, the dynamics of a group of individuals may be difficult to grasp.

One may propose to combine SNA with additional insights from other areas of the social sciences. A prime candidate is the notion of gift exchange, as it is, according to Boulding (1981), the more general type of exchange as compared to market exchange (Van der Eijk et al., 2006). Exchanging gifts is, as Mauss (1954) has made abundantly clear, a highly ritualized and contextualized obligation no person in a community can escape from. As part of a community, anybody is obliged to (1) give (2) receive and (3) reciprocate (Mauss, 1954; cf. Dore, 1983; Gouldner, 1960; Malinowski, 1996; Sahlins, 1972; Van der Eijk et al., 2006). The closer people are, the more

customized gifts may be, as one understands better what the other's preferences, inclinations and ambitions are. A gift is then intimately related to the
person of the giver, and her view of the recipient. Rejecting a gift thus means
rejecting the giver. Not returning a gift, or not being able to return a gift,
means that the recipient remains indebted and thus possibly subordinated to
the giver. A mixture of motives may be involved in gift exchange, including
altruism, self-interest and power-seeking. It is important that the perceived
value of a gift is not mentioned, even when the parties involved know what it
is (Bourdieu, 1993). When in gift exchange equilibrium in valuation is
reached, it actually turns into a market exchange and the relation stops
(Schwartz, 1996). Relations can thus go sour and discontinue. Start of relations can also be understood in terms of gift exchange. Getting parties one
wants to relate with to be positioned in circumstances such that they will
accept a gift will start a relation. This has been documented in relation to
venture capitalists in Silicon Valley, for instance (Ferrary, 2003). Even though
a venture capitalist may be able to undertake a lucrative deal himself, bringing in others from an established core group of venture capitalists makes sure
that in future deals the initial giver will also be involved. Similar procedures
are also at work in spheres that are less complex and changing (Darr, 2003).

The theory of gift exchange, originating from anthropology, thus offers
suggestions for a better understanding of how and under what circumstances relations start and stop, and thus also of how relations function. It
therefore offers a possible answer to the 'action problem' SNA faces given
its emphasis on structure at the expense of agency. Additionally, the
concept of trust can be one of the elements to explain the positioning of
individuals within a network and the rationale for their dynamics over time.
Obviously this requires a sufficient degree of knowledge concerning the
individuals' motivations, social standing and social capabilities. These
topics are as yet underexplored in SNA. This area for future exploration
is, however, bound to meet conceptual and methodological difficulties.
Conceptually, satisfactorily dealing with the structure–agency *problema-
tique* has always riddled the social sciences. Methodologically, matching
information one has about the nature of the relations with the form of the
structure may be troublesome, especially as inevitably the element of time
is involved in the highly contextualized exchange of gifts.

6. Conclusion
As the realization dawns that action and people are socially embedded and
meaningful, the question arises how to understand such embeddedness.
The notion of embeddedness has drawn a great deal of attention since it
was suggested (Granovetter, 1985), and has also been criticized for its
metaphorical nature. Rather than suggest replacing it (Krippner et al.,

2004), we believe that SNA offers a way of understanding how individuals are related socially with others. Some even suggest studying markets as networks to gain a better understanding of their workings (White, 2002). Specifically the notion of graphically representing one's interaction network and the possibility of statistically exploring the different interaction patterns of the individuals involved is helpful. Certainly if a fruitful combination of the analysis of the structures of networks, the contents of the relations and the meanings that relations have for the people involved can be found and developed, SNA will be a way forward for understanding embeddedness from a structural perspective and for understanding who trusts whom. As such, a 'thick description' may emerge, along the lines Clifford Geertz (1973) suggests, of social interaction.

Note

1. For instance, the International Network of Social Network Analysis; the Sunbelt conference; *Social Networks – An International Journal of Structural Analysis*, respectively.

References

Aalbers, R., O. Koppius and W. Dolfsma (2006), *On and Off the Beaten Path: Transferring Knowledge through Formal and Informal Networks*, Lund University: CIRCLE Working Papers 2006/8.

Borgatti, S., M.G. Everett and L.C. Freeman (2002), *Ucinet 6 for Windows*, Harvard: Analytic Technologies.

Boulding, K.E. (1981), *A Preface to Grant's Economics: The Economics of Love and Fear*, New York: Praeger.

Bourdieu, P. (1993), 'The production of belief: contribution to an economy of symbolic goods', in P. Bourdieu, *The Field of Cultural Production*, Cambridge: Polity Press, pp. 74–111.

Bouty, I. (2000), 'Interpersonal and interaction influences on informal resource exchanges between R&D researchers across organizational boundaries', *Academy of Management Journal*, **43** (1), 50–65.

Brass, D.J. and M.E. Burkhardt (1992), 'Centrality and power in organizations', in N. Nohria and R.G. Eccles (eds), *Network and Organizations: Structure, Form and Action*, Boston, MA: Harvard Business School Press, pp. 191–215.

Burt, R.S. (1992), '*Structural Holes': The Social Structure of Competition*, Cambridge, MA: Harvard University Press.

Burt, R.S. (1997), 'The contingent value of social capital', *Administrative Science Quarterly*, **42**, June, 339–65.

Burt, R.S. (2000), 'The network structure of social capital', in R.I. Sutton and B.M. Staw (eds), *Research in Organizational Behavior*, Vol. 22, Greenwich, CT: JAI Press, pp. 345–423.

Burt, R.S. (2004), 'Structural holes and good ideas', *American Journal of Sociology*, **110** (2), 349–99.

Campbell, K.E., P.V. Marsden and J.S. Hurlbert (1986), 'Social resources and socioeconomic status', *Social Networks*, **8**, 97–117.

Coleman, J.S. (1988), 'Social capital in the creation of human capital', *American Journal of Sociology*, **94**, supplement, 95–120.

Coleman, J.S. (1990), *Foundations of Social Theory*, Cambridge, MA and London: Belknap Press of Harvard University Press.

Contractor, N., S. Wasserman and K. Faust (2006), 'Testing multi-theoretical multilevel hypotheses about organizational networks: an analytic framework and empirical example', *Academy of Management Review*, **31** (6), 681–703.

Dacin, M.T., M.J. Ventresca and B.D. Beal (1999), 'The embeddedness of organizations: dialogue and directions', *Journal of Management*, **25** (3), 317–56.

Darr, A. (2003), 'Gifting practices and inter-organizational relations: constructing obligations networks in the electronics sector', *Sociological Forum*, **18** (1), 31–51.

Dore, R. (1983), 'Goodwill and the spirit of market capitalism', *British Journal of Sociology*, **34** (4), 459–82.

Ferrary, M. (2003), 'The gift exchange in the social networks of Silicon Valley', *California Management Review*, **45** (4), 120–38.

Freeman, L.C. (1978/9), 'Centrality in social networks: conceptual clarification', *Social Networks*, **1** (3), 215–39.

Freeman, C. (1991), 'Networks of innovators: a synthesis of research issues', *Research Policy*, **20**, 499–514.

Geertz, C. (1973), *The Interpretation of Cultures*, New York: Basic Books.

Giuliani, E. and M. Bell (2005), 'The micro-determinants of meso-level learning and innovation: evidence from a Chilean wine cluster', *Research Policy*, **34** (1), 47–68.

Gould, R.V. and R. Fernandez (1989), 'Structures of mediation: a formal approach to brokerage in transaction networks', *Sociological Methodology*, **19**, 89–126.

Gouldner, A.W. (1960), 'The norm of reciprocity: a preliminary statement', *American Sociological Review*, **25**, 161–78.

Granovetter, M. (1973), 'The strength of weak ties', *American Journal of Sociology*, **78**, 1360–80.

Granovetter, M. (1982), 'The strength of weak ties: a network theory revisited', in P.V. Marsden and N. Lin (eds), *Social Structure and Network Analysis*, Beverly Hills, CA: Sage Publications, pp. 105–310.

Granovetter, M. (1985), 'Economic action and social structure: the problem of embeddedness', *American Journal of Sociology*, **91** (November), 481–510.

Granovetter, M. (1985 [1992]), 'Problems of explanation in economic sociology', in N. Nohria and R.G. Eccles (eds), *Networks and Organizations: Structure, Form, and Action*, Boston, MA: Harvard University Press, pp. 25–56.

Granovetter, M. (1995), *Getting a Job: A Study of Contacts and Careers*, Chicago, IL: University of Chicago Press.

Hansen, M. (1999), 'The search-transfer problem: the role of weak ties in sharing knowledge across organization subunits', *Administrative Science Quarterly*, **44**, 82–111.

Hoang, H. and B. Antoncic (2003), 'Network-based research in entrepreneurship: a critical view', *Journal of Business Venturing*, **18**, 165–87.

Homans, G.C. (1951), *The Human Group*, London: Routledge & Kegan Paul.

Ibarra, H. and S.B. Andrews (1993), 'Power, social influence, and sense-making: effects of network centrality and proximity on employee perceptions', *Administrative Science Quarterly*, **38**, 277–303.

Kijkuit, B. and J. van den Ende (2007), 'The organizational life of an idea. Integrating social network, creativity and decision-making perspectives', *Journal of Management Studies*, **44** (6), September, 863–82.

Krippner G., M. Granovetter, F. Block, N. Biggart, T. Beamish, Y. Hsing, G. Hart, G. Arrighi, M. Mendell, J. Hall, M. Burawoy, S. Vogel and S. O'Riain (2004), 'Polanyi symposium: a conversation on embeddedness', *Socio-Economic Review*, **2** (1), 109–35.

Latour, B. (1987), *Science in Action: How to Follow Scientists and Engineers Through Society*, Milton Keynes: Open University Press.

Leydesdorff, L. and W. Dolfsma (2007), 'The local citation environment of the *Journal of Evolutionary Economics*', Working Paper.

Madhaven, R. and R. Grover (1998), 'From embedded knowledge to embodied knowledge: new product development as knowledge management', *Journal of Marketing*, **62**, 1–12.

Malinowski, B. (1996), 'The principle of give and take', in A.E. Komter (ed.), *The Gift: An Interdisciplinary Perspective*, Amsterdam: Amsterdam University Press, pp. 15–17.

Marsden, P.V. (1990), 'Network data and measurement', *Annual Review of Sociology*, **16**, 435–63.

Marsden, P.V. (2002), 'Egocentric and sociocentric measures of network centrality', *Social Networks*, **24**, 407–22.

Mauss, M. (1954 [2000]), *The Gift: Forms and Functions of Exchange in Archaic Societies*, New York: W.W. Norton.

Merton, Robert K. (1968), 'The Matthew effect in science', *Science*, **159** (3810), 56–63.

Moody, J. and D.R. White (2003), 'Structural cohesion and embeddedness: a hierarchical concept of social groups', *American Sociological Review*, **68** (1), 103–27.

Nonaka, I. and D. Teece (eds) (2001), *Managing Industrial Knowledge: Creation Transfer and Utilization*, London: Sage Publications.

de Nooy, W., A. Mrvar and V. Batagelj (2005), *Exploratory Social Network Analysis with Pajek*, New York: Cambridge University Press.

Obstfeld, D. (2005), 'Social networks the tertius lungens orientation, and involvement in innovation', *Administrative Science Quarterly*, **50**, 100–130.

Ouchi, W.G. (1980), 'Markets, bureaucracies, and clans', *Administrative Science Quarterly*, **25** (1), 129–41.

Podolny, J. and K. Page (1998), 'Network forms of organization', *Annual Review of Sociology*, **24**, 57–76.

Powell, W.W. (1990), 'Neither market nor hierarchy: network forms of organization', *Research in Organizational Behavior*, **12**, 295–336.

Powell, W.W., K.K. Koput and L. Smith-Doerr (1996), 'Inter-organizational collaboration and the locus of innovation: network of learning in biotechnology', *Administrative Science Quarterly*, **41**, 116–45.

Sahlins, M.B. (1972), *Stone Age Economics*, Chicago, IL: Aldine.

Schulz, M. (2003), 'Pathway of relevance: exploring inflows of knowledge into subunits of multinational corporations', *Organization Science*, **14** (4), 440–59.

Saxenian, A. (1994), *Regional Advantage: Culture and Competition in Silicon Valley and Route 128*, Cambridge, MA: Harvard University Press.

Schwartz, B. (1996), 'The social psychology of the gift', in A.E. Komter (ed.), *The Gift: An Interdisciplinary Perspective*, Amsterdam: Amsterdam University Press, pp. 69–80.

Simon, H.A. (1976), *Administrative Behavior*, New York: The Free Press.

Strogatz, S. (2001), 'Exploring complex networks', *Nature*, **410**, 268–76.

Swedberg, R. (ed.) (2005), *New Developments in Economic Sociology*, Cheltenham, UK and Northampton, MA, USA: Edward Elgar.

Thornton, P.H. (2001), 'Personal versus market logics of control: a historically contingent theory of acquisition', *Organization Science*, **12** (3), 294–311.

Thornton, P.H. and K.H. Flynn (2003), 'Entrepreneurship, networks and geographies', in Z.J. Acs and D.B. Audretsch (eds), *Handbook of Entrepreneurship Research*, Dordrecht: Kluwer Academic, pp. 401–36.

Van der Eijk, R., W. Dolfsma and A. Jolink (2006), 'No black box and no black hole: from social capital to gifts', Working Paper.

Warren, R.L. (1967), 'The interorganizational field as a focus for investigation', *Administrative Science Quarterly*, **12** (3), 396–419.

Wasserman, S. and K. Faust (1994), *Social Network Analysis*, New York: Cambridge University Press.

White, H.C. (2002), *Markets from Networks. Socioeconomic Models of Production*, Princeton, NJ: Princeton University Press.

23 Communication in the economy: the example of innovation
Stefan Kesting

Innovation

The classical notion and definition of innovation in economics originate in the works of Joseph Alois Schumpeter. Schumpeter emphasized that truly welfare-enhancing economic development is not based on a smooth adjustment from a slightly disturbed equilibrium to another, but is based on revolutionary innovations (Schumpeter, 1934, p. 64). He defined innovation as new combinations that lead to new products, new ways of production, discoveries of new resources, new organizational methods of running the business enterprise and entry into new markets (ibid., p. 66). In the process of innovation path-breaking eminent inventions and discoveries (technical, managerial or others) are picked up by radical individuals called entrepreneurs and turned into commercial successes. Schumpeter assumed the 'new' was somehow emerging out of the blue or floating around (ibid., p. 88). The distinctive role of the entrepreneur is to turn radically away from traditions, customs and routines and to commit her- or himself to push for change. This distinctive communicative and innovative role of the entrepreneur was more recently highlighted by Deirdre McCloskey. She calculates that about a quarter of national income is produced by *persuasive talk* (including, e.g., advertising, McCloskey and Klamer, 1995, p. 194). In her book *Knowledge and Persuasion in Economics* she collects a bulk of evidence for the economic significance of persuasion under the heading *The Economy as a Conversation*. McCloskey (1994, p. 370) uses the example of Donald Trump to point to the power of persuasion and *the art of felicitous speech acts* to close deals. For McCloskey, this power of persuasion is the outstanding characteristic of Schumpeter's entrepreneur, for it is he or she who persuades banks to invest in innovations (ibid., p. 372). Schumpeter explicitly and analytically distinguishes between the entrepreneur and the investor or banker: 'He stands between those who wish to form new combinations and the possessors of productive means' (Schumpeter, 1934, p. 74). According to Schumpeter, whilst persuading the investor to lend him or her money, the entrepreneur also shifts the burden of uncertainty towards the provider of financial funds: 'It also settles the question whether the ordinary shareholder as such is an entrepreneur, and disposes of the conception of the entrepreneur as risk bearer' (ibid., p. 75).

Schumpeter offers a set of motives as an alternative, or more precisely supplement to the neoclassical one of profit maximization (ibid., p. 93). This set of motives elucidates why the entrepreneur is more willing and able than others to take the radical turn. However, while constructing his theory of *creative destruction* (he also discussed creative *accumulation*: Schumpeter, 1942, pp. 31 and 32), he left two elements not fully explained: the origin of the new[1] and how the entrepreneur actually manages to transform the new combination into a commercial success. At least concerning the first of the two tasks, Schumpeter did not develop a distinctive microeconomic theory of dynamic entrepreneurial activity.[2]

Apart from some recent theoretical contributions that discuss structural and institutional factors supporting the flow of 'good ideas' across 'structural holes' (Burt, 2004), or the storage, decoding and transmission costs involved in communicating knowledge, depending on the particular governance structure (Dolfsma, 2005), several scholars of innovation have used a theory of communicative action to bridge these theoretical gaps. The dynamic process of innovation leading to improvements in economic development cannot be fully understood without considering the basic human capability of communication.

Communication

Adam Smith based his argument about the human urge to trade goods and services on the basic human capacity to talk. He considered exchange as analogous to communication. From his 'Lectures on Jurisprudence' (1978 [1762–66]) it is known that Smith considered the human propensity to speak and converse with others as the origin of the propensity to truck and barter, bargain and exchange (McCloskey and Klamer, 1995, p. 193). According to him, this is at the very heart of the economic process and of the division of labour.

The classical treatment of communication in the social science literature (Watzlawick et al., 1967) distinguishes three basic elements in verbal exchange:

- Information is obtained in conversation (the 'syntactic' aspect of communication).
- New ideas emerge in dialogues and debates (the 'semantic' aspect of communication).
- Institutional change is initiated and implemented on the basis of public disputes (the 'pragmatic' aspect of communication).

Based on the literature in economics on the topic, I derived four ideal-type modes of communication. Since language is a multidimensional device for different kinds of human interaction, it can be used: (a) to persuade others to work according to one's own material interests (strategic); (b) to convince others of one's own value judgements, which are not necessarily an expression of self-interest (opinionated); (c) to obtain information to serve one's self-interest or form one's own value judgement[3] (informational); or (d) to create mutual understanding, to find common ground concerning world-views (*Weltanschauungen*), among participants in discourse and thereby alter former beliefs and perceptions, and possibly invent new ideas during the course of a conversant process of recombination (dialogical) (see Kesting, 2008). All four modes are relevant and useful in interpreting and understanding processes of innovation.

Albert Hirschman explicitly introduced speech acts as a means for innovation to economics in his book *Exit, Voice, and Loyalty* (1970). Hirschman distinguishes exit (market) and voice (discourse) options that members of societies and organizations have to express and change some malfunctioning, slack or bad quality in the service or products of those social entities. Hirschman thoroughly analyses the complex relation of these two options. What distinguishes his conception of voice from McCloskey's strategic interpretation of persuasion, however, is the attitude of loyalty attached to speech. Especially in cases where voice is either used or required to bring about social inventiveness, Hirschman writes, loyalty to the social entities in question is necessary, because voice may ask for considerable effort compared to exit (cf. Hirschman, 1970, p. 80). Hence, what Hirschman means by voice is the dialogical mode of communication (d) or at least the opinionated mode (b) and not the strategic mode (a).

Hirschman describes such a strategic mode of communication in his book *The Rhetoric of Reaction*. He shows that certain rhetorical figures used in public debates about intended reforms by proponents of conservative as well as progressive political ideas are used to refute and destroy opponents' arguments without taking them seriously or engaging in a process of argumentation that might lead to a common understanding. Hirschman demonstrates that these rhetorical figures are not employed to persuade others to find a good solution for all, but instead to close the argument by undermining the validity and credibility of the other position. He reviews and interprets historical debates to demonstrate how the opinionated and often strategic use of language works in practice. While uncovering the rhetorical figures, his intention is 'to move public discourse beyond extreme, intransigent postures of either kind, with the hope that in the process our debates will become more "democracy friendly"' (Hirschman, 1991, p. 168).

The syntactic element or strategic mode of speech acts underlies George Akerlof's argument about 'lemons' (1970), that is, an asymmetry of information that leads to a favourable bargaining position of the seller compared to the buyer of second-hand cars. This asymmetry of information, often in reference to Herbert Simon's 'bounded rationality' (Simon, 1997), and combined with an assumption of opportunistic behaviour, leads to the principal–agent problem (Furubotn and Richter, 1997) and the development of a theory of transaction costs in new institutional economics (NIE) (Furubotn and Richter, 1997; North, 1993, 1994, 1996; Williamson, 1981, 1991, 2000). An article written from the perspective of NIE which comes closest to a theory of communicative action employing at least the informational mode is Arthur Denzau and Douglass North's discussion of 'mental models' (Denzau and North, 1994). However, a quite similar theory that can be seen as pioneering the communicative theory of innovation in economics had already been developed more than 40 years earlier by Kenneth Boulding (1997 [1956]).

The image and integrative power
Kenneth Boulding's theory of *the image* contains an alternative microeconomic approach compared to the neoclassical one which is, apart from terminology and one crucial theoretical difference, quite similar to Denzau and North's (1994) mental models approach (for a detailed comparison, see Kesting, 2008). Neoclassical theory tends to regard 'talk as cheap' (Farrell, 1995); in other words communication is useless amongst strategic self-interested actors because lies and truthful statements cannot be distinguished.[4] Boulding's image clearly departs from this assumption and is to the contrary solidly based on communication as a means of understanding. A short and at the same time inclusive definition of the image can be found in an article by Warren Samuels: 'The fundamental role of the image is to define the world. The image is the basic, final, fundamental, controlling element in all perception and thought. It largely governs our definition of reality, substantively and normatively, in part as to what is actual and what is possible' (Samuels, 1997, p. 311). Hence, instead of rational maximization, the image carried in our heads largely governs our behaviour in a semantic and pragmatic way (Watzlawick et al., 1967): 'The behavior is response to an image, not a response to a stimulus, and without the concept of an image the behavior cannot possibly be understood' (Boulding, 1997 [1956], p. 43). Economic transactions are embedded in a process of 'imagination' that incorporates value judgements: 'The image of value is concerned with the *rating* of the various parts of our image of the world, according to some scale of betterness or worseness. We, all of us, possess one or more of these scales. It is what the economists call a welfare function' (ibid., p. 11).

It is an unresolved issue whether the image remains stable or changes depending on the experiences of the individual and the influence on it of outside messages (Samuels, 1997, p. 312). How does our image, containing our value judgements, preferences and welfare perception, change, and how do others influence that process? Boulding insists that human beings communicate with each other via symbols (i.e. communication that can become independent of the communicator) as well as face to face (cf. Boulding, 1997, p. 88), and that communication constitutes and changes our images: 'It is this symbolic image and the communications which establish it and which change it which constitutes the peculiar quality of human society, a quality which no animal society shares' (ibid., 44).[5] Samuels highlights the linguistic character of the image, too: 'Images are linguistic phenomena for mankind. Language is the material of images. Having an image reducing it to words, talking about it – all this involves the use of language' (Samuels, 1997, p. 317). Image and language alike are at the same time intra- and inter-individual, and their change takes place via correspondence of these levels: 'The basic bond of any society, culture, subculture or organization is a "public image" that is, an image the essential characteristics of which are shared by the individuals participating in the group . . . Indeed, every public image begins in the mind of some single individual and only becomes public as it is transmitted and shared' (Boulding, 1997 [1956], p. 64). However, there is not one single public image; there are many public images (ibid., p. 132). In fact, a culture is nothing else than a group of people sharing a certain public image. What has this micro-theory of behaviour guided by individual and public images, which are stabilized or changed through communication, to contribute to the development of an alternative approach to innovation?

What we regard as a *new combination* in the Schumpeterian sense is a value-laden public image with the help of which we try to change and improve economic processes and their outcomes. Our image also helps us on the individual level to deal with uncertainty (Boulding, 1997 [1956], p. 87). On the collective level the novel creation is attained by a

> process of the mutual modification of images both relational and evaluational in the course of mutual communication, discussion, and discourse. The course of the discussion is punctuated by decisions which are essentially temporary in nature in the sense that they do not close the discussion, although they do, of course, have the effect of modifying it. In one sense, in a successful political process all decisions are interim. We live in a perpetual state of unresolved conflict. A decision is partial resolution of conflict. It should never be a complete resolution. (Ibid., p. 103)

According to Boulding the new is not only created, but also propagated and implemented in processes of communication that change public imagination. A good example of such a change of public sentiment and economic practice through a communicative process is Viviana Zelizer's 'The domestic production of money' (Zelizer, 1997). Based on written discourse material ranging from theatre plays, law reviews, magazine articles, reports in newspapers on court cases and home economics literature, she demonstrates the slowly shifting ideological notion of how a woman's access to 'a dollar of her own' widened from dole to household allowance and pin money to joint account and finally to earnings in the USA between 1870 and 1930. Zelizer shows how public argument was used to ensure the temporary legitimate resolution of 'allowance' or 'joint account' until a new round of discourse moved a step further forward towards emancipation.

Such processes are not free of conflict. The explanatory advantage of such an image/communication-based theory of innovation is not only that it includes changing preferences[6] and interdependence of individuals, but also that it allows for welfare-enhancing effects through social learning.

Boulding not only dealt with the impact of language and image on innovation, but also with the related topics of conflict resolution and power. Whereas the image represents a micro foundation for the Schumpeterian theory of *new combinations* and the Austrian process of innovation and discovery (Hayek, 1969), his view of conflict resolution can be interpreted as a complementary form of coordination (Boulding, 1962, 1974). However, it is an alternative view to Schumpeter's rather militaristic notion of *creative destruction*. Boulding in general is very much interested in a consensus-oriented development of society. As he writes in his book *Three Faces of Power*: 'Economic development is fundamentally a learning process and learning is on the whole non-conflictual, though it has some conflictual elements in the elimination of error and a possible threat to personal identity which this may involve' (Boulding, 1990, p. 196). Conflict is in most cases unproductive for him.

Inspired by John Kenneth Galbraith's book *The Anatomy of Power*, Boulding defines three forms of power: personal destructive power (threat); personal productive power (exchange); and personal integrative power (Boulding, 1990, p. 79). Boulding provides the following definition for the latter: 'Integrative power depends very much on the power of language and communication, especially on the powers of persuasion' (ibid., p. 221). 'Integrative power often rests on the ability to create images of the future and to persuade other people that these are valid' (ibid., p. 122). Integrative power influences via the creation of images based on communication while other power forms are either threats or bribes. Additionally, he points out that integrative power 'is the most dominant and significant form of power' (ibid., p. 10, and see Boulding, 1990, p. 110) compared to the other two forms.

Integrative power particularly rests on the use of language and is enhanced by a variety of emotional relations, which Boulding mentions in his book on power and which according to him can be ordered on a scale that reflects their intensity: reciprocity, respect for each other, the wish and willingness to learn from each other, sympathy for each other, and love for each other. Integrative power, however, must not always be consensus-oriented or inclusive. Boulding points out several ways in which it can be used during a conflict against others: (1) in a network or group that was built up by integrative power, some persons may achieve a powerful position or status; (2) 'Language can be a powerful weapon of destruction in putting people down, in complaining, in nagging, in recriminating' (Boulding, 1990, p. 81); (3) it can be used to stigmatize and exclude people: 'The power of social exclusion is a very important aspect of the overall integrative system' (ibid., p. 85); (4) the ability to persuade people can be used to manipulate them: 'Unfortunately, what is convincing is not always true, and what is true is not always convincing' (ibid., p. 119). Nevertheless, integrative power is a consensus-oriented concept.[7] According to Boulding this is 'the power to be accepted, respected, legitimated, loved, and to form part of a larger network' (ibid., p. 79). More so than market or hierarchy, the network can be regarded as the ideal type of governance for encapsulating communicative action and integrative power (Thompson, 2003).

Networks
To create new combinations they first have to be imagined, often while communicating in groups or teams (Penrose, 1959; Nonaka and Konno, 1998). These images may none the less differ from individual to individual. They are, however, also connected via integrative power, which is based on emotional bonds and communication: 'Integrative power within such a network may be a gradual process of a person gathering respect from the other people in the network through communication and the formation of images of that person in the minds of the other network members' (Boulding, 1990, p. 114). Via integrative power (networks) intersubjective public images are formed and changed.

This dialogical mode of communication is the microeconomic foundation that explains the creative and innovative advantage of networks and clusters compared to other governance structures (Foss, 2006; Granovetter, 1992, 2000, 2005; Granovetter and McGuire, 1998; Nooteboom, 1999; Porter, 1990, 1998; Saxenian, 2000; Thompson, 2003).

A theory of communicative action
The specific innovative productivity of speech that brings about a specific kind of rationality and thus allows the creation of mutual benefits during a transaction can further be clarified by drawing on Habermas's theory of communicative action. Although Habermas is not an economist and his

behavioural pattern of communicative action is not directed at the economic realm, his theory can none the less contribute to Hirschman's and Boulding's attitudinal and procedural concepts of communicative action.

Communicative action in Habermas's sense is not only oriented to success, efficiency, or personal goals, but also to reaching an understanding among the participants of a discourse and is coordinated 'through cooperative achievements of understanding among participants. In communicative action, participants are not oriented primarily to their own success, but to the realization of an agreement which is the condition under which all participants in the interaction may pursue their own plans' (Habermas, 1995, p. 385; Biesecker, 1997, p. 220). Communicative action is based on language and operates in the process of reciprocal exchange. This procedural exchange of arguments during which participants learn to understand each other's motivations, underlying norms and opinions is called *discourse* by Habermas. In discourse, participants are required to learn from each other and to change their own attitudes towards the world in general or towards certain problems occurring within it.[8]

So far, Habermas's concept of *communicative action* or *discourse* is similar to the creation of a public image (Boulding, 1997 [1956]) and the procedural conflict resolution of *reconciliation* described by Boulding (1962). What Habermas adds is what might be called a procedural *communicative rationality*[9] that helps to differentiate three basic types of arguments (speech acts) that can be criticized or defended, grounded in their specific rationality. Habermas argues that communicative rationality occurs inevitably during discourse, which is evident if we thoroughly consider the intersubjective meaning of illocutions. While locution means just saying something, that is an undirected statement, illocution is a speech act directed towards another person, such as an order, a promise or a confession. The success of an illocution is a common understanding, while a perlucution according to Habermas is a speech act with a clear goal (it follows Weber's *Zweckrationalitaet* – utilitarian rationality). It is meant to result in a strategically intended effect at the receiving end (Habermas, 1995, pp. 388–90). However, if we try to persuade during discourse (i.e. an illocution), we suppose that the other person can be convinced by our arguments and may accordingly change his or her mind. When we do this, however, we implicitly concede that exactly the same might happen to us but in the opposite direction. That is to say, we would admit the superiority of the other's arguments and change our minds.[10] The philosophical underpinning of the argument is that participants in a dialogue logically have to allow for mutual understanding to occur or they will commit a 'performative contradiction'. To assume opportunism or strategic behaviour in dialogue is what Apel and Habermas would call a *performative contradiction* (Habermas, 1995 [1981]).

What is true for persuasion in one direction of influence will in turn also be true for learning in the other direction. If you try to receive information (useful ideology or mental models, for instance[11]) from a person, you assume that people are capable of learning. Vice versa you should assume that the other will also be able to learn from whatever information you provide in the process of communication.

The communicative rationality of speech acts is not only instrumental, like the utilitarian rationality of economic man, but threefold. As Adelheid Biesecker put it (quoting and translating Habermas):

> They [speech acts, S.K.] are not simply grounded in knowledge of the object world (as in empirical thinking), but also in the norms of the society in which the discourse is taking place (Habermas's social world) and the values of the partners in the discourse (Habermas's subject world). Communicative rationality, therefore, has three dimensions: An action [or a statement, S.K.] is rational if it is objectively true, socially right and subjectively sincere. (Habermas, 1995, p. 149, translated in Biesecker, 1997, p. 220)

The participants in a discourse use their shared experiences (made in their life-world) as background and reservoir to test the validity of arguments along the three just-mentioned dimensions of rationality. In a certain discourse situation, the discussants refer to their shared experiences, which contain all opinions and world-views taken for granted, to begin a cooperative process of interpretation and new combination. During this process, some elements of their experiences will remain untouched or stable, while others will become a matter of doubt and may change. Because discourse, as a form of social coordination, is linked both to the social and to the subjective worlds, it has the capacity to integrate a number of seemingly irreconcilable values. Such integration is limited during a neoclassical transaction or an Austrian market process because these concepts are based merely on instrumental rationality. Here values have to be reflected monetarily in supply or demand to influence the outcome. Communicative rationality may lead to the development of creative solutions to conflicts or problems discussed in the economy or in society. This establishes the special innovative productivity of the discursive process.[12]

Philosophically, a strong Kantian, *a priori* emphasis on reason is apparent in discourse ethics. This bright side or optimistic view of discourse is probably as one-sided as the dark side or pessimistic view of interpreting it as solely strategic (see Kesting, 2005, 1998). Empirically both opportunistic behaviour (manipulation, betrayal, false and broken promises etc.) and mutually rewarding cooperation are possible and observable in actual transactions and processes of innovation. They are a complex mix of exploration and exploitation (Nooteboom, 2000, p. 304). Trials to reconcile the bright and the dark side will be discussed in the following sections.

The powers of persuasion

Like Habermas, Elster (1998) thinks along a rather strict theoretical dichotomy of two modes of communication: *arguing* and *bargaining*. On the one hand there is the exchange of rational arguments to deliberate ends and means, in the process possibly transforming the preferences of participants. On the other hand there is bargaining, where the outcome of the process results from the bargaining power of the parties – that is, the resources that enable them to make credible threats and promises.

In his book *Between Facts and Norms* (1999), however, Habermas shows awareness of the fact that both modes are intertwined in concrete discourses in the public sphere. I am unable here to do justice to Habermas's extensive treatment and explanation of the complex philosophical and sociological relation between communicative action in the public sphere and the constitutional, legal and parliamentary political system of Western democracies in his aforementioned book. My purpose is merely to highlight the way in which he conceptualizes the transformation of communicative action into communicative power. The public sphere and deliberative politics within it is a problem-solving debate and a conflict of interests at the same time. Even actors, who have little strategic power (to bribe, buy or have easy access to media or impose a threat), can turn communicative action into communicative power, that is a countervailing power against opponent strategically powerful actors (Habermas, 1999, p. 381). The emergence of organizations of consumer activists is a good example of such a process of empowerment. An important figure for consumer activism in the USA is Ralf Nader. After publishing his book *Unsafe At Any Speed* about the dangers of driving a Chevrolet Corvair, the Harvard-educated lawyer set up the Center for Study of Responsive Law and the Project for Corporate Responsibility in 1969.

By the end of the 1970s he had spawned a series of organizations, staffed by young professionals, nicknamed 'Nader's Raiders'. Naderism is adamant on the role of information, which should be free and fair. His ideas have spread all over the world (Lang and Gabriel, 2005, pp. 46–8).

In discussing philosopher Hannah Arendt's power theory Habermas writes:

> But discursively produced and intersubjectively shared beliefs have, at the same time, a *motivating* force. Even if this remains limited to the weakly motivating force of good reasons, from this perspective, the public use of communicative freedom also appears as a generator of power potentials. (Habermas, 1999, p. 147)

Discussing the work of Elster, Habermas concludes: 'The results of deliberative politics can be understood as communicatively generated power
that competes, on the one hand, with the social power of actors with credible threats and, on the other hand, with the administrative power of
officeholders' (ibid., p. 341). A good chance for communicative power to
have an impact on the course of social development appears especially in
moments of crisis. Habermas explains:

> even in more or less power-ridden public spheres, the power relations shift as
> soon as the perception of relevant social problems evokes a *crisis consciousness*
> at the periphery. If actors from civil society then join together, formulate the rele-
> vant issue, and promote it in the public sphere, their efforts can be successful,
> because the endogenous mobilization of the public sphere activates an otherwise
> latent dependency built into the internal structure of every public sphere, a
> dependency also present in the normative self-understanding of the mass media:
> the players in the arena owe their influence to the approval of those in the gallery.
> (Ibid., p. 382)

In other words, communication used to express a latent and problematic
issue that is perceived as legitimate will be able to withstand power used by
an opposing group. Hence there is an arena for communicative innovative
processes in the public sphere where powers of persuasion are used.

Galbraith's perspective on power shows a remarkable resemblance to
Habermas's. However, more so than Habermas he emphasizes the contingency of the effect of power and the importance of establishing shared
beliefs or images. He stresses that power is neither positive nor negative. In
his 1983 book *Anatomy of Power* he explains: 'Power can be socially malign;
it is also socially essential' (Galbraith, 1983, p. 13). The author distinguishes three forms of power: first, condign power, which proceeds from
threat; second, compensatory power, which is based upon reward; and
finally, conditioned power, which, 'in contrast, is exercised by changing
belief. Persuasion, education, or the social commitment to what seems
natural, proper, or right causes the individual to submit to the will of
another or of others' (ibid., pp. 5 and 6).

Of course conditioned power is the interesting one for the topic of this
chapter because condign and compensatory power are not based on communication, but must be backed by either force or material rewards,
whereas Galbraith's third category describes a language-based form of
power. Galbraith identifies each form of power with a certain source of
power (personality, property and organization) and elaborates the complex
relation between sources and forms, with considerable overlap and interdependence. However, he makes the empirical observation that modern
industrial societies are in the age of organization and therefore conditioned
power is the dominating form of power of our time (Galbraith, 1983,

pp. 54 and 115). Conditioned power can be understood as communicative action in Habermas's sense, when a group or organization uses discourse to reach a common understanding, and later publicly defends this consensus. One might say the members of an organization develop a persuasion to allow them to fight for that particular new idea much more powerfully than any person could do alone. Thus conditioned power is consensus-oriented as well as conflict-oriented. It describes the transition from Habermas's communicative action to communicative power.

Galbraith writes that indirect conditioned power is an often implicit, unnoticed, subconscious influence, as part of the framework of values that surrounds and influences all members of society (traditions, patriarchy), whereas direct conditioned power is the observable, explicit attempt to persuade and influence others.[13] Hence Galbraith's conditioned power is used in overt, covert and latent conflicts (Lukes, 1974). Dugger's theory of corporate hegemony for instance, is built upon Galbraithian thought,[14] and can be interpreted as conditioned power in the extreme. Dugger seems to suggest that the persuasive powers of modern corporations are so large and all-encompassing that they dominate all other conditioning influences. This, however, means that Galbraith's insistence on the contingency of the effects of conditioned power due to 'diffusion' and 'illusion' is lost.

Interesting, and a little confusing at first, is Galbraith's conclusion from his analysis of the workings of conditioned power: 'As we have sufficiently seen, organization and the associated role of social conditioning are basic to all modern exercise of power. At the same time, and paradoxically, they bring not only the modern concentration of power but also its *personal diffusion*' (Galbraith, 1983, p. 183).

The diffusion of power that Galbraith mentions results from his concept of *countervailing power* and his persuasion that conditioned power is often not in fact power (as an influence on someone), but only an illusion of power. Galbraith explains:

> There are few manifestations of power in modern times that expend such costly and committed energy as the cultivation of belief and the resulting exercise of power through advertising. However, partly because advertising is a wholly ostentatious attempt to capture belief, it is not a fully reputable way of winning it. It regularly invites its own resistance and disapproval. (Ibid., p. 30)

Whether an advertising campaign is able to catch the attention of consumers is uncertain. It can go unnoticed, have the desired effect or even be perceived as revolting. Advertising as a form of direct conditioning can be based on an illusion of its persuasive effect or have unintended consequences.

In other words, attempts at *creative destruction* with the aim of replacing an old product by a new one or conquering and expanding the market via a marketing campaign may be completely futile. They might meet considerable resistance because disapproval may also result from countervailing direct conditioned power issued by consumer activists or environmentalists. The case of Brent Spar[15] (Post et al., 2002), where Greenpeace successfully campaigned against Royal Dutch Shell, shows the general openness to direct conditioned power and the related openness of public discourse concerning its results and decisions.

Hence, from Galbraith's and Habermas's theories we gather that dialogical practice can, but may not, generate or strengthen communicative power. In other words, if it is used successfully in a public debate, it will change the minds of people participating in it and thereby also change the range of ideas, norms and ideologies that constitutes a process of innovation.

Routines
Moreover, such a theory of communicative innovation as developed above is apparent as an undercurrent in Richard Nelson and Sidney Winter's concept of routines. In their book *An Evolutionary Theory of Economic Change* (1982) they describe organizational routines as an analogue of individual skills and as an important part of a company's memory and therefore its knowledge. They stress the importance of routines for the smooth operation of any organization and highlight their tacit knowledge component. Skills and routines allow for an automatic and habitual response and, hence, for fast and efficient handling of all kinds of challenges and tasks (Nelson and Winter, 1982, p. 97). However, before a routine can run automatically the right one has to be picked. Nelson and Winter point to the importance of language when reasoning about choosing a particular skill for a particular task and about how to change and learn skills: 'It is, as we have emphasized, difficult or impossible to use language to characterize the "inner workings" of a skill, but words serve quite well in thinking and communicating about skills considered as units of purposive behaviour' (ibid., p. 85). Managers or any outside observers need well-defined descriptions of professional skills to ensure an efficient application in the production process. Moreover, about problem-solving skills and learning they write: 'In the exercise of these cognitive skills, an important role is played by language and, in particular, by the names of other skills that may or may not be possessed by the planner or problem solver' (ibid., p, 86). Vagueness about the right word or the right skill for the circumstances might lead to *semantic* ambiguity (ibid., p. 88).

At the level of the organization, appropriate routines are coordinated and 'triggered' by a constant stream of signals and messages, which can be interpreted as a form of language:

For organization members in such roles, there are additional requisites of knowing the job that parallel the ones involved in receiving and interpreting such messages . . . the abilities to speak and write the natural language of the society to which the organization belongs, but also the important additional requirement of command of the organizational dialect. (Nelson and Winter, 1982, p. 102)

Especially because of their tacit knowledge component and because they constitute socially shared knowledge, routines as part of the organizational memory are founded on explicit and implicit forms of communication:

To view organizational memory as reducible to individual member memories is to overlook, or undervalue, the linking of those individual memories by shared experiences in the past, experiences that have established the extremely detailed and specific communication system that underlies routine performance. (Ibid., p. 105)

They point out that 'Innovations in organizational routine similarly consist, in large part, of new combinations of existing routines' (ibid., p. 130); however, in their discussion of heuristics and search routines, they do not consider debate, argument and discussion to pool knowledge, to reach workable conclusions and to find appropriate solutions. Surprisingly, nor do Nelson and Winter discuss the role of communication and use of ordinary language when it comes to control, replication and imitation of routines. Such a 'linguistic turn' is equally absent when they 'review the behavioral foundations of the evolutionary approach' (Nelson and Winter, 2002, p. 25) in an article tracing 20 years of theoretical development since their book was first published.

Scripts
However, this next analytical step is taken by Bart Nooteboom, who especially in one of his articles (Nooteboom, 1999) and his book *Learning and Innovation in Organizations and Economies* (2000), replaces Nelson and Winter's 'routine' with the equivalent but analytically improved concept of a script: 'A script is a knowledge structure that fits predictable, conventional or frequently encountered situations . . . . People in organizations know how to act appropriately because they have a working knowledge of their organizational world' (Gioia and Poole, 1984, p. 450). In business companies scripts are, for instance, attached to performance appraisals, selection interviews and conversations with the boss. They also underlie meetings and decision-making processes. 'A script is a schema held in memory that describes events or behaviors (or sequences of events or behaviors) appropriate for a particular context' (ibid.). Such a schema can be broken down into nodes: 'The actions of people, in turn, based on their cognition are substituted into nodes of organizational scripts, where the nodes represent

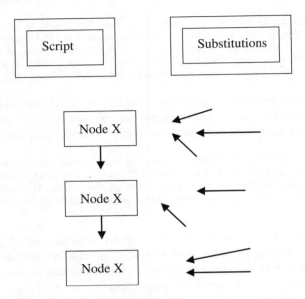

Source: Figure 6.1 in Nooteboom (2000, p. 126).

Figure 23.1   A script, nodes and substitutions

tasks and organizational scripts represent "routines" or "performance pro-grams" ' (Nooteboom, 2000, pp. 126 and 127). A script is like a prescriptive image for a particular action sequence. The individual steps to be taken are the nodes shown in Figure 23.1. However, it is also the reflective image of a sequence of actions that allows participants to deliberate and discuss alternative moves (substitutions).

Nooteboom illustrates the concept for the script at the example of dining according to two alternative scripts: 'In a restaurant script, the nodes repre-sent successive activities of entering, sitting down, ordering, eating, paying and leaving. Each can be done in different ways [substitutions]. For ex-ample, paying by cash, by cheque, bank card, credit card, or chip card' (Nooteboom, 2000, p. 126). An alternative script is for a self-service restau-rant, where 'the sequence of nodes is different: in contrast with the service restaurant, one generally pays before sitting down and eating' (ibid., p. 128).

Nooteboom argues that such scripts have to be seen as developed and applied in processes of 'interactive emergence' that are innovative dis-courses in the Habermasian sense:

> Knowledge and meaning constitute repertoires from which we select combina-tions in specific contexts, which yield novel combinations that may shift repertoires of knowledge and meaning. Such shifts of knowledge and meaning

occur in interaction with the physical world, in technical tinkering, and in social interaction, on the basis of discourse (cf. Habermas's (1982, 1984) notion of 'communicative action') (ibid., p. 121).

In other words, participants involved in a particular sequence of actions such as a production process or a science project develop a script in a communicative exchange of ideas and constantly alter and improve it in debating with each other. Nooteboom explicitly subscribes to *methodological interactionism* as a basis for understanding communicative action, a methodology that will 'replace both methodological individualism of economics and the methodological collectivism of (some) sociology with methodological interactionism' (ibid., p. 303).

Nooteboom explains how innovation in scripts and routines changes through the change of meaning in metaphor and by the hermeneutic circle. According to him, and quite similar to Boulding's concept of the image, using a metaphor allows one to take a different perspective or point of view:

> Things that seemed the same are now seen as different, and things that seemed different are now seen as the same. To effect such a break is, I propose, the function of metaphor, which carries over a feature from one word to another and thereby sheds a different light, which might cause us to form a novel concept by redistribution of features. (Ibid., p. 140)

He continues, 'Metaphor also plays an important role in reducing cognitive distance, in making something intelligible from one cognitive framework to another, by expressing something from one framework in terms of the other' (ibid., p. 145). However, in this process of understanding and new combination we are enabled and constrained at the same time by existing language and by scripts, as can be illustrated in the hermeneutic circle:

> Gadamer (1977) is the recognized 'father' of hermeneutics. The basic notion, according to him, is that, like an institution more generally, language provides an 'enabling constraint' (my term not Gadamer's). It enables us to interpret and understand but thereby also constitutes a prejudice, and interpretation that we construct and impose rather than an objective meaning that we find. (Ibid., p. 142)

Conclusion

As we have seen, quite a number of economists refer, sometimes explicitly, sometimes implicitly, to communication when they analyse particular aspects of innovation. Moreover, they usually start from some descriptive notion of verbal, symbolic or media-based human interaction without providing a clear definition of what communication actually is. To gain a deeper understanding of the micro processes of discovering and constructing the surprisingly *new*, however, it is important to start from a well-defined idea of communication as such, as Nooteboom does.

Communication between individual actors might be successful or unsuccessful. One prominent theoretical approach tends to stress that communicative action may lead to mutual understanding of a situation and, hence, productive consensus (Habermas, 1995; Biesecker, 1997).

Other scholars highlight that conflict can be seen as useful, inspiring and productive for reaching a common understanding (Boulding, 1990; Galbraith, 1983).

Other widely used approaches emphasize that discourse is manipulating (Dugger, 1989; and Foucault, 1983) or highlight, based on a notion of bounded rationality and an assumption of opportunisic behaviour among actors, that all communication is costly (Williamson, 1991; Denzau and North, 1994).

Demonstrating that for analytic purposes a more levelled approach proves to be more fruitful, some scholars try to combine the optimist and pessimist perspective on communicative action (Elster, 1998; Flyvbjerg, 1998).

What all these concepts of communication have in common is that they put particular forms of human interactive relations at the centre stage of their analysis of the process of persuasion and do not separate the question of how communication as such allows for the discovery or construction of the *new* from its anthropological and socio-economic foundation.

Notes

1. Although Schumpeter developed some interesting thoughts on this (Schumpeter, 2005), he did not publish these ideas in his lifetime.
2. Nooteboom highlights this shortcoming of Austrian eonomics in general: 'it deserts us when it comes to the clinch of understanding how knowledge shifts in interaction between "different minds thinking different things", because the black boxes of the minds of individuals and the knowledge of firms remain closed' (2000, pp. 73–4), and: 'But note that Schumpeter also was unable to endogenize creation in the form of invention (cf. Witt, 1993a): innovation was the realization of potential offered by invention' (ibid., p. 63).
3. This mode of communicative action is used by the uncertainty-ridden actor in Denzau and North's theory of shared mental models to save transaction costs (Denzau and North, 1994).
4. Notable exceptions to this perspective are Frank (1988), who discusses the long-term utility of signalling honesty, and Rubinstein (2000), who tries to apply economic theory to linguistics.
5. In his book *A Preface to Grants Economics* Boulding (1981) emphasizes the role of communication in exchange and gift relationships, and actually conceives of market exchange as a subset of gift exchange, explicitly taking communication into account.
6. For a case study of innovation involving preference change, see Dolfsma (2004).
7. It bears a great deal of resemblance to Habermas's concept of *communicative power* (Habermas, 1999).
8. The open attitude towards arguments of the other, which is implied here as a precondition, was called *democratic ethos* by one of Habermas's critics: 'The time has come for Habermas to acknowledge what pragmatists – especially Dewey and Mead – emphasized long ago: there is no democracy – in *theory* or in *practice* – *without a democratic ethos*' (Bernstein, 1996, p. 1146).

9. To develop this type of rationality, Habermas draws on George Herbert Mead and two generations of ordinary-language philosophy including the *speech act theory* of John L. Austin and John R. Searle.
10. The discourse concept developed by Bill Waller and Linda Robertson shows some similarities to Habermas's (Waller and Robertson, 1991, p. 1035).
11. See Denzau and North (1994) and my critical interpretation in Kesting (2008).
12. I am indebted to Biesecker and Ulrich, who developed an economic theory based on Habermas's work, which they termed *Practical Social Economics* (Biesecker, 1997; Ulrich, 1987, 1997).
13. 'Conditioned power is the product of a continuum from objective, visible persuasion to what the individual in the social context has been brought to believe is inherently correct. As we have seen, such power can be explicit, the result of a direct and visible attempt to win the belief that, in turn, reflects the purposes of the individual or group seeking or exercising the power. Or the belief can be implicit in the social or cultural condition; submission to the authority of others reflects the accepted view of what the individual should do. As one moves from explicit to implicit conditioning, one passes from obtrusive, ostentatious effort to win belief to an imposed subordination that is unnoticed – taken for granted. And, an important point, the social acceptance of conditioned power rises steadily as one moves in this direction from explicit to implicit conditioning' (Galbraith, 1983, p. 29).
14. Compare for example Dugger (1989) and his critique of Galbraith's work in Dugger (2001).
15. In 1995, the oil corporation Shell announced that it would send its outworn oil rig Brent Spar to the bottom of the Atlantic Ocean and faced tremendous opposition (a public campaign including a boycott of filling stations) which was organized by Greenpeace. At the end of that public conflict, Shell had to give in and scrapped the oil rig on shore.

References

Akerlof, G.A. (1970), 'The market for "lemons": quality uncertainty and the market mechanism', *Quarterly Journal of Economics*, **84**, 488–500.

Bernstein, R.J. (1996), 'The retrieval of the democratic ethos', *Cardozo Law Review*, **17** (4–5), 1127–46.

Biesecker, A. (1997), 'The market as an instituted realm of action', *Journal of Socio-Economics*, **26** (3), 215–41.

Boulding, K.E. (1962), *Conflict and Defence: A General Theory*, Lanham, MD: University Press of America.

Boulding, K.E. (1974), 'The communication of legitimacy', in K.E. Boulding (ed.), *Collected Papers: Toward a General Social Science*, Vol. IV, Boulder, CO: Colorado Associated University Press, pp. 239–43.

Boulding, K.E. (1981), *A Preface to Grants Economics: The Economy of Love and Fear*, New York: Praeger.

Boulding, K.E. (1990), *Three Faces of Power*, Newbury Park, CA: Sage.

Boulding, K.E. (1997 [1956]), *The Image: Knowledge in Life and Society*, Ann Arbor, MI: The University of Michigan Press.

Burt, R.S. (2004), 'Structural holes and good ideas', *American Journal of Sociology*, **110** (2), 349–99.

Denzau, A.T. and D.C. North (1994), 'Shared mental models: ideologies and institutions', *Kyklos*, **47** (1), 3–31.

Dolfsma, W. (2004), *Institutional Economics and the Formation of Preferences: The Advent of Pop Music*, Cheltenham, UK and Northampton, MA, USA: Edward Elgar.

Dolfsma, W. (2005), 'Towards a dynamic (Schumpeterian) welfare economics', *Research Policy*, **34**, 69–82.

Dugger, W.M. (1989), *Corporate Hegemony*, New York/Westport, CT/London: Greenwood Press.

Dugger, W.M. (2001), 'Progress denied: the unravelling of The New Industrial State', in M. Keaney (ed.), *Economist with a Public Purpose: Essays in Honour of John Kenneth Galbraith*, London and New York: Routledge, pp. 183–97.

Elster, J. (ed.) (1998), *Deliberative Democracy*, Cambridge: Cambridge University Press.

Farrell, J. (1995), 'Talk is cheap', *American Economic Review (Papers and Proceedings)*, **85** (2), 186–90.

Flyvbjerg, B. (1998), 'Habermas and Foucault: thinkers for civil society?', *British Journal of Sociology*, **49** (2), 210–33.

Foss, N.J. (2006), 'The emerging knowledge governance approach: challenges and characteristics', DRUID Working Papers, 06-10.

Foucault, M. (1983), 'The subject and power', in H.L. Dreyfus and P. Rabinow (eds), *Michel Foucault: Beyond Structuralism and Hermeneutics*, Chicago, IL: University of Chicago Press, pp. 208–26.

Frank, R.H. (1988), *Passions within Reason: The Strategic Role of the Emotions*, New York: W.W. Norton.

Furubotn, E.G. and R. Richter (1997), *Institutions and Economic Theory: The Contribution of New Institutional Economics*, Ann Arbor, MI: University of Michigan Press.

Galbraith, J.K. (1983), *The Anatomy of Power*, Boston, MA: Houghton Mifflin.

Gioia, D.A. and P.P. Poole (1984), 'Scripts in organizational behavior', *The Academy of Management Review*, **9** (3), 449–59.

Granovetter, M. (1992), 'Economic institutions as social constructions: a framework for analysis', in R. Swedberg (ed.) (1996), *Economic Sociology*, Aldershot, UK, and Brookfield, USA: Edward Elgar, pp. 269–77.

Granovetter, M. (2000), 'The economic sociology of firms and entrepreneurs', in R. Swedberg (ed.), *Entrepreneurship: The Social Science View*, Oxford and New York: Oxford University Press, pp. 244–75.

Granovetter, M. (2005), 'The impact of social structures on economic outcomes', *Journal of Economic Perspectives*, **19** (1), 33–50.

Granovetter, M. and P. McGuire (1998), 'The making of an industry: electricity in the United States', in M. Callon (ed.), *The Laws of the Markets*, London and Keele: Blackwell Publishers/*The Sociological Review*, pp. 147–73.

Habermas, J. (1995 [1981]), *Theorie des kommunikativen Handelns*, Vol. 1, Frankfurt am Main: Suhrkamp.

Habermas, J. (1999 [1992]), *Between Facts and Norms*, Cambridge, MA: The MIT Press.

Hayek F. von (1969), 'Der Wettbewerb als Entdeckungsverfahren', in F. von Hayek (ed.), *Freiburger Studien, gesammelte Aufsätze*, Tübingen: J.C.B. Mohr (Paul Siebeck), pp. 249–65; English translation as: F. von Hayek, 'Competition as a discovery process', in F. von Hayek (ed.), *New Studies in Philosophy, Politics, Economics and the History of Ideas*, Chicago, IL: University of Chicago Press, pp. 179–90.

Hirschman, Albert O. (1970), *Exit, Voice, and Loyalty: Responses to Decline in Firms, Organisations, and States*, Cambridge, MA and London: Harvard University Press.

Hirschman, Albert O. (1991), *The Rhetoric of Reaction: Perversity, Futility, Jeopardy*, Cambridge, MA and London: The Belknap Press of Harvard University Press.

Kesting, S. (1998), 'A potential for understanding and the interference of power: discourse as an economic mechanism of coordination', *Journal of Economic Issues*, **32** (4), 1053–78.

Kesting, S. (2005), 'Countervailing, conditioned and contingent – the power theory of John Kenneth Galbraith', *Journal of Post-Keynesian Economics*, **28** (1), 3–23.

Kesting, S. (2008), 'Mental models as language-transmitted means of power', in K. Nielsen and C.A. Koch (eds), *Institutionalism in Economics and Sociology: Variety, Dialogue and Future Challenges*, Cheltenham, UK and Northampton, MA, USA: Edward Elgar (forthcoming).

Lang, T. and Y. Gabriel (2005), 'A brief history of consumer activism', in R. Harrison, T. Newholm and D. Shaw (eds), *The Ethical Consumer*, London: Sage, pp. 39–53.

Lukes, S. (1974), *Power: A Radical View*, Basingstoke, UK: Macmillan.

McCloskey, D.N. (1994), *Knowledge and Persuasion in Economics*, Cambridge: Cambridge University Press.

McCloskey, D.N. and A. Klamer (1995), 'One quarter of GDP is persuasion', *American Economic Review (Papers and Proceedings)*, **85** (2), 191–5.

Nelson, R.R. and S.G. Winter (1982), *An Evolutionary Theory of Economic Change*, Cambridge, MA: Belknap Press.

Nelson, R.R. and S.G. Winter (2002), 'Evolutionary theorizing in economics', *Journal of Economic Perspectives*, **16** (2), 23–46.

Nonaka, I. and N. Konno (1998), 'The concept of "Ba": building a foundation for knowledge creation', *California Management Review*, **40** (3), 40–54.

Nooteboom, B. (1999), 'Innovation, learning and industrial organisation', *Cambridge Journal of Economics*, **23**, 127–50.

Nooteboom, B. (2000), *Learning and Innovation in Organizations and Economies*, Oxford and New York: Oxford University Press.

North, D.C. (1996 [1990]), *Institutions, Institutional Change and Economic Performance: Political Economy of Institutions and Decisions*, Cambridge: Cambridge University Press.

North, D.C. (1993), 'Institutions and Economic Performance', in U. Mäki, B. Gustafsson and C. Knudsen (eds), *Rationality, Institutions, and Economic Methodology*, London and New York: Routledge, pp. 242–61.

North, D.C. (1994), 'Economic performance through time', *American Economic Review*, **84** (3), 359–68.

Penrose, E.T. (1959), *The Theory of the Growth of the Firm*, Oxford: Oxford University Press.

Porter, M.E. (1990), 'The competitive advantage of nations', in M.E. Porter (1999), *On Competition*, Boston, MA: Harvard Business Review Book Series, pp. 155–95.

Porter, M.E. (1998), 'Clusters and the new economics of competition', *Harvard Business Review*, November–December, 77–90.

Post, J.E., L.E. Preston and S. Sachs (2002), *Redefining the Corporation: Stakeholder Management and Organizational Wealth*, Stanford, CA: Stanford University Press.

Rubinstein, A. (2000), *Economics and Language: Five Essays*, Cambridge: Cambridge University Press.

Samuels, W.J. (1997), 'Kenneth Boulding's *The Image* and Contemporary Discourse Analysis', in W.J. Samuels, S.G. Medema and A.A. Schmid (eds), *The Economy as a Process of Valuation*, Cheltenham, UK and Lyme, USA: Edward Elgar, pp. 299–327.

Saxenian, A. (2000), 'The origins and dynamics of production networks in Silicon Valley', in R. Swedberg (ed.), *Entrepreneurship: The Social Science View*, Oxford and New York: Oxford University Press, pp. 308–31.

Schumpeter, J.A. (1934 [1911]), *The Theory of Economic Development*, Cambridge, MA: Harvard University Press.

Schumpeter, J.A. (1942), *Capitalism, Socialism and Democracy*, New York: Harper & Row.

Schumpeter, J.A. (2005), 'Development', *Journal of Economic Literature*, **43** (1), 108–20.

Simon, Herbert (1997), *An Empirically Based Microeconomics*, Cambridge, New York and Melbourne: Cambridge University Press.

Smith, A. (1978) [1762–66], *Lectures on Jurisprudence*, Oxford: Oxford University Press, in German as: A. Smith (1996), *Vorlesungen über Rechts- und Staatswissenschaften*, Sankt Augustin: Academia Verlag.

Thompson, G.F. (2003), *Between Hierarchies and Markets: The Logic and Limits of Network Forms of Organization*, Oxford and New York: Oxford University Press.

Ulrich, P. (1987), *Transformation der ökonomischen Vernunft: Fortschrittsperspektiven der modernen Industriegesellschaft*, Bern: Paul Haupt.

Ulrich, P. (1997), *Intergrative Wirtschaftsethik: Grundlagen einer lebensdienlichen Ökonomie*, Bern: Paul Haupt.

Waller, W.T. and L.R. Robertson (1991), 'Valuation as discourse and process – or, how we got out of a methodological quagmire on our way to purposeful institutional analysis', *Journal of Economic Issues*, **25** (4), 1029–48.

Watzlawick, P., J.H. Beavin and D.D. Jackson (1967), *Pragmatics of Human Communication*, New York: W.W. Norton.

Williamson, O.E. (1981), 'The modern corporation: origins, evolution, attributes', *Journal of Economic Literature*, **19**, 1537–68.
Williamson, O.E. (1991), 'Comparative economic organization: the analysis of discrete structural alternatives', *Administrative Science Quarterly*, **36**, 269–96.
Williamson, O.E. (2000), 'The New Institutional Economics: taking stock, looking ahead', *Journal of Economic Literature*, **38**, 595–613.
Zelizer, V. (1997), 'The domestic production of money', in *The Social Meaning of Money*, Princeton, NJ: Princeton University Press, Chapter 2.

24 Methodological approaches in economics and anthropology
Pranab Bardhan and Isha Ray

Economics and anthropology are often seen as extremes along the social science continuum, and the methodological differences between them have rendered interdisciplinary work especially challenging. Our goal in this chapter is not to 'resolve' these methodological divides, but to understand what is important to each discipline, and see the divides in the light of that understanding. There are some foundational dichotomies that broadly divide mainstream economists from mainstream social and cultural anthropologists, and in this chapter we explore the role of these dichotomies.

Crossing the boundaries between economics and anthropology

There have always been some economists and anthropologists who have engaged constructively with the work of the other group. Sahlins argued that the marginalist principles of modern economics were inadequate to explain the gift- and network-based economies of older societies (Sahlins, 1972 [2004]). Geertz (1978) showed that the intense bargaining and client cultivation of markets in Morocco were the result of poorly distributed information and noisy communication networks. Sen placed freedom and individual dignity at the core of his welfare economics (Sen, 1999). Appadurai has engaged in a series of dialogues between his 'enfranchisement' and Sen's 'entitlements', his 'capacities' and Sen's 'capabilities' (Appadurai, 2004). Douglas introduced the framework of cultural theory into traditionally economic concepts such as risk and consumption (Douglas, 1992; Douglas and Isherwood, 1996).

The last two decades have seen a revival of workshops, papers and books on crossing the boundaries between economics, anthropology and sociology. *Conversations between Economists and Anthropologists* (Bardhan, 1989) brought together economists and anthropologists to discuss and compare their analytical methods. That first 'econ–anthro' dialogue focused on diverse approaches to the measurement of economic change in rural India, such as data collection through large *n* surveys versus intensive village-level studies, and the inability of quantitative macro surveys (favored in economics) to capture 'dynamics, processes and relations' (the domain of anthropology). The book illustrates both 'unsuspected areas of potential agreement' and 'legitimate rock-bottom differences' between the two disciplines, particularly as applied to issues of rural development.

In 1997, in a collection of essays on models of the household in developing countries (Haddad et al., 1997), economists and anthropologists contributed their understandings of household bargaining and resource allocation. Anthropological work on the separate spheres of decision-making within households is largely responsible for the recent shift in economics from the unitary model where household members have a joint utility function, to the binary model where the utility functions are gender-specific. In 2001, the 'Qualitative versus Quantitative' (or 'Q2') theme was discussed in a workshop convened by Ravi Kanbur.[1] Particular attention was paid to how (and if) borrowing from 'quant' methods could make 'qual' methods more generalizable and comparable, and to how 'qual' could explicate relationships between variables and so introduce context into 'quant' research. In 2002, the journal *World Development* published several papers on development economics and the 'other' social sciences,[2] in which John Harriss, Cecile Jackson and Howard White critiqued the too-powerful role of economics in development circles, and made the case that sociology, anthropology and politics should be equal players in development policy. The dominant impressions from many of the Q2 and the *World Development* papers are that (1) cross-disciplinary work on social problems is critical and (2) the onus is mostly on the economists to change.

Two recent additions to cross-boundary conversations between economists and anthropologists are Rao and Walton (2004) and Henrich et al. (2004). In *Culture and Public Action*, Rao and Walton reject the stereotypes of economic development being forward-looking and progressive while culture is backward-looking and static. Several contributors to the volume discuss the role of culture in enabling and even defining the goals of development. In *Foundations of Human Sociality*, Henrich and his co-authors, mostly economists and anthropologists, present new findings about human social behavior from a series of experimental games conducted in 'traditional' cultures around the world. The results showed huge variances among these societies, mostly not in line with the predictions of economic theory.

Over time, economists have modified their behavioral premises about, for example, the probability of collective action to protect common resources, based on the results of anthropological case studies (Bromley and Cernea, 1989; Ostrom and Gardner, 1993; Sethi and Somanathan, 1996). Some anthropologists have gone to their field sites ready to test economists' hypotheses on who cooperates and why, and with what degree of fairness or selfishness (as in Henrich et al., 2004). However, many economists and anthropologists remain divided on their views of human agency, on what constitutes data, on how to interpret their respondents' words, and on what constitutes a good, or even adequate, explanation.

The key dichotomies

Explicitly methodological differences between economics and anthropology include quantitative versus qualitative (referring to the nature of data and their analysis), and aggregative versus particular (referring to how the data are used to illuminate social situations). However, as several researchers have concluded, the social sciences are most often split along deeper lines, such as: how do economists and anthropologists view human agency and individual choice? What do economists and anthropologists seek to explain? (Some anthropologists would argue that they do not try to explain, but rather to 'translate' or 'interpret'.) We address these questions via the dichotomies of autonomy versus embeddedness, outcomes versus processes and parsimony versus complexity.

Autonomy versus embeddedness

The debate over whether individuals are best understood as autonomous agents within the constraints of social structures, or as products of the structures that bound their agency, is an old one. 'Men make their own history,' wrote Marx, 'but they do not make it just as they please; they do not make it under circumstances chosen by themselves . . .' (Marx, 1852).[3] Who could disagree? What largely separates economists from anthropologists, then, is the question of what is a meaningful construct of agency given what we want to explain. Three particularly contentious constructs that economists use are methodological individualism, optimizing behavior and exogenous preferences.

For (non-Marxist) economists, the individual is the unit of analysis and his or her 'rational' choices under a set of constraints are what must be explained. Societal characteristics reflect the aggregated result of individual choices and decisions – a point of view known as methodological individualism. Methodological individualism as an analytical concept comes in several versions (Bhargava, 1993; Basu, 2000, pp. 253–4), the most constraining of which have been critiqued from within economics itself (e.g. Arrow, 1994). Methodological individualism does not imply that all social characteristics are reducible to individual characteristics – many norms and practices can emerge as the unintended consequences of thousands of uncoordinated decisions (Schelling, 1978; Sugden, 1989). But economics is fundamentally a social science that explains social phenomena, such as cooperation or trade, in terms of individual choices and motives.

In most economic analyses, individuals are self-regarding – they try to do the best they can for themselves given their economic endowments, their

information sets, and their tastes and preferences. In recent years economists have recognized that a person could exhibit reciprocal rather than
self-regarding behavior, and be selfish to those who were selfish to him but
generous to those who were generous to him (Rabin, 1993; Charness and
Rabin, 2002). Nevertheless, the default assumption in much of microeconomics is that people are exclusively self-regarding. Economists are concerned that frequent deviations from this assumption might open the doors
to an 'anything goes' mentality.

Finally, tastes and preferences in economic analysis are exogenously
given and stable. Why some but not all members of a community have
cooperative propensities, or why lay people around the world cared about
the Bamiyan Buddhas, are not questions within the domain of mainstream
economics. Methodological individualism, utility maximization and exogenous preferences together create what might be called a 'thin' theory of
human action (Taylor, 1988), but it is this thinness that gives microeconomic models their precision, parsimony and predictive power. As Frank
Knight wrote over 60 years ago, the non-economic social sciences are quite
different from economics in that economics is at core a science of conceptual ideals, and not a 'descriptive science in the empirical sense at all'
(Knight, 1941, p. 252). Much theoretical and empirical economic analysis
consists of being precise about the conditions under which particular outcomes might or might not emerge.

With few exceptions, social and cultural anthropologists find the three
characteristics unsatisfactory as an account of human agency. In particular, the notion of exogenous preferences, formed and held at the individual
level, has been widely critiqued. Bourdieu famously argued that preferences
reflect the inner workings of culture and power in a society, that preferences
are formed just as much by the desire for social differentiation as by the
inherent properties of the preferred object (Bourdieu, 1979). In a similar
vein, Appadurai has critiqued survey research methods that treat the
household as an autonomous choice-making unit, because reciprocal relationships between households are central to the choices made by their individual members (Appadurai, 1989, p. 254). More recently, Klamer has
argued that social values and preferences are formed through dialogue,
negotiation and learning – far from being stable, they are constantly being
reassessed (Klamer, 2004). For most meaningful interactions, the individual as the locus of 'given' preferences is not a recognizable object of anthropological inquiry. The critique of exogenous preferences is one aspect of
the broader discomfort with the economist's individual agent. Individuals
have agency, certainly, say anthropologists, but they are situated, embedded
beings rather than autonomous beings who view life as a series of constrained optimization problems.

The operationalization of 'embeddedness' has a rich tradition in anthropology. Polanyi (1954) argued that individuals are characterized by relationships of reciprocity rather than utility-maximizing motives. Even ostensibly market interactions were embedded in, and inseparable from, larger social and political commitments. Dalton (1969), writing in the tradition of Polanyi, pointed out that in the economy viewed as a cluster of individuals the emphasis is on the choices exerted by each economic agent, whereas in the economy viewed as a system of rules into which 'each of us is born' such explicit choice-making is not the analytical framework. Geertz (1963) and Scott (1976) framed peasant societies in South-east Asia as moral economies rather than utilitarian economies. In a moral economy, individuals act not to advance their own well-being, but to make sure that resources and risks are pooled so that everyone has a part in the system. Interactions within local communities are not simply the aggregate effect of individual interests, but the living out of shared understandings of fairness or justice. Moral economy analyses have subsequently been critiqued from within the discipline as being naïve about how power permeates the social fabric. These critics argue that what appears to be a moral economy could be, at least in part, a manifestation of long-standing inequalities or hegemonic control. Embeddedness in reciprocity is in fact embeddedness in unequal relations, and multiple and overlapping notions of identity and interest (Hart, 1997).

Recent literature on economic sociology on the notion of identity in economic and non-economic activities has shown that the non-economic identities of individuals (such as belonging to a team or army unit) strongly influence their behavior in economic spheres (Granovetter, 1985; Akerlof and Kranton, 2005). There are many reasons for this, such as the personal rather than monetary rewards and punishments, and the nuanced nature of the information that social networks can provide. Granovetter (2005) argues that social identities and 'the interaction of the economy with non-economic aspects of social life' affect costs, benefits, techniques and market performance. Economists put their predictive power at risk by ignoring the embeddedness of economic life within the larger social dynamic.

Partly in response to the criticisms of Granovetter (1985) and others of the 'undersocialized conception of man', economists have begun to incorporate social or group effects on the preferences, constraints and beliefs of individual agents (and their aggregate outcomes). Following Manski (1993), one can distinguish between two aspects of an agent's interactions with her community or neighborhood: one is 'contextual' and the other 'endogenous'. The contextual factors are group-specific effects on individuals and are based on characteristics of the group to which the individual belongs. For example, the quality of education (or medical attention) that a female child receives may depend on ethnic or religious characteristics of the community or neighborhood. The endogenous effect relates to reflexive interdependence of behavioral choices of group members. For example, through peer group effects the educational effort of one student influences, and is influenced by, the effort of her friends. The same interdependence occurs in peer pressure for loan repayments in Grameen Bank-type experiments. These (and other) effects of group dynamics and social structures on the economy are part of a growing literature in economics.

Of embeddedness in values, commitments, power and norms, the one intrinsically collective concept that has gained real traction in economics is that of norms. By definition, and unlike preferences or habits, norms cannot be held at the individual level. Basu (2000) makes a strong argument that economists should build norms explicitly into their models, lest they embed them unconsciously instead. He divides norms that are useful for economic analysis into three categories: rationality-limiting, preference-changing and equilibrium-selecting (Basu, 2000, pp. 72–3). A rationality-preventing norm restricts a person from doing things, such as stealing her neighbor's newspaper, even if such an action would increase her utility. Preference-changing norms are those that become internalized into the utility function – the norms become preferences or cause too much guilt or shame if they are violated (see Elster, 1989). Equilibrium-selecting norms help people to choose from among multiple equilibria, such as driving on the right side of the street in the USA but on the left side in the UK. Most of the economic literature is on this third type of norm, which may or may not benefit everyone or even anyone, but once such norms take hold, no one individual has an incentive to deviate from them.[4]

How norms emerge and why they persist are two different questions. Mainstream economic analysis, true to its methodologically individualist roots, explains the emergence of norms as the aggregate (and frequently unintentional) effect of many individual decisions. For instance, Sugden (1989) shows that cooperative norms in the use of driftwood can emerge, 'spontaneously' and without explicit coordination, among the users' group. Once norms have emerged, however, they often persist because it is at least in some individuals' interest to sustain them, or in no one's interest to diverge from them. Or norms of restraint in resource use could evolve and be stable if there are at least some members in the community who are willing to punish rule-violators, even if sanctioning imposes material costs on the punishers (Sethi and Somanathan, 1996). In short, norms, once the domain of anthropology, are now firmly on the economists' agenda.

The remarkable influence of Michel Foucault in contemporary anthropology has led anthropologists to view cooperation- or order-sustaining norms with a critical eye. Foucault argued that governance consisted of certain arts and practices such as measurement, observation and education, through which individuals were 'made' into disciplined and governable 'subjects' (Foucault, 1991). The acceptance of these disciplinary forces circulated through society at large in the mutual enforcement of norms and of legitimated political and cultural discourses. Looking at economists' models of repeated games and the enforcement of cooperation through 'shared' norms, anthropologists would certainly ask not only how these norms emerged, but how their emergence revealed the dynamics of power working through everyday practices, and how the norms enforced the *status quo* – in short, how norms ensured the 'normality' of the ostensibly free individual. There is little room for the economist's autonomous agent in this framework.

Outcomes versus processes

'Economics is mainly about outcomes; anthropology is mainly about processes.' So begins Michael Lipton's review of *Conversations* in the journal *World Development*, 1992. Lipton goes on to acknowledge that models reach their outcomes through processes such as making choices, bargaining and so on. But these are modeled processes – economists rarely conduct empirical investigations of processes themselves. Anthropologists, in contrast, while interested in, for example, the outcomes of social relationships, are most concerned with 'the structure and function of the relationships themselves' and with the processes of exchange or the exercise of power that they generate. The implication is that empirical research in economics samples outcomes (such as the distribution of farm-gate prices), and does not usually sample, and so may gloss over, processes (such as how relationships between farmer and trader are structured, particularly off the equilibrium path, or how they evolve over time).

Outcomes in economic analysis have two characteristics – they serve as predictions (including predicting backward to understand changes that took place in history), and (when possible) they describe equilibrium points in the economy. Prediction is valuable in thinking about social change, and the sharp predictions of economics make it more influential in policy circles than the 'softer' social sciences. But anthropologists are concerned that economists' assumptions and models are too simple to be socially useful, and that prediction of a phenomenon under a given set of constraints is too readily conflated with justification of an existing institutional set-up. Yet others argue that in situations of rapid social and economic change, only the obvious can be 'predicted'. Whether prediction is or is not an explanation, or whether understanding the process is as important as predicting the outcome, are questions that relate to the nature and purpose of explanation in the social sciences.[5] We concentrate here on causal explanations, which are important in both economics and in anthropology.[6]

Causal explanations draw upon repeated empirical observations of the event and its supposed cause, as well as upon theories of the underlying mechanisms that supposedly produce the explained event. In economic theorizing, the causal arrow from cause C to event E is clearly specified. It is built into the model specification, and the model (in theory) stands or falls or wobbles on the basis of the accuracy of its predictions. Attributing causation in a regression analysis is a more complex matter – real data naturally create real problems. The causal arrows are not specified in statistical models; they have to be inferred from the strength and significance of the correlation between the dependent variable and the relevant independent variables. Of course, correlation on its own, however strong, cannot pass for causation. Because of the complexity of real-world data (and because of most researchers' reliance on secondary data), the most common problems econometricians struggle with are sample selection, endogeneity or reverse causality, and omitted variable bias. Economists' attempts at determining causes through hypothesis-testing have in recent years become much more rigorous, particularly through creative use of instrumental variables, and through random evaluations of interventions.

Social and cultural anthropologists explain social phenomena primarily by way of the case-study method.[7] These studies are well equipped to, and often do, investigate causal processes directly. An anthropologist's case study could include a small number of cases, compare two cases, or even conduct within-case analysis of a single case of interest (Ragin, 1987). On the one hand the few-cases method restricts the researcher's ability to generalize beyond his or her study site. On the other hand, anthropologists generally have a better insight into the wellsprings of human behavior, since they regularly live with the respondents, observe their practices, participate in some fashion in their daily lives, and can ask people why they took some action.[8] When the contributors to *Foundations* discovered that their respondents routinely undermined the predictions of bargaining theory, they were able to ask them explicitly about their motives. It was thus discovered that the way the games were played mirrored everyday interactions among the players (Henrich et al., 2004). There are also cases where many alternative causal paths may lead to the same outcome (sometimes called the 'equifinality' problem), and the case-study method may be better equipped to handle these. Some political scientists use what George (1979) calls 'process-tracing', which focuses on an analytical narrative of sequential processes in a causal chain within a particular case (and not on correlations of data across cases).

Case studies, however, are also prone to selection bias, omitted variable bias and (especially) endogeneity, and these errors and biases are often not addressed in the studies. Both sociologists and economists run regressions to statistically measure social effects, but often pay little attention to these possible biases. The proliferating literature on 'social capital' provides many examples of these methodological problems.[9] As we have noted before, one needs in this context to distinguish the effects of choices of others (which are endogenous or what Manski calls 'reflexive') versus the characteristics of others (Manski's 'contextual' effect) on an individual. The endogenous effect gives rise to statistical identification problems[10] which can vitiate the standard causal inferences on the group effects. There is also a self-selection problem since we, at least partly, choose the group or the community we are a part of. In this choice, issues of an individual's endogenous construction of shared identity and its self-reinforcing features are salient. Models with social interaction can also generate multiple equilibria. This raises the possibility that two communities with similar observable characteristics can exhibit different aggregate behaviors. This means we have to be careful about analyzing social effects on aggregate outcomes by simply referring to group-specific characteristics. In aggregating, one should also keep in mind that measured individual returns from a social network may be poor indicators of aggregate externalities. Individual returns will exceed aggregate returns when the network allows some individuals to capture rents at the expense of others in a competitive environment; in contrast, they will underestimate aggregate returns when the positive externalities generated by the social network cannot be fully appropriated by the network insiders.

While anthropologists are better at telling us *how* a variable mattered to the outcome, economists are often better at measuring *how much* it mattered. One creative way in which to combine the strengths of the two disciplines is 'participatory econometrics' (Rao, 2002). This approach includes participatory appraisals, focus group discussions, participant observation and structured surveys in the design of which the respondents participate. While labor- and skill-intensive, such hybrid approaches are likely to yield better insights into causal processes than traditional econometrics, and be more generalizable than traditional case studies.

One of the strengths of anthropologists' concern with process is the ability to explain the multiple ways in which power operates within a society. Economists are also interested in understanding power relations, and much work on the effect of inequality on social cooperation and economic growth has been done by economists.[11] But economists usually model power asymmetries as a standing condition, operationalize them as measurable inequalities, and then work through their consequences for the relevant economic agents. This leads them to overemphasize the material benefits and costs of asymmetry, and to underemphasize the symbolic and disciplining dimensions of power, where power and authority are regularly articulated through diverse institutions.

Anthropologists have brought a much richer understanding of power to the social-theoretic literature. First, as we mentioned, power has symbolic as well as material dimensions, which have to be revealed in the course of observation and analysis (Li, 1996; Mosse, 1997). Second, an understanding of power is incomplete without an understanding of the resistance that oppression can generate, and the history of resource struggles, for example, is replete with such resistance. From struggles to retain the right to use common forest resources in Indonesia (Peluso, 1992), to the protests to stop the displacement of tribal people along the Narmada River (Baviskar, 1995), the exercise of power has generated collective actions that can only be understood as *movements and processes*.

Finally, power is not only the ability to make someone do something that is not in the doer's interest – which is what economics can analyze. It is also, at its most subtle and perhaps most pervasive, the ability to frame the terms of public discussion such that the powerless do not even recognize their powerlessness (Lukes, 1974). The ascendance of critical social theory has brought the issues of language and framing into the core of current anthropology. This discursive turn reflects the influence of post-structuralism, whose starting point is not 'the objective truth' but rather the multiple and coexisting interpretations of social problems. In this framework, 'truths are statements within socially produced discourses rather than objective "facts" about reality' (Peet and Watts, 1996, p. 13). The ways in which different groups and individuals use concepts such as 'immigration' or 'invasive species', and the politics of such representations, become the foci of analysis.[12]

Anthropological research in the wake of critical theory thus undermines the 'naturalness' of familiar categories by revealing how all such categories and regimes are socially constructed, and by so doing, undermines the regimes of power that naturalize these categories. By rejecting the 'community' or the 'local' as pre-existing starting points, for example, Gupta and Ferguson (1997) argue that the researcher is free to explore the feelings, dynamics and processes that go into 'the construction of space as place and locality in the first instance'. The policy and the political implications of either accepting or interrogating these categories are sharply different. Many economists would probably agree that 'the way a question is framed often reveals the accommodation being reached' (Dasgupta, 2002, p. 63), but framings and discourses as instruments of social control are far from central to economic analysis. Such uses of power can only be uncovered through process analysis, and as of now they are squarely in the anthropologists' corner.

Parsimony versus complexity

We have just shown that the explication of the multiple ways in which power works in a society is a strong suit for anthropology. Many economic models allow social structures and cultural norms to emerge from millions of disaggregated individual decisions, with no explicit role for power in the emergence. Each individual choice may be reasonable but together the choices may create an inefficient, unjust or indeed a horrible society. Dasgupta argues that this feature is an achievement of modern economics,

> because it does not rely on postulating predatory governments, or thieving aristocracies, or grasping landlords. This is not to deny their existence, but you don't *need* an intellectual apparatus to conclude that a defenseless person will be robbed if there is an armed robber bent on robbing her. (Dasgupta, 2002, p. 71, our italics)

In a similar spirit, discussing von Thünen's pioneering work on agricultural land use, Krugman shows that a complex and historicized theory of power *was not needed* to explain how land was allocated in the von Thünen model – the assumption of self-interested behavior and strategic interaction was sufficient to allow the spatial pattern of land use to emerge (Krugman, 1995, p. 75). The point that we do not need a particular assumption to explain a particular outcome is an expression of the principle of parsimony, also known as that of 'Occam's Razor'. If there are two theories with equal explanatory power, we should choose the one with the fewer assumptions. This has been a guiding principle for model-building in the physical sciences.

It may not, however, be reasonable to assume that simplicity provides an insight into a particular society, which is a historically evolved system, with layers of change and modification building upon what was already there before it. This is the argument against parsimony that Francis Crick makes with respect to biology, 'While Occam's Razor is a useful tool in the physical sciences, it can be a very dangerous implement in biology. It is . . . rash to use simplicity and elegance as a guide in biological research' (Crick, 1988, p. 138). So why has parsimony been embraced by economics, which is not, after all, a physical science?

The first and most obvious reason is that economics looks for patterns in economic life that, while not universal, are widely generalizable. If, despite differences in culture, norms and values, a similar-enough set of behaviors can be observed in many places and over time, then a small set of simple assumptions may be sufficient to explain them. The most critical element of parsimony has been the assumption of the self-regarding choice-making individual – usually but not always simplified to a utility-maximizing agent. This one assumption, allied in modern economics to strategic interaction, has given economics its theoretical generalizability and practical policy relevance. This assumption is being seriously questioned by experimental and behavioral economists, but even here they look for systematic departures from the canonical model so that, for example, other-regarding behavior can be formalized and utilized for suitable generalizations.

The second and less obvious reason for parsimony in economic theory is the modeler's aesthetic sense. Parsimonious theories explain many observations with few assumptions, and this feature has come to be regarded as elegant. The conventional argument in all the social sciences, including economics, is that empirical tests are the final judges of whether a theory or hypothesis is a good one. Of course, the conditions under which the hypothesis holds – the *ceteris paribus* condition – should be as precisely specified as possible, so the tests conducted are relevant ones. However, there are disagreements among economists about how to test particular theories, about whether in a particular case the *ceteris paribus* condition was (approximately) met, about model specification, and so on. All the social sciences have running debates about what the 'data' show, and as a result, more than in the natural sciences, several competing and conflicting theories and hypotheses coexist within each discipline. In these circumstances, despite official agreement on the importance of empirically informed theorizing in economics, if there appear to be trade-offs between elegance and relevance, parsimony is likely to be the guiding principle (Klamer, 1988, p. 245).

Parsimonious explanations are not particularly favored in anthropology. There are two important and related reasons for this – the role of the anthropologist in her research and the methodological philosophies of major schools of anthropology. Anthropology as a discipline has a history of being concerned with non-Western non-capitalist economies, with a mission to explore the particular and the unique, and to translate other 'lifeworlds' into social-scientific discourse. There was a time when this mission was not especially progressive, let alone emancipatory – rather, it served to cement colonial stereotypes or exoticize other cultures (see, e.g., Asad, 1991). Today, however, the role of the anthropologist in research is conceived in a more complex way than that of the economist. For example, an empirical economist adopts the role of a neutral observer when in the field, gathering data about her subjects while remaining at all times a dispassionate outsider. Some anthropologists are in this category, but an increasing number are not willing to admit the possibility of a wholly neutral position. The attention to the formation of the subject at the intersection of power and knowledge has made researchers conscious of the asymmetries implicit in conducting surveys and interviews, which then purport to 'represent' their respondents to the wider world. Thus these researchers see themselves as empathetic rather than neutral observers, or interpreters of speech and action 'from the inside', or even as partners in their respondents' aspirations and struggles (Blaikie, 2000, p. 52).

Moreover, the epistemological position of major schools of anthropology is not to focus just on the seen and heard, but to look for hidden meanings, to listen for the unspoken, to interpret culture from the insider's perspective (Geertz, 2000) – in short, to 'make strange the familiar'. The traditional concern of anthropology with the particular and the unique has also made the genealogical approach of Foucault (1980, 1997) especially influential in this discipline. The genealogical approach argues that societies change through a series of power struggles and that there is no overarching or predictable trajectory to this unfolding. There are no universalizable evolutionary laws, no 'grand theories' of change as such. The methodological consequence of this framework is that the role of the social scientist is to reveal the *contingent* course that has shaped a society, and through this method, to contest notions of necessary orders and structures.[13] This is a very different project from that of economics – if anything, the project is to complicate rather than to simplify, question the unquestioned, and be wary of neat and tidy 'parsimonious' explanations.

The difference between a parsimonious and a complicating approach has had enormous consequences for the role of economics and anthropology in policy circles. In formulating causal explanations, the parsimony principle leads economists to insulate the effect of one variable, controlling for others, so that they can measure its direct effect. Anthropologists throw into the analysis a much larger set of factors to capture the essential multidimensionality of action – without telling us what the effect of each factor by itself will be. A cause may never be attributable to one factor; the symbolic and the material may be considered inseparable in judging effect. The economist's approach is needed if we want to use the research results to guide policy advice. We would want to know about the impact of a particular policy that largely has an impact on one variable (e.g. property rights). We could legitimately argue that too much inseparability and too much multidimensionality would make policy advice impossible, and could lead to an accumulation of possibly relevant factors without providing clues about how to sort the accumulated evidence.

Anthropologists acknowledge that policy advice requires simplifying assumptions and generalizable conclusions, and detailed analyses of complex situations are not conducive to either. But they could legitimately argue that policies are implemented in unequal social, cultural and economic settings, and that the impacts of these inequalities are more complex than policy analysts realize, or may even want to know. Simplification for the sake of policy could lead to new methods of social control (Li, 2002). And parsimonious explanations of central tendencies could lead to the further marginalization of the already marginal, particularly in terms of learning about omitted variables (Rao, 2002).

Conclusion
In this chapter we have argued that one of the key barriers to interdisciplinary work between economists and anthropologists is differences in methodology and epistemology – in what the two disciplines consider important to explain, and how they evaluate the criteria for a good explanation. We have highlighted three dichotomies that are emblematic of some of these differences: autonomy versus embeddedness, outcomes versus processes and parsimony versus complexity. A discussion of dichotomies is, of course, just one possible opening into a fruitful conversation between economists and anthropologists. We hope our discussion leads at least some economists and anthropologists critically to examine the assumptions and modes of analysis that may sometimes go unquestioned within each discipline.

Notes
1. The papers from the conference can be read at http://www.q-squared.ca/papers01.html. Accessed 15 February 2007.
2. *World Development*, **30** (3), 2002.
3. While Marx was referring to what economists somewhat crudely would call a constrained optimization equilibrium, the historian François Furet would suggest multiple equilibria and unintended consequences when he said, 'Men make history but do not know which one' (Furet, 1978).
4. It should be noted that all three norm families are considered constraints in economics – they are exogenous to the individual and they restrict her feasibility set.
5. A set of classic readings in epistemology and the nature of explanation can be found in Rosenberg (1988).
6. Some anthropological explanations such as symbolic interactionism are non-causal in nature.
7. The term 'case study' could imply that the case in question belongs to a family of cases with similar or generalizable characteristics. There are anthropologists who view their work as explaining what is particular or unique about a situation, and who therefore reject the 'case' terminology.
8. David Szanton points out that the immersion in the field that is often a rite of passage in social and cultural anthropology is itself a form of 'embeddedness'.
9. For a critical assessment of this literature see Durlauf and Fafchamps (2004).
10. For a discussion of the econometric issues involved, see Brock and Durlauf (2001).
11. See, for example, the papers from the *MacArthur Research Network on Inequality and Economic Performance*: http://globetrotter.berkeley.edu/macarthur/inequality/.
12. In anthropological writings, these questions are often phrased in a somewhat disembodied or agent-less manner: 'How does this issue get represented? How does it get used? How does discourse get reproduced?'
13. In contrast, we may note that while sociologists do consider Foucault to be a key social theorist, the structuralist roots of sociology have made him far less central to that discipline than to anthropology.

References

Akerlof, George and Rachel Kranton (2005), 'Identity and the economics of organizations', *Journal of Economic Perspectives*, **19**, 9–32.

Appadurai, Arjun (1989), 'Small-scale techniques and large-scale objectives', in Pranab Bardhan (ed.), *Conversations between Economists and Anthropologists: Methodological Issues in Measuring Economic Change in Rural India*, New Delhi: Oxford University Press, pp. 250–82.

Appadurai, Arjun (2004), 'The capacity to aspire: culture and the terms of recognition', in V. Rao and M. Walton (eds), *Culture and Public Action*, Stanford, CA: Stanford Social Sciences, pp. 59–84.

Arrow, Kenneth J. (1994), 'Methodological individualism and social knowledge', *American Economic Review*, **84**, 1–9.

Asad, Talal (1991), 'Afterword – from the history of colonial anthropology to the anthropology of western hegemony', in George W. Stocking (ed.), *Colonial Situations: Essays on the Contextualization of Ethnographic Knowledge*, Madison, WI: University of Wisconsin Press, pp. 314–24.

Bardhan, Pranab (ed.) (1989), *Conversations between Economists and Anthropologists: Methodological Issues in Measuring Economic Change in Rural India*, New Delhi: Oxford University Press.

Basu, Kaushik (2000), *Prelude to Political Economy: A Study of the Social and Political Foundations of Economics*, Oxford and New York: Oxford University Press.

Baviskar, Amita (1995), *In the Belly of the River: Tribal Conflicts over Development in the Narmada Valley*, Delhi and New York: Oxford University Press.

Bhargava, Rajeev (1993), *Individualism in Social Science: Forms and Limits of Methodology*, Oxford: Oxford University Press.

Blaikie, Norman (2000), *Designing Social Research*, Malden, MA: Blackwell.

Bourdieu, Pierre (1979), *Distinction: A Social Critique of the Judgment of Taste*, London: Routledge.

Brock, W. and S. Durlauf (2001), 'Interaction-based models', in J. Heckman and E. Leamer (eds), *Handbook of Econometrics*, Vol. 5, Amsterdam: Elsevier, pp. 3297–380.

Bromley, D.W. and M.M. Cernea (1989), 'The management of common-property natural resources: some conceptual and operational fallacies', World Bank Discussion Papers No. 57. Washington, DC: The World Bank.

Charness, Gary and Matthew Rabin (2002), 'Understanding social preferences with simple tests', *Quarterly Journal of Economics*, **117**, 817–69.

Crick, Francis (1988), *What Mad Pursuit: A Personal View of Scientific Discovery*, New York: Basic Books.

Dalton, George (1969), 'Theoretical issues in economic anthropology', *Current Anthropology*, **10**, 63–102.

Dasgupta, Partha (2002), 'Modern economics and its critics', in Uskali Mäki (ed.), *Fact and Fiction in Economics: Models, Realism and Social Construction*, Cambridge: Cambridge University Press, pp. 57–89.

Douglas, Mary (1992), *Risk and Blame: Essays in Cultural Theory*, London and New York: Routledge.

Douglas, Mary and Baron Isherwood (1996), *The World of Goods: Towards an Anthropology of Consumption*, London and New York: Routledge.

Durlauf, S. and M. Fafchamps (2004), 'Social capital', Working Paper, University of Wisconsin, Madison.

Elster, Jon (1989), *The Cement of Society: A Study of Social Order*, New York: Cambridge University Press.

Foucault, Michel (1980), *Power/Knowledge: Selected Interviews and Other Writings, 1972–1977*, ed. and trans. Colin Gordon, Sussex: Harvester.

Foucault, Michel (1991), 'Governmentality', in G. Burchell, C. Gordon and P. Miller (eds), *The Foucault Effect: Studies in Governmentality*, London: Harvester Wheatsheaf, pp. 87–104.

Foucault, Michel (1997), *The Essential Works of Michel Foucault, 1954–1984*, ed. Paul Rabinow, New York: New Press, distributed by W.W. Norton.

Furet, François (1978), *Penser la Révolution Française*, trans. Elborg Forster, Paris: Editions Gallimard.

Geertz, Clifford (1963), *Agricultural Involution: The Process of Ecological Change in Indonesia*, Berkeley, CA: University of California Press.

Geertz, Clifford (1978), 'The bazaar economy: information and search in peasant marketing', *American Economic Review*, **68**, 28–32.

Geertz, Clifford (2000), *Local Knowledge: Further Essays in Interpretive Anthropology*, New York: Basic Books.

George, Alexander L. (1979), 'The causal nexus between cognitive beliefs and decision-making behavior', in L.S. Falkowski (ed.), *Psychological Models in International Politics*, Boulder, CO: Westview Press, pp. 95–124.

Granovetter, Mark (1985), 'Economic action and social structure: the problem of embeddedness', *American Journal of Sociology*, **91**, 481–510.

Granovetter, Mark (2005), 'The impact of social structure on economic outcomes', *Journal of Economic Perspectives*, **19**, 33–50.

Gupta, Akhil and James Ferguson (1997), 'Beyond culture: space, identity and the politics of difference', in Akhil Gupta and James Ferguson (eds), *Culture, Power, Place: Explorations in Critical Anthropology*, Durham, NC: Duke University Press, pp. 33–51.

Haddad, Lawrence, John Hoddinott and Harold Alderman (1997), *Intrahousehold Resource Allocation in Developing Countries: Models, Methods, and Policy*, Baltimore, MD: Johns Hopkins University Press.

Hart, Gillian (1997), 'From rotten wives to good mothers: household models and the limits of economism', *IDS Bulletin*, **28**, 14–25.

Henrich, Joseph, Robert Boyd, Samuel Bowles, Colin Camerer, Ernst Fehr and Herbert Gintis (eds) (2004), *Foundations of Human Sociality*, Oxford: Oxford University Press.

Klamer, Arjo (1988), *Conversations with Economists*, Totowa, NJ: Rowman & Allanheld.

Klamer, Arjo (2004), 'Cultural goods are good for more than their economic value', in V. Rao and M. Walton (eds), *Culture and Public Action*, Stanford, CA: Stanford Social Sciences, pp. 138–62.

Knight, Frank (1941), 'Economics and anthropology', *Journal of Political Economy*, **49**, 247–68.

Krugman, Paul (1995), *Development, Geography and Economic Theory*, Cambridge, MA: MIT Press.

Li, Tania M. (1996), 'Images of community: discourse and strategy in property relations', *Development and Change*, **27**, 501–27.

Li, Tania M. (2002), 'Engaging simplifications: community-based resource management, market processes and state agendas in upland Southeast Asia', *World Development*, **30**, 265–83.

Lipton, Michael (1992), 'Economics and anthropology: grounding models in relationships', *World Development*, **20**, 1541–6.

Lukes, Steven (1974), *Power: A Radical View*, London: Macmillan.

Manski, C. (1993), 'Identification of endogenous social effects: the reflection problem', *Review of Economic Studies*, **60**, 531–42.

Marx, Karl (1852) (1981 printing), *The Eighteenth Brumaire of Louis Bonaparte*, New York: International Publishers.

Mosse, David (1997), 'The symbolic making of a common property resource: history, ecology and locality in a tank-irrigated landscape in South India', *Development and Change*, **28**, 467–504.

Ostrom, Elinor and R. Gardner (1993), 'Coping with asymmetries in the commons: self-governing irrigation systems can work', *Journal of Economic Perspectives*, **7**, 93–112.

Peet, Richard and Michael Watts (1996), *Liberation Ecologies: Environment, Development, Social Movements*, New York: Routledge.

Peluso, Nancy (1992), *Rich Forests, Poor People: Resource Control and Resistance in Java*, Berkeley, CA: University of California Press.

Polanyi, Karl (1954), *The Great Transformation*, Boston, MA: Beacon.
Rabin, Matthew (1993), 'Incorporating fairness into game theory and economics', *American Economic Review*, **83**, 1281–302.
Ragin, Charles (1987), *The Comparative Method: Moving beyond Qualitative and Quantitative Strategies*, Berkeley, CA: University of California Press.
Rao, Vijayendra (2002), 'Experiments in participatory econometrics', *Economic and Political Weekly*, 18 May.
Rao, Vijayendra and Michael Walton (eds) (2004), *Culture and Public Action*, Stanford, CA: Stanford Social Sciences.
Rosenberg, Alexander (1988), *Philosophy of Social Science*, Boulder, CO: Westview Press.
Sahlins, Marshall (1972 [2004]), *Stone Age Economics*, London and New York: Routledge.
Schelling, Thomas (1978), *Micromotives and Macrobehavior*, New York: W.W. Norton.
Scott, James (1976), *The Moral Economy of the Peasant*, New Haven, CT: Yale University Press.
Sen, Amartya (1999), *Development as Freedom*, New York: Knopf.
Sethi, Rajiv and E. Somanathan (1996), 'The evolution of social norms in common property use', *American Economic Review*, **86**, 766–88.
Sugden, R. (1989), 'Spontaneous order', *Journal of Economic Perspectives*, **3**, 85–97.
Taylor, Michael (1988), 'Rationality and revolutionary collective action', in M. Taylor (ed.), *Rationality and Revolution*, Cambridge: Cambridge University Press, pp. 63–97.

PART VIII

FINANCE, MONEY AND POLICY

Chapter 25: 'Saving, stock market investments and pension systems', by Martha A. Starr

Saving, investments and pensions are avenues by which households build up claims to future income and consumption. Such claims are important in a number of respects: they broaden people's options, reduce their insecurities about material living standards, and enhance their ability to live with dignity in old age. As such, understanding the multiplicity of factors that shape how people save, invest and acquire pension rights is important for understanding their access to well-being and the ways in which social arrangements improve or undercut that access. This chapter reviews social economic perspectives on these macroeconomic issues, highlighting contributions of existing research and identifying fruitful directions for future work.

Chapter 26: 'Monetary policy', by Sheila C. Dow

Mainstream theory and monetary policy practice have been identified as converging on a 'new consensus'. There are dissenting voices – monetarists continue to focus on monetary aggregates, while Keynesians focus on the non-neutrality of money and consider a wider range of monetary policy instruments. The interest rate is nevertheless seen by all as the predominant tool of monetary policy. Each approach can be distinguished by the mechanisms of transmission of monetary policy, as the official interest rate affects expectations in asset markets and asset pricing on the one hand, and real social experience on the other. It is argued here that there is a disconnect between these two broad channels of transmission; it is through the latter that monetary policy has its real effects. Current issues in the literature are considered, notably those surrounding credibility, expectations and the relevance of monetary aggregates, and unresolved issues for the future are outlined.

Chapter 27: 'Banking, finance and money: a social economics approach', by L. Randall Wray

This chapter briefly summarizes the orthodox approach to banking, finance and money, and then points the way towards an alternative based on social economics. It argues that the alternative approach is better fitted to the historical record, and also sheds more light on the nature of money in modern economies. In orthodoxy, money is something that reduces transaction costs, simplifying 'economic life' by lubricating the market mechanism. However, the orthodox story of money's origins is rejected by most serious scholars outside the field of economics as historically inaccurate. By contrast, this chapter locates the origin of money in credit and debt relations, with the money of account emphasized as the numeraire in which credits and debts are measured. Importantly, the money of account is chosen by the state, and is enforced through denominating tax liabilities in the state's own currency. The alternative view of money leads to quite different conclusions regarding monetary and fiscal policy, and it rejects even long-run neutrality of money. It also generates interesting insights on exchange rate regimes and international payments systems.

Chapter 28: 'Global finance and development: false starts, dead ends and social economic alternatives', by Ilene Grabel

The chapter explores the contribution of social economics to finance and development. It presents a brief account of the mainstream neoclassical approach to finance and traces its historical development. It demonstrates that the failures of this approach stem from key weaknesses in the neoclassical approach. Finally, the chapter considers a range of heterodox contributions to the debate over finance and development that draw on themes and presumptions that are central to social economics. Many of these contributions share something with social economics, emphasize the connections between economic and non-economic institutions and practices, and foreground normative goals that reach far beyond (and often reject) the neoclassical commitment to efficiency. We also find in these accounts particular concern for those worst off, for the ways in which financial arrangements can exacerbate or ameliorate inequality, and a concern with the effect of financial arrangements on political voice and on national policy autonomy.

25 Saving, stock market investments and pension systems
Martha A. Starr

Saving, stock market investments and pensions are avenues by which households build up claims to future income and consumption. Such claims are important in a number of respects: they broaden people's options, reduce their insecurities about material living standards, and enhance their ability to live with dignity in old age. As such, understanding the multiplicity of factors that shape how people save, invest and acquire pension rights is important for understanding their access to well-being and the ways in which social arrangements improve or undercut that access.

Saving

In the traditional life-cycle view of saving, households maximize utility over the life cycle, resulting in a profile whereby they borrow when young, save in mid-life, and spend down their assets when older; then total household saving is aggregated up from the behavior of independent households. Social economists share the criticisms of this perspective found in other fields, including feminist economics, behavioral economics, post-Keynesian economics, and economic methodology, which include: (1) the representation of households as monolithic, ignoring issues of gender and power within the household (Ferber and Nelson, 1993; Floro and Seguino, 2003); (2) conceptualizing cognition as general-purpose and powerful, rather than an assembly of special-purpose processes subject to limitations (Simon, 1955; Thaler, 1994; Dietz and Stern, 1995); (3) ignoring possibilities that differential saving across the income distribution may push aggregate supply out of balance with aggregate demand (Hobson, 1910; Ryan, 1935; Yunker, 1997; Froud et al., 2001), and (4) more generally, the problem of refuting a theory of behavior that only needs people to act 'as if' the theory explains their behavior (Davis, 2003).

Other alternative views of saving are more specific to social economics. First, whereas traditional theory takes preferences involved in consumption and saving to be given, social economics emphasizes how important social and cultural factors are in shaping how people perceive and value alternatives and decide among them (O'Boyle, 1994; Davis, 2003; Lee and Keen, 2004). Issues of potential importance here include socio-cultural

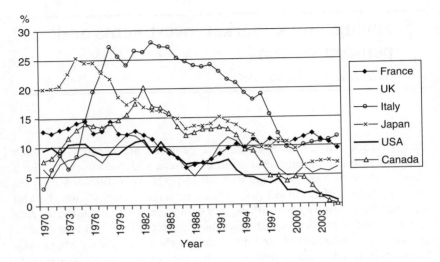

Source: OECD.

Figure 25.1   Household saving as a percentage of disposable income

norms that favor high consumption (Veblen, 1994 [1899]; Duesenberry, 1949; Schor, 1999; Shipman, 2004), the role of advertising in promoting spending (Galbraith, 1958), and public discourses of values such as thrift and self-control (Ryan, 1935; Tucker, 1991; Starr, 2007). Some evidence suggests that such factors have contributed to the slide in household saving rates in many OECD countries the past 25 years (see Figure 25.1): notably, studies using survey data for the USA show a broad-based decline in saving across all socio-demographic groups, consistent with a general cultural phenomenon such as an increase in the discount rate (Bosworth et al., 1991; Parker, 1999).[1] More work should be done to understand relations between preferences, culture and economic forces, and the ways in which they may fuel problems of unsustainable consumption in industrial countries (Norgaard, 1995; Røpke, 1999; Jackson, 2004).

A second departure from the standard approach concerns the *a priori* framing of consumption and saving as matters of autonomous households looking after themselves. Clearly, ties with broader networks of family, friends and neighbors, and with voluntary and community organizations, at least potentially provide a wealth of extra resources that people can call on in times of need, and to which they may contribute. Thus Guerin (2003) speaks of the need for putting a 'radical socialness' into our understanding of consumer behavior. Mainstream discourse is not oblivious to this point, as the large literature on strategic versus altruistic transfers attests.[2] However, for social economists the question is not whether people are 'essentially' social or 'essentially' self-interested – but rather how, when and why social dimensions of behavior come to be favored (Lutz, 1990; Davis, 2003).

Third, whereas the traditional view makes no distinction between wants and needs, the acceptance of 'needs' in the social framework (involving both social and biophysical dimensions) adds complexity to the analysis of saving behavior.[3] In the traditional view, the level of a household's income does not affect its saving: both low- and high-income households save to smooth consumption over the life cycle, so the savings behavior of the former will just be a scaled-down version of that of the latter, as long as their lifetime earnings profiles have the same shape. However, if needs must be met before income can be allocated to saving, certain groups of people may find it impossible to save. Thus, within populations of wealthy countries, we would expect to find little saving among households with low incomes, many mouths to feed, uninsured medical expenses and so on; across countries, we would expect saving rates to be lower among countries with relatively poor populations. While both of these implications are supported by the data (Friend and Schor, 1959; Leff, 1969; Bunting, 1991; Paxson, 1996; Huggett and Ventura, 2000), the role of needs in explaining them remains to be established. Thus, for example, Hubbard et al. (1995) argue that low-income households in the USA fail to save, not because of inability to do so, but rather because asset-based means-testing for social insurance programs effectively penalizes saving; the policy implication that low saving can be 'solved' by removing disincentives would just increase hardship if failure to save in fact reflected inability to do so. Understanding how needs are involved in inability to save is particularly important for policies related to pensions and social security, as will be discussed below.[4]

Stock market investments
Social economic analysis of stock markets highlights that, rather than being forums for exchange whose origin and position can be taken for granted, stock markets are institutions, constructed and regulated by people, that need to be seen in terms of the social and economic relations in which they are situated. There are three dimensions to looking at the stock market through a social lens.

The first concerns the conduct of the market itself. Standard narratives of how financial markets work can give such minimal attention to human and social factors that they can resemble descriptions of how atoms behave in particle accelerators, more than representations of activities organized and carried out by humans. Yet trading is carried out by people whose reasons for behaving may or may not include considerations other than making the most possible amount of money, and whose behavior is shaped by legal and institutional constraints and socially determined rules. Thus Abolafia (1996) studied the social dynamics among traders in stock, bond and future markets, highlighting the importance of social and institutional factors in understanding how these markets work, including 'the strength and efficacy of reputational and trust networks among buyers and sellers, the shifting balance of power among stakeholder groups in the market, the strength and efficacy of institutionalized norms and rules of exchange, and the role of state intervention in shaping market relations' (ibid., p. 190). Also of interest to social economists are ethical dimensions of financial transactions and their intersection with law and regulation; see, for example, John Ryan (1935) on speculation, and Phillip O'Hara (1998) on insider trading.[5]

Second, stock markets are associated with a way of structuring relations of production that shapes the distribution of power and wealth in industrial societies. An important issue here is the separation of ownership and control associated with the growth of large-scale enterprises: from the mid-nineteenth century on, railroads and mass-production businesses required such great amounts of capital that large pools of investors were needed to finance them, and responsibility for managing operations was delegated to executives (Veblen, 1908; Berle and Means, 1932). This separation is potentially a source of efficiency problems in so far as incentives of managers may be imperfectly aligned with those of shareholders (Fama and Jensen, 1983). But it also creates important equity problems, in that it bestows considerable power and authority on a privileged executive class. Concerns about equity flared in the 1990s when average CEO pay skyrocketed, reaching 300 to 500 times the earnings of average workers in the USA (see Figure 25.2).[6] Social economics has valuable insights to offer on the question of whether such extraordinary income differentials should be tolerated on ethical grounds. For example, the 1986 Pastoral Letter of the US Catholic Bishops argues that people do not have a right to unlimited incomes when the needs of others are unmet.[7] John Ryan (1916, pp. 226–7) argued that most cases of large profits arise in markets that are uncompetitive in structure or conduct, and so should be addressed by enforcing appropriate economic policies; but when large profits are fairly earned, they should be paid out to 'active workers, from the president of the concern down to the humblest day laborer, [since] this arrangement would return the surplus to those who had created it and would prove a powerful stimulus to sustained and increased efficiency'. More work could be done to use such insights to develop conceptually rigorous approaches to the ethics of CEO pay.

The structuring of relations of production associated with stock markets also entails an exclusion of employees and communities from power or

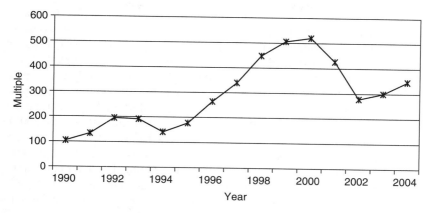

Source: Author's computations using *Business Week*'s annual Executive Pay Scoreboard (usually published in April) and the Bureau of Labor Statistics (2004) data on average weekly earnings of production workers (multiplied by 52 to convert to an annual basis).

Figure 25.2 *Average CEO pay as a multiple of average earnings of production workers, 1990–2004*

voice in control of the productive process – something Jon Wisman (1988) had identified as a central problem of industrial democracies. Framing the employees of a firm as doing nothing other than supplying labor services denies that part of the value of the firm's capital was created by its employees (US Catholic Bishops, 1986). It also both conceals and reinforces the problem that worklife in large organizations can have limited intrinsic value: when what is needed of a worker is defined by his/her position in the complex structure of the firm's operations, there may be minimal opportunities for creative contribution, self-development, self-expression or realization of self-worth.

Thus a number of schemes have been explored as ways of fostering more participatory forms of organization that acknowledge and promote workers' integral contributions. The most comprehensive is the idea of worker-owned and -managed firms, in which employees run all aspects of the firm's operations; they may also build ties with surrounding communities (see Ellerman, 1986, 1993; Gunn, 2000). Other schemes entail less radical changes in organizational form while still aiming to insert workers into the discourses of owners and managers. These include employee stock ownership plans (ESOPs), whereby workers can buy stock in the company; profit-sharing plans, in which workers get a bonus linked to firm performance; and stock options, which permit employees to buy company stock at a favorable price in a specified period of time.[8]

Available research suggests that these kinds of participatory programs tend to be associated with greater employee well-being – although to bring about appreciable improvements, they are best combined with broader efforts to restructure decision-making within the firm (Freeman et al., 2000; Morehouse et al., 2000, p. 70). Interestingly, when used blatantly as incentive devices, stock ownership and profit-sharing schemes can actually erode productivity and morale; rather, they seem to work best when they underline the intrinsic value of work (Frey, 1997a, 1997b; Arocena and Villanueva, 2003). However, an undesirable consequence of such schemes is that they create a strong positive correlation between workers' labor earnings and their financial assets. Thus, for example, when the Color Tile Company went bankrupt in 1997, workers both lost their jobs and saw the value of their retirement accounts plummet, since the latter were invested overwhelmingly in company stock (Wiatrowski, 2000; Muelbroek, 2002).[9]

Thus, other schemes hold up broad-based, diversified stock ownership as a means of shifting workers out of subordinate, excluded positions in relations of production – and into positions where they can share its fruits more fully. In the USA, ideas such as those in Kelso and Adler's (1958) *Capitalist Manifesto* and Speiser's program for a Universal Stock Ownership Plan have figured into public discourse about how to humanize the economy and improve its moral footing, although the profound sorts of changes they advocate make them difficult to get off the ground (Morehouse et al., 2000). More recently, in transition economies it was hoped that 'voucher privatization' would pave the way to a participatory capitalism in which the benefits of free market growth would be widely distributed. For the most part, these schemes failed to work as planned, as the general public sold its asset claims (whose values were then highly uncertain) to small groups of investors (Black et al., 2000).

Even so, stock ownership has been rising in the industrial world due to ongoing trends: the growth of mutual funds, the introduction of tax-deferred retirement accounts with investment options, and a long period of rising prices (Guiso et al., 2002). Stock ownership is most widespread in the USA, where almost half of all households owned stock in some form in 1998, up from one-third in 1989 (Bertaut and Starr, 2002, p. 190).[10] Still, this increased ownership has had a negligible effect on relations of production because it involves no change in participation in decision-making, and because stock ownership remains strongly concentrated in the high end of the wealth distribution; for example, in the USA, two-thirds of the value of total stock owned by households was held by those in the top 5 percent of the wealth distribution in 1998 (ibid., p. 196). This illustrates that the idea, expressed for example by Marshall in 1923 (p. 68), that ownership of stock by 'multitudes of small capitalists' would 'strengthen the position of the middle classes relatively to the working classes on the one hand and to the wealthy classes on the other' has never been very close to the truth.

A third dimension of stock markets of social economic interest is the role of ethical and social factors in decisions of investors. Starting with efforts to promote divestment from South Africa during the apartheid era (Lashgari and Gant, 1989), a growing segment of stock market investors has come to make investment decisions based in part on the ethics of a company's products and/or business practices, in addition to considerations of risk and return. 'Socially responsible investing', or SRI, as it is known, had initially involved staying away from companies of certain types: those that profit from addiction (tobacco, alcohol, gambling), deal in means of violent force (weapons, defense services), exploit sweatshop labor, operate in countries that abuse human rights, have poor labor practices, treat animals inhumanely, use environmentally unsound production methods, and/or produce products with adverse environmental effects (Bruyn, 1991). Now SRI also involves 'positive' as well as 'negative' screening, that is, deliberately seeking out and favoring companies that use socially responsible practices or produce products that are socially beneficial. In the USA in 2003, about $2 trillion was managed with social responsibility taken into account, representing about 11 percent of the value of financial assets under professional management; while foundations, church pensions and charities represent an important part of the social investment movement, SRI funds are increasingly being offered as an investment option in 401(k)-type retirement plans (Social Investment Forum, 2003). To date, only a few economic studies have investigated the effects of SRI on companies' behavior. Teoh et al. (1999) found that, although the South African boycott did not push down the stock prices of targeted companies (apparently because institutional investors bought stock that socially concerned investors were unloading), targeted companies did shut down their South African operations, leading the authors to conclude that SRI should be thought of as a 'powerful and effective means to achieve social change'. More economic research on the effects of SRI would be valuable.[11]

Pension systems

As the fields fear drought in autumn, so people fear poverty in old age.
                                                                 Chinese proverb

Before the advent of old-age pension systems, the lives of older people were often ones of insecurity and deprivation: decreasingly able to work, but not necessarily having savings or the care of family members to fall back on, many older people reduced their spending to minimal levels, in line with their limited means. Addressing the problem of old-age poverty was a central concern of social insurance programs put in place by industrial democracies over the course of the twentieth century. As US president Franklin Delano Roosevelt said upon signing the Social Security Act of 1935:

> The civilization of the past hundred years, with its startling industrial changes, has tended more and more to make life insecure . . . We can never insure 100% of the population against 100% of the hazards and vicissitudes of life, but we have tried to frame a law which will give some measure of protection to the average citizen and to his family against the loss of a job and against poverty-ridden old age.[12]

Public pension programs have been highly effective in reducing poverty in old age; in the USA, for example, the poverty rate among people aged 65 and older fell from 30 percent in the mid-1960s, when social security benefits were made more generous, to about 10 percent in the early 2000s (Figure 25.3).[13] Because most public-pension systems replace only 40–60 percent of the worker's pre-retirement pay,[14] some private employers also provide pension coverage to close the gap. Private pensions may be either *defined-benefit* plans, which provide a set monthly amount paid indefinitely based on years of service and salary level, or *defined-contribution* plans, where the employer and/or employee contribute to a retirement account, usually on a tax-deferred basis.[15] The importance of private pensions in retirement income varies considerably across countries, in part reflecting

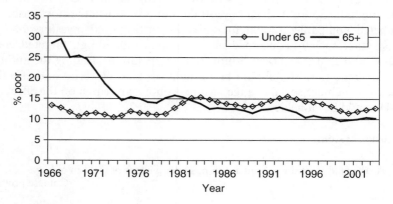

Source: US Census Bureau, Current Population Survey, Annual Social and Economic Supplements.

Figure 25.3   Poverty rates by age, US population, 1966–2003

differences in the ability of organized labor to win pension promises from employers; uniformly, however, men are more likely than women to be covered under private pension plans.[16]

An important policy issue concerns the expectation that in coming years, public pension schemes will become increasingly difficult to sustain fiscally due to population aging. Slowing rates of population growth and rising life expectancies have increased the shares of older people in the populations of industrial countries (see Figure 25.4); with such trends expected to continue well into the twenty-first century, expenditures on pensions are expected to become increasingly burdensome relative to national output (OECD, 2003). There is much debate, however, about whether radical measures are required to address this problem. Possible changes under discussion include reducing early retirement options (a particularly important possibility in Europe since such options are widely used), increasing the normal retirement age, notching up payroll taxes used to finance pension payments, and scaling back payments to wealthy retirees. Measures of a more radical nature favor increasing reliance on private saving for retirement. The outcomes of this policy debate are important because many people depend heavily on public pensions for income during retirement; for example, in the USA in 2001, more than one-fifth of workers aged 55 to 64 had no retirement savings other than social security (Weller and Wolff, 2005).

While much economic research explores effects of pensions and social security on labor supply, saving behavior and fiscal balance, contributions

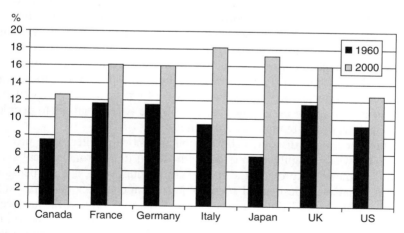

Source: World Bank, *World Development Indicators.*

Figure 25.4 Share of population aged 65 and older

from social economics have tended to emphasize issues of *values* in retirement income policies. In general, public pensions have represented the kind of constructive social intervention that social economists tend to support: they have reduced material and psychological insecurities, they have advanced people's abilities to live a dignified old age, they have taken the burden off people to carry out complicated life-cycle planning, and they have reinforced ideas that pooling resources and managing them together can advance the common good. Thus, not surprisingly, social economists tend to object to the types of 'pension reforms' advocated by the World Bank and implemented in the UK and Chile, which aim to replace fixed-income pensions with mixed systems centered around individual accounts (Niggle, 2000, 2003; Dixon and Hyde, 2003; Ervik, 2005). Because returns to saving into such accounts are uncertain, they recreate insecurities about living standards in old age, which have anyway been much aggravated by concerns about rising healthcare costs.

Several ideas from social economics could be usefully integrated into the academic and policy discourses of public pension programs. First, while most evaluations of policy changes examine how the latter would affect people's incomes during retirement, taking into consideration that returns to saving are uncertain, they do not consider the extent to which people's well-being declines because of that uncertainty. Thus social economists can valuably insist that measures of well-being that reflect adverse effects of insecurity be used for policy evaluation, rather than simple income measures.[17]

Second, evaluations of policy changes examine how they affect individuals or households, without taking social preferences into account – that is, they neglect the fact that people are not only concerned with their own well-being, but also want the social context within which they live to reflect certain worthy social principles, such as preventing avoidable deteriorations in well-being, offering fair access to resources and opportunities, and extending support to people in genuine need.[18] In other words, policy evaluations need to factor in that the character of the system matters to people, not just how they fare materially within it.

Third, economic discourse about public pensions privileges the profession's knowledge highly, taking for granted that its rigorous, logical analytical frameworks provide the only valid avenue for designing pension systems that meet designated social objectives and fiscally add up. Yet a corollary of aggrandizing the strengths of economic frameworks has been a counterproductive obfuscation of weaknesses, especially concerning unresolved issues of behavioral assumptions upon which these frameworks depend. Some studies find patterns of wealth accumulation among households to be consistent with the life-cycle model of saving, suggesting that people can be expected to save for retirement satisfactorily on their own (Hubbard et al. 1995); other studies argue that, left to their own devices, people balance consumption today against consumption in the distant future in ways that disfavor the latter, so that they benefit from pension systems in which saving is done for them (Sheffrin and Thaler, 1988; Choi et al., 2006). Here it is not clear that economic knowledge is being well served by adversarial contests to determine the *one true way* to describe how people prepare themselves for retirement (or not); on the contrary, our inability to nail down this one true way suggests that strategies towards retirement may instead be plural, with some people engaging in deliberative forward-looking behavior and others using other kinds of heuristics. If we reject the old hypothesis of a unitary universal behavior as too simple, then we need to ask fundamental questions about how people acquire strategies towards consumption and saving (e.g. instruction, imitation, learning-by-doing) and about avenues by which strategies spread within populations (e.g. through family upbringing, social networks and/or the media). The work of authors such as Boyd and Richerson (1985), Axtell and Epstein (1999), Bowles and Gintis (2004) and Bisin et al. (2004) are highly relevant here.

Finally, analyses of pensions are based on a highly naturalized view of retirement that can be fruitfully interrogated. In particular, analyses take for granted that the life-course is divided into a period dominated by work while 'young' and a period dominated by leisure while 'old'. While there are some 'natural' elements to this, as when declining physical prowess reduces abilities to do physical labor, changes in the nature of work and lengthening life expectancies have transformed retirement from a few years of relief from physical toil, into a stretch of one to three decades that people must infuse with personal meaning themselves; that doing so is not necessarily easy is suggested by the fact that depressive symptoms are much more common among older people than they are in the population as a whole.[19] A highly insightful contribution here comes from Dugger (1999), who argues that, by structuring work in a hierarchical way such that an inflow of younger workers pushes older workers 'up or out', corporations create and maintain conditions under which people who are willing and able to work are induced to retire prematurely. After showing that alternative ways of organizing work could greatly attenuate the fiscal problems that public pensions are expected to face, Dugger (ibid., p. 84) concludes that 'If reform is really needed, what is called for is adjustment in the way work is organized, not abandonment of security for the elderly.' This highlights the importance of understanding 'problems' of pension policy in terms of the broader social forces and relations from which they arise.

Acknowledgement
I am grateful to Adam Seitchik of Trillium Asset Management for his valuable insights on socially responsible investing.

Notes

1. Another factor contributing to the decline in saving has been rising prices of assets owned by households, namely homes and stocks (Parker, 1999; Lusardi et al., 2001; de Serres and Pelgrin, 2003).
2. See, e.g., Behrman et al. (1995) or Altonji et al. (1997).
3. See Haines (1990), O'Boyle (1993) and Trigg (2004) for discussion of 'needs'.
4. Beverly and Sherraden (1999) consider institutional approaches for promoting saving among low-income households.
5. See also Williams et al. (1989).
6. Multiples also rose in other industrial countries, though not to the same extent as in the USA. See Conyon and Murphy (1998) for comparison of the USA and the UK.
7. The US Catholic Bishops (1986, p. 24) write, 'Support of private ownership does not mean that anyone has the right to unlimited accumulation of wealth . . . "No one is justified in keeping for his exclusive use what he does not need, when others lack necessities".' The second sentence quotes from Pope Paul VI's encyclical, *On the Development of Peoples* (March 1967). See also Barrera (1997).
8. According to the US Bureau of Labor Statistics (2004), in 2003, 5 percent of private workers participated in an ESOP at their current workplace, 5 percent received cash profit-sharing bonuses, 26 percent participated in a deferred profit-sharing plan, and 8 percent had access to stock options.
9. As Bowles and Gintis (1996) point out, this problem of increasing risk to workers would not be such a problem if the distribution of wealth were more equal.
10. For comparison, for the most recent year for which data were available, the share of households owning stock directly or indirectly was 34 percent in the Netherlands (1997), 32 percent in the UK (1997–98), 19 percent in Germany (1993) and 19 percent in Italy (1998). See Guiso et al. (2002, p. 11).
11. See also Elliott and Freeman (2000) and Rock (2003). There is a substantial body of financial research on SRI, including Sauer (1997), Statman (2000), and Derwall et al. (2005).
12. Presidential Statement, 14 August 1935.
13. As incomes have risen around the world, so too has the number of countries with public pension systems: as of 1999, 167 countries had such systems, up from 33 in 1940 (US Social Security Administration, 1999). Programs are most comprehensive in advanced industrial countries, where over 90 percent of the workforce is eligible for benefits. Coverage is much less complete elsewhere; for example, public pensions cover 10 percent of the workforce in Zambia, 30 percent in Korea, and 50 percent in Brazil (US Census Bureau, 2001, p. 117).
14. However, some countries have more generous benefits – as in Greece, Italy, Portugal and Spain, which have average replacement rates above 80 percent (OECD, 1998).
15. While coverage under defined-benefit plans has been falling in recent years, coverage under defined-contribution plans has been rising. Wolff (2003) finds that this shift has made the distribution of pension wealth increasingly unequal.
16. See Behrendt (2000) for cross-country evidence on both of these points.
17. Rejda and Haley (2005) provide a proposal for a broad index of economic insecurity which includes income security in old age.
18. Bowles and Gintis (1999) discuss this point with regard to welfare form.
19. Summarizing available research, the US Surgeon General reports that 8–20 percent of the over-65 population has symptoms of depression; see US Department of Health and Human Services (1999), ch. 5.

References

Abolafia, Mitchel Y. (1996), *Making Markets: Opportunism and Restraint on Wall Street*, Cambridge, MA: Harvard University Press.

Altonji, Joseph G., Fumio Hayashi and Lawrence J. Kotlikoff (1997), 'Parental altruism and inter vivos transfers: theory and evidence', *Journal of Political Economy*, **105** (6), 1121–66.

Arocena, Pablo and Mikel Villanueva (2003), 'Access as a motivational device: implications for human resource management', *Kyklos*, **56** (2), 199–221.

Axtell, Robert and Josh Epstein (1999), 'Coordination in transient social networks: an agent-based computational model of the timing of retirement', in Henry Aaron (ed.), *Behavioral Dimensions of Retirement*, Washington, DC: Brookings Institution Press, pp. 161–86.

Barrera, Albino (1997), 'Degrees of unmet needs in the superfluous income criterion', *Review of Social Economy*, **55** (4), 464–86.

Behrendt, C. (2000), 'Private pensions – a viable alternative? Their distributive effects in a comparative perspective', *International Social Security Review*, **53**, 3–26.

Behrman, Jere R., Robert A. Pollak and Paul Taubman (1995), *From Parent to Child: Intrahousehold Allocations and Intergenerational Relations in the United States*, Chicago, IL: University of Chicago Press.

Berle, Adolf and G.C. Means (1932), *The Modern Corporation and Private Property*, New York: Commerce Clearing House.

Bertaut, Carol and Martha Starr (2002), 'Household Portfolios in the U.S.', in Luigi Guiso, Michael Haliassos and Tullio Jappelli (eds), *Household Portfolios*, Cambridge, MA: MIT Press, pp. 181–218.

Beverly, Sondra G. and Michael Sherraden (1999), 'Institutional determinants of saving: implications for low-income households and public policy', *Journal of Socio-Economics*, **28** (4), 457–73.

Bisin, Alberto, Giorgio Topa and Thierry Verdier (2004), 'Cultural transmission, socialization and the population dynamics of multiple state traits distributions', Working Paper, New York University, September.

Black, B., R. Kraakman and A. Tarassova (2000), 'Russian privatization and corporate governance: what went wrong?', *Stanford Law Review*, **52**, 1731–808.

Bosworth, Barry, Gary Burtless and John Sabelhaus (1991), 'The decline in saving: evidence from household surveys', *Brookings Papers on Economic Activity*, **1**, 183–241.

Bowles, Samuel and Herbert Gintis (1996), 'The distribution of wealth and the viability of the democratic firm', in Ugo Pagano and Robert Rowthorn (eds), *Democracy and Efficiency in the Economic Enterprise*, London and New York: Routledge, pp. 82–97.

Bowles, Samuel and Herbert Gintis (1999), 'Is inequality passé? *Homo reciprocans* and the future of egalitarian politics', *Boston Review*, **23** (6), 4–10.

Bowles, Samuel and Herbert Gintis (2004), 'The evolution of strong reciprocity: cooperation in heterogeneous populations', *Theoretical Population Biology*, **65**, 17–28.

Boyd, R. and P. Richerson (1985), *Culture and the Evolutionary Process*, Chicago, IL: University of Chicago Press.

Bruyn, Severyn (1991), *The Field of Social Investment*, Cambridge: Cambridge University Press.

Bunting, David (1991), 'Savings and the distribution of income', *Journal of Post Keynesian Economics*, **14** (1), 3–22.

Bureau of Labor Statistics (2004), *National Compensation Survey: Employee Benefits in Private Industry in the United States*, Summary 04-04 (March).

Choi, James, David Laibson, Brigitte Madrian and Andrew Metrick (2006), 'Saving or retirement on the path of least resistance', in Ed McCaffrey and Joel Slemrod (eds), *Behavioral Public Finance*, New York: Russell Sage, pp. 304–54.

Conyon, Martin and Kevin Murphy (1998), 'The prince and the pauper: CEO pay in the U.S. and U.K.', *Economic Journal*, **110** (November), F640–71.

Davis, John (2003), *The Theory of the Individual in Economics: Identity and Value*, London and New York: Routledge.

460   *The Elgar companion to social economics*

de Serres, Alain and Florian Pelgrin (2003), 'The decline in private saving rates in the 1990s in OECD countries: how much can be explained by non-wealth determinants?', OECD Economic Studies, No. 36, pp. 117–53.
Derwall, Jeroen, Nadja Guenster, Rob Bauer and Kees Koedijk (2005), 'The eco-efficiency premium puzzle', *Financial Analysts Journal*, **61** (2), 51–64.
Dietz, Thomas and Paul Stern (1995), 'Toward a theory of choice: socially embedded preference construction', *Journal of Socio-Economics*, **24** (2), 261–79.
Dixon, John and Mark Hyde (2003), 'Public pension privatization: neo-classical economics, decision risks and welfare ideology', *International Journal of Social Economics*, **30** (5/6), 633–51.
Duesenberry, James (1949), *Income, Saving, and the Theory of Consumer Behavior*, Cambridge, MA: Harvard University Press.
Dugger, William (1999), 'Old age is an institution', *Review of Social Economy*, **57** (1), 84–98.
Ellerman, David (1986), 'The employment contract and liberal thought', *Review of Social Economy*, **44** (1), 13–39.
Ellerman, David (1993), 'Capital markets and worker ownership', in William Lafferty and Eliezer Rosenstein (eds), *International Handbook of Participation in Organizations*, Vol. 3, Oxford and New York: Oxford University Press, pp. 344–62.
Elliott, K.A. and R.B. Freeman (2001), 'White hats or Don Quixotes? Human rights vigilantes in the global economy', NBER Working Paper No. 8102 (January).
Ervik, Rune (2005), 'The battle of future pensions: global accounting tools, international organizations and pension reforms', *Global Social Policy*, **5** (1), 29–54.
Fama, Eugene and Michael Jensen (1983), 'The separation of ownership and control', *Journal of Law and Economics*, **26** (2), 301–25.
Ferber, Marianne and Julie Nelson (eds) (1993), *Beyond Economic Man: Feminist Theory and Economics*, Chicago, IL: University of Chicago Press.
Floro, Maria S. and Stephanie Seguino (2003), 'Does gender matter for aggregate saving? An empirical analysis', *International Review of Applied Economics*, **17** (2), 147–66.
Freeman, Richard, Morris Kleiner and Cheri Ostroff (2000), 'The anatomy of employee involvement and its effects on firms and workers', NBER Working Paper No. 8050 (December).
Frey, Bruno S. (1997a), 'On the relationship between intrinsic and extrinsic work motivation', *International Journal of Industrial Organization*, **15** (4), 427–39.
Frey, Bruno S. (1997b), *Not Just for the Money: An Economic Theory of Personal Motivation*, Cheltenham, UK and Lyme, USA: Edward Elgar.
Friend, Irwin and Stanley Schor (1959), 'Who saves?', *Review of Economics and Statistics*, **41** (2), 213–48.
Froud, Julie et al. (2001), 'Accumulation under conditions of inequality', *Review of International Political Economy*, **8** (1), 66–95.
Galbraith, J.K. (1958), *The Affluent Society*, New York: Houghton Mifflin.
Guerin, Bernard (2003), 'Putting a radical socialness into consumer behavior analysis', *Journal of Economic Psychology*, **24** (5), 697–718.
Guiso, Luigi, Michael Haliassos and Tullio Jappelli (eds) (2002), *Household Portfolios*, Cambridge, MA: MIT Press.
Gunn, Christopher (2000), 'Markets against economic democracy', *Review of Radical Political Economics*, **32** (3), 448–60.
Haines, Walter W. (1990), 'Wants and metawants: Marshall's concern for higher values', *International Journal of Social Economics*, **17** (9), 17–24.
Hobson, John (1910), *The Industrial System*, London: Longmans, Green & Co.
Hubbard, R. Glenn, Jonathan Skinner and Stephen Zeldes (1995), 'Precautionary saving and social insurance', *Journal of Political Economy*, **103**, 360–99.
Huggett, Mark and Gustavo Ventura (2000), 'Understanding why high income households save more than low income households', *Journal of Monetary Economics*, **45** (2), 361–97.
Jackson, Tim (2004), 'Negotiating sustainable consumption: a review of the consumption debate and its policy implications', *Energy & Environment*, **15** (6), 1027–51.

Lashgari, Malek and David Gant (1989), 'Social investing: the Sullivan principles', *Review of Social Economy*, **47** (1), 74–83.

Lee, Frederic and Steve Keen (2004), 'The incoherent emperor: a heterodox critique of neo-classical microeconomic theory', *Review of Social Economy*, **62** (2), 169–99.

Leff, Nathaniel (1969), 'Dependency rates and savings rates', *American Economic Review*, **59** (5), 886–96.

Lusardi, Annamaria, Jonathan Skinner and Steven Venti (2001), 'Saving puzzles and saving policies in the United States', NBER Working Paper No. 8237 (April).

Lutz, Mark (1990), 'Social economics in the humanist tradition', in Mark Lutz (ed.), *Social Economics: Retrospect and Prospect*, Boston, MA: Kluwer Academic.

Marshall, Alfred (2003 [1923]), *Money, Credit and Commerce*, Amherst, NY: Prometheus Books.

Morehouse, Ward, Stuart Speiser and Ken Taylor (2000), 'The universal capitalism movement in the United States', *Review of Social Economy*, **58** (1), 63–80.

Muelbroek, Lisa (2002), 'Company stock in pension plans: how costly is it?', Harvard Business School Working Paper 02-058.

Niggle, Christopher (2000), 'The political economy of Social Security reform proposals', *Journal of Economic Issues*, **34** (4), 789–810.

Niggle, Christopher (2003), 'Globalization, neoliberalism and the attack on social security', *Review of Social Economy*, **61** (1), 51–71.

Norgaard, Richard (1995), 'Beyond materialism: a coevolutionary reinterpretation of the environmental crisis', *Review of Social Economy*, **53** (4), 475–92.

O'Boyle, Edward J. (1993), 'On need, wants, resources and limits', *International Journal of Social Economics*, **20** (12), 13–26.

O'Boyle, Edward J. (1994), '*Homo socio-economicus*: foundational to social economics and the social economy', *Review of Social Economy*, **52** (3), 286–313.

O'Hara, Phillip Anthony (1998), 'Capital and inequality in today's world', in Doug Brown (ed.), *Thorstein Veblen in the Twenty-first Century: A Commemoration of The Theory of the Leisure Class (1899–1999)*, Cheltenham, UK and Northampton, MA, USA: Edward Elgar, pp. 171–88.

Organisation for Economic Co-operation and Development (1998), *Maintaining Prosperity in an Ageing Society*, Paris: OECD.

Organisation for Economic Co-operation and Development (2003), 'Policies for an ageing society: recent measures and areas for further reform', Economics Department Working Paper No. 369 (November).

Parker, Jonathan A. (1999), 'Spendthrift in America? On two decades of decline in the U.S. saving rate'. NBER Working Paper No. 7238.

Paxson, Christina (1996), 'Saving and growth: evidence from micro data', *European Economic Review*, **40** (2), 255–88.

Rejda, George and Joseph Haley (2005), 'Construction of an economic index to measure the causes of economic insecurity', *Forum for Social Economics*, **34** (1–2), 9–30.

Rock, Michael (2003), 'Public disclosure of the sweatshop practices of American multinational garment/shoemakers/retailers: impacts on their stock prices', *Competition and Change*, **7** (1), 23–38.

Røpke, Inge (1999), 'The dynamics of willingness to consume', *Ecological Economics*, **28** (1), 399–420.

Ryan, John A. (1916), *Distributive Justice: The Right and Wrong of our Present Distribution of Wealth*, New York: Macmillan Company.

Ryan, John A. (1935), *A Better Economic Order*, New York: Harper & Brothers.

Sauer, David A. (1997), 'The impact of social-responsibility screens on investment performance: evidence from the Domini 400 Social Index and Domini Equity Mutual Fund', *Review of Financial Economics*, **6** (2), 137–49.

Schor, Juliet (1999), *The Overspent American: Why We Want What We Don't Need*, New York: HarperCollins.

Sheffrin, Hersh M. and Richard H. Thaler (1988), 'The behavioral life-cycle hypothesis', *Economic Inquiry*, **26** (4), 609–43.

462 *The Elgar companion to social economics*

Shipman, Alan (2004), 'Lauding the leisure class: symbolic content and conspicuous consumption', *Review of Social Economy*, **62** (3), 277–89.
Simon, Herbert (1955), 'A behavioral theory of rationality', *Quarterly Journal of Economics*, **69** (1), 99–118.
Social Investment Forum (2003), *2003 Report on Socially Responsible Investing Trends in the U.S.*, Washington, DC: Social Investment Forum.
Starr, Martha A. (2005), 'Spending, saving and self-control', *Review of Radical Political Economy*, **39** (2), 214–29.
Statman, Meir (2000), 'Socially responsible mutual funds', *Financial Analysts' Journal*, **56** (3), 30–39.
Thaler, Richard (1994), 'Why do people save? Psychology and savings policies', *American Economic Review*, **84** (2), 186–92.
Trigg, Andrew (2004), 'Deriving the Engel curve: Pierre Bourdieu and the social critique of Maslow's hierarchy of needs', *Review of Social Economy*, **62** (3), 393–406.
Tucker, David M. (1991), *The Decline of Thrift in America: Our Cultural Shift from Saving to Spending*, Westport, CT and London: Greenwood, Praeger.
US Catholic Bishops (1986), 'Economic justice for all: pastoral letter on Catholic social teaching and the US economy', 13 November, available at: http://www.usccb.org/sdwp/international/EconomicJusticeforAll.pdf, accessed 2 January 2008.
US Census Bureau (2001), 'An aging world, 2001', International Population Reports P95/01-1 (November).
US Department of Health and Human Services (1999), *Mental Health: A Report of the Surgeon General*, Rockville, MD: US Department of Health and Human Services, National Institutes of Health.
US Social Security Administration (1999), 'Social Security programs throughout the world, 1999', SSA Publication No. 13-11805.
Veblen, Thorstein (1908), 'On the nature of capital', *Quarterly Journal of Economics*, **22** (4), 517–42.
Veblen, Thorstein (1994 [1899]), *The Theory of the Leisure Class*, New York: Penguin Books.
Weller, Christian and Ed Wolff (2005), *Retirement Income: The Crucial Role of Social Security*, Washington, DC: Economic Policy Institute.
Wiatrowski, William (2000), 'Putting stock in benefits: how prevalent is it?', *Compensation and Working Conditions*, Fall, 2–7.
Williams, Oliver, Frank Reilly and John Houck (eds) (1989), *Ethics and the Investment Industry*, Savage, MD: Rowman & Littlefield.
Wisman, Jon (1988), 'Economic reform for humanity's greatest struggle', in Kenneth B. Taylor (ed.), *Capitalism and the Evil Empire: Reducing Superpower Conflict through American Economic Reform*, New York: Horizons Press, pp. 63–80.
Wolff, Edward N. (2003), 'The devolution of the American pension system: who gained and who lost?', *Eastern Economic Journal*, **29** (4), 477–95.
Yunker, James A. (1997), 'The adverse economic consequences of extremely high capital-wealth inequality', *Journal of Post Keynesian Economics*, **19** (3), 387–422.

26 Monetary policy
Sheila C. Dow

Introduction

The theory of monetary policy has gone through marked changes over the last 50 years, with the focus changing in turn from liquidity (in the Radcliffe approach) to the money supply and money targeting (in the monetarist approach) to the money supply and inflation targeting (the new classical approach) to the current emphasis on the interest rate within an inflation-targeting framework, relying heavily on the forward-looking expectations of market participants (the new Keynesian approach). This last approach has been dubbed the 'new consensus', reflecting a convergence of view among theorists and also a convergence between theorists and policy-makers. This view is also embedded in the institutional arrangements for monetary policy, whereby policy is made by a committee within an independent central bank. Yet there are still alternative viewpoints, notably the continuing emphasis by monetarists on monetary aggregates, and the Keynesian focus on the interdependence of real and financial variables. There is, further, some evidence of a weakening of the consensus, as doubts emerge as to the capacity of interest rate policy to control inflation.

The theoretical analysis and much of the policy analysis are couched in macroeconomic terms, that is, in terms of variables which aggregate individual experience, and emphasize outcomes rather than processes. Macroeconomic analysis illuminates general relationships between data series, providing a clue to possible underlying relationships at the level of experience, at the same time as capturing something of the macroeconomic backdrop of individual experience. The latter is important in particular for the formation of expectations that guide social and individual action. Yet further analysis is required in order to attempt to uncover the causal processes that underpin real experience. This is the main argument of critical realists, that focusing on event regularities distracts from real causal mechanisms which underpin processes within an open social system (Lawson, 1997).

The purpose of this chapter is to consider the theory of monetary policy in terms of real social experience. Monetary policy provides a particularly interesting case study, in that a significant channel for monetary policy is to influence expectations, as a means of influencing real behaviour. Other channels directly affect real experience; a rise in mortgage rates following a rise in the official rate, for example, reduces household disposable income and therefore the capacity of (particularly low-income) households to maintain their standard of living. Or banks may be less willing to lend to finance the start-up of a new business, for example. Yet the conventional view in recent years has been that ideally monetary policy will have minimal impact on real experience, operating rather through price-setting behaviour according to an inflation target. In what follows I focus on the distinction between transmission of monetary policy which does not directly affect social reality, and that which does.

Of course, monetary policy-making is itself a real social experience for policy-makers. In attempting to influence real behaviour, they employ theoretical ideas, conveyed with the rhetoric of expertise, to communicate with market players. They also do so within an institutional framework which itself reflects a particular set of ideas (in particular the neutrality of money). Yet, as Niebyl (1946) has demonstrated, ideas, institutional design and real practice can get out of phase with each other (reflecting power relations), to the detriment of effective monetary policy. I shall explore how this has occurred in modern times.

I start by reviewing the theoretical literature on monetary policy, focusing on the transmission mechanisms implied, and also the more eclectic central bank literature. The issues as currently perceived are then reviewed, drawing out the extent to which monetary policy has its effect at the level of financial markets rather than real experience. Finally I outline the outstanding issues for monetary policy theory and practice that remain to be addressed.

The evolution of the theory of monetary policy

The theory of monetary policy against which monetarism reacted in the 1970s was Keynesian. The role of monetary policy had been seen as providing a stable financial backdrop for investment planning, so that the focus was on low and stable interest rates, without reference to monetary aggregates. Keynes (1936), and his interpreters Minsky (1975), Davidson (1972, 2002) and Chick (1973, 1983) saw money as non-neutral (i.e. interdependent with the real economy) at a range of levels. Money arises through the creation of credit which is a counterpart to spending plans, while the demand for money depends on a variety of real, nominal and expectational factors. So money is non-neutral (i.e. it can affect real variables) in the short-run operation of the economy, and is non-neutral in the long run, which is a series of short runs. It is also non-neutral in the long run in a more fundamental way. Money is a social relation that is integral to the functioning of a capitalist economy, facilitating debt and labour contracts, and in general providing a refuge from uncertainty, as the asset of most stable value. Thus money is integral to the real activity of consuming, producing, employing and so on. Monetary policy, which is designed to influence monetary relations in some way, was therefore addressed at the functionality of market processes, that is, at the level of real experience.

The monetarist argument promoted by Friedman (1968) was that this policy of aiming for financial stability had allowed growth of the money supply in such a way as to cause inflation, disrupting monetary stability. A strong statistical correlation between nominal income and the money supply was interpreted in terms of a causal link from money to nominal income (through prices). Monetary policy should therefore be addressed to controlling monetary aggregates as a way of controlling inflation. While Friedman (1953) had argued that it was predictive success by which theories should be judged, not their content, he nevertheless articulated a transmission mechanism. The transmission of an attempt to reduce inflation by reducing growth of the money supply (relative to a stable demand for money) was that expenditure on goods, services and assets would all be curtailed directly by attempts to restore money balances, or indirectly by the counterpart to monetary tightening, a rise in interest rates. Given the crucial assumption that the norm was full employment ensured by market competition, a fall in money supply growth would feed through into a fall in the growth of prices rather than output. Money was neutral. The term 'real' was reserved for deflated values.

But implementation of monetarist policy proved to be problematic, not least since the process of controlling the money supply itself proved to be difficult. Aggregates of real deposit totals are difficult to control directly, far less the new money assets that banks introduce (in line with Goodhart's Law[1]), in turn far less the perceived liquidity which is the variable that most affects expenditure plans according to Radcliffe (1959). The evident real effects of the introduction of monetarism in the USA and the UK in 1979 (increasing unemployment) encouraged amendment to theory to allow money to be non-neutral in the short run (due to slow market adjustment), although long-run neutrality was preserved.

In the meantime new classical theory had reintroduced expectations into the analysis, in the form of the rational expectations hypothesis. Agents are modelled as forming expectations in exactly the same way as the model; rational expectations theorists argue that this is an 'as if' assumption, accepting that it does not reflect the real process of expectations formation. The focus was then on the speed of expectations adjustment: the greater the speed, the closer was money to being neutral. This development had two major impacts on the theory and practice of monetary policy. First, Sargent and Wallace (1975) put forward the policy-ineffectiveness theorem, by which active monetary policy could not have any real effect even in the short run if agents are rational and employ the same stochastic model as the policy-maker – only a random monetary policy could have any impact. All policy-makers could do was to set – and announce – a rate of growth of money and this would feed through to inflation directly, as prices were adjusted automatically to that rate of growth, since rational expectations (on the part of wage- and price-setters) would be based on the idea of money's neutrality. Ideally there would be no real impact.

The second strand of thinking was expressed by Kydland and Prescott (1977) and Barro and Gordon's (1983) time-consistency argument, that monetary policy needed to provide a credible basis for expectations. This encouraged the search for optimal policy rules which could be followed by central banks, with the full knowledge of market participants. The Taylor (1993) rule was arrived at by empirical analysis of historical data for the USA as what appeared to have guided monetary policy, and was turned round in the theoretical literature to be an optimal rule for policy. This rule specified monetary tightening if actual output was high relative to full employment output and if inflation was high relative to target inflation (the differences being the 'output gap' and 'inflation gap', respectively). The aim was to achieve an equilibrium official interest rate with output at the full employment level and inflation at the target level.

These ideas fed into a change in institutional framework for those central banks that were not independent of government. In Europe in particular, as part of the institutional arrangements for European Monetary Union, there was a requirement for central banks to be independent of government, including withdrawal of the requirement to administer government debt. The norm now is for monetary policy to be made by a committee, with a view to achieving an inflation target set by government. This separation institutionally embeds the idea of monetary neutrality: it is based on confidence that central banks can control inflation in a way that is separable from the real economy, which is the business of government. The requirement to bear in mind the government's goals for output and employment does, however, apply to many central banks.

While the Taylor rule may have been consistent with US policy, central banks themselves are unwilling to express their decisions (at least in public) in relation to any rule, not least because it has proved difficult to operationalize such concepts as the output gap (Goodhart, 1999). The inflation target itself acts as the nominal anchor. Indeed, central banks have become explicit about the various forms of uncertainty they face. The most fundamental of these is model uncertainty: uncertainty as to the best model to use as the basis for policy-making. Here we see a divergence between the theoretical literature and the central banking literature: the theoretical literature generally presumes that there is such a thing as a correct model, but that policy-makers face stochastic errors in identifying it (see, e.g., Hansen and Sargent, 2004). This follows from the mainstream literature's inattention to fundamental uncertainty (unquantifiable risk) as opposed to quantifiable risk (Dow, 2004). Policy-makers themselves tend to discuss the limitations of modelling in a wider sense and emphasize the role of judgement (see, e.g., Bank of England, 1999).

The Taylor rule in fact fitted well with the emerging new Keynesian approach to monetary policy, which carries forward many features of new classical analysis (such as rational expectations, and the monetarist view that monetary policy acts on prices through its influence on aggregate demand), but emphasizes the welfare-reducing effects of information asymmetries in the labour market and financial markets. The new Keynesian Phillips curve reflects wage-bargaining which leads to sticky prices that persist over time, encouraging a forward-looking interpretation of monetary policy by price-setters, further focusing analysis on expectations. Market behaviour thus factors in expectations of the consequences for inflation of current monetary policy announcements. Further, the new Keynesian approach reintroduced the welfare-enhancing effects of low and stable inflation. While new classicals had seen inflation as independent of the real economy, now low inflation targets are seen as another element of supply-side policy.

This emphasis on expectations has encouraged increasing transparency in monetary policy-making (see Geraats, 2002 for a review). The mainstream theoretical literature has generally been in favour of central banks revealing the thinking behind their decisions as a way of ensuring that market expectations are as consistent as possible with those of the central bank. This is aimed at minimizing the real consequences of monetary policy. Given the inflation target, and the central bank's credibility in achieving it, monetary policy is no longer a matter of shocks (the only way of having any effect, according to new classical analysis), but of promoting consistency of expectations. As a result, there is now a lively literature on central bank communication (see, e.g., Amato et al., 2000). But central bankers themselves have encouraged doubts about transparency which follow from their greater awareness of the uncertainties they face about the state of the economy and the effects of policy (see, e.g., Mishkin, 2004; Eusepi, 2005).

It is the expectations of financial markets that have been pivotal, since it is these that react most immediately to policy announcements (although there is awareness of their relevance also for expectations in labour markets, and property markets). Indeed, the Monetary Policy Committee of the

Bank of England explicitly incorporates financial market expectations of monetary policy (derived directly from asset-pricing) into the forecasts on which their policy is based. There is a presumption that efficient financial markets will then feed through any rise in the official rate to yields on other assets with longer term. The official rate is now generally (in the USA, the UK and the euro area, for example) the 'repo rate', which is the rate implied by short-term sale and repurchase agreements between banks and the central bank.

But in the meantime, the new Keynesian focus on imperfections in financial markets has encouraged some to analyse the channelling of monetary policy through the credit market, emphasizing more the segmentation of financial markets, at least for some borrowers. In particular, if borrowers cannot substitute other forms of finance for bank loans, then the reaction of banks to a change in the repo rate is all the more powerful. This in turn has drawn attention to structural matters, with the credit channel behaving differently in countries with different banking structures, for example (de Bondt, 2000). Since the interest rate is now the main policy instrument, it follows that the money supply is endogenous, encouraging attention to the supply of credit of which money is the counterpart. Endogenous money has long been a tenet of Post-Keynesian monetary theory. While the new Keynesian analysis has focused on information asymmetries in the credit market, the post-Keynesian structuralists have focused more widely on the factors that influence supply of credit within different institutional arrangements. This approach is distinct from horizontalist post-Keynesians, who see the banks as more passive in the face of credit demand (see Dow, 2006). Horizontalists are so called because they posit a horizontal money supply curve, at the official rate (see, e.g., Moore, 1988).

The feedthrough of policy from the repo market to actual financial conditions, quite apart from wage- and price-setting behaviour, is therefore not as straightforward as the conventional aggregative macroeconomic analysis has presumed. Indeed, the diversity of channels by which monetary policy is transmitted to those who set prices has become a focus of concern among those who express doubts about the effectiveness of the current approach to monetary policy. Even central banks have made it apparent that they are not confident about their understanding of the transmission mechanism. Further doubts refer to the capacity to meet the inflation target, but also to the absence of any damaging effects on output and employment, which is characteristic of mainstream theory. Post-Keynesians, who have consistently anticipated real effects of monetary policy, have been demonstrating this empirically (see, e.g., Arestis and Sawyer, 2004).

Current issues

Credibility

The general mainstream consensus is that the current approach to monetary policy has been reasonably successful, in that inflation targets have been more or less met (Bernanke et al., 1999), but there are growing concerns about whether this success is likely to continue. In the UK, for example, at the time of writing (February 2007), inflation has come uncomfortably close to the ceiling of the target range at a time of monetary tightening. While energy prices are falling back and immigration is exerting downward pressure on wages, labour costs nevertheless have shown some signs of accelerating. The actual inflation experienced by households (the Retail Price Index, or RPI, which includes taxes and housing costs) and which is most commonly used as the benchmark for wage settlements, is running significantly ahead of the inflation index to which the 2 per cent target applies (the Consumer Price Index, or CPI). The MPC's credibility is under threat. If the central bank successfully persuades economic actors that inflation is under control, then that is factored into wage settlements, contributing to control of inflation. But if expectations take hold of above-target inflation, then wage settlements reflect this, making it much more difficult to meet the target.

We saw just this scenario in Germany following unification, which disrupted labour market norms, and damaged the Bundesbank's reputation for inflation control. If it becomes apparent that the central bank is not in fact in a position to control inflation (other than by persuasion), then real experience was in this case an effective challenge to the conventional neutral-money theory. It was an unfortunate accident of history that, in the meantime, the EU had adopted the Bundesbank model for its own central bank, in the expectation that this would deliver the same success as the Bundesbank had experienced under more favourable conditions.

Central banks have recently become more explicit about their need to improve and update their understanding of the transmission mechanism (e.g. Federal Reserve Bank of New York, 2002). This concern is made explicit in the concept of model uncertainty (uncertainty as to which is the best way to model the economy and the effects of monetary policy), a concept that has also spawned a series of central bank research publications (Dow, 2004). Indeed, this is just one of the many uncertainties that central banks face, such as data uncertainty, which have been expressed by central bankers in a more modest presentation of their capability to control inflation than was customary in the past (see, e.g., King, 2004). While the mainstream theoretical literature purports to address these uncertainties, it provides minimal guidance for central bankers since the formal mathematical approach employed cannot handle fundamental uncertainty. These efforts to persuade the public not to expect too much of central bankers could be seen as an effort to maintain credibility in the face of reduced success in targeting inflation. Alternatively it could be seen as evidence that central bankers themselves simply accept the limits to the scope for monetary policy to control inflation.

The virtual world of expectations

Arguably financial markets do not operate in the belief that central banks can actually control inflation, as mainstream theory suggests, although the neutral-money rhetoric is commonplace among commentators (Forder, 2006). While mainstream theory has advocated a convergence of analytical understanding between policy-makers and markets, an alternative inter-pretation of real market behaviour is that markets are motivated solely by the need to correctly anticipate changes in the repo rate. Their concern with central bank analysis is therefore not so much with whether it correctly explains real economic behaviour but with the signals it sends about mon-etary policy. Financial markets in this sense can be said to operate in a virtual world of economic analysis, where the operative reality is the cost of borrowing liquidity and corresponding movements in asset prices and the exchange rate. The relevant context is financial markets – real experi-ence is only relevant in so far as it encourages policy-makers to change the repo rate. Nevertheless, the outcome, in the form of the cost and availabil-ity of credit, can have real consequences that may or may not influence inflation.

But there is also a more direct channel for transmitting monetary policy through expectations. Not only is the aim to influence expectations in financial markets, but also expectations in labour markets, the housing market and among consumers. Public pronouncements by policy-makers can achieve headline news about the inflation rate against which wage settle-ments are to be made. Further, predictions about the housing market, if per-suasive, can be self-fulfilling in terms of house prices, but also in terms of perceived wealth; headline predictions of a weakening in the housing market, for example, can dampen consumer demand directly and also dampen banks' valuation of collateral for consumer loans. The fact of a rise in the repo rate can raise expectations of rising borrowing costs (although the con-nection is not a necessary one), and thus of falling disposable income, that consumption plans are curtailed. Similarly, the expectation among firms of rising borrowing costs, and associated weakening consumer demand, can adversely affect plans for investment and/or expanding production. If expec-tations are 'rational' (in the rational-expectations-hypothesis sense of coming to the same conclusions as the central bank), then the inflation target is achieved with minimal real consequences. But the monetarist transmission mechanism would allow some real consequences in the short run as one means by which monetary policy is transmitted.

Expectations therefore can have real consequences. And sometimes reality breaks through, confounding expectations. Indeed, this is what post-Keynesian analysis would suggest, since expectations are subject to uncertainty, and can vary, and since money is seen as inherently non-neutral, being integral to economic relations. Thus, for example, depending on the banks' reactions, a fall in the repo rate may not feed through into lower borrowing costs, or a rise in the rate may reduce the availability of credit, at whatever cost, to households facing debt problems. Reality can also break through in asset markets themselves. Quantitative risk-based valuations cannot take account of the possibility of a structural crisis, yet such crises do occur. The current possibility of a structural crisis, given the high leveraging of household debt and the opaqueness of risk in the credit derivatives market, poses a real issue for monetary policy.

There has been debate as to whether monetary policy-makers should be concerned with asset prices. Inflation in the housing market in particular has attracted policy-makers' attention because of its expansionary effect on consumer demand. This has also drawn attention to the risks attached to a potential turnaround in house values, and the consequences for consumer demand. Since speculation in the housing market is related to speculation in other assets (having taken off in the wake of weakness in equities in 2001), there is a more general awareness of risks of more general instability in asset markets. Further, the development of the credit derivatives market has involved the bundling and selling of default risks in such a way that it is virtually impossible to assess how far risks in any portfolio are spread. For monetary policy, the issue is that a rise in the repo rate, and the policy pronouncements around such a rise, hold the potential to destabilize asset markets, causing multiple defaults, and inducing a recession.

Financial instability has not been a feature of the mainstream transmission mechanism, although it is featuring increasingly in central bank commentary and the discussion among media experts of monetary policy. However, the Keynes/Radcliffe approach to monetary policy placed financial stability at its heart. If strong and stable investment is the key to macroeconomic progress, then firms require a stable financial environment to encourage investment in spite of uncertainty about its outcome. This focus on financial stability was built on by Minsky (1982), whose financial instability hypothesis addressed the dangers posed by increasing financial fragility as unreasonably confident expectations of asset price rises took hold in a boom, encouraging excessive credit creation. In particular, when gearing is high and there is reliance on capital gains for covering borrowing costs, markets are vulnerable to any rise in borrowing costs.

With the focus now on inflation targeting, against a backdrop of rising asset prices and rapid credit expansion, there is therefore a risk that its dramatic effects on asset markets could induce a global recession. Palley (2006) points out that, while central banks have increasingly learned to increase liquidity in order to limit downturns in asset prices in crisis situations, this creates a moral hazard in favour of the kind of asset price inflation that threatens financial stability. He goes on to argue, along Minskian lines, for inflation targeting to be supplemented by a regulatory approach to limiting the credit expansions which facilitate asset price inflation.

Monetary policy, monetary aggregates and fiscal policy

As Forder (2006) explains, the view continues to be widespread that money, and thus monetary policy, are neutral, in the long run if not in the short run. But, even without structural instability in asset markets, monetary policy addressed to an inflation target has been shown empirically to have real effects, not only in the short run but also in the long run (Arestis and Sawyer, 2004). Monetary policy is transmitted to the rest of the economy by altering the terms of borrowing and lending, and of buying and selling across the exchanges. The real effects on production, employment, investment and consumption then follow, with producers' responses in setting the prices of goods and services determining the effect on inflation. Expectations play an important part. But if money is not in fact neutral, then expectations will reflect this, and cannot be counted on to deliver neutrality.

This set of chains is complex, indirect and context-dependent, in terms of the overall conjuncture, but also in terms of particular market segments. The real effect of a rise in the repo rate on borrowing and borrowing costs is therefore indirect. It depends on banking structure, and on the market power of borrowers (which also determines the availability of alternative forms of finance). Such a perspective follows naturally from an application of the Keynesian view of money as integral to the workings of a market economy.

However, within the mainstream central banking literature there is an emerging debate on the merits of returning attention to monetary aggregates on the one hand (as in Laidler, 2006, and the ECB conference in December 2006 on 'The role of money: money and monetary policy in the twenty-first century') and analysing monetary policy purely in real terms, and in relation to fiscal policy, on the other (notably as in Woodford, 2003). While post-Keynesians emphasize the interdependence of the monetary and the real, therefore, the mainstream debate is dichotomized between thinking of inflation as a monetary phenomenon on the one hand and inflation as a real phenomenon on the other. The European Central Bank, or ECB, has been most consistent in retaining monetary analysis as one of its 'two pillars' analytical approach, but other central banks have been drawing attention lately to monetary aggregates (as in the MPC's *Inflation Report*). Tighter monetary policy is being justified in part by the accelerating growth in monetary aggregates.

But meanwhile Woodford has synthesized the new consensus in a model apparently without money and without the banks whose liability most money is. This explicitly Wicksellian analysis focuses on the bank rate in relation to the natural rate of interest, but gives it much more general application than did Wicksell (Laidler, 2006; Mehrling, 2006). The aim of monetary policy is that the repo rate doesn't deviate from the natural rate, so that there is nothing to transmit. This natural rate corresponds to society's time rate of discount and the real long-term return on capital. In a neutral-money model with perfect markets, trading ensures that the real bank rate converges to the natural rate, where the rate of inflation is arbitrary. Where there are market imperfections, and thus monetary policy has real effects, the central bank's task is to set the nominal rate in such a way as to promote convergence of actual rates to the natural rate, in the process setting the rate of inflation. This monetary policy requires the support of a Ricardian fiscal policy, reflecting an emerging renewed interest in fiscal policy in relation to monetary policy.

So the theoretical literature, as represented by Woodford (2003), emphasizes the real (as opposed to nominal) economy, with inflation simply one supply-side variable. Yet central banks still, to some degree or other, retain a focus on monetary variables (see, e.g., Bank of England, 2007, p. 10). The resulting conflicting analyses within central banks has contributed to diversity of opinion, and thus uncertainty, in monetary policy-making. As doubts have emerged about the capacity for central banks to routinize monetary policy based on modelling, attention has shifted to the decision-making framework, and the communication of decision-making. There is minimal debate now about central bank independence, which institutionalizes the widely held idea of money's neutrality. Yet there is debate about the size and composition of monetary policy committees, the frequency of meetings, the publication of deliberations and of voting patterns. This debate reflects the fact that, quite apart from what goes into the making of the repo rate decision, the manner in which the decision is communicated can have profound effects on expectations, and thus on the transmission of monetary policy to prices, but also to real output, expenditure and employment.

The future of monetary policy
It is conventional now to see the interest rate as the single policy instrument addressed to an inflation target. Yet the increasing emphasis on central bank communications has raised the possibility that it is these that in fact have become the main instrument, addressing expectations directly (see, e.g., Bank of England, 2007, p. 3). Certainly these expectations are held with respect to central bank actions, but a circularity has emerged between central bank forecasts based on market forecasts of what the central bank will do. Further, the transmission channel from central bank pronouncements directly to price- and wage-setting is increasingly emphasized. The current analysis of transparency and communication is thus likely to continue.

The focus on the interest rate dates back to Poole's (1970) discussion of the interest rate and the money supply as the two alternatives. But historically central banks have used a wider range of instruments, in particular credit controls and other portfolio restrictions. Credit controls became less feasible as banking systems became more sophisticated and thus more able to evade them. Rather than aiming at a direct effect on the capacity of firms and households to borrow (and thus spend), the real consequences were rather the availability of new financial instruments for investors. But post-Keynesian analysis, drawing on Minsky's financial instability analysis, would suggest that a strategy is required to address directly the massive expansion of credit (particularly for households, and also to finance the credit derivatives market) that currently threatens financial stability. This could take the form of limiting the multiple of earnings allowed for mortgage loans, and increasing the transparency of the credit derivatives market so that risk is more easily identified by investors. The key regulatory instrument introduced to deal with a similar problem in the 1980s, capital adequacy ratios, suffer from the flaw that banks are not capital-constrained in a rising market.

Financial innovation has served to fuel the scope for financial instability. The derivatives market evolved initially as a means of firms hedging against risk (in the form of futures contracts on currencies in which they traded, for example). But past experience of excessive credit expansion in the 1970s and 1980s, the resulting bad debts, and the imposition of capital adequacy requirements aimed at preventing a recurrence of excessive credit expansion, all encouraged banks to become proactive in a range of non-traditional functions to protect their profits. One of these functions was engagement in the derivatives market, which was taking on a life of its own, independent of the needs of producing firms. Credit derivatives started as a means for banks to protect themselves against risk of default by borrowers; the risk could be sold off. But now banks themselves are actively engaging in this market too, as traders with a view to profit-making. The market is notoriously opaque, such that it is extremely difficult to identify actual risk embodied in a derivative which bundles up risk from a range of borrowers (where their risks may or may not be correlated, or even double counted when these bundles are repackaged in further derivatives). This market is adding significantly to the fragility of the global financial system.

The relationship between financial stability and monetary stability could indeed become a key issue. The latter has lately been seen as the primary concern of central banks, to such an extent that bank supervision has in some cases (such as the UK) been moved to a separate institution. There is potential for conflict between the two. For example, feeding liquidity into the market to defuse a fall in asset prices would run counter to attempts to tighten liquidity with an eye to an inflation target. Nevertheless, this is an area where reality can force the issue. There is a distinct possibility of another global financial crisis which would threaten the economic process in a more fundamental way than inflation, so that financial stability would need to be given priority. Although such a crisis would have its origins in the virtual world of financial markets, it would have real effects if it sparked off a global recession, with declining output, employment and living standards.

A financial crisis, leading to a recession, is precisely what the Keynesian approach to monetary policy is designed to avoid. Keynes was not concerned to curtail economic expansion as such, but to prevent recession. Booms therefore had to be managed in such a way as to prevent a build-up of financial instability. A stable macroeconomy with steady growth requires stable financial conditions. In times of instability, money is preferable to real assets whose value is uncertain, making it more difficult for firms to finance investment.

A financial crisis is an extreme case of unquantifiable risk, that is uncertainty. Central banks have increasingly been referring to uncertainty as being relevant to their analysis, and indeed to economic behaviour more generally (see, e.g., Bank of England, 2007, pp. 12–13). Since the methodology of the mainstream literature means that it cannot address uncertainty (only quantifiable risk), it is not providing adequate guidance. The post-Keynesian literature does have the theory from which to provide guidance. But this literature also challenges the predominant view on the neutrality of money and the related separation of monetary policy from fiscal policy as well as bank supervision. It remains an issue how far the mainstream rhetoric, which dominates the public discourse, will preclude attention to this alternative literature. But if post-Keyensians are right that it is not in fact in the power of central banks to control inflation, and developments are such that central bank credibility is seriously dented, then reality might force a rethink about the theory of monetary policy.

Acknowledgement

The chapter has benefited from helpful comments from Alberto Montagnoli.

Note

1. Goodhart's Law states that, whenever the authorities try to control money by one definition, the financial sector innovates to create new money assets, so that that definition of money is no longer adequate.

References

Amato, Jeffery D., Stephen Morris and Hyun Song Shin (2002), 'Communication and monetary policy', *Oxford Review of Economic Policy*, **18**, 495–503.
Arestis, P. and M. Sawyer (2004), 'Can monetary policy affect the real economy?', *European Review of Economics and Finance*, 7–30.
Arestis, P. and M. Sawyer (2006), 'The nature and role of monetary policy when money is endogenous', *Cambridge Journal of Economics*, **30**, 847–60.
Bank of England (1999), *Economic Models at the Bank of England*, London: Bank of England.
Bank of England (2007), 'Evidence to the House of Commons Treasury Committee', *The Monetary Policy Committee of the Bank of England: Ten Years On*, Vol. II, pp. 1–14.
Barro, R. and D. Gordon (1983), 'Rules, discretion and reputation in a model of monetary policy', *Journal of Monetary Economics*, **12**, 101–21.
Bernanke, B.S., T. Laubach, F.S. Mishkin and A.S. Posen (1999), *Inflation Targetting: Lessons from the International Experience*, Princeton, NJ: Princeton University Press.
de Bondt, G.J. (2000), *Financial Structure and Monetary Transmission in Europe*, Cheltenham, UK and Northampton, MA, USA: Edward Elgar.
Chick, V. (1973), *The Theory of Monetary Policy*, Oxford: Blackwell.
Chick, V. (1983), *Macroeconomics After Keynes*, Oxford: Philip Allan.
Davidson, P. (1972), *Money and the Real World*, London: Macmillan.
Davidson, P. (2002), *Financial Markets, Money and the Real World*, Cheltenham, UK and Northampton, MA, USA: Edward Elgar.
Dow, S.C. (2004), 'Uncertainty and monetary policy', *Oxford Economic Papers*, **56**, 539–61.
Dow, S.C. (2006), 'Endogenous money: structuralist', in P. Arestis and M. Sawyer (eds), *A Handbook of Alternative Monetary Economics*, Cheltenham, UK and Northampton, MA, USA: Edward Elgar, pp. 35–51.
Eusepi, S. (2005), 'Central bank transparency under model uncertainty', *Federal Reserve Bank of New York Staff Reports*, No. 199.
Federal Reserve Bank of New York (2002), 'Financial innovation and monetary transmission', Proceedings of a conference sponsored by the Federal Reserve Bank of New York, 5 and 6 April 2001, *Economic Policy Review*, **8** (1).
Forder, J. (2006), 'Monetary policy', in P. Arestis and M. Sawyer (eds), *A Handbook of Alternative Monetary Economics*, Cheltenham, UK and Northampton, MA, USA: Edward Elgar, pp. 224–41.
Friedman, M. (1953), 'The methodology of positive economics', in *Essays in Positive Economics*, Chicago, IL: Chicago University Press, pp. 3–43.
Friedman, M. (1968), 'The role of monetary policy', *American Economic Review*, **58**, 1–17.
Geraats, P.M. (2002), 'Central bank transparency', *Economic Journal*, **112**, F532–65.
Goodhart, C.A.E. (1999), 'Central bankers and uncertainty', *Bank of England Quarterly Bulletin*, February, 102–16.
Hansen, L.P. and T.J. Sargent (2004), *Robust Control and Economic Model Uncertainty*, Princeton, NJ: Princeton University Press.
Keynes, J.M. (1936), *The General Theory of Employment, Interest and Money*, London: Macmillan.
King, M. (2004), 'What fates impose: facing up to uncertainty', *Eighth British Academy Annual Lecture*.

Kydland, F. and E. Prescott (1977), 'Rules rather than discretion: the inconsistency of optimal plans', *Journal of Political Economy*, **87**, 473–92.

Laidler, D. (2006), 'Woodford and Wicksell on interest and prices: the place of the pure credit economy in the theory of monetary policy', *Journal of the History of Economic Thought*, **28** (2), 151–9.

Lawson, T. (1997), *Economics and Reality*, London: Routledge.

Mehrling, P. (2006), 'Mr Woodford and the challenge of finance', *Journal of the History of Economic Thought*, **28** (2), 161–70.

Minsky, H.P. (1975), *John Maynard Keynes*, London: Macmillan.

Minsky, H.P. (1982), *Inflation, Recession and Economic Policy*, Armonk, NY: M.E. Sharpe, and Brighton: Harvester.

Mishkin, F.H. (2004), 'Can central bank transparency go too far?', NBER Working Paper No. 10829, Cambridge, MA: National Bureau of Economic Research, Inc.

Moore, B.J. (1988), *Horizontalists and Verticalists: The Macroeconomics of Credit Money*, Cambridge: Cambridge University Press.

Niebyl, K. (1946), *Studies in the Classical Theories of Money*, New York: Columbia University Press.

Palley, T.I. (2006), 'Monetary policy in an endogenous money economy', in P. Arestis and M. Sawyer (eds), *A Handbook of Alternative Monetary Economics*, Cheltenham, UK and Northampton, MA, USA: Edward Elgar, pp. 242–57.

Poole, W. (1970), 'Optimal choice of policy instruments in a simple stochastic macro model', *Quarterly Journal of Economics*, **84**, 197–216.

Radcliffe, Lord (1959), *Report of the Committee on the Working of the Monetary System*, Cmnd 827. London: HMSO.

Sargent, T.J. and N. Wallace (1975), ' "Rational" expectations, the optimal monetary instrument, and the optimal money supply rule', *Journal of Political Economy*, **83**, 241–54.

Taylor, J.B. (1993), 'Discretion versus policy rules in practice', *Carnegie–Rochester Conference Series on Public Policy*, **39**, 195–214.

Woodford, M. (2003), *Interest and Prices*, Princeton, NJ: Princeton University Press.

27 Banking, finance and money: a social economics approach
L. Randall Wray

This chapter will briefly summarize the orthodox approach to banking, finance and money, and then will point the way toward an alternative based on social economics. It will be argued that the alternative approach not only fits the historical record better, but also sheds more light on the nature of money in modern economies. While the orthodox approach presumes that money really does not matter (at least in the long run, when it is supposed to be 'neutral'), the alternative stresses that money is perhaps the most important institution in an economy organized along capitalist principles. Further, rather than relegating money to a 'thing' that lubricates the market mechanism, a social economic perspective emphasizes social relations – credit and debt, power and sovereignty. Finally, the alternative view of banking, finance and money also leads to different conclusions regarding the appropriate scope for monetary and fiscal policy.

1. The state of orthodox thinking on the subject

For decades economics students were introduced to the topic of money and banking through a story about the evolution of money from the supposed earliest origins in barter and on to our present 'fiat' money. For example, Paul Samuelson presents the 'historical states of money' as follows:

> Inconvenient as barter obviously is, it represents a great step forward from a state of self-sufficiency in which every man had to be a jack-of-all-trades and master of none . . . Nevertheless, simple barter operates under grave disadvantages . . . In all but the most primitive cultures, men do not directly exchange one good for another. Instead they sell one good for money, and then use money to buy the goods they wish . . . Money does simplify economic life. If we were to reconstruct history along hypothetical, logical lines, we should naturally follow the age of barter by the age of commodity money. Historically, a great variety of commodities has served at one time or another as a medium of exchange: cattle, . . . tobacco, leather and hides, furs, olive oil, beer or spirits, slaves or wives, copper iron, gold, silver, rings, diamonds, wampum beads or shells, huge rocks and landmarks, and cigarette butts. The age of commodity money gives way to the age of paper money . . . Finally, along with the age of paper money, there is the age of bank money, or bank checking deposits. (Samuelson, 1973, pp. 274–6)

It is more important to recognize the underlying view on the nature of money represented in this quote than to take the history seriously (even Samuelson offers the caveat that the history is 'hypothetical, logical'). Money is something that reduces transactions costs, simplifying 'economic life' by lubricating the market mechanism (Friedman, 1969). Indeed, this is the unifying theme in virtually all orthodox approaches to banking, finance and money: banks, financial instruments and even money itself originate to improve market efficiency (Klein and Selgin, 2000).

Essentially, orthodox economists turn the evolution of money into a 'natural' phenomenon:

> Although economists allow that money is a human invention assuming different forms in different times and places, they adopt an evolutionary perspective that de-emphasizes money's contingency and its ultimate foundation in social convention. As capitalist economies became more complex, money 'naturally' assumed increasingly efficient forms, culminating in the highly abstract, intangible money of today. (Carruthers and Babb, 1996, p. 1558)

An innate propensity to 'truck and barter' is taken for granted; this instinct leads naturally to the development of markets organized through a self-equilibrating relative price system. It is then 'natural' to choose a convenient medium of exchange to facilitate impersonal market transactions. The ideal medium of exchange is a commodity whose value is natural, intrinsic – free from any hierarchical relations or social symbolism. As Hilferding put it:

> In money, the social relationships among human beings have been reduced to a thing, a mysterious, glittering thing the dazzling radiance of which has blinded the vision of so many economists when they have not taken the precaution of shielding their eyes against it. (Quoted in Carruthers and Babb, 1996, p. 1556)

Simmel put it more concisely: money supposedly transforms the world into an 'arithmetic problem' (quoted in Zelizer, 1989, p. 344). The underlying relations are 'collectively "forgotten about"' in order to ensure that they are not explored (Carruthers and Babb, 1996, p. 1559).

The value of each marketed commodity is then denominated in the commodity chosen as the medium of exchange through the asocial forces of supply and demand. Regrettably, nations have abandoned the use of intrinsically valuable money in favor of 'fiat' monies that cannot provide a relative price anchor. Monetary growth rules, prohibitions on treasury money creation, balanced budget requirements and the like (not to mention currency boards and dollar standards for developing nations) are all attempts to remove discretion from monetary and fiscal authorities, to make fiat money operate as if it were a commodity, thereby restoring the 'natural', asocial, monetary order.

Money and banking textbooks also reduced discussion of the money supply to 'an arithmetic problem' based on the 'deposit multiplier' identity. The central bank would increase the supply of bank reserves and banks would respond by increasing loans and deposits by a fairly stable multiple (Brunner, 1968). Hence the growth of the money supply was supposed to be 'exogenously controlled' by the central bank. Since money is mostly used for transactions purposes, it can be linked to nominal GDP through the equation of exchange. If 'real' GDP grows at a 'natural rate' (determined by supply-side factors such as technological advance and growth of inputs), and given stable velocity, then there will be a close relation between growth of the money supply and changes to the price level. This is, of course, the foundation to the monetarist approach and led to the famous call by Milton Friedman for the central bank to target reserves and thereby money growth in order to control inflation. By the late 1970s this view came to dominate policy-making and actually led to attempts by central bankers to target monetary aggregates.

At the same time, the rational expectations hypothesis was merged with old 'classical' theory and monetarism to create what came to be called new classical theory. The most important conclusion was that money would be neutral in the short run, as well as the long run, so long as policy was predictable. In practical terms, this meant that an announced and believable policy could bring down inflation rapidly merely by reducing money growth rates, and with no unemployment or growth trade-off. In a sense, money became irrelevant.

While I shall not explore modern theories of finance in detail, developments there mirrored the evolution of mainstream economic theory in the sense that finance also became irrelevant. So long as markets are efficient, all forms of finance are equivalent. Financial institutions are seen as intermediaries that come between savers and investors, efficiently allocating savings to highest-use projects. Evolution of financial practices continually reduces the 'wedge' between the interest rate received by savers and that paid by investors – encouraging more saving and investment. Domestic financial market deregulation (under way since the mid-1960s in the USA) as well as globalization of international financial markets plays a key role in enhancing these efficiencies and, hence, in promoting growth. The key conclusion is that if market impediments are removed, finance becomes 'neutral'.

To be sure, a wide range of objections has been raised to these extreme conclusions, including existence of credit rationing, of sticky wages and prices, and of complex input–output relations – all of which could leave money non-neutral in the short run (see Gordon, 1990 for a summary.) These have been collected under the banner of new Keynesianism, but it is usually conceded that they do not constitute a coherent theoretical challenge to new classical theory. Another challenge came from real business cycle theory, which made money even less important, but it had to adopt assumptions that almost all economists regard as highly unrealistic. As Mankiw (1989) mused, mainstream economists were left with the uneasy choice of internal consistency (new classical or real business cycle approaches) or empirical relevance (new Keynesianism). The economics student faced a series of seemingly unrelated special-purpose models that shed little light on money, banking and finance.

By the end of the 1980s, orthodox policy-making was also in disarray as it appeared that central banks could not control the money supply and that money was not closely linked to nominal GDP (alternatively stated as that velocity had become unstable). Further, it did seem to many that money matters, in the sense that monetary policy affects unemployment and growth in fairly predictable – even if moderate – ways. Without money rules to guide them, central banks cast about for alternatives.

Over the course of the 1990s, orthodox economists developed a 'new monetary consensus' (NMC) to monetary theory and policy formation. There are several versions, but perhaps the best known includes an equation for output gap (the percentage point gap between actual and potential output), a dynamic version of a Phillips curve relating inflation to the gap, and a monetary policy (Taylor-like) rule. These can be set out as:

$$Y^*_t = a Y^*_{t-1} + b E_t(Y^*_{t+1}) - c[R_t - E_t(p_{t+1})] + x_t \qquad (27.1)$$
$$P_t = d(Y^*_t) + w1 p_{t-1} + w2 E_t(p_{t+1}) + z_t \text{(note } w1 + w2 = 1) \qquad (27.2)$$
$$R_t = r^* + E_t(p_{t+1}) + f Y^*_{t-1} + g(p_{t-1} - p^*), \qquad (27.3)$$

where Y^* is the output gap, R is the nominal interest rate target, r^* is the 'natural' or equilibrium real interest rate, p is inflation, and p^* is the inflation target (x and z are stochastic shocks) (see Meyer, 2001). Note that the nominal interest rate target is set taking into account the output gap and the difference between actual and desired inflation. This then feeds into the IS (investment/saving)-like demand gap equation based on the presumption that the nominal rate less expected inflation (the 'real rate') influences demand.

According to the NMC, in the long run only the supply side matters, while in the short run, both supply-side and demand-side variables matter. Unlike the 1960s version of Keynesian economics, fiscal policy is given a small role to play on the demand side (although government can influence the supply side, e.g. through its tax policy). Hence monetary policy is given the larger role to play in affecting demand and hence growth. In the long run, money is neutral, but a variety of transmission avenues has been posited to allow money to influence demand in the short run.

The NMC rejects a simple monetarist transmission mechanism (from monetary aggregates to spending). Rather, it is recognized that central banks operate mostly with interest rate targets, but these are supposed to affect demand directly (interest elasticity of spending) and indirectly (portfolio effects). The money supply, in turn, results from an interaction of central bank policy, portfolio preferences of market participants, and the demand for credit. There is substantial consensus that the central bank has a strong, albeit short-run, impact on demand. When the economy grows too fast, threatening to set off inflation, the central bank dampens demand by raising interest rates; when it grows too slowly (causing unemployment and raising the specter of deflation), the central bank lowers rates to stimulate demand.

Private banks and financial markets play an accommodating role, following the central bank's lead. When the central bank announces that it will tighten, financial market participants drive interest rates up, choking off credit demand and reducing spending, cooling the economy and dissipating inflationary pressures. The NMC encourages central bank transparency because effective monetary policy requires cooperation of financial markets; this, in turn, requires consistency of expectations so that central bank intentions are quickly incorporated in expectations and thus in market behavior. For example, when the central bank raises nominal interest rates to fight inflation, if there are consistent expectations, markets quickly lower their inflation forecasts. This makes the real interest rate (nominal rate less expected inflation) rise even more, depressing demand and spending, allowing actual inflation to fall. The shared expectations make policy more effective. Further, policy changes are implemented only gradually to avoid disruptive 'surprises' that could generate instability. In this way, the central bank can slow growth and inflation through a limited series of small interest rate hikes – avoiding the problems created in the early 1980s when the Federal Reserve Board (the Fed) raised overnight interest rates above 20 percent in its attempt to fight inflation.

2.   Development of an alternative to orthodoxy

The orthodox story of money's origins is rejected by most serious scholars outside the field of economics as historically inaccurate (see Davies, 1994; Cramp, 1962; Heinsohn and Steiger, 1983, 1989; Hudson, 2001; Ingham, 2000, 2005; Keynes, 1914; Maddox, 1969; Robert, 1956; Wray, 2004). While there is evidence of ceremonial exchange in primitive society, there is nothing approximating money-less markets based on barter (outside trivial cases such as POW camps). Further, the orthodox sequence of 'commodity (gold) money' and then credit and fiat money does not square with the historical record. Written records of credits and debits pre-date precious metal coins by thousands of years. Indeed, financial accounting was highly sophisticated and much more 'efficient' for market transactions than use of coins, which developed thousands of years later, indicating that it is highly unlikely that coinage developed to facilitate exchange. Finally, historians and anthropologists have long disputed the notion that markets originated spontaneously from some primeval propensity; rather they emphasize the important role played by authorities in creating and organizing markets (Polanyi, 1971).

Still, orthodox economists do not insist on the historical accuracy of their story, but instead use it to shed light on what they believe to be the nature of money and the proper role for government to play. Perhaps the most interesting aspect of the orthodox story is that it completely ignores the overriding feature of the monetary landscape: in almost every case, a money of account (or 'currency') is associated with a nation-state. However, again, we can set aside historical accuracy and ponder the implications for our understanding of the 'nature' of money. In the orthodox story, money is a handy medium of exchange and government enters the picture as an interloper that abandons 'natural' gold money in favor of 'unnatural' fiat money that is imposed on markets. The obvious danger is that money then has no backing, nothing to guarantee its value relative to marketed commodities. This is why orthodox policy is so concerned with inflation control. In addition, and related to this, the orthodox story downplays all social relations – including power. The main exception to this would be reference to state legal tender laws that force market participants to accept the state's currency, and reserve ratios that are required of banks. With a fiat money, this is said to provide seigniorage to government. Still, government has at best a quasi-legitimate role, but this is tempered by a strong inclination to mismanage a fiat money that in the long run is neutral, but in the short run can distort market signals.

Is there an alternative, social economic, view?

To be sure, we shall never 'know' the origins of money. For one reason, it is not clear what we want to identify as money. Money is social in nature, consisting of a complex social practice that includes power and class relationships, socially constructed meaning and abstract representations of social value. As Hudson (2004) rightly argues, ancient and even 'primitive' society was no less complex than today's society, and economic relations were highly embedded within social structures that we little understand. At best, our story about money's origins identifies what we believe to be important about money by singling out past institutionalized behaviors that appear similar to those today that we wish to identify as 'money'. While the alternative view *is* more consistent with the historical record, such as it exists, the essential point is that it sheds light on an alternative approach to finance, banks and money.

To that end, we would locate the origin of money in credit and debt relations, with the money of account emphasized as the numeraire in which credits and debts are measured. The store of value function could also be important, for one stores wealth in the form of others' debts. On the other hand, the medium of exchange function is de-emphasized; indeed, credits and debits could pre-date a functioning market. Some have suggested that we can locate the origins of credit and debt relations in the elaborate system of tribal wergild[1] designed to prevent blood feuds (Innes, 1913, 1914, 1932; Goodhart, 1998, 2005; Grierson, 1977, 1979; Wray, 1998, 2004). Wergild fines were paid directly to victims and their families, and were socially established and levied by public assemblies. Note that fines were not levied in a unit of account but rather in terms of a particular item that was both useful to the victim and more or less easily obtained by the perpetrator.

As Hudson (2004) reports, the words for debt in most languages are synonymous with sin or guilt, reflecting these early reparations for personal injury. Originally, until one paid the wergild fine, one was 'liable', or 'indebted', to the victim. The words for money, fines, tribute, tithes, debts, manprice, sin and, finally, taxes are so often linked in language as to eliminate the possibility of coincidence. It is almost certain that wergild fines were gradually converted to payments made to an authority. This could not occur in an egalitarian tribal society, but had to await the rise of some sort of ruling class. As Henry (2004) argues for the case of Egypt, the earliest ruling classes were probably religious officials, who demanded tithes (ostensibly, to keep the gods happy). Alternatively, conquerors required payments of tribute by a subject population. Tithes and tribute thus came to replace wergild fines, and fines for 'transgressions against society', paid to the rightful ruler, could be levied for almost any conceivable activity (see Peacock, 2003). Eventually, taxes would replace most fees, fines and tributes.

A key innovation was the transformation of what had been the transgressor's debt to the victim to a universal 'debt' or tax obligation imposed by and payable to the authority. The next step was the standardization of the obligations in a unit of account. At first, the authority might have levied a variety of fines (and tributes, tithes and taxes) in terms of goods or services to be delivered, one for each sort of transgression. Denominating payments in a unit of account would simplify matters, but as Grierson (1977, 1979) remarked, development of a unit of account would be conceptually difficult (see also Henry, 2004). It is easier to come by measures of weight or length – the length of some anatomical feature of the ruler (from which comes our term for the device used to measure short lengths), or the weight of a quantity of grain. It is certainly not a coincidence that all the early money units (mina, shekel, livre, pound) were taken over from grain weights. For example, Hudson links the early monetary units developed in the temples and palaces of Sumer in the third millennium BC to the 'monthly consumption unit, a "bushel" of barley, the major commodity being disbursed' (Hudson, 2004, p. 111).

Once we had the universal unit of account, credits and debts could be denominated in 'money'. In a particularly insightful pair of articles, A. Mitchell Innes (1913, 1914) developed what might be called a credit theory of money (see also Gardiner, 2004; Ingham, 2000, 2004a, 2004b.) He mocked the view that 'in modern days a money-saving device has been introduced called *credit* and that, before this device was known all purchases were paid for in cash, in other words in coins' (Innes, 1913, p. 389). Instead, he argued, 'careful investigation shows that the precise reverse is true' (ibid.). Rather than selling in exchange for 'some intermediate commodity called the "medium of exchange"', a sale is really 'the exchange of a commodity for a credit'. Innes called this the 'primitive law of commerce': 'The constant creation of credits and debts, and their extinction by being cancelled against one another, forms the whole mechanism of commerce . . .' (ibid., p. 393). The market, then, is not viewed as the place where goods are exchanged, but rather as a clearinghouse for debts and credits. On this view, debts and credits and clearing are the general phenomena; trade in goods and services is subsidiary – one of the ways in which one becomes a debtor or creditor (or clears debts).

Finally, banks emerge to specialize in clearing:

> Debts and credits are perpetually trying to get into touch with one another, so that they may be written off against each other, and it is the business of the banker to bring them together. This is done in two ways: either by *discounting bills*, or by *making loans*. (Ibid., p. 402)

> There is thus a constant circulation of debts and credits through the medium of the banker who brings them together and clears them as the debts fall due. This is the whole science of banking as it was three thousand years before Christ, and as it is to-day. (Ibid., p. 403)

Banks are not intermediaries between 'savers and investors' but rather allow creditors and debtors to clear accounts with third-person – bank – liabilities. If 'A' has a debt to 'B', A does not have to find one of B's IOUs to settle the debt, but rather can clear accounts using a bank's liability. The debtor, A, writes a check on the bank, accepted by the creditor, B, which can use it to cancel any debt owed to the bank. The bank accepts its own IOU and clears it against B's IOU, the bank's asset.

Another important activity of banks is to operate clearing facilities between the state and its taxpayers: the taxpayer does not have to get hold of a government liability to pay taxes, because the treasury accepts bank liabilities in payment. This then leads to a deduction of bank reserves. In this way, bank reserves are not viewed as the 'raw material' from which banks are able to make loans (as in the orthodox deposit multiplier story), but rather as the government liability held by banks to facilitate clearing with the government for their customers. In addition, reserves are used by banks for net clearing with one another, for example, when debtor A and creditor B use different banks. Rather than seeing government currency and reserves ('high-powered money', HPM, or monetary base) as a 'fiat money' with no backing, the alternative approach insists that even government money can be viewed as a set of credits and debts. On the government's balance sheet, HPM is a liability; on the holder's balance sheet, HPM is an asset.

What backs the government liability? Orthodoxy responds 'nothing', and insists that is the fundamental problem with 'fiat' money. For a more satisfying answer, we need to explore the 'very nature of credit throughout the world', which is 'the right of the holder of the credit (the creditor) to hand back to the issuer of the debt (the debtor) the latter's acknowledgment or obligation' (Innes, 1914, p. 161). Any issuer of a debt must accept its own debt back in payment, and Innes explains quite clearly that the government is no exception:

> The holder of a coin or certificate has the absolute right to pay any debt due to the government by tendering that coin or certificate, and it is this right and nothing else which gives them their value. It is immaterial whether or not the right is conveyed by statute, or even whether there may be a statute law defining the nature of a coin or certificate otherwise. (Ibid.)

Government money – like any liability – must 'reflux' back to the issuer. Still, money *is* different, because it is 'redeemable by the mechanism of taxation' (ibid., p. 15): '[I]t is the tax which imparts to the obligation its 'value' . . . A dollar of money is a dollar, not because of the material of which it is made, but because of the dollar of tax which is imposed to redeem it' (ibid., p. 152). In other words, what 'stands behind' the state's currency is the tax system, and the state's obligation to accept its own currency in payment of taxes. There is sovereign power behind state money – the power to impose fees, fines, tithes, or, ultimately, taxes (Bell, 2004; Knapp, [1924] 1973; Lerner, 1943, 1947; Parguez, 2002; Wray, 1998).

Of course, saying that dollars have value because the government imposes a dollar tax does not mean that only those with tax liabilities will accept dollars; nor does it even mean that anyone accepting a dollar in payment is consciously thinking of the tax liability that can be removed by paying dollars. People also accept bank liabilities (checks drawn on banks) without realizing that the issuing bank must accept its own check to pay down a loan it has made – the person accepting the check probably uses another bank and may not have any outstanding bank loans at all. However, if a bank began to refuse to accept its own liabilities in payment, these would very quickly lose all value (and the bank's officers would just as quickly be taken to court). Similarly, so long as a government imposes a dollar tax on at least some of its citizens, and so long as it requires payment in the form of its dollar liabilities (even where banks play an intermediating role), this will be sufficient to ensure that the dollar will be desired – by someone. (We do not need to make the stronger case that the tax liability is a *necessary* condition for acceptance of dollar currency, but only that it is a *sufficient condition*.) And just as a bank's liabilities will be accepted even by those who are not bank debtors, a government's currency will be accepted by those with no current tax liabilities – and even by those with no conscious thought of tax liabilities.

3. New directions and policy implications of the alternative approach

The alternative view of money leads to quite different conclusions regarding monetary and fiscal policy. It rejects even long-run neutrality of money, although it might downplay the short-run effectiveness of monetary policy. It also generates interesting insights on exchange rate regimes and international payments systems. In this section I shall outline only briefly directions for alternative thinking about policy, focusing on the government budget constraint, on central bank control of money and inflation, and on international financial flows and exchange rate regimes.

Fiscal policy

It is commonly believed that fiscal policy faces a budget constraint according to which its spending must be 'financed' by taxes, borrowing (bond sales), or 'money creation'. Since many nations prohibit direct 'money creation' by the government's treasury, it is supposed that the last option is possible only through complicity of the central bank – which could buy the government's bonds, and hence finance deficit spending by 'printing money'. Actually, a government that issues its own currency spends exclusively by crediting bank accounts – using banks as 'agents' of government, as discussed above – while tax payments result in debits to bank accounts. Deficit spending by government takes the form of net credits to bank accounts. Those receiving net payments from government usually hold banking system liabilities while banks hold reserves in the form of central bank liabilities (we can ignore leakages from deposits – and reserves – into cash held by the non-bank public as a simple complication). While there are fairly complex coordinating procedures followed by the central bank and treasury, the logical point is that deficit spending by the treasury results in net credits to banking system reserves (see Bell, 2000, 2001; Bell and Wray, 2003; Wray, 1998 for detailed analyses.)

If these net credits lead to excess reserve positions, overnight interest rates will be bid down by banks offering the excess in the overnight interbank lending market. Unless the central bank is operating with a zero interest rate target, declining overnight rates trigger automatic open market bond sales to drain excess reserves. Hence, on a day-to-day basis, the central bank intervenes to offset undesired impacts of fiscal policy on reserves when they cause the overnight rate to move away from target. The process operates in reverse if the treasury runs a surplus, which results in net debits of reserves from the banking system. This puts upward pressure on overnight rates that is relieved by open market purchases. When fiscal policy is biased to run deficits (or surpluses) on a sustained basis, the central bank will run out of bonds to sell (or will accumulate too many bonds, offset on its balance sheet by a treasury deposit exceeding operating limits). Hence policy is coordinated between the central bank and the treasury to ensure that the treasury will begin to issue new securities as it runs deficits (or retire old issues in the case of a budget surplus). Again, these coordinating activities can be varied and complicated, but they are not important to our analysis. When all is said and done, a budget deficit that creates excess reserves leads to bond sales by the central bank (open market) and the treasury (new issues) to drain all excess reserves; a budget surplus causes the reverse to take place when the banking system is short of reserves.

Bond sales (or purchases) by the treasury and central bank are, then, ultimately triggered by deviation of reserves from the position desired by (or required of) the banking system, which causes the overnight rate to move away from target (if the target is above zero). Bond sales by either the central bank or the treasury are properly seen as part of monetary policy designed to allow the central bank to hit its target, rather than as a government 'borrowing' operation. The interest rate target is exogenously 'administered' by the central bank. Obviously, the central bank sets its target as a result of its belief about the impact of this rate on a range of economic variables that are included in its policy objectives. In other words, setting this rate 'exogenously' does not imply that the central bank is oblivious to economic and political constraints it believes to reign.

In sum, the notion of a 'government budget constraint' applies only *ex post*, as a statement of an identity that has no significance as an economic constraint. Ultimately, it is certainly true that any increase of government spending will be matched by an increase of taxes, an increase of high-powered money (reserves and cash), and/or an increase of sovereign debt held. But this does not mean that taxes or bonds actually 'financed' the government spending. Government might well enact provisions that dictate relations between changes to spending and changes to tax revenues (a balanced budget, for example); it might require that bonds are issued before deficit spending actually takes place; it might require that the treasury have 'money in the bank' (deposits at the central bank) before it can cut a check; and so on. These provisions might constrain government's ability to spend at the desired level. However, economic analysis shows that they are self-imposed and are not economically necessary – although they may well be politically necessary.

What is the significance of this? It means that the state can take advantage of its role in the monetary system to mobilize resources in the public interest, without worrying about 'availability of finance'. It still must worry about 'availability' of real resources: are resources underutilized? If not, increased government use of resources means that other activities will have to be curtailed – a trade-off that should be carefully evaluated. But in the normal situation in which significant portions of social resources are underutilized, the government can use the monetary system to put them to work, simply through its spending that is 'financed' by crediting bank accounts. If this results in a budget deficit, that is no cause for alarm.

Monetary policy
Turning to conventional views on money, as discussed above there is a long-held belief that the central bank can and should control the money supply. Innes (like Tooke and others before him – see Wray, 1990) made a very strong case that attempts to control the issue of bank notes (or, today, the quantity of deposits issued by banks) is fundamentally misguided:

> To attempt the regulation of banking by limiting the note issue is to entirely misunderstand the whole banking problem, and to start at the wrong end. The danger lies not in the bank note but in imprudent or dishonest banking. Once insure that banking shall be carried on by honest people under a proper understanding of the principles of credit and debt, and the note issue may be left to take care of itself. (Innes, 1913, p. 407)

This argument can be carried through to the 'money supply' as a whole: the rate of growth of any monetary aggregate provides no information of use to policy-makers – whether we are talking of HPM, M1, M2, or any broader monetary measure (see Moore, 1988). The quantity of an outstanding 'money stock' is simply an aggregation of some portion of the quantity of credits (and, equally, debts) outstanding at some point in time. It can grow through time either because the rate of creation of new credits (and debts) has risen, or because the rate of 'retirement' of credits (that is, matching credits and debts to clear them) has fallen. Either of these can result from a variety of circumstances, and correlation with some measure of the 'value' of money (as measured by an index of prices of a selected basket of marketed commodities) could be entirely coincidental.

Further, even if the link between 'money growth' and 'inflation' were more than coincidence, which policy might constrain 'money growth' is far from unambiguous. Direct 'credit controls' that constrained lending for, say, real-estate purchases could be effective in cooling overheated housing construction markets, which *could* reduce the growth of a price index that included housing prices, and could *perhaps* reduce the growth of some monetary aggregate. However, it is hard to see why the usual tool used by modern central banks – rate hikes – would generally result in lower money growth and inflation (however defined). Interest rate changes have multifarious effects on spending, income distribution, solvency and hence financial stability, and costs. For example, rate hikes will shift the distribution of income from debtors to creditors, which has complex – perhaps offsetting – effects on spending (consumption, investment, government and foreign sector). While it is generally believed that rate hikes reduce borrowing and spending, lowering aggregate demand and thus price pressures, this could be offset if not overwhelmed by the effects of higher interest costs on businesses that have to finance wages, inventories and capital projects. Finally, government is a net payer of interest in most nations, and as rates rise, its spending rises – increasing interest income and presumably spending of the non-government sector. It is no wonder that empirical studies have not been able to find consistent evidence in favor of the conventional views of interest rate–spending–inflation relations.

In conclusion, even if there is a link between 'money' and 'inflation' (however defined), it is not at all clear that conventional monetary policy has any predictable effect on inflation (or spending). This does mean that money is neutral, for money is key to the production process in a capitalist economy. But it does cast serious doubt on the NMC call for fine-tuning of 'demand gaps' through use of monetary policy.

Exchange rate policy
There is a great deal of confusion over international 'flows' of currency, reserves and finance, much of which results from failure to distinguish between a floating versus a fixed exchange rate. For example, it is often claimed that the USA needs 'foreign savings' in order to 'finance' its persistent trade deficit that results from US consumers who are said to be 'living beyond their means'. Such a statement makes no sense for a sovereign nation operating on a flexible exchange rate. For example, a US trade deficit results when the rest of the world (ROW) wishes to net save in the form of dollar assets. From the perspective of the ROW, exports to the

USA reflect the 'cost' imposed on citizens of the ROW to obtain the 'benefit' of accumulating dollar-denominated assets. From the perspective of the USA as a whole, the 'net benefit' of the trade deficit consists of the net imports that are enjoyed. In contrast to the conventional view, it is more revealing to think of the US trade deficit as 'financing' the net dollar saving of the ROW – rather than thinking of the ROW as 'financing' the US trade deficit. If and when the ROW decides it has a sufficient stock of dollar assets, the US trade deficit will disappear.

Note that these arguments are predicated on adoption of a floating exchange rate. A country that operates on a gold standard, or a currency board, or a fixed exchange rate is constrained in its ability to use the monetary system in the public interest, because it must accumulate reserves of the asset(s) to which it has pegged exchange rates. This leads to significant constraints on both monetary and fiscal policy because they must be geared to ensure a trade surplus that will allow accumulation of the reserve asset. This is because such reserves are required to maintain a credible policy of pegging the exchange rate. On a fixed exchange rate, if a country faces a current account deficit, it will need to depress domestic demand and wages and prices in an effort to reduce imports and increase exports. In a sense, the nation loses policy independence to pursue a domestic agenda. Floating the exchange rate effectively frees policy to pursue other, domestic, goals such as maintenance of full employment.

4. Conclusions

To put it as simply as possible, the state chooses the unit of account in which the various money things will be denominated. In all modern economies, it does this when it chooses the unit in which taxes will be denominated and names what is accepted in tax payments. Imposition of the tax liability is what makes these money things desirable in the first place. And those things will then become the high-powered money-thing (HPM) at the top of the 'money pyramid' used for ultimate clearing. The state then issues HPM in its own payments – in the modern economy by crediting bank reserves, and banks, in turn, credit accounts of their depositors.

Of course, most transactions that do not involve the government take place on the basis of credits and debits, that is, privately issued credit money. This can be thought of as a leveraging of HPM. However, this should not be taken the wrong way – there is no fixed leverage ratio (as in the orthodox deposit multiplier story). Further, in all modern monetary systems the central bank targets an overnight interest rate, standing by to supply HPM on demand ('horizontally') to the banking sector (or to withdraw it from the banking sector when excess reserves exist) to hit its target. Thus, both the central bank and treasury supply HPM. The central bank either buys assets or requires collateral against its lending, and it may well impose other 'frown' costs on borrowing banks. Hence, while central bank provision of HPM provides a degree of 'slop' to the system, HPM is never dropped from helicopters – as Friedman famously assumed. In any case, the central bank and treasury coordinate to ensure the banking system has the amount of reserves required/desired using bond sales and purchases to adjust reserves to allow the central bank to hit its rate target.

Likewise, the privately supplied credit money is never dropped from helicopters. Its issue puts the issuer simultaneously in a credit and debit situation, and does the same for the party accepting the credit money. For example, a bank creates an asset (the borrower's IOU) and a liability (the borrower's deposit) when it makes a loan; the borrower simultaneously becomes a debtor and a creditor. Banks then operate to match credits and debits while net clearing in HPM. Borrowers operate in the economy to obtain bank liabilities to cancel their own IOUs to banks, to others in the private sector, and to government. Banks act as intermediaries in this clearing process.

There is an important hierarchical relation in the debt/credit system, with power – especially in the form of command over society's resources – underlying and deriving from the hierarchy. The ability to impose liabilities, name the unit of account, and issue the money used to pay down these liabilities gives a substantial measure of power to the authority. There is, thus, the potential to use this power to further the social good, although misunderstanding or mystification of the nature of money results in an outcome that is far below what is economically feasible as government is 'constrained' by the principles of 'sound finance'.

Far from springing from the minds of atomistic utility maximizers, money is a social creation. The private credit system leverages state money, which in turn is supported by the state's ability to impose social obligations, mostly in the form of taxes. While it is commonly believed that taxes 'pay for' government activity, actually obligations denominated in a unit of account create a demand for money that, in turn, allows society to organize social production, partly through a system of nominal prices. Much of the public production is undertaken by emitting state money through government purchase. Much private sector activity, in turn, takes the form of 'monetary production', or M–C–M' as Marx put it, that is, through monetary purchase of required inputs with a view to realizing 'more money' from the sale of final product. The initial and final purchases are mostly financed on the basis of credits and debits – that is, 'private' money creation. Because money is fundamental to these production processes, it cannot be neutral. Indeed, it contributes to the creation and evolution of a 'logic' to the operation of a capitalist system, 'disembedding' the economy to a degree never before encountered (Heilbroner, 1985; Wray, 1990, p. 54). At the same time, many of the social relations can be, and are, hidden behind a veil of money. This becomes most problematic with respect to misunderstanding about government budgets, where the monetary veil conceals the potential to use the monetary system in the public interest.

By emphasizing the importance of the link between the 'fiat' (or state) unit of account and public finance, the alternative approach to money points to new directions for monetary, fiscal and exchange rate policies that stand in stark contrast to the orthodox view of money as little more than a market lubricant. There is still much research to be undertaken to further develop a truly social economic approach to these issues, but a good place to start is with the nature of sovereign power and credit–debt relations.

Note

1. Alternative spellings include wergeld or weregild. 'In ancient Germanic law the amount of compensation paid by a person committing an offense to the injured party or, in case of death, to his family' (Encyclopedia Britannica article, www.britannica.com/eb/article-9i076562/wergild).

References

Bell, Stephanie (2000), 'Do taxes and bonds finance government spending?', *Journal of Economic Issues*, **34**, 603–20.
Bell, Stephanie (2001), 'The role of the state and the hierarchy of money', *Cambridge Journal of Economics*, **25** (2), 149–63.
Bell, Stephanie and L. Randall Wray (2003), 'Fiscal impacts on reserves and the independence of the Fed', *Journal of Post Keynesian Economics*, **25** (2), 263–71.
Bell, Stephanie, John F. Henry and L. Randall Wray (2004), 'A Chartalist critique of John Locke's theory of property, accumulation, and money: or is it moral to trade your nuts for gold?', *Review of Social Economy*, **62** (1), 51–65.
Brunner, Karl (1968), 'The role of money and monetary policy', *Federal Reserve Bank of St Louis Review*, **50** (July), 9.
Carruthers, Bruce G. and Sarah Babb (1996), 'The color of money and the nature of value: greenbacks and gold in post-bellum America', *American Journal of Sociology*, **101** (6), 1556–91.
Cramp, A.B. (1962), 'Two views on money', *Lloyds Bank Review*, July, p. 1.
Davies, G. (1994), *A History of Money from Ancient Times to the Present Day*, Cardiff: University of Wales Press.
Friedman, Milton (1969), *The Optimal Quantity of Money and Other Essays*, Chicago, IL: Aldine.
Gardiner, Geoffrey W. (2004), 'The primacy of trade debts in the development of money', in L.R. Wray (ed.), *Credit and State Theories of Money: The Contributions of A. Mitchell Innes*, Cheltenham, UK and Northampton, MA, USA: Edward Elgar, pp. 128–72.
Goodhart, Charles A.E. (1998), 'Two concepts of money: implications for the analysis of optimal currency areas', *European Journal of Political Economy*, **14**, 407–32.
Goodhart, Charles A.E. (2005), 'Review of credit and state theories of money: the contributions of A. Mitchell Innes', *History of Political Economy*, **37** (4), 759–61.
Gordon, Robert J. (1990), 'What is New-Keynesian economics?', *Journal of Economic Literature*, **28** (3), 1115–71.
Grierson, Philip (1977), *The Origins of Money*, London: Athlone Press.
Grierson, Philip (1979), *Dark Age Numismatics*, London: Variorum Reprints.

494   *The Elgar companion to social economics*

Heilbroner, Robert (1985), *The Nature and Logic of Capitalism*, New York and London: W.W. Norton and Co.
Heinsohn, Gunnar and Otto Steiger (1983), *Private Property, Debts and Interest or: The Origin of Money and the Rise and Fall of Monetary Economics*, Naples, Italy: University of Bremen.
Heinsohn, Gunnar and Otto Steiger (1989), 'The veil of barter: the solution to the "task of obtaining representations of an economy in which money is essential" ', in J.A. Kregel (ed.), *Inflation and Income Distribution in Capitalist Crises: Essays in Memory of Sydney Weintraub*, New York: New York University Press, pp. 175–201.
Henry, John (2004), 'The social origins of money: the case of Egypt', in L.R. Wray (ed.), *Credit and State Theories of Money: The Contributions of A. Mitchell Innes*, Cheltenham, UK and Northampton, MA, USA: Edward Elgar, pp. 79–98.
Hudson, Michael (2001), 'Public-sector vs. individualistic (and debt vs. barter) theories of the origins of money', manuscript.
Hudson, Michael (2004), 'The archaeology of money: debt versus barter theories of money's origins', in L.R.Wray (ed.), *Credit and State Theories of Money: The Contributions of A. Mitchell Innes*, Cheltenham, UK and Northampton, MA, USA: Edward Elgar, pp. 99–127.
Ingham, Geoffrey (2000), 'Babylonian madness: on the historical and sociological origins of money', in John Smithin (ed.), *What Is Money*, London and New York: Routledge, pp. 16–41.
Ingham, Geoffrey (2004a), 'The emergence of capitalist credit money', in L.R. Wray (ed.), *Credit and State Theories of Money: The Contributions of A. Mitchell Innes*, Cheltenham, UK and Northampton, MA, USA: Edward Elgar, pp. 173–222.
Ingham, Geoffrey (2004b), *The Nature of Money*, Cambridge: Polity Press.
Ingham, Geoffrey (ed.) (2005), *Concepts of Money: Interdisciplinary Perspectives from Economics, Sociology, and Political Science*, Cheltenham, UK and Northampton, MA, USA: Edward Elgar.
Innes, A.M. (1913), 'What is money?', *Banking Law Journal*, May, 377–408.
Innes, A.M. (1914), 'The credit theory of money', *Banking Law Journal*, January, 151–68.
Innes, A.M. (1932), *Martyrdom in Our Times: Two Essays on Prisons and Punishment*, London: Williams & Norgate.
Keynes, J.M. (1914), 'What is money?', *Economic Journal*, **24** (95), 419–21.
Keynes, J.M. (1930), *A Treatise on Money*, Vols I and II (1976), New York: Harcourt, Brace & Co.
Keynes, J.M. (1982), *The Collected Writings of John Maynard Keynes, Volume XXVIII*, ed. Donald Moggridge, London and Basingstoke: Macmillan.
Klein, Peter G. and George Selgin (2000), 'Menger's theory of money: some experimental evidence', in John Smithin (ed.), *What Is Money?*, London and New York: Routledge, pp. 217–34.
Knapp, Georg Friedrich ([1924] 1973), *The State Theory of Money*, Clifton, NJ: Augustus M. Kelley.
Lerner, Abba P. (1943), 'Functional finance and the federal debt', *Social Research*, **10**, 38–51.
Lerner, Abba P. (1947), 'Money as a creature of the state', *American Economic Review*, **37**, 312–17.
Maddox, Thomas (1969), *The History and Antiquities of the Exchequer of the Kings of England in TwoPeriods*, Vols I and II, 2nd edn, New York: Greenwood Press.
Mankiw, N. Gregory (1989), 'Real business cycles: a New Keynesian perspective', *The Journal of Economic Perspectives*, **3** (3), 79–90.
Meyer, L.H. (2001), 'Does money matter?' The Homer Jones Memorial Lecture, Washington University, St Louis, MO: Federal Reserve Bank.
Moore, Basil J. (1988), *Horizontalists and Verticalists: The Macroeconomics of Credit Money*, Cambridge: Cambridge University Press.
Parguez, Alain (2002), 'A monetary theory of public finance', *International Journal of Political Economy*, **32** (3), 80–97.
Peacock, Mark S. (2004), 'State, money, catallaxy: underlaboring for a chartalist theory of money', *Journal of Post Keynesian Economics*, **26** (2), 205–25.

Polanyi, Karl (1971), 'Aristotle discovers the economy', in Karl Polanyi, Conrad M. Arensberg and Harry W. Pearson (eds), *Trade and Market in the Early Empires*, Chicago, IL: Regnery Co., pp. 60–94.

Robert, Rudolph (1956), 'A short history of tallies', in A.C. Littleton and B.S. Yamey (eds), *Studies in the History of Accounting*, Homewood, IL: Richard D. Irwin, pp. 75–85.

Samuelson, Paul (1973), *Economics*, 9th edn, New York: McGraw-Hill.

Wray, L. Randall (1998), *Understanding Modern Money: The Key to Full Employment and Price Stability*, Cheltenham, UK and Northampton, MA, USA: Edward Elgar.

Wray, L. Randall (1990), *Money and Credit in Capitalist Economies: The Endogenous Money Approach*, Aldershot, UK and Brookfield, USA: Edward Elgar.

Wray, L. Randall (ed.) (2004), *Credit and State Theories of Money: The Contributions of A. Mitchell Innes*, Cheltenham, UK and Northampton, MA, USA: Edward Elgar.

Zelizer, Viviana A. (1989), 'The social meaning of money: "special money"', *American Journal of Sociology*, **95** (2), 342–77.

28 Global finance and development: false starts, dead ends and social economic alternatives
Ilene Grabel

Social economics entails a commitment to a range of interlinked principles that make it particularly appropriate as a basis for thinking critically but also productively about development. Now more than ever, in the face of widening global inequality in wealth ownership, incomes and meaningful opportunities, the social economic commitment to the value-ladeness of all economic inquiry, the ethical imperative to engage in ameliorative practice, appreciation of the embeddedness of the economy (and economic actors) in social relations and institutions, and to holistic theorizing are particularly vital as we seek to theorize and design policy interventions that can bring about basic economic justice in the developing world. Central to the social economics tradition is the imperative to study ways of strengthening the weak and assisting the poor (Dugger, 1977, p. 300), wherever on the globe they reside. The internationalism of this commitment to improving the circumstances of the poor flows directly from the foundational constructs of interconnectedness and holism, as well as from the understanding of economics as a fundamentally moral science directed to social improvement.

For many working within this tradition, social economics entails an understanding of economists *qua* activists and educators with an ethical obligation to help society understand its possible alternative paths (Waters, 1990, p. 102). This understanding of the profession, however, does not imply that the economist is an omniscient figure standing above other social actors, as is the case in the dominant mainstream (i.e. neoclassical) approach (Lutz, 1999, p. 105). The theoretical precepts and commitments of social economics enable those working within this tradition to shed light on contemporary debates concerning the spillover effects of policies in wealthy countries on conditions in developing countries and over the efficacy of policies adopted by developing countries. The work of Nobel Laureates Gunnar Myrdal and Amartya Sen stand as notable exemplars of social economic research in development.

The social economic principles and commitments described above bear with particular force on the matter of the connections between global finance and economic development. Over the past several decades, mainstream economic theorists and policy entrepreneurs have presented an unambiguous and even simplistic account of the means by which financial flows can be put in service of development. The general contours of this prescription, which entails a rather steadfast commitment to 'financial liberalization', are fairly well known. But this prescription has met with repeated failures across the developing world, and among the postsocialist transitional economies. As a consequence, the prescription has been amended repeatedly in order to account for these failures without sacrificing the economic science that founds the prescription, or its most central features.

In this chapter I explore the contribution of social economics to the matter of finance and development in several steps. First, I present a fairly brief account of the mainstream neoclassical approach to finance and trace through its historical development since the early 1970s. In the next substantive section of the chapter I attempt to demonstrate that the failures of this approach stemmed from key weaknesses in the neoclassical approach. Among other things, I argue that this approach fails to recognize the embeddedness of financial arrangements in broader political and social contexts, and that these contexts shape decisively the consequences that these arrangements have on economic outcomes. Moreover, I argue that the refusal of this approach to recognize the interpenetration of the normative and the positive leaves its proponents in the grasp of ideological forces that they do not themselves recognize, which leaves them with no avenue but to reach for *ad hoc* adjustments to the theory to which they adhere rather than look beyond its confines for alternative explanations of events and sources of policy prescription.

The chapter then turns to a range of important heterodox contributions to the debate over finance and development that have emerged in the wake of the repeated and consequential failures of the financial liberalization prescription. I focus in this section on contributions that in some way or other draw on themes (and presumptions) that are central to social economics. We shall find that many of these contributions, coming as they do from the ranks of institutionalists, post-Keynesians, Marxists and other traditions that share something with social economics, emphasize the connections between economic and non-economic institutions and practices, and they foreground normative goals that reach far beyond (and often reject) the neoclassical commitment to efficiency. We shall find in these accounts particular concern for those worst off, and the ways in which financial arrangements can either exacerbate or work to ameliorate economic inequality. We shall also find in these approaches a concern with the effect of financial arrangements on political voice (in the sense of

Albert Hirschman, 1986) and on national policy autonomy *vis-à-vis* external actors and domestic rentiers.

1.   State of the literature: the evolution of the financial liberalization ideal[1]
The neoclassical approach to finance and development has predominated in the academy and policy circles for several decades. During that time advocates of this approach have offered significant amendments to the initial theory and prescription. These are viewed simply as marking the natural evolution of a maturing science that only began to explore the connections between finance and development in a systematic way in the early 1970s.[2]

First-generation financial liberalization theory: the McKinnon–Shaw hypothesis
Following the publication of what became seminal works by Ronald McKinnon and Edward Shaw (published separately in 1973), neoclassical economists began to argue that active regulation of financial systems in accordance with a state's development goals was counterproductive. This regulation – which they notably termed 'financial repression' – was the norm under import substitution industrialization strategies from the end of World War II until the mid-to-late 1970s. Financial systems were dominated by banks whose decisions were influenced by governments (rather than by capital markets) and were characterized by some combination of controls on interest and foreign exchange rates and credit allocation, state imposition of non-interest-bearing reserve requirements, restrictions on the presence of foreign financial institutions and investors, and controls over international private capital inflows and outflows.

In the view of McKinnon and Shaw and their theoretical descendants, active state involvement in the financial sector has a number of adverse consequences. The maintenance of artificially low interest rates encourages domestic savers to hold funds abroad, and encourages current consumption rather than saving in domestic financial institutions. This aggravates inflationary pressures. Moreover, low savings rates also suppress bank lending activity. Thus financial repression retards domestic investment and impedes employment and economic growth. In this account, then, economic stagnation and poverty are linked rather directly back to financial policy regimes that are ostensibly designed to promote development.

Neoclassical economists extended the critique of financial repression beyond these macroeconomic matters. They maintain that active state involvement in finance fragments domestic financial markets, with only a small segment of politically connected borrowers gaining access to scarce low-cost credit. Disenfranchised borrowers must resort to unregulated, 'informal' lenders who often charge exorbitant interest rates, or otherwise have to manage in the face of unmet needs for capital. Entrepreneurship, employment creation and growth thereby suffer. These negative effects are disproportionately experienced by the poor as the burden of scarce credit hits them hardest since they rarely have access to alternative, lower-cost sources of credit, such as the finance available on international capital markets or from international banks.

In view of the above, neoclassical economists from McKinnon and Shaw onward argued that developing countries must 'liberalize' their domestic financial systems. A liberalized financial system with a competitive capital market is seen to be central to the promotion of high levels of savings, investment, employment, productivity, foreign capital inflows and growth. From this perspective, liberalized systems serve the interests of the poor and the disenfranchised (as well as other groups) by increasing access to capital with attendant benefits for employment, investment and growth.

Neoclassical economists maintain that domestic financial liberalization not only increases the level of investment, but also increases its efficiency by allocating funds across investment projects according to rate-of-return criteria and via what are seen as objective or 'arm's-length' practices. Domestic financial liberalization is seen to improve the overall efficiency of the financial system by eliminating the wasteful and corrupt practices that flourish under financial regulation, and by subjecting borrowers and firm managers to market discipline. Market discipline and a reduction in cor-ruption are seen to improve the operating performance of financial institu-tions, and consequently enhance the prospects for financial stability.

In the neoclassical view, liberalization has other benefits. Not least, it encourages financial innovation, which reduces transactions costs while enhancing allocational efficiency. Investment and financial stability are pro-moted by new opportunities to diversify and disperse risk. By increasing the availability of finance, liberalization also eliminates the need for infor-mal finance, and allows borrowers to utilize forms of finance that are most appropriate to their investment project.

Neoclassical economists see the finance provided through internationally integrated, liberal capital markets as preferable to bank loans because the former is understood to have a greater ability to disperse risk, is allocated according to efficiency and performance criteria, is cheaper than other forms of external finance (such as bank loans), and is highly liquid. The liq-uidity attribute is seen as especially desirable because it places firm man-agers under the threat of investor exit (or higher capital costs) if they underperform. Internationally integrated capital markets are also seen to give the public and private sector access to capital and other resources (such as technology) that are not being generated domestically. Thus neoclassical economists maintain that an increase in private capital inflows will inaugurate a virtuous cycle by increasing the nation's capital stock, productivity, investment, growth and employment. All of these benefits redound to the benefit of society as a whole. But the poor may benefit particularly because higher levels of investment increase employment, especially in the technologically advanced firms that are financed by foreign investment. Sales of government bonds to foreign investors increase the resources available for public expenditure since these are rather scant thanks to problems with tax collection and the myriad demands on budgets.

Internationally integrated capital markets are also seen by neoclassical economists to increase efficiency and policy discipline. The need to attract private capital flows and the threat of capital flight are powerful incentives for the government and firms to maintain international standards for 'good policy', macroeconomic performance and corporate governance. Specifically, neoclassical economists maintain that governments seeking to attract international private capital flows are more likely to pursue anti-inflationary policies and anti-corruption measures because foreign investors value price stability, transparency and the rule of law. The discipline that is enforced by financial integration is essential because of the commonly held view that public officials are inherently corrupt and/or incompetent (everywhere, but especially in developing countries). Note also that the poor are seen to benefit from stable prices and transparency since they are less able than the rich to hedge against inflation or extract benefits from corrupt regimes.

Out of the laboratory and into the real world
What became known as the McKinnon–Shaw hypothesis proved to be immediately and immensely influential, not least because of the rhetorical power attached to the concepts of 'repression' and 'liberalization'. By the early 1980s, the financial systems of many developing countries had been abruptly and radically liberalized in 'shock therapy' programs. Among the most ambitious and well-studied efforts to operationalize the McKinnon–Shaw hypothesis were the Southern Cone countries of South America. Uruguay experimented with liberalization from 1973 to 1983, Chile from 1974/75 to 1983, and Argentina from 1976/77 to 1983. Implementation differed across countries with respect to the sequence of liberalization. For example, Chile liberalized trade prior to finance, while Uruguay liberalized in the reverse order. In each of these cases, however, full financial liberalization occurred swiftly, ranging from several months to less than two years. Rarely are social scientists afforded a laboratory in which to test their hypotheses. But in a space of ten years, McKinnon–Shaw witnessed several thorough practical tests of their ideas.

Within five years of their initial liberalization, countries in the Southern Cone experienced severe financial and macroeconomic difficulties. With soaring interest rates,[3] waves of bank failures and other bankruptcies, extreme asset price volatility and extensive loan defaults, the real sector entered deep and prolonged recessions. Widespread loan defaults and bank distress necessitated massive bailouts of struggling financial institutions. Moreover, the assumed benefits of financial liberalization (e.g. increases in savings and investment, reductions in capital flight) failed to materialize.

Post hoc theoretical revisionism in the sequencing argument
While these events seemed to call into question the liberalization prescription, neoclassical theorists remained committed to it. In what I have elsewhere termed 'neoclassical revisionism', these theorists modified the original thesis to take account of what they now recognized as troublesome and previously overlooked attributes of developing economies (cf. McKinnon 1973 with 1989 and 1991). Through these *post hoc* theoretical extensions (including sequencing, credibility and coherence, all of which are examined below), the liberalization prescription was repeatedly rescued from empirical refutation.

In self-critical assessments of the original prescription, neoclassical economists (including McKinnon, 1989) concluded that sudden liberalization was not viable. A consensus emerged that a 'second-best' strategy had to be found, one that was more attuned to the features of developing-country economies. Neoclassical theorists began to incorporate new developments in macroeconomic theory – which focused on the uniqueness of financial markets – into their *ex post* assessments of the early experiences with financial liberalization. For instance, neoclassical economists began to take seriously new theoretical work that argued that high real interest rates could exacerbate moral hazard and adverse selection in lending. By the mid-1980s, neoclassical theory also reflected the insight that financial markets were unique in their ability to adjust instantaneously to changes in sentiments, information and so on. Goods markets, on the other hand, adjusted sluggishly. Thus, given these differences, financial markets could not be reformed in the same manner and in the same instant as other markets. Instead, a broad-based program of economic reform had to be sequenced. Successful reform of the real sector came to be seen as a prerequisite for financial reform: firewalls – in the form of temporary financial repression – had to be maintained during the first stage of liberalization in order to insulate the economy from financial disruptions.

But this insight about divergent adjustment speeds produced another: different aspects of reform programs may work at cross-purposes. This conflict has been termed the 'competition of instruments'. For present purposes the most important competition of instruments relates to the 'Dutch disease effect' whereby the real-currency appreciation generated by the opening of the capital account undermines the competitiveness of domestic goods, causing a deterioration of the current account. The second-best liberalization strategy requires that trade liberalization occur in the context of an appropriate degree of temporary financial repression. During a transition period following trade liberalization, the capital account is to be managed through the retention of capital controls (especially limiting inflows). Finally, the capital account is to be opened only after domestic financial markets have been liberalized.

Advocates of sequencing generally find their case strengthened following financial crises, as these are seen as a consequence of premature external financial liberalization. Indeed, had the East Asian financial crisis of 1997–8 not intervened, the IMF was poised to modify Article 6 of its Articles of Agreement to make the liberalization of international private capital flows a central purpose of the Fund and to extend its jurisdiction to capital movements. The Asian financial crisis did cause some neoclassical economists to step away from a blanket endorsement of external financial liberalization. Following the East Asian crisis, some studies, even by IMF staff, acknowledged that certain techniques to manage international capital flows can prevent undue financial volatility, *provided* that capital controls are temporary and that the rest of the economy is liberalized (Prasad et al., 2003; Kuczynski and Williamson, 2003). Even in these more nuanced and cautious minority views, however, there remains a strong commitment to the idea that liberalization is the *ultimate goal* for *all* developing countries – it is only a question of managing the timing appropriately.

Some neoclassical economists reject arguments for sequencing because of the problems introduced by this strategy (such as the possibility that it gives time for interest groups to mobilize to block liberalization). Neoclassical economists who nevertheless argue for sequencing today tend to add several non-economic factors to the menu of prerequisites, for example appropriate governance, institutions, the rule of law, and the protection of property rights.

Revisionism redux: the credibility and coherence arguments
The financial liberalization prescription was modified further in the mid-to-late 1980s to take into account the policy environment in which liberalization is to occur. This new focus is manifested in discussions of the appropriate macroeconomic conditions for liberalization. Of particular importance is the determination whether the liberalization program is credible (see Grabel, 2000 on credibility). At issue are the perceptions of the

economic actors in the affected economy concerning the viability of the proposed policies. An inconsistent liberalization program is one that the public believes is likely to be reversed. Such policies are likely to be sabotaged, as the public engages in behavior (e.g. capital flight) that undermines the success of the program.

How could economic policy be developed in this new, complex environment, in which the success of policy depends critically on agents' perceptions of its viability? There seemed to be two choices: one could shade policy toward existing popular sentiments; or one could implement 'correct' policy, one that respected the principles of neoclassical theory. The former option was ruled out of court on the simple grounds that incorrect policy could not possibly retain credibility in the wake of the disruptions that would inevitably attend it. The latter, on the other hand, would induce credibility as it proved itself uniquely capable of promoting development, even if it were unpopular in the short run. Hence a correctly specified policy would impel rational agents to act 'properly', at once achieving growth and the credibility necessary to sustain itself. On this account, financial liberalization could only be credibly implemented in an economy in which budget deficits are closed, inflation is tamed, and in which exchange rates reflect fundamentals (McKinnon, 1991, ch. 3).

In the last several years, neoclassical economists and members of the policy community have begun to raise the issue of policy coherence in explaining the success or failure of liberalization programs (see Grabel, 2007 on coherence). The intuition behind the concept of policy coherence is simple: any individual economic policy (such as financial liberalization) will only yield beneficial outcomes if it is nested in a broader policy environment that is consistent or coherent with its objectives. From this perspective, then, previous efforts to liberalize finance have failed to promote growth because of inconsistencies between financial and other economic and social policies. These new discussions of policy coherence are pointing neoclassical theory back toward McKinnon and Shaw's early work in so far as they provide a theoretical justification for across-the-board and abrupt liberalization in developing economies.

2. Social economic responses: main issues and policy implications

What neoclassical theorists view as a simple and altogether desirable evolution of financial liberalization theory, social economists (and those working within other heterodox traditions) recognize as something else: as a series of *ad hoc* theoretical adjustments designed to prevent the disconfirmation and even collapse of the financial liberalization agenda. The effect of these *ad hoc* adjustments is to repress this recognition, to block the realization that would otherwise emerge that the financial liberalization mission was flawed from the start, and has by now proven its deficiencies beyond the academy in the real world of development practice.

In what follows, I subject the neoclassical case for financial liberalization to critical scrutiny from the perspective of social economics and other heterodox traditions. To date, social economists have not studied financial liberalization in the developing world (though a few social economists have examined broader schemes of liberalization, privatization and structural adjustment in the developing world, e.g., Lutz, 1999, ch. 9; Thanawala, 1996; Mobekk and Spyrou, 2002; Rider, 1996; Currie, 2006 is an exception in so far as she studies financial crises). From the social economic perspective, I identify two important failings with the liberalization prescription. First, the frequent resort to revisionism lends an ideological character to the neoclassical case for liberalization. Second, liberalization's advocates fail to appreciate the importance of national specificities, path-dependence and the embeddedness of actors and institutions. This leads them to conclude that the failure of this prescription stems from improper implementation, rather than from the inappropriateness of the model itself and from the futility of efforts to graft it on to diverse national contexts. I shall also show that other heterodox traditions, particularly post-Keynesian economics, identify additional failings with the neoclassical case that are resonant with social economics.

Ad hoc revisionism as ideology
The refusal of the neoclassical approach to recognize the interpenetration of the normative and the positive leaves its proponents in the grasp of ideological forces that they do not themselves recognize, which means that they have no avenue but to reach for *ad hoc* adjustments to the theory to which they adhere rather than look beyond its confines for alternative explanations of events and sources of policy prescription. For this reason, the neoclassical case for financial liberalization has been subject to several bouts of revisionism, without ever challenging the basic underlying myth that liberalized finance is the ideal to which developing countries must aspire, no matter the cost.

In so far as it can always be asserted *ex post* that the environment in which financial liberalization failed was not credible or that financial liberalization policy was not consistent (i.e. coherent) with other policies, it is possible to insulate financial liberalization from critique. Thus, for neoclassical economics, the failure of financial liberalization to achieve its chief goals does not stem from the inappropriateness of the policy or from the underlying theoretical framework that gives rise to it. Rather, policy failure is explained by the presence of all manner of distortions that characterize the economy, by political uncertainty, by the public's lack of confidence in the capacity of policy-makers.

Polanyi (1944) wrote precisely of this phenomenon when discussing the propensity of advocates of free markets (in general) to explain their failure as stemming from insufficient liberalization rather than from the failure of markets themselves:

> Its apologists [i.e. defenders of market liberalization] are repeating in endless variations that but for the policies advocated by its critics, liberalism would have delivered the goods; that not the competitive system and the self-regulating market, but interference with that system and interventions with that market are responsible for our ills. (Ibid., p. 143)

This strategy leaves the neoclassical argument for financial liberalization immune to any substantive empirical refutation. It is the impossibility of testing (and therefore rejecting) its central propositions, combined with its self-understanding as the uniquely adequate and objective positive economic science, that imparts to this approach its ideological content.

The ideological content of the neoclassical case for financial liberalization emerges even more directly in the credibility argument. A proposition stating that credible policies are more likely to succeed is, on its face, innocuous. But upon closer examination we see that this proposition carries with it a particularly ideological and troubling claim about the unique truthfulness of the neoclassical case.

The credibility thesis can be reduced to a simple set of propositions: (1) an economic policy will garner credibility only to the degree that it is likely to survive; (2) an economic policy is likely to survive only to the degree that it attains its stated objectives; (3) an economic policy is likely to attain its stated objectives only to the degree that it reflects and operationalizes the true theory of market economies; (4) a policy reflects the true theory of market economies only to the degree that it is neoclassical. The exclusionary, dissent-suppressing maneuver that has been undertaken here is captured in propositions (3) and (4). Non-neoclassical economic theories are ruled out of court on the grounds that they could not possibly meet the unforgiving 'credibility' test, because they could not possibly be true. Hence policy regimes founded upon non-neoclassical theories must collapse, with deleterious social and economic consequences.

The recent effort to incorporate coherence into examinations of policy regimes shares with the credibility literature a strong ideological content. In principle, the concept of coherence (like credibility) is empty of substantive content; that is, coherence does not in and of itself entail a commitment to any particular kind of policy regime. Hence deployment of this concept can be entirely benign. But if the concept is intrinsically open-ended, in practice it has come to be understood by neoclassical economists and by the key multilateral institutions/organizations (namely, the International Monetary

Fund, World Bank and World Trade Organization) in a way that biases policy prescription in a very particular direction. The concept of policy coherence has been invoked to legitimize ambitious and comprehensive liberalization schemes. It is used to validate the common, dangerous and incorrect view that neoliberal policies represent the only viable path to development for all countries. Like credibility, then, it serves to close off consideration of any and all other paths to development.

That policy coherence must entail liberalization has been contradicted by historical and cross-country experience (see Chang, 2002). Chang and Grabel (2004) (and many other scholars) demonstrate that there exist multiple paths to development, and that high levels of economic growth that are feasible, sustainable and stable can be achieved via an array of heterogeneous strategies. While any one country's policies must exhibit a degree of internal coherence in order to succeed, the evidence is clear that the alternative policy regimes need not cohere around liberalization.

Embeddedness, resilience, path-dependence and the failure of financial liberalization
From the perspective of social economics, there are a number of related factors that help to explain the failures of financial liberalization in the developing world. The neoclassical approach rejects the idea that financial arrangements and financial actors are embedded in a constellation of historically contingent political and social relationships that may enable development along all sorts of non-neoliberal paths. This view explains why neoclassical economists approach the task of financial reform as if it merely involves grafting the liberalized financial model that predominates in the USA and the UK on to the economies of the developing world. But the matter of financial reform is not nearly as uncomplicated as neoclassical theory suggests.

Social economics foregrounds the concepts of social embeddedness, institutional resilience/stickiness and path-dependence as key attributes of all economies, and hence as critical factors that must be taken account of by those considering structural reform programs. These understandings suggest that any one program of financial reform cannot be expected to perform uniformly across diverse national contexts, and that any effort to transplant financial arrangements will be fraught with all manner of unintended and undesirable consequences. In particular, institutional stickiness helps to account for the fact that new market-oriented financial institutions tend to function eerily like their dirigiste predecessors following liberalization, and that old, dysfunctional behaviors (such as corruption) reappear in new forms in a reformed environment. Finally, the recognition of specificity and embeddedness in social economics implies that a uniform set of financial arrangements could not possibly be viable, let alone suitable, for all countries at all times.

Heterodox views[4]

Among heterodox traditions, post-Keynesians have been most directly engaged in discussions of financial liberalization in developing countries. On the most abstract theoretical level, these economists argue that liberalized markets are not efficient in the ways that neoclassical theory claims. These critics argue that there is no demonstrated empirical or historical relationship between a market-based allocation of capital and satisfaction of growth and social objectives. This is not surprising since the allocation of capital in market-based systems relies on private financial returns as the singular yardstick of investment success. The private financial return on an investment can be quite different from its social return, where the latter refers to the promotion of important social goals (such as poverty reduction, equality and economic security) not reducible to economic efficiency narrowly defined.

Despite the claims of neoclassical economists, a market-based allocation of capital is not a magic cure for inefficiency, waste and corruption. Liberalization frequently changes the form, but not the level, of corruption or inefficiency. The situation of Russia after financial liberalization exemplifies this point, but the country is by no means exceptional in this regard (on Russia, see Kotz, 1997). For instance, research on Nigeria, South Korea and South America describes quite persuasively the corruption that so often flourishes following financial liberalization (Crotty and Lee, 2004; Lewis and Stein, 1997). Thus financial liberalization does not resolve the problems of corruption and the lack of transparency that frequently operate to the detriment of the poor.

Liberalized financial markets are at least as apt as governments to allocate capital in an inefficient, wasteful or developmentally unproductive manner. In many developing countries, market-based allocations of domestic capital and increased access to international flows following liberalization financed speculation in commercial real estate and the stock market, the creation of excess capacity in certain sectors, and allowed domestic banks and investors to take on positions of excessive leverage, often involving currency and locational mismatches that culminated in crises.

Neoclassical economists often herald the disciplining effects of capital markets, arguing that the threat of investor exit and corporate takeovers creates pressure to improve corporate governance. We know that the exit and takeover mechanisms are well developed in the markets of the USA and UK. But there is simply no evidence to support the case that these mechanisms have, on balance, been beneficial. Indeed, numerous studies find that the threat of investor exit shortens the time horizon of managers, and takeovers have increased concentration and induced job losses. The case that developing-country firms and consumers benefit from enhancing possibilities for exit and takeover by liberalizing financial markets is therefore without merit.

There is a large body of empirical evidence demonstrating that domestic financial liberalization has unambiguously failed to deliver most of the rewards claimed by its proponents (see Grabel, 2003b, and references therein). For instance, domestic savings have not responded positively to domestic financial liberalization. Moreover, the liberalization of domestic and international financial flows has not promoted long-term investment in the types of projects or sectors that are central to development and to the amelioration of social ills, such as unemployment, poverty and inequality. Financial liberalization has created the climate, opportunity and incentives for investment in speculative activities and a focus on short-term financial as opposed to long-term developmental returns. Granted, the creation of a speculative bubble may temporarily result in an increase in investment and overall economic activity. But an unsustainable and financially fragile environment, or what Grabel (1995) terms 'speculation-led development', is hardly in the long-term interest of developing countries. Such an environment certainly does not improve the situation of the poor – indeed it worsens their conditions of life, as we shall see.

One channel by which the speculation-led development induced by financial liberalization worsens the situation of the poor is by increasing income and wealth inequality and by aggravating existing disparities in political and economic power. This is because only a very small proportion of the population is situated to exploit the opportunities for speculative gain available in a liberalized financial environment. Speculation-led development often creates a small class of rentiers who maintain greater ties to financial markets abroad than to those in their own country, and it is also associated with a shift in political and economic power from non-financial to financial actors. In such an environment, the financial community and powerful external actors such as the IMF become the anointed arbiters of the 'national interest' and the judges of precisely what constitutes sound, sustainable economic and social policies (Grabel, 2003c). This means that macroeconomic policies that advance the interests of the financial community (such as those that promote low inflation, high interest rates, fiscal restraint, etc.) are justified on the basis that they serve the broader public interest when this is simply not the case.

The range of acceptable policy options is further constrained by the threat or actuality of capital flight, itself made possible by the liberalization of international capital flows. This dynamic of 'constrained policy autonomy' (Grabel, 1996b) means that the political voice of rentiers and the IMF are empowered over those of other social actors (such as the poor and middle class, export-oriented industrialists and agricultural producers) in discussions of macroeconomic policy. In practice, this means that macroeconomic policies exhibit a restrictive bias that favors rentiers and the IMF. Research by Braunstein and Heintz (2006) shows that such policies have a negative effect on the poor and on women.

The speculation-led development induced by financial liberalization also worsens the situation of the poor through its effect on financial fragility, and ultimately on the prevalence of currency, banking and generalized financial crises. There is now a large body of unambiguous empirical evidence that shows that the liberalization of domestic and international financial flows is strongly associated with banking, currency and financial crises (see Grabel 2003b, and references therein; Weller, 2001). Since the Southern Cone crises of the mid-1970s, we have seen financial crises on the heels of liberalization in a great many developing countries, such as Russia, Nigeria, Jamaica, Korea, Thailand, Indonesia, Mexico and Turkey.

Contrary to the neoclassical view, the increase in liquidity that is associated with liberalization and the creation of internationally integrated capital markets increases the level of financial and economic volatility. In addition, the removal of restrictions on international private capital inflows and outflows introduces the possibility of the Dutch disease or, alternatively, of sudden, large capital outflows (i.e. capital flight) that place the domestic currency under pressure to depreciate. Capital flight often induces a vicious cycle of additional flight and currency depreciation, debt-service difficulties and reductions in stock (or other asset) values. In this manner, capital flight introduces or aggravates existing macroeconomic vulnerabilities and financial instability. These can culminate in a financial crisis which, as we have seen, impairs economic performance and living standards (particularly for the poor and the politically weak) and often provides a channel for increased external and rentier influence over domestic decision-making.

Numerous recent cross-country and historical studies demonstrate conclusively that there is no reliable empirical relationship between the liberalization of international capital flows and performance in terms of inflation, growth or investment in developing countries (e.g. Eichengreen, 2001). Moreover, studies also show that the liberalization of international capital flows is associated with increases in poverty and inequality, although the authors of these studies take care to point out that it is difficult to isolate the negative effects of financial liberalization from those associated with broader programs of economic liberalization (involving, for instance, the simultaneous adoption of trade and labor market liberalization). With this caveat it mind, it is worth noting that Weller and Hersh (2004) find that capital and current account liberalization hurt the poor in developing countries in the short run (see Epstein and Grabel, 2006, for further discussion). The poor are harmed by international financial liberalization through a chain of related effects that have been established in several studies. Increased short-term international financial flows (especially portfolio flows) are often associated with a greater chance of financial crisis (Weller, 2001), especially in more liberalized environments (Demirgüc-Kunt and Detragiache, 1999); financial crises have disproportionately negative consequences for a country's poor (Baldacci et al., 2002), not least through labor market effects (Eichengreen et al., 1996); and the poor are the first to lose under the fiscal contractions and the last to gain when crises subside and fiscal spending expands (Ravallion, 2002).

Cornia (2003) argues that of the six components of what he terms the 'liberal package', liberalization of international private capital flows appears to have the strongest impact on widening within-country inequality. He finds that the next most important negative effects on the poor derive from domestic financial liberalization, followed by labor market deregulation and tax reform. Finally, Weisbrot et al. (2001) conclude that there is a strong *prima facie* case that structural and policy changes implemented during the last two decades, such as financial liberalization, are at least partly responsible for worsening growth and health and other social indicators.

Inequality among countries has also increased during liberalization, partly as a result of the concentration of international private capital flows.[5] The United Nations Development Program (UNDP) finds that in 1960 the countries with the richest 20 percent of the world's population had aggregate income 30 times that of those countries with the poorest 20 percent of the world's population. By 1980, that ratio had risen to 45 to one; by 1989, it stood at 59 to one; by 1997, it rose to 70 to one (UNDP, 2001, 1999). In the era of intensified commitment to liberalization, then, inequality between the richest and the poorest countries nearly doubled.

The theoretical insights and empirical findings summarized above have prompted heterodox economists to articulate a range of alternatives, many of which are deeply consistent with the premises and value commitments of social economics. For all branches of heterodox economics, financial liberalization is at a dead end. The task now must be not to give it new life through some new theoretical amendment, but to find and advocate for genuine alternatives that promise human development of a sort that has been obstructed by financial liberalization.

3.   New directions for future research on post-financial liberalization regimes

Heterodox economists have in the last few years begun to move beyond the task of explaining the failures of financial liberalization to thinking seriously about the nature of post-liberalization regimes. Three pertinent questions confront advocates of a post-financial liberalization agenda. (1) What are the principle objectives of financial systems in developing countries? (2) What types of financial arrangements might best serve the goals of substantive equality and human development, while also engaging private actors? And (3) how can global financial rules and national financial arrangements provide space for local financial institutions and practices that meet local needs? In what follows, I offer some thoughts on these questions with the hope of stimulating research and debate on these critical issues within social economics and other heterodox traditions.

Performance objectives for financial systems in developing countries
Several heterodox economists have attempted to articulate goals for financial systems in developing countries. I now summarize three such contributions.

In regard to the goals of the domestic financial system, Chang and Grabel (2004) submit that regulation should be guided by one fundamental consideration: the domestic financial system should operate in the service of sustainable, stable and equitable economic development. The chief function of the financial sector in developing countries is to provide finance in adequate quantities and at appropriate prices for those investment projects that are central to this kind of development. Chang and Grabel argue that all financial reforms should be evaluated against the extent to which they achieve this aim. Domestic financial reforms that improve the functioning of the financial system along other dimensions (such as liquidity, international integration etc.) should be seen as secondary to its primary developmental goal.

The most important way in which the financial system can serve appropriate economic development is through the provision of long-term finance. Long-term finance is necessary to the success and viability of most projects that are central to economic development (e.g. investment in infrastructure and the promotion of infant industries). In his research on the US financial system, Nobel Laureate James Tobin (1984) used the term functional efficiency to refer to the ability of the financial system to provide finance for long-term investment. The concept of functional efficiency contrasts with the more conventional (neoclassical) notion of efficiency that focuses on the pricing mechanism. Any proposed financial reform in the developing world should be evaluated based on its ability to contribute to the critical objective of functional efficiency.

Grabel (2003b) argues that capital controls should maximize the net developmental benefits of international private capital flows by focusing on three objectives. First, a program of well-designed capital controls should promote financial stability, and thereby prevent the economic and social devastation that is associated with financial crises. Second, policies should promote desirable types of investment and financing arrangements (i.e. those that are long term, stable and sustainable, and that create employment opportunities, improve living standards, promote income equality, technology transfer and learning-by-doing) and discourage less desirable types of investment/financing strategies. Finally, capital controls should enhance democracy and national policy autonomy by reducing the potential for speculators and various external actors to exercise undue influence (and even veto power) over domestic decision-making and/or control over national resources.[6]

Epstein and Grabel (2006) argue that financial systems in developing countries should be restructured so that they directly promote 'pro-poor economic growth' rather than hope, as does neoclassical theory with its decidedly unjust 'trickle-down' approach, that reforms that target the wealthy will eventually redound to the benefit of the poor. Pro-poor economic growth would involve designing a far-reaching program of institutional and financial policy reform that is guided by a very particular set of goals. In this view, the financial system should mobilize savings that can be used for productive investment and employment creation; create credit for employment generation and poverty reduction at modest and stable real interest rates; allocate credit for employment generation and help the poor to build assets, including in agriculture and in small- and medium-sized enterprises and in housing; provide long-term credit for productivity-enhancing innovation and investment and provide financing for public investment; help to allocate risks to those who can most easily and efficiently bear those risks; contribute to the economy's stabilization by reducing vulnerability to financial crises, pro-cyclical movements in finance, and by helping to maintain moderate rates of inflation; and aid the poor by providing basic financial and banking services.

Towards a post-financial liberalization policy agenda
In the last few years, heterodox economists have begun to articulate a post-financial liberalization agenda. This emerging body of work is wide ranging, and space constraints preclude anything more than a brief treatment of this literature. This research is founded on the following four propositions. (1) There is no single, correct template for financial policy in

developing countries. (2) It is the task of national policy-makers to design and implement those financial policies that are consistent with human and economic development objectives, reflect the priorities of diverse social groups, and take account of the needs of the disenfranchised. (3) Policy-makers in developing countries have the right to engage in policy experimentation. (4) The rights and priorities of members of the financial community and external actors are no more important than those of other domestic social actors.

Beyond the general themes articulated above, we see in the heterodox literature presentation of a diverse array of policies toward internal and external financial flows. Discussion of the specifics of these policies is beyond the scope of this chapter, but for the sake of illustration I highlight below a few policies that have been proposed. I direct interested readers to the original sources for specific discussions of policy (e.g. Chang and Grabel, 2004; Epstein and Grabel, 2006; Epstein et al., 2004; Grabel, 2003a, 2003b, 2004, and references therein).

For instance, in Grabel (2004) I make a case for what I term a 'trip wire–speed bump' regime. This regime is essentially a system of graduated, transparent capital controls that are activated whenever information about the economy indicates that controls are necessary to prevent nascent macroeconomic fragilities from culminating in serious difficulties or even in a crisis. In this view, measures that reduce financial instability and the likelihood of crises can protect living standards and economic growth, while also protecting policy autonomy by making it less likely that external actors can trade influence over policy for financial assistance.

Many heterodox (and even some mainstream) economists have written favorably of the controls over international private capital inflow utilized in both Chile and Colombia during much of the 1990s (e.g. Agonsin, 1998; Ariyoshi et al., 2000; Eichengreen, 1999; Ffrench-Davis and Reisen, 1998; Grabel, 2003a; Prasad et al., 2003). These Chilean-style capital controls, as they have come to be known, had the effect of lengthening the time horizons of foreign investors and of shifting the composition of international capital flows towards FDI and away from debt and portfolio investment. Many heterodox economists have also noted that Malaysia's use of far more stringent (though shorter-lived) capital controls following the East Asian crisis of 1997–8 (and also in 1994) demonstrates the positive role that capital controls can play in promoting financial stability and economic stabilization and in protecting policy autonomy.

Other studies have argued that restrictions on currency convertibility and ceilings or surcharges on foreign debt levels can enhance financial stability and policy autonomy (Grabel, 2003a); that 'developmentalist' central banks have a central role to play in the achievement of pro-poor economic growth; that variable asset-based reserve requirements can promote stability and facilitate the flow of funds to projects of the highest developmental and social priority; and that programs that forge linkages between informal and formal financial institutions, support microfinance institutions, and establish specialized lending institutions can enhance the ability of the financial system to serve diverse constituencies (Epstein and Grabel, 2006).

The foregoing has demonstrated that the neoclassical financial liberalization prescription has been marked by false starts and is now at a dead end. As a consequence, the opportunity now exists for social economists to make substantial contributions to post-liberalization development policy. Progressive and feasible financial institutions and practices must be founded on the ethical, holistic and normative commitments of the social economics tradition.

Acknowledgment
I thank George DeMartino for useful suggestions.

Notes
1. This section draws heavily on Grabel (1994, 1995, 1996a, 2000, 2003a, 2003b, 2007); Epstein and Grabel (2006); Chang and Grabel (2004). See these works for further discussion and citations to relevant literature.
2. Writing in finance and development certainly pre-dates the 1970s, but serious study in this area only began in the early 1970s with the publication of McKinnon and Shaw's work.
3. Ramos (1986) reports that real deposit rates peaked at 9, 29 and 27 percent in Chile, Argentina and Uruguay, respectively, while real lending rates in these countries peaked at 27, 127 and 40 percent.
4. Discussion in this subsection draws heavily on work cited in note 1, especially Grabel (1995, 2003a, 2003b).
5. Data on international private capital flows show that despite the growth of portfolio and foreign direct investment (PI and FDI, respectively) flows to developing countries during the 1990s, their share of global private capital flows is still rather small and remains highly concentrated in a few large countries (World Bank, 2005). With regard to concentration of FDI, Brazil, China, India, Mexico and the Russian Federation received just over 60 percent of net FDI inflows to all developing countries in 2004, and China accounted for one-third of the net FDI inflows that went to all developing countries. Low-income countries in 2003/4 received about 11 percent of the net FDI and the same percentage of the portfolio equity flows that went to all developing countries. China, India and South Africa together accounted for 82 percent of all portfolio equity flows that went to developing countries in 2004, and China alone accounted for almost 40 percent of the net PI that went to all developing countries.
6. See Epstein et al. (2004) for discussion of the extent and means by which financial arrangements in Chile, Colombia, Taiwan, India, China, Singapore and Malaysia achieved these three objectives during the 1990s.

References
Agosin, Manuel R. (1998), 'Capital inflows and investment performance: Chile in the 1990s', in R. Ffrench-Davis and H. Reisen (eds), *Capital Flows and Investment Performance: Lessons from Latin America*, Paris: UN/ECLAC Development Centre of the OECD.

Ariyoshi, Akira, Karl Habermeier, Bernard Laurens, Inci Otker-Robe, Jorge Ivan Canales-Kriljenko and Andrei Kirilenko (2000), 'Capital controls: country experiences with their use and liberalization', IMF Occasional Paper No. 190.

Baldacci, E., L. de Mello and G. Inchauste (2002), 'Financial crisis, poverty and income distribution', paper presented at the IMF conference on Macroeconomic Policies and Poverty Reduction, Washington, DC, 14–15 March.

Braunstein, Elissa and James Heintz (2006), 'Gender bias and central bank policy: employment and inflation reduction', PERI Working Paper (www.peri.umass.edu).

Chang, Ha-Joon (2002), *Kicking Away the Ladder*, London: Anthem Press.

Chang, Ha-Joon and Ilene Grabel (2004), *Reclaiming Development: An Alternative Economic Policy Manual*, London: Zed Books.

Cornia, Giovanni Andrea (2003), 'Globalization and the distribution of income between and within countries', in Ha-Joon Chang (ed.), *Rethinking Development Economics*, London: Anthem Press, pp. 325–45.

Crotty, James and Kang-kook Lee (2004), 'From East Asian miracle to neoliberal mediocrity: the effects of liberalization and financial opening on the post-crisis Korean economy', unpublished paper, University of Massachusetts, Political Economy Research Institute (www.peri.umass.edu).

Currie, Carolyn (2006), 'A new theory of financial regulation: predicting, measuring and preventing financial crises', *Journal of Socio-Economics*, **35**, 48–71.

Demirgüc-Kunt, A. and E. Detragiache (1999), 'Financial liberalization and financial fragility', in B. Pleskovic and J. Stiglitz (eds), *Annual World Bank Conference on Development Economics 1998*, Washington, DC: World Bank, pp. 303–31.

Dugger, William (1977), 'Social economics: one perspective', *Review of Social Economy*, **35** (3), 299–310.

Eichengreen, Barry (1999), *Toward a New International Financial Architecture*, Washington, DC: Institute for International Economics.

Eichengreen, Barry (2001), 'Capital account liberalization: what do cross-country studies tell us?', *World Bank Economic Review*, **15** (3), 341–65.

Eichengreen, Barry, Andrew Rose and Charles Wyplosz (1996), 'Exchange rate mayhem: the antecedents and aftermath of speculative attacks', *Economic Policy*, **21** (21), 249–312.

Epstein, Gerald and Ilene Grabel (2006), 'Financial policies for pro-poor growth', study prepared for the United Nations Development Program (UNDP), International Poverty Centre, Global Training Programme on Economic Policies for Growth, Employment and Poverty Reduction.

Epstein, Gerald, Ilene Grabel and Jomo KS. (2004), 'Capital management techniques in developing countries: an assessment of experiences from the 1990s and lessons for the future', G24 Discussion Paper No. 27, New York and Geneva: United Nations.

Ffrench-Davis, R. and H. Reisen (eds) (1998), *Capital Flows and Investment Performance: Lessons from Latin America*, Paris: UN/ECLAC Development Centre of the OECD.

Grabel, Ilene (1994), 'The political economy of theories of "optimal" financial repression in the Third World', *Review of Radical Political Economics*, **26** (3), 47–55.

Grabel, Ilene (1995), 'Speculation-led economic development: a post-Keynesian interpretation of financial liberalization in the Third World', *International Review of Applied Economics*, **9** (2), 127–49.

Grabel, Ilene (1996a), 'Financial markets, the state and economic development: controversies within theory and policy', *International Papers in Political Economy*, **3** (1), 1–42.

Grabel, Ilene (1996b), 'Marketing the Third World: the contradictions of portfolio investment in the global economy', *World Development*, **24** (11), 1761–76.

Grabel, Ilene (2000), 'The political economy of "policy credibility": the new-classical macroeconomics and the remaking of emerging economies', *Cambridge Journal of Economics*, **24** (1), 1–19.

Grabel, Ilene (2003a), 'Averting crisis: assessing measures to manage financial integration in emerging economies', *Cambridge Journal of Economics*, **27** (3), 317–36.

Grabel, Ilene (2003b), 'International private capital flows and developing countries', in Ha-Joon Chang (ed.), *Rethinking Development Economics*, London: Anthem Press, pp. 325–45.

Grabel, Ilene (2003c), 'Ideology, power and the rise of independent monetary institutions in emerging economies', in Jonathan Kirshner (ed.), *Monetary Orders: Ambiguous Economics, Ubiquitous Politics*, Ithaca, NY: Cornell University Press, pp. 25–52.

Grabel, Ilene (2004), 'Trip wires and speed bumps: Managing financial risks and reducing the potential for financial crises in developing economies', G-24 Discussion Paper No. 33, New York and Geneva: United Nations.

Grabel, Ilene (2007), 'Policy coherence or conformance? The new World Bank–IMF–WTO rhetoric on trade and investment in developing countries', *Review of Radical Political Economics*, **39** (3), 335–41.

Hirschmann, Albert (1986), *Rival Views of Market Society*, New York: Viking.

Kotz, David (1997), *Revolution from Above*, London: Routledge.

Kuczynski, P.-P. and John Williamson (eds) (2003), *After the Washington Consensus*, Washington, DC: Institute for International Economics.

Lewis, P. and H. Stein (1997), 'Shifting fortunes: the political economy of financial liberalization in Nigeria', *World Development*, **25** (1), 5–22.

Lutz, Mark (1999), *Economics for the Common Good*, London and New York: Routledge.

McKinnon, Ronald (1973), *Money and Capital in Economic Development*, Washington, DC: Brookings Institution.

McKinnon, Ronald (1989), 'Macroeconomic instability and moral hazard in banking in a liberalizing economy', in P. Brock, M. Connolly and C. Gonzalez-Vega (eds), *Latin American Debt and Adjustment*, New York: Praeger, pp. 99–111.

McKinnon, Ronald (1991), *The Order of Economic Liberalization: Financial Control in the Transition to a Market Economy*, Baltimore, MD: Johns Hopkins University Press.

Mobekk, Eirin and Spyros Spyrou (2002), 'Re-evaluating IMF involvement in low-income countries: the case of Haiti', *International Journal of Social Economics*, **29** (7), 527–37.

Polayni, Karl (1944), *The Great Transformation*, Boston, MA: Beacon Press.

Prasad, Eswar, Kenneth Rogoff, Shang-Jin Wei and M. Ayhan Kose (2003), 'Effects of financial globalization on developing countries: some empirical evidence', www.imf.org/external/np/res/docs/2003/031703.htm.

Ramos, Joseph (1986), 'Rise and fall of capital markets in the Southern Cone', Helen Kellogg Institute for International Studies Working Paper No. 81, University of Notre Dame.

Ravallion, M. (2002), 'Who is protected? On the incidence of fiscal adjustment', paper presented at the IMF Conference on Macroeconomic Policies and Poverty Reduction, Washington, DC, 14–15 March.

Rider, Christine (1996), 'Ethical policy making in the transition economies', in Edward O'Boyle (ed.), *Social Economics*, London: Routledge, pp. 178–90.

Shaw, Edward (1973), *Financial Deepening in Economic Development*, New York: Oxford University Press.

Thanawala, Kishor (1996), 'Solidarity and community in the world economy', in Edward O'Boyle (ed.), *Social Economics*, London: Routledge, pp. 75–89.

Tobin, J. (1984), 'On the efficiency of the financial system', *Lloyds Bank Review*, **153**, 1–15.

United Nations Development Program (UNDP), various years, *Human Development Report*, Oxford: Oxford University Press.

Waters, William (1990), 'Evolution of social economics in America', in Mark Lutz (ed.), *Social Economics: Retrospect and Prospect*, Boston/Dordrecht/London: Kluwer Academic Publishers, pp. 91–117.

Weisbrot, M., D. Baker, E. Kraev and J. Chen (2001), 'The scorecard on globalization 1980–2000', Center for Economic Policy Research, September, www.cepr.net/globalization/scorecard_on_globalization.htm.

Weller, C. (2001), 'Financial crises after financial liberalisation: exceptional circumstances or structural weakness?', *Journal of Development Studies*, **38** (1), 98–127.

Weller, C. and A. Hersh (2004), 'The long and short of it: global liberalization, poverty and inequality', *Journal of Post Keynesian Economics*, **26** (3), 471–504.

World Bank (2005), *Global Development Finance*, Washington, DC: World Bank.

PART IX

THE STATE

Chapter 29: 'The welfare state and privatization', by Robert McMaster

The welfare state has been, and continues to be, a prominent focus for arguments over economic efficiency, and individual freedom and dignity. Neoliberalism associates the welfare state with an erosion of individual freedom and dignity as well as inefficiency. It stimulates a dependency culture that stymies economic dynamism. Only with privatization with its promotion of the market will efficiency and individual freedom and dignity be realized. As Amartya Sen observed, this is a particular conceptualization of dignity and freedom, where freedom-achievements are coupled with welfare-achievements. Social economics challenges this conceptualization and its basis for undermining the welfare state. Social economists stress the importance of human dignity within the social provisioning process that is the economy, and associate dignity partly with freedom from humiliation and humiliating institutions. On this basis the privatization of welfare state activities does not furnish a convincing platform for the enhancement of individual dignity.

Chapter 30: 'The states of social economics', by Charlie Dannreuther and Oliver Kessler

This chapter explores what the meaning of state might be for social economics. It begins by asserting that social economics is concerned with representing the many social aspects of everyday life that influence economics. This plurality of approaches means that there are many approaches to the state in social economics, and this assumption provides the focus for our chapter. The first part of the chapter therefore examines how the state has been separated from everyday economics through the distinction between public and private spheres. This boundary is shown to be central to the maintenance of domestic and international hierarchies, and remains an important assumption in economics. A discussion of the political economy of representation helps us to understand the social process that maintains this boundary and demonstrates how the new representations of economic life developed in social economics can lead to change in government structures. This has implications for the agency of the state, and the following section shows how economic change can be explained endogenously rather than through exogenous variables such as globalization. The conclusion outlines the implications that these observations might have for social economics and the state.

29 The welfare state and privatization
Robert McMaster

That any sane nation, having observed that you could provide for the supply of bread by giving bakers a pecuniary interest in baking for you, should go on to give a surgeon a pecuniary interest in cutting off your leg, is enough to make one despair of political humanity.

George Bernard Shaw, *The Doctor's Dilemma*, 1911[1]

Introduction

The 'Great Capitalist Restoration' (Stanfield and Stanfield, 1996) from the 1970s/1980s onward is predicated upon powerful convictions centring on economic efficiency and development, and the freedom and dignity of the individual. Indeed, so powerful are these convictions that they exude the aura of conventional wisdom. The welfare state has been, and continues to be, a prominent locus for these arguments. Yet there is some ambiguity concerning the nature of the 'welfare state' and what is meant by 'privatization'. It is beyond the parameters of this chapter to furnish a comprehensive account of the complexities of this contested terrain, but none the less, some attempt will be made to furnish definitions that act as entry points to the principal focus of the discussion. This relates to an aspect of the second claim noted above: dignity. Neoliberalism embeds dignity in a particular conceptualization of individual freedom. In this literature, as Sen (1993) observed, freedom-achievements are associated with welfare-achievements. For example, Wiseman (1991) contests that if 'welfare' is identified with the 'existence of caring feelings', then the market is revealed as the conduit not only to greater welfare and individual freedom, but also to care and dignity.

Social economists also stress the importance of human dignity within the social provisioning process that is the economy. This has led Wisman (2003, p. 442) to observe that the scope of social economics encapsulates as its primary task the analysis of the requisites of 'the good and just society'.[2] Hence, in contrast to much of the underlying economic rationale for the 'Great Capitalist Restoration', or neoliberalism, there is an explicit recognition that the Humean fault line between the positive and normative is more illusory than real. In setting out to investigate parameters of Wisman's 'good and just society' explicit recognition of human needs (O'Boyle, 2005) and the contours of 'living standards' (Figart, 2007) are both necessary if not sufficient. Drawing from this literature, this chapter argues that the patterns of welfare state reform, primarily through some form of privatization, are not as persuasively related to the enhancement of human dignity as its advocates suggest.

Of necessity this chapter is general in nature as it endeavours to address important conceptual issues. The following section considers the analytical terrain by briefly reviewing some definitional issues. Thereafter the rationale for 'privatization' and recent trends in associated approaches are noted, and a contrasting social economics perspective is advanced.

Some old questions: what are the 'welfare state' and 'privatization'?
This section initially reflects upon some prominent considerations underlying the constitution of the welfare state, and follows this with a similar analysis of privatization.

From a recent well-known mainstream economic perspective Barr (1992, p. 742) observes:

> Defining the welfare state continues to baffle writers, and, as with poverty, much effort has been wasted in the search. The term is used as a shorthand for the state's activities in four broad areas: cash benefits; health care; education; and food, housing, and other welfare services.

Barr's reference to fields of activities reflects the standard conceptualization of merit goods and, from a mainstream perspective, introduces an overtly normative set of considerations since the defining feature of merit goods is grounded in the attenuation of consumer sovereignty. The foregoing range of activities keys into issues of justice, usually considered in terms of equity, where each individual is assumed to have some *right* to access these entities in order to sustain a basic, or what is deemed to be some minimum, standard of living: in effect some *welfare* (and avoidance of poverty).

Barr's review then considers the nature of welfare state regimes broadly in terms of a bifurcation between universal coverage and last resort, or safety net. The former is claimed to resemble a more European (and possibly Canadian and Antipodean) frame, whilst the latter is more typical of the USA. Barr readily acknowledges that such a portrayal is at best approximate, but the point is, in effect, conveyed in an albeit simple model of rights of access. Within these ideal types there remains considerable variety in terms of the extent of state provision, usually classified in terms of delivery, regulation and finance.

By contrast, Esping-Andersen (1999) emphasizes the state's role in decommodifying (men's) labour power. In essence this represents an attempt to capture social and economic reproduction and shifts across the so-called private–public boundary. Within this he identifies four typologies of welfare regimes: liberal type, where there is a minimal role for the state and labour power is most commodified; conservative, where there is a key role for the voluntary sector and there is risk-pooling within particular social strata as opposed to universally; social democratic, with the highest level of decommodification, where there is a extended role for the state in risk bearing and generous levels of universal benefits; and familial, typified by a residual welfare state and reliance on extended family. Esping-Andersen's typologies form the basis for the identification of geographical welfare regime blocs, such as familial with Southern Europe, liberal with North Atlantic, and social democratic with Northern Europe, and so forth.

While Esping-Andersen's work has been influential in the social sciences, with the exception of economics, his typology has been subject to persuasive and sustained criticisms. Fine (2002) and Jessop (2002), for example, argue that Esping-Andersen's approach is highly reductionist, emphasizing one dimension of commodification and focusing on an outdated model of gender roles that assumes a sole male breadwinner in a nuclear household. Fine (2002, p. 208) states: 'his [Esping-Andersen's] . . . welfare regimes have increasingly proven to be an analytical and empirical strait-jacket . . .'. From the perspective advanced here, the most compelling area of criticism relates Esping-Andersen to mainstream economic approaches such as Barr's. Apart from Esping-Andersen's flirtation with a Beckerian-style household, his typological approach shares mainstream economics' accent on risk management. Indeed, he observes: 'social policy means the public management of social risks' (Esping-Andersen, 1999, p. 36). This centring of market failure is redolent of mainstream economics' presumption that markets are the natural mode of socio-economic governance. Arguably it relegates historical context to a one-dimensional account of the economy.

Certainly in mainstream accounts the alleged objectives of welfare states are revealing, if not unsurprising. Barr (1992) and Snower (1993) are examples of those who claim authority in stating the objectives of the welfare state in terms of efficiency, equity and administrative feasibility; indeed, Barr (1992, p. 745) asserts that this is common to all 'social institutions'. There is no reference to any definitive statements or historical context to justify the supposition that the objectives of welfare states do indeed resemble those, and, moreover, remain fixed through real time. Framing objectives in this manner, as is argued below, furnishes legitimacy to the notion of (welfare) state failure.

Alternative conceptualizations of the welfare state that resonate with a more social economic approach have been advanced by, among others, Fine (2001), Jessop (2002) and O'Hara (2000). Explicit in these authors' analyses is the view that the economy is a social provisioning process subject to endogenous evolutionary change in historical time. Historical contingencies play a key analytical role, as do social factors. Hence, as with well-known political economic approaches (such as Gough, 1979; O'Connor, 2002), the state, when incorporating 'welfare state' activities, is frequently argued to be inherently contradictory, subject to periodic bouts of crises, and an integral part of the architecture of capitalism. This offers a much broader vista that explicitly incorporates issues of power, history and social structure. Hence, in more radical explanations the capitalist welfare state both preserves and retains power for the capitalist elite and simultaneously diffuses that of the working class and the poor.

Of particular relevance here is the delineation of the Keynesian welfare state (KWS) that arose following World War II. The KWS emerged as a support of Fordism and its reproduction, enabling the expansion of mass consumption through Keynesian demand management. This was accompanied by the extension of welfare rights, particularly through the expansion of education, social security entitlements and healthcare coverage, such as those initiated in the UK under the auspices of the Beveridge reforms.[3] Contrary to mainstream economic analysis, the state is not viewed as a substitute for the market, but a critical element within a capitalist *system*.

The foregoing begs the question as to what constitutes privatization in this complementary schema between state and market. Again, the conceptualization of privatization is subject to ambiguity, arguably albeit of less significance than the typology of the welfare state. None the less, the two are intimately linked in policy discussion. A narrow interpretation of privatization could be represented by reference to ownership transfers from the state, or public sector, to the private sector (see Florio, 2004). However, such a reliance on the full-scale transfer of property rights does not capture the institutional richness of privatization, especially in the context of the welfare state. A broader typology is advanced here based on privatization as a multidimensional concept that centres on some attenuation in the degree of state provision (McMaster, 2002).[4] This draws upon a literature prominent in the 1980s that sought to define the nature of privatization as a key element of neoliberal reform, and, to paraphrase Margaret Thatcher, by doing so furnish some means of evaluation of the extent to which the 'frontiers of the state had been rolled back'. Heald (1984) provides a sound example of such endeavours. He categorizes privatization: ownership transfers; deregulation and liberalization; tendering and contracting out, and de-subsidization, including greater recourse to user fees. All involve greater recourse to market mechanisms and hence are expected to increase the extent of commodification.

An enormous literature examining and outlining the emerging nature of privatization has grown since the 1980s. That privatization is a global phenomenon engendered by supranational bodies such as the World Bank and the International Monetary Fund is obvious.[5] What is less obvious, and is a core concern of social economists, is whether this global phenomenon improves the living standards of the most vulnerable in society and enhances human dignity. This chapter focuses particularly on the latter, and the following sections trace contrasting economic approaches to this.

The economic rationale: welfare state failure and the privatization nirvana
The economic case for the reform of the welfare state is well documented and known. It is usually associated with the rise of neoliberalism, and in the mainstream economics literature is typified by the growth in the public choice school, the Chicago school, and to a lesser extent new institutional economics.[6] In the mainstream literature the crux of the case for reform/ privatization revolves around the argument that (welfare) state failure is more extensive, and hence economically damaging, than market failure. This directly challenges the old Pigovian conventional wisdom fostered by price-theoretic micro models of externalities and market structure. The twin, yet disparate, influences of the Coase theorem and public choice models of bureaucracy effectively undermined the Pigovian model. This, combined with the breakdown of the Keynesian consensus in the 1970s, afforded neoliberal approaches an unparalleled opportunity for academic growth and political influence (Harvey, 2005). Of course the Friedmanite monetarist mantra may have been diminished with the advent of new Keynesianism, recourse to evolutionary game theory and the 'third way', but arguably the tenor of the analytical framework and reference points remain largely intact (see, e.g., Arestis and Sawyer, 2001; Fine, 2002).

Concisely, new institutionalist and public choice arguments highlight endemic agency problems arising from information asymmetries in state activities. This supply-side failure is also accompanied by demand-side failure traceable to similar information failings, resulting in widespread money illusion. In short, rational agents are subject to profound informational problems that generate incentive misalignments and inherent inefficiencies. The solution is clear: vertically disintegrate state activities by contracting out social welfare services and efficiency improvements will be achieved, or at least the stifling ineptitude of state bureaucracies overcome. In effect this position advocates some form of commodification of welfare state services in order to create exchange values that reveal the 'true' worth of such activities (for examples see Niskanen, 1994; Mueller, 2003).

The exigency of the case is partly grounded in Baumol's (1993) study of the sluggish productivity of education and health services in the USA.[7] Baumol argued that such activities are not amenable to productivity growth given the heterogeneity of the production process and relatively high levels of labour intensity. His analysis has been refashioned to buttress the case that the public sector acts as a drag on growth and economic development. *Prima facie*, married to the crowding-out argument (see Bacon and Eltis, 1976), Baumol's 'cost disease' thesis culminates in a strong analytical construct fundamentally questioning a statist metric.

Of course the welfare state is also deemed to adversely affect the efficient workings of the labour market, generating distortions and dependency. Familiar arguments regarding the adverse incentive effects of generous welfare provision indicate an obvious preference for supply-side labour reform and the erosion of benefits.[8] The risk-bearing emphasis shifts from the KWS to the individual. From the perspective of the arguments presented here three pertinent points emerge: the neoliberal/new right stress on individual responsibility continues to be relevant in 'third way' accounts; the advance of a 'Schumpeterian competition state' (Jessop, 2002), and a move to promote a particular view of individual dignity.

Taylor-Gooby (1999, 2001) notes that the work of Anthony Giddens (and the mind-set of the current UK government) advocates an attenuation in the role of the (welfare) state and greater responsibility by individuals and communities in the provision of 'well-being'. Accordingly the state is responsible for ensuring equality of opportunity, as opposed to outcomes, and individual rights (to welfare) are accompanied by responsibilities (Giddens, 1998). Such an association is hardly surprising given the close relationship between New Keynesianism and Giddens's work (Arestis and Sawyer, 2001; Giddens, 1998). Arestis and Sawyer convincingly argue that new Keynesianism is heavily influenced by monetarism and new classicism, especially through its reliance on the non-accelerating inflation rate of unemployment (NAIRU), market failure and endogenous growth theory.[9]

The thrust of this literature is that an expansive state represents a retardation of economic and individual development. Earlier contributions, such as those of the public choice school, portray the market and state in adversarial terms. In contrast, more recent new Keynesian-influenced approaches are predisposed to notions of social capital that enable consideration of appropriate spheres for alternative governance frames – state, market and community. Again, though, the state is cast as inferior to the dynamism of the market, being consigned at best a supporting role. Reference to endogenous growth theory reveals an important sphere for a reformed (welfare) state: buttressing the 'new knowledge economy'. Concisely, endogenous growth theory centres on the importance of knowledge and information to both human capital and productivity, and hence economic growth: knowledge and information are in effect factors of production. As with public choice and new institutional economics, it allows that knowledge and information are subject to imperfections. However, unlike the public choice model these imperfections occur in the private sector since knowledge and information are accorded some features of public goods, chiefly non-excludability and non-rivalry in consumption. The state, then, should be cast in the role of encouraging knowledge provision to address underprovision problems. Crucially, education and training are keys to sustainable growth, and should be ensured by the state.

For Jessop (2002) the globalizing 'knowledge economy' represents a transformation in the nature of capitalist modes of production from Fordist mass production to post-Fordist processes, where the latter are described in terms of increasing flexibility, especially of the labour force, and changes in transactions based on information and communications technologies (see also Pietrykowski, 1999). Jessop (2002, p. 99) explains: 'In ideal-typical terms and in contrast to Fordism, [post-Fordism's] virtuous cycle would be based on flexible and networked production; growing productivity based on some combination of economies of scope, economies of networks and process innovations . . .'.

Similar to O'Connor (2002), Jessop's analysis suggests that labour flexibility can entail positive outcomes for some groups in terms of job enrichment and multi-skilling, but for others it can entail de-skilling, low wages and indigence resulting from the outsourcing of tasks, especially in the context of globalization. Moreover, in the commitment to ongoing innovation, corporate structures are becoming flatter, more decentralized and flexible, while organized around what are considered to be core competencies with extensive outsourcing of production (Jessop, 2002). It is this emphasis on innovation that lends Jessop to employ the Schumpeterian adjective.

Given the foregoing emphases on endogenous growth, the 'knowledge economy', and the 'third way', the greater role accorded to the individual is manifest in the new shape of the (welfare) state (Taylor-Gooby, 2001), most evidently as embodied in the noted transfer in burden of (labour market) insecurity from the state to the individual. The stress on training as a means of developing human capital may be seen as a reconfiguration of welfare provision where the state's role is reduced. Jessop argues that this reorientation is typified by a repertoire that: subordinates social policy to economic policy; exerts downward pressure on 'social wages'; shifts from welfarist to workfarist modes, and exhibits a propensity to shift from state intervention to correct for market failure to public–private partnerships, or some form of self-organizational governance to address both state and market failures. Thus, and at the risk of being overly concise, Jessop convincingly argues that the Schumpeterian competition state (or the third way) focuses on individual innovation on the supply side, and economic policies should be tailored to promote the production of knowledge and entrepreneurship. This economic stance dominates social policy where citizens' automatic rights to welfare benefits are eroded; that is, there is a downward pressure on 'social wages' (Jessop, 2002; Navarro et al., 2004). In essence this refers to social security benefits and state pensions, among others. In terms of the former, Peck and Theodore (2000) note that in generic terms welfare-to-work reforms compel welfare benefit recipients to enrol in (re)training programmes in order to receive benefits and to be better equipped for the uncertainties of a flexible labour market. However, training programmes tend to be confined to low-skilled areas, and the element of compulsion

> creates contingent welfare as a means of enforcing contingent work. Welfare ceases to exist as a temporary shelter from the vagaries of low-wage labour markets. In addition to exerting a downward pull on wages and regulatory standards, such models recall the workhouse principle in standing as a reminder of the (individual) price to be paid for unemployment. (Peck and Theodore, 2000, pp. 134–5)

The provision of pensions is a prominent case where reform is tailored towards retrenchment with amendments to the indexation of pensions (from average wage increases to inflation) and from intergenerational transfers to redistributions of income over the life cycle via savings through prefunded schemes. Again the general transfer of uncertainty from the state to the individual is manifest. Conventional economic wisdom represents an ageing population as the (demand-side) source of increased expenditures on healthcare and social support. Yet as Dugger (1999) and Jackson (2001, 2006) contest, the conventional view is predicated on a simplistic association between ageing and state expenditures. Jackson and Dugger offer important insights into the social construction of age. Physical ageing is a continuous process, yet the delineation between young and old is to some degree founded on what can appear to be capricious grounds.[10] Jackson (2001, p. 206) argues:

> The divisions within most people's life cycles – education, work, retirement – are socially constructed. This man-made periodization of ageing both reflects and reinforces social attitudes to the elderly; the retired are seen as being dependent on younger age groups even when physically capable and receiving no public pensions or health care.

Insightfully, Jackson (2006, p. 464) further argues:

> At the ideological level, technical change and population ageing provide depoliticised accounts of why it is essential to curtail the welfare state. Economic effects have been exaggerated and portrayed as natural and inevitable, in order to deflect attention from the choices behind policy reforms.

From the perspective advanced here the foregoing prompts an arguably distinct view of individual dignity. The shift in responsibility and risk-bearing from the state to the individual and the increasing recourse to market- and 'community'-based governance are common to economic discourses in this area, from public choice to new Keynesianism. In short, here dignity is associated with individual autonomy, responsibility and freedom from stigma. Yet not all of these elements are accorded the same footing. Barr (1992) observes that an objective of the welfare state (listed as objective 9, well behind efficiency – accorded objective 1 status) is that benefits and services *should* be provided in a manner that 'preserves' an individual's dignity and be without stigma. He cites Beveridge, who considered that by making contributions an individual can feel that (s)he is receiving benefits not as charity, but as a right. Beveridge's reference to rights is at the foundation of the KWS: citizenship of a state entitles an individual to benefits. But, as noted, the KWS has eroded and is, arguably, being reconfigured into, to paraphrase Jessop, a Schumpeterian variant. It is hard to disagree with Barr's reference to, and invocation of, Beveridge, but it prompts the question as to whether the privatization that has accompanied the evolution of the welfare state is compatible with such a rendering of dignity, or whether the other elements are recasting its meaning.

The influential Mont Pelerin Society[11] at its inaugural meeting in 1947 declared in its statement of aims:

> The central values of civilization are in danger. Over large stretches of the earth's surface the essential conditions of human dignity and freedom have already disappeared. In others they are under constant menace from the development of current tendencies of policy [from the KWS to the encroachment of Communism] . . . Even that most precious possession of Western Man, freedom of thought and expression, is threatened by the spread of creeds which, claiming the privilege of tolerance when in the position of a minority, seek only to establish a position of power in which they can suppress and obliterate all views but their own.
>
> [The Society] holds further that they [threats to individual freedom] have been fostered by a decline in the belief in private property and the competitive market, for without the diffused power and initiative associated with these institutions [absolute moral standards, rule of law and private property] it is difficult to imagine a society in which freedom may be effectively preserved.

This crystallizes the evocative conceptualization of dignity as indelibly embedded in a particular negative view of individual freedom (see Berlin's, 1958, seminal dichotomization). Drawing from Sen (1993), individual autonomy in decision-making and immunity from encroachment are integral domains of what he terms as the process aspect of individual freedom that is readily associated with a Hayekian and neoliberal stance. In the extreme, markets, by incorporating the notion of voluntary exchange, represent the *only* arrangement where trading and trading possibilities symbolize both the exercise and expression of free choice and choice sets respectively. A powerful case is that the extension of this mechanism for facilitating the 'freedom to choose' to the activities of the de-individualizing, repressive and dependency-generating KWS represents what Sen (1993) referred to as the association between welfare-achievements, in terms of efficiency and hence living standards, and freedom-achievements. As noted, in this light, a truncated or residual welfare state should be confined to ensuring the efficient operation of markets in welfare services (see, e.g., Wiseman's, 1991, references to care). Accordingly the linkage between welfare-achievements and freedom-achievements furnishes a positive veneer on the latter given the standard economics assumption that the former rests in the domain of the positive. In such circumstances Jackson's allusion, noted above, to the de-politicization of the retrenchment of the welfare state is confirmed: privatizing welfare is 'scientific', and moreover, the promotion of human dignity exhibits an objective aura.

The welfare state, privatization and individual dignity: a social economics perspective

From a social economics perspective dignity is not necessarily served with the neoliberal promotion of markets in welfare and the individualization of the burden of uncertainty of indigence that the Schumpeterian model prompts. The analytical entry point for social economists as to the meaning and purpose of economics is social provisioning, which, as Figart (2007) observes, is closely tied with social reproduction as it engages with the study of the organization of economic activities as mediated by culture, ideology and institutions. It therefore goes beyond material provisioning, embodying emotional, social and interpersonal activities (Figart, 2007). This lends itself to contemplating the individual as profoundly socially embedded (Davis, 2003), makes no pretensions that economics is ideology-free (Wilber, 2004), and seeks to address issues of individual living standards, poverty and dignity: more generally, what constitutes the 'good and just society' (Wisman, 2003).

Davis's (2006) recent observations on the nature of dignity are highly informative. He draws from Avishai Margalit's *Decent Society* and the work of Bernard Williams in conceiving that dignity is not only grounded in negative (or process) freedom, but that it is also embedded in integrity. Two types of integrity are distinguished: personal and moral. Personal differs from moral in that the former concerns the coherence of a person's character and the latter concerns whether this character is virtuous. The latter depends on the former. Davis is interested in the association between personal integrity and identity. Referring to Williams's work, he considers that personal integrity is the product of an individual's 'identity-conferring commitments'. According to this line of argument individuals make various types of commitments to others, and the commitments an individual most strongly identifies with help establish this individual's integrity. In this way, Davis argues, individuals engage in some sort of reflexive self-construction. It is this self-construction, or sense of self, that is the key to appreciating dignity.

An individual is socially embedded through their capacity to express a 'we-intention' (Davis, 2003). Employing 'we' language is more demanding than 'I' language as it involves a collective intention; that is, an individual expressing shared intentions effectively speaks for all those to whom that 'we' language applies; therefore some consideration must be given to whether the intention expressed accurately reflects the intentions of those to whom it applies. In this respect individuals are socially embedded – in effect by (socially) embedding others 'in' themselves by expressing an intention which they believe is held by others as well. This is important in appreciating the interconnectedness of the personal and social aspects of dignity.[12]

For Davis, the sense of self and the social aspect of the individual contribute to an individual's sense of dignity: dignity possesses personal and social qualities embodied in feelings of self-esteem and self-respect. Self-esteem, associated with the personal aspect of dignity, arises from an individual's feelings and self-opinion. Self-respect, the social aspect of dignity, is a matter of how an individual believes that (s)he is entitled to regard themselves in virtue of their membership of social constituencies. On the one hand, then, dignity is similar to pride in that pride is an expression of self-esteem; on the other hand, dignity is an expression of the respect individuals feel towards themselves as human beings derived from personal and moral integrity that arises from being 'an accepted member of a community equal in certain basic rights' (Davis, 2006, p. 78).

From the foregoing synopsis it is apparent that a decent society is one that ensures decent living standards that embody human dignity. This, as Figart notes, goes beyond possession of privately owned commodities and the provision of public goods; it embraces human flourishing and addresses human needs (O'Boyle, 2005). The conception of human flourishing is allied to the capabilities approach advanced by Amartya Sen and Martha Nussbaum, among others (see, e.g., Putnam, 2003). Capabilities refer to the abilities or freedoms to enjoy 'valuable functionings'. Levine (2004, p. 102) describes this further: 'The central element in this way of thinking is that we are poor not primarily because we lack goods, but because we lack the ability to be and do things that are essential to leading a human life.'

Putnam (2003) argues that Nussbaum is more forthright than Sen in furnishing characteristics of what she terms 'central human capabilities'. These capabilities essentially amount to rights of opportunity; they include life (including freedom from premature mortality) and bodily health (including reproductive health, adequate nourishment and shelter) and bodily integrity (freedom from violence, rights to mobility and choice in reproductive matters). These are important and contested points, and a reflection of a more general point that freedom from poverty should be seen as a human right.

In terms of human needs, the literature draws upon the classic contributions of Karl Marx and Thorstein Veblen in arguing that there is a *need* for work as sources of self-expression, identity and belonging (see, e.g., Levine, 2004; O'Boyle, 2005). For work to encompass freedom it must engage with the individual's skills and creativity, and not alienate or bore. Hence for Levine poverty is a developmental failure, or a failure to develop skills: without skills there is a loss of identity, which is a further manifestation of poverty and a loss of dignity.

The intention here is by no means to provide a comprehensive review of a rich literature; it is more to provide a flavour. Concisely, a social economics perspective stresses the centrality of the socially embedded individual and the complexities of human needs for dignity and ability to flourish, both of which are viewed as human rights. The considerable question is begged as to whether recent privatizations of welfare states – the transformation of the KWS into a Schumpeterian variant – serve to enhance the capability to promote human rights in this way. Does shifting responsibility from the state to the individual afford the individual opportunities to flourish? Does the neoliberal emphasis on the assignation of human dignity with negative freedom provide a basis for the attainment of a privatization-led utopia, where freedom and efficiency furnish human dignity? In themselves these are massive issues, although the general thrust of the social economics literature is to query the basis of such claims.

Given the limitations of space, the remainder of this section seeks to examine through social economics lenses whether the conditions of increasing commodification (of welfare state activities) are compatible with the advancement of human dignity.

Prima facie, references to the 'decent society' are embodied by Davis's (2006, p. 81) statement: 'Making human dignity a central value of socio-economic policy, then, means changing social institutions to *eliminate* humiliating institutions' (emphasis added). Humiliation is defined as the violation, or undermining, of dignity. Systematic humiliation, as an outcome of a system of institutions, erodes individuals' self-respect by either denying them membership or attenuating their status (Davis, 2006).

Freedom *from* such institutions is, from a neoliberal standpoint, afforded by the market. Each agent is imbued with inalienable rights to exchange: exchange is the voluntary exercise of free will, free choice and autonomy (O'Neill, 1998). Moreover, as noted, the state as Leviathan, generating dependencies and infringing individual liberties, autonomy and choice, renders both it and the 'welfare state' as a set of humiliating institutions.

This neoliberal frame, however, is subject to an intractable problem instituted in the nature of commodification. Perhaps the most notable contributions to the conceptualization of 'the commodity' are furnished by Karl Marx (1990) and Karl Polanyi (1944). Succinctly, both believed that the defining feature of commodities was exchange value: a commodity is an entity that may be potentially monetized (Fine, 2002); is produced for sale in a market (Polanyi, 1944; Jessop, 2002), and therefore property rights to the entity can be defined and transferred.

In Marx's and Polanyi's analyses, the notion of the commodity also warrants examination of the processes of commodification and decommodification. Marx allied commodification with the valorization of labour power, and indeed narrowly construed commodification refers to the buying and selling of entities through market exchange, where previously such activity was not marketable. A broader interpretation incorporates the metaphorical representation of exchange as commodity (market) exchange (Radin, 1996). A more literal interpretation refers to the social context of markets, whereas a metaphorical rendering is broader and embodies market rhetoric which conceives of human attributes as fungible, owned assets (Radin, 1996; Fine, 2002; O'Neill, 1998). Given this, Beckerian-inspired approaches can be conceived as metaphorical connotations of ubiquitous commodification. Further, mainstream economics' reliance on the market as an epistemological (and ontological) entry point(s) and meta-narrative inculcates the notion of the market as the 'natural' mode of socio-economic activity. Through social economics lenses this is unnecessarily reductionist and hastens misplaced utopian solutions.

Whilst privatization involves increasing commodification, it is analytically attractive to conceive of some sort of continuum of commodification (see, e.g., Radin, 1996). *Pace* Esping-Andersen, such conceptual considerations are multidimensional, multi-polar, and hence not suitable for two-dimensional representation. Following Radin, goods may demonstrate incomplete commodification in the narrow sense in that activities may have a coexistence of market and non-market interactions, and/or entities may have a socially acknowledged and legitimate non-monetizable aspect. Drawing from and augmenting Radin's (1996, ch. 8) highly informative analysis, conceptually complete commodification involves the conjunction of four dimensions: fungibility; commensurability; monetization; and objectification. Fungibility, commensurability and monetization are closely related but distinct notions.[13] Fungibility concerns the exchangeability of entities while maintaining their value for the proprietor, whereas commensurability relates to the valuation of entities such that they may be arrayed on a continuous scale. Monetization obviously concerns matters of the ready convertibility of the entity into money. Indeed, possession of the entity is equivalent to possessing money. Importantly, the foregoing emphasizes the centrality of exchange or instrumental value. In Kantian terms, the entity lacks any intrinsic deontological worth.

This is perhaps further underscored by considerations of objectification. For Nussbaum (1995, p. 257), treating something as an object implies seven notions: instrumentality, where the object is treated as a tool for the purposes of another; denial of autonomy, where the object is treated as lacking in autonomy and self-determination; inertness, where the object is treated as lacking in agency; fungibility; violability, where the object is treated as lacking in boundary-integrity, that is, it is possible to decompose the object; ownership, or property rights to the object, and denial of subjectivity, where the object can be treated as if devoid of experience or feelings, or they need not be considered.

The inherent features of objectification patently do not lend themselves to the promotion of human dignity and rights. Although processes of commodification are neither necessary nor sufficient for objectification, they do not retard orientations towards objectification. Arguably this is unproblematic for certain exchanges, such as those where voluntary exchange occurs for unnecessary material goods. However, welfare state activities are frequently profoundly relational, and the economic rationale of increasing commodification coupled with privatization is incapable of theoretically accommodating this. Commodification, and its analytic heuristic, denotes a particular form of social construction and process of valuation of things that can be apprehended as commodities. It is this specific social arrangement that founds a particular means of valuation that is highly contested for some activities. However, as noted, for some commentators, markedly Becker, all aspects of social interaction are, and can be, treated as commodities in rhetorical terms. Radin (1996, p. 6) contests:

> [U]niversal commodification implies extreme objectification. Commodities are socially constructed as objects separate from the self and social relations. Universal commodification assimilates personal attributes, relations, and desired states of affairs to the realm of objects by assuming that all human attributes are possessions bearing a value characterisable in money terms, and by implying that all these possessions can and should be separable from persons to be exchanged through the free market.

Feminist and social economics is replete with misgivings over the complete commodification of care (see, e.g., Folbre, 1995; Davis and McMaster, 2007). In its extreme, neoliberalism hardly seems to provide a convincing template for the enhancement of human dignity, at least from a social economics perspective. Its economics, in the main, assumes that, epistemologically, concepts from care to knowledge and labour can be reduced to commodities, and accordingly connections between agents in these fields are identical: the natural schema for commodities is the market. Yet standard economics is ill equipped to furnish a comprehensive conceptualization of markets (Jackson, 2007), and therefore fails to provide an adequate theoretical platform for an investigation of the ramifications of the evolution of the welfare state following privatization initiatives.

That markets in welfare activities, from pension provision to healthcare and education, augment processes of commodification, and hence objectification, seems inescapable. From the social construction of dependency, as in the cases of age and the flexible labour markets of the post-Fordist economy, neoliberal programmes seem inherently contradictory: markets are depicted as the conduits of individual freedom and dignity, yet through increasing commodification promote objectification traits that undermine human autonomy and dignity via the vilification and isolation of societies' most vulnerable. To be sure, the KWS had bureaucratic and institutional structures that did not necessarily endorse human flourishing, but the central contradiction of the KWS is that simultaneously it did provide some basis for the expansion of positive freedoms and hence dignity that also served the accumulation requirements of capitalism. The evolution in the structure of accumulation has fostered an impression of extended freedoms (Harvey, 2005), yet this has been attained on an altar of humiliation for many. As John Kenneth Galbraith (2005, p. 11) wryly observed in his final work:

> Reference to a market system is . . . without meaning, erroneous, bland, benign. It emerged from a desire for protection from the unsavoury experience of capitalist power and . . . the legacy of Marx, Engels and their devout and exceptionally articulate disciples. No individual firm, no individual capitalist, is now thought to have power; that the market is subject to skilled and comprehensive management is unmentioned even in most economic teaching. Here the fraud.

Notes

1. Cited by Barr (1992, p. 741).
2. There is an obvious parallel here with prominent institutionalist writers, such as Veblen, Commons and Ayres. Veblen spoke of 'enhancing human life', Commons 'reasonable value', and Ayres a 'reasonable society'.

3. These rather concise observations are intended to furnish only a generic representation of the KWS, and are in no way intended to provide a comprehensive account. Jessop and Fine are among those authors who stress the distinctive traits of the KWS across countries and regions. Indeed, Jessop frames his analysis in terms of the KWNS, where 'N' denotes national.

4. Not all necessarily weaken the role of the state; for instance, in some instances of water privatization in the UK the role of the state was enhanced from a previous arm's-length relationship with nationalized bodies to a more proactive regulation of privatized concerns (see Maloney, 2001).

5. The emergence of this became known by international economist John Williamson's phrase 'The Washington Consensus'.

6. The Austrian school of thought is also a major contributor to this literature. The Austrian case was especially prominent during the socialist calculation debate of the 1920s and 1930s, and latterly through the work of Hayek and the establishment of the Mont Pelerin Society, which transcended methodological differences between the Austrians and more neoclassical schools.

7. Baumol's rendition is based on an earlier study he conducted with William Bowen in the 1960s into the performing arts, which they concluded were subject to the 'cost disease of the personal services'.

8. Trade union reform in the form of curbing power is also evident from this type of approach.

9. At first sight this may seem incompatible with monetarist and new classical explanations of market properties, such as self-equilibration around the 'natural rate'. Arestis and Sawyer's appeal is that a fixed point in new Keynesian analysis is a modification of the natural rate hypothesis where NAIRU is based on variables outside the labour market, such as firms' pricing decisions and productive capacity. Moreover, market failures may be associated with information failures of the type alluded to in the text, as well as Pigovian sources.

10. The importance of indigence and consumption patterns on health status is stressed by numerous authors and bodies (as examples, see the World Health Organization, 2002; Fine, 2002). With adjustments in diet, lifestyle and preventive screening, a concentrated morbidity pattern may emerge at the end of individuals' lives. Hence reduced morbidity rates would act to further attenuate the presumed impact of population ageing on medical expenditure.

11. The Society was founded by, among others, Friedrich Hayek. Among its prominent members are Nobel Laureates Milton Friedman, James Buchanan, George Stigler, Maurice Allais, Ronald Coase, Gary Becker and Vernon Smith (in addition to Hayek himself). Other notable economists include Harold Demsetz, Ludwig von Mises and Thrainn Eggertsson.

12. This goes well beyond the strictures of mainstream economics. For instance, Wiseman (1991) and Lindbeck et al. (1999) are among those who attempt to capture social norms either within a given utility function or within a family of utility functions governed by some meta-function. Thus individuals may be behaving rationally even if they do not maximize utility, or indeed behave in a fashion that is costly to themselves – as in some forms of altruism. In this interpretation norms become tradable within an overall utility calculation. Accordingly they only possess an instrumental value, rendering any deontic aspect redundant. From a social economics approach this seems unduly reductionist (see Davis, 2003).

13. Each of Radin's *indicia* are logically separable and do not reduce to one another. For instance, objectivity may be a necessity for the other *indicia*, but is not sufficient: it could potentially be the case that improper subordination arising from power relations and not commodification results in objectification. Further, commensurability need not entail money equivalence: witness neoclassical economics' references to non-reducible utility functions.

References

Arestis, P. and M. Sawyer (2001), 'The economic analysis underlying the "third way"', *New Political Economy*, **6**, 255–78.

Bacon, R. and W. Eltis (1976), *Britain's Economic Problem: Too Few Producers*, London: Macmillan.

Barr, N. (1992), 'Economic theory and the welfare state: a survey and interpretation', *Journal of Economic Literature*, **30**, 741–803.

Baumol, W.G. (1993), 'Health care, education and the cost disease', *Public Choice*, **77**, 17–28.

Berlin, I. (1958), 'Two concepts of liberty', Inaugural Lecture, University of Oxford, October, http://www.hss.bond.edu.au/phil12-205/Berlin%20Liberty2.pdf.

Davis, J.B. (2003), *The Theory of the Individual in Economics: Identity and Value*, London and New York: Routledge.

Davis, J.B. (2006), 'The normative significance of the individual in economics: freedom, dignity, and human rights', in B.J. Clary, W. Dolfsma and D.M. Figart (eds), *Ethics and the Market: Insights from Social Economics*, London: Routledge, pp. 69–83.

Davis, J.B. and R. McMaster (2007), 'The individual in mainstream health economics: a case of persona non-grata', *Health Care Analysis*, **15**, 195–210.

Dugger, W.M. (1999), 'Old age is an institution', *Review of Social Economy*, **57**, 84–98.

Esping-Andersen, G. (1999), *The Social Foundations of Post-Industrial Economies*, Oxford: Oxford University Press.

Figart, D.M. (2007), 'Social responsibility for living standards', Presidential Address to the Association for Social Economics, Chicago, January.

Fine, B. (2002), *The World of Consumption: The Material and Cultural Revisited*, 2nd edn, London: Routledge.

Florio, M. (2004), *The Great Divestiture: Evaluating the Welfare Impact of the British Privatizations 1979–1997*, Cambridge, MA: MIT Press.

Folbre, N. (1995), '"Holding hands at midnight": the paradox of caring labor', *Feminist Economics*, **1**, 73–92.

Galbraith, J.K. (2005), *The Economics of Innocent Fraud*, London: Penguin Books.

Giddens, A. (1998), *The Third Way: The Renewal of Social Democracy*, Cambridge: Polity Press.

Gough, I. (1979), *The Political Economy of the Welfare State*, London and Basingstoke: Macmillan.

Harvey, D. (2005), *A Brief History of Neoliberalism*, Oxford: Oxford University Press.

Heald, D. (1984), 'Privatisation: analysing its appeal and limitations', *Fiscal Studies*, **5**, 36–46.

Jackson, W.A. (2001), 'Age, health and medical expenditure', in J.B. Davis (ed.), *The Social Economics of Health Care*, London and New York: Routledge pp. 195–218.

Jackson, W.A. (2006), 'Post-Fordism and population ageing', *International Review of Applied Economics*, **20**, 449–67.

Jackson, W.A. (2007), 'On the social structure of markets', *Cambridge Journal of Economics*, **31**, 235–53.

Jessop, B. (2002), *The Future of the Capitalist State*, Cambridge: Polity Press.

Levine, D.P. (2004), 'Poverty, capabilities and freedom', *Review of Political Economy*, **16**, 101–15.

Lindbeck, A., S. Nyberg and J.W. Weibull (1999), 'Social norms and economic incentives in the welfare state', *Quarterly Journal of Economics*, **114**, 1–35.

McMaster, R. (2002), 'The analysis of welfare state reform: why the "quasi-markets" narrative is descriptively inadequate and misleading', *Journal of Economic Issues*, **36**, 769–94.

Maloney, W.A. (2001), 'Regulation in an episodic policy-making environment: the water industry in England and Wales', *Public Administration*, **79**, 625–42.

Marx, K. (1990), *Capital*, Vol. 1, London: Penguin.

Mont Pelerin Society, http://www.montpelerin.org/.

Mueller, D.C. (2003), *Public Choice III*, Cambridge: Cambridge University Press.

Navarro, V., J. Schmitt and J. Astudillo (2004), 'Is globalisation undermining the welfare state?', *Cambridge Journal of Economics*, **28**, 133–52.

Nussbaum, M.C. (1995), 'Objectification', *Philosophy and Public Affairs*, **24**, 249–91.
Niskanen, W.A. (1994), *Bureaucracy and Public Economics*, Aldershot, UK and Brookfield, USA: The Locke Institute/Edward Elgar.
O'Boyle, E.J. (2005), '*Homo Socio-Economicus*: foundational to social economics and the social economy', *Review of Social Economy* (Special Issue: The Best of the Review of Social Economy, 1944–1999), **63**, 483–507 (originally published in 1994).
O'Connor, J. (2002), *The Fiscal Crisis of the State*, New Brunswick, NJ: Transaction Books (updated, originally published 1973).
O'Hara, P.A. (2000), *Marx, Veblen, and Contemporary Institutional Political Economy: Principles and Unstable Dynamics of Capitalism*, Cheltenham, UK and Northampton MA, USA: Edward Elgar.
O'Neill, J. (1998), *The Market: Ethics, Knowledge and Politics*, London: Routledge.
Peck, J. and N. Theodore (2000), ' "Work first": workfare and the regulation of contingent labour markets (commentary)', *Cambridge Journal of Economics*, **24**, 119–38.
Pietrykowski, B. (1999), 'Beyond the Fordist/post-Fordist dichotomy: working through the second industrial divide', *Review of Social Economy*, **57**, 177–98.
Polanyi, K. (1944), *The Great Transformation: The Political and Economic Origins of Our Time*, Boston, MA: Beacon Press.
Putnam, H. (2003), 'For ethics and economics without the dichotomies', *Review of Political Economy*, **15**, 395–412.
Radin, M.J. (1996), *Contested Commodities*, Cambridge, MA: Harvard University Press.
Sen, A. (1993), 'Markets and freedoms: achievements and limitations of the market mechanism in promoting individual freedoms', *Oxford Economic Papers*, **45**, 519–41.
Snower, D.J. (1993), 'The future of the welfare state', *Economic Journal*, **103**, 700–717.
Stanfield, J.R. and J.B. Stanfield (1996), 'Reconstructing the welfare state in the aftermath of the great capitalist restoration', in W.M. Dugger (ed.), *Inequality: Radical Institutionalist Views on Race, Gender, Class, and Nation*, Westport, CT: Greenwood Press, pp. 127–39.
Taylor-Gooby, P. (1999), 'Markets and motives: trust and egoism in welfare markets', *Journal of Social Policy*, **28**, 97–114.
Taylor-Gooby, P. (2001), 'Risk, contingency and the third way: evidence from the BHPS and qualitative studies', *Social Policy and Administration*, **35**, 195–211.
Wilber, C.K. (2004), 'Ethics and social economics', ASE Presidential Address, January 2004, *Review of Social Economy*, **62**, 425–39.
Wiseman, J. (1991), 'The welfare state: a public choice perspective', in D. Wilson and T. Wilson (eds), *The State and Social Welfare: Objectives of Policy*, London: Longman, pp. 55–72.
Wisman, J.D. (2003), 'The scope and promising future of social economics', *Review of Social Economy*, **61**, 425–45.
World Health Organization (2002), *World Health Report: Reducing Risks, Promoting Healthy Life*, http://www.who.int/whr/2002/en/index.html.

30 The states of social economics
Charlie Dannreuther and Oliver Kessler

Introduction

Let us assume that social economics is mainly about real people. These people love and hate, laugh and cry, daydream and dysfunction. Of course a few of them do manage to act like modern men of reason and make egoistic self-maximizing decisions or follow the paths laid before them by institutional procedures, norms and careers. But most of them are more rounded individuals whose behaviour is better explained by approaches that treat individuals as *homo sapiens* and so are genuinely meta-disciplinary (i.e. that goes beyond disciplinary defined theory). As such an approach, social economics therefore tries to explain the relationship between economics and lived experiences. It is this ontology of life that differentiates social economics from other approaches in economics and social science.

This chapter argues that if social economics seeks to provide a different way of representing economic activity, then it needs to problematize and engage with the notion of the state. Many views of the state start from an *a priori* given distinction of public and private spheres through which the state is defined in terms of a person or a subject with wants, needs, interests and an 'objective function'. However, if social economics is about the relationship between people engaged with economic activity first and then the state, such a framework is of limited use. If social economics wants to capture fully the role of the state in economic practices, it needs to leave the confines of this public–private distinction behind to examine the processes that influence the relationship between the state and the real people as its economic subjects. This means that social economics must explore how representations of social life have been shaped by the state, the arenas in which particular notions of subject are constituted and asserted by the state, and the role of the extension of the public sphere in this process. Understood as a set of political practices, the 'unity' of the state results from social processes that implicitly or explicitly deny the complexity of everyday life. From a social economics perspective economic actors cannot be seen as autonomous and atomistic nor simply determined by the social institutions with which they are associated. Rather, they are constituted through a variety of interactions with social relations. Only by transcending the public–private distinction can social economics treat the state as a social concept.

We argue in four steps. The first section reconstructs the current approach to the state. Within the social sciences, it is common to frame the concept 'state' by dividing the world into a public and a private sphere. With this distinction, the state is separated from everyday life and given a particular function within society that is analogous to the individual. Seeing the state as a person leads the discussion on to the material practices of the state in administration, public policy and bureaucracy, and how it is the performance of these roles, through institutionalized rules, norms and procedures, that gives the state its personality. The second section discusses the political economy of representation to show how the changing contours of state-hood stretch the analogy linking individuals with the state. The third section emphasizes that once the public–private distinction is gone and the state loses its actor-like status, many of the ways that the state represents its activities and justifies its actions are undermined. Fourth, this is most obvious in the failure of the state to account for the changing identities of its political subjects. The conclusion suggests lessons for writing about the relationship between the state from a social economics perspective.

1.   The delineation of public and private spheres

It is common within the social sciences to frame the boundaries of 'the nation-state' by separating the public from the private sphere (Habermas, 1991). Through this division into different spheres, approaches to the nation-state distinguish the boundaries of legitimate and illegitimate state actions, representation, and even the range of possible debate from illegitimate ones. In this way the state, and the sphere of public action, is separated from the everyday private life of society as a whole.

> For peculiar to the modern State is the creation of its own autonomous space in which its permanent personnel, who staff state institutions, manoeuvre by playing off interest groups, classes, or factions against one another and against other states. The basis of the State's power as an executive authority is found in its set of administrative, policing and military organizations, all of which are founded by resources that are extracted from the individuals in the society within which the state exercises legitimate jurisdiction. (Coleman, 1996, p. xiii)

This public–private distinction has enabled modern public debate about the state to be informed predominantly by the professionalized knowledge of the Weberian bureaucrat. Public bureaucracies, such as welfare states, were launched in the name of the people to help them cope with markets as they went about their lives (Polanyi, 1957). Similarly ministries and bureaucracies are organized with the intention that they serve the citizens of the state in accordance with universal principles such as accountability and public service. As well as embodying the professional public roles that legitimate the authority of the state, civil servants, politicians and representatives have also been attributed ways of behaving that are more moral and virtuous than those beyond the public sphere. Many of the activities of the public sphere have been justified by providing citizens with their rights (Marshall, 1964).

Modern theories of the state that start with the distinction have tended to begin their definitions of states by prescribing their actions according to principles rather than to practices. This creates a problem as the concept of the state precedes an analysis of its role in everyday life. Citizens are aware of this discontinuity when they assert that their rights have been infringed: their ideal of the state has not been upheld by its practices. If new policies do not address the problem, then the state is 'corrupt' or 'wrong' or 'out of touch', and in each of these accusations lies an assumption of the state. Throughout the twentieth century, a period when the modern bureaucratic state grew beyond any previous form, there have been regular claims that states, and politics more generally, have failed (Hayek, 1944; Gray, 1994).

The separation of the public sphere from the private life of its citizens has presented the moral superiority of the state over its subjects. Public office has exonerated many political actors from the legal sanctions with which their citizens are obliged to comply. The International Criminal Court (ICC) has challenged this assertion through its prosecutions of heads of state responsible for various heinous crimes. But the ICC is new, and for centuries heads of governments have been protected from prosecution by their office for many acts that their citizens could not perform. In great wars of the twentieth century, the conceptual status of the state as antecedent to its citizens justified the use of nuclear weapons despite the inevitable loss of life that this would entail. Judges are given the authority to take resources from, imprison or even kill people according to the operation of the state systems in which they hold authority. States and those acting on their behalf are therefore given superior positions because of the antecedence and separation of the state: states exist before the office-holder (and even the office) and this legitimates the exercise of extraordinary powers.

For citizens, certain responsibilities are fulfilled both when in contact with the public sphere but more often through the daily activities of their lives. States placed certain responsibilities on citizens in their own private spheres. The integrative welfare states of the early twentieth century favoured workers over peasants and men over women. In Chile, for example, industrialization was driven by a technocratic elite largely isolated from political forces (Silva, 1994). The social compromises that accompanied the push for industrialization under President Ibáñez in the 1930s sidelined agricultural workers and women. The Popular Front government cemented male-headed nuclear families materially and ideologically, making it difficult for women to make independent political or economic claims. The reason for this inequality between men and women was the greater role that male workers, and specifically miners, played in the national economic interest. They were considered more important workers, were attributed greater voice, and so were more effectively able to demand political and economic entitlements. During this period there was a greater need to signal to industrial workers that their interests were being met through the redistribution of resources through various political and social rights. Mechanisms and social institutions were established to fulfil this promise that formalized both the procedures for redistributing wealth and the bias in favour of men (Dannreuther and Gideon, 2007). In other words, twentieth-century governments regulated labour markets according to an implicit division of labour in the private sphere: men would go to work and women would stay at home. The bias of this male-breadwinner model clearly placed significant obligations on women in the household (Gottfried, 2000; Gideon, 2006; Elson, 1991). But it was justified by the distinction between the private and public sphere, with states daring to make only limited policy interventions into the family.

In return for sustaining these distinctions, states would grant certain rights. Access to these rights has always set an important boundary in society. Rights apply only to a select public of citizens for whom the privilege is derived solely from the accidental incident of their birth. The special status of this state/subject relationship is evident to any immigrant who discovers, at border crossings or social security offices, that states and democracies have their limits beyond which the rights they protect do not extend (Kymlicka, 2007; Ferrera, 2005).

What we can see is how this allocation of resources and rights to one person over another is normalized through the concept of the modern state. The public sphere was sustained because the relationship between the state and the subject was contained within historically defined boundaries. The boundaries of modern states differentiated them from other states as well as from their citizens and private spheres. At their most abstract, these boundaries were defined according to principles and rights, institutionalized and enacted through secondary and tertiary law and norms of behaviour, and associated by historical record, memory and geography (Searle, 2005). Such boundaries provide the foundations for the hierarchy of state authority that is used to delimit the personality of the state. And this hierarchy and allocation of rights are tacitly presupposed when neoclassical theory takes this public–private distinction as vantage point to conceptualize the state in analogy to an individual where the state acts, intervenes, kills, raises taxes, produces, solves collective action problems – and might fail and go bankrupt.

The invocation of the public–private distinction as the constitutive and delimiting boundary for analysis of the state reveals assumptions about the state as an actor. It is essentialist, in that the agency of the state is made possible only through the assumption of an ordered public sphere, which as we have noted requires considerable effort to maintain. In distinction to the order of the state, the private sphere has to organize itself to make credible representations through the collective interests or shared experiences of groups (Bentley, 1908; Truman, 1958; Olson, 1965). The distinction between public and private is positivist as pluralist views of the state demonstrate state action as a consequence of the interests of groups. Pluralist (or group theory) notions of the state therefore share the positivist philosophy of science on which neoclassical economic thought is based (Dahl, 1961). Rather than seeing the state as a sphere of action created and sustained by social processes in turn supported through and by interactions with society, economic theorists derive the meaning of statehood by observing the actions of politicians. The state is therefore able to behave as an individual with observable consequences of its actions against which theories of public choice can be objectively tested.

Social economics as the study of economic activity within societies needs to step beyond these confines and develop its own understanding of the state. If social economics is interested in the changing contours of the state–society relationship, and thus in the changing meaning of the state for everyday economic practices, it cannot start with a pre-given understanding of the public which presents the separation of the state from society *a priori*. Rather, it needs to develop a conceptual framework from which historically contingent constellations and meanings of public and private and thus of the state–society divide result from interactions. As Bourdieu observes:

> Everything economic science posits as given, that is, the range of dispositions of the economic agent which ground the illusion of the ahistorical universality of categories and concepts employed by that science, is, in fact, the paradoxical product of a long collective history, endlessly reproduced by individual histories which can be fully accounted for only by historical analysis. (Bourdieu, 2005, p. 5)

Such a historical analysis is compatible with the strength and promise of a social economics understanding of the state, which is grounded in its commitment to a plurality of approaches. Social economics has some good reason to react suspiciously to views of the state based on pre-given hierarchies or ideologies. Yet the question as to how to approach the state within social economics requires caution. To frame the discussion in terms of what the state 'is' in social economics would lead to the identification of various conceptualizations of statehood that will pitch definitions against each other on the assumption that some common ground or tentative working definition will be found. We think this is not a fruitful path. As there is no hegemonic approach to social economics, there should not be 'the' social economic approach to the state. Rather social economics should understand the state as a series of contradictory perspectives supporting both conservative and radical notions of authority, and assuming pluralism while often critiquing liberalism. We propose a more reconstructive approach that examines the historically changing contours of a state–society divide where 'theories' of the state always represent current social conditions and forces. This view of statehood moves beyond the 'state as a person' position. Rather, the state is presented as a diversity of practices that then constitute public life from private life. This is most clearly seen in the role that representation plays in formalizing public experiences over private ones through a familiar set of political procedures.

2.   The political economy of representation

One of the key roles of the state is the regulation of legitimate forms of representation. Through this the state manages access across the public–private divide. The right of the citizen to vote, the terms on which the political parties compete, the choice of methodologies to produce national accounts, and the regulation of lobby groups are all dependent on the authority of the state. By regulating the main channels of representation, the state was able to define and manage the boundary between politics and the economy, and thus the public from the private. It could thereby set priorities in economic policy and select and structure its interaction with economic groups.

With this distribution of voices and silences, the state interacts with economic and social forces in ways that are not defined by prices alone. Representation is thus beyond the confines of neoclassical theorizing. That does not mean that neoclassical economists have not tried to come to terms with what they call rent-seeking and lobbying. But neoclassical approaches strip away the complexity of the relationship through which the state is embedded within its society. Representation is a deeply cultural and social phenomenon that defines the boundary between public and private spheres. Group theorists, who present the political process as the interaction of pluralist lobby groups, contain the state within a tightly defined set of rules and locate the bulk of political life within the public sphere of civil society. Social democrats and other corporatist approaches extend the role of the state to the regulation of representation by granting monopolies of representation to specific organizational bodies (Schmitter, 1974). These institutional approaches (of corporatist and or national capitalisms) highlight the various channels and compromises through which states interact with their economies, making the study of economic representation an area of interest for social economists.

Social economics' focus on economic institutions and cultural dimensions of economic value has therefore revealed a competing ontology for economics to one based on methodological individualism. It has demonstrated that economic values are instituted socially by more than one set of actors according to a host of symbolic as well as material influences. Social economics' ontology of socially embedded economic activity indicates a competing view of the state to that of neoclassical economics. If people are not seen as maximizing individuals but as living messy lives, and if they are not separated from the public sphere but constituted in part through their relationship with it, then social economics will present a view of the state that is not easily conflated into narrow group interests or neatly regulated representative organizations. Indeed, social economics is far more likely to explore the social and psychological origins of authority (Milgram, 1974) and its impact on political life (Michels, 1962) than assuming it as a precondition of political life. Social economics is therefore likely to be somewhat reticent to the state as a grand project, focusing more on pragmatic and localized concerns. As Petit observes, 'an implicit ontology of the people and the relation between the people and the state often shapes how we think in normative terms about politics' (Petit, 2005, p. 157).

The economic value of political representation can be seen in a brief comparison between two forms of capitalist accumulation in the twentieth century. During the period of sustained economic growth that characterized the post-World War II period, representative practices in many states described the hierarchical and ordered form of political representation termed corporatism. The social interests of trade unions and business were given preferential political influence in the political process. Their special status reflected the core economic relations that sustained wealth accumulation under the mass-production technologies of the day. The redistribution of wealth from capitalist to worker was managed through the mechanism of the state to ensure that there was sufficient popular demand to keep the production lines moving at a profitable rate. While such Fordist compromises are often associated with corporatist welfare compromises of West Europe (Grant, 1985; Schonfeld, 1965; Cawson, 1985; Hall, 1986; Berger and Dore, 1996; Schmidt, 2002), they were also practised in Latin American states during periods of state-led national integration (Silva, 1998). The state played a vital role in enabling these systems to persist by providing the focal point for the representation and mediation of economic interests.

The certainties of national redistributive economies were shattered by powerful new forms of representation that challenged the hermetically sealed public sphere of corporatism. New social movements arose in the 1970s and 1980s that revealed alternative representations of economic behaviour. The green movement articulated the ecological cost to economic expansion that Kapp had expressed in the academic sphere and in the political sphere (Kapp, 1950). Feminist economics identified gender bias in the economy and argued for greater awareness of the unvalued care economy (Elson, 1991). Others directly challenged the virtue of consensus politics, ridiculing welfare states as nanny states and challenging the 'tyranny of the minority' (Olson, 2000). The agendas of these new social movements fitted the attack on the redistributive state led by political leaders like Reagan, Thatcher and Kohl, but not solely for the promotion of free market neoliberalism. Groups that characterized the new social movements of the 1970s and 1980s focused on issues that were often presented as structural problems. These included the environment, feminism and sexual freedom, ethnicity and identity and a range of issues that explicitly contradicted the social conservatism of the neoliberal agenda of politicians such as Reagan (USA), Thatcher (UK), Kohl (Germany) and later Bolkestein (Netherlands and EU). These new social movements did not seek to simplify the representation of society from the collective actions of trade unions into the isolated actions of individuals. Rather they wanted to introduce greater complexity into the representation of society by recognizing greater diversity than could be accommodated in the redistributive agendas of the welfare state.

Other changes in macroeconomic governance also offered alternatives to parliamentary economic control. Monetarist economics reduced the need for the institutional infrastructure that had orchestrated demand management policies, and relied instead on independent central banks and deregulated financial markets. Regional trading blocs, such as the EU's Single Market programme, regulated product markets according to common standards. Decision-making processes, such as subsidiarity and co-decision, and implementation instruments, such as directives and preliminary rulings, allowed the development of a Single European Market based upon common standards by being sensitive to national variations. In doing so, the EU Commission, the EU institution that devised and led the strategy of the Single Market Programme, challenged the distinction of national economic hierarchies and privileged other ways of coordinating economic relations. Societies no longer had to be organized as nationally homogeneous populations, but according to multiple ethnicities and subnational regional identities and other allegiances. Small industrial regions also demonstrated that economic prosperity could be generated through the flexibility that trust from social networks could provide (Piore and Sabel, 1984; Nooteboom, 1999). This idea of social capital demonstrated that socially held values could contribute to competitiveness and so needed to be acknowledged and represented (Woolcock, 1998; Putnam, 2000; Dolfsma and Dannreuther, 2003). As new political issues such as the environmental denigration demonstrated the damage that national compromises could do (Beck, 1999), the credibility of national representations was diluted. The political infrastructure of redistributive politics had been designed to promote social integration by removing social forms of inequality (Fraser, 1995).

The distinction between public and private that had been orchestrated through national representative traditions and realized through technocratic executive institutions began to wane. The collective memories of crisis that had sustained core political compromise began to fade and new forms of conflict based around gender, race, sexuality and identity emerged. This new politics of recognition challenged the nation-state as the main sphere of political action. Social structures that encroached upon the private sphere, such as patriarchy and racism, were not addressed effectively by the mechanisms of redistribution (Fraser, 1995). As the end of the cold war transformed the international political arena, arguments that had sustained the virtue of the collective provision of welfare services were replaced by the morality of the individualistic responsibility and citizenship (Kymlicka and Norman, 1994; Sterba, 1994). While the economic logic of organized capitalism had begun to unravel some years before (Lash and Urry, 1988), the political logic of the state's monopoly of representation was challenged from below, from above and from within.

3.   The agency of the state

Nation-states had been able to secure considerable support for their actions by appealing to large parts of society. Traditional defenders of the nation-state, such as aristocracy and military, allied with modern supporters, such as social welfare reformers, to provide a flexible and resilient social system around the collective idea of the nation. Once defined, national interests could be identified and pursued through the mechanisms and apparatus of the state to provide clear evidence of state intervention. The state could therefore exercise its influence through the regulation of markets, through legal mechanisms and institutions, or through direct intervention, in the form of subsidies, nationalized industries or the specific direction of companies. The agency of the state can clearly be seen once the assumption of a public–private distinction, one incompatible with social economics, has been made. As we have shown above, social economics' focus on everyday life distinguishes the private sphere of behaviour from the public sphere through the process of representation. Social economics' various evolutionary and institutional methodologies are particularly helpful in demonstrating how the history of national economies has informed the ability and ways in which states act. In this section we shall explore how these two distinctions can help us to understand the changes to the state associated with globalization.

Let us begin to understand the problem of state agency in social economics from two well-known starting-points. The first is to see the actions of the state as the consequence of interested groups and individuals, and the second is to see the actions of the state as undistinguishable from society. The two sides of these positions, aired in a famous debate between Miliband and Poulantzas, helped to clarify the role of the state from instrumentalist and structuralist positions (Miliband, 1970, 1973; Poulantzas, 1976, 1978). Miliband argued that the state's administrative apparatus was an instrument of control for a particular set of interests, Poulantzas that it reflected the social relations that prevailed in society. A key point of divergence was in the problematic of the subject: Poulantzas criticized Miliband for originating the action of the state in individuals, albeit elite ones. Rather than seeing ruling-class participation in the state as the cause of state action in support of capitalist accumulation, Poulantzas argued that ruling-class participation in policy was an effect of the accumulation process and the objective relation that this produced with the state. Miliband was accused of effectively using the tools of pluralism to tell a story of elite domination and in doing so undermining the credibility of his position.

While many in the field of social economics may dismiss these modern and thoroughly twentieth-century debates, the focus on state administration and on the problematic of the subjects is of enormous importance these days. During the 1980s a number of authors argued for greater understanding of the organization of the state, suggesting that state–society relations were influenced through its organizational structure, rather than through the instrumentalism of elite or other groups. But in doing so they also dislocated the state from its social relations and, as Poulantzas had predicted, opened up the theorization of the state to bourgeois social science. In its most virulent form, this came from management science, and specifically March and Olson's 1984 *American Political Science Review* piece called 'The New Institutionalism: organizational factors in political life'. The New Institutionalism explicitly separated theories of the state from their ideological foundations. March and Olson's manifesto claimed to be anti-contextualism, anti-reductionism, anti-utilitarian, anti-functionalism and anti-instrumentalism (March and Olson, 1984, pp. 735–8). In line with other approaches that sought to 'bring the state back in', this focus on organizations was explicitly meso level, with only a brief and secondary debate over the relative autonomy of the institutions of the state from its society (Krasner, 1984; Nordlinger, 1981). The 'meso level' dominated political science in the 1990s, with various brands of institutionalism (historical institutionalism, rational choice institutionalism, sociological institutionalism, constructivism) spreading over political science's sub-disciplines of international relations, public policy and political economy (Hall and Taylor, 1996; Immergut, 1998; Wendt, 1999). This meso-level analysis challenged the grand narratives that had been associated with state theories. But it did so at the expense of locating the state in its society. The analysis of state behaviour became focused on rules and norms within state institutions and policy spheres, but without explaining their relevance to the experiences of people on the street.

This literature released the theorization of the state from its ideological compass by introducing empiricism as an alternative claim to truth. In conjunction with an increase in public policy literature approaches, the analysis of economic policy decisions came to be increasingly dominated by questions of methodology (e.g. 'when is a norm a norm and not a rule?') rather than the normative dimensions of the debate. The de-politicization of policy analysis began from within the academy and focused on 'objective analysis' rather than normative political theory to breed what one commentator has described as 'technically competent barbarians' in the political science community (Rothstein, 2005). Not only did institutional analysis explode the notion that the state was a homogeneous actor; it also rendered any reason to act meaningless. When the entire political science community failed to predict the end of the cold war, they looked to new ways of conceptualizing states and their relation with their societies, their economies and each other.

4.   Globalization, the 'great debate' and the place of the subject

By the 1990s, political scientists knew that 'institutions mattered', but beyond this suffered a collective confusion over the role for their discipline. Gone were the great organizing ideologies of the twentieth century and with them their comforting methodological prescriptions. Just as it had become clear that there were many, and not just one, forms of capitalism on the planet, so it was also clear that there were common experiences across the world of technological change and transition in the public sphere. What is surprising is that these complex and diverse phenomena should be explained by so many through one epoch-defining word: globalization. There is insufficient space in this entire volume to begin tracking the use of the term globalization, its meanings and the careers that it has sustained (Cammack, 2007). It has been discussed in many different disciplinary contexts and transcended the academic world into the policy and then the daily facts of people's lives. It is most often associated with changes brought on by external forces, such as technological change or the exercise of international and supranational bodies on sovereign states. So overwhelming has its influence been that it has been used to justify a wealth of political and economic reform, and radically transformed the relationship between subject and the state. But if we explore globalization as a change in the relationship between the state and society as outlined, we see that globalization was symptomatic not of a range of external forces but of a different way of constructing the state–subject relationship. Globalization describes a shift in the representative processes that relate the public to the private sphere.

Much of this is evident in the changes that we already associate with globalization. One of the main tenets of globalization is the challenge presented to the primacy of the state by various regional and non-state actors. This dissolution of the public–private distinction compromises the domestic and international hierarchies built upon it that we have described above. Globalization also embraced a plurality of new voices in the practical world, by shaking up old convictions, and in the intellectual world, through the variety of approaches it could accommodate. Many of these new representations of life have been associated with the role of new social movements and lobby groups that have pushed their way into the worlds of public and international affairs. Globalization has been closely associated with organizational change, in both public and private spheres, as have notions of competitiveness, innovation and entrepreneurship. These are all terms that have been used to redefine the relationship between the state and the economy. Competitiveness councils emerged in the early 1990s just before the debate on globalization grew, while the constant references to change and individual responsibility have replaced the collective representations of society that characterized the twentieth century with the individualism of the twenty-first.

Whereas much of the effort of modern state theory was to define and justify a system of order based upon and between states, the common theme of globalization is to revisit the assumptions of public and private separation upon which this phenomenon of statehood was constructed. The notion that the state could serve as 'the' box within which key social relations could be represented was both derisible and oppressive, depending on the perspective engaged. With so many representations of life, and the ways that it contributed to economic prosperity, why did the state have the exclusive right to regulate the representation of economic value?

Social economics' focus provides a far more useful starting-point to understand the political phenomena associated with globalization than the phenomena itself. Because globalization begins with the nation-state as its organizing principle and then seeks to explain its demise or reformation, the discipline of political science is vulnerable to repeating the assumptions of a predetermined state and its inherent public–private distinctions. It therefore has to seek exogenous forces of change to explain the changes associated with globalization, otherwise the integrity of the state could no longer be the starting-point of its enquiry. This is why information technology constructs a form of causality that complements the other idealized fallacies of globalization, such as (neo) liberalism or statism, that prevail in debates over globalization and change.

What is, for social economists, far more remarkable than the phenomenon of globalization is that nation-states exist in the first place. That the daily routines through which life is exercised should be appropriated into a set of institutionalized processes that are then given the powers of life and death should seem to be bizarre if it were not so tragic. But social economics shows that this process has been central to the reproduction of the nation-state through the identification, reification and formalization of economic value in regulated markets. For some such as Giddens and Baumann, the popular realization that states are constituted rather than constant describes a new event reflecting a hyper or liquid stage of modernity (Giddens, 1973). Thus Baumann describes this 'great war of recognition' as definitive of a new stage of 'liquid modernity' that takes place beyond the nation-state:

> In the 'solid stage' of modernity the actions classified as 'economic' took place inside the political and cultural cocoon of the nation-state, simultaneously a greenhouse and an internment camp. All the factors of economic activity having been similarly confined, 'solid modernity' was an era of mutual dependency, mutual engagement, production and servicing of mutually binding and durable bonds. The defining trait of 'liquid modernity' is, on the contrary, dis-engagement. (Baumann, 2001, p. 139)

As Baumann observes, in the absence of the coordinating resource of the nation-state, economic and political life is redefined. Networks have emerged that fail to respect the geographical underpinnings of the state. Lawyers rather than elected members of parliaments have become central agents for change in the pursuit of various human and economic rights. Thus international courts provide the direction while governance experts provide the capabilities for realizing the foreign policy objectives of major international players. This privatization of political agency has followed the extension of the right to trade into once public services from heavy industry to welfare provision that has challenged the very integrity of the separation between public and private spheres. While once associated with the New Right of the 1980s, it is organizations such as the WTO and the EU that define these boundaries today. The EU's service directive initially failed because it sought to replace domestic labour market regulation with the country of origin principle. It also challenged the state provision of core welfare services in the services of a general interest.

550 *The Elgar companion to social economics*

This real and theoretical dissolution of the bond between the state and society acted in two ways. First, it separated the state from the broader normative justifications that had characterized the extension of its powers through much of the twentieth century. Second, it reunited society with collective action through new political agendas. These issues, such as the environment, the nature of work, and, since 9/11, security, were presented as 'everyday' concerns and the responsibility of each individual, rather than the great historical trajectories taken on by the modern state. States are now far more explicitly concerned with how they regulate the lives of their subjects (Amin, 2005), providing work–life balance policies to help them run their family lives, and extending closed circuit television to ensure that they behave well when outside. Without the normalizing influence of the state, engagements in all areas of life have become unpredictable and contingent, spawning a vast interest in the politics of risk.

The traditional conception of the modern *subject* has been fundamentally challenged by this redefinition of the state with notion of the given individual – and individuality – as vantage points now seeming quaintly dated. White nicely describes this traditional modern notion of the subject:

> *he* is conceived as *disengaged* from his social background and oriented toward *mastery* of the world that confronts him; nevertheless, he can *discover*, by the light of *reason, universally applicable principles of justice*, grounded in some *foundationalist account* of God, nature, or progress, that can become the object of an *agreement* with other individuals. (White, 2003, p. 209)

Despite the fact that this liberal concept of the subject is common in economic theory, it is in stark contrast to many of the core concerns of social economics: gender, embeddedness, contingency, performativity, relativism, post-positivism and difference, all primary concerns of social economics challenge the liberal notion of the subject. If social economics holds true to its basic convictions, it needs to challenge this idea of pre-given agents including the state. Rather, what social economics provides is a variety of explanations as to how economic value can be generated without representing economic actors in the modern form described above. With a notion of the subject so problematized, the theorization of the state also needs to be reconsidered. To offer such an account, the next section discusses the concept of power in more detail as we are convinced that a deeper discussion of power in social economics could advance the understanding of the relationships that link state and society.

Conclusions

The chapter has argued that social economics already has much to say about the state. It argued that in order to take the role of the state in structuring the economic practices of everyday life seriously, social economics needed to step beyond the idea of the state as a person and problematize the public–private distinction upon which the various boundaries of the state have been constructed. We then explored how these distinctions have been sustained through a political economy of representation, an area of state–economy relations in which social economics has a vital contribution to make. The following section linked this to everyday life by demonstrating how social economics can provide an alternative explanation of the challenges to the nation-state that are often associated with the less clearly defined term of globalization, and then illustrated this further through a discussion of the regulatory state, globalization's exemplary form of state.

Throughout the discussion, power relations have been central to explaining how notions of the subject are central to understanding the reproduction of societal and everyday relations. The discussion of power is clearly an area where social economics has a significant contribution to make. Many in social economics are familiar with Foucault's family of critiques of modern notions of control. The power of these critiques has been drained both through repetition and as events demonstrate the limits of relativism. But social economics has the potential to generate fruitful discussions of power through its engagement with economics at a disciplinary level. Rather than talking across meanings, social economics is able to explore how representation and reality constitute the state through different processes and norms that are based in everyday transactions and at many different levels of interaction.

There is therefore no conclusive position that we can offer to the question 'What is the state in social economics?' Rather, the multiplicity of perspectives that pervade social economics will always generate a variety of understandings and critiques of the power that the state exercises and the legitimacy that this will provide. This plurality is the strength of the approach. There are, however, a few assumptions that have underpinned this discussion of the states of social economics that may be worth identifying.

The first observation is that social economics debates on the state can be strengthened through interdisciplinary as well as multidisciplinary perspectives. This means that as well as employing conceptual and methodological tools from, for example, political and international relations, social economics can also benefit from exploring how these techniques converge and diverge from their own more familiar resources. Using relatively rugged concepts such as 'power' and 'subject', and, for that matter, 'state', enables comparison of disciplinary assumptions that are all too often left unspoken. It has the added advantage of enriching the discussion as a whole.

The second point is that discussions of social economics need to be contextualized. For this chapter we have contextualized the contribution of social economics through a historical discussion of the political economy of representation and a comparative one on globalization. The benefit of relativism has been to demonstrate the diversity of life and its contributions to society and happiness. The limits are that it offers little response to oppressive regimes, which must also have a place under relativist ideals. War fear and financial insecurity all help us to understand why authoritarian regimes are on the ascendant. But what is the alternative advocated by social economists? Social economics' tendency to start from lived experience has brought it close to communitarian debates. But while the assumptions of organization do not focus solely on the separation between public and private, they do tend to rehearse Bourdieu's collective history. As well as a caveat, this is also an invitation to revisit, as we have done, 'outdated' conceptions of the state.

Finally, because social economics is not built on a singular body of knowledge, it lacks a coherent definition. We have found it useful to begin with everyday life as the core interest of social economics, and in writing considered that as the point from which we have made each of our arguments in this chapter. But this cannot be the only starting or ending point of social economics as it merely avoids the problem of collective behaviour and destabilizes organization. Despite the potential dangers of disciplinary centralization and hierarchy, exploring the underlying concepts of social economics is an important and ongoing exercise. This volume should, in short, be the springboard for many other incursions into the meaning of social economics.

References

Amin, Ash (2005), 'Local community on trial', *Economy and Society*, **34** (4), 612–33.
Baumann, Zygmunt (2001), 'The great war of recognition', *Theory, Culture and Society*, **18** (2–3), 137–50.
Beck, Ulrich (1999), *World Risk Society*, London: Polity.
Bentley, Arthur (1908), *The Process of Government: A Study of Social Pressures*, Chicago, IL: Chicago University Press.
Berger, Suzanne and Ronald Dore (eds) (1996), *National Diversity and Global Capitalism*, Ithaca, NY: Cornell University Press.
Bourdieu, Pierre (2005), *The Social Structure of the Economy*, London: Polity.
Cammack, Paul (2007), 'RIP IPE', *Papers in the Politics of Global Competitiveness*, **7**, May, http://hdl.handle.net/2173/12264.
Cawson, Alan (1985), *Organized Interests and the State: Studies in Mesocorporatism*, Beverly Hills, CA: Sage.
Coleman, Janet (1996), 'Preface', in Janet Coleman (ed.), *The Individual in Political Theory and Practice*, Oxford: Clarendon Press, pp. ix–xviii.
Dahl, Robert (1961), *Who Governs? Democracy and Power in an American City*, New Haven, CT: Yale University Press.
Dannreuther, Charlie and Jasmine Gideon (2007), 'Entitled to health? Social protection in health – Chile's Plan AUGE', unpublished mimeo.
Dolfsma, Wilfred and Charles Dannreuther (2003), *Globalisation, Social Capital and Inequality: Contested Concepts, Contested Experiences*, Cheltenham, UK and Northampton, MA, USA: Edward Elgar.

Elson, Diane (1991), 'Male bias: an overview', in Diane Elson (ed.), *Male Bias in the Development Process*, Manchester: Manchester University Press, pp. 164–90.

Ferrera, Maurizio (2005), *The Boundaries of Welfare: European Integration and the New Spatial Politics of Social Protection*, Oxford: Oxford University Press.

Fraser, Nancy (1995), 'From redistribution to recognition? Dilemmas of justice in a "post-socialist" age', *New Left Review*, **21** (2), 68–93.

Giddens, A. (1973), *Capitalism and Modern Social Theory: An Analysis of the Writings of Marx, Durkheim and Max Weber*, Cambridge: Cambridge University Press.

Gideon, Jasmine (2006), 'Integrating gender issues into health policy', *Development and Change*, **37** (2), 329–52.

Gottfried, Heidi (2000), 'Compromising positions: emergent neo-Fordisms and embedded gender contracts', *British Journal of Sociology*, **51** (2), 235–59.

Grant, Wyn (1985), *The Political Economy of Corporatism*, London: Macmillan.

Gray, John (1994), *Beyond the New Right: Markets, Government and the Common Environment*, London: Routledge.

Habermas, Jürgen (1991), *The Structural Transformation of the Public Sphere: An Inquiry into a Category of Bourgois Society*, Cambridge, MA: MIT Press.

Hall, Peter (1986), *Governing the Economy: The Politics of State Intervention in Britain and France*, Oxford: Oxford University Press.

Hall, Peter and Rosemary Taylor (1996), 'Political science and the three new institutionalisms', *Political Studies*, **44** (5), 936–57.

Hayek, Friedrich, (1944), *The Road to Serfdom*, Chicago, IL: Chicago University Press.

Immergut, Ellen (1998), 'The theoretical core of the new institutionalism', *Politics and Society*, **26** (1), 5–34.

Kapp, K. William (1950), *The Social Costs of Private Enterprise*, Cambridge, MA: Harvard University Press and Oxford University Press.

Kapp, K. William (1978), *The Social Costs of Business Enterprise*, Nottingham: Spokesman.

Krasner, Stephen (1984), 'Approaches to the state: alternative conceptions and historical dynamics', *Comparative Politics*, **16** (2), 223–46.

Kymlicka, Will (2007), *Multcultural Odysseys: Navigating the New Politics of Diversity*, Oxford: Oxford University Press.

Kymlicka, Will and Wayne Norman (1994), 'Return of the citizen: a survey of recent work on citizenship theory', *Ethics*, **104** (2), 352–81.

Lash, Scott and John Urry (1988), *The End of Organized Capitalism*, London: Sage.

March, James G. and Mancur Olson (1984), 'The new institutionalism: organizational factors in political life', *American Political Science Review*, **78** (3), 734–49.

Marshall, T. (1964), *Class, Citizenship and Social Development*, Westport, CT: Greenwood Press.

Michels, Robert (1962), *Political Parties*, New York: Free Press.

Milgram, Stanley (1974), *Obedience to Authority: An Experimental View*, London: Pinter & Martin.

Milliband, Ralph (1970), The capitalist state: A reply to Nicos Poulantzas', *New Left Review*, **59** (1), 53–60.

Milliband, Ralph (1973), 'Poulantzas and the capitalist state', *New Left Review*, **82** (1), 83–92.

Nooteboom, Bart (1999), 'Innovation, learning and industrial organisation', *Cambridge Journal of Economics*, **23** (2), 127–50.

Nordlinger, Eric A. (1981), *On the Autonomy of the Democratic State*, Cambridge, MA: Harvard University Press.

Olson, Mancur (1965), *The Logic of Collective Action: Public Goods and the Theory of Groups*, Cambridge, MA: Harvard University Press.

Olson, Mancur (2000), *Power and Prosperity*, New York: Basic Books.

Petit, Philippe (2005), 'Rawls's political ontology', *Politics, Philosophy & Economics*, **4** (2), 157–74.

Piore, Michael and Charles Sabel (1984), *The Second Industrial Divide*, New York: Basic Books.

Polanyi, Karl (1944), *The Great Transformation: The Political and Economic Origins of Our Time*, Boston, MA: Beacon.

Polanyi, Karl (1957), *The Great Transformation*, Boston, MA: Beacon Press.
Poulantzas, Nicos (1976), 'The capitalist state: a reply to Milliband and Laclau', *New Left Review*, **95**, 63–83.
Poulantzas, Nicos (1978), *State, Power, Socialism*, London: Verso.
Putnam, Robert D. (2000), *Bowling Alone: The Collapse and Revival of American Community*, New York: Simon & Schuster.
Rothstein, B. (2005), 'Is political science producing technically competent barbarians?', *European Political Science*, **4** (1): 3–13.
Schmidt, Vivien (2002), *The Future of European Capitalism*, Oxford: Oxford University Press.
Schmitter, Philippe C. (1974), 'Still the century of corporatism?', *Review of Politics*, **36** (1), 85–131.
Searle, John (2005), 'What is an institution?', *Journal of Institutional Economics*, **1** (1), 1–22.
Shonfield, Andrew (1965), *Modern Capitalism: The Changing Balance of Public and Private Power*, Oxford: Oxford University Press.
Silva, Patricio (1988), 'The state, politics and peasant unions in Chile', *Journal of Latin American Studies*, **20** (2), 433–52.
Silva, Patricio (1994), 'State, public technocracy and politics in Chile, 1927–1941', *Bulletin of Latin American Research*, **13** (3), 281–97.
Sterba, James (1994), 'From liberty to welfare', *Ethics*, **105** (1), 64–98.
Truman, David (1958), *The Governmental Process: Political Interests and Public Opinion*, New York: Alfred Knopf.
Wendt, Alexander (1999), *Social Theory of International Politics*, Cambridge: Cambridge University Press.
White, Steven (2003), 'After critique: affirming subjectivity in contemporary political theory', *European Journal of Political Theory*, **2** (2), 209–26.
Woolcock, Michael (1998), 'Social capital and economic development: toward a theoretical synthesis and policy framework', *Theory and Society*, **27** (2), 151–208.

PART X

LAW AND THE ECONOMY

Chapter 31: 'Law and social economics: a Coasean perspective', by David Campbell and Matthias Klaes

The use of economic insights to elucidate legal doctrine has become so widespread that 'law and economics' is now one of the principal forms of jurisprudence. Most influential in this field has been what has become known as the Chicago school, typically identified with the work of Richard Posner. Although Posner must take the greatest credit for the wide reception of law and economics, it is essential to recognize that there are now many claimants to the use of law and economics beyond, or even in outright opposition to, Posner. This raises the question of why those interested in social economics would want to claim law and economics rather than reject it. For us, the basic answer to this lies in the work of Ronald Coase, who has vigorously distanced himself from Posnerian law and economics. Our contention is that law and economics represented by Posner is not only not exhaustive of law and economics without Chicago, but also does not help us to come to terms with what Chicago has produced that is very worthwhile.

Chapter 32: 'Social law and economics and the quest for dignity and rights', by Mark D. White

The economic approach to the law, or 'law and economics', is a straightforward extension of the core principles of neoclassical economics to legal issues. As such, social economists would be expected to be critical of many assumptions and tenets of the field, yet surprisingly few have written on it. In this chapter, White surveys the existing commentary from social economists regarding law and economics, and then details some shortcomings of the field from the perspective of respecting fundamental human rights and dignity. He concludes by suggesting several ways that social economists can work to improve the economic study of law, specifically by modifying the evaluative efficiency criterion and the deterministic model of choice that are standard in law and economics.

31 Law and social economics: a Coasean perspective
David Campbell and Matthias Klaes

Introduction

Iudex non calculat: before the 1960s, legal doctrine, in the common law tradition at least, had developed largely innocent of insights from economics. But during the subsequent half-century, the use of such insights to elucidate legal doctrine has become so widespread, albeit far more so in the USA than in other jurisdictions (Landes and Posner, 1993; Ogus, 1995; Symposium, 1991), that 'law and economics' is now one of the principal forms of jurisprudence, as is evidenced by the large number of existing introductions to the subject (Bowles, 1982; Cooter and Ulen, 2004; Hirsch, 1988; Malloy, 1990b; Mercuro and Medema, 1997; Mercuro and Ryan, 1984; Polinsky, 1989; Posner, 2007; Shavell, 2004; Veljanovski, 1982, 2006).

Much of the intellectual substance of modern law and economics derives from the application of microeconomic principles to legal reasoning, informed by what the main currents of economic analysis have argued since the time of Ricardo: compared to alternative institutional arrangements, properly functioning markets yield superior allocative outcomes in terms of aggregate wealth. Law and economics largely accepts the depiction of markets in neoclassical welfare economics, and uses perfect markets as the basic yardstick with which to compare alternative forms of allocating goods.

There is, of course, a serious and well-known problem in doing this. With suitably restrictive assumptions on how individuals and markets behave, the economic efficiency of perfect markets can be established with great rigour in modern welfare economics. But there is no hope that those assumptions can ever hold in any empirical situation. One therefore finds that in the history of economic thought there has run, parallel to the mainstream neoclassical tradition and in response to its abstraction from the detailed institutional context, various dissenting lines that stress the economic significance of that context. In particular, circa 1890–1920, an 'institutional economics' gained prominence in the USA (Gruchy, 1987; Hodgson, 1998), in which detailed description of economic institutions, particularly of their legal constitution (Commons, 1924), took precedence over abstract rigour (Veblen, 1958).

It is this focus on the pivotal role of formal and informal social institutions that constitutes the distinguishing characteristic of social economics *vis-à-vis* mainstream economic thought. Social economists interested in legal issues have therefore displayed some scepticism towards fields such as law and economics, which draw their analytical strength from the mainstream tradition, turning to institutionalism and its analysis of the sphere of law instead. What social economic scholars cannot afford to ignore, however, is the fact that law and economics has had a far greater impact on jurisprudence than social economic or socio-legal approaches (Ayres, 1997). While we would thus like to acknowledge that the institutionalist literature is clearly relevant to those interested in law and economics (Goldberg, 1976; Hovenkamp, 1990; Medema et al., 2000), we shall not further explore this literature, but refer the reader to Mark White's chapter in this *Companion* (chapter 32). Instead, we shall focus our discussion on the obstacles that have hindered those sympathetic to social economic approaches to law grasping what is important in law and economics, the chief one of which is a far too sweeping identification of law and economics with the unapologetically neoliberal outlook of the (second-generation) Chicago school.

Current state of the field
The field of law and economics obviously includes works of a general jurisprudential nature, but it has developed predominantly within the core law subjects. Posner's (2007) deservedly highly influential textbook, in which a general part merely precedes substantial treatments of the core subjects, clearly expresses this. Although this has been a major reason for the success of Posner's book, what immediately strikes those sensitive to social economic issues is how uneven the contribution of Posnerian law and economics to the various core subjects has been. Law and economics has obvious relevance to contract, where the action being discussed is 'economic' in an uncontroversial way, and some fine theoretical (Goetz and Scott, 1980; Posner and Rosenfeld, 1977; Trebilcock, 1993) and empirical (Joskow, 1985, 1987, 1988) work has been produced, particularly on the topic of remedies, which had been neglected in 'black letter' approaches to the law (Barton, 1972; Birmingham, 1970; Farnsworth, 1970; Polinsky, 1983; Shavell, 1980). Law and economics' direct relevance extends to commercial and company law and related topics, and also straddles the 'private–public divide' to cover state intervention in economic affairs, so thereby obtains for a large sphere of modern society (Samuels, 1971).

However, outside this sphere, the relevance of law and economics becomes less clear. For example, law and economics had one of its first great successes in the tort scholarship which Guido Calabresi developed following Coase's (1988, p. 96) insistence that the tort of negligence cannot seek to completely prevent accidents but must establish the socially acceptable level of harm (Calabresi, 1970; Calabresi and Bobbitt, 1978). But a disquiet has crept into one's reading of much of the subsequent scholarship. One now commonly comes across risk calculations conducted in purely economic terms (Posner, 1972) which cannot fully capture what is at issue in negligence cases (England, 1980; Steiner, 1976; Veljanovski, 1981, pp. 125–33). The Learned Hand formula so widely elaborated in law and economics discussions of torts states that 'if the probability be called P; the injury L; and the burden B; liability depends on whether B is less than L multiplied by P: ie whether B<PL' (*United States v. Carroll Towing Co.* at 173 per Learned Hand J.). The power of Learned Hand lies in combining apparently contradictory considerations in a formula, but, of course, taken too far, this becomes misleading. The cost of personal injury is a matter of the value placed on the lives lost or damaged, and therefore what goes into L (and much of B) is a value judgement which economics cannot ultimately determine, as Learned Hand (*Conway v. O'Brien* at 612), Coase (1988, p. 154) and Calabresi (Calabresi and Hirschoff, 1972, p. 1080) themselves were perfectly well aware.

Turning to other subjects, disquiet can turn to outright concern. The application of law and economics to crime through the 'deterrence hypothesis' (Ehrlich, 1973, 1975, 1979) turns on the claim that there is a 'market' for crime such that potential offenders can be deterred by setting penalties at such a level (including death) that the increase in the sum of the offender's utilities by offending is smaller than the decrease in that sum from threat of apprehension. This hypothesis clearly is a mathematically sophisticated version of Bentham's felicific calculus (Becker, 1968, p. 209), and so is subject to the well-known criticisms of utilitarianism. Of these, the most damaging is that the decision to offend is robbed of moral significance when it is reduced to a technical matter of choice of the optimal utility-maximizing action, though the very concept of a crime essentially involves an element of normativity. Basing criminal law on the deterrence hypothesis would mean that much of it would turn into a sort of private law (Becker, 1968, p. 198), where criminality would no longer be defined by the nature of the committed offence but by the inability of offended parties to seek recompense.

That it is unwise to flatten out all the moral and political issues involved in the definition of a crime as an act punishable by the state by a purportedly purely technical treatment of these issues should be obvious (Klevorick, 1983). Take that subset of crimes that in effect redistributes resources from the relatively rich to the relatively poor. Since resources in those cases end up in the hands of those for whom they have a higher marginal value, it is not immediately obvious, on the 'economic' view, why these crimes would be defined as harms at all. It is by no means impossible to see why this is so, but Becker's (1968, p. 171) own reason, that the expenditure of resources in executing crimes is a deadweight loss which should be prevented, clearly fails to come to terms with what surely is the central contribution of modern criminology, that the 'labelling' of deviance is an *explanandum*, not an *explanans*.

Let us regard Becker's work benignly as an abstract exercise aimed at teasing out the intellectual and moral limits of pushing economic analysis beyond its traditional market context into other areas. From the perspective of social economics, this has helped to make these limits visible to a larger audience. Still, since the enormous contribution of the Chicago school now hardly needs to be stressed (Duxbury, 1994, 1995), one can say without qualification that some contributions to Chicagoan law and economics have insufficiently considered whether the economic approach is appropriate to all the issues to which it has been applied, and have just driven on regardless.

This strain is typically identified with Richard Posner, the most influential writer on law in the common law world in the second half of the twentieth century (Baker, 1975, 1978, 1980; Buchanan, 1974; Campbell, 1994; Heller, 1976; Horwitz, 1980; Hovenkamp, 1995; Krier, 1974; Leff, 1974; Liebhafsky, 1976; Malloy, 1990a; Markovits, 1975; Samuels, 1976; Scherer, 1977; Tribe, 1972). Where some would have preferred a more circumspect reflection on the wider implications of law and economics (cf. Michelman, 1979; Polinsky, 1974), Posner has made the economic approach to legal issues pioneered by Becker and others easily comprehensible by translating it into widely accessible prose, largely doing away with the rather hard mathematical economics (Posner, 1990, pp. 367–70, 1993a). Posner has shown little hesitation in applying the law and economics approach to a very wide range of issues both legal and tangential to law (Philipson and Posner, 1993; Posner, 1988, 1995), with at times astonishing audacity; as, for example, when pursuing the implications of Becker's (1960, pp. 210–15) notion that children are 'consumer durables' through to the actual advocacy of running adoption as an auction (Landes and Posner, 1978; Posner, 1987).

Though clearly variants of some common arguments in jurisprudence, Posner's most important claims, to which he has given an original twist that has provoked much debate, have been that the common law is 'efficient' (Ehrlich and Posner, 1974; Landes and Posner, 1976, 1979, 1980; Posner, 1973, 1993b) and 'wealth maximizing' (Posner, 1979b, 1980a, 1980b). The common law is claimed to display an intrinsic evolutionary tendency towards efficiency which makes it innately superior to legislation

(Goodman, 1978; Higgins and Rubin, 1980; Priest, 1977, 1980; Priest and Klein, 1984; Rubin, 1977, 1982; Rubin and Bailey, 1994). Further, it is argued that the operation of the courts and common law reasoning can usefully be viewed as a market evolving towards an equilibrium in adjudication, in that bad rules will give way because they, rather than better rules, produce costs which it is worthwhile to litigate to remove. The decisions reached by this process of continual improvement are, it has also been claimed, wealth-maximizing, for by confining itself to disputes thrown up by those who thereby demonstrate an effective demand for their solution, the common law addresses problems that did need solving, and therefore those solutions will enhance welfare. The point is that common law is preferable to legislation, which has no such intrinsic necessity to be efficient or wealth-maximizing, as it is 'politically' driven.

These notions of efficiency and wealth maximization have led to some worthwhile proposals for the reform of legal procedure (Caspar and Posner, 1976; Posner, 1973, 1985). They have done so because they do hit on some important general points. That economic reasoning has usefully informed and should inform some legal decisions is why law and economics is worth bothering about. More than this, that the law does work itself pure is an idea with a long, productive history in jurisprudence. It is clearly valuable to have provoked such a volume of discussion of these themes. At the end of that discussion, however, it remains unclear what has been gained by the specifically Posnerian emphasis on efficiency and wealth maximization.

The efficiency claim assumes a correlation between a party's ability to get to court and the welfare-enhancing significance of the party's case, and justified doubt about that correlation is the main reason for state subsidy of legal advice and for the statutory reform (and much aggressive judicial shifting) of the substantive common law (Atiyah, 1990, pp. 151–8; Michelman, 1978, 1980). The introduction of realistic variables, such as, not entirely surprisingly, the ability to pay fees, into the evaluation of the efficiency claim shows that '[t]he conclusion that disruptive precedents automatically stimulate litigation that leads to their displacement by clearer decisions is a fragile one' (Bayes, 1996, p. 2). What one needs to do is compare the fitness of the common law and legislation in specific cases, but though doing this will be assisted by healthy scepticism about the prospects of successful legislation, what it fundamentally requires is an open-mindedness that can follow only by rejecting a compulsion to find the common law efficient which the efficiency notion elevates into some sort of ineluctable spirit of that law (Cooter and Kornhauser, 1980, p. 157; Cooter and Rubinfeld, 1989; Epstein, 1980; Fried, 1980; Greenawalt, 1977; Kenny, 1982, pp. 50–55; Symposium, 1980).

Posner began to proselytize the efficiency claim despite being conscious of 'our inability to explain in an entirely convincing way why the common law should be efficient' (Posner, 1979a, p. 294), and, after seeing wealth maximization subjected to a decade of calumny, to his credit he eventually allowed that 'It may be impossible to lay solid philosophical foundations under wealth maximisation' (Posner, 1990, p. 384). However, to a man of his stamp this hardly means that a congenial idea should be given up, and he has stuck to this one (Posner, 1993c) by concluding that what is at fault is not wealth maximization but thought. Wealth maximization is right, Posner now outright asserts, 'and it would be a mistake to allow philosophy to deflect us [from this], just as it would be a mistake to allow philosophy to alter our views on infanticide' (Posner, 1990, p. 384).

Main issues: a Coasean perspective

Although Posner must take the greatest credit for the wide reception of law and economics, it is essential to recognize that there are now many claimants to the use of law and economics beyond, or even in outright opposition to, Posner (Campbell, 1994; Symposium, 1989a, 1989b, 1997). The question really is why social economists would want to claim law and economics rather than reject it, and for us, the basic answer to this lies in the work of Ronald Coase (Ellickson, 1989; Medema, 1998; Schlag, 1986), who has vigorously distanced himself from Posnerian law and economics (Coase, 1993, p. 96). Our contention is that law and economics represented by Posner is not only not exhaustive of law and economics outside Chicago, but also does not help us to come to terms with what Chicago has produced that is very worthwhile.

Coase himself held a view of the scope of economics sympathetic to Becker (Coase, 1988, p. 12; 1994, pp. 40–41; cf. Campbell and Harris, 1993, pp. 177–80). He has looked forward to economics unifying 'contiguous disciplines' (Coase, 1977) along socio-biological lines so that all human action and higher animal behaviour can be analysed as 'choice' (Coase, 1988, pp. 2–4) within broadly competitive systems. This 'unified science' was to be mathematized after what Coase believes is the methodological essence of the natural sciences (Coase, 1994, p. 14). He also believes that the US economy, alongside other advanced capitalist systems, is sufficiently competitive to allow successful application of the main insights from neoclassical price theory, albeit reformulated to properly address the costs of transacting (Coase, 1937, 1960).

Coase has never substantiated his claim about the broadly competitive nature of the advanced economies, and his position on this point has plausibly been described as an 'act of faith' (Pratten, 2001, p. 629, n. 2). However, his claim for the competitiveness of the economy stands in sharp contrast to the carefully formulated methodological stance that informs his work, where the demand for empirical evidence holds a pivotal place. Coase's basic contribution to law and economics, which requires a 'new' institutional economics of industrial organization (Coase, 1972, 1984; cf. Williamson, 1975, ch. 1), is an economic analysis of institutions based upon a form of the regulatory perspective, albeit a form in which the considerable strengths of competitive forces, when they are furnished with a space in which to work, are duly recognized (Campbell, 1996a; Klaes, 2005; Campbell and Klaes, 2005).

The general outlines of Coase's perspective on economic institutions are familiar territory in social economics. A brief summary shall suffice here. Coase's initial question was: if markets are efficient, why are there firms at all? Analysed as a question of allocative efficiency, the answer must be that, in certain circumstances, the firm is a cheaper way of organizing production than the market (Coase, 1988, pp. 37–47). In other words, there is a cost attached to organizing market transactions (cf. Klaes, 2008b). In particular, empirical markets have positive transaction costs and so must be weighed against alternatives, of which the firm and the state have been the most thoroughly analysed. After Coase, we can say that mainstream economic analysis, which typically assumes a market with zero transaction costs, should be balanced by an appreciation of the importance of the institutional structure of transactions, including those made in a market. This has given rise to, for example, a highly interesting law and economics of the corporation (e.g. Williamson, 1996, 1993a, 1985, 1975). A related discussion of the concept of contract has emerged which is particularly rich because it has been able to draw on the criticism of the classical theory of contract within legal scholarship. The nascent formulation of an alternative 'relational' theory of contract (Campbell, 1990, 1996b; Campbell and Harris, 1993; Feinman, 1983) led by Ian Macneil (1974, 1980) is the most substantial development in legal doctrine to which this new economic institutionalism has so far contributed (Macneil, 1978).

Having focused our discussion not on the established, if heterodox, institutional traditions in economics, but rather on teasing out what in mainstream law and economics may be valuable to social economics, we have thus come full circle, for we have identified a promising institutionalist agenda at the centre of the mainstream project itself. What is progressive in this 'new' institutionalism runs counter to the reversal of Coase's thrust by his purported disciples in Chicago (Williamson, 1987, pp. 313–18, 1993b), and is in fact closer to the established institutional traditions in economics than the 'new' versus 'old' dichotomy might suggest (Rutherford, 1994; Medema, 1996; cf. Hutchison, 1984).

The Chicago-inspired reversal of Coase's thrust has perhaps been most pronounced in relation to what has become known as the 'Coase theorem', the principal way in which Coase's work was first taken up in law and economics. As we have said, for Coase the fundamental aim of tort is the establishment of the socially acceptable level of harm. Take the perceived harm to a nearby settlement of environmental pollution emanating from a factory. According to Coase, any response to this harm should comparatively assess the net benefits to society associated with different levels of pollution, including the *status quo*. In a world of perfect markets and thus of zero transaction costs, this calculation would be best left to those markets, since they would ensure that the rights to pollute were allocated to their most highly valued uses. It is a feature of the operation of perfect markets that reaching an optimal allocation does not depend on the initial distribution of property rights. In other words, it would not matter whether the factory initially had a right to pollute, or whether those affected by pollution had the right to prevent the pollution, since either way, trade between both parties would ensure the optimum allocation of pollution rights. It is this proposition that lies at the heart of what has been called the Coase theorem.

We do not propose to deal here with all the many meanings of this theorem (e.g. Cooter, 1987; Daly, 1974; Zerbe, 1980), nor with the very large theoretical (e.g. Frech, 1973, 1979; Maloney, 1977; Schulze and d'Arge, 1974) and substantial empirical literature it has generated (e.g. Crocker, 1971; Ellickson, 1991; Johnston, 1973; Kelman, 1979; Vogel, 1987). But even when concentrating on the most sensible meaning of the Coase theorem, it is apparent that it has become a silly way of saying something initially quite simple and already part and parcel of received microeconomic theory, though prior to Coase not widely recognized as such. Expressing the irrelevance of the initial allocation of property rights under perfect markets by means of convoluted references to a Coase theorem is therefore best abandoned (Cooter, 1982; Fried, 1978, ch. 4; Kennedy, 1981; Mishan, 1971; Regan, 1972; Tribe, 1973).

More importantly, however, far from encapsulating the central insight of Coase's contribution to the emerging law and economics literature (cf. Medema, 1999), the point that, in a world of perfect markets with zero transaction costs, property rights are essentially without significance (provided that they are honoured in the first instance), is itself of no practical significance, since in economies as we know them, transaction costs are far from negligible, and hence the allocation of property rights is of the utmost importance. It is this point that constitutes Coase's core contribution to law and economics (Medema and Zerbe, 2000; Medema, 2002), and it is only recently that the implications of this insight are being taken seriously.

With the ubiquity of positive transaction costs, markets will always 'fail' if measured against the yardstick of perfect markets. Crucially, though, non-market order has its own costs. Awareness of market failure must therefore be complemented with an awareness of 'government failure' (Coase, 1964, p. 195). Coase undoubtedly was anxious to stress the costs of regulation, but there is nothing in his framework of analysis *per se* that authorizes a bias against state governance (Calabresi, 1968, p. 73, 1991, pp. 1211–12). What comparative institutional analysis does authorize is an informed choice between alternatives, none of which are costless, and valuable debate has taken place on these lines (Calabresi and Melamed, 1972; Burrows, 1981).

Law and economics has played a substantial part in calling into question the very size and structure of government. Making good the democratic deficit of the modern state and restraining that state's growth have been increasingly identified as a problem of extending 'quasi-markets' to services formerly provided by the state (Osborne and Gaebler, 1992), and of remodelling the remaining state apparatuses so that they mimic markets in order to facilitate public choice. The power of these works over property rights and their analogues lies in the way they have identified widespread regulatory failures and so have revived the plausibility of some market-based solutions. Their shortcoming is that many of them tend to substitute for the careful evaluation of alternative governance structures recommended by Coase a blithe recitation of formulaic market solutions to complicated problems (Trebing, 1976; Williamson, 1986, p. 259). The exposure of the unworkability of some of these (Bryden, 1978; McKean, 1970) is proving to be a protracted and painful process (e.g. the debate in Shoup, 1971; Demsetz, 1971; Daly and Giertz, 1975; cf. Schlicht, 1996).

Emerging avenues: institutional 'direction'
Coasean law and economics is based on an even-handed and empirically informed comparative institutional analysis of feasible market and non-market forms of economic coordination. It is important to realize that, on the conceptual level, Coase's work displays an essentially regulatory thrust, which, rather than proceeding from an *a priori* presumption in favour of market coordination, in fact accords primacy to what is best called the 'principle of institutional direction' (Campbell and Klaes, 2005). To appreciate this point, it is necessary to re-examine Coase's mature work centred on 'The problem of social cost' (Coase, 1960) in the light of the central argument of his much earlier work, 'The nature of the firm' (Coase, 1937).

'The nature of the firm' is widely acknowledged to be a compelling criticism of the conventional treatment of the firm in economics. A further dimension of the paper is much less well recognized: its intervention in the contemporaneous debate about the role of planning in socialism (Campbell and Klaes, 2005). Coase's (1937) views of planning in the economic system are in fact in open opposition to the position that Hayek (1933, 1935) famously advocated in the planning debate:

> [t]hose who object to economic planning on the grounds that the problem is solved by price movements can be answered by pointing out that there is planning within our economic system which is quite different from . . . individual planning . . . and which is akin to what is normally called economic planning. (Coase, 1937, p. 35)

Coase is claiming that an entrepreneur controls his firm according to the same principles that a socialist planner would have to adopt when centrally administering the economy. Of course, this should not be read as a call for state planning to replace the market system. The analogy between the proposal to run the state as a big factory and the evident success of large capitalist corporations rather serves to qualify Hayek's scepticism regarding the possibility of successful large-scale planning *per se*. What Coase pointed out was that 'direction', as a form of hierarchical (but entrepreneurial) planning, was evidently able to complement decentralized market coordination, due to the relative imperfections inherent in both modes of economic coordination.

Coase's (1937) emphasis on 'direction' emerges in 'The problem of social cost' (Coase, 1960) when he draws attention to another aspect of 'planning' that places it beyond the simplistic opposition between 'state' and 'market' (Campbell, 1999). Coase (1960) demonstrates that the definition of property rights is of crucial importance to markets that exhibit positive transaction costs. This leads him to define 'economic regulation' as 'the establishment of the legal framework within which economic activity is carried out' (Coase, 1977, p. 5). Hence, for Coase the question can never be whether or not to regulate a market, since the institution of market exchange as such rests on regulatory input, or 'institutional direction' (Campbell and Klaes, 2005), that is, 'direction' in the sense of Coase (1937), but applied to the market as an instituted entity.

This concept of regulation has important policy implications, for even when market governance is identified as the more efficient mode of coordination, such governance, according to Coase, relies on planned decision-making, not just at the level of any firms participating in the market, but also at the collective level. Crucially, though much less appreciated in this context, this collective planning goes beyond the definition of a regulatory framework for market exchange, which, traditionally conceived, would merely amount to an *ex ante* specification of the rules of the market game. Once fixed, these would define the possible moves within that game. But any revision, any binding reinterpretation of these rules would amount to a move in that very game itself, with direct allocative implications. And this is, of course, what happens in the real world of permanent legislative change, ongoing clarification and redefinition of the law by the judiciary, and constant rewriting of administrative rules at all levels of governmental bureaucracy.

Coase's conception of the competitive economy addresses the fundamental conjunction between 'direction' and competition at all levels. According to 'The nature of the firm', effective planning must rely on competition. 'The problem of social cost' adds to this that competition itself is unthinkable without planned decision-making at the level of the collective about the specification and distribution of rights (logically prior to the market). Therefore, economic policy cannot extricate itself from a continuing process of institutional direction which underlines any regime even of market governance.

It is clear that the Coasean perspective does not as yet offer a comprehensive and fully formulated theory of institutional direction (Klaes, 2005). The most promising developments at the intersection of social economics and legal studies seek to combine the institutional insights we have claimed are at the heart of modern law and economics with institutional traditions that, until recently, have largely operated in separation from, if not in opposition to, those law and economics. The rise of a neo-behaviourist economics is encouraging in this regard, but, as yet, it clearly does not go far enough to embrace social economic perspectives (Klaes, 2008a). Appreciation of the subtle relationship between the social and psychological dimensions of choice, and therefore also of transacting and contracting in the legal sense, will require acknowledgement of the role of the symbolic, expressive and outright narrative elements in the interaction between those dimensions and individual identity. Promising starting-points for the required shift may be found in 'expressive' theories of choice (e.g. Anderson, 1993) and their reception in socio-legal and in particular feminist studies (Hadfield, 1998), provided one approaches them with a Coasean caution towards any 'paternalist' interventionism that remains residually embedded in at least some of these departures (Campbell, 2005).

Cases

Conway v. O'Brien 111 F. 2d. 611 (1940).
United States v. Carroll Towing Co 159 F. 2d. 169 (1947).

References

Anderson, E. (1993), *Value in Ethics and Economics*, Cambridge, MA: Harvard University Press.

Atiyah, P.S. (1990), *Essays on Contract*, rev. edn, Oxford: Clarendon Press.
Ayres, I. (1997), 'Never confuse efficiency with a liver complaint', *Wisconsin Law Review*, 503–20.
Baker, C.E. (1975), 'The ideology of the economic analysis of law', *Philosophy and Public Affairs*, 5, 3–48.
Baker, C.E. (1978), 'Posner's privacy mystery and the failure of economic analysis of law', *Georgia Law Review*, 12, 475–95.
Baker, C.E. (1980), 'Starting points in economic analysis of law', *Hofstra Law Review*, 8, 939–72.
Barton, J.H. (1972), 'The economic basis of damages for breach of contract', *Journal of Legal Studies*, 1, 277–304.
Bayes, C.W. (1996), 'A note on the efficiency of the common law', unpublished, Department of Economics, East Carolina University, Greenville, NC, USA.
Becker, G.S. (1960), 'An economic analysis of fertility', in Ansley J. Coale et al. (eds), *Demographic and Economic Change in Developed Countries*, Princeton, NJ: Princeton University Press, pp. 209–40.
Becker, G.S. (1968), 'Crime and punishment: an economic approach', *Journal of Political Economy*, 76, 169–217.
Birmingham, R. (1970), 'Breach of contract, damage measures and economic efficiency', *Rutgers Law Review*, 24, 273–92.
Bowles, R. (1982), *Law and the Economy*, Oxford: Martin Robertson.
Bryden, D.P. (1978), 'Environmental rights in theory and practice', *Minnesota Law Review*, 62, 163–228.
Buchanan, J.M. (1974), 'Good economics – bad law', *Virginia Law Review*, 60, 483–92.
Burrows, P. (1981), 'Nuisance, legal rules and decentralised decisions: a different view of the cathedral crypt', in P. Burrows and C.J. Veljanovski (eds), *The Economic Approach to Law*, London: Butterworths, pp. 151–66.
Calabresi, G. (1968), 'Transaction costs, resource allocation and liability rules: a comment', *Journal of Law and Economics*, 11, 67–73.
Calabresi, G. (1970), *The Cost of Accidents*, New Haven, CT: Yale University Press.
Calabresi, G. (1991), 'The pointlessness of Pareto: carrying Coase further', *Yale Law Journal*, 100, 1211–37.
Calabresi, G. and P. Bobbitt (1978), *Tragic Choices*, New York: W.W. Norton.
Calabresi, G. and J.T. Hirschoff (1972), 'Toward a test for strict liability in torts', *Yale Law Journal*, 81, 1055–85.
Calabresi, G. and A.D. Melamed (1972), 'Property rules, liability rules and inalienability: one view of the cathdral crypt', *Harvard Law Review*, 85, 1089–128.
Campbell, D. (1990), 'The social theory of relational contract: Macneil as the modern Proudhon', *International Journal of the Sociology of Law*, 18, 75–95.
Campbell, D. (1994), 'Ayres *versus* Coase: an attempt to recover the issue of equality in law and economics', *British Journal of Law and Society*, 21, 434–63.
Campbell, D. (1996a), 'On what is valuable in law and economics', *Otago Law Review*, 8, 489–514.
Campbell, D. (1996b), 'The relational constitution of the discrete contract', in D. Campbell and P. Vincent-Jones (eds) (1996), *Contract and Economic Organisation*, Aldershot: Dartmouth Publishing, pp. 40–66.
Campbell, D. (1999), 'The "hybrid contract" and the merging of the public and private law of the allocation of economic goods', in D. Campbell and N.D. Lewis (eds), *Promoting Participation: Law or Politics?*, London: Cavendish Publishing, pp. 45–73.
Campbell, D. (2005), 'Afterword: feminism, liberalism and utopianism in the analysis of contracting', in L. Mulcahy and S. Wheeler (eds), *Feminist Perspectives on Contract Law*, London: Cavendish, pp. 161–73.
Campbell, D. and D. Harris (1993), 'Flexibility in long-term contractual relationships: the role of co-operation', *Journal of Law and Society*, 20, 166–91.
Campbell, D. and M. Klaes (2005), 'The principle of institutional direction: Coase's regulatory critique of intervention', *Cambridge Journal of Economics*, 29, 263–88.

Caspar, G. and R.A. Posner (1976), *The Workload of the Supreme Court*, Chicago, IL: American Bar Foundation.

Coase, R.H. (1937), 'The nature of the firm', in *The Firm, the Market and the Law*, Chicago, IL: University of Chicago Press, pp. 33–55.

Coase, R.H. (1960), 'The problem of social cost', in *The Firm, the Market and the Law*, Chicago, IL: University of Chicago Press, pp. 95–156.

Coase, R.H. (1964), 'The regulated industries: discussion', *American Economic Review (Papers and Proceedings)*, **54**, 194–7.

Coase, R.H. (1972), 'Industrial organisation: a proposal for research', in *The Firm, the Market and the Law*, Chicago, IL: University of Chicago Press, pp. 57–74.

Coase, R.H. (1977), 'Economics and contiguous disciplines', in *Essays on Economics and Economists*, Chicago, IL: University of Chicago Press, 1994, pp. 34–46.

Coase, R.H. (1984), 'The new institutional economics', *Journal of Institutional and Theoretical Economics*, **140**, 229–31.

Coase, R.H. (1988), *The Firm, the Market and the Law*, Chicago, IL: University of Chicago Press.

Coase, R.H. (1993), 'Coase on Posner on Coase', *Journal of Institutional and Theoretical Economics*, **149**, 96–8.

Coase, R.H. (1994), *Essays on Economics and Economists*, Chicago, IL: University of Chicago Press.

Commons, J.R. (1924), *The Legal Foundations of Capitalism*, New York: Macmillan.

Cooter, R.D. (1982), 'The cost of Coase', *Journal of Legal Studies*, **11**, 1–33.

Cooter, R.D. (1987), 'The Coase theorem', in J. Eatwell et al. (eds), *The New Palgrave*, vol. 1, London: Macmillan, pp. 457–60.

Cooter, R.D. and L. Kornhauser (1980), 'Can litigation improve the law without the help of the judges?', *Journal of Legal Studies*, **9**, 139–63.

Cooter, R.D. and D.L. Rubinfeld (1989), 'Economic analysis of legal disputes and their resolution', *Journal of Economic Literature*, **27**, 1067–97.

Cooter, R.D. and T. Ulen (2004), *Law and Economics*, 4th edn, Boston, MA: Pearson, Addison Welsey.

Crocker, T.D. (1971), 'Externalities, property rights and transaction costs: an empirical study', *Journal of Law and Economics*, **14**, 451–64.

Daly, G. (1974), 'The Coase theorem: assumptions, applications and ambiguities', *Economic Inquiry*, **12**, 203–13.

Daly, G. and J.F. Giertz (1975), 'Externalities, extortion and efficiency', *American Economic Review*, **65**, 997–1001.

Demsetz, H. (1971), 'Theoretical efficiency in pollution control: comment on comments', *Western Economic Journal*, **9**, 444–6.

Duxbury, N. (1994), *Law, Economics and the Legacy of Chicago*, Hull: Hull University Law School.

Duxbury, N. (1995), *Patterns of American Jurisprudence*, Oxford: Clarendon Press.

Ehrlich, I. (1973), 'Participation in illegal activities: a theoretical and empirical investigation', *Journal of Political Economy*, **81**, 521–65.

Ehrlich, I. (1975), 'The deterrent effect of capital punishment: a question of life and death', *American Economic Review*, **65**, 397–417.

Ehrlich, I. (1979), 'The economic approach to crime: a preliminary assessment', in S. Messinger and E. Bittner (eds), *Criminology Review Yearbook*, vol. 1, Beverly Hills, CA: Sage, pp. 25–60.

Ehrlich, I. and R.A. Posner (1974), 'An economic analysis of legal rulemaking', *Journal of Legal Studies*, **3**, 257–86.

Ellickson, R.C. (1989), 'The case for Coase and against "Coaseanism"', *Yale Law Journal*, **99**, 611–30.

Ellickson, R.C. (1991), *Order Without Law: How Neighbours Settle Disputes*, Cambridge, MA: Harvard University Press.

Englard, I. (1980), 'The system builders: a critical appraisal of modern American tort theory', *Journal of Legal Studies*, **9**, 27–69.

Epstein, R.A. (1980), 'The static conception of the common law', *Journal of Legal Studies*, **9**, 253–75.

Farnsworth, E.A. (1970), 'Legal remedies for breach of contract', *Columbia Law Review*, **70**, 1145–216.

Feinman, J. (1983), 'Critical approaches to contract law', *UCLA Law Review*, **30**, 829–60.

Frech, H.E. (1973), 'Pricing of pollution: the Coase theorem in the long run', *Bell Journal of Economics and Management Science*, **4**, 316–19.

Frech, H.E. (1979), 'Extended Coase theorem and long-run equilibrium', *Economic Inquiry*, **17**, 254–68.

Fried, C. (1978), *Right and Wrong*, Cambridge, MA: Harvard University Press..

Fried, C. (1980), 'The laws of change: the cunning of reason in moral and legal history', *Journal of Legal Studies*, **9**, 335–53.

Goetz, C.J. and R.E. Scott (1980), 'Enforcing promises: an examination of the basis of contract', *Yale Law Journal*, **89**, 1261–322.

Goldberg, V.P. (1976), 'Commons, Clark and the emerging post-Coasean law and economics', *Journal of Economic Issues*, **10**, 877–93.

Goodman, J.C. (1978), 'An economic theory of the evolution of the common law', *Journal of Legal Studies*, **7**, 393–406.

Greenawalt, K. (1977), 'Policy, rights and judicial decision', *Georgia Law Review*, **11**, 991–1053.

Gruchy, A.G. (1987), *The Reconstruction of Economics: An Analysis of the Fundamentals of Institutional Economics*, New York: Greenwood Press.

Hadfield, G.K. (1998), 'An expressive theory of contract: from feminist dilemmas to a reconceptualisation of rational choice in contract law', *University of Pennsylvania Law Review*, **146**, 1235–85.

Hayek, F.A. (1933), 'The trend of economic thinking', *Economica*, **40**, 121–37.

Hayek, F.A. (ed.) (1935), *Collectivist Economic Planning*, London: Routledge.

Heller, T.C. (1976), 'The importance of normative decisionmaking: the limitations of legal economics as a basis for legal jurisprudence', *Wisconsin Law Review*, 385–502.

Higgins, R.S. and P.H. Rubin (1980), 'Judicial discretion', *Journal of Legal Studies*, **9**, 129–38.

Hirsch, W.Z. (1988), *Law and Economics: An Introductory Analysis*, 2nd edn, Boston, MA: Academic Press.

Hodgson, G.M. (1994), 'The return of institutional economics', in N.J. Smelser and R. Swedberg (eds), *The Handbook of Economic Sociology*, Princeton, NJ: Princeton University Press, pp. 58–76.

Hodgson, G.M. (1998), 'The approach of institutional economics', *Journal of Economic Literature*, **36**, 166–92.

Horwitz, M.J. (1980), 'Law and economics: science or politics?', *Hofstra Law Review*, **8**, 905–12.

Hovenkamp, H. (1990), 'The first great law and economics movement', *Stanford Law Review*, **42**, 993.

Hovenkamp, H. (1995), 'Law and economics in the United States', *Cambridge Journal of Economics*, **19**, 331–52.

Hutchison, T.W. (1984), 'Institutional economics: old and new', *Journal of Institutional and Theoretical Economics*, **140**, 20–29.

Johnston, R.L. (1973), 'A decision-making process for the California coastal zone', *Southern California Law Review*, **46**, 513–64.

Joskow, P.L. (1985), 'Vertical integration and long-term contracts: the case of coal-burning electric generating plants', *Journal of Law, Economics and Organisation*, **1**, 33–80.

Joskow, P.L. (1987), 'Contract duration and relationship specific investments: empirical evidence from coal markets', *American Economic Review*, **77**, 168–85.

Joskow, P.L. (1988), 'Price adjustment in long-term contracts: the case of coal', *Journal of Law and Economics*, **31**, 47–83.

Kelman, M. (1979), 'Consumption theory, production theory and ideology in the Coase theorem', *Southern California Law Review*, **52**, 669–98.

Kennedy, D. (1981), 'Cost–benefit analysis of entitlement problems: a critique', *Stanford Law Review*, **33**, 387.

Kenny, P. (1982), 'Economic analysis and efficiency in the common law', in R. Cranston and A. Schick (eds), *Law and Economics*, Canberra, Australia: Law Department, Research School of Social Sciences, ANU, pp. 42–58.

Klaes, M. (2005), 'Historical economics and evolutionary economic policy: Coasean perspectives', in K. Dopfer (ed.), *Economics, Evolution and the State*, Cheltenham, UK and Northampton, MA, USA: Edward Elgar, pp. 78–96.

Klaes, M. (2008a), 'Rationality and its bounds: re-framing social framing', in M.C. Galavotti, R. Scazzieri and P. Suppes (eds), *Reasoning, Rationality and Probability*, Stanford, CA: CSLI Publications.

Klaes, M. (2008b), 'Transactions costs, history of', in S. Durlauf and L. Blume (eds), *The New Palgrave Dictionary of Economics*, 2nd edn, London: Palgrave Macmillan.

Klevorick, A.K. (1983), 'On the economic theory of crime', *Nomos*, **27**, 289–309.

Krier, J.E. (1974), 'Review of *Economic Analysis of Law* by Richard A Posner', *University of Pennsylvania Law Review*, **122**, 1664–705.

Landes, E.M. and R.A. Posner (1978), 'The economics of the baby shortage', *Journal of Legal Studies*, **7**, 323–48.

Landes, W.M. and R.A. Posner (1976), 'Legal precedent: a theoretical and empirical analysis', *Journal of Law and Economics*, **19**, 249–307.

Landes, W.M. and R.A. Posner (1979), 'Adjudication as a private good', *Journal of Legal Studies*, **8**, 235–84.

Landes, W.M. and R.A. Posner (1980), 'Legal change, judicial behaviour and the diversity jurisdiction', *Journal of Legal Studies*, **9**, 367–86.

Landes, W.M. and R.A. Posner (1993), 'The influence of economics on law: a quantitative study', *Journal of Law and Economics*, **36**, 385–424.

Leff, A.A. (1974), 'Economic analysis of law: some realism about nominalism', *Virginia Law Review*, **60**, 451–82.

Liebhafsky, H.H. (1976), 'Price theory as jurisprudence: law and economics Chicago style', *Journal of Economic Issues*, **10**, 23–43.

Macneil, I.R. (1974), 'The many futures of contract', *Southern California Law Review*, **47**, 691–896.

Macneil, I.R. (1978), 'Contracts: adjustment of long-term economic relations under classical, neo-classical and relational contract law', *Northwestern University Law Review*, **72**, 854–905.

Macneil, I.R. (1980), *The New Social Contract*, New Haven, CT: Yale University Press.

Malloy, R.P. (1990a), 'Is law and economics moral? Humanistic economics and a classical liberal critique of Posner's economic analysis', *Valparaiso University Law Review*, **24**, 147–61.

Malloy, R.P. (1990b), *Law and Economics*, St Paul, MN: West Publishing.

Maloney, T.T. (1977), 'The Coase theorem and long-run industry equilibrium', *Quarterly Review of Economics and Business*, **17**, 113–18.

Markovits, R.S. (1975), 'A basic structure for micoeconomic policy analysis in our worse-than-second-best world: a proposal and related critique of the Chicago approach to the study of law and economics', *Wisconsin Law Review*, 950–1080.

McKean, R.N. (1970), 'Products liability: some implications of changing property rights', *Quarterly Journal of Economics*, **84**, 611–26.

Medema, S.G. (1996), 'Ronald Coase and American institutionalism', *Research in the History of Economic Thought and Methodology*, **14**, 51–92.

Medema, S.G. (1998), *Coasean Economics*, Boston, MA: Kluwer.

Medema, S.G. (1999), 'Legal fiction: the place of the Coase theorem in law and economics', *Economics and Philosophy*, **15**, 209–33.

Medema, S.G. (2002), 'George Stigler and the Coase theorem', *American Journal of Economics and Sociology*, **61**, 638–41.

Medema, S.G. and R.O. Zerbe Jr (2000), 'Educating Alice: lessons from the Coase theorem', *Research in Law and Economics*, **19**, 69–112.

Medema, S.G., N. Mercuro and W.J. Samuels (2000), 'Institutional law and economics', in B. Bouckaert and G. De Geest (eds), *The Encyclopedia of Law and Economics*, Cheltenham, UK and Northampton, MA, USA: Edward Elgar, pp. 418–55.

Mercuro, N. and S.G. Medema (1997), *Economics and the Law: From Posner to Postmodernism*, Princeton, NJ: Princeton University Press.

Mercuro, N. and T.P. Ryan (1984), *Law, Economics and Public Policy*, Greenwich, CT: JAI Press.

Michelman, F.I. (1978), 'Norms and normativity in the economic theory of law', *Minnesota Law Review*, **62**, 1015–48.

Michelman, F.I. (1979), 'A comment on "Some uses and abuses of economics and law"', *University of Chicago Law Review*, **46**, 307–15.

Michelman, F.I. (1980), 'Constitutions, statutes and the theory of efficient adjudication', *Journal of Legal Studies*, **9**, 431–61.

Mishan, E.J. (1971), 'Pangloss on pollution', *Swedish Journal of Economics*, **73**, 113–20.

Ogus, A.I. (1995), 'Law and economics in the United Kingdom: past, present and future', *Journal of Law and Society*, **22**, 26–34.

Osborne, D.E. and T. Gaebler (1992), *Reinventing Government: How the Entrepreneurial Spirit is Transforming the Public Sector*, Reading, MA: Addison-Wesley.

Philipson, T.J. and R.A. Posner (1993), *Private Choices and Public Health: The AIDS Epidemic in an Economic Perspective*, Cambridge, MA: Harvard University Press.

Polinsky, A.M. (1974), 'Economic analysis as a potentially defective product: a buyer's guide to Posner's economic analysis', *Harvard Law Review*, **87**, 1655–81.

Polinsky, A.M. (1983), 'Risk sharing through breach of contract remedies', *Journal of Legal Studies*, **12**, 427–44.

Polinsky, A.M. (1989), *An Introduction to Law and Economics*, 2nd edn, Boston, MA: Little, Brown.

Posner, R.A. (1972), 'A theory of negligence', *Journal of Legal Studies*, **1**, 29–96.

Posner, R.A. (1973), 'An economic approach to legal procedure and judicial administration', *Journal of Legal Studies*, **2**, 399–458.

Posner, R.A. (1979a), 'Some uses and abuses of economics in law', *University of Chicago Law Review*, **46**, 281–306.

Posner, R.A. (1979b), 'Utilitarianism, economics and legal theory', *Journal of Legal Studies*, **8**, 103–40. A revised version is given in R.A. Posner, *The Economics of Justice*, Cambridge, MA: Harvard University Press, 1981, pp. 48–87.

Posner, R.A. (1980a), 'The ethical and political basis of the efficiency norm in common law adjudication', *Hofstra Law Journal*, **8**, 487–507. A revised version is given in R.A. Posner, *The Economics of Justice*, Cambridge, MA: Harvard University Press, 1981, pp. 81–115.

Posner, R.A. (1980b), 'The value of wealth: a comment on Dworkin and Kronman', *Journal of Legal Studies*, **9**, 243–52.

Posner, R.A. (1985), *The Federal Courts: Crisis and Reform*, Cambridge, MA: Harvard University Press.

Posner, R.A. (1987), 'The regulation of the market in adoptions', *Boston University Law Review*, **67**, 59–72.

Posner, R.A. (1988), *Law and Literature*, Cambridge, MA: Harvard University Press.

Posner, R.A. (1990), *The Problems of Jurisprudence*, Cambridge, MA: Harvard University Press.

Posner, R.A. (1993a), 'Gary Becker's contributions to law and economics', *Journal of Legal Studies*, **22**, 211–15.

Posner, R.A. (1993b), 'What do judges and justices maximise?', *Supreme Court Economic Review*, **3**, 1–41.

Posner, R.A. (1993c), 'What do judges and justices maximise?', 3 *Supreme Court Economic Review* 1.

Posner, R.A. (1995), *Aging and Old Age*, Chicago, IL: University of Chicago Press.

Posner, R.A. (2007), *The Economic Analysis of Law*, 7th edn, New York: Aspen.

Posner, R.A. and A.M. Rosenfeld (1977), 'Impossibility and related doctrines in contract law', *Journal of Legal Studies*, **6**, 83–118.

Pratten, S. (2001), 'Coase on broadcasting, advertising and policy', *Cambridge Journal of Economics*, **25**, 617–38.

Priest, G.L. (1977), 'The common law process and the selection of efficient rules', *Journal of Legal Studies*, **6**, 65–82.

Priest, G.L. (1980), 'Selective characteristics of litigation', *Journal of Legal Studies*, **9**, 399–421.

Priest, G.L. and B. Klein (1984), 'The selection of disputes for litigation', *Journal of Legal Studies*, **13**, 1–55.

Regan, D.H. (1972), 'The problem of social cost revisited', *Journal of Law and Economics*, **15**, 427–37.

Rubin, P.H. (1977), 'Why is the common law efficient?', *Journal of Legal Studies*, **6**, 51–63.

Rubin, P.H. (1982), 'Statute law and common law', *Journal of Legal Studies*, **11**, 205–23.

Rubin, P.H. and M.J. Bailey (1994), 'The role of lawyers in changing the law', *Journal of Legal Studies*, **23**, 807–31.

Rutherford, M.C. (1994), *Institutions in Economics: The Old and the New Institutionalism*, Cambridge: Cambridge University Press.

Samuels, W.J. (1971), 'Interrelations between legal and economic processes', *Journal of Law and Economics*, **14**, 435–50.

Samuels, W.J. (1976), 'The Chicago school of political economy: a constructive critique', in W.J. Samuels (ed.), *The Chicago School of Political Economy*, East Lansing, MI: Division of Research, Graduate School of Business Administration, Michigan State University, pp. 1–18.

Scherer, F.M. (1977), 'The Posnerian harvest: separating the wheat from the chaff', *Yale Law Journal*, **86**, 974–1002.

Schlag, P. (1986), 'An appreciative comment on Coase's "The problem of social cost": a view from the left', *Wisconsin Law Review*, 919–62.

Schlicht, E. (1996), 'Exploiting the Coase mechanism: the extortion problem', *Kyklos*, **49**, 319–30.

Schulze, W. and R.C. d'Arge (1974), 'The Coase proposition, information constraints and long-run equilibrium', *American Economic Review*, **64**, 763–72.

Shavell, S. (1980), 'Damage measures for breach of contract', *Bell Journal of Economics*, **11**, 466–90.

Shavell, S. (2004), *Foundations of Economic Analysis of Law*, Cambridge, MA: Belknap Press.

Shoup, D.C. (1971), 'Theoretical efficiency in pollution control: comment', *Western Economic Journal*, **9**, 310–17.

Steiner, J.M. (1976), 'Economics, morality and the law of torts', *Toronto Law Journal*, **26**, 227–52.

Symposium (1980), 'Efficiency as a legal concern', *Hofstra Law Review*, **8**, 485–770.

Symposium (1989a), 'Post-Chicago law and economics', *Chicago–Kent Law Review*, **65**, 3–191.

Symposium (1989b), 'Non-Posnerian law and economics', *Hamline Law Review*, **12**, 195–410.

Symposium (1991), 'Economic analysis in civil law countries: past, present, future', *International Review of Law and Economics*, **11**, 261–342.

Symposium (1997), 'Law and society and law and economics: common ground, irreconcilable differences, new directions', *Wisconson Law Review*, 375–637.

Trebilcock, M.J. (1993), *The Limits of Freedom of Contract*, Cambridge, MA: Harvard University Press.

Trebing, H.M. (1976), 'The Chicago school versus public utility regulation', *Journal of Economic Issues*, **10**, 97–126.

Tribe, L.H. (1972), 'Policy science: analysis or ideology', *Philosophy and Public Affairs*, **2**, 66–110.

Tribe, L.H. (1973), 'Technology assessment and the fourth discontinuity: the limits of instrumental rationality', *Southern California Law Review*, **46**, 617–60.

Veblen, T. (1958), *The Theory of Business Enterprise*, New York: Mentor Books.

Veljanovski, C.J. (1981), 'The economic theory of tort liability: toward a corrective justice approach', in P. Burrows and C.J. Veljanovski (eds), *The Economic Approach to Law*, London: Butterworths, pp. 125–50.

Veljanovski, C.J. (1982), *The New Law and Economics*, Oxford: Centre for Socio-legal Studies.
Veljanovski, C.J. (2006), *The Economics of Law*, 2nd edn, London: Institute of Economic Affairs.
Vogel, K.R. (1987), 'The Coase theorem and California animal trespass law', *Journal of Legal Studies*, **16**, 149–87.
Williamson, O.E. (1975), *Markets and Hierarchies*, New York: Free Press.
Williamson, O.E. (1985), *The Economic Institutions of Capitalism*, New York: Free Press.
Williamson, O.E. (1986), *Economic Organisation*, Sussex: Harvester Wheatsheaf.
Williamson, O.E. (1987), *Antitrust Economics*, Oxford: Basil Blackwell.
Williamson, O.E. (1993a), 'The evolving science of organisation', *Journal of Institutional and Theoretical Economics*, **149**, 36–63.
Williamson, O.E. (1993b), 'Transaction cost economics meets Posnerian law and economics', *Journal of Institutional and Theoretical Economics*, **149**, 99–118.
Williamson, O.E. (1996), *The Mechanisms of Governance*, Oxford: Oxford University Press.
Zerbe, R.O. (1980), 'The problem of social cost in retrospect', *Research in Law and Economics*, **2**, 83–102.

32 Social law and economics and the quest for dignity and rights
Mark D. White

The economic approach to law, otherwise known as 'law and economics', is by many measures the most successful instance of economic imperialism, the application of economic principles to an 'outside' field.[1] However, law and economics is very closely tied to traditional, neoclassical economics, both in terms of its consequentialist standard of efficiency, embodied (variously) in Pareto optimality and Kaldor–Hicks efficiency, and its utility-maximizing economic agent, his choices completely determined by his preferences and constraints. But most social economists take issue with these foundational concepts, both of which reflect a basic ignorance of, or negligence to consider, the humanity and dignity of the persons economists purport to be modeling. This leads neoclassical economists to consider well-being to be just the sum of utilities, with no regard for how those utilities were obtained or their distribution, and to treat the individual as just a cog in the legal machine to be manipulated by policy as a means to furthering the end of efficiency.

In the first section of this chapter, I shall introduce the brief social economics literature discussing law and economics. In the second section, I shall outline several key issues of interest to social economists regarding law and economics, focusing on the consequentialist foundations of the field and the resulting ignorance of fundamental human rights and dignity therein. Finally, I shall suggest several future areas of research in law and economics, such as including rights and dignity into the evaluative toolbox of law and economics, and incorporating moral motivation and true agency into the models of individual decision-making used in law and economics.

1. State of the literature
Social economists have not spent much time and energy writing about law and economics. The reason seems fairly clear: the field of law and economics represents an application of the worst features of neoclassical economics to an institution of critical importance to human flourishing in society. Law and economics scholars analyze the effect of laws on human behavior in the most reductionist, mechanistic way possible, and then evaluate the

optimality of these laws on an impersonal scale of efficiency that benefits some persons at the cost of others' well-being and rights. Social economics, on the other hand, is more concerned with the humanity and dignity of persons in the economy, and would be skeptical regarding an approach to legal studies that minimizes those aspects of legal actors. Since their outlook is far removed from that of neoclassical law and economics, social economists understandably have felt little need to devote scarce time to discussing it – but this is also a strong reason to focus anew on the issue.[2]

Perhaps the most important work directly criticizing law and economics from a social economics viewpoint is Steven Medema's 1993 article, 'Is there life beyond efficiency? Elements of a social law and economics'. Medema starts by acknowledging the pluralistic nature of social economics, and then cites Mark Lutz as identifying a 'profound interest in values and the process of valuation in order to more fully understand both economic behavior and the possibilities of improving the economic system' (Lutz, 1990, p. ix), though the preferred values chosen for emphasis will of course differ among social economists. He explains that social economists should be interested in law because it is inextricably linked not only to the economy, but more broadly to the distribution of rights, wealth and power in society. He then highlights the same two aspects of neoclassical law and economics that are emphasized in the current chapter, the efficiency norm and the assumption of utility-maximizing individuals, and outlines some disagreements social economists may have with them. Medema notes that besides occasional criticism, 'little work has been done in formulating an approach to law and economics from an explicit social economics perspective' (Medema, 1993, p. 138). Unfortunately, this is as true now as it was when he wrote it in 1993, save for some work specifically on the economics of crime from the viewpoint of social economics (discussed below).

A seminal critique cited by Medema is by economist Mark Lutz and psychologist Kenneth Lux in their 1988 book *Humanistic Economics: The New Challenge*. Lutz and Lux spend most of their chapter on economic imperialism discussing law and economics, 'the most dangerous thrust of the imperialist movement' (ibid., p. 182). They start with the paper that is universally acknowledged as the foundation of modern law and economics, Ronald Coase's 'The problem of social cost' (1960), emphasizing the concepts of reciprocal harm and instrumental rights used therein. They then turn to Richard Posner, the main defender of the normative foundations of law and economics, focusing on his justification for wealth maximization (his preferred variant of Kaldor–Hicks efficiency), and identifying problems with it, such as wealth constraints and hypothetical compensation. They call for the replacement of standard efficiency concepts with 'social welfare maximization and social justice maximization', which emphasize distributional concerns and personal rights, respectively (ibid., p. 192), but again, little has been done to advance this project in developing an alternative efficiency standard for a social law and economics.[3] (These issues are discussed at greater length in Section 2.)

An important exception to social economists' neglect of law and economics is the modest body of work on the economics of crime, specifically regarding the model of choice used to represent the decision to commit crimes. Danziger and Wheeler (1975) construct a model of individual behavior based on income inequality and allegiance to social contract; as they explain,

> crime is the product of malevolent interdependence; the potential criminal is concerned not only with his own income, but with how this income compares to that of his reference group . . . Economic calculations and malevolent interdependence are both necessary conditions for crime, but neither is sufficient, since the propensity to commit crime varies also with the individual's allegiance to the social contract. (Ibid., p. 119)[4]

Fadaei-Tehrani and Green (2002) recommend that sociological and psychological factors be incorporated in the economic model as psychic phenomena (but do not explicitly discuss ethical factors *per se*). Finally, White (2005) develops a model of criminal behavior based explicitly on Kantian ethics, including a character parameter (similar to Danziger and Wheeler's index of social contract allegiance) that can represent moral feeling, respect for the law, or weakness of will. Despite these tentative steps, more work clearly needs to be done in this area, as well as on a social economic approach to the law in general.[5]

2.   Main issues and implications

Efficiency and consent: Kaldor–Hicks and Pareto
The ethical foundations of law and economics are utilitarian, ultimately based on the writings of Bentham (1781) and Beccaria (1764), and the criticisms of utilitarianism are well known.[6] However, most law and economics scholars reject hedonic utilitarianism, based on comparisons of pleasure and pain, and prefer either economics-oriented proxy measures, such as the wealth maximization of Posner (1983), or formal theories of the good, such as the preference-satisfaction of Kaplow and Shavell (2002) (albeit with a very selective view of which preferences are to considered).[7] Most law and economics scholars do not concern themselves with these foundational issues, and simply adopt either Pareto optimality or Kaldor–Hicks efficiency as their evaluative standard. But there are many ethical problems with both of these concepts that concern social economists, several of which I

discuss below, such as the blatant inequities built into the Kaldor–Hicks standard and the lack of true consent in the Pareto criterion, both of which violate basic norms of human dignity.

Kaldor–Hicks efficiency endorses a change in policy or law if and only if the gains to those who benefit from the change exceed the losses to those who are harmed, ensuring a net benefit overall. This is sometimes justified with the concept of hypothetical compensation: if Group A benefits (in monetary terms) more than Group B loses, then Group A can (hypothetically) compensate Group B for their total losses, leaving them in the same position they were before the change, with Group A still experiencing residual benefit. If such compensation actually occurred, the situation would be a Pareto improvement (since Group B benefits and Group A is not harmed, at least in financial terms), so changes approved by Kaldor–Hicks efficiency are often called 'potential Pareto improvements'.

There are numerous ethical difficulties with this picture. First, hypothetical compensation does not make those harmed by the change any better off; it will buy a hypothetical cup of coffee, nothing more. Law and economics scholars will claim either that the responsibility for compensation lies with politicians, not economists, or that the transaction costs of arranging for compensation prohibit its use. Neither argument holds up to scrutiny, because arrangements for compensation should be included in any proposed change in policy or law that by design will harm members of society. If economists truly want Pareto improvements, they will personally see to it that compensation is arranged, and not shift the burden to politicians. The excuse of high transaction costs is not valid, though all too often used to justify injustices in the name of efficiency. Such costs are simply part of the overall policy proposal, and if compensating those harmed by the proposal is too costly, that should cast doubt on the policy itself, not the practice of compensation.

Also, Kaldor–Hicks efficiency compares benefits and losses in monetary terms, which grants the illusion of metrical stability, but there are several familiar problems with this. First, these benefits and losses are based on willingness-to-pay, itself a hypothetical measure with no verifiability. Second, even if the willingness-to-pay figures are taken to be accurate, those with more resources will be able to pledge higher amounts in support of their preferences regarding the proposal, lessening the ability of the poor to influence policy outcomes. Third, the standard (if often ignored) assumption of diminishing marginal utility of income also shifts the balance of power away from the poor, and may end up approving projects that, in non-monetary terms, result in net harm rather than net benefit.[8] For instance, if Group A pledges $5 million to support a project, and Group B pledges $4 million, but Group B is composed of poorer citizens, then it is very possible that Group B's pledge represents more of a sacrifice to its members than Group A's nominally larger pledge. In monetary terms, the project results in $1 million of net benefit, but in terms of well-being and relative sacrifice, it may be a net loss. As Coleman writes, this system is 'normatively prejudiced in a particularly insidious way: namely, it turns out that what is efficient depends on what people are willing to pay, [which] in turn depends on what they are capable of paying. In short, the greater one's wealth, the more likely one is to increase it' (Coleman, 1984b, p. 662).[9]

Finally, hypothetical compensation can be seen as a strategic ploy to hitch Kaldor–Hicks to Pareto's wagon, since Pareto has practically been elevated to sainthood by neoclassical economists.[10] However, Pareto efficiency is more objectionable than it may seem, depending on its precise relationship to consent, an integral aspect of respect for the dignity of persons.[11] If the Pareto criterion is merely a restatement of a consent requirement, then it's harmless, but redundant; a voluntary transaction is Pareto-improving because both parties consent, but any moral approval given to the transaction will be based on the consent, not the Pareto judgment based upon it. On the other hand, if it is left to others to determine if at least one party is better off and no party is worse off, and the focus of evaluation goes beyond monetary factors, then we have potential problems, mainly with the latter judgment of 'no harm'. Even if no party is harmed in absolute monetary terms, or even if all parties benefit, some may feel that they have been hurt in relative terms, or be offended morally by some aspect of the change or the outcome of it. For instance, if Sue feels her co-worker Bill is receiving a higher raise than he deserves, she may feel that she has been made worse off in comparison, even if she received a raise also. Or, low-income taxpayers may resent a drop in income tax rates that lowers everybody's tax bill by 10 percent, which lowers high-income taxpayers' payments by a greater absolute amount. For this reason, Pareto is no less subject to estimation and valuation problems than Kaldor–Hicks.[12]

The basic problem with Pareto is that it attempts to circumvent consent by allowing policy-makers merely to infer its existence. If they argue that no party is made worse off by a policy, particularly in financial terms, then they cannot imagine any reason why those parties would not consent to it. But consent, unlike estimates of value made by third parties, can be based on more than just material well-being – 'the fact of self-interest in no way constitutes an actual consent' (Dworkin, 1980b, p. 276) – and may be above mere preferences. Jules Coleman (1984a) recognizes that there are some people who place an infinite value on their right to consent, and will feel injured by any coerced transaction, no matter how beneficial in material terms, denying any forced Pareto improvements. Law and economics scholars will again claim that transaction costs prohibit them from obtaining actual consent from the parties affected by the policy, but if the policy endangers basic rights of the parties involved, transaction costs do not justify coercive policies based on Pareto calculations.

Unlike Pareto, the Kaldor–Hicks criterion explicitly condones harm to some parties, as long as greater benefit accrues to others, with no serious thought given to actual compensation. Since it is usually assumed that those who lose from a policy proposal would not consent to it (in the absence of actual compensation), some law and economics scholars, such as Posner (1983) and Kaplow and Shavell (2002), justify the Kaldor–Hicks criterion by recourse to hypothetical consent, which holds that even those who lose from a particular policy proposal would consent to the Kaldor–Hicks test in general because on the average, they will benefit from such decisions over time.[13] Of course, this assumes that each person is equally likely to gain from any given proposal, but as we saw before, Kaldor–Hicks decisions based on willingness-to-pay are biased towards more wealthy participants in the process, so the less wealthy may not be able to reasonably expect an overall benefit in the long run. And even if all parties were made better off in the long run, we are back to a Pareto situation, where consent cannot be inferred automatically from self-interest, for reasons discussed above.

In summary, the two evaluative criteria most often used by law and economics scholars, Pareto optimality and Kaldor–Hicks efficiency, both deny human agents their dignity by circumventing any requirement that policymakers obtain their consent before engaging in policies that may violate essential rights. Kaldor–Hicks explicitly (and Pareto inadvertently) endorses policies that benefit some persons at the expense of others, and with no justification based on desert or blame.[14]

The Coase theorem and instrumental rights

One of the foundational concepts of neoclassical law and economics is the Coase theorem, derived from Coase's 1960 paper 'The problem of social cost', the most common version of which states that if rights are fully and clearly assigned, and transaction costs are zero (or sufficiently low), then, regardless of the initial assignment of rights, a legal dispute will ultimately be solved, between the parties involved, in the (most) efficient manner possible. Taken in isolation from later developments, the Coase theorem is simple, elegant and brilliant. Let's say Alice is playing music too loudly for her neighbor Brad, who likes to spend quiet evenings reading social economics. There are two options: Alice can turn down the music, which she would do for no less than $25, and Brad can wear earplugs, which he would do for no less than $30. We will assume that Alice and Brad can costlessly come to an agreement, and that one of them has an unambiguous and undisputed right to determine the volume of Alice's music. If Brad has the right to quiet, then Alice will turn her music down, at a subjective cost of $25, because the alternative, paying Brad to wear earplugs, is costlier. If Alice has the right to play her music as loud as she pleases, then Brad can wear earplugs, at a subjective cost of $30 to him, but he will more likely pay Alice $25 to turn down her music. So no matter who has the controlling right, the result will be that Alice lowers the volume of her music, which is the more efficient (least-cost) option out of the two suggested.[15]

That much is uncontroversial from an ethical point of view. This basic application of the Coase theorem relies on voluntary transactions that reflect each party's subjective valuation of the available options, and results in unqualified Pareto improvements, since actual consent is guaranteed. The ethical problems begin when law and economics scholars ponder the alternatives when the necessary conditions for the Coase theorem are not met: if transaction costs are too high for the parties to bargain on their own, or rights are not clearly assigned at the outset (which implies high transaction costs as well). In either case, the standard assumption is that the parties will take their dispute to court, and a judge will decide what the result will be if the right-holding party is clear, or who has the right if it isn't.

According to law and economics, the judge should 'mimic the market' and try to determine what the agreement the parties would arrive at if they could bargain with low transaction costs. This is a lot of information for a judge to handle, and involves the same problems of estimation of costs and benefits discussed earlier in the context of Kaldor–Hicks efficiency (appropriately, since that is in essence the criterion the judge would be using). If rights are clearly assigned, then the judge has only to determine the most efficient solution, and order the party without the right to pay for it. There are several dangers implicit in this: the more specific, economic danger is the possibility of an incorrect solution from the judge that ends up in an inefficient solution, although it is possible the parties can negotiate around this (if transaction costs fall enough to allow it). The more general, moral danger is one we have seen before, namely the use of transaction costs to justify a coerced solution.

What if rights are not clearly assigned? The judge still determines the efficient solution, and then vests the right in whichever party values it the most (according to the judge's estimates), the reasoning being that this party would purchase the right anyway (in the absence of transaction costs), and judicial fiat saves the transaction costs of negotiating over it. Note that the assignment of the right is not based on any moral claim based on desert, but rather on relative estimated valuations, with all the attendant problems discussed previously. Reasonable persons can argue over whether

Alice or Brad has the right to control the volume of Alice's music, but few (outside law and economics) would claim that this right should be assigned according to who would pay more for it. According to the figures I gave, Brad should have the right, since it is worth $30 to him, and only $25 to Alice. (And even this assumes that their incomes are equal, as well as their marginal utilities of income.) Tweak the numbers a bit, and the right would go to Alice. Whatever criteria they may use to determine who has the right in this situation, social economists would not make that decision with a calculator.

This example illustrates a general theme of law and economics that ties it closely to its utilitarian roots: the instrumental nature of rights. As far as law and economics scholars are concerned, the rights of individuals are secure only in so far as no one else values them more. As seen in the example above, law and economics adherents regard rights as merely a means to maximize efficiency. They would argue that with low transaction costs and a clear initial assignment of rights, those rights will eventually be sold to the parties that value them most, so if judges, legislatures, or regulatory agencies can nudge things along a little more quickly, what's the problem? Of course, we know the problems, one practical and the other ethical: it is impossible for anyone besides the parties involved to have all of the information necessary to make accurate decisions, and even if this information were known, individuals should not be forced to relinquish their deserved rights, even in the name of efficiency.[16] Human dignity mandates that persons be accorded at least a minimal level of respect, which can take the form of rights or claims against others. Such rights can include negative rights, such as rights to one's person and property, and rights to freedom of thought, or positive rights, such as rights to security, food, or employment. These are not simply legal rights, to be granted or retracted at the will of the state, but moral rights, guaranteed to each person by virtue of his or her dignity.[17]

Ronald Dworkin (1977) has taken the lead in emphasizing the negligence of intrinsic rights in law and economics. He sees that a respect for the dignity of persons implies that their rights should 'trump' any considerations of policy in the name of efficiency, or at the very least, represent a strong counterweight to any such proposals. In law and economics, on the other hand, rights are secondary to efficiency, implying that dignity of some is sacrificed for the 'well-being' of all, and 'the institution of rights, and particular allocations of rights, are justified only insofar as they promote social wealth more effectively than other institutions or allocations' (Dworkin, 1980a, p. 243). For instance, Posner claims (in a very Orwellian fashion) that economics *does* recognize absolute rights: 'the economist recommends the creation of such rights . . . when the cost of voluntary transactions is low . . . But when transaction costs are prohibitive, the recognition of absolute rights is inefficient' (1983, p. 70). Dworkin also points out that law and economics scholars (Posner, specifically) do not apply this reasoning only to 'less important rights, like the right to an injunction in nuisance or to damages in negligence', but to 'determining the most fundamental human rights of citizens, including their right to life and to control their own labor rather than be slaves to others' (Dworkin, 1980a, p. 252), not to mention a woman's 'right to determine her sexual partners' (Posner, 1983, p. 71).[18]

Examples of the instrumental approach to rights can be found in all areas of law and economics. For instance, a central concern of the economic approach to tort law (in which a private party who suffered harm sues to recover damages) is the minimization of accident costs through the choice of optimal liability rules (Shavell, 1987). The question here is: when a person causes harm to another person, under what circumstances should the first person be required to compensate the second for her harm? In other words, under what circumstances does the victim have a right to compensation for her injuries? The two basic rules of liability are strict liability and negligence: under strict liability, the injurer is always responsible for harm caused, regardless of any precautions taken, and under negligence, the injurer is responsible for harm caused only if she took insufficient care. There are many arguments for either strict liability or negligence based on justice and rights, to be sure, but the economic approach considers the issue one of efficiency: which rule will minimize accidents costs, understood as the sum of harm, costs of precaution, and costs of the legal system. The rights of victims to compensation are held hostage to utilitarian calculations rather than evaluated according to principled arguments based on rights and justice.[19]

Another example comes in the economics of contract law, in which a central issue is 'efficient breach', or when it is optimal for one party to break the terms of a contract unilaterally.[20] Like the tort case, the policy issue is the optimal determination of remedies (damages) so that the party who desires to breach will only do so when it is efficient overall, bringing private incentives in line with public interests. (Optimal liability rules can be couched in the same language.) Payment of expectation damages, which compensate the party opposed to the breach for any losses resulting from non-performance, is the economically optimal rule in simple cases, but it denies the 'losing' party any right to enforce the breaching party's contracted performance. Under the alternative remedy of specific performance, the non-breaching party has the right to enforce the contract as written, and can sell that right to the party who wants to breach if an agreement can be reached (*à la* the Coase theorem). This preserves the right of both parties to maintain the contract both agreed to, but whether specific performance is recommended in law and economics is again a question of efficiency, not rights. Generally, social economists may disagree over what and whose rights are to recognized, respected and enforced, but few would endorse an efficiency-based method for solving these problems.

The special case of the criminal law

Perhaps the one area in which law and economics most obviously shows its brute utilitarian values and denial of absolute rights is criminal law. In the economic approach to criminal law, or 'the economics of crime' for short, the sole purpose of criminal enforcement and punishment is the efficient deterrence of future crime, not the punishment of wrongdoers, the pursuit of justice, or the expression of community outrage. Words such as 'guilt', 'blame' and 'wrongdoing' are not used in the literature on economics of crime – in fact, writers in the field have to bend backwards to explain why crimes are 'wrong' and merit societal resources devoted to prevent them. For instance, to law and economics scholars, the criminal status of theft is not due to the fact that a property right is violated – property rights are supported only in so far as they lead to efficient outcomes, so they cannot justify anything *a priori*. After all, if Jim values Kathy's car more than she does, then Jim's theft of the car will result in a more Kaldor–Hicks efficient outcome, all else the same. (Of course, Jim may not value the car more than Kathy, but given the relative incomes of thieves and those from whom they steal, diminishing marginal utility of income implies that the case described above may be common, if not the norm.)

But law and economics scholars *know* in their hearts that theft is wrong (for any number of reasons, none of them based on efficiency, I would guess), and it would be a embarrassment if they could not explain why. But the true embarrassment is in the explanations they have come up with, which have nothing to do with the common-sense idea of crime as a category of moral wrong. The simplest law and economics explanation is that theft leads to an inefficient private allocation of resources devoted to preventing it, primarily in the form of security expenditures, but also abstaining from purchases out of fear of losing them to theft.[21] The absurdities abound: first, in this 'ideal' efficient state of affairs with no private or public measures taken to combat theft, theft would of course prosper, which would inevitably lead to tremendous public outcry. (After all, it is doubtful that the common citizen, not schooled in neoclassical economics, would accept the efficiency of having their property stolen.) Second, this analysis implies that it is the security measures taken by private citizens, rather than theft itself, that are the source of the inefficiency, and therefore *they* should be criminalized. And finally, if private expenditures taken against theft are inefficient, what explains the public expenditures toward the same end, such as the costs of police officers, prosecutors and judges who deal with suspected thieves? (One answer may be the public outcry mentioned earlier, but that begs the question of what justifies the public outcry – 'theft is efficient, don't you see?')

A more general economic explanation of the category of crime, due to Alvin Klevorick, is based upon the type of transaction deemed acceptable by society. He writes that society establishes a 'transaction structure . . . [which] sets out the terms or conditions under which particular transactions or exchanges are to take place under different circumstances' (Klevorick, 1985b, p. 908). Crimes are understood in this analysis as crossing the boundaries of the transaction structure instituted by society, and therefore deserve public resources devoted to preventing them.[22] While this theory is preferable to the simplistic one presented previously, we still need to know what end is served by the chosen transaction structure; if the answer is efficiency (as Posner would say), then as with all utilitarian arguments, the result is wholly contingent on the particular calculation used to get it. In fact, Klevorick's more general point is that even given his suggested economic definition of crime, we still need a political theory of rights to support it (Klevorick, 1985a, pp. 301–4).

It does not take a social economist, uniquely dedicated to the inclusion of ethical values in economic modeling and discourse, to recognize that the transaction structure theory, while elegant, misses the boat. Responding not only to the transaction structure idea but to all law and economics theorizing about crime, Coleman writes that 'such a theory has no place for the moral sentiments and virtues appropriate to matters of crime and punishment: guilt, shame, remorse, forgiveness, and mercy, to name a few. *A purely economic theory of crime can only impoverish rather than enrich our understanding of the nature of crime*' (1985, p. 165, emphasis added).[23] Another prominent legal scholar, Herbert Morris, subtly indicts the law and economics approach, which 'subordinates principle to the realization of social goals, a mode of thinking that focuses, not upon exculpation of the innocent and conviction of the guilty, that is, upon justice, but upon keeping social disruption at an acceptable level' (Morris, 1988, p. 73).[24] Unfortunately, such criticism too rarely comes from economists, but most often from legal scholars and moral philosophers (many of whom also criticize the efficiency norm in the economics of private law as well).

3. New directions

While other scholars criticize the explanatory power of law and economics, social economists would more likely focus on the normative aspects, such as those I pointed out in the last section. In particular, a renewed and retargeted focus on dignity and rights would require a re-evaluation of the efficiency norm and consequently the economic understanding of both private and public law, as well as a rethinking of the deterministic model of consequentialist rational choice used to represent agents' decision-making in law and economics (and neoclassical economics at large).

Goals and purpose: efficiency and beyond

Due to the utilitarian nature of the efficiency norm, which obscures the difference between persons and ignores their inherent dignity, we need an alternative criterion on which to judge legal and policy decisions. Efficiency has a clear technical advantage over richer alternatives – it is simple. But simplicity is no virtue if it comes at the expense of realism, precision, or ethics. Quantification of costs and benefits that are ultimately subjective in nature lends welfare economics an air of pseudo-scientism, for the sake of which they exclude that which cannot be quantified. This inevitably leads to a neglect of exactly what social economists find lacking in law and economics: recognition of the immeasurable, incomparable and inviolable dignity embodied in human beings.

The most essential role that economics has to play in legal studies is to recommend how scarce resources are to be allocated to achieve the purpose of the legal system. It is not by accident that economists claim that this purpose is to promote efficiency, and neither is it an accident that lawyers bought into it so quickly. George Fletcher writes that 'American law professors have been receptive to economic analysis of the Kaldor/Hicks variety because the culture of American law has long had strong ties to utilitarian thought' (1996, p. 162). Elsewhere, he attributes economics' success in tort law to the 'scientific image' granted by the formal, multi-step process of the cost minimization model, which thereby 'basks in the respectability of precision and rationality . . . Yet associating rationality with multistaged argumentation may be but a spectacular lawyerly fallacy – akin to the social scientists' fallacy of misplaced concreteness (thinking that numbers make a claim more accurate)' (Fletcher, 1972, p. 573).

But the purpose of the legal system does not have to be efficiency, or, for that matter, any utilitarian goal. For instance, many legal scholars think the purpose of the tort system is to ensure corrective justice, which holds that victims of wrongful harm are entitled to compensation from their injurers as a matter of right.[25] A tort system based on corrective justice may lead to lower accident costs, but that is not its primary purpose. Likewise, some think that the criminal justice system should not be geared primarily toward efficient deterrence of future crimes, but instead punishment of ones actually committed, a stance generally known as retributivism.[26] Again, a retributivist criminal justice system may lead to more efficient deterrence as well, but that would be a secondary concern. Finally, the purpose of the court system, rather than arriving at efficient outcomes, can be to arrive at truth and justice, even though cases may still be decided efficiently. Justice, right, truth – these are all immeasurable and not quantifiable, but are none the less core concepts of a liberal society, and they challenge the analytically straightforward, but normatively unsatisfying, efficiency goal that dominates neoclassical law and economics, and that social economists find offensive on many levels.

By rejecting the evaluative standards of Kaldor–Hicks efficiency and inferred Pareto improvements, a social economic approach to prescriptive law and economics might seem to hinder any change at all. After all, Kaldor–Hicks is usually promoted as a workable compromise in the face of the inapplicability of a strict Pareto standard (especially when the issue is reallocation of scarce resources). But unanimous, actual consent should not be seen as a hurdle to social change, but a precondition to any defensible proposal and an achievement to be lauded. Ideally, policy-makers should address their constituents, explain the benefits and costs of a proposal, and discuss the implications with them. Only if this is done, and consent is freely given, is respect given to the persons affected by the change. It is not that change in general will be stymied, but rather that changes that take advantage of one group of citizens for the benefit of another will be checked, and changes that benefit all – or at least are approved by all – will be adopted.

Rational choice, ethics and the will

Combining Bentham's reform-minded utilitarianism, John Austin's sanction theory of law, and Oliver Wendell Holmes's theory of the 'bad man', we have in law and economics a field seemingly custom-made for the standard assumptions of neoclassical economics – self-interested agents responding to incentives (legal sanctions as 'prices') designed to bring about behavior leading to maximal welfare or well-being.[27] I want briefly to discuss two problems with this approach, one focused on ethics, and the other on the deterministic nature of choice, and suggest ways to deal with each (separately and together).

Economists, especially social economists, have been incorporating various types of ethical behavior into models of decision-making for some time, often based on non-consequentialist or deontological concepts such as commitment, duty and obligation, that transcend preference rankings.[28] We saw the importance of deontological choice divorced from preferences in the discussion of Pareto above, in which someone may object to a proposed change, based not on her preferences but rather on her sense of justice or fairness. Also, concepts such as duty and obligation play an important role in determining persons' reactions to changes in the law, and therefore influence predictive and normative results in law and economics. But unfortunately, this approach has not yet made significant inroads into law and economics, with the exception of the literature on social norms (in so far as those norms are grounded in ethics).[29] However, several scholars writing on ethics and economics have commented on the link to law, primarily in reference to criminal behavior.[30] Much more work needs to be done incorporating an explicit moral sense into the choice models used in law and economics. For instance, to use the two examples above, how would optimal liability rules change if potential injurers were ethically motivated to take precautions against harm? Or how would optimal remedies change in contract disputes if parties to a contract behaved according to some code of ethics? Finally, with reference to crime, how would optimal enforcement and penalties change if citizens were assumed to obey the law to some extent without the threat of legal sanctions?

Also at issue is the deterministic nature of choice in economic modeling. *Homo economicus* does not have any true choice, because all of his decisions follow directly and unswervingly from his preferences and constraints – he has no agency in a meaningful sense. This is the standard model of choice among philosophers as well, usually traced back to David Hume, but is increasingly criticized of late. One such critic is philosopher R. Jay Wallace (1999), who refers to the Humean model as the 'hydraulic conception', in which the various influences on choice interact like vectors of force, with the strongest one determining the final direction of action. In other words, no agency is involved, because there is no room for human volition in this picture, only the impersonal interaction of predetermined preferences and fixed constraints. The contrasting view, in which persons have true agency, can also be interpreted as implying the existence of a true will (White, 2007), which is also linked to human dignity by many philosophers (such as Kant).

This deterministic depiction of choice is integral to law and economics, in both its positive and normative guises. In positive analysis, it allows theorists to suppose a direct and precise causal link between legal and policy changes and behavioral responses. The analogy to price effects is obvious: if grocers raise the price of bananas by 25 percent, market research can predict the size of the resulting drop in purchases of bananas, according to the estimated elasticity of demand for them. But when a criminal penalty is changed, the process is more complicated (ignoring practical issues such as how this knowledge is spread). Not only does the moral aspect of the agent's decision-making process interfere with the predicted result, but also the possibility of desire-independent reasons which by definition are not included in the standard model of rationality. These reasons are part of what philosopher John Searle (2001) calls 'gaps' in the decision-making process, one of which exists between judgment and decision, and another between decision and action. These gaps, which by their very nature are impossible to model, as they represent breaks in the deterministic process, can also be understood as the seat of the will. Although the effects of these factors can be studied and estimated, they can never be understood, and therefore changes in them are essentially unpredictable.[31]

Of course, any problem with the positive analysis of law and economics flows into the normative analysis as well. In order for economists to calculate optimal legal rules or sanctions, they need reliable predictions of behavioral effects of those rules or sanctions, and as we saw, the existence of true choice and desire-independent reasons makes this impossible. Furthermore, the link between preferences and well-being, always shaky at best, is completely ripped asunder if choices can no longer be assumed to derive deterministically from preferences. So efficiency is further damaged as an appropriate goal for law and economics, opening the door for a goal, function, or purpose more in line with human dignity.

Notes

1. For an excellent introduction to the various schools of law and economics, see Mercuro and Medema (2006). I limit my comments to neoclassical law and economics, the most prominent school; the chief proponent thereof is Richard Posner (1983, 1998a), with more recent statements such as Kaplow and Shavell (2002).
2. Law and economics scholars also usually adhere strongly to the distinction between positive and normative economics, which many social economists eschew. Katz (1996) argues interestingly that this positivism in law and economics is one reason some legal scholars cannot accept the economic approach either.
3. Though not a social economist, Zerbe (2001) argues for an amended Kaldor–Hicks criterion that explicitly includes factors such as the psychological nature of benefits and costs, transaction costs (including the costs of compensation for losses), income distribution, regard for others and rights.
4. They go on to make policy recommendations (such as income redistribution) that ignore the role of guilt and blame in punishing crime; see the discussion of crime below, and also Tullock (1975).
5. The 'law and society' movement also shares some concerns with social economics; see Donohue III (1988) and Johnston (1990) for criticism of law and economics from this perspective.
6. See Smart and Williams (1973) for a canonical debate over utilitarianism.
7. See Hoffman and O'Shea (2002), Kornhauser (2003) and White (2004b). Of course, basing any social decision on preference-satisfaction immediately raises many issues with linking preferences to well-being, including the social construction of preferences, other-regarding preferences, manipulated preferences and the like. See Nussbaum (1997, pp. 1209–11) for a unique statement of these problems, and Adler and Posner (1999, 2000) for a sophisticated analysis of such problems within cost–benefit analysis (Kaldor–Hicks efficiency).
8. This problem is exacerbated if we introduce different marginal utilities of income for different persons, but this less common assumption is not necessary to illustrate the current problem.
9. See also Baker (1975) and Leff (1974, pp. 477–81).

10. For example, Kaplow and Shavell (2001) is a six-page article in the *Journal of Political Economy*, a top-ranked mainstream economics journal, with a title presumably meant to be self-evidently condemning: 'Any non-welfarist method of policy assessment violates the Pareto principle'.

11. On non-utilitarian defenses of Paretianism, including arguments from consent, see Coleman (1980b, pp. 122–9). But as he points out elsewhere, 'because securing unanimous consent is not necessary for a change to *constitute* a Pareto improvement, the *justification* of the Pareto criteria cannot require universal consent' (1982, p. 1119). Arguing against positing a preference for consent, he writes, 'if autonomy or consent is reducible to utility or preference satisfaction, it is impossible to defend policies that maximize preference satisfaction on autonomy grounds. Such a move simply bases the pursuit of utility on the pursuit of utility. Yet it was the desire to defend Paretianism on nonefficiency grounds that motivated the argument in the first place' (1984a, p. 139).

12. Calabresi (1991) interprets the 'strict' Pareto test as including 'not only material, emotional, and psychological well-being . . . but also what might be called preferences or judgments' (p. 1215, fn. 14), such as envy and resentment, but criticizes the less strict financial interpretation for not guaranteeing consent when such non-pecuniary factors are decisive. (See also Lawson, 1992, pp. 86–8.)

13. For discussion of the internal logic and normative power of hypothetical consent, see Coleman (1980b, pp. 118–21), Dworkin (1980b, pp. 275–80), Kronman (1980, pp. 236–8), Brudney (1991) and Wennberg (2004).

14. Coleman (1980a, 1980b) provides a thorough comparison of Pareto and Kaldor–Hicks efficiency, as does Calabresi (1991, pp. 1221–7). Due to space limitations, I cannot discuss the voluminous literature criticizing the efficiency norm in general, and Richard Posner's wealth maximization in particular; for this, see the aforementioned Coleman pieces, plus Dworkin (1980a), Weinrib (1980), Kronman (1980) and Veljanovski (1981), just to cite a few.

15. The party who bears the cost of the solution does, of course, depend on the assignment of the right.

16. One could argue that if one party values a right at $100, but does not want to sell to another party who values it at $200, the potential seller's valuation is incorrect, and is actually higher than $200, which explains the decision. But the reluctant seller may have other reasons not to sell that are immeasurable in monetary terms, such as a personal dislike for the buyer that drive him to block a sale at any price. It is not that he now values the right at infinite value; rather he has something akin to a desire-independent reason not to sell (White, forthcoming).

17. These statements conflict starkly with legal positivism, a philosophical precondition for neoclassical law and economics, which denies any pre-legal, natural rights (or 'nonsense upon stilts', in Jeremy Bentham's words).

18. Posner must be given credit for recognizing some limitations of this approach: when discussing the economic analysis of rape law, which is not conclusively supportive of an unqualified prohibition, he admits 'the fact that any sort of rape license is even thinkable within the framework of the wealth-maximization theory that guides so much of the analysis in this book is a *limitation on the usefulness of that theory*' (1998a, p. 238, emphasis added).

19. As recognized by Lutz and Lux (1988), the denial of intrinsic rights also grounds the doctrine of reciprocal causation (credited primarily to Coase), in which both parties are judged to have contributed causally to an injury. 'The question is commonly thought of as one in which *A* inflicts harm on *B*, and what has to be decided is, How should we restrain *A*? But this is wrong. We are dealing with a problem of a reciprocal nature. To avoid the harm to *B* would be to inflict harm on *A*' (Coase, 1960, p. 96). But from his written examples, Coase did seem to believe in unidirectional harm, and some claim he was positing reciprocal causation merely to simplify matters and show that any intrinsic rights were irrelevant to the efficient solution being reached (Epstein, 1973; Coleman, 1980a, p. 81; Page, 1986). For counterarguments to reciprocal causation, see Mishan (1967); Epstein (1973); Fletcher (1972); Coleman (1980a).

20. See Mercuro and Medema (2006, pp. 138–44).
21. Usher lists 'four efficiency costs of the existence of theft: loss of [social value of] labour of the thief, loss of the labour of the victim who protects himself, destruction of product [lost in act of theft], and deadweight loss in underproduction of stealable goods' (1987, p. 237).
22. Klevorick's argument is more complex than this; see Coleman (1985) and Fletcher (1985) for commentary. His theory builds on previous work by Calabresi and Melamed (1972) and Posner (1985, p. 1195): 'The major function of criminal law . . . is to prevent people from bypassing the system of voluntary, compensated exchange . . . in situations where, because transaction costs are low, the market is a more efficient method of allocating resources than forced exchange.'
23. This statement foreshadows Coleman's more recent work on the economics of tort law, which he criticizes for (among other things) not accounting for the bilateral relationship between injurer and victim. Coleman (2001) suggests that a corrective justice interpretation better explains the institutional aspects of tort law, without arguing for corrective justice on normative grounds.
24. Of course, 'acceptable' would mean 'efficient', as in Richard Posner's lament that retributivist punishments may be suboptimal, 'but this is not say that there would be too much crime. There might rather be too little' (1983, p. 215).
25. For instance, both Weinrib (1995) and Wright (1995) explain tort law with a Aristotelian–Kantian conception of corrective justice, while Finnis (1980, pp. 178–9) grounds his explanation of tort law on Aquinas's idea of commutative justice. Coleman (2001) goes even further, and argues that tort law does not serve corrective justice instrumentally, but rather embodies it, and the practice of tort law helps define corrective justice.
26. See Alexander (2002, pp. 816–20) for a brief overview of the various types of retributivism, and White (2006, pp. 244–7) for more detailed criticism of economic theories of punishment from the viewpoint of Kantian retributivism.
27. Austin (1832) defined law as commands backed by threats; this theory was roundly criticized in Hart (1961), but still lingers in common discourse. Holmes famously wrote that to understand law, 'you must look at it as a bad man, who cares only for the material consequences which such knowledge enables him to predict' (1897, p. 459). Mark Lutz criticizes this line of thinking in law and economics: 'a law as such will have no effect on personal conduct but only the probability of punishment making illegal behavior more costly . . . In other words, obedience to the law is wholly contingent upon calculations of self-interest' (Lutz, 1999, p. 160).
28. For a sampling, see Sen (1977), Margolis (1982), Etzioni (1988), Minkler (1999), van Staveren (2001), Brekke et al. (2003), and White (2004a); see White (forthcoming) for a discussion of deontological choice models in economics.
29. See Mercuro and Medema (2006, ch. 6) on the various approaches to integrating social norms into law and economics.
30. For instance, see Dowell et al. (1998) and White (2005, pp. 363–4; 2006, pp. 244–9) for approaches to explaining the price/sanction distinction, also modeled by Cooter (1984). See also Nussbaum (1997, pp. 1211–12) on moral behavior and law, and Dau-Schmidt (1990) and Cooter (1998), both of whom argue that the criminal law can shape preferences.
31. Besides neoclassical law and economics, this critique has yet-unexplored ramifications for behavioral law and economics, which criticizes key rationality assumptions made in the standard literature. For a summary of behavioral law and economics, see Jolls et al. (1998); see Posner (1998b) and Rostain (2000) for criticism.

References

Adler, Matthew D. and Eric A. Posner (1999), 'Rethinking cost–benefit analysis', *Yale Law Journal*, **109**, 165–247.
Adler, Matthew D. and Eric A. Posner (2000), 'Implementing cost–benefit analysis when preferences are distorted', *Journal of Legal Studies*, **29**, 1105–47.

Alexander, Larry (2002), 'The philosophy of criminal law', in Jules Coleman and Scott Shapiro (eds), *The Oxford Handbook of Jurisprudence and Philosophy of Law*, Oxford: Oxford University Press, pp. 815–67.

Austin, John (1832), *The Province of Jurisprudence Determined*, ed. W. Rumble, Cambridge: Cambridge University Press, 1995.

Baker, C. Edwin (1975), 'The ideology of the economic analysis of law', *Philosophy and Public Affairs*, **5**, 3–48.

Beccaria, Cesare ([1764] 1986), *On Crimes and Punishments*, trans. David Young, Indianapolis: Hackett.

Bentham, Jeremy ([1781] 1988), *The Principles of Morals and Legislation*, Buffalo, NY: Prometheus Books.

Brekke, K.A., S. Kverndokk and K. Nyborg (2003), 'An economic model of moral motivation', *Journal of Public Economics*, **87**, 1967–83.

Brudney, Daniel (1991), 'Hypothetical consent and moral force', *Law and Philosophy*, **10**, 235–70.

Calabresi, Guido (1991), 'The pointlessness of Pareto: carrying Coase further', *Yale Law Journal*, **100**, 1211–37.

Calabresi, Guido and A. Douglas Melamed (1972), 'Property rules, liability rules, and inalienability: one view of the cathedral', *Harvard Law Review*, **85**, 1089–128.

Coase, Ronald H. (1960), 'The problem of social cost', *Journal of Law and Economics*, **3**, 1–44.

Coleman, Jules L. (1980a), 'Efficiency, auction and exchange', reprinted in *Markets, Morals, and the Law*, Cambridge: Cambridge University Press, 1988, pp. 67–94.

Coleman, Jules L. (1980b), 'Efficiency, utility and wealth maximization', reprinted in *Markets, Moral and the Law*, Cambridge: Cambridge University Press, 1988, pp. 95–132.

Coleman, Jules L. (1982), 'The normative basis of economic analysis: a critical review of Richard Posner's "The economics of justice" ', *Stanford Law Review*, **34**, 1105–31.

Coleman, Jules L. (1984a), 'The foundations of constitutional economics', reprinted in *Markets, Moral and the Law*, Cambridge: Cambridge University Press, 1988, pp. 133–50.

Coleman, Jules L. (1984b), 'Economics and the law: a critical review of the foundations of the economic approach to law', *Ethics*, **94**, 649–79.

Coleman, Jules L. (1985), 'Crimes, kickers and transaction structures', reprinted in *Markets, Moral and the Law*, Cambridge: Cambridge University Press, 1988, pp. 153–65.

Coleman, Jules L. (2001), *The Practice of Principle: In Defence of a Pragmatist Approach to Legal Theory*, Oxford: Oxford University Press.

Cooter, Robert (1984), 'Prices and sanctions', *Columbia Law Review*, **84**, 1523–60.

Cooter, Robert (1998), 'Models of morality in law and economics: self-control and self-improvement for the "bad man" of Holmes', *Boston University Law Review*, **78**, 903–30.

Danziger, Sheldon and David Wheeler (1975), 'The economics of crime: punishment or income redistribution', *Review of Social Economy*, **33**, 113–31.

Dau-Schmidt, Kenneth G. (1990), 'An economic analysis of the criminal law as a preference-shaping policy', *Duke Law Journal*, 1–38.

Donohue III, John J. (1988), 'Law and economics: the road not taken', *Law & Society Review*, **22**, 903–26.

Dowell, Richard S., Robert S. Goldfarb and William B. Griffith (1998), 'Economic man as a moral individual', *Economic Inquiry*, **36**, 645–53.

Dworkin, Ronald (1977), *Taking Rights Seriously*, Cambridge, MA: Harvard University Press.

Dworkin, Ronald (1980a), 'Is wealth a value?', in *A Matter of Principle*, Cambridge, MA: Harvard University Press, 1985, pp. 237–66.

Dworkin, Ronald (1980b), 'Why efficiency?', in *A Matter of Principle*, Cambridge, MA: Harvard University Press, 1985, pp. 267–89.

Epstein, Richard A. (1973), 'A theory of strict liability', *Journal of Legal Studies*, **2**, 151–204.

Etzioni, Amitai (1988), *The Moral Dimension: Toward a New Economics*, New York: The Free Press.

Fadaei-Tehrani, Reza and Thomas M. Green (2002), 'Crime and society', *International Journal of Social Economics*, **29**, 781–95.

Finnis, John (1980), *Natural Law and Natural Rights*, Oxford: Oxford University Press.

Fletcher, George P. (1972), 'Fairness and utility in tort theory', *Harvard Law Review*, **85**, 537–73.

Fletcher, George P. (1985), 'A transaction theory of crime?', *Columbia Law Review*, **85**, 921–30.

Fletcher, George P. (1996), *Basic Concepts of Legal Thought*, New York: Oxford University Press.

Hart, H.L.A. (1961), *The Concept of Law*, Oxford: Oxford University Press.

Hoffman, David A. and Michael P. O'Shea (2002), 'Can law and economics be both practical and principled?', *Alabama Law Review*, **53**, 335–417.

Holmes, Jr, Oliver Wendell (1897), 'The path of the law', *Harvard Law Review*, **10**, 457–78.

Johnston, Jason Scott (1990), 'Law, economics, and post-realist explanation', *Law & Society Review*, **24**, 1217–54.

Jolls, C., C.R. Sunstein and R. Thaler (1998), 'A behavioral approach to law and economics', *Stanford Law Review*, **50**, 1471–550.

Kaplow, Louis and Steven Shavell (2001), 'Any non-welfarist method of policy assessment violates the Pareto principle', *Journal of Political Economy*, **109**, 281–6.

Kaplow, Louis and Steven Shavell (2002), *Fairness Versus Welfare*, Cambridge, MA: Harvard University Press.

Katz, Avery Wiener (1996), 'Positivism and the separation of law and economics', *Michigan Law Review*, **94**, 2229–69.

Klevorick, Alvin (1985a), 'The economic analysis of crime', in J.R. Pennock and J.W. Chapman (eds), *Criminal Justice: Nomos XXVII*, New York: New York University Press, pp. 289–344.

Klevorick, Alvin (1985b), 'Legal theory and the economic analysis of torts and crimes', *Columbia Law Review*, **85**, 905–20.

Kornhauser, Lewis A. (2003), 'Preference, well-being, and morality in social decisions', *Journal of Legal Studies*, **32**, 303–29.

Kronman, Anthony T. (1980), 'Wealth maximization as a normative principle', *Journal of Legal Studies*, **9**, 227–42.

Lawson, Gary (1992), 'Efficiency and individualism', *Duke Law Journal*, **42**, 53–98.

Leff, Arthur Allen (1974), 'Economic analysis of law: some realism about nominalism', *Virginia Law Review*, **60**, 451–82.

Lutz, Mark A. (1990), *Social Economics: Retrospect and Prospect*, Boston, MA: Kluwer Academic Publishers.

Lutz, Mark A. (1999), *Economics for the Common Good: Two Centuries of Social Economic Thought in the Humanistic Tradition*, London and New York: Routledge.

Lutz, Mark A. and Kenneth Lux (1988), *Humanistic Economics: The New Challenge*, New York: The Bootstrap Press.

Margolis, Howard (1982), *Selfishness, Altruism, and Rationality: A Theory of Social Choice*, Cambridge: Cambridge University Press.

Medema, Steven G. (1993), 'Is there life beyond efficiency? Elements of a social law and economics', *Review of Social Economy*, **51**, 138–53.

Mercuro, Nicholas and Steven G. Medema (2006), *Economics and the Law: From Posner to Post-Modernism and Beyond*, 2nd edn, Princeton, NJ: Princeton University Press.

Minkler, Lanse (1999), 'The problem with utility: toward a nonconsequentialist/utility theory synthesis', *Review of Social Economy*, **57**, 4–24.

Mishan, E.J. (1967), 'Pareto optimality and the law', *Oxford Economic Papers*, **19**, 255–87.

Morris, Herbert (1988), 'The decline of guilt', *Ethics*, **99**, 62–76.

Nussbaum, Martha C. (1997), 'Flawed foundations: the philosophical critique of (a particular type of) economics', *University of Chicago Law Review*, **64**, 1197–214.

Page, T. (1986), 'Responsibility, liability, and incentive compatibility', *Ethics*, **97**, 240–62.

Posner, Richard A. (1983), *The Economics of Justice*, 2nd edn, Cambridge, MA: Harvard University Press.

Posner, Richard A. (1985), 'An economic theory of the criminal law', *Columbia Law Review*, **85**, 1193–231.

Posner, Richard A. (1998a), *Economic Analysis of Law*, 5th edn, New York: Aspen Law & Business.

Posner, Richard A. (1998b), 'Rational choice, behavioral economics, and the law', *Stanford Law Review*, **50**, 1551–75.
Rostain, Tanina (2000), 'Educating Homo economicus: cautionary notes on the new behavioral law and economics movement', *Law & Society Review*, **34**, 973–1006.
Searle, John R. (2001), *Rationality in Action*, Cambridge, MA: MIT Press.
Sen, A.K. (1977), 'Rational fools: a critique of the behavioural foundations of economic theory', reprinted in *Choice, Welfare and Measurement*, Cambridge, MA: Harvard University Press, 1982, pp. 84–106.
Shavell, Steven (1987), *Economic Analysis of Accident Law*, Cambridge, MA: Harvard University Press.
Smart, J.J.C. and Bernard Williams (1973), *Utilitarianism: For and Against*, Cambridge: Cambridge University Press.
Tullock, Gordon (1975), 'The economics of crime: punishment or income redistribution – comment', *Review of Social Economy*, **34**, 81–2.
Usher, D. (1987), 'Theft as a paradigm for departures from efficiency', *Oxford Economic Papers*, **39**, 235–52.
van Staveren, Irene (2001), *The Values of Economics: An Aristotelian Perspective*, London: Routledge.
Veljanovski, Cento G. (1981), 'Wealth maximization, law and ethics – on the limits of economic efficiency', *International Review of Law and Economics*, **1**, 5–28.
Wallace, R. Jay (1999), 'Addiction as defect of the will: some philosophical reflections', reprinted in G. Watson (ed.), *Free Will*, 2nd edn, Oxford: Oxford University Press, 2003, pp. 424–52.
Weinrib, Ernest J. (1980), 'Utilitarianism, economics, and legal theory', *The University of Toronto Law Journal*, **30**, 307–32.
Weinrib, Ernest J. (1995), *The Idea of Private Law*, Cambridge, MA: Harvard University Press.
Wennberg, Mikko (2004), 'Modeling hypothetical consent', *Rechtstheorie*, **35**, 71–86.
White, M.D. (2004a), 'Can *homo economicus* follow Kant's categorical imperative?', *Journal of Socio-economics*, **33**, 89–106.
White, M.D. (2004b), 'Preaching to the choir: a response to Kaplow and Shavell's *Fairness Versus Welfare*', *Review of Political Economy*, **16**, 507–15.
White, M.D. (2005), 'A social economics of crime (based on Kantian ethics)', in M. Oppenheimer and N. Mercuro (eds), *Law & Economics: Alternative Economic Approaches to Legal and Regulatory Issues*, Armonk, NY: M.E. Sharpe, pp. 351–73.
White, M.D. (2006), 'A Kantian critique of neoclassical law and economics', *Review of Political Economy*, **18**, 235–52.
White, M.D. (2007), 'Does *homo economicus* have a will?', in Barbara Montero and Mark D. White (eds), *Economics and the Mind*, London: Routledge, pp. 143–58.
White, M.D. (forthcoming), 'Deontology', in Jan Peil and Irene van Staveren (eds), *Handbook of Economics and Ethics*, Cheltenham, UK and Northampton, MA, USA: Edward Elgar.
Wright, Richard W. (1995), 'Right, justice, and tort law', in David G. Owen (ed.), *Philosophical Foundations of Tort Law*, Oxford: Oxford University Press, pp. 159–82.
Zerbe, Jr, Richard O. (2001), *Economic Efficiency in Law and Economics*, Cheltenham, UK and Northampton, MA, USA: Edward Elgar.

PART XI

THE LONG VIEW

Chapter 33: 'Technology and long waves in economic growth', by Alfred Kleinknecht and Gerben van der Panne

As early as 1930, Simon Kuznets illustrated that macroeconomic growth is composed of individual industry life cycles that can be described by logistic curves. Schumpeter (1939) argued that the start of such life cycles by major innovative breakthroughs does not come about randomly over time. Major breakthroughs tend to cluster in a 50-year rhythm. The Schumpeterian cluster hypothesis has been received with scepticism by authors such as Kuznets, Solomou, Freeman and Soete, or Verspagen and Silverberg. Our inspection of time series of 'basic innovations' leads us to conclude that Schumpeter's cluster hypothesis has a degree of realism.

Chapter 34: 'Analysing regional development: from territorial innovation to path-dependent geography', by Frank Moulaert and Abid Mehmood

This chapter gives an overview of models that can be used to analyse regional development as well as to design policies and strategies for the future of regions and localities. It evaluates the analytical and policy relevance of these models, and offers some recommendations for a more structural realist approach to spatial development analysis. Section 2 provides an overview of territorial innovation models (TIM), which theorize local and regional development from a new regionalism point of view, and explains why they fall short of 'realist' regional development analysis, strategy and policy design. Section 3 then makes a plea for a return to the 'old' institutionalist and structuralist tradition of regional development analysis. Finally, Section 4 makes some methodological recommendations, focusing on contemporary spatial development analysis within a framework of integrated regulationist, cultural political economy and network theoretical approaches, and taking full cognizance of the structural-institutional, scalar and cultural dimensions of development processes and strategies.

Chapter 35: 'Radical institutionalism', by William M. Dugger

Radical institutionalism is largely a US, English-speaking school of socioeconomic thought. However, it is not closed-minded or xenophobic, being highly critical of the biased geopolitical and *laissez-faire* content of the 'Washington Consensus'. Its immediate origins were the social movements of the 1960s and it is commited to the peaceful approach to change. It rejects the validity of the positive–normative split promoted by neoclassical economics. Reducing corporate power, inequality and war, and expanding social nurturing, equality and abundance, are its social goals. In working towards transforming rather than reforming the modern economy, radical institutionalism follows Thorstein Veblen more closely than his cofounder of institutionalism, John R. Commons. Radical institutionalism is critical of the market, insisting that democratic policy-making and economic planning are needed in addition to and as substitutes, complements and supports for market processes.

Chapter 36: 'Exploitation and surplus', by Phillip Anthony O'Hara
The purpose of this chapter is to examine the various meanings and interpretations of exploitation as it relates to the problem and realization of surplus value. After a brief interlude on a neoclassical interpretation of exploitation, three main approaches are analysed that link specifically to surplus. The first is the traditional Marxist theory of labour power being remunerated with a wage, while labour produces in addition a surplus value. The second approach extends the analysis further to the social foundations of the political economy, including elements such as trust, sociality and familial capital. The third approach links to social structures of accumulation, and the institutional basis of exploitation, and surplus production and realization. A brief interlude examines the nature of systems to reduce or eliminate exploitation.

33 Technology and long waves in economic growth
Alfred Kleinknecht and Gerben van der Panne

1. Introduction

Many people have accepted the existence of the classical business cycle of seven to ten years in length, sometimes also referred to as the 'Juglar cycle'. The idea, however, that there may be a (regular) long-term variation in the speed of economic growth of some 50 years, with 20–25 'good' years being followed by 20–25 'bad' years (the so-called Kondratieff wave) has always remained controversial among economists and economic historians. It is tempting to give some credit to the concept of Kondratieff waves, as it could explain why the dark period between 1929 and World War II has been followed by an unprecedented 'Golden Age' of capitalism, lasting up to the early 1970s. After the mid-1970s, there was a growing perception that the good times were *passé*, but after the mid-1990s, with an upward shift in US productivity growth, we suddenly had euphoria about a 'new economy'.

It is surprising to note that many adherents of the 'new economy' did not seem to be aware that many of their observations fitted nicely into the old-fashioned concept of the Kondratieff wave. Ignorance of history can be misleading. Once the hype was over (after the crash of the NASDAQ index in spring of 2000), many believed that the 'new economy' story was fake. From the viewpoint of a possible long wave in economic life, however, one tends towards a more positive evaluation. It could well be that, in the years ahead of us, the diffusion of ICT will foster restructuring of the economy, productivity growth and numerous (incremental and radical) product and service innovations in a broad range of sectors, as did railways, electricity or automobiles in the past. A bold prediction to be derived from a Schumpeter–Kondratieff perspective will be that, after 2020, ICT will have reached the stage of a 'normal', mature industry, with normal growth and normal profit rates, following a calm neoclassical regime, after its wild Schumpeterian phase from the 1990s onwards. In future years, we may look back to the present days as having been quite a 'good' period. This chapter does not intend to speculate about the future, however, but will sketch what can be learnt from the past.

The three most important early contributors to the theory of Kondratieff long waves were Van Gelderen (1913), De Wolff (1924, 1929) and Kondratieff

(1926).[1] Kondratieff became the most famous of the three, as two of his major articles were translated from Russian into German (1926, 1928) and, later, into English.[2] The studies by Van Gelderen and De Wolff, which were published earlier, anticipated many of Kondratieff's arguments, but were published only in the Dutch language and therefore remained relatively unknown outside the Netherlands. In his *History of Economic Analysis*, Schumpeter coined a term for the approximately 50-year-long waves, calling them 'Kondratieff waves' and this has become generally accepted.

The early contributions by Van Gelderen, De Wolff and Kondratieff were quite similar in their content and they were based on fairly simple observations. Long waves of about 50 years were, at the time, easily observable from two types of time series: price indices and interest rates. (Wholesale) price indices showed long periods of inflation and deflation, each lasting approximately 20–25 years. Similar fluctuations were found in real interest rate series. At those times, periods of rising prices were considered 'good times' as rising prices indicated that demand was larger than supply. Deflationary periods were 'bad times' as supply seemingly exceeded demand. The pioneers of long-wave studies therefore believed that what they observed were fluctuations in the general rhythm of economic life that affected not only prices and interest rates but also the 'real' economy.

One of the first contributors sceptical about this belief was Garvy (1943), arguing that it was doubtful whether Kondratieff's long waves could indeed be found in time series for the real economy, for example production and trade. This gave rise to concerns about whether Kondratieff's long waves were a 'real' (and not just a monetary) phenomenon. During a renewed rise in interest in long waves in later periods, several authors engaged in econometric analyses of time series. We discuss their contributions briefly below. Even more serious concerns were raised by Kuznets (1940) in his discussion of the work by Schumpeter (1939), the latter being one of the 'believers' in long waves. The contribution of Kuznets is remarkable and merits closer inspection.

2.   The Kuznets–Schumpeter discussion

Simon Kuznets, in his 1930 *Secular Movements in Production and Prices*, was the first to demonstrate that macroeconomic growth was built up of numerous s-shaped industry life cycles. These life cycles followed breakthrough innovations that initiated new industries:

> In many industries there comes a time when the basic technical conditions are revolutionized . . . In all these cases we observe a revolutionary invention or discovery applied to the industrial process which becomes the chief method of production . . . When such a change occurs, the industry grows very rapidly. The innovation is rarely perfect at the start, and further improvements take place

continually after the main invention or discovery. The use of the continually improving and cheapening commodity spreads to larger areas, overcoming obstacles that may have limited demand in the past . . . But with all this, after a time the vigorous expansion slackens and further development is not so rapid. (Kuznets, 1930, p. 10)

At the time, Kuznets believed breakthrough innovations to be *randomly* distributed over historical time. Nine years later, in his *Business Cycles*, Schumpeter (1939) proposed that these life cycles were not randomly distributed on the time axes but tended to occur in clusters, an idea that had already been formulated by Kondratieff (1926). Clustering implies that, at any point in time, several of these industry life cycles tend to be in the same stage (i.e. slow start, or rapid expansion, or saturation). This might give rise to fluctuations in real economic growth at the macro level. A year later, in a famous review article of Schumpeter's *Business Cycles*, Kuznets (1940) articulated severe criticism: Schumpeter had failed to give a satisfactory explanation of why innovations should cluster, and why the alleged Kondratieff waves should occur, and Schumpeter had also failed to give any serious empirical underpinning for his speculative construct.

Kuznets's criticism was tough and, at the time (in 1940), it was credible. As a consequence, Schumpeter and his theory became *passé*. From then to the late 1970s, little was published on Kondratieff long waves or on Schumpeterian innovation clusters. In the wake of a Schumpeter renaissance during the 1980s and 1990s, however, various scholars have reinvestigated Schumpeter's cluster-of-innovation hypothesis, but the discussion remained controversial. In this chapter we give a brief historical sketch of this discussion and, thereafter, we address analyses of time series of major innovations that have been produced by other authors. We do not undertake econometric analyses of *economic* time series, as this has been done quite thoroughly by other authors (the best contributions coming from Reijnders, 1984, 1990, 1992; Bieshaar and Kleinknecht, 1984; Metz, 1992). We conclude, in our final section, that there is something to be said in favour of a rehabilitation of Schumpeter's (1939) cluster-of-innovations hypothesis.

3. Requirements of a (long) cycle theory

When discussing the realism of the Schumpeter–Kondratieff long-wave hypothesis, one needs first to remember that any such theory will need to fulfil demands such as those formulated by Kuznets:

To establish the existence of cycles . . . requires first a demonstration that fluctuations of that approximate duration recur, with fair simultaneity, in the movements of various significant aspects of economic life . . . and second, an

> indication of what external factors or peculiarities of the economic system proper account for such recurrent fluctuations. Unless the former basis is laid, the cycle type distinguished cannot be accepted as affecting economic life at large . . . Unless the second, theoretical, basis is established there is no link that connects findings relating to empirical observations of a given type of cycles . . . with the broader realm of already established knowledge. Neither of these bases has ever been satisfactorily laid for the Kondratieff cycles . . . The prevalence of such fifty-year cycles in volumes of production . . . in employment, in physical volume of trade, has not been demonstrated; . . . Nor has a satisfactory theory been advanced as to why these 50-year swings should recur . . . (Kuznets, 1940, p. 267)

It is hard to deny that this statement by Kuznets was realistic at that time (i.e. in 1940). During the Schumpeter renaissance of the 1980s, several authors tried to meet the above-quoted demands made by Kuznets. A first strand of research related to time-series analyses of industrial production or national product data of advanced countries. While some authors (among whom were Van Ewijk, 1981, 1982; Solomou, 1986) arrived at sceptical results, others were affirmative of Kondratieff waves. In an important but sparsely noticed *Social Science Information* article, Reijnders (1984) formulated a criticism of authors such as Van Ewijk (1981, 1982), who had transformed original time series into trend-free series by using first differences. According to Reijnders, such a transformation is not as innocent as it may look when first seen: transformation into first differences will increase the noise in the series and it may also favour the discovery of 'waves' that are half as long as the waves that are really in the series.

In 1990, Reijnders demonstrated the existence of Kondratieff long waves in real output series. Independently, Metz (1992) applied a novel method of de-trending economics series and also concluded that Kondratieff long waves exist. In our judgement, both authors have given a satisfactory answer to Kuznets's above-quoted first demand: to show that wave-like movements, corresponding to the periodization of Kondratieff, have indeed occurred in important indicators of general economic performance.

4.   Breakthrough innovations: random walk or clustering?

This leaves us with Kuznets's second demand: what are the causal mechanisms behind such fluctuations? Without a satisfactory theory, one could argue that observed movements in economic time series are due to historically unique or accidental factors and they can therefore not be considered as 'cycles'. In other words, if there is no evidence of an 'endogenous' cycle mechanism, there are no reasons to expect such movements to be repeated in the future.

During the Schumpeter renaissance of the 1980s, a second strand of research focused on finding theoretical explanations for long waves.

Particular attention was given to Schumpeter's (1939) hypothesis that innovations cluster in historical time. Mensch (1979) was the first to rediscover the old Schumpeterian argument that major breakthrough innovations ('basic innovations') would be introduced into the market discontinuously in time, that is, with a roughly 50-year rhythm. This implies that several industry growth cycles initiated by such 'basic innovations' would tend to pass simultaneously through the same stages: slow introduction, rapid take-off, or saturation thus being a cause of fluctuations in macroeconomic growth. Mensch also provided data on 'basic innovations' that should prove the realism of Schumpeter's cluster hypothesis. A few years later, however, Freeman, Clark and Soete (Clark et al., 1981; Freeman et al., 1982) provided a tough criticism of Mensch's innovation series. Their criticism related to problems of precise timing of the introduction years of 'basic innovations', to Mensch's sampling procedures, and, in particular, to the inclusion or exclusion of certain doubtful cases.

Another round of discussion was initiated by Solomou's (1986) *Cambridge Journal of Economics* article, arguing that there was little evidence of Schumpeterian clusters of innovations. He received a reply in the same journal. In a critical re-examination of times series of three different authors, Kleinknecht (1990) concluded that, using an appropriate timing of waves (close to the original dating by Kondratieff, 1926), there was evidence of clusters of major innovations. In a quite recent contribution in the same journal, however, Silverberg and Verspagen (2004) again raised doubts about the realism of Schumpeter's cluster-of-innovations hypothesis. The remainder of this chapter will be dedicated to an appraisal of their criticism.

The testing of Schumpeter's cluster-of-innovations hypothesis was essentially based on three time series of 'basic innovations': one by Mensch (1979), one by Haustein and Neuwirth (1982) and one by Van Duijn (1983). Freeman et al. (1982) criticized the series by Mensch and made some amendments and updates to his twentieth-century data. Below, we use an amended version of the Mensch data. Obviously, in collecting cases of 'basic' innovations, there remains some room for judgement about what is 'basic'. Probably everybody would agree that cases such as the first successful application of the steam engine, the first commercial bicycle or photography should be included. However, what about cases such as 'refined steel/Bessemer steel', the 'first portable camera' or 'reinforced concrete'? There clearly is room for personal judgement. This is also evident from the fact that the data collections by Mensch, Haustein and Neuwirth, and Van Duijn do not show much overlap. Figure 33.1 shows that 44 cases of basic innovation are named in all three sources. Forty-eight cases have been included in two out of three sources and 119 cases are named in only one source, being ignored by the other two data collectors.

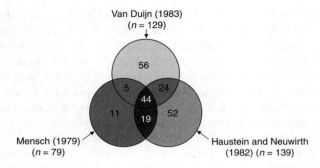

*Figure 33.1   Overlap between three samples of basic innovations
            (1861–1968)*

The discrepancies in data collection decisions shown in Figure 33.1 can be due to using different historical sources or due to the different personal judgements made by the data collectors. It should be beyond doubt that really famous historical cases of breakthrough innovations are named in numerous historical sources and therefore have a high chance of being picked up by more than one data collector. Moreover, with respect to 'classical' cases of breakthrough innovations, data collectors will differ little in their decision to have them included. It seems realistic to assume that the 44 cases that are named in all three data series are 'safe' cases of basic innovations, the inclusion of which requires little debate. The 48 cases that come back in at least two out of the three sources will probably also cover fairly safe cases. However, the 119 cases that have been included in only one out of the three sources are likely to cover more doubtful cases. The last group may be cases that are named in only few technical history records and therefore have less chance of being discovered by data collectors. And if they had been discovered, the data collectors may have had doubts about whether or not to consider them as 'basic' innovations.

In his appraisal of the evidence, Kleinknecht (1990) therefore decided to introduce some weighting procedure, giving more weight to fairly safe cases, that is, those picked up by more than one of the three data collectors, than to the less safe cases, that is, those found in only one of the three sources. Silverberg and Verspagen (2004) complain that Kleinknecht's weighting procedure 'introduces an element of extreme arbitrariness' (ibid., p. 676). We disagree with them for the following reasons: first, Silverberg and Verspagen's decision *not* to apply any weighting is, in a sense, also arbitrary. Not using explicit weights implies that all cases, safe or doubtful, receive the same weight. Second, they use only the Van Duijn and the Haustein and Neuwirth data, omitting the (amended) Mensch data. Third,

Table 33.1 Mean numbers of breakthrough innovations per year according to various sources

	Series of 'basic innovations' by three authors			Three versions of merging the three series		
	Van Duijn (1983)	Haustein and Neuwirth (1982)	Mensch (1979)[a]	Version 1*	Version 2**	Version 3***
1861–81	0.95	1.00	–	2.80	0.90	2.35
1881–1901	1.10	1.45	–	3.50	1.05	2.35
1901–27	0.96	0.81	0.48	2.19	0.58	1.38
1927–62	1.66	1.51	1.28	4.09	1.00	2.63
1962–	0.33	1.07	0.57	1.40	0.20	0.40
Chi-square	9.4	7.6	10.9	10.6	12.1	12.3
Levels of significance	0.053	0.106	0.004	0.032	0.016	0.015

Notes:
[a] Twentieth-century data by Mensch as revised by Clark et al. (1981) and Freeman et al. (1982).
* Adding up all cases from the three sources. This implies that cases named in all three sources, the most reliable ones, are counted three times; cases named in two of the three sources are counted twice and single cases are counted once.
** We omit the least reliable cases, i.e. those named in only one out of three sources. Cases named in two out of three sources (or in three out of three sources) are counted once.
*** As in version 2, but cases named in two sources are counted twice; cases named in three sources are counted three times.

as will be seen below, the outcomes of our test of the significance in mean numbers of innovations between time periods are not sensitive to alternative ways of applying weights. It is, however, important that some weights are applied.

Silverberg and Verspagen are right in one point of their criticism: Solomou (1986) and Kleinknecht (1990) applied t-tests of differences in mean innovation rates for predefined periods. These tests assume that the data are normally distributed. Silverberg and Verspagen are probably right that they are not. In Table 33.1 we therefore apply a test that does not assume normal distribution: the Kruskal–Wallis test.

From Table 33.1 it can be seen that there are differences in mean numbers of innovations across time periods that follow the classical dating of Kondratieff waves with a 12-year lag.[3] It should be noted, however, that the evidence is not clear-cut if the individual series by the three authors are tested separately. The differences in mean innovation rates in the Van Duijn series just fail to be significant at a 95 per cent level; the Haustein and Neuwirth series fails even at a 90 per cent level of significance. This is not surprising, given that these series cover many uncertain innovation cases that are not included in the series of the other two data collectors (see Figure 33.1). This underlines our plea for introducing some form of weighting procedure.

Whatever weighting we apply, version 1, 2 or 3 (see the explanation in the footnote of Table 33.1), it turns out that differences in mean numbers of innovations for the predefined periods are highly significant according to the Kruskal–Wallis test, which does not require the observations to be normally distributed (Newbold, 1995). It is interesting to note that version 1, which still includes the cases from one source only, has a slightly lower level of significance, while significance levels of versions 2 and 3, excluding these less safe cases, are higher. As a control, we also tested a series that consists exclusively of less safe cases, that is, those named in only *one* of the three sources. As expected, this series, not documented here, was found to show *no* significant differences in innovation rates across predefined Kondratieff periods. These outcomes support the view that, taking the classical dating by Kondratieff as a reference, there is a 12-year lagged fluctuation in the innovation series.

5.   Concluding discussion

In his 1930 *Secular Movements in Production and Prices*, Simon Kuznets gave substantial empirical support to the idea that macroeconomic growth is built up of a series of individual industry life cycles. Each of these life cycles follows some breakthrough innovation. After the initial breakthrough, the basic concept will be developed via large series of subsequent improvement innovations, aiming at quality improvement as well as at cost reduction via incremental innovations. As David Landes has noted in his classic *The Unbound Prometheus* (1969), it is the large stream of subsequent improvements that push the new industry into a virtuous circle of productivity gains, price reductions and expansion of demand. In the course of time, however, improvements are subject to the law of diminishing returns, and therefore, at some time, expansion will slacken.

We argued above that there is something to be said in favour of Schumpeter's (1939) hypothesis that breakthroughs may be clustered on the time axes. One of Schumpeter's arguments for clustering over time was that various breakthrough innovations may be technically linked. A breakthrough in one field will enable breakthroughs elsewhere.

Another argument may be related to the concept of opportunity costs: once a new industry life cycle is under way, there will be high gains in terms of productivity and quality improvements, translating into high growth of demand and profits. This is likely to attract talent and capital to the new industry. As long as the 'bandwagon' of this new industry is rolling strongly, there are high opportunity costs for developing uncertain new break-throughs elsewhere. This may explain why, once new growth industries show rapid expansion, investors will concentrate on incremental innovation within these industries rather than trying to achieve radical break-throughs in other, still uncertain, areas. However, once the stream of improvement innovations is subject to diminishing returns, increasing saturation of demand and declining profits will lower the opportunity costs of switching to completely new technological trajectories. Of course, such a switch will involve uncertainty. The history of breakthrough innovations is full of trial and error, false starts, dead ends and new departures, and all this takes real, historical, time. It appears plausible that the period between the (gradual) saturation of earlier technological trajectories and the take-off of new ones might well have the length of a Kondratieff period of weak growth of some 20 years, leaving open the question of whether, in the course of the current IT revolution, wave periods may become shorter.

Finally, it is tempting to interpret the recent hype around a 'new economy' in this theoretical context. The rise of ICT and an associated increase of productivity growth in the USA might well be part of a new upswing of the Schumpeter–Kondratieff wave. Temporary spurts in economic growth due to a temporarily higher speed of technical change fit into the neoclassical theory of economic growth that considers 'technical change' as a main driver of long-run economic growth. At the same time, however, for a neoclassical economist, trained in general equilibrium thinking, it is hard to accept the idea that the capitalist system will *endogenously* bring about long-run fluctuations in economic growth.

There is therefore enough room for further scepticism and discussions. Clearly, various propositions around the Schumpeter–Kondratieff wave need further investigation. Students of Kondratieff long waves meet several problems that explain why consensus has not yet been reached. First, many important historical time series are of limited length and, notably during the eighteenth and early nineteenth centuries, of poor quality. Second, all series were seriously disturbed by events such as the Napoleonic Wars and the two world wars, causing outliers. Outcomes of econometric time-series analyses are sensitive to treatment of these outliers. Third, we have the problem of how to develop indices of major technological breakthroughs, data collection not being free of personal judgement. All this is likely to feed a continued debate between believers and non-believers in Kondratieff long waves.

Notes

1. A review that includes some other precursors of long-wave theory can be found in Kleinknecht (1987).
2. An exhaustive survey of the literature (in German) has been given by Spree (1991, pp. 3–138).

3. When counting average numbers of innovations per Kondratieff period, I realized that my earlier count of numbers of basic innovations (Kleinknecht, 1990) and the counting documented here differ slightly in several cells, although both countings are based on the same original sources.

References

Bieshaar, H. and A. Kleinknecht (1984), 'Kondratieff long waves in aggregate output: an econometric test', *Konjunkturpolitik*, **30**, 279–303.
Clark, J., C. Freeman and L. Soete (1981), 'Long waves and technological developments', in D. Petzina and G. van Roon (eds), *Konjunktur, Krise, Gesellschaft*, Stuttgart: Klett-Cotta, pp. 132–69.
De Wolff, S. (1924), 'Prosperitäts- und Depressionsperioden', in O. Jenssen (ed.), *Der Lebendige Marxismus: Festschrift für Karl Kautsky*, Jena: Thuringer Verlagsanstalt.
De Wolff, S. (1929), *Het Economisch Getij*, Amsterdam: J. Emmering.
Freeman, C., J. Clark and L. Soete (1982), *Unemployment and Technical Innovation: A Study of Long Waves in Economic Development*, London: Pinter.
Garvy, G. (1943), 'Kondratieff's theory of long cycles', *Review of Economics and Statistics*, **25**, 203–20.
Haustein, H.D. and E. Neuwirth (1982), 'Long waves in world industrial production, energy consumption, innovations, inventions and their identification by spectral analysis', *Technological Forecasting and Social Change*, **22**, 53–89.
Kleinknecht, A. (1987), *Innovation Patterns in Crisis and Prosperity. Schumpeter's Long Cycle Reconsidered*, London: Macmillan and New York: St Martin's Press.
Kleinknecht, A. (1990), 'Are there Schumpeterian waves of innovation?', *Cambridge Journal of Economics*, **14**, 81–92.
Kondratieff, N.D. (1926), 'Die langen Wellen der Konjunktur', *Archiv für Sozialwissenschaften und Sozialpolitik*, **56**, 573–610.
Kuznets, S. (1930), *Secular Movements in Production and Prices*, Boston, MA: Houghton Mifflin.
Kuznets, S. (1940), 'Schumpeter's business cycles', *American Economic Review*, **30**, 257–71.
Landes, D. (1969), *The Unbound Prometheus*, Cambridge: Cambridge University Press.
Mensch, G. (1979), *Stalemate in Technology*, Cambridge, MA: Ballinger.
Metz, R. (1992), 'A re-examination of long waves in aggregate production series', in A. Kleinknecht, E. Mandel and I. Wallerstein (eds), *New Findings in Long-wave Research*, London: Macmillan and New York: St Martin's Press, pp. 80–119.
Newbold, P. (1995), *Statistics for Business and Economics*, London: Prentice-Hall.
Reijnders, J.P.G. (1984), 'Perspectivistic distortion. A note on the approximation of trends and trend-cycles', *Social Science Information*, **23**, 411–26.
Reijnders, J.P.G. (1990), *Long Waves in Economic Development*, Aldershot, UK and Brookfield, USA: Edward Elgar.
Reijnders, J.P.G. (1992), 'Between trends and trade cycles: Kondratieff long waves revisited', in A. Kleinknecht, E. Mandel and I. Wallerstein (eds), *New Findings in Long-wave Research*, London: Macmillan and New York: St Martin's Press, pp. 15–44.
Schumpeter, J.A. (1939), *Business Cycles*, New York: McGraw-Hill.
Silverberg, G. and B. Verspagen (2004), 'Breaking the waves: a Poisson regression approach to Schumpeterian clustering of basic innovations', *Cambridge Journal of Economics*, **27**, 671–93.
Solomou, S. (1986), 'Innovation clusters and Kondratieff long waves in economic growth', *Cambridge Journal of Economics*, **10**, 101–12.
Spree, R. (1991), 'Lange Wellen wirtschaftlicher Entwicklung in der Neuzeit. Historische Befunde, Erklärungen und Untersuchungsmethoden', *Historische Sozialforschung/Historical Social Research*, No. 4 (Supplement), 3–138.
Van Duijn, J.J. (1983), *The Long Wave in Economic Life*, London: Allen & Unwin.
Van Ewijk, C. (1981), 'The long wave – a real phenomenon?', *De Economist*, **129**, 324–72.
Van Ewijk, C. (1982), 'A spectral analysis of the Kondratieff-Cycle', *Kyklos*, **35**, 468–99.
Van Gelderen, J. (pen-name J. Fedder) (1913), 'Springvloed', *De Nieuwe Tijd*, **18**, 253–450.

34 Analysing regional development: from territorial innovation to path-dependent geography
Frank Moulaert and Abid Mehmood

1. Introduction

With the rise (or the 'return'?) of 'Regionalism', the study of regional development and policy has once again become a major focus in social science spatial analysis. To benefit fully from the long tradition of research in this field (say starting with the German historical school in the nineteenth century), an equilibrated use of 'old' and 'new' epistemological stances and of 'back to basics' regional analysis is needed – the latter being a plea by Lovering (2001).[1]

Over the last 20 years regional development has been addressed mainly through the bird's-eye view of territorial and especially regional innovation models, the spearheads of the so-called 'new regionalism' movement. These models, discussed in section 2 as Territorial Innovation Models (TIMs) (a generic or family name for industrial district, *milieu innovateur*, learning region, among others; see section 2 for details), were a significant advance on neoclassical regional growth analysis because they enabled the filling of the 'black box' – the institutional dynamics of development – traditionally left untouched by neoclassical economics. However, territorial innovation models go only half-way in solving the analytical problems in regional development and policy analysis.

The epistemological reductionism of TIMs (a capitalist market economic ontology: collapse of past and future perspectives, empirical and normative stances, institutions and structure, cultural and economic norms) means a backwards step compared to previous regional *development* theories. Therefore, section 3 argues in favour of a return to the 'old' institutionalist tradition of regional development analysis (German historical school, Gunnar Myrdal, François Perroux, the French school of disequilibrated spatial development, radical geographers of the 1970s, etc.). Indeed, these theories are more advanced in distinguishing the analytical features of regional development from its design strategy: by combining these analytical features with recent insights from cultural political economy and relational economic geography, these theories could be made useful relatively easily for the analysis of regional development and policy in this era of globalization. The final section is devoted to methodological reflections about the study of regional development. It dwells on contemporary attempts to accomplish new syntheses (based on territorial embeddedness, relational complexity, strategic coupling), and explicitly chooses to connect cultural political economy, regulationist and 'empowered' network approaches in order to underpin regional development and policy analysis today. Such a connection should lead to the definition of a structural-realist meta-theoretical framework within which more issue-focused spatial theories can be brought into use.

2.　Territorial innovation models: what are they telling us?[2]

Territorial Innovation Models (TIMs) are models of regional innovation in which *local institutional dynamics* play a significant role as catalysts (especially positive) in innovative development strategies. Most of these models address the following features of development and innovation as well as the relationships between them: the core of the innovation dynamics, the role of institutions, the view of regional development, culture, the types of relations among agents and the types of relationships with the environment. Three main families of TIM can be identified.[3] The first contains the *milieu innovateur* and the industrial district model. The French model *milieu innovateur*, which was the basis for the synthesis produced by GREMI (Aydalot, 1986), stresses the role of endogenous institutional potential in producing innovative dynamic firms. The same basic idea is found in the industrial district model, which focuses even more on the role of cooperation and partnership within the innovation process (Becattini, 1987). The second TIM family contains models belonging to the tradition of the systems of innovation: a translation of institutional coordination principles found in sectoral and national innovation systems onto the regional level (Edquist, 1997) or, more properly, an evolutionist interpretation of the regional learning economy within the regional space (Cooke, 1996; Cooke and Morgan, 1998). The third TIM tradition stems from the Californian school of economic geography: the new industrial spaces (Storper and Scott, 1988; Saxenian, 1994). In addition, there is a residual category, encompassing 'spatial clusters of innovation', which is not really another TIM family, as it has little affinity to regional analysis but lies close to Porter's clusters of innovation. All these models share a large number of key-concepts that have been used in regional economics or analysis for a long time, or that have been borrowed from other disciplines, especially in social science.

　　Table 34.1 summarizes the meaning of territorial innovation and its features in most of these models.[4] The learning region model has not been included because it can be considered as an essential synthesis of the features of many of the other TIMs.

Table 34.1 Views of innovation in territorial innovation models

Features of innovation	*Milieu innovateur* (Innovative milieu) (MI)	Industrial district (ID)	Model Regional innovation systems (RIS)	New industrial spaces (NIS)
Core of innovation dynamics	Capacity of a firm to innovate through relationships with other agents of the same milieu	Capacity of actors to implement innovation in a system of common values	Innovation as an interactive, cumulative and specific process of R&D (path-dependency)	A result of R&D and its implementation; application of new production methods (JIT etc.)
Role of institutions	Very important in the research process (university, firms, public agencies etc.)	Institutions are 'agents', enabling social regulation, fostering innovation and development	As in the NIS, definitions vary according to authors. But all agree that the institutions lead to a regulation of behaviour, both inside and outside organizations	Social regulation for the coordination of interfirm transactions and the dynamics of entrepreneurial activity
Regional development	Territorial view based on *milieux innovateurs* and on agent's capacity to innovate in a cooperative atmosphere	Territorial view based on spatial solidarity and flexibility of districts (flexibility as an element of innovation)	View of the region as a system of 'learning by interacting/and by steering regulation'	Interaction between social regulation and agglomerated production systems
Culture	Culture of trust and reciprocity links	Sharing values among ID agents – trust and reciprocity	The source of 'learning by interacting'	Culture of networking and social interaction

Table 34.1 (continued)

		Model		
Features of innovation	*Milieu innovateur* (Innovative milieu) (MI)	Industrial district (ID)	Regional innovation systems (RIS)	New industrial spaces (NIS)
Types of relations among agents	The role of the support space: strategic relations between the firm, partners, suppliers and clients	The network is a social regulation mode and a source of discipline, enables coexistence of cooperation and competition	The network is an organizational mode of 'interactive learning'	Interfirm transactions
Types of relations with the environment	Capacity of agents to modify their behaviour according to changes in environment. Very 'rich' relations: third dimension of support space	Relationships with environment impose some constraints and new ideas. Must be able to react to changes in the environment. 'Rich' relations. Limited spatial view of environment	Balance between inside specific relations and environment constraints. 'Rich' relations	Dynamics of community formation and social reproduction

Source: Moulaert et al. (1999).

Most TIMs stress the instrumentality of institutions in the economic restructuring and improved competitiveness of regions and localities. But in none of these models is reference made to improving non-economic dimensions and non-market-led sections of regional and local communities, unless such improvements could contribute in some way to the competitiveness of the territory. According to the TIM, quality of life in local and regional communities depends on growth of prosperity and will appear as a positive externality of higher economic growth; no distinction is made between well-being and growth, or between community culture and business climate.

There is no doubt that TIMs take a significant step forward when compared to orthodox models of spatialized economic 'development' (e.g. neoclassical regional growth models) in that they recognize the explicit role of institutions (including firms) and their learning processes as key factors in economic development. In this way, they fill the 'black box' of the neoclassical model of the firm and its networks which disregards the institutional dynamics of innovative agents, and considers only the logic of rational economic agency. TIMs are therefore more socially sophisticated than neoclassical regional growth models, for they perceive institutional dynamics (culture, learning organizations, networks) as improving the market-competitiveness of the local economy. (In orthodox development discourse, one could say that they make 'development' functional to 'growth': the neo-classical adage turned upside down!) But at the same time TIMs reflect a societal ontology with a restricted view of economic development: innovation and learning will improve the market-economic performance of a region or a locality, and in this way will contribute to the achievement of other developmental goals (economic, social, political, cultural).

In other words: implicitly, TIMs do not consider either the multifunctionality or the allocative diversity of the economy – an economy that is in reality much broader than the capitalist market economy – or the other existential (non-economic) spheres of local and regional communities, such as the natural environment, the social–cultural (artistic, educational, social services) and the socio-political sphere. Despite their devotion to institutional dynamics, they are sworn to a market-based economic ontology and technological view of development. They blatantly overlook the past and present role of the structural mechanisms of growth and decline, even and uneven interregional exchange and development mediated by these institutions and their strategic agencies (cf. Holland, 1976). One could argue that in the TIM view of institutionalization, the 'lightness of being' of the rationalist behavioural perspective transforms the institutional complexity of the real world and its development paths into self-evident pathbreaking strategic behaviour – thus rationalizing history as if it were organically engineering the innovative future!

Another ontological aspect of the market-economist and instrumentalist view of institutional dynamics inherent in TIMs is the narrow view of regional economic development policy. In tune with the TIM ontology, economic policy sectors are honed by prioritizing technological innovation and rationalist learning procedures, while other sectors are geared towards market-led economic policy. Cultural, educational, transportation, urban development policies and so on all become more or less subjugated to market competitiveness and lose the *raison d'être* and policy purpose specific to their own logic in contributing to the cultural, educational and environmental emancipation of human beings and their social groupings (Moulaert and Nussbaumer, 2005).

Finally TIMs suffer from what we could call a 'localist trap'. For a variety of reasons, they regard regional and local development strategies using endogenous resources as the appropriate answer to the uneven and unequal consequences of globalization and strategies of global players. This position waters down into a naïve misjudgement of the role of the latter and into an unbalanced view of how realistic regional development strategies should take into account both global players and especially their 'focal firms' (see Coe et al., 2004 on the global production network perspective); at the same time this denial of the 'evil of the global' leads to an unrealistic understanding of the power of endogenous resources (in Lacanian terms: the denial of the impact of the Real) and how these have been managed. It would, for example, be interesting to apply this perspective to Hassink and Lagendijk's (2001) observations on the 'scant attention to interregional dimension of learning', contrasting with the strong focus on regional learning in regional development analysis. In its most extreme reading the 'localist trap' also means that TIMs are defined in economic and political isolation from the outside world. Old insights (see Section 3) that TIMs can only be successful thanks to economies of scale (and not only of scope, as TIMs do recognize) and high-value-added trade networks, and that regions and localities are competitors within a wider economy and polity – with the risk that in absence of appropriate national and supranational development policies only a limited number among them will succeed – seem to have been forgotten. True, contemporary new regionalism analysis is more realistic about this and 'places increased weight on extra-local dynamics shaping economic growth within regions' (Coe et al., 2004, p. 469), but it remains an enigma why today, in order to bring 'new regionalism' back to this level of geographical complexity, established verities of the 1970s about path-dependency and the meaning of wider spatial scales for development had to be reinvented from scratch.

These ontological positions of TIMs have inspired at least two major epistemological miscarriages that affect these models' utility for regional development and policy analysis, and generate a need for significant revisions.

First, TIMs do not manage to disentangle normative from analytical perspectives in regional development research. The most significant consequence of this is that 'intentionality of change in agency' (e.g. innovative strategies, improved organizational learning) is taken as the main driving force of actual regional development. This leads recurrently to a situation in which real-life strategies are analysed as 'imagineered' future behaviour, as if the past and present of regional development can be explained only as the result of rational innovative behaviour within effectively organized learning processes (Moulaert and Sekia, 2003).

Second, despite TIMs' significant contribution to reinstitutionalizing the study of territorial development, their analysis of institutional dynamics is framed by the instrumental interpretation of 'territorial institutions for market-led growth' and by what Hess (2004) calls an 'over territorialized view of embeddedness'. This leads, for example, to either an overdeterministic explanation of the role of globalization – the global shapes the local institutions – or a naïve understanding of the width of the manoeuvring space left to endogenous strategies within the global economy and society.[5]

To overcome these epistemological flaws in the explanation of regional development and policy, we turn in Section 3 to 'older' and/or more 'cultured' theories that offer clearer explanations of the relationship between past, present and future; agency, structure and institutions; institutions and culture; and development and policy.

More recent attempts to overcome the devotion to local endogeneity have been made by the 'strategic coupling' approach (Coe et al., 2004), the revisiting of 'relational economic geography' (Yeung, 2005), the contextualization of the territorial embeddedness approach (Hess, 2004) and the path-dependent definition of local development strategies (Cox, 2004). These we deal with in Section 4 as a spring-board for the presentation of our own analytical synthesis.

3. Old-timers on regional development

We have seen in Section 2 that in contemporary literature on regional development 'new regionalism' and TIMs are playing the first violin. But we noticed that these models suffer from ontological and epistemological flaws: they use idealized categories of design strategies for future development also as key categories in the analysis of the structural and institutional dynamics of the past; and they prototype regional development policy as almost exclusively targeting improved competitiveness. To this end they search for good or best practice combinations of technology and organization, supported by regional and local institutional catalysts. Most contributions from new regionalism refer to a path-dependency of regional development which is usually limited to the continuity of culture patterns and modes of social association between innovative agents and which does not consider the constraining or incapacitating impact of the historical paths followed by the so-called 'abstract' structures of the capitalist economy (division of labour, wage–labour relationship, competition between capital and market structures).

In this section we briefly survey 'old timers', which in their days did not suffer from the institutional instrumentalism and selective a-historicism we have observed in TIMs. We successively look at historicism, the schools of disequilibrated growth, and radical economic geography. In the latter part of the section, we also turn to recent contributions in cultural political economy that can be considered as bringing a new dimension to regional development analysis.

3.1   Historicism and territorial development

The German historical school (GHS) has been the basis of the development of twentieth-century economic growth and development theory.[6] GHS contributions to a better understanding of the *Nazionalökonomie* and the various analyses of the stages of economic growth have had a major impact on later national and regional development theory and analysis. However, post-World War II 'stages of growth' theory can be only indirectly connected to the GHS, mainly because the German literature was not well known to Rostow and others, and also because of the influence of the British classical school on the rise of the 'stages of economic growth' analyses which transformed the reading of historical development into a time-series record of economic growth performance indicators (see Hoselitz, 1960). A significant difference between the GHS and the classical economists is that the GHS had already offered a real theory of economic dynamics (e.g. the idea of cumulative causation) whereas the classical economists provided principles only for economic dynamics (such as the role of the changes in the division of labour following Adam Smith) while maintaining the view of an organic tendency towards equilibrium both of the economy and among its agents.[7] The GHS contributed to the making of territorial development analysis in the following three ways:

The recognition of the growing role of the state and industrialization
Nussbaumer (2002) demonstrates that significant numbers of ideas found in post-World War II literature on local and regional development were already present to some extent in the writings of the GHS. For example, the

focus on the social dynamics of development, connected to the building of the nation-state from the different German (regional) states; social relations between the nation-state and economic development; and the culturally embedded socio-economic organization of economic activities, have all been active features of discussion in the GHS literature.

Space as a historical category   Gustav Schmoller's writings (1884, 1905) have applied historical embeddedness to spatial analysis. Using an anthropological perspective, he showed how society appropriated space through the development of institutions that organize it according to the needs of the population. In other words: spatial institutions materialize the social relations that are developed in a community. Therefore the evolution of needs and the economic system implies a transformation of the institutional configuration of space. The relative importance of institutional levels varies according to their relevance for the development of the (regional, local) community. However, institutional evolution is not uniformly harmonious but produces conflicts. Power relations, both within and between institutions, form part of a dialectical movement. The interrelations between economic actors illustrate the political dimension of development; for instance, those who try to influence policies by integrating town councils, and political powers that try to orient and promote economic activities (see also François Perroux and Gunnar Myrdal, next subsection). Space, considered from the perspective of its appropriation through (re)institutionalization, is embedded in the movement of history.

Spatial and territorial approach   The GHS territorial approach to development was mainly developed by Gustav Schmoller. He showed how competition and cooperation within and between institutions are important in creating opportunities for political intervention and for interaction between political action and the transformation of the economic system. This idea, linked to the emphasis on the combination of development factors necessary to generate development and the recognition that social relations within a group or community are part of the development process, leads to an analysis of development that links market mechanisms to social interaction.

3.2   Embedded regional development and cumulative disequilibrium
In the 1960s (or late 1950s) the simultaneous discovery of the difficulties of development in the South and of regional and local problems of development in industrialized countries due to massive transformation of the industrial system (Hirschman, 1984) highlighted the significance of spatial scales of development and their diversified political and economic dynamics.

However, it would be illusionary to think that a smooth interparadigmatic path of scientific progress led from the GHS scholars to the spatial development analysts of the 1960s. In the first half of the twentieth century a rupture in the analysis of spatial development (and location) came with the rise of neoclassical location and central place theory. There were many reasons for this paradigmatic discontinuity, of which we cite only the few most important: (1) US scholars' (who until the interbellum still frequently trained at German universities) disapproval of German imperial policy – especially under the Nazi regime – led to a loss of interest in the GHS that was strongly focused on the role of institutions in general and the state *par excellence*; (2) the euphoric spread of positivist scientific methods in social science – finally social science becomes 'real science'! Positivist methodology development was invigorated by the rise of formal (algebraic) location analysis, already present at the end of the nineteenth century, especially in Germany, which began to overrule the GHS approach by the second quarter of the twentieth century.

Gradually, by the 1930s but especially after World War II, a growing separation occurred between pseudo-classical or neoclassical location theory and regional growth theory on the one hand, and institutionalism-rooted regional development theory on the other. The latter includes authors such as Gunnar Myrdal (1957), Albert Hirschman (1958) but also François Perroux (1955, 1983, 1988). Perroux is remembered especially for his analysis of the relationships between economic agglomeration on the one hand (growth poles within geographical space) and externalities (technological, pecuniary) and power relations on the other; his growth pole and regional development analysis adopts a strong institutional perspective and shows how unevenness in economic relations is institutionally confirmed, with only well-established public policy being capable of countering uneven development.

An interesting novel presentation of Myrdal's work on spatial socio-economic development is given by Meardon (2001, p. 49), who argues:

> In sum, Myrdal's theory of agglomeration was part of a holistic alternative research program. Its main components were a critique of predominant economic theory, the development and interdisciplinary application of the concept of cumulative causation, and the proposal of public policies intended to reduce international, interregional, and even interracial inequalities – all founded upon explicitly stated value premises.

For our purpose the 'application' of his cumulative causation framework to regional and interregional development is of particular interest. Myrdal discusses cumulative causation in terms of a tension between backwash and spread effects. He explains how agglomerations often originate as a consequence of either a single or a few economic initiatives (historical accidents) but that their development and dominance over lesser centres is a result of ever-increasing internal and external economies in the growth centres. Cultural and political processes play a significant part in this, and the increasing inequality between growth and lesser centres can only be overcome by active and sustained public initiative (Myrdal, 1957).

The confrontation between these institutionalist regional development analyses and the new regionalism is instructive and shows how the latter has simplified the 'regional world' into an agency space combining institutional and economic engineering – far removed from the real spaces of cumulative causation of growth and development in leading regions and localities, where political power-broking and unequal exchange-based trade and investment networks play a significant part. This analysis of Myrdal and others also provides arguments explaining why worldwide maybe a thousand rather than a million TIMs will flourish within the real global world and how successful regions will extort resources (human capital, innovative ideas, finance capital) from less successful or poorer regions.[8]

3.3 Political economy of regional development

The political economy of regional development examines the deployment of the relations of production both within and as reproduced by the 'systems of regions'. The most interesting analytical frameworks have been developed quasi simultaneously by Doreen Massey (1984) and Alain Lipietz (1977). Both look at the articulation between the (spatial) hierarchy of the division of labour on the one hand and the reproduction of regional inequality on the other. Later contributors such as Markusen (1983) and Hudson (2001) have broadened the concept of social relations and its role in the analysis of the regionalization process and thus attributed more value to non-reductionist interpretations of regional development; and Sum (2006) has valorized the potential of a more culture-enhanced approach to regional development. These and other authors have stressed the need for better articulation of the different social processes through which space is constantly reproduced – and thus *de facto* executing Lefèbvre's concept (1974) in which he distinguishes between perceived, conceived and lived space and paves the way for a more counter-hegemonic, lived-diversity-based approach to spatial development strategies.

The spatial division of labour In his book *Le capital et son espace*, Alain Lipietz (1977) develops a Marxist theory of regional development. It combines an explanation of the regional inequality problem in terms of the condition of the rural economy in France with a spatial division of labour model of manufacturing and service activities across the space-economy. To do so Lipietz analyses 'interregionality' ('les rapports qui s'établissent entre régions inégalement développées au sein d'une zone d'intégration articulée en circuits de branches desservant un marché unique',[9] p. 84) on the basis of the flows or circuits of the branches of production. For this purpose he examines the articulation between 'pre'-capitalist relations of production – especially as materialized in traditional agriculture – and the capitalist relations of production as expressed in manufacturing (especially Fordist) branches of production. Lipietz analyses explicitly both the development of, and the articulation between, modes of production within the complexity of state–capital relations (i.e. the complexity of national social formations, regional armatures and the overarching 'imperialist multinational bloc'). He establishes a hierarchical typology of regions: central, intermediary and peripheral. His original empirical basis for this work is the spatial development of industry in relation to agriculture in France; later he completes his analysis using evidence from the regional development of the service sector, which he considers as a further though partial expression of the permanent laws of capital accumulation (concentration, agglomeration of capital, de-skilling of direct producers etc.) and which he links to the deskilling industrialization of metropolitan regions both internally and at their peripheries (Lipietz, 1980, p. 68).

Doreen Massey's analysis of divisions of labour and the reproduction of uneven spatial development in the UK has strong parallels with Lipietz's in France. Massey:

> If the social is inextricably spatial and the spatial impossible to divorce from its social construction and content, it follows not only that social processes should be analysed as taking place spatially but also that what have been thought of as spatial patterns can be conceptualised in terms of social processes . . . The primary social process which the geography of jobs reflects is production. The spatial distribution of employment, therefore, can be interpreted as the outcome of the way in which production is organised over space. (Massey, 1984, p. 67)

Then Massey develops the argument that the social relations of production are necessarily deployed in space and in a variety of forms, which she calls spatial structures of production. Such spatial structures, although often similar across social spaces, should never be considered as archetypes, deterministically reproduced through the reproductive dynamics of capitalism. Instead the geographical forms of the organization of production should be examined empirically. In capitalist production systems two distinct types of hierarchies quite often overlap and reinforce each other: (1) the managerial hierarchy – comparable to Hymer's control structure linking headquarters to subsidiaries and branch plants (Hymer, 1972); (2) the hierarchy of the production process itself with R&D (often) separated from it; and R&D itself consisting of the production of technically more complex components (engineering) and the final assembly of commodities. Massey stresses that in most cases a country's national economic geography – perceived as the ensemble of geographical forms of the organization of the economy – 'reflects its position in the international political economy, the international division of labour' (ibid., pp. 82–3).

Both Lipietz and Massey keep underlining that the reproduction of social space is not a one-way outcome of the organization and reproduction of the capitalist production system. Massey: 'Spatial structures are established, reinforced, combated and changed through political and economic strategies and battles on the part of managers, workers and political representatives' (ibid., p. 85). Political struggle will ultimately determine these forms. However, national territories and their spatial organization significantly reflect the unevenness embedded in the corporate hierarchies, be it manufacturing firms (Hudson, 2001) or service providers and their networks (Martinelli and Moulaert, 1993). But the material outcome of this use of space will ultimately depend on capital–labour relations within the regional system, the strength of the unions and the strength of the class-balance of the state apparatus.

Cultural and socio-political dimensions of regional development Note that these analyses of regional development, although attaching significant importance to social relations and regulation (especially by the state), still employ an economic interpretation of social relations and their spatial forms. Later work, often influenced by Lefèbvre (1974), such as the regulationist analysis of spatial development (Leborgne and Lipietz, 1990; Moulaert et al., 1988; Moulaert and Swyngedouw, 1989; Moulaert, 1996) and gender and diversity literature (see, e.g., Blunt and Wills, 2000), broadens the whole idea of social relations in space, and shows how different conceptions of space lead to a better understanding of regional development, its potential opportunities and how these feed into the development paths and visions of past and present.

Lefèbvre's generic work on the production of (social) space has had a determining influence on spatial analysis across most disciplines. In his Marxist approach to space, Lefèbvre contrasts perceived, conceived and lived space, and addresses the spatial character of each of them by distinguishing spatial practices, representations of space, and representational spaces. Although he stresses the relations of production and their spatial deployment when applying these trialectics to capitalist society, his approach, more than that of Lipietz and Massey, leaves all doors open to look beyond 'abstract' space created by capitalist dynamics, and to include (other than production) social relations, representations of space and representational spaces involved in the reproduction of society and the interaction between hegemonic and counter-hegemonic movements. However, Lefèbvre never breaks the links between production relations and other social relations in society.

Over the last 15 to 20 years several contributions to regional development analysis have used a broader perspective on social relations, encompassing empirical complexity as well as the role of culture and social diversity in their interpretation. We cite here four contributions in particular:

1. *Markusen's (1983) work on regionalism and regional development.* Markusen explains how territorially defined regions are relevant to political economists when conflicts in social relations of production are perceived as regional conflicts by the actors involved. She calls this perception *regionalism*, 'the espousal of a territorial claim by some social group', or in the case of a political movement, 'the political claim of a territorially identified group of people against one or several mechanisms of the State . . .'. Although 'regionalism' for Markusen is clearly a subjective and experiential term, it can also refer to objective social dynamics that cause territorial differences in social formations. In this way it may refer to the different social relations and institutions that embody or govern relationships within the human community: the household, the state and cultural institutions.

    Because the term *region*, warns Markusen, 'connotes a territorial, not social, entity', its use can lead to a number of analytical errors. First, region might be confused with all social relations that are territorially based. As such, a class conflict or a conflict between cultural groups might be wrongly perceived as a conflict between regions (Markusen gives a number of examples). Second, it is probable that the existing territorially defined regions (state, cultural identity, natural habitat etc.) are only partially relevant to the spatiality of the social relations determining the dynamics of social reality in the region.

    Although Markusen explains very well how territorially defined regions can be an issue in political economy, a regional issue itself can only be fully understood if the spatial expression of the social relations – that is, the spatial organization of which the region forms a part – is fully understood also. Markusen's framework recognizes the diversity of social relations – beyond strict confinement to (social) relations of production – and thus is highly significant for the analysis of the spatial nature of social and economic development within and across regions and localities.

2. *Gender and diversity*. The inclusion of gender and diversity (using a multi-ethnic perspective, for example), together with the role of the wage–labour relationship in the analysis of regional development, has enriched the understanding of the role of female and migrant labour in regional labour markets (Massey, 1984), the uneven reproduction of patriarchal professional hierarchies (Mullings, 2005) and the design of alternative emancipation and spatial development strategies (Blunt and Wills, 2000).

3. *Regulation approach and local/regional development*. The 'territorialization' of the regulationist approach has reinvigorated the debate on the analytical (and strategic) weaknesses of regulation theory and contributed to overcoming them (Leborgne and Lipietz, 1990; Moulaert et al., 1988; Moulaert and Swyngedouw, 1989; Moulaert, 1995). Reformulating regulationism, after a refreshing territorial bath, is meant to enable this at first national social formation-oriented analytical framework to address regional development. The revisited regulationist approach includes: (i) an articulated time-space approach to subsequent modes of development and their concrete forms; (ii) a greater focus on the impact of non-economic structural dynamics on regional and local development; (iii) the broadening of the reading of regulatory dynamics from 'pure economic' and 'state agency' to different types of formal and informal regulation; (iv) redefining the role of agency and behavioural codes within the broader definition of institutional dynamics; (v) a reading of social reproduction at the local and regional level which is both extensive and respecting of diversity, and is in tune with recent insights on the role of culture, gender and diversity in spatial development strategies, institutionalization and structural transformations; (vi) the recognition of power relations together with social and political struggle as critical analytical categories in regulation theory (Moulaert et al., 2000). These improvements to the regulationist approach – already either made effective or else in progress – within the territorial regulationist approach resonate with most of the concerns about the one-track approach of political economy, that is, overemphasis on the determinist explanatory power of the social relations of production, and how to overcome them. One major exception is the role of discourse both in reproducing culture and as a 'real' strategy, which has been a concern of the cultural political economy approach to socio-economic development.

4. *Cultural political economy and discourse*. Recent work on the relationships between culture, discourse, identity and hegemony (CDIH) has laid the foundations for an improved integration of two analyses: the analysis of social and cultural embedding of agency and the social

construction of institutional change (the 'pure' cultural turn in social science) as well as the more 'structural–materialist' social science analysis stressing the historical specificity and material effectivity of economic categories and practices as applied by, for example, the regulation approach or the strategic-relational approach (Sum, 2006, 2005; Jessop, 2001; Jessop and Sum, 2006; Sum and Jessop, 2007). According to Sum (2006, p. 6),

> The CDIH model [within the cultural political economy approach] seeks to develop a more balanced approach that pays due attention to the material–discursive nature of social relations, albeit based on a more open conception of social structure [Smart, 1986; Fairclough, 1992; Jessop, 1990; Gibson-Graham, 1996], as well as to the strategic-discursive moment that is associated with the textual or semiotic aspects of social relations and their emergent properties.

Over the last few years cultural political economy (CPE) approaches have enriched regional development analysis by focusing on the role of discourse and identity-building in defining regional and urban policy and interpreting 'histories' of regions and cities. The most promising of these applications are based on the integration of critical discourse analysis into variants of the regulation approach that retain strong residual elements of the Marxist critique of political economy. In this way, CPE takes the cultural turn, with its emphasis on discursive–strategic questions, in the analysis of socio-economic development without sacrificing the lessons of a materialist–structural analysis of the historically specific socio-economic dynamics of capitalist economies. Following Sum (2005), this integration examines the development of economic imaginaries and associated *grand narratives* at various *interlocked spatial scales*; and also explores how these imaginaries and narratives facilitate the emergence and consolidation of not only hegemonic systems (of which they are also an important moment) but also of counter-hegemonic movements. Economic imaginaries involve spatio-temporal horizons of action and are institutionalized in specific spatio-temporal matrices and, as such, have major implications for spatial development. In particular, they have a significant impact on how regulation and strategic agency are reproduced at the regional and local level. Moreover, the modes by which grand discourses are reproduced via struggles at the *global and national scales* are highly relevant in coming to grips with the role of discourse in reproduction and accumulation at the local and regional level. Interesting illustrations of this approach are Hajer (1995), Sum (2002) on Hong Kong, Gonzalez (2005, 2006) for the Basque Country and Bilbao (Northern Spain),

Raco (2003) on Scotland, McGuirk (2004) on Sydney, and Moulaert et al. (2007) in relation to urban redevelopment policy in Milan, Antwerp, Vienna and Naples.

4. Methodological prospects: breaking through the time-space constraints of relational geography?

Over the last 15 to 20 years the literature on regional development and regional development policy has been dominated by the new regionalism approach and its territorial innovation models, of which the most popular today is the learning region. Although new regionalism did reintroduce the role of institutional dynamics and path-dependency into regional development analysis, unfortunately its analytical potential soon became constrained by a contemporary reading of the historical and institutional foundations of development, thus reducing path-dependency to the reproduction of specific assets and institutions within local and regional communities. At the same time, the scalar geography of this approach overplayed the role of the local and regional territory at the expense of interdependencies with other spatial scales. By doing so, the opportunities or constraints stemming from globalization were often miscalculated, and the critical role of supraregional governance – with still currently an important role for the national state – overlooked. As a consequence, TIMs have become idealized icons of development dreams instead of much-needed models addressing the politics and policy of the possible (Novy and Leubolt, 2005; Swyngedouw, 2005).

4.1 Beyond new regionalism

Recently several attempts have been made to overcome some of the flaws of new regionalism models. We address consecutively the approaches of strategic coupling, of social embeddedness and of relational geography.

Coe et al. (2004, p. 469) explain how the *strategic coupling approach* offers a way out of the localist trap overshadowing the TIMs:

> Drawing upon a global production networks (GPN) perspective and deriving insights from both the new regionalist and GCC (Global Commodity Chain) and GVC (Global Value Chain) literatures, our approach focuses on the dynamic 'strategic coupling' of global production networks and regional assets, an interface mediated by a range of institutional activities across different geographical and organizational scales. Our contention is that regional development ultimately will depend on the ability of this coupling to stimulate processes of value creation, enhancement and capture.

Although the strategic coupling approach offers a major corrigendum to the most localist among the TIMs, it is not really as successful as it claims in analysing regional development as a set of relational processes.

Although we support a process view of regional development, in our opinion processes involve more than relational dynamics as analysed in the relational geography approach. Two other recent contributions from (economic) geography have scrutinized 'spatial' relationships in development. The 'social embeddedness' approach attempts to bypass the limits of territorial embeddedness – often implicitly assumed in many TIMs. Hess (2004) seeks to do so by illuminating the concept of 'embeddedness', first by explaining the evolution of embeddedness in Karl Polanyi's work and then moving on to Granovetter's distinction between relational and structural embeddedness, with 'the former describing the nature or quality of dyadic relations between actors, while the latter refers to the network structure of relationships between a number of actors' (ibid., pp. 170–71). Two observations should be made on Hess's synthesis of the 'rescaled' embeddedness approach: it overcomes the local-scale bias of embeddedness in a positive way (social embeddedness occurs at related spatial scales); but unfortunately it clings to an 'interactive' interpretation of social structure – in fact it uses a definition of social structure as 'interactively constructed', not historically and 'societally' reproduced.

A similar observation can be made about Yeung's (2005) critical survey article on relational economic geography, which is both illuminating and debate provoking. Yeung – inspired by Jessop (2001) – rightly points out that the recent relational turn in economic geography is mainly a thematic one and that an ontological–epistemological relational turn is still to come. He connects the recent popularity of relational thought in economic geography partially to the analytically limited (presumed) structural determinism of social relations of production (and spatial division of labour; see Section 3.3.1 above) that leaves little room to analyse mid-range institutionalization and micro agency. He compares three recent thematic turns in relational geography: (1) regional and local development as a function of synergized relational assets; (2) relational embeddedness in networks; and (3) relational scales. (1) coincides largely with the theoretical approach used in the new regionalism/TIM approach while (2) matches the 'social embeddedness' line of analysis summarized and revisited by Hess. But (3) in our opinion offers a misunderstanding of the meaning of the scalar articulation approach. Swyngedouw, Peck, Brenner and others do not offer a relational geography approach – at least not in the interactive interpretation of relationality which Yeung attributes to these authors – but make a successful attempt to overcome the scalar problem of the reproduction of social relations in space (see especially Swyngedouw, 1997). To do so, they improve mainly on the territorialized version of the regulation approach which, although it provides the analytical key to the spatial articulation approach, strangely enough is not mentioned in Yeung's article. This observation is not just hair-splitting, but points to a significant distinction between the meanings of 'relationality' in the different 'relational turns' examined by Yeung: for the authors of the scalar articulation approach, relationality refers to social relations in the political economy meaning of the term, and not to interactive dynamics as meant in both the new regionalism or social embeddedness thematic turn. A real 'methodological' relational turn should clarify this distinction, as it should also clarify the distinction in relationality between objects and as social processes. In the political economy and the regulation approach, for example, social relations are not relations between objects but are social processes that are historically and spatially articulated. As a consequence, therefore, they cannot be changed as a rule through the action of individual actors but through social forces such as (counter-) hegemonic movements, institutionalization processes, cultural upturns and so on. And they are different ontologically and epistemologically from the type of relationality studied in mainstream network analysis. More careful study is therefore needed of the types of relationality that are relevant to economic geography.

4.2 Towards a meta-theory for regional development analysis
To re-equilibrate the framework of regional development analysis, a return is necessary to the 'old' interpretation of institutional dynamics and structural relations. But to lead a comprehensive analysis of regional development these (rediscovered) structures as time-and-place robust institutions and mediated social structures should be combined with an interactionist view of relations between 'development' agents and a cultural perspective on their agency and institutionalization. To achieve this synthesis it could be worthwhile combining an empowered network perspective (Moulaert and Cabaret, 2006) with a 'culturalized' regulation perspective – an integration of a regulation approach with a cultural political economy perspective (Jessop and Sum, 2006; Moulaert et al., 2007), which together would offer a meta-theoretical framework that could host various contributions from old and new institutional and political economy approaches to regional development.

Our support for this meta-theoretical integration is based on our agreement with relational (socio-) economic geography that relationality has many dimensions: interaction, embeddedness and scalar articulation; at the same time our endeavour is a reaction against the 'networkish' interpretation of relationality inherent in most relational geography applications, which stress the central role of agents as architects of networks and their institutions while overlooking the role of structural relations – as processes – in the reproduction of agency networks and their institutions. To calibrate this reaction, we appeal to a regulation approach but one upgraded from a

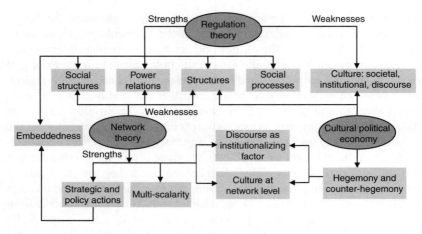

Figure 34.1   A meta-theory for regional development analysis: regulation, network and CPE approaches

cultural political economy perspective, as argued in Section 3. Figure 34.1 and the subsequent discussion reflect how a meta-theoretical foundation can be established.

Moulaert and Cabaret (2006, p. 54) argue that using the network metaphor as a concept for analysing real-life situations as basically the interaction between agents and the resulting outcomes is a logical intellectual ambition:

> Human life, organizations and agencies are based on interactions between human beings that are to a large extent networked amongst themselves. Agents (individuals, organizations) develop and share cultures, modes of communication, principles of (network) action and ways of building institutions. These institutions will of course not just be the outcome of voluntary institutional engineering within the networks, but will also depend on the interaction between the network dynamics, the network environment and the development paths of the society and communities to which the network belongs. Thus network theory is useful in modeling strategies and policy actions in regional and local development.

Better than 'structural' social theories, the network metaphor, by looking at cognitive processes, the role of network culture and the production of discourse, offers a natural link to cultural political economy. However, most current network theories defend reductionist rational approaches to human behaviour, stress the role of procedures in information-gathering, exchange and institution-building, but deal very poorly with social structures, power and power relations. To overcome this weakness, regulation theory can step in.

Although regulation theory, like Marxism, primarily looks at economic (strategic) behaviour, its theorizing of social and political structure as social relations focused on power relations and institution-building as a social process is relevant to 'empowering networks' within society. Similarly, property relations, labour–capital relations, finance capital, the state as an extended logic of capital and so on play a direct role in most networks embedded in the socio-economic world. In network terminology, this means that stakeholders hold significantly unequal stakes, the decision-making space is limited or uneven, and, in extreme cases, the outcome of negotiation processes is known beforehand, because the structural–institutional impact of the logic of capital and politics is so influential. By using the embeddedness metaphor of Polanyi and Granovetter, therefore, we could not only embed the network analysis of strategic behaviour and policy-making by leading regional and local agents within the regulationist approach of social relations, but also use that approach to study the reproduction of the economic, political, social and cultural structures of the region and its localities (Moulaert and Swyngedouw, 1989).

These structures – together with the networks embodying their microdynamics – would then become 'encultured', under the cultural political economy's revisiting of social analysis by looking at the role of culture, identity and discourse and how they affect social forces and strategic agency. As indicated in Section 3, the work of Sum (2005, 2006) in particular has been bridge-building in this respect. Inspired by Jessop (1990) and Anglo-Foucauldian theorists such as Rose and Miller (1992) and Dean (1999), Ngai-Ling Sum has designed a heuristic device that links the macro- and microprocesses – especially stressing the role of discourse – of hegemony and counter-hegemony-making. In six interrelated moments that highlight the discursive dimensions of social relations and individual and collective agency, she provides the concepts necessary to analyse the relationship between 'real' and 'cultural' articulation via the examination of struggles involved in the material–discursive practices of everyday life. As shown in cited case studies (Section 3), this adds real value to the understanding of culture and discourse in regional and local development and policy.

We label the integration tripod of network theory, regulation approach and cultural political economy as a 'meta-theoretical framework' because it provides an ontology and epistemology of spatial development analysis, but does not expand the specific theories that shed light on the various dimensions and questions of regional and local development. To this end, we should return to the survey of theories in Sections 2 and 3 which offer specific intelligence on each of these dimensions: Myrdal on economic and political factors and mechanisms of centre–periphery relations; Hirschman on the significance of political processes in regional development; Lipietz on the links between the reproduction of economic structure and the state apparatus; Markusen on the role of social and political movements in the regionalization process; and many others. Looking at these theories within this newly defined triangular field of 'social relations–networks of agents–cultural dynamics' may offer a wind of change – yet one redolent of the prickling dust of historical manuscripts that are badly needed today but have rested for too long on library shelves – in addressing regional development and policy.

Notes

1. This chapter deals with regional development, not regional growth theories. Although there are affinities between the analytical traditions, we have no space to deal with both and prefer to address the more 'quality features'-oriented development theories. As a consequence we shall not, for example, present the debate on new economic geography and regional endogenous growth models (see, e.g., Fujita et al., 1999).
2. This section is based on Moulaert and Nussbaumer (2005). Copyright granted by Sage Publications.
3. For details see Moulaert et al. (1999).
4. For more details see Moulaert et al. (1999). See also MacKinnon et al. (2002), who among other critical observations point out how the learning region model underemphasizes the articulation among spatial scales in learning dynamics.
5. In an authoritative Roepke lecture Peter Dicken has shown that the interplay between states and firms in a global economy still looks to a large extent like an international economy, in which major national political and economic agents seek to implement their particular national agendas (Dicken, 1994).
6. The GHS also played a significant role in the genesis of location theory; this is not developed here. See Nussbaumer (2002).
7. We should also keep in mind that the theory of stages of economic growth also had an influence on Lösch's theory of system of regions (Lösch, 1938).
8. See also Williams et al. (2004) on the relationship between migration flows and uneven development in contemporary Europe.
9. The relations which establish themselves between unequally developed regions at the heart of a process of articulated integration between production circuits serving a unique market.

References

Aydalot, P. (1986), *Milieux innovateurs en Europe* (*Innovative 'Milieux' in Europe*), Paris: GREMI.
Becattini, G. (1987), *Mercato e forze locali: il distretto industriale*, Bologna: Il Mulino.
Blunt, A. and J. Wills (2000), *Dissident Geographies: An Introduction to Radical Ideas and Practice*, Harlow, UK: Pearson Education.
Coe, N.M., M. Hess, H.W.C. Yeung, P. Dicken and J. Henderson (2004), ' "Globalizing" regional development: a global production networks perspective', *Transactions of the Institute of British Geographers*, **29**, 468–84.
Cooke, P. (1996), 'Reinventing the region: firms, clusters and networks in economic development', in P. Daniels and W. Lever (eds), *The Global Economy in Transition*, Harlow, UK: Longman.
Cooke, P. and K. Morgan (1998), *The Associative Region*, Oxford: Oxford University Press.
Cox, K.R. (2004), 'Globalization and the politics of local and regional development: the question of convergence', *Transactions of the Institute of British Geographers*, **29**, 179–94.

Dean, M. (1999), *Governmentality: Power and Rule in Modern Society*, London: Sage.
Dicken, P. (1994), 'The Roepke lecture in economic geography. Global–local tensions: firms and states in the global space-economy', *Economic Geography*, **70** (2), 101–28.
Edquist, C. (ed.) (1997), *Systems of Innovation: Technologies, Institutions and Organizations*, London: Pinter.
Fairclough, N. (1992), *Discourse and Social Change*, Cambridge: Polity.
Fujita, M., P. Krugman and A.J. Venables (1999), *Spatial Economy: Cities, Regions, and International Trade*, Cambridge, MA: MIT Press.
Gibson-Graham, J.K. (1996), *The End of Capitalism*, Oxford: Blackwell.
Gonzalez, S. (2005), 'The politics of the economic crisis in the Basque Country and Spain during the 1980s', *Space and Polity*, **9** (2), 93–112.
Gonzalez, S. (2006), 'Scalar narratives in Bilbao. A cultural politics of scales approach to the study of urban policy', *International Journal of Urban and Regional Research*, **30**, 836–57.
Hajer, M. (1995), *The Politics of Environmental Discourse: Ecological Modernization and the Policy Process*, Oxford: Oxford University Press.
Hassink, R. and A. Lagendijk (2001), 'The dilemmas of interregional institutional learning', *Environment and Planning C: Government and Policy*, **19** (1), 65–84.
Hess, M. (2004), ' "Spatial" relationships? Towards a reconceptualization of embeddedness', *Progress in Human Geography*, **28** (2), 165–86.
Hirschman, A.O. (1958), *The Strategy for Economic Development*, New Haven, CT: Yale University Press.
Hirschman, A.O. (1984), 'The on and off connection between political and economic progress', *The American Economic Review*, **84** (May), 343–8.
Holland S. (1976), *Capital versus the Regions*, London: Macmillan.
Hoselitz, B.F. (1960), *Theories of Economic Growth*, New York: Free Press.
Hudson, R. (2001), *Producing Places*, New York: Guilford Press.
Hymer, S. (1972), 'The multinational corporation and the law of uneven development', in J.N. Bhagwati (ed.), *Economics and the World Order*, London: Macmillan.
Jessop, B. (1990), 'Regulation theories in retrospect and prospect', *Economy and Society*, **19** (2), 153–216.
Jessop, B. (2001), 'Institutional re(turns) and the strategic relational approach', *Environment and Planning A*, **33**, 1213–35.
Jessop, B. and N.-L. Sum (2006), *Beyond the Regulation Approach: Putting Capitalist Economies in their Place*, Cheltenham, UK and Northampton, MA, USA: Edward Elgar.
Leborgne, D. and A. Lipietz (1990), *Fallacies on Open Issues about Post-Fordism*, Paris: CEPREMAP Working Papers (Couverture Orange), no. 9009.
Lefèbvre, H. (1974 [2004]), *The Production of Space*, Oxford: Blackwell.
Lipietz, A. (1977), *Le capital et son espace*, Paris: Maspero.
Lipietz, A. (1980), 'Le tertiaire, arborescence de l'accumulation capitaliste: prolifération et polarisation', *Critiques de l'Economie Politique*, July–September, 17–69.
Lösch, A. (1938), 'The nature of economic regions', *Southern Economic Journal*, **5**, 71–8.
Lovering, J. (2001), 'The coming regional crisis (and how to avoid it)', *Regional Studies*, **35** (4), 349–54.
MacKinnon, D., A. Cumbers and K. Chapman (2002), 'Learning, innovation and regional development: a critical appraisal of recent debates', *Progress in Human Geography*, **26** (3): 293–311.
Markusen, A. (1983), 'Regions and regionalism', in F. Moulaert and P. Willson (eds), *Regional Analysis and the New International Division of Labor*, Boston, MA: Kluwer Nijhoff.
Martinelli, F. and F. Moulaert (1993), 'The location of advanced producer services firms: theory and illustrations', *Geographische Zeitschrift*, **81**, 1–17.
Massey, D. (1984), *Spatial Divisions of Labour: Social Structures and the Geography of Production*, London: Macmillan.
McGuirk, P. (2004), 'State, strategy and scale in the competitive city: a neo-Gramscian analysis of the governance of "global Sydney" ', *Environment and Planning A*, **36** (6), 1019–43.

Meardon, S.J. (2001), 'Modelling agglomeration and dispersion in city and country: Gunnar Myrdal, François Perroux, and the new economic geography', *American Journal of Economics and Sociology*, **60** (1), 25–57.
Moulaert, F. (1996), 'Rediscovering spatial inequality in Europe. Building blocks for an appropriate "regulationist" framework', *Society and Space*, **14** (2), 155–79.
Moulaert, F. and K. Cabaret (2006), 'Planning, networks and power relations: is democratic planning under capitalism possible?', *Planning Theory*, **5** (1), 51–70.
Moulaert, F. and J. Nussbaumer (2005), 'The social region: beyond the territorial dynamics of the learning economy', *Journal of European Urban and Regional Studies*, **12** (1), 45–64.
Moulaert, F. and F. Sekia (2003), 'Territorial innovation models: a critical survey', *Regional Studies*, **37** (3), 289–302.
Moulaert, F. and E. Swyngedouw (1989), 'Survey 15: A regulation approach to the geography of flexible production systems', *Environment and Planning D: Society and Space*, **7**, 327–45.
Moulaert, F., J.-C. Delvainquière, C. Demazière et al. (2000), *Globalization and Integrated Area Development in European Cities*, Oxford: Oxford University Press.
Moulaert, F., F. Sekia and J.B. Boyabe (1999), 'Innovative region, social region? An alternative view of regional innovation', IFRESI Discussion Paper, Lille.
Moulaert, F., E. Swyngedouw and P. Wilson (1988), 'The geography of Fordist and post-Fordist accumulation and regulation', *Papers of the Regional Science Association*, **64**, 11–23.
Moulaert, F., F. Martinelli, S. Gonzalez and E. Swyngedouw (2007), 'Social innovation and governance in European cities: urban development between path dependency and radical innovation', *European Urban and Regional Studies*, **14** (3), 195–209.
Mullings, B. (2005), 'Women rule? Globalization and the feminization of managerial and professional workspaces in the Caribbean', *Gender, Place and Culture*, **12** (1), 1–27.
Myrdal, G. (1957), *Economic Theory and Underdeveloped Regions*, London: Duckworth.
Novy, A. and B. Leubolt (2005), 'Participatory budgeting in Porto Alegre: social innovation and the dialectical relationship of state and civil society', *Urban Studies*, **42** (11), 2023–36.
Nussbaumer, J. (2002), 'Le rôle de la culture et des institutions dans les débats sur le développement local: la contribution de l'Ecole Historique Allemande' [The role of culture and institutions in the debates on local development: the contribution of the German Historical School], unpublished PhD thesis, Lille: University of Lille I, Faculty of Social Science.
Perroux, F. (1955), 'Note sur la notion de "pôle de croissance"', *Economie Appliquée*, **8**. Republished and translated in D.L. McKee, R.D. Dean and W.H. Leahy (eds), *Regional Economics*, New York: The Free Press, 1970, pp. 93–103.
Perroux, F. (1983), *A New Concept of Development: Basic Tenets*, London: Croom Helm.
Perroux, F. (1988), 'The pole of development's new place in a general theory of economic activity', in B. Higgins and D.J. Savoie (eds), *Regional Economic Development: Essays in Honour of François Perroux*, Boston, MA: Unwin Hyman, pp. 48–76.
Raco, M. (2003), 'Governmentality, subject-building and the discourses and practices of development in the UK', *Transactions of the Institute of British Geographers*, **28**, 75–95.
Rose, N. and P. Miller (1992), 'Political power beyond the state: problematics of government', *British Journal of Sociology*, **43**, 173–205.
Saxenian, A. (1994), *Regional Advantage: Culture and Competition in Silicon Valley and Route 128*, Cambridge, MA: Harvard University Press.
Schmoller, F.G. (1884), 'Das Merkantilsystem in seiner historischen Bedeutung: Städtische, territoriale und staatliche Wirtschafts-politik', *Jahrbuch für Gesetzgebung, Verwaltung und Volkswirtschaft im Deutschen Reich*, VIII, 15–61.
Schmoller, F.G. (1905), *Principes d'economie politique (Principles of Political Economy)*, Paris: V. Giard et E. Brière.
Smart, B. (1986), 'The politics of truth and the problem of hegemony', in D. Couzens Hoy (ed.), *Foucault: A Critical Reader*, Oxford: Basil Blackwell, pp. 157–73.
Storper, M. and A.J. Scott (1988), 'The geographical foundations and social regulation of flexible production complexes', in J. Wolch and M. Dear (eds), *The Power of Geography*, London: Allen & Unwin, pp. 21–40.
Sum, N.-L. (2002), 'Globalization and Hong Kong as an entrepreurial city strategies: contested visions and the remaking of city governance in (post-)crisis Hong Kong', in J. Logan

(ed.), *The New Chinese City: Globalization and Market Reform*, Oxford: Blackwell, pp. 74–91.

Sum, N.-L. (2005), *From the Regulationist Approach to Cultural Political Economy*, DEMOLOGOS Working Paper (http://demologos.ncl.ac.uk/wp/wp 1/disc.php, December 2005).

Sum, N.-L. (2006), *Culture, Discourse, Ideology, and Hegemony*, DEMOLOGOS Working Paper (http://demologos.ncl.ac.uk/wp/wp 2/disc.php, August).

Sum, N.-L. and B. Jessop (2007), *Towards a Cultural Political Economy*, Cheltenham, UK and Northampton, MA, USA: Edward Elgar.

Swyngedouw, E. (1997), 'La reconstruction de la choréographie espace/temps de la monnaie mondiale', *Espaces et Sociétés*, **88–9**, 53–90.

Swyngedouw, E. (2005), 'Governance innovation and the citizen: the Janus face of governance-beyond-the-state', *Urban Studies*, **42** (11), 1991–2006.

Williams, A.M., V. Balaz and C. Wallace (2004), 'International labour mobility and uneven regional development in Europe: human capital, knowledge and entrepreneurship', *European Urban and Regional Studies*, **11** (1), 27–46.

Yeung, H. Wai-Chung (2005), 'Rethinking relational economic geography', *Transactions of the Institute of British Geographers*, **30** (1), 37–51.

35 Radical institutionalism
William M. Dugger

Introduction: there be beasties down below

Robert Lekachman provides an appropriate introductory quotation:

> American institutionalism has been diverse, interdisciplinary, critical of society,
> concerned unashamedly with equity, and, inevitably, all of this said, less intel-
> lectually tidy than the ordered but visibly irrelevant universe of respectable
> theory. (Lekachman, 1979, p. i)

On the surface, economics is steadfast in its pro-market stance. In the textbooks, all is smoothed out and calm. Also, it often seems as if all is for the
best in this best of all possible worlds (Hodgson, 1991). Nevertheless, below
the surface of the Panglossian science, sharp criticism of the economic
order is brewing. Way down in the lower strata of the discipline, discontent
is astir. All manner of wondrous beasties (schools of heterodox economics)
roam an underground of the discipline. One of them is radical institutionalism, a form of socio-economics.

> Radical institutionalism is a processual paradigm focused on changing the direc-
> tion of cultural evolution and changing the outcome of social provisioning in
> order to promote the full participation of all. (Dugger, 1989b, p. 126)

The word 'processual' was coined to emphasize the processes of change and
to distinguish institutionalism from the equilibrium analysis of neoclassical economics, and 'social provisioning' is used to emphasize that institutionalism includes social and cultural factors in its study (Gruchy, 1987).
Changing the course of social evolution to move it in more egalitarian and
peaceful directions that allow for greater participation of the excluded is
the principal desire of *radical* institutionalists. Violent revolution is not
acceptable to folks who were strongly influenced by the non-violent civil
rights movement and by the 1960s peace movement. The radical adjective
applies because this institutionalist discourse has returned to its fundamentals – to its roots in Thorstein Veblen – and because these particular
institutionalists think that the current economic system needs to be transcended, not just reformed.

Will this beastie break through the tranquil surface of economics?
Should the authorities be alerted against an outbreak of pluralism?

(Further discussion of the institutionalist underground is in Dugger, 1992b.) The rest of this chapter is in three sections: (1) state of the literature; (2) new directions taken; and (3) issues and implications.

1. State of the literature

Preliminaries
Veblen is the founder of institutionalism (Veblen, 1899, 1904, 1919, 1921, 1923). Radical institutionalists are more traditional on this point and emphasize Veblen more than do other institutionalists (Dugger, 1988, 1995). Veblen looked toward replacing capitalism based on absentee corporate owners and an inegalitarian society with some form of socialism based on the technically adept workers managing their own enterprises in an egalitarian society. Veblen also looked toward replacing neoclassical economics, with its preconceptions of normality and equilibrium, with a Darwinian approach relying on the preconceptions of variation and evolution (Hamilton, 1953). In broader circles, Veblen is known best for his critical analysis of conspicuous consumption and emulation (Veblen, 1899), as well as his critique of the predatory practices of corporate business (Veblen, 1904; Stabile, 1982; Dugger, 2006). Numerous social critics have followed Veblen's lead. (A recent social critique that is Veblenian in spirit is in Hahnel, 2005.) In narrower economic circles Veblen is best known for his critical analysis of neoclassical economics (Veblen, 1919) and for his promotion of institutional reconstruction. Veblen stood for replacing capitalism with an industrial republic planned by the 'engineers' (Veblen, 1921).

The liberal reformer John R. Commons is usually included as a co-founder of institutionalism. He differed from Veblen significantly, in terms of basic orientation. While Veblen wished to replace capitalism, Commons wished to reform it; and while Veblen wished to replace neoclassical economics, Commons wished to add institutionalism to it. Commons worked on collective bargaining and the regulation of capitalist excesses (Commons, 1934).

Commons's emphasis on reform led him to work out a unique and highly useful approach to social provisioning. He made the economic transaction his unit of analysis and explained that serious disputes between transactors required some kind of sovereign power to resolve. Sovereign power is usually the state, and when the state exercises its sovereignty effectively, a set of working rules is established that maintains the going concerns in the economy. As new disputes arise and are resolved, the economy's set of working rules evolves (Commons, 1934). Commons put more emphasis on reforming the working rules of capitalist enterprises and institutions than on replacing them (Dugger, 1979).

Radical institutionalism leans more toward Veblen than Commons. It began further growth and differentiation as a discourse in the tumultuous 1960s. During the same period in the USA the emergence of the Association for Evolutionary Economics and the Union for Radical Political Economics contributed to the development of radical institutionalism.

The radical institutionalist literature fits into a broader context of US economic discourse. Soon after World War II John Gambs wrote that Keynes

> [P]romises something that cannot be resisted: full employment and high levels of consumption without serious disruptions of our institutions. Veblen promises the possibility of an even brighter future: a utopian industrial republic – but only alternatively and possibly at great cost. Attainment of the industrial republic requires a dislocation of our accustomed way of life, perhaps sharp conflicts, and exposes us to the possibility of regression towards barbarism. (Gambs, 1946, p. 3)

Gambs concluded the contrast he drew between Veblen and Keynes with a prophecy: 'The next decade or two will clarify that issue. Those years will probably tell whether the plans of Keynes can be achieved in contradiction to the prophecies of Veblen' (ibid.). Keynes, of course, stood for stabilization policy, for reducing unemployment and for dampening the swings in the business cycle. He wanted to make capitalism good (Keynes, 1936).

In the next two decades after World War II Keynes and stabilization policy won out over Veblen and institutional reconstruction. Many institutional economists adjusted their thinking to correspond more closely to the liberal Keynesian discourse that had come to dominate economics (not Douglas Dowd, however: see Dowd, 1958). Clarence Ayres argued that just as absolute monarchy had been reformed in the UK into limited monarchy, so absolute capitalism should be reformed in the USA into limited capitalism. Ayres argued that the reform did not require replacing capitalism with socialism. Instead, it required limiting capitalism by redistributing wealth more equally. Redistribution would limit the inequity and instability of capitalism without subjecting us all to the difficulties of more radical change (Ayres, 1946). Reform was stressed by most institutionalists working in the 1950s and early 1960s. Institutional adjustment was their major theme (see Thompson, 1967). Keynes, however, was soon pushed into the underground and neoclassical economics was restored to dominance in the mainstream of the discipline.

Most institutionalists continued working in the tradition of Keynesian reform. In the meantime, more radical themes were emerging. Three themes have served as rallying points for radical institutionalism. Those who rallied to these themes did not deny the significance of Keynesian theory or the efficacy of Keynesian stabilization policy. Rather, they made Keynesian theory another plank in their platform supporting the transcendence of corporate capitalism.

First theme: the problem of corporate power

Corporate power is a problem, even in neoclassical economics, when it means monopoly power (but see Adams and Brock, 1991). Radical institutionalists object to monopoly power, recognizing along with almost everyone else that it drives up prices to consumers while it restricts output and employment. Radical institutionalists also recognize that market power goes even further than that – it can make people sick. The first person to use in print the phrase 'radical institutional' explained that the market power of the corporations that dominated the processed food industry in the USA was a growing menace to the public health (Junker, 1982). In his article, which was 20 years before its time, Junker argued that the market power of some food processors was making it possible for them to sell us food that was contributing to a number of significant health problems.

But concerns go much further than market power. Large corporations are powerful in society because they control huge financial and managerial resources. Their widespread control of resources leads to major concern with how this scale of corporate power can change political institutions and laws to benefit higher corporate circles at the expense of the rest of society (Fusfeld, 1979). The USA proudly displays its democracy for the entire world to emulate; and it should be proud of its democratic institutions. Nevertheless, US democracy presents radical institutionalists with a puzzle. '[T]he political institutions of the United States are among the most democratic in the world; yet the policies of its government – local, state, and federal – have consistently and increasingly been bent to the interests of the few' (Dowd, 1997, p. 258. See also Fusfeld, 1979).

Corporate power in the USA also raises concern about the distribution of income. Corporate executives have pushed their own incomes up, even at the expense of corporate shareholders (Bebchuk and Fried, 2004). Furthermore, the top Federal tax rate on capital gains and dividends has been lowered to just 15 percent (latest tax cut for shareholders by the George W. Bush Administration). In a democratic society these developments are alarming. But in the USA, they should not be unexpected.

> In a capitalist society it is to be expected that the most powerful in the business world will wish and be able to design many of the laws within which they function, that their political power will be greatly disproportionate to their percentage of the population. (Dowd, 1997, p. 255)

This quotation from Dowd describes individual power in a system of corporate capitalism. The corporation also possesses social power in its own right as an institution (Dugger, 1989a). The powerful corporation is a hegemonic institution. Its hegemony refers to a hierarchy of institutions in which the ends of institutions lower down in the hierarchy have become the means for institutions higher up in the hierarchy. This makes the lower institutions subordinate to the higher ones and hollows out the meaning and importance of the subordinate institutions, while it fills in the meaning and importance of the dominant one. In this way the family's objectives of raising healthy children and providing nurturance to family members is turned into the means used by corporations to acquire an ample supply of trained and productive employees as well as an ample supply of revenue from corporate sales to eager family consumers. (See Brown, 2002 for additional radical institutional analysis of hegemonic processes.) The reduction of meaning and value reduces the family, subordinating it to the corporation and hollowing it out. Similar hierarchical means-and-ends relations exist between the corporation and the school, church and even the state. Of course, these relations are or can be contested and overturned on a broad scale. Corporate hegemony certainly is not universal. It is not inevitable.

Hegemony contrasts with pluralism and should cause concern not only among those of us who value the power and influence of their own favored institutional order such as the church or nation, but also among those who value pluralism itself. For example, in *Habits of the Heart*, Bellah et al. criticize radical individualism, but much of what they say applies with equal force to corporate hegemony (Bellah et al., 1986).

Another, related, view of corporate power sees it locked into a contest for dominance with groups that come together to oppose it. Instead of hegemony emerging, there emerges a system of countervailing power (Galbraith, 1956). In two additional books, Galbraith explained that the US economy was a contested terrain in which opposing centers of countervailing power struggle for money and dominance (Galbraith, 1967, 1970). In this struggle, corporate management (the technostructure) tries to plan the production and distribution of goods and services through a revised sequence in which production determines consumption instead of the other way around. Corporate power is dominant, and society has become unbalanced, with too much emphasis on private production and consumption and too little on public needs. But corporate power is not universal. Areas of market competition remain. Furthermore, unions, consumer organizations and social movements of various sorts mount offensives against entrenched corporate power, sometimes successfully and sometimes not.

Summing up his own view of the implications of corporate power, Daniel Fusfeld argued that more was needed than just a patching up of the cracks and the compromises that make the modern economic system work better. Then he stated:

The far more difficult task is to restructure our economic institutions in the direction of a humane society. We need more than prosperity, economic growth, and stable prices. We need a redistribution of wealth to achieve greater equality and freedom. We need a world at peace. These goals will not be achieved unless we can take the guns away from the generals and power from the managerial elite. We must disperse economic power and governmental authority. We must move to nothing less than a revolutionary transformation of our economic and political institutions. (Fusfeld, 1979, p. 157)

Second theme: the wrong direction of social evolution
The direction of social evolution in the USA has moved toward more inegalitarian domestic institutions and more warlike foreign policies (Dowd, 1977, 1997). This did not have to be the case. The tumultuous 1960s included not only the war in Indochina, but President Lyndon Johnson's war on poverty as well. Radical institutionalists agreed that we should declare war on poverty, but unlike the war in Indochina, the war Johnson was waging against poverty was merely a 'popgun war'. According to David Hamilton, Johnson's war on poverty was not weakening the institutional support of poverty because it was not replacing the system of status and power that made poverty seem legitimate. If its legitimacy was not destroyed, poverty itself would remain (Hamilton, 1967, 1968, 1970, 1971) Sadly, Hamilton's critique was right on the mark. The war on poverty did succeed in redistributing some income and in establishing effective training programs and community development programs. But the war on poverty wound down before it changed the system of status and power that supported inequality and poverty in the first place. (Some recent debates and developments are in Widerquist et al., 2005.)

The end of the cold war between the USA and the USSR promised an enormous peace dividend for both countries and for all humanity. Sadly, payment of that peace dividend is still pending. The Soviets collapsed and the standard of living enjoyed in the majority of the newly transitioning economies is still recovering. The USA has grown its economy but has also become bogged down in expensive and bloody wars in Iraq and Afghanistan. In the year 2007, most of the people in the USA want peace, but their leaders seem unable or unwilling to deliver. Aggregate demand remains high. The stock markets reach new highs. So do the Middle East casualties.

Third theme: the promise of a better life
Neither war nor poverty is inevitable. In an age of corporate power, the market can no longer be relied on as the exclusive foundation of the economy. It can no longer be counted on to provide a natural economic harmony, if it ever could. Instead, the modern, high-tech economy could

benefit significantly from a democratic system of national economic planning. Call it indicative planning or call it anything you want, but when adapted to the unique conditions encountered in each national economy, it could add significantly to productivity and welfare. It could supplement the market by providing a democratic government with policies for pursuing a whole range of public objectives, including full employment without war, balanced growth and price stability (Gruchy, 1939, 1972, 1984; Dugger, 1987).

Left to its own devices, even the modern economy is unstable. It is still plagued by business cycles. The instabilities and uncertainties of the cycle are its natural state. Booms and busts are not aberrations. Nevertheless, the business cycle is not inevitable and can be tamed by peaceful government policies that take us beyond the instabilities of corporate capitalism (Sherman, 1991).

Corporate power and corporate capitalism are not the only ways to operate the economy. We did not start out with capitalism and the corporation. In fact, humans have organized their social provisioning in many different ways. Economies and societies have been evolving for many centuries, and unless we blow ourselves up, will continue doing so (Sherman, 2006; Dugger and Sherman, 2000, 2003). These, too, will pass. The corporation and capitalism will be replaced with something else. And, since evolution is open-ended, the choices human beings make today will determine the kind of future their progeny will enjoy tomorrow. The future could be very bright – or not. Humans could even resolve their differences non-violently.

2. New directions taken
Specifying the new directions taken by radical institutionalists is like herding stray cats – fun but associated with a low probability of success. Nevertheless, let us try. The literature of radical institutionalism seems to be moving in two new directions: exploring nurturance in the social economy and exposing the scandal of inequality and poverty in the modern world of potential abundance.

Nurturance
Nurturance is caring for others, particularly rearing children, and usually is performed in some form of family or in some privileged social space that resembles the family. Nurturance involves more love than exchange and is recognized as more important (privileged) than exchange. The most frequent nurturing relations are between parents and children, but nurturing also takes place between grandparents and grandchildren, between adult children and elderly parents, and between spouses, also between friends. Critiques of nurturance can sink into reactionary fulminations against

change in general: 'Bring back the good old days when families were much stronger, children more obedient, and parents more loving.' Such rants do not promote understanding and play no role in the radical institutionalist literature.

Instead, two aspects of nurturance are being explored in radical institutionalism. First is the problem of a nurturance gap in the social economy (Stanfield, 1992, 1995; Folbre, 1994, 2001). Second is the role of nurturance in the social structure of accumulation (O'Hara, 1995, 1998).

The two aspects are related. A nurturance gap in the social economy implies an inadequacy or pending crisis in the social structure of accumulation. The reverse is also the case: a crisis in the social structure of accumulation that provides for nurturance implies some kind of nurturance gap or breakdown in the social economy. Nevertheless, when nurturance is looked at as an important part of the social structure of accumulation, the resulting analysis draws more on the contemporary Marxist literature on social structures of accumulation. On the other hand, when nurturance is looked at as a kind of gap in the social economy, the resulting analysis draws more on the anthropological tradition of Karl Polanyi (Polanyi, 1944). Of course, this difference is not absolute, but a matter of degree (O'Hara, 2000, pp. 219–40).

The existence of a nurturance gap means that a society is not providing adequately for the rearing of children or for the care of the elderly, or for the care of adults. Not enough social space or personal time for love? Neglect of children results in widespread social deterioration when the neglected generations of the past take their place as the leading generations of the future. Neglect of the elderly results in the hardening of social relations in general as people are given object lessons of what happens to those who have fallen behind in the race for money, status and power – they end up in warehouses for the dying. Spurred on by the object lessons provided by care for the elderly, the race is run more feverishly. When adults have no loving relations with other adults, further hardening of social relations takes place. Given a large enough nurturance gap, for enough generations, and the loveless (nurtureless) society will resemble the rush for the exits in the suburban mega-church parking lot after Sunday's sermon of self-help and individual uplift.

Nurturance is also important in terms of maintaining social structures of accumulation (SSA). The theory and terminology of SSA are still very new, but we can say that SSA are sets of institutions that emerge and facilitate a renewal of profits and capital accumulation after a period of difficulty or crisis. The set of institutions may be referred to in the singular as a social structure of accumulation, thereby emphasizing the entire set of institutions as a unified whole; or the individual institutional orders may be referred to in the plural as social structures of accumulation, thereby emphasizing each institutional order as a separate structure. An SSA is made up of different institutional structures such as the family, the workplace, the state, the working class and the corporation. When the relations between the structures and/or within the different structures reach an impasse or crisis such that profits collapse and accumulation ceases, a long wave of development within capitalism comes to an end. Only if a new SSA emerges that can facilitate renewed profits and accumulation will another long wave of development resume (Kotz, et al., 1994; O'Hara, 2000).

Dialectics and crisis are emphasized more in classical Marxian than in Veblenian (radical institutionalist) analysis (Veblen, 1919, pp. 409–56). Be that as it may, SSA theory provides a bridge between Marxian and Veblenian forms of analysis, as both are attempts at radical theories of institutional change. Furthermore, SSA theory makes room for emphasizing the importance of nurturance in the social economy (O'Hara, 2000, pp. 120–36, 219–40). A stable SSA requires a reliable flow of new workers, socialized into the ways of proletarian life required by the SSA, possessed of a certain level of honesty and industry as well as certain sets of skills and general knowledge – all essential to the SSA. Peaceful and stable behavior must be inculcated into succeeding generations. Ample flows of consumer spending and predictable responses to advertising and salesmanship are also essential (no dropping out and joining hippie communes). None of this is instinctual. All of it is learned during some form of nurturing, even down to the smallest detail of proper behavior in long checkout lines at the supermarket (no cutting in front or fist-fighting, no shoplifting; keep a smiley face – prescribed medication helps but no self-medication). Parents and other nurturing adults have had to teach all of us these things, and many more, so that we can fit into the SSA without a hitch. If the nurturing breaks down, hitches immediately develop. Then we will have to say, in all honesty, that whenever two or more are gathered together surely a fight will break out.

The family, or something that performs its nurturance services, is one of the indispensable structures in the social structure of accumulation. It is a weak structure in the contemporary SSA. An indicator of that weakness is the falling fertility rate in the developed capitalist countries. In most of the countries, the fertility rate has fallen so low that they are failing to reproduce themselves. They must outsource production and entice immigrant labor to fill the ranks of their working class. The fertility rate is also falling in the less developed countries, as they are finding their place in the global social structure of accumulation. The total fertility rate (births per woman) has fallen from 2.3 in 1970–75 to 1.7 in 2000–2005 for high-income countries. Over the same period, it has fallen from 6.0 to 3.9 for low-income countries (United Nations Development Programme, 2006, p. 300).

Inequality/abundance

Considerable work has been done on the broader aspects of social inequality, with attention paid to sexism, racism, classism and nationalism. Radical institutionalists recently have been looking at inequality and abundance as a kind of pair, condemning the inequity and waste of inequality, particularly in a world where abundance is within our grasp, and examining the mixed blessings of abundance, particularly in a world of run-away consumerism (Peach and Dugger, 2006).

> *Abundance* does not mean that goods are free. *Abundance* means adequacy, not satiation. The level of adequacy is not constant but is relative to the progress made in the community's joint stock of knowledge. In a Stone Age community there is a lower level of adequacy than in a Space Age community. (Ibid., p. 693)

Many of the great economists from different schools of thought and from different political positions have argued that abundance was possible, not in the far distant future but now, within our grasp. John Kenneth Galbraith proclaimed:

> To furnish a barren room is one thing. To continue to crowd in furniture until the foundation buckles is quite another. To have failed to solve the problem of producing goods would have been to continue man in his oldest and most grievous misfortune. But to fail to see that we have solved it, and to fail to proceed thence to the next task, would be fully as tragic. (Galbraith, 1970, p. 268)

The economics of scarcity should not continue its intellectual monopoly of the discipline. The creation of abundance for all, regardless of race, gender, class or nation, should not be excluded from economic discourse as utopian (Peach and Dugger, 2006).

Abundance looked at from a different angle becomes consumerism run amuck in which modern capitalism inculcates an insatiable drive to realize unlimited potential consumption – a drive to always go beyond, never be satisfied, always to want more. Our culture drives us to perpetual self-improvement, which causes deep personal distress and fear of not measuring up to the always-higher standards. We cannot just *be* ourselves. We must always *become* better. And so, we are always driven and unhappy. No matter how much progress our community makes, we can never be satiated. But the drive for satiation can destroy us and our environment (Brown, 2002).

Equality is the way out (Dugger, 1996). Equality means more than just the removal of race, gender, sexual orientation and ethnic origin as discriminatory characteristics in our competitive race for money, power and status. It means transcending the race itself. Drawing from John C. Livingston's critique of affirmative action and meritocratic elitism (Livingston, 1979), Marc Tool states

> To 'choose equality' is not only to affirm the worth of each person but to recognize that only through social action as public policy can the potential instrumental merit of people be assured and acknowledged. I am suggesting that 'worthiness' implies, among other things, the human rights to be and to belong, to work at meaningful pay, to have unfettered access to health care, and to become as fully trained and educated as our interests and abilities will permit. (Tool, 1996, p. 124)

Janice Peterson makes an important feminist point to consider along with Tool's discussion of equality:

> Radical institutionalism and feminism share a devotion to equality and full participation. The experiences of women all over the world suggest, however, that it is critical to carefully consider the meaning of these concepts. For increased participation to end the subordination of women it must mean the transformation of existing institutions. Simply adding women into existing structures is not sufficient and may even result in further exploitation. (Peterson, 1994, p. xiii; see also Waller and Jennings, 1990)

3. Issues and implications

Issues that need attention
Many issues lie underdeveloped by radical institutionalists. Only a select few will be mentioned here. The radical institutionalist literature still needs a great deal of work on racism (Shulman, 1996). Of course, a radical institutionalist produced the classic study on racism in the USA – the famous Swedish socialist Gunnar Myrdal (Myrdal, 1944). Nevertheless, more work is needed. William A. Darity Jr and Samuel L. Myers Jr have helped. Neither author closely associates with radical institutionalism. But both should, because they explain the persistent racial disparity in the USA in terms of historical deprivations – seizure of property, exclusion from opportunity, and containment in limited social and physical space. Furthermore, they suggest a radical policy to deal with the disparity – racial redistribution of wealth (Darity and Myers, 1998).

It is not that radical institutionalists disagree with Darity and Myers, for they do not. Instead, their attention has mainly been elsewhere. Dugger and Sherman, for example, have tried to reclaim evolutionary theory for the left by taking it away from social Darwinism and socio-biology. Evolutionary theory does not place a cap on human potential *à la* Malthus. Instead, in the social sciences, evolutionary theory carries a more optimistic message – societies evolve through endogenous change and that change is open-ended. It can involve significant improvement in the human condition, if we play our cards right. It can also involve deterioration, if we do not. Properly understood, evolutionary theory in the social sciences is a part of post-Marxism (Sherman, 2006) and of radical institutionalism (Dugger, 2006; Dugger and Sherman, 1997, 2000, 2003). Perhaps they should have paid as much attention to racial inequality as to social evolution.

Environmental quality has been addressed by virtually all radical institutionalists, but usually in the context of some other issue. Doug Brown ties environmental deterioration directly to consumerism run amuck. He argues that a society based on the perpetual pursuit of insatiable material desires cannot possibly be sustained by its environment (Brown, 2002).

Phillip Anthony O'Hara discusses different forms of capital, including 'ecological capital', in terms of global capital and inequality. He defines ecological capital as a dynamic stock of ecological and biological resources. He distinguishes between ecological, human, social and private business capital. Furthermore, he analyzes the trade-offs made between accumulation and destruction of the different forms, particularly the trade-off between the accumulation of private business capital and the destruction of ecological capital (O'Hara, 1998). O'Hara, Brown and others do fine jobs, but much more work needs to be done on environmental quality, particularly global warming. One interesting series of questions could begin with, 'Are radical institutionalists red or green?' 'Must we choose between red and green?' 'Can we be checkered?'

Another important underdeveloped issue is globalization. Radical institutionalism is not isolationist, but cosmopolitan. So the important question is, 'What kind of globalization should be supported?' Globalization from below, which favors third world workers and families must be preferred to globalization from above, which favors powerful multinational corporations at the expense of the underlying populations and their supporting institutions. Globalization that relies on Bretton Woods institutions is little more than an acceptance of the present process of globalization from above (Dugger, 2005). William K. Tabb has done a good job exploring globalization (Tabb, 2002). However, as with Darity and Myers, Tabb is not closely associated with radical institutionalism, even though he should be.

The last underdeveloped issue to be mentioned here is the relation between the market and the corporate planning system, as first raised by John Kenneth Galbraith in terms of the revised sequence, discussed above. Of course, significant areas of the developed economies are still competitive, and control of markets is often hotly contested. None the less, Galbraith emphasized, a not insignificant part of the market system is influenced by corporate planning. In the markets so influenced, exactly how has the revised sequence worked itself out in terms of supply, demand, the price mechanism and market clearing? Absent corporate power, information flows from consumers (demand) to producers (supply). The revised sequence does not require complete corporate dominance of the flow of information in the market. But in the revised sequence, at least some information flows in the opposite direction – from producer to consumer. If producers have some influence over what consumers want and that influence is exercised through advertising and management of information, then how is an excess supply or an excess demand cleared from that particular market? How is market balance restored?

Many questions are raised: in particular, if excess supply plagues a market, does the exercise of corporate power alter the market adjustment process so as to reduce the role of the neoclassical price mechanism? To what extent can more advertising and better information management substitute for a price cut when excess supply needs to be cleared out of the market? Can a horizontal merger or two do the trick? How about more government spending in the glutted market? Is a universal theory of market adjustment even possible in an economy where corporate producers can influence demand through advertising and information management? In an economy where antitrust action is exercised with political discretion? In an economy where governments can spend on the pet projects of powerful interests? In an economy where exchange rates can be manipulated to encourage or discourage imports and exports? To what extent and in what particular ways does the introduction of economic and political discretion into market adjustment processes curtail the universality of the old laws of supply and demand? A great deal of additional research is needed. But neoclassical price theory is no longer adequate, if it ever was.

Furthermore, if producers can influence consumer wants, then neoclassical welfare theory is no longer adequate either, if it ever was. The optimality of market outcomes is seriously challenged, if consumer wants are affected by what producers want to sell. Consumer/worker welfare is not necessarily increased when they work more in order to buy what producers have encouraged them to want in the first place. Consumer/worker behavior loses its authenticity and spontaneity to the extent that the revised sequence allows producers to create additional wants instead of just satisfying existing ones. In other words, consumers begin losing their sovereignty when producers become powerful enough to begin manipulating them through advertising, information management and political influence. Consumer surplus loses meaning.

Some new progress has been made in understanding collective action and discretion in the market system. A new theorem has been proposed: 'The free market is impossible.' It explores the essential roles of the state in the market, particularly in the context of globalization (Dugger, 2005, 1992a). Frederic S. Lee makes much further progress. He puts together administered pricing, mark-up pricing and normal costing along with considerable empirical material to provide a microeconomic foundation for post-Keynesian macroeconomics (Lee, 1998). Marc R. Tool brings together corporate power and human agency to forge a discretionary theory of costs and prices that can assign responsibility for market results. In Tool's analysis, markets become products of human collective action instead of the mechanical implementation of natural law (Tool, 1995).

Failures or opportunities?
These and related issues require further research. Radical institutionalists are spread too thin. They have failed to cover the field adequately. That is most unfortunate. But each failure is an opportunity. It represents an open area of economic inquiry, just waiting for adequate empirical exploration and theoretical formulation. In fact, there are far more opportunities for meaningful work than there are radical institutionalists pursuing them. So if you are looking for meaningful challenges, here they are.

References

Adams, Walter and James W. Brock (1991), *Antitrust Economics on Trial: A Dialogue on the New Laissez-Faire*, Princeton, NJ: Princeton University Press.
Ayres, C.E. (1946), *The Divine Right of Capital*, Boston, MA: Houghton Mifflin.
Bebchuk, Lucian and Jesse Fried (2004), *Pay Without Performance: The Unfulfilled Promise of Executive Compensation*, Cambridge, MA: Harvard University Press.
Bellah, Robert, Richard Madsen, William M. Sullivan, Ann Swidler and Steven M. Tipton (1986), *Habits of the Heart*, Berkeley, CA: University of California Press.
Brown, Doug (2002), *Insatiable Is not Sustainable*, London: Praeger.
Commons, John R. ([1934] 1961), *Institutional Economics: Its Place in Political Economy*, Madison, WI: University of Wisconsin Press.
Darity, William A. Jr and Samuel L. Myers Jr (1998), *Persistent Disparity: Race and Economic Inequality in the United States since 1945*, Cheltenham, UK and Northampton, MA, USA: Edward Elgar.
Dowd, Douglas F. (ed.) (1958), *Thorstein Veblen*, Westport, CT: Greenwood Press.
Dowd, Douglas F. (ed.) (1977), *The Twisted Dream: Capitalist Development in the United States since 1776*, 2nd edn, Cambridge, MA: Winthrop Publishers.
Dowd, Douglas F. (1997), *Blues for America: A Critique, A Lament, and Some Memories*, New York: Monthly Review Press.
Dugger, William M. (1979), 'The reform method of John R. Commons', *Journal of Economic Issues*, **13** (June), 369–81.
Dugger, William M. (1984), *An Alternative to Economic Retrenchment*, Princeton, NJ: Petrocelli Books.
Dugger, William M. (1987), 'An institutional theory of economic planning', *Journal of Economic Issues*, **21** (4), 1649–75.
Dugger, William M. (1988), 'Radical institutionalism: basic concepts', *Review of Radical Political Economics*, **20** (Spring), 1–20.
Dugger, William M. (1989a), *Corporate Hegemony*, New York: Greenwood Press.
Dugger, William M. (ed.) (1989b), *Radical Institutionalism: Contemporary Voices*, Westport, CT: Greenwood Press.

Dugger, William M. (1992a), 'An evolutionary theory of the state and the market', in William M. Dugger and William T. Waller, Jr (eds), *The Stratified State: Radical Institutionalist Theories of Participation and Duality*, Armonk, NY: M.E. Sharpe, pp. 87–115.

Dugger, William M. (1992b), *Underground Economics: A Decade of Institutionalist Dissent*, Armonk, NY: M.E. Sharpe.

Dugger, William M. (1995), 'The changing concepts of inquiry', *Journal of Economic Issues*, **29** (December), 1013–27.

Dugger, William M. (ed.) (1996), *Inequality: Radical Institutionalist Views on Race, Gender, Class, and Nation*, Westport, CT: Greenwood Press.

Dugger, William M. (2005), 'Dugger's theorem: the free market is impossible', *Journal of Economic Issues*, **39** (June), 309–24.

Dugger, William M. (2006), 'Veblen's radical theory of social evolution', *Journal of Economic Issues*, **40** (September), 651–72.

Dugger, William M. and Howard J. Sherman (1994), 'Marxism and institutionalism compared', *Journal of Economic Issues*, **28** (March), 101–27.

Dugger, William M. and Howard J. Sherman (1997), 'Institutionalist and Marxist theories of evolution', *Journal of Economic Issues*, **31** (December), 991–1009.

Dugger, William M. and Howard J. Sherman (2000), *Reclaiming Evolution: A Dialogue between Marxism and Institutionalism on Social Change*, London: Routledge.

Dugger, William M. and Howard J. Sherman (eds) (2003), *Evolutionary Theory in the Social Sciences*, 4 vols, London: Routledge.

Folbre, Nancy (1994), *Who Pays for the Kids? Gender and the Structures of Constraint*, London: Routledge.

Folbre, Nancy (2001), *The Invisible Heart: Economics and Family Values*, New York: The New Press.

Fusfeld, Daniel R. (1979), 'The rise of the corporate state in America', in Warren J. Samuels (ed.), *The Economy as a System of Power*, New Brunswick, NJ: Transaction, pp. 139–60.

Gambs, John S. (1946), *Beyond Supply and Demand: A Reappraisal of Institutional Economics*, Westport, CT: Greenwood Press. Reprinted 1976.

Galbraith, John Kenneth (1956), *American Capitalism: The Concept of Countervailing Power*, rev. edn, Boston, MA: Houghton Mifflin.

Galbraith, John Kenneth (1967), *The New Industrial State*, Boston, MA: Houghton Mifflin.

Galbraith, John Kenneth (1970), *The Affluent Society*, 2nd edn, revised, New York: The New American Library.

Gruchy, Allan G. (1939), 'The concept of national planning in institutional economics', *Southern Economic Journal*, **6** (October), 121–44.

Gruchy, Allan G. (1972), *Contemporary Economic Thought*, Clifton, NJ: Augustus M. Kelley, pp. 287–339.

Gruchy, Allan G. (1984), 'Uncertainty, indicative planning and industrial policy', in Marc R. Tool (ed.), *An Institutionalist Guide to Economics and Public Policy*, New York: M.E. Sharpe, pp. 177–98.

Gruchy, Allan G. (1987), *The Reconstruction of Economics: An Analysis of the Fundamentals of Institutional Economics*, Westport, CT: Greenwood Press.

Hahnel, Robin (2005), *Economic Justice and Democracy: From Competition to Cooperation*, New York: Routledge.

Hamilton, David (1953), *Newtonian Classicism and Darwinian Institutionalism: A Study of Change in Economic Theory*, Albuquerque, NM: University of New Mexico Press.

Hamilton, David (1967), 'The political economy of poverty: institutional and technological dimensions', *Journal of Economic Issues*, **1** (4), 309–20.

Hamilton, David (1968), *A Primer on the Economics of Poverty*, New York: Random House.

Hamilton, David (1970), 'Reciprocity, productivity and poverty', *Journal of Economic Issues*, **4** (1), pp. 35–42.

Hamilton, David (1971), 'The paper war on poverty', *Journal of Economic Issues*, **5** (3), 72–9.

Hodgson, Geoffrey M. (1991), 'Economic evolution: intervention contra Pangloss', *Journal of Economic Issues*, **25** (2), 519–33.

Junker, Louis J. (1982), 'Nutrition and economy: some observations on diet and disease in the American food power system', *The Review of Institutional Thought*, **2** (December), 27–58.

Keynes, John Maynard (1936), *The General Theory of Employment, Interest and Money*, New York: Harcourt, Brace.

Kotz, David M. et al. (1994), *Social Structures of Accumulation: The Political Economy of Growth and Crisis*, Cambridge: University of Cambridge Press.

Lee, Frederic S. (1998), *Post Keynesian Price Theory*, Cambridge: Cambridge University Press.

Lekachman, Robert (1979), 'Foreword', in Warren J. Samuels (ed.), *The Economy as a System of Power*, New Brunswick, NJ: Transaction, pp. i–ii.

Livingston, John C. (1979), *Fair Game? Inequality and Affirmative Action*, San Francisco, CA: W.H. Freeman and Co.

Myrdal, Gunnar [1944] (1969), *An American Dilemma: The Negro Problem and Modern Democracy*, 2 vols, New York: Harper & Row.

O'Hara, Phillip Anthony (1995), 'Household labor, family, and macroeconomic instability in the United States, 1940s–1990s', *Review of Social Economy*, **52**, 89–120.

O'Hara, Phillip Anthony (1998), 'Capital and inequality in today's world', in Doug Brown (ed.), *Thorstein Veblen in the Twenty-First Century*, Cheltenham, UK and Northampton, MA, USA: Edward Elgar, pp. 171–88.

O'Hara, Phillip Anthony (2000), *Marx, Veblen, and Contemporary Institutional Political Economy: Principles and Unstable Dynamics of Capitalism*, Cheltenham, UK and Northampton, MA, USA: Edward Elgar.

Peach, Jim and William M. Dugger (2006), 'An intellectual history of abundance', *Journal of Economic Issues*, **40** (September), 693–706.

Peterson, Janice (1994), 'Introduction', in Janice Peterson and Doug Brown (eds), *The Economic Status of Women under Capitalism*, Cheltenham, UK and Brookfield, VT: Edward Elgar, pp. x–xvii.

Polanyi, Karl (1944), *The Great Transformation: The Political and Economic Origins of Our Time*, Boston, MA: Beacon Press.

Sherman, Howard J. (1991), *The Business Cycle: Growth and Crisis under Capitalism*, Princeton, NJ: Princeton University Press.

Sherman, Howard J. (2006), *How Society Makes Itself: The Evolution of Political and Economic Institutions*, Armonk, NY: M.E. Sharpe.

Shulman, Steven (1996), 'Radical inequality and radical institutionalism: a research agenda', in William M. Dugger (ed.), *Inequality: Radical Institutionalist Views on Race, Gender, Class, and Nation*, Westport, CT: Greenwood Press, pp. 251–71.

Stabile, Donald R. (1982), 'Thorstein Veblen and his socialist contemporaries: a critical comparison', *Journal of Economic Issues*, **16** (March), 1–28.

Stanfield, James Ronald (1992), 'Economy and society at the close of the American century', *Review of Social Economy*, **50** (December), 366–73.

Stanfield, James Ronald (1995), *Economics, Power and Culture: Essays in the Development of Radical Institutionalism*, New York: St Martin's Press.

Tabb, William K. (2002), *Unequal Partners: A Primer on Globalization*, New York: The New Press.

Thompson, Carey C. (ed.) (1967), *Institutional Adjustment: A Challenge to a Changing Economy*, Austin, TX: University of Texas Press.

Tool, Marc R. (1995), *Pricing, Valuation and Systems: Essays in Neoinstitutional Economics*, Aldershot, UK and Brookfield, USA: Edward Elgar.

Tool, Marc R. (1996), 'Choose equality', in William M. Dugger (ed.), *Inequality: Radical Institutionalist Views on Race, Gender, Class, and Nation*, Westport, CT: Greenwood Press, pp. 103–26.

United Nations Development Programme (2006), *Human Development Report 2006*, New York: Palgrave Macmillan.

Veblen, Thorstein [1899] (1975), *The Theory of the Leisure Class*, New York: Augustus M. Kelley.

Veblen, Thorstein [1904] (1975), *The Theory of Business Enterprise*, Clifton, NJ: Augustus M. Kelley.

Veblen, Thorstein (1919), *The Place of Science in Modern Civilization and Other Essays*, New York: B.W. Huebsch.
Veblen, Thorstein [1921] (1965), *The Engineers and the Price System*, New York: Augustus M. Kelley.
Veblen, Thorstein [1923] (1964), *Absentee Ownership and Business Enterprise in Recent Times: The Case of America*, New York: Augustus M. Kelley.
Waller, William and Ann Jennings (1990), 'On the possibility of a feminist economics: the convergence of institutional and feminist methodology', *Journal of Econonmic Issues*, **24** (June), 612–22.
Widerquist, Karl, Michael Anthony Lewis and Steven Pressman (eds) (2005), *The Ethics and Economics of the Basic Income Guarantee*, Burlington, VT: Ashgate.

36 Exploitation and surplus
Phillip Anthony O'Hara

Introduction

Exploitation has a number of meanings in social economics, ranging from 'reasonably utilizing a resource for advantage', 'unfairly utilizing a resource for advantage', to 'illegally utilizing a resource for advantage'. The type of exploitation examined in this chapter could be described in any of these ways, depending on the perspective of the social scientist. Indeed, various authors utilize 'exploitation' in one or more of these three ways, variously emphasizing the more positive and others the more normative elements of the social process. Many authors, however, examine exploitation without the concept of surplus or profit (e.g. Wertheimer, 1996), and these works are not part of this chapter. Specifically, this work links exploitation with surplus, in particular surplus product, surplus value or profit.[1]

A surplus in social economics is that portion of a product or financial arrangement left over after costs. Typically, for businesses it represents revenue minus costs of wages, materials and depreciation. Every society has a surplus, in the sense that, from time to time, the total production exceeds the necessary consumption of 'the people'. However, the surpluses of some societies are larger than others. For instance, the surplus of hunter-gatherer societies may be only seasonal or cyclical, since such people prefer leisure and/or they fail to have the productive capacity to produce a sustainable surplus. In any case, there is not usually a large parasitic class to support from the surplus (Sanderson, 1991, pp. 250–51). A surplus becomes more necessary in class societies, such as slavery, feudalism and capitalism. The historical rationale for capitalism is the production of a large surplus through technological change and industrial reorganization. According to many social scientists it produces a surplus through the exploitation process. And so it is with capitalism that this chapter begins the analysis of surplus and exploitation.

There are four main interpretations of surplus and exploitation from a social perspective. The first is the Pigou–Robinson neoclassical view where labour does not receive its marginal product. The second is the traditional Marxian view, based on a monetary theory of (labour) value.[2] The third is a more socially embedded social economics view, where trust and sociality are an important part of the explanation. And the fourth is a social structure of accumulation view, based on institutions and history. These four interpretations are examined in this chapter in successive sections. Afterwards we examine the nature of relatively egalitarian systems and whether they depend upon exploitation or not. A conclusion follows.

Neoclassical exploitation of labour
Exploitation of labour is not a theme that is very common in neoclassical economics, since workers are usually assumed to be paid their marginal productivity. For instance, if workers are paid a wage equal to the marginal product of their labour, then it is usually concluded that they are being paid an adequate remuneration according to their level of productivity. But there are a few traditions, and even empirical evidence, to support some degree of exploitation and greater surplus when conditions are not consistent with workers being paid their marginal product. Usually this tradition follows that of the Arthur Cecil Pigou (1877–1959) and Joan Robinson (1903–83) literature.[3]

Joan Robinson (1933), in some respects following Pigou, for instance discussed a number of situations in which workers were not being paid according to their marginal productivity, leading to exploitation and higher surplus (super-profit) for corporations. The first case is where there is a monopoly firm or a number of firms enjoying partial monopoly profit. With monopoly power, the marginal net productivity of these firms will be lower than the marginal physical product of labour when valued at commodity price (1933, ch. 25). The exploitation is thus due to a lack of competition in industry, leading to above-normal profit and wages not commensurate with workers' marginal productivity. If competitive conditions were instituted, output would rise, and the price of the commodity would decline to the even lower level of workers' marginal product. No worker exploitation would now occur, although workers' wages themselves would probably have declined, along with the rate of profit. Thus, in this analysis, eliminating exploitation probably does not likely lead to workers' improved conditions of pay.

The second case of neoclassical labour exploitation and higher surplus is where firms have effective monopsony power over labour. Joan Robinson provides some examples, such as the existence of a 'gentleman's agreement' among firms not to bid up wages in response to a relative insufficiency of supply, which effectively gives these firms a form of monopsony power. Here the wage equals the supply price of labour but is less than the marginal physical product of labour. Hence exploitation exists because workers are not given a fair remuneration, leading to a higher rate of surplus or super-profit.

The third example is where there are cultural or social reasons for workers to reside in an area, despite a low wage, when they could just as easily move to higher-wage areas. They prefer not to change location, due to geographical advantages in the form of family and friends, environmental factors or upbringing. They may also not move to higher-wage areas because of lack of information or ignorance (Robinson, 1933, p. 297). This leads to a relative oversupply of labour, or relative inelasticity of labour supply to other areas. In this case, wages are lower than workers' marginal physical product times price. Minimum wages will eliminate such exploitation, but may also lead to lower surplus, output and employment.

Some empirical evidence has been garnered by scholars as to whether such neoclassical exploitation exists in reality. Richard Vedder and Lowell Gallaway (1985), for instance, illustrate that such exploitation does not seem to have existed in the USA between 1820 and 1920. Milan Zafirovski (2003), on the other hand, studied comparative data for the late 1990s and found varying rates of neoclassical exploitation ranging from high (UK, Australia, Canada) to medium (Japan, Netherlands, USA) to low (Norway, Switzerland, Finland). The consolidation of neoliberalism (Washington Consensus) is said to have raised the rate of exploitation as workers are not being remunerated in accordance with productivity due to greater power being given to corporations *vis-à-vis* labour.

Traditional Marxian view of surplus and exploitation
While the neoclassical vision of exploitation operates only when conditions of perfect competition do not prevail, Marxists start their analysis of exploitation under competitive assumptions (Marx, 1867). This view of surplus and exploitation starts off by explaining that under an advanced capitalist system there is a monetary expression of surplus and exploitation. In other words, the generation of the surplus through the process of exploitation mediates the spheres of production, circulation (exchange and movement) and distribution through the various social classes. The institutional conditions of existence of a surplus and exploitation are the first things to ascertain. These include:

1. Perfect competition exists in product markets, labour markets and money markets. It may be assumed to begin with that prices equal values, wages equal the value of labour power, and all surplus is distributed to capitalists.
2. There is control of the means of production in the hands of an elite social class of various industrial capitalists, who include the managers of enterprises in the commanding heights of industry. The means of production have been handed down through an array of processes linked to inheritance and conquest. Inheritance and conquest have enabled the reproduction of families who have established cultural,

educational and business networks that reproduce differential control
over the means of production, distribution and exchange. These means
of production are socially controlled by this class of privileged people,
who own the factories, machinery, buildings, computers, raw materials
and other inputs into production. This leaves the majority of the population who live off the fruits of their labour power; that is, their ability
to create value and hence to contribute directly to material and market relationships. This majority forms various classes of producers,
depending on the historical phase of capitalist development, such as
the workers at the point of production of mining, manufacturing,
transportation, infrastructure, agriculture and services. In the contemporary form of capitalism this may take the form of the lower and
middle ranks of the segmented labour market.

3.   There are also various institutional conditions of existence of
exploitation and surplus generation. For instance, it is necessary to
employ various non-productive agents to promote circulation (sales)
and other functions necessary for exploitation. These include accoun-
tants, marketing divisions, sales workers, education, health, police and
defence. These institutional supports provide unproductive labour
that may indeed be critical to the reproduction of surplus value more
generally conceived. Such unproductive labour enables the long-term
generation of the conditions of existence of surplus value and thus
exploitation.

The production of surplus value requires various markets, such as the
labour market, commodity market, financial system and global systems of
supply and demand that propel the circuit of social capital, upon which
surplus value depends. This is shown in Figure 36.1.

Here the supply of money (M) (from financial institutions and retained
earnings) is used to purchase commodity (C) inputs into the production
process, including means of production (MOP) and labour power (LP).
This is followed by the production process ($\ldots P \ldots$) where value-added
is potentially generated. If the value-added is zero, then total value is 'C',
but if surplus product is generated, this is shown as 'c'. However, before the
surplus product can become surplus value, it must satisfy the 'Keynes
problem', that of being sold in the commodity market for money. If the

$$M \longleftrightarrow C \,(MOP, LP) \ldots P \ldots C + c \longleftrightarrow M + m$$

Figure 36.1   The circuit of social capital

total money revenue is equal to '*M*', then only the costs of production are met; but if a surplus value is generated, then '*m*' is positive and exploitation has been successful. Afterwards, it is still necessary to reproduce the circuit of social capital further, as more money is reinvested into the circuit (as shown by the arrow) (Marx, 1885). This circuit relates to agricultural, mining, manufacturing, high-technology and most service sectors of the economy.

The monetary theory of exploitation states that surplus value is generated in a monetary form and that the total product produced comprises constant capital (K), variable capital (V) and surplus value (SV) in the three departments of means of production (department 1), consumer goods production (department 2) and luxury good production (department 3):

$$k1 + v1 + sv1$$
$$k2 + v2 + sv2$$
$$k3 + v3 + sv3$$
$$\overline{K + V + SV = \Sigma GDP}$$

Accordingly, the social rate of exploitation (rate of surplus value) is defined as sv/v, the organic composition of capital is $k/(k + v)$, and the rate of profit $s/(k + v)$, with the corresponding macro formulas also applying.

Surplus value is thus the process whereby labour power is exploited socially by capital in the pursuit of profit. More specifically, labour power is exchanged for wages, and surplus value is distributed between industrial capitalists (as profit), interest and charges (financial institutions), and rent (for rentiers). Exploitation occurs as capitalists are able to pay workers wages, but then extend their workday beyond this to produce a surplus product which is then sold on the market at a price that generates a surplus.

It is critical to the exploitation process that there be an array of markets, especially two: one, the payment of wages (variable capital) in exchange for labour power; and the other for selling the final commodity on the market in exchange for money (total price or value). If total revenue exceeds the wage and capital inputs, then a surplus is produced, which then is expressed as profit, but may also be shared as interest and rent. A critical part of the story is that total labour equals total value of price produced and then realized on the market – workers create this value – but they are only paid their wages, which fall short of total revenue. Thus exploitation occurs because the dominant class of owners and controllers of capital have a monopoly hold on the means of production, whereas workers have little or none and thus must sell their labour power for wages. This monopoly power in ownership and social networks thus enables capitalists to exploit workers, who receive wages according to competitive conditions of labour. If the ownership of the means of production, distribution and exchange were equally endowed by the whole population, and they were included in decision-making, then exploitation of this type could not exist.

Exploitation is thus the most pervasive element in the generation of surplus value. It is justified through market ideology and entrepreneurial assumptions of creativity. The 'free' existence of the individual under capitalism is the dominant enabling myth underlying this process. The state also supports the process through various legal apparatuses that protect private property, plus police, armies and intelligence forces. The schools and universities also play their role in legitimizing exploitation. When markets are assumed to be the dominant relationships of the economy it is easy to mystify the generation of surplus value, and fail to understand the nature of the veil over which we are taught that workers receive the full value of their production.

Surplus value is then distributed throughout the economy on the basis of various laws of competition and innovation. Through competition, for instance, the surplus value produced by the least efficient firm with the greatest amount of labour employed is redistributed to the most efficient with the smallest labour employed. Thus innovation does not generate surplus value *per se* but enables surplus value to be distributed from workers in inefficient sectors to firms in more efficient ones. Competition may also encourage firms to quickly put into practice the latest innovations, thus leading to higher organic compositions of capital $(k/(k + v))$, and lower rates of profit $(s/k + v)$. This occurs through an increase in depreciation of capital as firms are forced through competition to introduce the latest forms of technology even if in the long run their profit rate will decline.

Many authors have related these processes of exploitation and the production of surplus value to national income accounts. For instance, O'Hara (2006a) has done this for China, and the results are shown in Table 36.1.

Studying the trends and nature of these variables reveals a quite obvious process of development. The Chinese authorities have recently set in motion a form of social capitalism, which has encouraged competition, globalization and the expansion of capital accumulation. It has utilized the capitalist mode of production and reproduction to stimulate industrialization, in the context of a high degree of competition for Chinese products on the world market. Expanding capital accumulation and thus raising the share of investment in GDP to over 40 per cent raises labour productivity to successively high levels.

This has the ramifications of reducing the rate of profit from the previously very high rate of 47 per cent to the still high (in global terms) but

Table 36.1 Rate of economic surplus, exploitation, organic composition of capital and profit: China, 1978–2002[4]

	1978	1984	1990	1996	2002
Economic surplus/GDP	0.32	0.28	0.25	0.24	0.24
Rate of exploitation (sv/v) (%)	56	46	40	39	41
Organic composition of capital ($k/(k+v)$)	0.16	0.16	0.18	0.20	0.24
Rate of profit ($s/(k+v)$) (%)	47	40	33	32	32

Source: Adapted from O'Hara (2006a).

moderate by Chinese standards of around 32 per cent. John Knight and Shi Li (2005) point out that during the period of central planning the state-owned enterprises were 'highly profitable' since they employed a price-scissors policy of 'keeping industrial prices high and agricultural prices low in order to finance industrialization' (ibid., p. 206). But during the period of reform from 1978 onwards, greater competition reduced margins and cut profit rates in both state and many private firms. The profit rate was reduced through the incessant expansion of capitalist production, especially the continual investment and replacement of labour by capital in the ongoing process of global competition. Substituting capital for labour raises labour productivity, but it also reduces the productivity of capital as the rate of investment rises faster than GDP. The higher capital/labour ratio translates into a higher organic composition of capital, which thus reduces the rate of profit. Chinese enterprises are, in this sense, poorly managing their capital investments and relying more on accumulation and substitution of capital for labour rather than capital improvements (through innovation and knowledge) *per se*.

China is thus exploiting workers at a lower rate than previously, but nevertheless the exploitation process forms the foundation of profit, accumulation and growth of the Chinese system of capitalism.

Social and cultural view of exploitation and surplus
The traditional Marxian view of surplus and exploitation can be extended somewhat to provide a more social and cultural perspective on the matter. Much of this vision emanates from Thorstein Veblen and other social economists. Veblen (1899), for instance, believed that the net product (surplus product) is created not just from workers being exploited, but also from the use of social knowledge and institutions. In other words, the system functions of knowledge, trust and circulation create some of the surplus product, and demand also may contribute to it by transforming surplus

product into surplus value or profit. Institutions, in general, may thus contribute to the surplus by performing public-goods functions that generate long-term profit.

This can be shown by extending the circuit in various ways, such as by the introduction of the world economy, the state, the corporation, and so on (see O'Hara, 2001).[5] We seek to extend the circuit through the introduction of family relations, trust and association, and cultural factors via a more complex 'systemic circuit of social capital' (SCSC), as illustrated in Figure 36.2.

The SCSC illustrates, first, how the reproduction of social and material relations of production and circulation (exchange) are embedded in a system of 'cultural relations', which constitutes the way of life of the community, including the differential norms, mores and practices of the people. Culture also includes the relations of status, ceremony as well as class, ethnicity and gender, which have regional variations and modes of uneven development. Second, the reproduction of the SCSC is embedded in a 'global environment' as well as 'governance relations' that embody the rules, laws and regulations channelling and directing the practices of individuals, corporations and groups. Third, the SCSC is embedded in a myriad of relations of 'trust and association' through global, regional, national, corporate, social, familial and individual processes.

Set within this broad institutional and social environment, the SCSC, more narrowly conceived, can be seen to 'begin' with a system of 'familial reproduction' (*FR*), which constitutes the roles, practices and forms of care

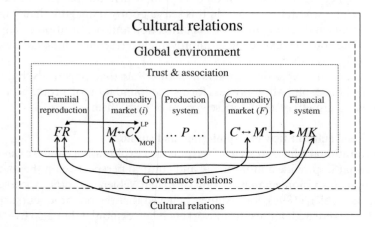

Source: O'Hara (2004).

Figure 36.2   Systemic circuit of social capital (SCSC)

that are embedded in households: between parents, children and others. Familial reproduction potentially enables the emergence of a stable environment for people to structure their social practices, and for personality and emotions to evolve. Closely linked to the family are relations, friends and community linkages. The trust and association developed in the family may help the market for intermediate (i) goods and services through enhancing the quality of labour power and conditioning consumption patterns and spending decisions.

The second dynamic structure of the inner SCSC includes decisions to exchange money for labour power and means of production in the market for intermediate goods and services. This involves agreements and relationships between capital and labour (or their representatives) in the distributive struggle over shares of national or international income. It also involves structures of competition and pricing in the market for capital goods and material inputs, including machinery, factories, oil, gas and other raw materials. Bottlenecks at this phase of the circuit can have a major negative impact on the reproduction process as a whole. Family relations, trust, association and culture can also affect these practices.

The third phase of the inner SCSC involves the direct production process, including the valorization of capital, which includes the production of surplus product. This involves all the major relations and processes associated with the ability of capital to subordinate labour and extract surplus labour through an array of technological, organizational, supervisory and governance structures. However, before the surplus product can become effective, it requires a fourth phase, that of the realization process through 'final' market demand (F). Without the ability of capitalism to create sufficient demand – through a combination of consumption, investment, government spending and/or net exports – the surplus value remains only potential rather than actual. Familial relations and trust are important to this process. And lastly, for the SCSC to be fully reproducible requires that corporate finance (M'), or endogenous money and credit through the financial system (MK), be (re)invested into the market for intermediate goods and services as well as through the system of familial reproduction. And so on *ad infinitum* as the circuit becomes reproduced through varying turnovers of capital.

This social way of viewing exploitation and surplus value recognizes that profit, interest and rent become a form of monopoly ownership income that is generated by exploiting the system-conditions of trust, institutions, knowledge and the environment. Business is thus able to exploit social value by controlling the means of production, distribution and exchange. Indirectly, this may be a form of worker exploitation because the workers are not sufficiently included as owners of capital and therefore are denied a share of the surplus. Underdeveloped nations similarly are exploited in this because they do not share in the global surplus created in part by the public goods of financial, civil, material and social relations generated in society.

Social structure of accumulation exploitation and surplus

A subset of the social explanation of exploitation and surplus is provided by the social structure of accumulation (SSA) school of political economy. It argues that institutions specifically provide the foundation for most of the long-term growth and development occurring in society (Gordon, 1998; Bowles et al., 1990). Therefore certain classes of people are able to exploit these institutions for their own benefit, and thereby gain a material and social advance on other classes.

For instance, most nation-states utilize the institutional spheres provided by family–community, production–distribution, state and governance, and trade and finance for reproducing surplus value. This system of institutions is shown in Figure 36.3.

The SSA approach to surplus and exploitation has two layers. The first layer says that exploitation in the short term is undertaken of workers by capitalists and their functionaries, resulting in the production of a surplus. The second layer says that the long-term conditions underlying exploitation are institutionalized through an array of social arrangements.

The family and community play a role in the reproduction of labour power, sociality and trust, upon which the rest of the institutions depend. The work of women is of special relevance here since they perform most of the household labour of child-rearing, non-market production and domestic psychological counselling. Research consistently demonstrates that men, even in egalitarian arrangements, tend to render such activities as 'females roles', and are therefore unable to contribute substantially to them (O'Hara, 2000, ch. 11). On this basis, without the coordinating power of women the reproduction of potential workers and capitalists would be severely hindered. Hence they produce what may be called an 'underlying institutional surplus' of social cooperation and connectedness that is necessary for long-term socio-economic reproduction. Periodically the family and community become dislocated as individualism, work and rapid social change upset established human relationships, and this can inhibit long-term growth, surplus and exploitation.

The state plays a critical role when directed to productive capital, such as education, infrastructure, communications, health and utilities. Historically, the state has provided a critical element of public goods and services that stimulate economies of agglomeration, human capital and the circulation of socio-economic activities. The state in the postwar period has also

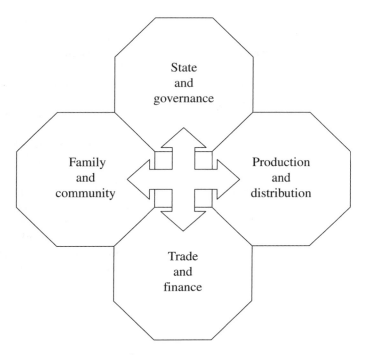

Figure 36.3   SSA system of institutions

specialized in providing countercyclical automatic and discretionary spending as well as prudential functions along with lender-of-last-resort facilities. The public-goods functions underlying these activities have historically been critical to the production of a social surplus, as well as to promoting stability in the conditions underlying exploitation in corporate relationships. However, when unproductive activities dominate, resulting in crowding out of private investment, this usually sees increasing reliance on handouts such as subsidies, benefits and general consumption that inhibit surplus generation and exploitation.

The corporate system historically has been critical to the provision of systems of management, organization and technological change underlying long-term accumulation. It has structured the labour process through an array of supervisors, overseers and labour relations personnel whose task it is to extract labour from labour power more effectively (Braverman, 1974). Specialist marketing, sales and R&D divisions can enhance the production, distribution and realization of surplus. The complex institutional layers within the corporation usually protect it from the market and help to reduce bankruptcy. Corporate contradictions, however, sometimes dominate as financial excesses, corporate crises, and conflict between capital and labour can lead to anomalous surplus production and reproduction.

Trade and finance are also critical to long-term growth and accumulation underlying the rate of surplus value or exploitation. The transformation of use values through transport itself creates surplus value and ensures the greater circulation of capital. Circulation routes through shipping, air and road transport enhance the spatial reproduction of capital. They also promote a greater degree of market penetration of countries and continents until now not much open to capitalist production. They thus promote the rate of exploitation and the turnover of capital, providing a double boost to profit.

And the finance system potentially stimulates the rate of turnover of surplus value, as well as ensuring the continuation of exploitation through production in the workplace. In this way it functions to enhance long-term reproduction. But it can also, as with most contradictions, inhibit long-term growth through an excessive expansion of fictitious capitals, such as speculative bubbles associated with share markets, property markets and high-tech markets. When finance thus dominates industry, this increases the degree of instability in the macro economy and thus inhibits surplus production and exploitation.

Overall, this social view of surplus and exploitation processes recognizes that public-goods functions can operate within institutions, and these social relationships are in essence the foundation of long-term profit and growth (O'Hara, 2006b). In this sense, individuals and groups of people are able to extract the surplus in the long run through exploiting the very institutions that propel progress and development. Hence exploitation is not simply concerned with one class versus another at the point of production, but also groups of people controlling the institutions themselves, including the media, political processes and the commanding heights of innovation.

Exploitation and surplus in egalitarian societies

The question now arises as to what might be the nature of exploitation and surplus in more egalitarian societies. Can socialism, for instance, exist without exploitation? If so, does it still produce a surplus? These are the critical questions that have led to many theories and solutions to the problems of moving from class to non-class societies. Four types of egalitarian societies are briefly examined here: profit-sharing systems of capitalism; state-based societies; worker cooperative-based societies; and trust-and-sociality structures.

The first type of more egalitarian system is the profit-sharing corporate system of democratic capitalism. Here, the corporation is controlled by private managers, CEOs and shareholders, while workers merely receive a share of the profits, according to the rate of profit and their position in the firm. For instance, a corporate system could be based on a method of distributing surplus to workers when the rate of profit is above 10 per cent. In this case, 30 per cent of the extra profit may be distributed to workers as bonuses, depending on the nature and position of the respective workers. In this case, both exploitation and surplus exist since the rate of exploitation may have simply declined from, say, 40 per cent to 30 per cent; or the profit-sharing arrangement may be a form of efficiency wages where productivity expands, along with total wages, such that the rate of exploitation may not change.

The second type of egalitarian system is where the state controls much of the surplus, either through higher corporate taxes or through controlling the dominant enterprises. In the case of the state owning and controlling dominant industries, it represents the collective capitalist (much of the former Eastern bloc). It therefore uses the institutions of business to extract surplus value and hence to exploit workers. However, the rate of exploitation also depends on what is done with the surplus. If the state utilizes it for further innovation, employment, education, health and infrastructure, as well as cultural venues and public transport, then some of the surplus may be redistributed to workers, thus lessening the rate of exploitation. But if the public utilities are financed purely in order to promote private investment, then the corporate system's exploitation of labour continues unabated.

The third type of egalitarian system is where there is an expansion of worker cooperatives as a systemic response to social needs of workers and production. This may result in a system such as the Mondragon group of companies, in the Basque area of Spain. Here, productivity is high since workers have control of decision-making, electing members of the board, which appoints managers; and supervisors are generally not needed since social factors enhance the commitment of workers to the collective concerns of production, distribution and exchange. A portion of the surplus is distributed to company tertiary institutions, medical assistance, banks and housing cooperatives. Here the workers are not exploited since they control the company's institutions, and the surplus is democratically distributed into productive and social institutions. Exploitation thus does not exist, even with a surplus, when the workers themselves make such decisions.

The fourth type of egalitarian system is one where there is a large degree of trust among the various groups and organizations; where community values and participatory decision-making extends beyond corporations and governments; and where people have few ceremonial needs to engage in conspicuous consumption and emulation through the market. This system is based on a strong level of social capital, which binds people together in such a way that they are socialized into considering other people's needs as well as their own. The environment and other species may also be included in the various accords and pacts that institutionalize the system of cooperative decision-making and sociality. In this system, economic activities play a secondary role to social and community pursuits, and the ideology of exploitation is not a critical part of its operational dynamics.

Conclusion

This chapter has examined four social perspectives on exploitation and surplus. The first is a neoclassical view of exploitation and super-profits based on labour not being remunerated according to workers' marginal productivity. However, generally exploitation is due to monopoly or monopsony conditions and inelastic labour supply curves, where raising the wage does not usually reduce such exploitation. The second view of exploitation is the traditional Marxian theory, which emphasizes the collective exploitation of workers forming the basis of capitalist development. Here, increasing wages usually does reduce exploitation. The third and fourth forms of exploitation are modifications and extensions to the traditional Marxian explanation. Thus the third and fourth types are both more socially oriented forms of exploitation – the third linking to cultural arrangements that impinge on trust and sociality, and the fourth forming part of the long-term reproduction of the conditions of existence of exploitation and surplus production in the social structure of accumulation approach. In both highly social perspectives it is possible for the dominant social classes to exploit the institutions for their own ends. Here the long-term surplus is reproduced through an array of institutional conditions and accords, as public goods or system-functions.

Then we examined four types of relatively egalitarian societies. The first has a profit-sharing facility, where exploitation still exists but there is a stimulus for workers to create a larger surplus. The second system is where the state produces and distributes the surplus. Under this system the rate of exploitation tends to be high if the state reinvests the surplus into production, distribution and exchange systems. But if the state recreates community through propelling cultural services, health, education and means of community involvement, it may reduce the rate of exploitation and even enhance social and economic democracy. The third system, though, is one where exploitation in production ceases, since workers control the firm, decide what to produce, and recreate community capital and production systems simultaneously. The fourth egalitarian system ceases altogether to reproduce exploitation, and the surplus takes on both material and immaterial forms. The surplus is produced collectively, taking into account the cultural and knowledge basis of society, and is regenerated into productive, educative, creative and communal forms of social reality.

Notes

1. This chapter links exploitation with surplus, but does not follow the rational choice Marxism of Roemer (1982) and Hahnel (2006). Rather, it follows a realist perspective, more if keeping with that of Baran (1957), Foster (1986), Danielson (1994), Davis (1992), Stanfield (1973). We argue that surplus value and economic surplus have a similar origin, but that economic surplus needs to argue specifically for the link, and the link is more indirect in some instances.
2. There is of course a large literature on the relationship between value and price in Marxian economics. This literature is important for social economics because it demonstrates that value may not equal price, or that they are situated in different planes or spheres. Some scholars equate value with price by using the monetary theory of labour values, and many develop a transformation procedure linking values and prices. There are numerous methods of transformation, such as that developed by Marx (1894), Shaikh (1977), the new method (see Rieu, 2006), and a *Rethinking Marxism* method (Ormazabal, 2006).
3. Paul Flatau (2001) argues, however, that while they have much in common, Pigou's and Robinson's theories of neoclassical exploitation are somewhat different from each other. Edward Chamberlin (1933) went further than Pigou and Robinson, and argued that under conditions of monopolistic competition 'all factors (not merely any one, say, labor) receive less than their marginal products' (p. 182).
4. The data in Table 36.1, including the economic surplus, organic composition of capital, rate of exploitation and rate of profit, are all estimated from the national accounts data. The 'economic surplus', for instance, called 'operating surplus' in the national accounts, is defined as 'a residual' and it 'reflects economy-wide business profit'. It is 'the return to the owners of the capital involved in a productive activity, and thus constitutes [in principle] the economy-wide return on equity'. Furthermore, 'surplus constitutes the return on' 'fixed and intangible assets'. The rate of exploitation is defined as the ratio of economic surplus/GDP divided by the ratio of labour share/GDP. The organic composition of capital is here specifically defined as the depreciation proportion of GDP divided by the depreciation and wages proportions of GDP. It does not include circulating capital but, nevertheless, is thought to be a good indicator of the trend direction of the organic composition of capital.
5. The project of modifying and extending the circuit of capital (CSC) is a critical one in contemporary political economy. This is because the CSC is a powerful tool of analysis, yet the contemporary economy is a complex one that requires expanding the linkages in the analysis. On some attempts to use the CSC to comprehend changes in capitalism, see Arthur and Reuten (1998). An interesting work linking surplus with exploitation and other processes is Boss (1990).

References

Arthur, Christopher J. and Geert Reuten (eds) (1998), *The Circulation of Capital: Essays on Volume Two of Marx's 'Capital'*, London: Macmillan.
Baran, Paul A. (1957), *The Political Economy of Growth*, New York: Monthly Review Press.
Boss, Helen (1990), *Theories of Surplus and Transfer: Parasites and Producers in Economic Thought*, Boston, MA and London: Unwin Hyman.
Bowles, Samuel, David M. Gordon and Thomas E. Weisskopf (1990), *After the Waste Land*, Armonk, NY and London: M.E. Sharpe.
Braverman, Harry (1974), *Labour and Monopoly Capital: The Degradation of Work in the Twentieth Century*, New York and London: Monthly Review Press.

Chamberlin, Edward Hastings (1933), *The Theory of Monopolistic Competition: A Re-orientation of the Theory of Value*, Cambridge, MA: Harvard University Press, 1962.
Danielson, Anders (1994), *The Economic Surplus: Theory, Measurement, Applications*, London and Westport, CT: Praeger.
Davis, John (1992), *The Economic Surplus in Advanced Economies*, Aldershot, UK and Brookfield, USA: Edward Elgar.
Flatau, Paul (2001), 'Some reflections on the "Pigou–Robinson" theory of exploitation', *History of Economics Review*, **33**, 1–16.
Foster, John Bellamy (1986), *The Theory of Monopoly Capitalism: An Elaboration of Marxian Political Economy*, New York: Monthly Review Press.
Gordon, David M. (1998), *Economics and Social Justice: Essays on Power, Labor and Institutional Change*, edited by S. Bowles and T. Weisskopf, Cheltenham, UK and Northampton, MA, USA: Edward Elgar.
Hahnel, Robin (2006), 'Exploitation: a modern approach', *Review of Radical Political Economics*, **38** (2), 175–92.
Knight, J. and S. Li (2005), 'Wages, firm profitability and labor market segmentation in urban China', *China Economic Review*, **16**, 205–8.
Marx, Karl (1867), *Capital, Volume 1 – The Process of Production of Capital*, Harmondsworth: Penguin, 1976.
Marx, Karl (1885), *Capital, Volume 2 – The Process of Circulation of Capital*, Harmondsworth: Penguin, 1978.
Marx, Karl (1894), *Capital, Volume 3 – The Process of Capitalist Production as a Whole*, Harmondsworth: Penguin, 1981.
O'Hara, Phillip Anthony (2000), *Marx, Veblen and Contemporary Institutional Political Economy*, Cheltenham, UK and Northampton, MA, USA: Edward Elgar.
O'Hara, Phillip Anthony (2001), 'Circuit of social capital', in P.A. O'Hara (ed.), *Encyclopedia of Political Economy*, London and New York: Routledge, pp. 84–7.
O'Hara, Phillip Anthony (2004), 'A new family–community social structure of accumulation for long wave upswing in the United States?', *Forum for Social Economics*, **34** (2), 51–80.
O'Hara, Phillip Anthony (2006a), 'A Chinese social structure of accumulation for capitalist long-wave upswing?', *Review of Radical Political Economics*, **38** (3), 397–404.
O'Hara Phillip Anthony (2006b), *Growth and Development in the Global Political Economy: Social Structures of Accumulation and Modes of Regulation*, London and New York: Routledge.
Ormazabul, Kapa M. (2006), 'The "quantitative approach to the Marxian concept of value"', *Rethinking Marxism*, **18** (1), 121–39.
Rieu, Dong-Min (2006), 'A reexamination of the quantitative issues in the new interpretation', *Review of Radical Political Economics*, **38** (2), 258–71.
Robinson, Joan (1933), *The Economics of Imperfect Competition*, 2nd edn, London and Basingstoke: Macmillan and St Martin's Press, 1969.
Roemer, John E. (1982), *A General Theory of Exploitation and Class*, Cambridge, MA: Harvard University Press.
Sanderson, Stephen K. (1991), *Macrosociology: An Introduction to Human Societies*, 2nd edn, New York: HarperCollins.
Shaikh, Anwar (1977), 'Marx's theory of value and the transformation problem', in Jesse Schwartz (ed.), *The Subtle Anatomy of Capitalism*, Santa Monica, CA: Goodyear, pp. 106–39.
Stanfield, James Ronald (1973), *The Economic Surplus and Neo-Marxism*, Lexington, MA: Lexington Books.
Veblen, Thorstein Bunde (1899), *The Theory of the Leisure Class: An Economic Study of Institutions*, London: Macmillan, 1981.
Vedder, Richard K. and Lowell E. Gallaway (1985), 'Productivity and wages in the American economy: a tale of two centuries', Working Paper, Ohio University, Department of Economics.

Wertheimer, Alan (1996), *Exploitation*, Princeton, NJ: Princeton University Press.
Zafirovski, Milan (2003), 'Measuring and making sense of labour exploitation in contemporary society', *Review of Radical Political Economics*, **35** (4), 462–84.

Index

Titles of publications are in *italics*.

Abolafia, M.Y. 450
abundance and inequality 641–2
accumulation of social capital 384
acquisitions and mergers 348–67
Acs, Z.J. 333, 334, 342, 343
action problem, SNA 401–2
ad hoc revisionism 504–6
agency of the state 545–7
agency theories of the firm 312–13
Akerlof, G. 178, 179, 180, 323, 409
Akkerman, T. 189
Alchian, A. 306, 309–10, 313, 315
alternative growth model, ethical
    implications 244–5
altruistic family 193
altruistic preferences 80–85, 112–13
Anatomy of Power, The 411, 416
Anderson, E. 272, 278, 282
Anderson, P. 46–7
Anker, R. 293, 294
anthropology and economics 427–40
anti-miscegenation laws 165
Appadurai, A. 427, 430
Arendt, H. 415
Arestis, P. 524
Arrow, K.J. 315, 336–7, 341, 379, 381
asset prices and monetary policy 471
association
    and social order 307–8
    and theory of the firm 314–16
Association for Social Economics
    (ASE) 4
atomistic individuals 92
Audretsch, D.B. 333, 334, 336, 338,
    339, 343, 342
Augier, M. 351
Aune, J.A. 280
Austin, J. 591
authority and cooperation 317–19
autonomy versus embeddedness
    429–33
Axelrod, R. 319

Ayres, C.E. 34, 39, 41, 160, 162, 163,
    634

Babb, S. 479
Banerjee, A.V. 118, 358
Banerjee, B. 183–4
banking 478–93
    evolution of 478–87
Bardhan, P. 427
bargaining power and growth 228
Barnard, C. 306, 316–19, 320, 324
Baron, J. 323
Barr, N. 520, 521
Barro, R. 466
Basu, K. 432
Baumann, Z. 549
Baumol, W.G. 523
Bayes, C.W. 561
Beck, U. 45, 49, 52
Becker, G.S. 178, 193, 270–71, 272, 560
Becker, H. 52
Beckert, J. 45
behavioural economics 350
    and the individual 97
behavioural theory of the firm 357
Bellah, R. 636
benefits, pulling forward 116–17
Between Facts and Norms 415
Beveridge 527
Bhattacherjee, D. 182
Biesecker, A. 414
Bikhchandani, S. 358, 359
biophysical conception of the economy
    14–15
Birchfield, V. 273
Blau, P. 259
blocked exchanges 278
Bonvin, J.-M. 150
Booth, D. 15
Boulding, K.E. 401, 409, 410, 411
Bound, J. 334
boundaries 2–3

667